PRACTICAL HANDBOOK FOR

Professional Investigators

THIRD EDITION

PRACTICAL HANDBOOK FOR

Professional Investigators

THIRD EDITION

RORY J. McMAHON, CLI, CFE

CRC Press
Taylor & Francis Group
Boca Raton London New York

CRC Press is an imprint of the
Taylor & Francis Group, an **informa** business

CRC Press
Taylor & Francis Group
6000 Broken Sound Parkway NW, Suite 300
Boca Raton, FL 33487-2742

First issued in paperback 2019

ISBN-13: 978-1-4398-8722-6 (hbk)
ISBN-13: 978-0-367-86681-5 (pbk)

Library of Congress Cataloging-in-Publication Data

McMahon, Rory J.
Practical handbook for professional investigators / Rory J. McMahon. -- Third Edition.
pages cm
Includes bibliographical references and index.
ISBN 978-1-4398-8722-6 (hardcover : alk. paper)
1. Private investigators--United States--Handbooks, manuals, etc. I. Title.

HV8093.M36 2013
363.28'9--dc23 2013014909

Visit the Taylor & Francis Web site at
http://www.taylorandfrancis.com

and the CRC Press Web site at
http://www.crcpress.com

To my brother, Daniel J. McMahon, who has been there for me throughout my life. His advice, guidance, and support have been a constant theme in my life, for which I will always be grateful.

In memory of my cousin, Chris Maguire Simmers, who passed on September 30, 2010, shortly after her 60th birthday. She was a beautiful person who brought much joy, love, and friendship to those who knew and cherished her. You may be gone, Chris, but you will never be forgotten.

Contents

Preface **xv**
Acknowledgments **xix**
The Author **xxi**

1 Introduction **1**

Job Outlook 1
Earnings 2

2 Skills Needed to Become a Successful Investigator **3**

Three Methods That Investigators Use to Obtain Information 3
What Is an Investigator? 3
Attributes of a Successful Investigator 4

3 Foundations of Investigation **9**

Types of Investigation 9
Assignments Performed by a Professional Investigator 11
Sources of Information 14
Missing Persons 27
Undercover Operations in Business Settings 34
Asset Protection—Loss Prevention—Access Control 36

4 Interviews, Interrogation, and Taking Statements **41**

Introduction to Interviews 41
Purpose of the Interrogation 45
Taking Statements 52

5 Legal Investigations **61**

The Legal Investigator 61
Structure of the U.S. Constitution 62
The Bill of Rights 64
Habeas Corpus 66
Criminal and Civil Procedure 66
The Concept of Crime 70
The Effective Limits of Criminal Law 70

The Authority to Arrest 71
Investigative Detention Short of Arrest—Stop and Frisk 71
Searches 72
Interrogating the Accused 72
The Trial 72
Legal Investigations 83
Role of the Legal Investigator 85
Evidence 85
Conducting Legal Investigations 89
Case Study: *United States v. Nancy Walter* 90
Case Study: *United States v. Pedro Huezo* 91

6 Fraud Investigation 97

Corporate Fraud 99
Economic Crime Schemes 103
White-Collar Crime 108
Corporate Crime 109
Boiler Rooms—Telemarketing Fraud 119
How to Conduct a Criminal Fraud Defense Investigation 130
"Eating the Elephant": Defense Investigations for Complex Fraud Cases 131
Case Studies 138
Appendix 6.1: Sample Activity Reports 148

7 Computer Crime 153

Computer Crimes 153
Computer Fraud 154
The Computer Crime Investigator 155
Investigative Methodology 156
Areas of Computer Abuse 156
Institutional Vulnerability 159
Appendix 7.1: Investigation of Computer Fraud 163
Appendix 7.2: Computer Crime 163
Appendix 7.3: The Internet and the World Wide Web 166
Computer Forensics 167

8 Criminal Investigation 175

The Investigative Function 175
Role of the Criminal Investigator 176
Reasons for Investigating Crime 179
Limitations on Solving Cases 180

Investigative Theory and Methods 180
Types of Evidence 181
Uses of Evidence 181
Development of a Set of Suspects 182
Methods of Investigation 182
Phases of the Investigation 184
Rules of Evidence 188
Role of the Police 194
Government Agencies 196
Nuts and Bolts 196
Conducting a Criminal Investigation 197
Investigator's Pretrial Responsibility 197
Case Studies 206
Component Method™ of Criminal Defense Investigation 212
Suggested Reading 214
Appendix 8.1: The Grand Jury 214

9 Death Investigation 219

DEAN A. BEERS, CLI

An Overview of Death Investigation 219
What Is Death? 220
Medicolegal Death Investigations in Criminal Cases 222
The Investigative Protocol 223
What Is Death Investigation? 224
Are All Deaths Autopsied, or What Determines an Autopsy? 225
Key Concepts to Review and Analyze 227
History of Decedent 233
Forensic Autopsy 235
Determine the Cause and Manner of Death 241
In Conclusion 245

10 Terrorism Investigations 247

DOUGLAS K. HAAS

Terrorism Defined 247
Types of Terrorism 248
Government Approach to Terrorism 249
Government Tactics 251
Entrapment 251
Criminal Activity by Terrorist 252
Your Client 254
Suggested Reading 254
Case Study: Terrorism Investigation 255

11 Insurance and Arson Investigation 263

Insurance 263
Risk 264
Probability 264
Ideal Requirements for Insurability 265
Insurance Contracts 266
Negligence 269
Insurance Adjusting 270
Types of Insurance 271
Government Regulation of Insurance 280
Insurance Fraud 284
Fire and Arson Investigation 287
Liability Claims Investigation 294
Appendix 11.1: Sample Investigative Report 295
Appendix 11.2: Sample Vehicle Fire Report 299
Appendix 11.3: Car Theft, Past, Present and the Future 302
Appendix 11.4: Car Insurance Scam 305

12 Domestic Investigations 311

Appendix 12.1: Sample Activity Report 314
Appendix 12.2: Indicators of Online Marital Infidelity 316

13 Due Diligence and Background Investigations 319

Due Diligence Investigations 319
Scope of Investigations 326
Content of Investigations 327
Legal Constraints 329
Preemployment Screening 331

14 Locates and Skip Tracing 333

The Basics of Skip Tracing 333
Relevant Federal and State Statutes 333
Beginning the Process 334
Skip Tracing Resources 335
Searching for Financial and Business Information 339
Searching for Legal Information 339
Search Engines 340
Other Internet Sites 344
Government Records 345
Appendix 14.1: IRB—Custom Comprehensive Report (Sample) 349
Appendix 14.2: Sample Forms 351

15 Surveillance 361

General Rules 361
Presurveillance 361
Foot Surveillance 362
Automobile Surveillance 362
Stakeouts 364
Tactics 365
Surveillance Equipment 366
Technical Surveillance 367
Practical Considerations 368
Procedures for Interception of Wire or Oral Communications 369
Appendix 15.1: Notes on Surveillance 369
Appendix 15.2: Glossary and Sample Logs 413
Glossary 413

16 Service of Process 417

Types of Service 417
Proof of Service 418
Pitfalls to Avoid 418
Service of Subpoenas for Witnesses in Federal Courts 418
Appendix 16.1: Florida Statutes Governing Service of Process 422

17 Testifying in Court 439

The Investigator Pretrial 439
The Investigator during Trial 439
Preparation of Witnesses by Investigator 440
Preparation of Evidence 441
The Investigator as a Witness 441
Trial Tactics Used by Attorneys 444
Testifying in Court for Law Enforcement Officers 445
Expert Witnesses 451
Tips for Testifying in Court 452
Your Rights as a Witness 455
Types of Evidence 457
Testifying as a Witness or Victim, or an Expert Witness 458

18 Ethics 463

Confidentiality and Privacy 464
Truth 464
Keep Informed 465

Promote Education and Advocacy 465
Business Conduct 465
Avoid Conflicts of Interest 466
Fair Representation to Clients 466
Treatment of Competitors 466
Legal Issues 467
Render Services That Match Your Qualifications 467
Reporting 468
Compensation 468
Advertising 468
Client Relations 469
Testimony 469
Equal Rights 469
Appendix 18.1: U.S. Association of Professional Investigators (USAPI) Code of Ethics 470
Appendix 18.2: Ethics 470
Appendix 18.3: Investigative Ethics 471
Appendix 18.4: Summary of the Rules of Professional Conduct 472

19 Finding a Niche 477

How to Find Your Niche 479
Double-Check Your Choices 481
Niche Markets in the Investigative Industry 481

20 Getting Licensed 483

21 Operating a Professional Investigative Agency 485

Choosing a Name 485
Form of Operation 485
Location 486
Pricing 487
Bookkeeping 487
Business Problems 488
Licenses and Permits 489
Taxes 489
Appendix 21.1: Tips for Operating Your Agency 502
Appendix 21.2: The Paperless Office 503
Appendix 21.3: Managing and Marketing Your Investigative Practice: An Interactive Discussion 505
Appendix 21.4: Case File Management 507
Appendix 21.5: "PI" Should Also Mean "Professional Image" 509

Appendix 21.6: Three Ways to Raise Prices without Losing Customers 514

22 Professional Associations 517

National Associations 517
Additional Specialty Associations of Interest 525
International Associations 525
State Associations 525
Appendix 22.1: Recommended Associations 528

Index 531

Preface

This book is designed for individuals studying to become investigators, as well as investigators of all types and with all levels of experience. I am pleased to share what my research and experience have taught me in 40 years as an investigator. I do not claim to have all the answers, because there is something new to be learned about investigations and people every day. From my perspective, this is one of the most attractive features of this career. This book is primarily for use in the academic realm for the many private and community colleges offering classes in investigation, and as a perspective that may be useful to professional investigators in terms of evaluating their approach to working cases. It is not meant to be a definitive thesis on how all investigations should be performed.

Most of my research was performed while I was a college teacher at a small private junior college in Fort Lauderdale, Florida, and during my 30-plus years as an investigator. Much has been borrowed from a wide variety of academic and professional sources over the years. I hope that the information will be useful to both students and professionals in the field of professional investigation.

I have turned to my friends and colleagues in the investigative community to contribute to this third edition and to bring expertise that is far superior to mine own in their individual fields.

Mark J. Murnan, CCDI, CFE, who contributed the "Eating the Elephant" article in Chapter 6, is a board-certified criminal defense investigator, a certified fraud examiner, a licensed private investigator, and president of Complete Legal Investigations, Inc. A former staff investigator for the Federal Public Defender, Southern District of Florida, Murnan has over 25 years' investigative experience in both public and private sectors, handling a complete range of criminal and civil cases, including white-collar fraud, first-degree murder, and allegations of sexual abuse and molestation. He has assisted counsel for adults and juveniles in both state and federal courts. He is an advisory board member and a certified instructor for the Criminal Defense Investigation Training Counsel and first vice president for the Florida Association of Licensed Investigators. He has offices in Palm Beach Gardens, Florida.

Dean Beers, CLI, wrote Chapter 9 on cause of death investigations, his area of specialty, to help those of you involved in homicide and other death-related investigations. I think that you will find his submission invaluable. I highly recommend that those of you who do legal investigation purchase his book *Practical Methods for Legal Investigations* (CRC Press, Boca Raton, Florida, 2011). He also wrote *Professional Locate Investigations* (Lulu Press, Raleigh, NC, 2006). Dean is a Certified Legal Investigator and Certified Criminal Defense Investigator, and expert in criminal defense homicide and civil equivocal death investigations. He is certified in Medicolegal Death Investigation and served as a forensic autopsy assistant. He has lectured and authored multiple articles and peer-reviewed white papers and provided expert testimony on private investigator protocols. Beers is the board chairman of the Professional Private Investigators Association of Colorado; Region 6 CLI Representative of the National Association of Legal Investigators (NALI), and has a column called Forensic Focus in *The Legal Investigator*, the trade magazine of NALI; is Region 5A Director of the National Council of Investigation and Security Services, faculty advisor for Criminal Defense Investigator Training Council; affiliate consultant member of the National Association of Medical Examiners, and holds additional memberships in the World Association of Detectives, International Association for Identification, and Mensa USA. Dean and his wife Karen, also a legal investigator and agency partner, developed "Death Investigation for Private Investigators," an online continuing education course for PIEducation.com and available at www.MedicolegalDeathInvestigations.com.

Doug Haas submitted Chapter 10 on terrorism investigation. Haas enjoyed a 29-year career as a law enforcement professional. He retired as a captain of detectives from the Fort Lauderdale Police Department, Florida. During his tenure with the Fort Lauderdale Police Department he served in various investigative and administrative positions. He was a homicide detective for several years, supervisor of a surveillance team, and intelligence supervisor. For 10 years he was the director of a federal, state, and local organized crime task force specializing in identifying, arresting, and prosecuting organized crime groups operating or having impact on the South Florida area. He then was offered a position with the Broward County Sheriff's Office as a lieutenant colonel/director of the Department of Organized Crime. Haas was a board member of an international organization of law enforcement executives dedicated to sharing intelligence and methods of operations concerning organized crime and terrorism. He has expertise in the areas of organized crime enforcement, terrorism, intelligence programs, interviewing techniques, and police procedures. Haas has maintained his many law enforcement contacts through lectures on the above topics as well as his activities as a consultant on security and investigative matters. He is an on-air personality and terrorism consultant for WSVN news in South Florida and Boston, Massachusetts. He has appeared on *20/20*, *60 Minutes*, and *NBC News*. In 1996, following his retirement from law enforcement, he joined McMahon & Associates Detective Division, where he was the chief investigator. He subsequently worked as an in-house investigator for law firms in Miami and Broward County.

Richard Harris has contributed to Chapter 11 on insurance and arson investigation. Rich was a fire chief in Michigan. Since he retired he has worked in the fire investigation field for the past 20 years, primarily as the best fire investigator I have ever seen, until health problems led to his inability to continue. I am indebted to him for his work over the many years and his continued contributions to my agency.

JP Merlano, who has been my go-to surveillance guy for many years, edited and added his wealth of knowledge for the Appendix in Chapter 15, based upon his many years of working these types of cases. JP does all of my surveillances when he is available, because he is the best that I have seen in 21-plus years of running my investigative agency. He owns and operates WildCard Investigations, Inc., based in Miami, Florida. He has been observing people from a distance and at close proximity for over 20 years and has worked over 3000 surveillance assignments. His philosophy is simple: "You are only as good as your last case." He is considered to be the leading authority in the surveillance realm. JP has also worked surveillance assignments for the Office of Inspector General in Washington, DC, and has testified as a factual witness in many cases. His agency has supported clients in areas such as defense of insurance carriers, self-insured's, third-party administrators, and encompassing both civil and criminal related matters.

Kitty Hailey, CLI, contributed Appendix 18.4 to Chapter 18, on ethics. Anyone interested in working as a professional investigator should purchase her book *Code of Professional Conduct* 2nd Ed. (Lawyers & Judges Publishing Co., Inc., Tucson, AZ, 2006) as well as *The Professional Investigator* (Writers Club Press, Bloomington, Indiana, 2002). Both books should be required references on the bookshelves of every professional investigator.

Longtime NALI (National Association of Legal Investigators) friend John Lajoie, CLI, contributed to Chapter 21, on operating a professional investigative agency, with the PowerPoint® presentation he offered at the 2011 FALI (Florida Association of Licensed Investigators) annual conference.

Paul Purcell contributed two sections to Chapter 21. He is an Atlanta-based professional investigator, specializing in security analysis and preparedness counseling, and is the vice president and license holder for the agency InfoQuest, and author of the Private Investigation Case Management System, "The Case File."

Acknowledgments

I would like to thank all of the professional investigators who helped me begin my career as an investigator, especially Bill Courtney, Kerry Farney, Kitty Hailey, Herb Simon, John Lajoie, Brian McGuinness, Bill Vincent, Jean Mignolet, Rene Champagne, as well as those involved with me in the formation of the Florida Association of Licensed Investigators and my friends and associates in the National Association of Legal Investigators. I also thank all of my students from 1990 to 2000, who have been the source of inspiration for my writing, and for whom I hope this book will be the culmination of all the areas of learning from their City College careers.

I thank my friends, clients, and associates who have been with me for many years, including Charlie Mangiaracina; Dan Christensen; Richard Harris; Doug Haas; Glenn and Bev Horowitz; Jack Toal; Rich Rubin; Mark Silverberg; Jim Mintz; Marc Fader; Terry Lenzner; Jeff Nason; Andrew Froman; Jeff Jacobs; Albert Levin; Allen S. Kaufman; Bruce Gertsman; Tom Sterner; Carlton Joyce; David Vine; Danny Waxler; JP Merlano; Tom Brooks, CLI; Reggie Montgomery, CLI; Michelle and Richard Weddle; and all of my past and present interns and other employees and investigator subcontractors. I would also like to thank my friends at the S2 Institute, which conducts online training of investigative courses. I am happy to be their primary instructor for the investigative classes. I wish to acknowledge and thank my close friend, and Irish brother, Tim (Tango) O'Rourke, and other S2 friends K.C. Pullen and Craig Gundry.

Finally, to my family, without whom I would be lost: Kelly, for her independence, loyalty to her friends and family, and dedication to her career; Tara, mother of my beautiful granddaughters, Elle, Caitlin, and Cameron, for her encouragement, her spirit and integrity, and her love and support; Conor, who has become a man and is discovering his own world; Joseph Patrick, my handsome and talented 12-year-old son; and my gorgeous wife, Fran, for her constant encouragement, support, and love.

Acknowledgments

[illegible]

The Author

Rory McMahon has been an "investigator" of some sort for most of his adult life. In 1973 as a probation officer in Westchester County, New York, he investigated and supervised persons convicted of state crimes. In 1978 he was appointed a federal probation officer in the Southern District of New York, which comprises New York City and the surrounding area, investigating and supervising persons convicted of federal crimes. He transferred to the Southern District of Florida in 1982, where he conducted pre-sentence investigations on persons convicted of federal crimes in Miami, and subsequently supervised convicted career criminals—primarily organized crime members, major narcotics traffickers, and white-collar offenders—as a member of the Special Offender Unit in Fort Lauderdale.

McMahon left government service in 1990 to become a private investigator, working a wide variety of investigations. In 1991 he opened a successful investigative agency based in Fort Lauderdale, Florida. He still owns and operates this agency today. He specializes in both fraud and legal investigations, and does work throughout the United States. He has also conducted training seminars, one-day fraud seminars in various cities in the United States. He has written articles that appeared in *PI Magazine* and various professional association newsletters (National Association of Legal Investigators [NALI], Florida Association of Licensed Investigators [FALI], Texas Association of Licensed Investigators [TALI], Professional Private Investigators Association of Colorado [PPIAC]) and journals throughout the world.

McMahon became a Certified Legal Investigator (CLI) in 1997, specializing primarily in legal investigations. In 1999 he became a Florida Certified Investigator (FCI). He currently serves as the second vice president of the Florida Association of Private Investigators (FALI). In 2009 he was selected FCI of the year. In 2000, he became a Certified Criminal

Defense Investigator, and in 2005 he became a Certified Fraud Examiner. Based upon his professional, academic, and personal experiences, he has written this book.

Introduction

1

Since the trial of O.J. Simpson, the business of professional investigation has gained a new level of respect among both the legal community and the public at large. The success of O.J.'s "Dream Team" was largely a result of the brilliant work of the defense investigators. The Dream Team found the witness who exposed Mark Fuhrman's racism. They fashioned successful responses to everything that the prosecution witnesses testified about.

From there we entered into the era of corporate fraud that has been unparalleled in history—Enron, Tyco, and HealthSouth have became synonymous with greed that would have embarrassed even Gordon Gecko (Michael Douglas in the movie *Wall Street*—"Greed is good"). From there, we moved into the era of the Ponzi schemers—Bernie Madoff, Scott Rothstein—and the era of mortgage fraud; Medicare/Medicaid fraud; and the "Pill Mills," unabashed sales of pain pills, such as oxycodone, to anyone with a pulse. Government allegedly entered a new era of accountability and oversight of corporate conduct in the banking sector and the accounting industry. All of this has been a great source of increased work for legal, fraud, and professional investigators.

The recession housing foreclosures, and financial setbacks caused by Wall Street, as well as the continuing greed of corporate executives coupled with the inability of politicians on all levels to come together to solve these problems does not bode well for the short term. However, Americans have always come together when times are bleakest. We have overcome the world-changing events of September 11, 2001, and I am confident that we will rise from the economic ashes in 2012; however, the need for professional investigators has never been greater.

Job Outlook

According to the *Occupational Outlook Handbook* published by the U.S. Bureau of Labor Statistics, employment of private detectives and professional investigators is expected to grow much faster than the average for all occupations through the year 2014. Demand for investigators is expected to be generated by fear of crime, increased litigation, and the need to protect confidential information and property. The proliferation of criminal activity on the Internet, such as identity theft, spamming, e-mail harassment, and illegal downloading of copyrighted materials, will increase the demand for investigators. Employee background checks will become standard for an increased number of jobs. Growing financial activity worldwide will increase the demand for investigators to control internal and external financial losses and to monitor competitors and prevent industrial spying. As crime continues to increase, more firms will hire or contract for the services of private detectives. Additionally, professional investigators will be needed to meet the need for information associated with criminal defense and litigation for companies and individuals.

According to a National Employment Matrix issued in 2011, total employment in the industry is expected to rise by 22 percent from 44.5 per thousand to 55.5 per thousand by 2018.

Earnings

Earnings of professional investigators vary greatly depending on employer, specialty, and the geographic area in which they work. According to studies conducted in May 2004, professional investigators averaged about $24,080 to $43,260 per year, earning an estimated $20,000 per year to start, with experienced investigators earning more than $58,000. Entry-level corporate investigators earn $40,000 to $45,000, with experienced corporate investigators earning $50,000 to $55,000. However, a successful self-employed PI can earn $100,000 and more.

Investigators bill their clients $50 to $350 per hour to conduct investigations. Most investigators, except those working for law firms and corporations, do not receive paid vacation or sick days, health or life insurance, retirement packages, or other benefits. Investigators are reimbursed for expenses and receive pay for mileage.

In my experience in South Florida, intern investigators earn from $15 to $35 per hour. Investigators with 2 or more years' experience earn from $35 to $75 per hour.

The potential earnings for those entering the field are unlimited. There has never been a greater need for these services than right now. Investigators are finally receiving the professional recognition that they deserve. Business is good, and the prospects for the future are incredible!

Skills Needed to Become a Successful Investigator

2

All investigations, regardless of type or purpose, depend on the gathering of factual information. Gathering factual information is the main purpose of any investigation, without which no case would be solved, no stolen property recovered, and no missing person located. Factual information in a concise written report is the product that we sell to our client.

Today's professional investigator must learn to think of him- or herself as a highly sophisticated camera with the lens always open, recording and observing everything. Regardless of the case, the investigator wants answers to the questions "who," "what," "when," "where," "how," and "why." The professional investigator is often the last hope for many people.

Three Methods That Investigators Use to Obtain Information

- Researching public records
- Interviewing individuals with relevant information
- Conducting surveillance of individuals to learn about their behavior

Investigators must use one, two, or all three of these methods in order to obtain the information needed by the client. To excel as an investigator, one must know how to do all three very well.

What Is an Investigator?

An investigator is a professional researcher who uses observation, inquiry, examination, and experimentation to obtain evidence and factual information upon which sound decisions can be made. In order to achieve success as an investigator, certain basic guidelines must be observed:

- Ask many questions when seeking information. Often, this means repeating questions in order to uncover discrepancies and following up on initial questions with more detailed ones. You can never gather too much information. It is easy to eliminate nonessential information later on.
- Recognize that suspects, criminals, and other subjects of investigation come from all walks of life and are represented by all races, both sexes, and an endless variety of lifestyles.
- When investigating the crime scene, do not commit yourself to the guilt or innocence of anyone at the scene whom you may question. Remember, your purpose is to gather facts; judgments will come later.
- Do not be overconfident. Be certain that you have gathered all the information. Before you conclude the investigation, ask yourself, "Is there more information I should attempt to obtain? Have I overlooked anything that could make a difference in the outcome of the investigation?"
- Do not jump to conclusions.
- Never take things for granted—make no assumptions about how much information is needed before you begin searching. False assumptions often lead to the loss of valuable information and evidence.
- Work with evidence you find at the scene. Examine all evidence carefully—pieces of paper, documents, tools, fragments of cloth, or personal items belonging to a possible suspect or other person involved in the incident that you are investigating. Any physical evidence can provide an important investigative lead.
- Develop informants and sources of information before you need them. No investigator can get along without sources, because they can provide shortcuts to many investigative problems.

Attributes of a Successful Investigator

The following attributes are the special qualities that will help you achieve success. And, in my humble opinion, if you possess the skills listed, not only will you be successful as an investigator, but more importantly, you will be successful as a human being.

Suspicion

Be cautious of obvious things and wary of persons who are quick to provide alibis and identification. Demand verification whenever possible.

Curiosity

Develop your own curiosity and follow up on it. Have the desire to learn the truth. An inquisitive mind is essential to the investigator.

Observation

Your five senses are important tools of the trade. It may be important for you to remember unusual things about an individual (i.e., his or her manner and posture or the way he or she dresses). Learn to observe details.

Memory

The ability to accurately recall the facts and events or the physical characteristics of a suspect is a valuable skill.

An Unbiased and Unprejudiced Mind

Bias and prejudice will result in a poor investigation, unfairness to suspects, and clouding of facts that need to be uncovered objectively. Do not let personal likes or dislikes interfere with investigations.

Ability to Play a Role

This skill is especially important for private investigators who work alone most of the time. Using his or her own identity could expose the investigator to recognition and danger. The ability to assume convincing identities is particularly valuable in surveillance, undercover activities, and a variety of confidential inquiries.

Persistence and Capacity for Hard Work

Many times, you will find yourself working late into the night to follow up a promising lead or question a particularly valuable witness.

Resourcefulness

An investigator must be able to adapt to all types of stressful situations that may demand technical or other skills.

Ability to Obtain the Cooperation of Others

In the course of your work, you will make many contacts. Some will be clients, some will be witnesses, some will be suspects, and some will be well-meaning citizens who can provide information. It is essential that you obtain cooperation from as many people as possible in order to secure the vital facts and information that you will need to conclude an investigation. You will need patience, courtesy, tact, and understanding. A suspect or witness who has been intimidated, frightened, or angered by an impatient investigator is of no value.

Interest in Your Work and Pride of Accomplishment

True success in any profession is based on sincere interest and pride in a job well done. The knowledge that your efforts can bring a criminal to justice, locate a missing loved one, or save a business large sums of money can bring you immense satisfaction.

Street Sense

You should have an intuitive understanding of the way the world works and how people move through it. This can be developed and refined. The more time you spend on the street and the more attention you pay to detail, the sharper your street sense will become. This can be learned and honed as you work in the investigative field.

Good Listening Skills

You need to be a good listener in order to effectively communicate. To be a good interviewer, you must be able to understand the person you are questioning. If you do not have good listening skills, you will never be an effective interviewer. Therefore, you will not be a successful legal or corporate investigator.

Ability to Put People at Ease

In order to convince people to submit to interviews, you need to be able to "schmooze," which means to make people feel comfortable talking to you. This is a necessary skill to have in order to conduct successful interviews.

Ability to Speak at the Level of the Audience

There is nothing that turns a person off quicker than someone speaking down to him or her or using language that is difficult to understand. You must be able to speak to anyone from a high school dropout to a professional doctor in language that is appropriate and understandable.

Understanding of Body Language

To know if a person is truthful in an interview situation, you must be able to read body language. As a legal investigator, you may interview a potential witness for 30 minutes. At the end of that time, you must gauge that person's honesty and credibility as a potential witness.

Good Manners

There is no excuse for rude behavior—at any time!

Flexibility

You must have the ability to adapt to whatever situation is presented.

Intuitive Understanding of Human Nature

People are people regardless of the circumstances you may be investigating. As investigators, we see people—our clients, subjects, and suspects—often at times of extreme emotional distress.

Self-Confidence

You need to believe in your ability to handle any situation.

Foundations of Investigation

3

Professional investigation combines the skills of both science and art. Given the proper knowledge, tools, and money to operate, few cases exist that cannot be solved if the investigator devotes the time and energy necessary to complete the assignment.

Professional investigators perform the following activities:

- Criminal and civil investigations
- Matrimonial or domestic relations investigations
- Negligence investigations
- Background and due diligence investigations
- Security
- Expert witness
- Electronic countermeasures—also called communication security sweeps (i.e., debugging)
- Corporate investigation
- Shopping services
- Skip tracing
- "Day in the life" productions
- Undercover investigation
- Process service

Types of Investigation

There are several types of investigation that will become part of your routine as an investigator.

Criminal Investigations

Professional investigators work for either the victim or the defendant or his attorney in criminal proceedings.

Serious crimes that may lead to arrest and conviction of a subject are the source of cases for the legal/criminal investigator. Burglary, theft, homicide, fraud, auto accidents, arson, kidnapping, and so on, are examples of activities for which violations of laws have taken place, and you may be called to investigate. These cases typically fall into two categories:

1. Felonies—serious crimes that may involve punishment by death or imprisonment in state or federal prison in excess of 1 year.
2. Misdemeanors—lesser crimes usually punishable by a fine or imprisonment, not to exceed 1 year, in a city or county jail.

Civil Investigations

Civil investigations pertain to anything involving lawsuits in which questions of money or property must be settled. Violations of the law are usually not involved. Divorce, bankruptcy, personal injury, negligence cases, and lawsuits of various types are examples of civil matters that may require investigation.

Civil Actions

An attorney or client may hire an investigator to prove either one of the parties to the suit is liable. Two terms an investigator must know are *plaintiff* and *defendant*.

1. The plaintiff is the party who brings a legal action—one who accuses another person of wrongdoing.
2. The defendant is the accused—the one who must defend him- or herself against charges brought by the plaintiff. While he or she may be accused of wrongdoing, the defendant is assumed innocent until proven guilty by the plaintiff and the plaintiff's attorney.

Negligence Investigations

This type of investigation is conducted either for the plaintiff's attorney to prove liability or for the defendant's company or business to prove the absence of liability or absence of a permanent serious injury. This can be accomplished through the use of surveillance (often video or photo), locating and interviewing witnesses, or trying to establish that a preexisting condition caused or was aggravated by the injury or that the defendant was at fault. A modest investigative fee often saves a client from having to pay a large monetary award.

Corporate Investigations

An investigator may monitor what is going on in a business, investigate fraud within or outside the company, and provide diligence investigations or preemployment screening.

General Investigations

This category includes a wide variety of investigative activities: location of witnesses and missing persons, serving of legal process, skip tracing, checks on employee dishonesty and fraud, security surveys, bodyguard work, surveillances, and so forth.

Personnel and Background Checks

This type of investigation is ordered by businesses and is undertaken in order to determine whether the character, history, financial status, and credentials of an individual make him or her a suitable candidate for a job, a position of public trust, a large loan, credit, and so on. Insurance companies investigate applicants; banks check on individuals applying for loans and also check the applicant's credit rating.

Security

Many private investigative firms offer a range of security services, including the following:

- Security surveys—to determine vulnerability and to suggest corrective measures against theft
- Celebrity protection
- Event protection or security (i.e., concerts)

Assignments Performed by a Professional Investigator

Insurance Claims/Insurance Fraud

This is the largest and most complex category and includes inflated claims on vehicular accidents, phony claims by individuals and organized fraud rings, hit and run (multicar) with phantom vehicle liability, staged accidents, phony and exaggerated personal injury claims, fraudulent income (disability claims), and paid or untruthful witnesses.

Witness Location

This involves researching public records (often the beginning of any investigation) and includes use of the following:

- Telephone books, records, and listings
- Cross-reference books

- Neighborhood and employment investigations
- Postal records Freedom of Information Act (FOIA)
- Public records, including search of microfiche; voter registration lists; birth, death, and marriage records; real property records; fictitious business files; municipal, county, state, and federal civil court records; state and federal criminal records; corporate and partnership filings; Department of Motor Vehicle (DMV) records; church, medical, and dental records; credit history records; union records; state licensing boards; and law enforcement agencies
- Trash (dumpster diving)—it is legal to take the trash once it is put out on the street for pickup, and this can be a very good source of information

Interviews and Statements

Witness, plaintiff, and defendant interviews are conducted, and statements and declarations are taken.

Service of Legal Process

Service of summons and complaint, service for civil subpoena for deposition, service for civil subpoena duces tecum, and service for civil subpoena for trial testimony are some of the assignments of investigators.

Malpractice Defense

Investigations are conducted for medical, dental, and legal malpractice cases.

Bank Fraud

Investigations are conducted of all aspects of bank fraud cases.

Employment Investigations

Pre-employment screening, business partner thefts and fraud, employee theft, and business and industrial espionage are investigated.

Worker's Compensation Claims

Investigations include neighborhood and employment canvas, medical background and previous claims history, and surveillance and photography/videotaping.

Private Family Investigations

Investigations are conducted involving theft and embezzlement of family funds, theft and embezzlement of trust and estates, and the location of missing persons and runaways.

Homicide, Suicide, and Missing Persons Investigations

Death investigations are conducted, including apparent death that may be staged for the collection of life insurance benefits.

Drug Investigations

Investigations are conducted of the transportation, purchase, and sale of illegal drugs using business and employment channels.

Reconstruction of Accidents; Vehicular and Personal Injury

Investigations are conducted of claims related to motor vehicle accidents and personal injuries claims.

Trademark and Patent Infringements

Investigations of protection of trademarks and patents are conducted.

Slip-and-Fall Accident Claims

Investigations are conducted of circumstances surrounding slip-and-fall accidents and resulting disability claims.

Domestic, Child Custody, or Divorce Cases

Surveillance is performed on cheating spouses and unfit parents. In cases of domestic abuse, interviews are conducted. In hidden asset cases, investigation is conducted to check finances.

Shopping Services

These services include monitoring employees in stores to make sure that all the sales money is put in the register and conducting drug screens on prospective employees. Also, investigators can act as spotters in bars who monitor the restaurants/bars for theft by employees, and they can provide constructive assessment of employee conduct.

Skip Tracing

Everyone is looking for someone. Skip tracing is the art of locating persons who don't want to be found.

"Day in the Life" Productions

"Day in the life" productions are used in bodily injury or malpractice claims where the plaintiff claims total or serious disability. Photos or videos of a day or a week of activity often convince the plaintiff to abandon the suit or at least settle for a substantially smaller award.

Undercover Investigations

Undercover investigations usually involve a business that tries to identify problems by hiring investigators to pose as employees.

Sources of Information

Your effectiveness as an investigator will depend largely on your ability to obtain information from the sources listed below.

Physical Evidence

Physical evidence includes identifiable objects and traces found at the crime or accident scene, including fingerprints, clothing and personal effects, photographs, tire marks, notebooks, identification cards, credit cards, weapons, tools, and so forth. The types, nature, and importance of physical evidence vary with each case.

Scientific Examinations

This type of evidence may be provided by laboratories maintained by law enforcement agencies, private investigative agencies, universities, corporations, and medical centers. Any type of physical evidence from blood samples to metal scrapings can be analyzed. These can be useful sources of information to an investigator.

Records and Documents

A great deal of information concerning a suspect, missing person, or wanted person can be found in records and documents of government and private agencies. In order to use these sources effectively, the investigator must know the type of information that a particular agency provides and how to obtain that information. In some states, information is available under the public records law (see FS 119 in the State of Florida). Only active criminal record information is exempt. Law enforcement records would, in most instances, be unavailable, except following a request for discovery information once a defendant has been arrested and charged with a crime. Two simple rules will help you in your search for information:

1. Take the time to learn the sources in your locality, and strive to develop new ones. Browse through listings under city, county, state, and federal governments in your telephone directory. Become familiar with titles and functions of the various agencies listed. Visit a public library, and become familiar with the various documents, references, and directories available. Help from a cooperative librarian can cut your search time substantially.
2. Develop sources of information before you need them. Remember, nobody but the court can force any person to produce records or divulge information except for public records. A smart investigator develops his sources carefully so that he can obtain information on a personal basis when he needs it.

Information from People

Despite all databanks, libraries, volumes of documents, and reports available today, people remain our primary sources of information. Cab drivers, reporters, clerical personnel, court employees, as well as specialists and highly placed professionals can provide information leading to the successful conclusion of a case. The experienced investigator understands the importance of people as resources and devotes a great deal of time to maintaining existing contacts and making new ones. As sources of information, people fall into two general categories: informants and clients.

Informants

Investigators classify their informants according to the type of information they are seeking. Informants are classified as victims, witnesses, or suspects, and are questioned for information concerning a specific event. Those classified as personal references are used to gather information in personnel investigations. Those making up still another group, experts or specialists, are able to provide specific technical information about their fields of expertise. Investigators sometimes find it necessary to use paid informants who have connections with the underworld to gather information about criminal activities.

Personal References Whenever an investigator is assigned to a personnel investigation, he will be interviewing personal references supplied by the subject. Naturally, the subject will select people who will give him or her good reviews. Such people generally tend to provide good news only. The investigator who does a thorough job will search for the neutral person, the one who will provide balanced information that points out the subject's weaknesses as well as his strengths. The best sources for such balanced information are professional people and former employers.

Experts Anyone with special knowledge because of a profession or hobby is a potential expert. Biologists, psychologists, teachers, doctors, historians, and reformed criminals all qualify as experts. Success in getting information from such sources depends on the investigator. Specialists are usually people whose knowledge is in great demand. The investigator should do his homework before interviewing the expert. First, the investigator should outline the information needed and write out some important questions. The investigator should come prepared with a notepad and a tape recorder. He should also acquire some knowledge of the subject so that he can talk intelligently to the source. Finally, he should be brief and to the point.

Paid Informants These people can be useful in gathering first-hand information on underworld activities: gambling, prostitution, drug offenses, and organized crime. Information provided by professional informants has frequently been instrumental in solving crimes that otherwise would have remained unsolved. Paid informants are a dangerous source of information and are often misused. They are overly relied on as sources of information by law enforcement. Remember, credibility is a major factor in all investigations. Paid informants' credibility must be proven before they can be relied upon as witnesses. If you use paid informants, you must take precautions to protect yourself and to safeguard your source. First, determine the informant's motive. Is the informant talking because he or she wants money or a reward? Is the informant's motive revenge against someone? Is he or she looking for some personal favor from you? Experienced investigators have learned that the informant who is primarily interested in money is the most reliable and can be used repeatedly.

After determining the informant's motive, you should plan on meeting privately with your informant. You should avoid close association in public. Avoid calling paid informants by slang terms such as rat, stoolie, squealer, or snitch.

Finally, protect your informant from possible danger. Never reveal the informant's identity or use any information that he or she gives you to his or her disadvantage. Offer privacy and protection, as well as money, in exchange for information.

Demeanor of the Investigator

Your success in obtaining information from a source will depend largely on your approach. Here are a few tips:

- Prepare for the interview by outlining the questions you want answered or the information you hope to obtain.
- Investigate the source, and verify his or her identity and stability.
- Make an appointment if your source is a busy person and you need more information than you can obtain in a phone call.
- If you must go through a secretary, it is very important not to divulge the nature of your business to the secretary.
- Identify yourself only to your source.
- Do not tell your informant too much. Never reveal any suspicions or personal feelings that you have about the case, because your attitude may slant the informant's answers.
- Conduct your business efficiently and politely.

Above all, remember that no one is required to give you information. Your own patience, tact, and determination will enable you to be successful in using people as sources.

Records and Documents as Investigative Sources of Information

Public Library

For the investigator, the public library has a great deal of valuable information, primarily in the form of directories. With the exception of city telephone directories, they are frequently overlooked. These sources are primarily professional membership directories and various employments listed by professional associations. The following is a brief list:

- The *American Medical Association Directory of Physicians* is issued by the American Medical Association (AMA). This provides names and addresses of all presidents and secretaries of all the county medical associations listed. Listings of hospitals, sanitariums, related institutions, and names of doctors by states and cities are provided.
- Directories of newspapers and periodicals provide a guide to newspapers and periodicals printed in the United States and its possessions. These directories also provide descriptions of states, cities, and towns in which they are published. This source is useful for interrogations of out-of-town suspects.
- *Lloyd's Register* lists all seagoing merchant and passenger ships of the world and their owners. Similar publications are *Lloyd's Register*

of Yachts and *Lloyd's Register of American Yachts,* which provide names and descriptions of yachts, their classification, and names and addresses of the owners.

- *Marquis Who's Who®* gives autobiographies of prominent people (www.marquiswhoswho.com).
- The *Directory of Hotel and Lodging Companies* is available as a computer spreadsheet issued monthly from the American Hotel & Lodging Association or Smith Travel Research. It lists hotels and lodging companies in the United States, Canada, Mexico, and other countries (www.ahla.com).
- *Baird's Manual of American College Fraternities* lists men's and women's organizations, professional fraternities, honor societies, local fraternities more than 50 years old, and inactive fraternities and sororities (www.greekpages.com).
- National, state, city, and county guidebooks and directories are also helpful. Among the most useful are *Baedecker's Guides* (although they are now outdated and no longer published), tourist guidebooks of all foreign countries, and congressional directories that provide biographical sketches of senators and representatives, listings of officers of the House and Senate, judicial and executive department personnel, foreign and diplomatic consular offices in the United States, and other valuable information.

Telephone Directories

Current and past telephone directories may be checked for variations in the spelling of a subject's name and telephone listings of all persons with the same last name. In large cities, also check suburban and outlying directories.

Cross-Reference Directories

These books have three separate types of listings. There is an alpha section that lists each party name (like a phone book). If the name is found, it will also give the subject's name and phone number. Polk directories will also list an occupation. In the address section, you can look up a listing if all you have is an address. It will tell you who lives there and the phone number. The number section lists all phone numbers by prefix. Once a number is located, it will give the name and address of the person to whom the number is listed. You may also use this directory to locate neighbors or parties nearby when trying to locate someone. As a rule, these directories do not contain unlisted numbers, but there are numerous exceptions.

Local Newspapers and Magazines

The daily paper is backed by an enormous behind-the-scenes operation and is a potential goldmine for investigators. The circulation department has the names and addresses of subscribers and lists of professional subscription advertisers. The classified ad department keeps on file the names, addresses, and telephone numbers of classified advertisers and the dates of each ad. Change of address for subscribers is on record as well. The newspaper morgue maintains a cumulative file on every person whose name has appeared in the newspaper. The library maintains all back issues of papers, many of which are stored on microfilm.

Become acquainted with local magazines published in your area. They report in depth on activities of prominent citizens in the community. Make the acquaintance of editors and investigative reporters who work for these publications, because they will prove useful to you.

City and County Business Licenses and Permit Offices

These records contain the name, address, phone, owner, type of business, date filed, and expiration or renewal date on a license.

Local Police and Fire Departments

Local law enforcement may know the subject and may even run a check for you if you approach them correctly. The fire department might tell you if they have ever received a fire zoning violation.

Fictitious Filings (DBA)

These records are kept by owner's name and cross-referenced by the business name. They will give you the name and address of any business the subject is involved in. Also, the names and addresses of all registrants and the dates of filing are available. For a small fee, this information can be certified for use as a court document.

Bureau of Vital Statistics

Records are maintained on deaths, births, and marriages. In addition to parties' names, these records will also show addresses, relatives, and witnesses.

Court Records

A county criminal court retains records of traffic citations and all misdemeanor charges. A county civil court retains records of marriages, evictions, and all civil suits with a dollar amount usually under $10,000. The microfiche contains listings (alpha) of both plaintiffs and defendants. It will give you the date filed, case number, and nature of the action. The Florida Circuit Court is broken down into two categories: the circuit criminal that handles all felony cases and the circuit civil that handles all civil suits over $15,000, divorce cases, foreclosures, and probates.

U.S. federal courts are also separated into criminal and civil. They also contain the bankruptcy court. All courts retain files and records considered to be public records and available to the public. There may be records available to you from other government agencies (FBI, CIA, etc.). You must file a request under the Freedom of Information Act (FOIA). There are also agencies that will do research for you in Washington, DC, and Canada.

City Hall

Property Assessor's Office Maps of real property are on file, including dimensions, addresses, owners, taxable value of property, and improvements.

Street Department Maps of the city are kept on file, showing widths of streets, locations of conduits, drains, sewers, and utility lines. Also listed are current street numbers, abandoned streets, and right-of-ways.

Building Department This department issues building permits, maintaining applicants on file, addresses of construction sites, amount and cost of construction, and the names of builders. Blueprints and diagrams showing construction details are also available.

Fire Marshal and Sanitary Engineer These are the officials who conduct inspections on businesses to check for possible violations of code. They have the right to inspect all premises.

Health Department Birth and death certificates are kept on file, as well as the records and statistics on outbreaks of communicable diseases, including sexually transmitted diseases.

Sanitation Department This department has access to all premises. Investigators may accompany workers and search the contents of garbage (although you have to pay them something for this privilege).

City Attorney This individual usually operates the consumer fraud division, which maintains files of complaints made by citizens against businesses suspected of fraud (State Attorney for criminal charges).

County Records Most records in the courthouse are public and available to anyone. The trick is to know where records are kept and what information they provide.

County Recorder's Office This office maintains official index records. All instruments are required to be recorded—all papers pertaining to real estate transactions, marriage certificates, contracts (prenuptial), petitions for separation and divorce decrees (lots of information contained), notice of lien and attachment on real estate, certified copies of decrees and judgments of courts of record, official bonds, and, occasionally, birth and death records.

Also available in the County Recorder's office is the General Index to Official Records. It is cross-indexed as to plaintiffs and defendants, grantors and grantees. The General Index shows the date that the instrument was filed, the defendants and the plaintiffs, the type of instrument, and the book and page of official records where the instrument may be found.

A death certificate, for example, contains the following information:

- Name, address, sex, age, race, birthplace, and birth date of the decedent
- Place, date, and time of death
- How long decedent has been in community
- Hospital, if death occurred there
- Social security number
- Marital status, occupation, parents' names, including mother's maiden name
- Death informant's name and address
- Medical certificate, if under a doctor's care at time of death
- Coroner's certificate that includes autopsy data, cause of death, and disposal of the body

County Clerk's Office This office may be checked for naturalization records, marriage license applications, petitions for divorce, and criminal files:

- The Naturalization Records and Record Book provides the names of applicants for citizenship, port and date of entry, manner of arrival, declaration of intent, and miscellaneous information relating to the naturalization process.
- Marriage license applications provide pertinent information about applicants.
- Petitions for divorce include information on the grounds or charges, place and date of marriage, children, and community property.
- Criminal files provide information about the complaint, the arresting officer's report, a description of preliminary proceedings, and other pertinent information.

County Auditor This office lists all county employees, occupations, and rates of pay. Records of all fiscal business of the county are also available.

Property Assessor's Office This office maintains plats or maps of real property in the county, with dimensions, addresses of owners, taxable values, and legal descriptions. Files also include information on buyers and sellers of the property.

County Tax Collector Records of names and addresses of property owners and legal descriptions of property are kept, as well as records of the amount of taxes paid on real and personal property, and whether or not taxes are delinquent.

Registrar of Voters or Board of Elections The affidavits of registration that include some biographical information on registrants are kept on file here. They have a file that lists registered voters according to precincts, and they maintain a roster of voters. Listings are maintained on microfiche and include subject's name, address, telephone number, date of birth, date registered, and voter registration number. This information is free. Also on file are the nomination papers of candidates for public office.

Medical Examiner or Coroner's Office Information is available on all deceased persons and includes the name or description, date of inquest (if any), property found on the deceased, cause of death, and notes regarding disposition of the body.

State Regulatory Agencies as Sources of Information

Examination of a subject's business, profession, or past or present employment may lead an investigator to one or more of these sources. For example, in the state of Florida we have the following agencies.

Department of Motor Vehicles

Information regarding operator's licenses, verification of certificates of title, motor or serial numbers, license plate, and vehicle ownership can be obtained.

Health and Rehabilitative Services

Social service agencies and state unemployment offices maintain information concerning individuals receiving assistance from these agencies. This information may be obtained for legitimate investigative purposes.

Professional and Licensing Bureaus (Department of State)

These bureaus set professional and vocational standards for the state and issue licenses or certificates to individuals who qualify. Professional and vocational groups licensed by such agencies include doctors, dentists, social workers, real estate agents and brokers, funeral directors, cosmetologists, contractors, pest control specialists, dry cleaners, chiropractors, accountants, teachers, architects, attorneys, and private investigators.

Florida Department of Law Enforcement (FDLE)

The FDLE maintains criminal records on all individuals who have been arrested in the state of Florida. In other states, a state police agency keeps criminal records of individuals arrested in that state.

Florida Department of Financial Services

Investigates all white-collar and fraud crimes reported to state agencies.

Florida Division of Alcoholic Beverages and Tobacco (ABT)

This agency governs the issuance of licenses to establishments that sell alcohol, tobacco, or firearms.

Federal Sources of Information

Many agencies of the federal government do not open their files or release information on request. However, as an investigator, you may find it possible to get information from the following agencies.

U.S. Postal Service

The U.S. Postal Service will supply forwarding addresses. There are two methods by which to obtain change of address information. The first is to obtain a court order for the release of the information (e.g., when working a legal investigation). The second method (cheap and slow) of obtaining an address is to simply address an envelope to the last known address of the subject. Under your return address write, "Address Correction Requested." On the line below that, write "Do Not Forward." When the post office receives this envelope, they will not deliver it but will note the person's new address and return the envelope to you.

Most post offices can supply you with copies of applications on file for customers of postage meters, bulk-mail permits, and business reply permits. You can also obtain information concerning the holder of a P.O. box, provided it belongs to a business.

U.S. Department of Homeland Security

The Department of Homeland Security is responsible for assessing the nation's vulnerabilities. It takes the lead in evaluating vulnerabilities and coordinating with other federal, state, local, and private entities to ensure the most effective response. The collection, protection, evaluation, and dissemination of information to the American public, state and local governments, and the private sector are central to this task.

U.S. Immigration and Customs Enforcement (ICE)

Records are maintained of all immigrants and aliens. Passenger and crew lists of all foreign vessels using U.S. ports are also kept on file.

Departments of the Army, Navy, Marines, and Air Force

Records are kept of all persons who are or have ever been in military service.

U.S. Coast Guard

A listing is kept of all persons serving aboard U.S. merchant ships.

Drug Enforcement Administration (DEA)

Records are maintained of all licensed handlers of narcotics and other drugs (physicians, pharmacists, and so on).

Bureau of Alcohol, Tobacco, and Firearms (ATF)

The alcohol tax unit keeps records of violations relating to the manufacture, storage, and sale of alcoholic beverages. This agency also enforces the National Firearms Act.

Federal Communications Commission (FCC)

Records are maintained of licensed holders for all broadcast communications media.

Federal Bureau of Investigation (FBI)

The FBI primarily serves as a clearinghouse for criminal identification records. On file are the following:

- Criminal records and fingerprints
- The national stolen property index, including stolen government property
- The national fraudulent check index
- Nonresident information on criminal offenses and subversive activities

Social Security Administration (SSA)

The original social security applications are maintained, and names are listed (maiden or married for women), along with addresses, sex, race, and parents' names and addresses, at time of application. Current records on cardholders show present employer.

Federal Aviation Administration (FAA) (Oklahoma City)

Records of all licensed pilots, all aircraft, and aircraft parts are maintained here.

Private Organizations and Agencies

Resources in this category are limitless. Subjects under investigation do not abandon lifetime interests and associations. They frequently keep in touch with organizations that have always served them, and in so doing they leave behind various records. The following are examples of private sources that can be valuable to investigators.

Telephone Companies

Local telephone companies publish geographical directories that list subscribers according to street address in addition to the regular telephone directories. They also maintain records of long distance phone calls.

Public Utility Companies (Gas, Electricity, and Water)

Applications for service usually contain the basic background information. Customers are usually filed according to address, rather than by name. Files include complete service history, number of meters in service, place of last service, and the names of persons who have had service at that address previously.

Credit Reporting Agencies

Most individuals and practically all businesses have credit reporting associations that maintain credit ratings and files on them. Attorneys, wholesalers, retailers, physicians, and so on, are among the many groups represented. The Retailers Credit Association is a national credit reporting organization that maintains files on individuals. On record is basic biographical and financial information on all individuals who apply for credit. Information on the credit rating and financial stability of businesses and individuals can be obtained only for a sound reason, because such organizations must protect privacy.

Private Sources of Information

Insurance Reporting Agencies

Agencies serving insurance companies and underwriters gather information on policy holders. They have detailed records of bad risks in all types of insurance. Of particular value to investigators is the National Auto Theft Bureau. Maintained by auto insurance companies, this agency investigates abandoned and wrecked vehicles, wrecking yards, and junkyards. They also maintain files on professional auto thieves and theft rings and have a national teletype communications network.

Transportation Companies

Taxicabs, limousine services, auto rental companies, and so on, have very useful information that may include a complete record of a trip with time, location, destination, and stops en route recorded. Drivers from limousine services frequently make useful informants.

Private Investigative Organizations

Many detective agencies may be willing to sell information that they have compiled during the course of investigations.

Real Estate Agencies

Information can be provided on residents and former residents of property; former addresses of residents; business, social, and character references; and handwriting samples.

Hospitals

Records of patients, illnesses, operations, scars, wounds, injuries, and complications are kept. Such information is often useful in establishing descriptions and identifications of subjects.

School Records

These are good sources of information on behavior, scholarship, family background, disciplinary actions, and financial status.

Personnel Offices

Valuable employment information can be obtained concerning the subject's employment history, successes and failures, and financial standings.

Moving Companies

Information may be provided as to where a subject has moved.

Shipping Companies

Records are maintained on all passenger lists. Included are names, addresses, ports of embarkation and disembarkation, and stateroom numbers.

Travel Agencies

Information can be provided concerning a subject's travel, including departure times, itinerary, and insurance beneficiaries.

Jewelers

Repair records and invoices are maintained that might provide leads to stolen jewelry.

Funeral Directors

Information about families of the deceased is on file here.

Missing Persons

Over one million people are reported missing each year. Many of these people are considered "skips"—a person who for whatever reason of his or her own chooses to leave a given area. You will find that no one disappears without a trace. If you, as the investigator, devote enough time and effort, and you follow the proper techniques and procedures, nearly everyone can be located. The three major exceptions to this rule are the very rich, the very criminal, and the very dead. Usually, the longer a person is gone, the easier it is to find the person. Most skips or missing persons eventually leave paper trails, verbal trails, or both.

Phase One—The Initial Interview

Every missing person case begins with an interview. The purpose of the interview is to develop a body of reliable information that is useful in an actual investigation. The client who is seeking the help of the investigator is likely to be emotionally upset and unable to provide accurate information without careful guidance from the investigator. The client may be thinking of the possibility of murder, kidnapping, serious personal harm to a loved one, and other unspoken fears. It is essential that your manner and approach be reassuring and professional. By remaining calm and comforting, you will be able to gather the vital information you will need to begin your investigation. (See Figure 3.1.)

Maintain an approach that helps the client remain calm. Project a personal image of professional competence. Allow the client time to relax before beginning a series of probing questions. Let your client know that you will follow an orderly logical procedure.

Keep in mind that most missing persons leave situations that they consider unbearable. Your client may not recognize or want to reveal the nature of the circumstances that led to the disappearance. In practical terms, this means you should not accept at face value the initial statements made by the client, such as, "everything was all right at home" prior to the disappearance. Get as complete a story as possible. Some clients may hesitate to divulge family problems, because they are reluctant to air "dirty laundry" or because they fear that police action and publicity could result. You must assure them that all information will be treated in the strictest confidence. As a private investigator, you function much as an attorney does, for the benefit of your client.

Give your client a quick preview of the kind of information that you will be seeking, and then proceed in an orderly fashion to interview him or her. You will be seeking information in three areas:

ASSETS SEARCH
PRELIMINARY DATA SHEET

CASE #:________________ DATE:________________ TYPE:________________

CLIENT:________________________________ TELE:________________

ADDRESS:________________________________ FAX:________________

OTHER ADDRESS:________________________________ O.TELE:________________

CASE NAME:________________________________ DOCKET #:________________

SUBJECT:____

DATE OF BIRTH:________________ SS#:________________ DL#:________________

ADDRESS:________________________________ TELE:________________

WORK:________________________________ TELE:________________

CELL/PAGER/OTHER TELE:________________________________

KNOWN ASSETS:

BANK ACCOUNTS:________________________________

____

PROPERTIES:________________________________

____

MISC:________________________________

____

PARENTS/SIBLINGS (relatives who would assist)________________________________

____

BEST FRIEND/PARAMOUR (friends who would assist)________________________________

____

LOCATIONS VISITED ON REGULAR BASIS________________________________

____

ATTORNEY:________________ TELE:________________ DEADLINES:________________

Figure 3.1 Assets search preliminary data sheet.

- Has this person run away or disappeared before?
- What was the motivating factor that caused the person to leave?
- What does the missing person look like?

Previous Disappearances

A surprising number of runaways are repeaters. Clients may not readily volunteer information about previous disappearances for fear of embarrassment. Be sure to ask if the missing person has run away before. If so, then the client can provide valuable information about probable destinations. Gather all the information you can about the previous incident. Take the opportunity to check police reports about the disposition of any previous disappearances.

Motive

Determining the motive is perhaps the most important step in a successful investigation. The majority of people who run away do so for predictable motives: family arguments, inability to meet financial obligations, mental or emotional disturbances, inability to cope with severe stress, and so on. However, your client will not volunteer this information without your guidance.

Other motives for disappearances can be far more serious because they involve criminal activity. Some people run away with stolen money. Others leave because they have been threatened with physical violence. Some intend to collect insurance through fraud. When the interview reveals such serious motives, police involvement may be necessary, and further detailed investigation will have to take place.

Description

During the initial interview, get a detailed description of the missing person. If possible, obtain a recent photograph. Keep in mind that the client may not be able to give you a satisfactory description because he or she is upset. Plan to get supplemental description from friends, associates, and schoolmates. A complete description includes the following elements:

- Physical appearance—height, weight, race, birthmarks, scars, characteristics, posture, manner of walking, and manner of speech
- Clothing worn and personal articles carried at the time of the disappearance
- Vehicle used—make, model, year, body style, license number, color, and condition of the vehicle used by the missing person

Phase Two—The Investigation

After you have completed the initial interview, you are ready to begin the actual investigation. As you uncover additional information and clues, you will need to speak with your client many times. These follow-up interviews will enable you to eliminate inaccurate information initially provided and concentrate on following clues provided by new information. The three steps you will follow during the actual investigation include the following.

Check the Bad News Sources

Before going ahead with an extensive and costly investigation, you must determine if the missing person has already been found. This means checking area hospitals and jails. If you suspect suicide or other foul play, check the medical examiner's office. If these sources reveal the missing person, then the investigation is complete. If they do not, then you have the basis for further investigation.

Check Personal Belongings

The personal belongings of the missing person can provide important clues to the disappearance. This is especially true with juveniles. The missing person's personal effects should be examined, including mail, clippings, items found in a purse or briefcase, items found in dresser drawers, and contents of an automobile glove compartment. With juveniles, notes scribbled in books and notebooks, sometimes passed to friends, can provide important clues.

Where foul play is suspected, the examination of personal effects is especially vital and should be pursued persistently. Remember, in cases involving possible criminal activity, your investigation will supplement or complement police efforts, and you will be expected to cooperate with the authorities.

Follow-Up Investigation

Although you may develop sufficient information from the initial interview and check of personal belongings to successfully proceed, there may be times when you need to do additional investigation. Such follow-up investigation may involve people associated with the missing person and aspects of the individual's life.

It may be necessary for you to dig deeply into the missing person's social activities, medical history, family history, and employment record. Investigation into these areas may reveal patterns of unbearable stress that motivated the individual to run away. Membership in clubs, special interest groups, unions, and professional associations may provide clues about the individual's interests and associations. Financial records and credit ratings may reveal money problems, a frequent cause for desertion. Records of local government offices, such as state employment offices, relief agencies, and the Department of Motor Vehicles, may provide clues to temporary residences.

Comments made by a missing person's friends can be significant. You learn that the person missed his or her last class, and friends add that he or she was acting strangely on the night the missing person was last seen. This can be an important clue in establishing the time of disappearance. Lifestyles are also significant. If the missing person is a gambler, pool player, gun collector, golfer, and so on, then his or her activities and associations provide additional clues as to his or her whereabouts.

Investigation into family history during the follow-up investigation may reveal marital difficulties. In the past, males made up the majority of those who deserted their families. Today, women are more frequently disappearing and leaving families and husbands. They are searching for a different kind of life. Frequently, deserters cannot be induced to return to their families if found. As an investigator, your role in such instances will be to determine the missing person's whereabouts and assure the client that the missing person is safe. Do not act as a marriage counselor. Reconciliation is a separate matter to be worked out between the involved parties.

Runaway Juveniles

Running away from home in search of adventure has always had a strong romantic appeal to many American kids. Many would-be Huck Finns took to the roads, not only to escape from home, but to search for adventure. In today's crowded world, running away offers none of the challenges it did in the past. Juvenile runaways can look forward to a life of extreme poverty, homelessness, crime, drug addiction, prostitution, and even early death. Parents, aware of the dangers the runaways face, are quicker to seek the help of private investigators in locating their children.

In dealing effectively with runaways, you need to know three things:

- Who the runaway is
- What motivated the child to run away
- How to conduct an investigation involving juvenile runaways

Today's Runaway—A Profile

Studies indicate that most runaways are between 14 and 16 years of age. Usually, the girls are older than the boys. The average juvenile runaway either goes home or is found in about 1 week. Knowing how to find the runaway rapidly is especially important, because the longer the child is away, the more likely he or she is to commit crimes.

Psychological research shows that runaways are likely to be hostile and defiant. They tend to behave impulsively and exhibit puzzling mood swings—extreme aggressiveness alternating with extreme passivity. Their behavior interferes with schoolwork, for which routine and discipline are required. Studies also show that home atmospheres left by these juveniles are not conducive to happiness. Finally, police records indicate that juvenile runaways more than any other juveniles have been involved in delinquent activities prior to running away.

Motives

Although children leave home for many reasons, including desire for independence, excitement, or adventure, the most common motive is desperation to get away from unbearable conditions. The following are the most common motives for running away.

Poor Home Conditions Alcoholic or drug-addicted parents; crowdedness; negative personalities of parents, stepparents, or others involved in running the household; physical or mental illness of family members; lack of affection; and so on may be contributing factors.

Desire to Avoid Criticism or Punishment Children who are reprimanded or are convinced they have disappointed or disobeyed their parents often run away to avoid dealing with the problem.

Rigid, Overstrict Home Discipline Youngsters who do not feel close to their parents due to rejection or strict discipline run away to escape their parents' demands, even though the infraction may be relatively minor.

Fear of Being Apprehended by the Police for an Offense The crime may be relatively minor, such as petty theft, a fight, or broken windows, but the runaway fears the offense will be regarded as more serious.

Lack of Security in New Surroundings Young people often find it difficult to adjust to the problem of establishing themselves in new communities or neighborhoods. They miss old friends and have difficulty making new ones.

Eloping Many older juveniles, especially girls, run away from home to get married. In most cases, the marriages are valid.

Conducting Investigations

As with other missing person cases, investigating juvenile runaways involves initial interviews, examination of personal belongings, and follow-up investigation. The investigator who is successful in locating runaway juveniles builds a body of information through interviews with parents, friends, and relatives which focuses on the runaway's home situation and on his or her involvement with friends and activities.

Home Situation Keep the following questions in mind as guidelines:

- Is there hostility between parents and child?
- Are parents demonstrating marital instability, including violent scenes?
- Are other household members showing continuous conflict?
- Does anyone in the household have physical or mental disorders, especially long-standing problems that could interfere with home life?

- Are there financial difficulties resulting in constant bickering or hardships that upset or humiliate family members, especially children?
- Is there alcoholism or drug addiction in the family?
- Was there a sudden change in the child's attitude, especially where his family was concerned? Did he or she suddenly become quiet or explosive, belligerent, or too submissive to be considered normal?
- Did his or her attitude toward studies, teachers, and so on, change recently?
- Did he or she stop talking about his or her friends? Did he or she suddenly abandon his or her old friends?

Friends, Activities, and So Forth Keep the following questions in mind as guidelines:

- Are the runaway's friends able to suggest clues to his or her activities, interests, previous behavior, or other details that would help you? An understanding attitude on the part of an investigator can bring cooperation, especially if those friends believe you are trying to help a runaway.
- Did the juvenile frequent neighborhood video arcades, beaches, picnic grounds, parks, sports centers, or hamburger stands?
- Do the juvenile's friends have recent photos that would be helpful to you?

Locating Runaways

Most runaways can be located relatively near home, even though credit cards, family autos, or even their own ability make it possible for them to go greater distances. As the runaway learns how to survive on his or her own (usually after several attempts), he or she is likely to be away longer and thus be more difficult to locate. The following locations can be used as temporary hiding places (harbors or shelters).

A Friend's House The runaway may be able to stay at a friend's house for several nights without arousing suspicion. The friend may tell his or her parents a convincing story about the visit. The home of a married friend is a more attractive shelter often used by a young female runaway.

All-Night Public Places These include grills and coffee shops, railway and bus depots, airports, Laundromats, and movie theaters. Runaways find them convenient first stops where their presence will not be noticed.

Lobbies, Vestibules, and Basements These places serve as very short-term stops, because food and bathroom facilities are not available.

Automobiles It is not unusual to find exhausted runaways asleep in parked or abandoned cars.

Vacant Buildings These may include apartments, commercial buildings, lumber yards, garden sheds, or unoccupied private residences.

Campgrounds, Parks, and Beaches In mild weather these are common stops for runaways. They can mingle freely with others without creating suspicion.

Skid Row Local and out-of-town runaways often seek shelter in the run-down parts of town. They may share a "crib" with other runaways or derelicts or flop in a cheap hotel.

Carnivals and Circuses Kids still run away to join the circus. Carnival people are friendly and sympathetic, so these places are considered good choices by many runaways.

The Located Runaway

Assuming you have located a missing juvenile, the first step you should take is to notify parents or guardians of the child's location, because they may have special instructions and will be anxious to know about the child's status.

Determine whether the child needs help. Does he or she display signs of illness or abuse? Attention to these needs puts you in a good position to talk to the runaway and get the complete story.

When speaking to the runaway, try to determine if he or she was involved in criminal activity (burglary, shoplifting, prostitution, etc.) or if he or she was victimized by adults in some way. Many young runaways have been seriously mistreated by sexual perverts and may need medical and psychological help. Others may have been persuaded to become members of gangs that commit serious crimes. At first, runaways may be unwilling to reveal details of their activities for fear of further punishment by parents or police, but with patience and skillful questioning, you can get these details.

Watch for discrepancies in any story. Be cautious about accepting details of a supposed kidnapping. Check the story carefully, and eliminate discrepancies to prevent you from falsely accusing someone.

Undercover Operations in Business Settings

Cover stories are an extremely important part of any undercover operation. The more complex the case and the greater the sophistication of the criminal suspects, the more attention must be given to the preparation of the cover story. An agent can only be as effective as his or her cover story is acceptable or believable. It must fit the role being played by the agent. There are three rules to observe on a cover story:

1. Keep it simple.
2. Keep it believable.
3. Keep it as close to the truth as possible.

Another trait that the good undercover agent would benefit from mastering is called "roping." The art of roping can be defined as the undercover agent gaining the trust and confidence of a suspect to the point where the suspect will disclose past or present criminal acts or, at least, will not hide them from the agent's view. Techniques used to accomplish roping must steer clear of entrapment and areas of illegality. A mature thief would never reveal him- or herself to a newcomer (the undercover agent) until he or she feels that the agent can be trusted or, at least, is not a threat. Therefore, if the agent can create the impression that he or she, too, is dishonest, the agent will have neutralized some of the thief's defenses.

In any company setting, one can usually identify two main groups of employees—those who are relatively "straight" and free from dishonesty and those who care little about the company and take advantage of every opportunity to further their own ends either through company expense or outright illegality.

In the initial stages of an undercover investigation, it is often necessary for the agent to gain and keep the goodwill of the "straights." Members of this group often possess invaluable information about the illegal activities of persons in the group. During this time, the agent, in effect, must walk a tightrope between the two groups so as not to be identified too closely with either one to the detriment of a future relationship with the other. Eventually, the agent will have to decide to swing away from the "straight" group in order to become completely accepted by the thieves in the plant. This switching over from one group to the other is accomplished through the art of roping. It usually results in the alienation of the original group, which is loyal to the company and not interested in stealing.

The last (and most important) requirement for the supervisor in an undercover case is that he or she maintain overall perspective on the entire case. The typical undercover case will involve the identification of various dishonest employees on the work force. This is usually done employee by employee. In other words, over a given time period, the undercover agent will gradually be able to identify more and more dishonest employees. It is up to the supervisor to ensure that the undercover agent does not become bogged down in a relationship with any one dishonest employee or group.

Asset Protection—Loss Prevention—Access Control*

Herbert Simon CPP†

Loss prevention (LP) is asset protection. The most important asset to protect is personnel, however, proprietary information and physical assets must also be secured. Asset protection begins at the workplace and it must travel with your employees. Offsite events such as seminars, conferences, training and awards programs, expose a corporation's personnel and proprietary information to threats that are effectively deterred at the office. Vulnerability increases greatly when a corporation's employees leave the home base's protection. Extensive preplanning and competent implementation is critical with regard to ensuring that the corporation's assets are protected and personnel safeguarded when both are transported from normal to detached venues.

Corporate LP professionals can secure their buildings, operating seamlessly with proper protective measures, but do the venues to which your employees travel use the same or even similar measures? Convention centers, conference locations and major hotels have security departments and loss prevention procedures, but never specific to a corporation's needs. Additionally, these venues are by nature accessible to the public. This unrestricted access creates exposure and risk. Within these venues a protected environment must be established. Through cooperation with a subcontracted LP professional, the meeting planner and the offsite facility's security professionals, the corporation's LP can coordinate appropriate access control, deny unauthorized individuals, and make an event secure.

Ensuring employee safety is always the primary assignment. Nothing is more significant than providing a risk-free working environment for conference attendees and employees. Protection of all assets, i.e., personnel, proprietary information, property, etc., is the ultimate goal. For a successful conference LP program, cooperation, coordination and communication are essential.

Corporate espionage is a genuine threat. As technology advances, so too do the tools used for espionage. Corporate America's competitive nature has made information protection a priority. Laptop computers, promotional literature, training manuals, product specifications must be secured at all

* One of the major areas of investigation for today's professional investigator is corporate investigations. This article is redacted and used with permission. It is published in its entirety in *Corporate Investigations*, 2nd ed., Montgomery, R.J. and Majeski, W.J., Eds., Lawyers & Judges, Tucson, AZ, 2005.

† Simon is vice president of R.J. Montgomery and Associates in Allendale, New Jersey. He has extensive experience in the Loss Prevention–Access Control industry as a result of his many years working with the pharmaceutical industry.

times. Research and development programs cost millions of dollars and the resulting information and products must be kept confidential. Allowing such information to be taken and used by others can be financially disastrous. Such intellectual and proprietary information is greatly exposed during corporate conferences.

By definition, LP must be proactive, not reactive. If a demonstration forms, protests, threats, violence or other "worst-case" scenarios, qualified LP professionals must handle these incidents.

While many convention centers and hotels have solid and effective in-house Security forces, using a LP professional is still strongly recommended. If the conference center does not have its own "in-house" officers and their sub-contracted Security is a private organization, then other arrangements must be made. It is NEVER recommended to use private, sub-contracted physical security "guards" for such assignments.

Identification Badges (ID)

In order to keep unauthorized persons out, it must first be determined who belongs. When all authorized attendees are wearing badges, the attendees themselves become aware of and alert for persons who are not wearing ID. Every supervisor, meeting planner, LP professional can firmly enforce the ID requirement. ID badges are an access control program's most fundamental and important component. The LP staff must wear badges that clearly identify themselves as such to the conference attendees.

- *ALL attendees must clearly display their ID badges at ALL times:* General sessions, breakout rooms, and during onsite social functions, breakfasts, lunches and dinners. It is strongly recommended that the event's ID not identify the corporation's name, any product or conference topic.
- *Photographic IDs* should be used whenever possible. Some meeting planners have purchased digital ID systems that can create photo ID at the conference with little disruption. The LP professional's job can be performed much more effectively when able to match a face on an ID to the bearer.
- *All ID badges must be protected.* Pre-made ID badges must never be placed on an unattended table. Lines leading to registration should not pass near the ID badges and attendees must never be allowed to "find" their own ID badges. It is strongly recommended that the LP professionals assist in the registration process. If desired, LP professionals can be stationed as "first contact." The LP professional will ask the attendee for photographic ID to confirm identity. If the attendee has no photographic ID, an inspection of identification documents

can be made in order to confirm the person is who they claim to be. Once the identification is confirmed, the attendee proceeds to regular registration to obtain the conference program and the event-specific ID badge.

Laptops

All employees are responsible for their own laptops. For some reason, however, responsibility is not always taken seriously at conferences. In the "field," an employee would never leave a laptop unattended, but at a conference the laptops are often found left on tables during breaks or lunches and in unsecured rooms. This is a serious matter. The laptop's purchase cost is inconsequential compared to the associated costs when a laptop goes missing, i.e., reloading software, lost productivity, retraining, etc. The proprietary information on an employee's laptop in the wrong hands can cripple a corporation. Everyone involved in a conference must understand the gravity of protecting these computers. A warning to this effect should be included on a separate page in the conference program.

- Laptops must NOT be left in any unsecured room. A room is considered secured if there is security personnel assigned to it or if the room is locked immediately following its vacancy and access is controlled.
- Laptops that are left in unsecured rooms will be removed by the LP professional and given to the meeting planner to be held until the owner comes to report its disappearance.
- The meeting planner should notify the laptop user's supervisor of the incident. LP should log the date, time, and location at which the laptop was found and to whom and when it was delivered.
- If laptops are being delivered to the conference location other than being hand-carried by attendees, it is critical that the laptops be secured when they arrive. LP and, if desired, the meeting planners, must coordinate with the conference facility's security director and receiving managers to secure the laptops. LP must control this laptop intake and transfer process from receiving dock to final destination.
- The locks for the rooms where laptops will be stored should be changed immediately prior to the conference commencement and keys as well as access, controlled.
- Some establishments have cables or other devices that can secure laptops to tables. If these are available, they should be used.

Conclusion

Corporate conferences celebrate successes, conduct training, continue education and bond employee attendees in fraternal comradeship. Cost for travel, housing, food and entertainment can be huge, and while a LP presence will increase the conference's budget, it is essential. As with most protection programs, the corporation's financial professionals will wonder why, following an "uneventful" conference, so much money had to be spent for loss prevention? The answer is that the conference was uneventful because the LP program worked! Achieving LP's objective is hard work; however, when attendees leave, having enjoyed a comfortable, safe and secure conference, the effort and protection afforded is priceless.

Conclusion

Interviews, Interrogation, and Taking Statements

4

For the purpose of this book, the working definition of an interview is the questioning of a person who has knowledge of a subject that is relevant to an investigation. Although the interview often resembles a conversation, it is a highly specialized form of conversation with a specific purpose.

Introduction to Interviews

All information can be categorized into two areas: trivial (irrelevant) and important information.

Important information is the who, what, when, where, why, and how (the five W's and H). Important information includes unusual observations at the scene, other unusual observations, and the interviewer's gut feelings about the subject noted during the interview.

Interviews, whether formal or informal, always involve a relationship between two people: the interviewer and the person being questioned (the interviewee). The interviewee must be convinced that talking to the investigator is the most important thing at that point in time. Investigators must convey interest in the interviewee without appearing forced or contrived, providing undivided attention and listening thoughtfully and with consideration to what the interviewee says.

There is considerable controversy about taking notes, tape recording, and using prepared notes during the interview. Note taking often interferes with the flow of the interview and observation of the significance of pauses, facial expressions, and body movements that will tip off the investigator to the believability of the person interviewed. Note taking versus recording statements will be discussed later in this chapter. In my opinion, it is better to record a statement than to take notes, providing the interviewee will permit the recording. However, when needed, note taking should be confined to facts that may be difficult to remember, such as family names, addresses, dates, telephone numbers, and so on.

Interviews need to maintain focus. Keep the interviewee focused on the issue under discussion and discourage rambling thoughts and comments. This can be accomplished by asking relevant questions to bring the focus of the interview back to the matter at hand. When possible, you should organize the interview questions in advance. You should have an outline of the material you wish to explore and the information you need to obtain and have a series of questions firmly fixed in your mind.

Strategies

Ask the interviewee to relate the series of events in his or her own words. The interviewee should be allowed to tell the entire story once without interruption. If the interviewee stops, nod your head or repeat a phrase that was used to stimulate him or her into continuing. It is not productive to ask questions that require only a yes or no answer. However, questions should be kept simple and easily understood by the interviewee.

Investigators should analyze the interviewee's behavior and body language for clues to truthfulness and honesty. Does the interviewee maintain eye contact or act fidgety? These clues to truth or deception will be discussed further in the section on body language.

The investigator also must strive to convey understanding and empathy with the interviewee. A nod or smile will help convey connection with the interviewee. Remember never to talk above the level of understanding of the person. Defining the purpose of the interview at the beginning of the conversation will help get the relationship off to a good start.

The presumption of every interview should be that the interviewee has information and material pertinent to the case. The investigator's task and intent should be to obtain all that information.

Role Playing

The investigator must be able to play the role that is required, depending on the circumstances, in order to promote the most open response to the interview.

During the early stages of the interview process, an investigator may realize that the witness, victim, or suspect has some personal problem (defense mechanism, fear, or other more conscious reaction) that prevents him or her from cooperating in the investigation. Some witnesses and victims are reluctant to cooperate because they fear for their personal safety or they fear their involvement will create an undue burden (time or money) on their families. In these instances, the investigator may attempt to calm the person by playing the role of a protector or benefactor. As a concerned listener, the investigator plays the role of an understanding stranger.

Common Interviewing Errors

The two most common interviewing errors are that the interviewer does not allow the interviewee to tell his own story, and the interviewer talks too much.

Interview Guidelines

The following strategies are important interview guidelines:

- The investigator must control the interview.
- Prior preparation is essential. Review the facts of the case and all available records and data before commencing the interview. Know what you are talking about.
- Carefully evaluate the subject of the interview.
- Play whatever role is required to facilitate the free flow of information.
- Tactfully select the best combination of strategies to use.
- Do not automatically discredit information that is unfavorable to your position.
- Remember that your responsibility is to gather the facts.

Empathy

Empathy is the feeling associated with emotional identification with another person. When used correctly, the concern (real or imagined) that results will facilitate the free flow of information. The interviewer should follow these guidelines: appear sincere, use a very understanding approach, have a nonjudgmental attitude, and be careful to disguise any negative feelings or lack of compassion for the interviewee.

Criminal Investigation Techniques

Questioning is divided into two broad classifications:

- The interview is conducted to learn facts from persons who may have knowledge of the wrongful act but are not themselves implicated.
- The interrogation is conducted to learn facts and to obtain an admission or confession of wrongful acts from persons who are implicated in them, to obtain a written, signed, and witnessed statement, and to establish the facts of a crime or develop information that will enable the investigator to obtain physical or other evidence to prove or disprove the truth of an admission or confession.

Purpose of an Interview

An interview is an informal questioning session to learn facts. The successful investigation of facts regarding criminal acts requires that the investigator be able to learn, through personal questioning, what the person interviewed has observed through his or her five senses: smell, sight, hearing, touch, and taste. Effective interviewing requires that the investigator make full use of his or her knowledge of human nature so that the interviewee will disclose all that he or she knows about the matter in question.

Preparation for an Interview

Interviews should be planned carefully to prevent repetition. The investigator must thoroughly review all the developments in the case prior to the interview. He must also consider the relationship of the interviewee to the investigation—that is, complainant, victim, witnesses, or informant. The effective interviewer combines his or her knowledge of human nature with available information about the person to be interviewed, such as education, character, reputation, associates, habits, and past criminal record. The investigator also should prepare by noting pertinent facts to be developed to detect and evaluate inconsistencies and discrepancies in the statements of the persons interviewed, and to require clarification of the statements, as necessary.

Control over Interviews

An investigator must maintain absolute control of the interview at all times. If the interviewee becomes so evasive as to obscure the purpose of the interview, effective results may be obtained by a more formal type of questioning, by taking notes, or by aggressiveness of the investigator. Although an investigator has no legal power to force a person being interviewed to disclose any information, he or she may, if clever, induce the interviewee to disclose whatever he or she knows.

Attitude and Demeanor of the Investigator

The investigator must establish a cordial relationship with the interviewee. The investigator should be friendly. The interviewee should be permitted to give an uninterrupted account while the investigator makes mental notes of omissions, inconsistencies, or discrepancies that will require clarification by later questioning. The investigator should avoid a clash of personalities, acts of undue familiarity, the use of profanity or violent expressions (kill, steal, murder), improbable stories, or distracting mannerisms like pacing the floor or fumbling with objects.

Types of Approach

The indirect approach in interviewing consists of discussions carried out in a conversational tone that permit the interviewee to talk without having to answer direct questions. The direct approach consists of direct questioning, as in an interrogation. The use of interrogation techniques often succeeds when the person interviewed fears or dislikes police officers, fears retribution from a criminal, desires to protect a friend or relative, or is unwilling to cooperate with the investigator. The talkative person should be allowed to speak freely and to use his or her own expressions but should be confined to the subject by appropriate questions.

Interviews of Complainants, Victims, and Witnesses

In interviewing complainants, the investigator should be considerate, understanding, tactful, and impartial, regardless of the motive for the complaint. When interviewing a victim, the investigator must consider his or her emotional state, particularly in crimes of violence. Frequently, victims have unsupported beliefs regarding the circumstances connected with the crime.

When interviewing a witness, the investigator must frequently assist the witness in recalling and relating facts exactly as he or she observed them. The emotions of witnesses before, during, and after the incident and when interviewed greatly affect their recall of events as they occurred. A frightened witness may recall events differently than a calm, unruffled person. Credibility of a witness is usually governed by his or her character and is demonstrated by his or her reputation for truthfulness.

During the interview, the investigator must continually evaluate the mannerisms and the emotional state of the interviewee in terms of the information developed. The manner in which a person relates his or her information or answers questions may indicate that he or she is not telling the truth or is concealing something. Evasiveness, hesitation, or unwillingness to discuss certain situations may signify a lack of cooperation. The relation of body movement to the emotional state of the person must carefully be considered by the investigator.

Purpose of the Interrogation

Interrogation is the questioning of a person suspected of having committed the act under investigation. The purpose of the interrogation of a suspect is to obtain an admission or confession of wrongful acts and to obtain a written, signed, and witnessed statement. The interrogation should only be conducted after sufficient information has been obtained and the background of the subject has been thoroughly explored.

The investigator should base his or her plan for interrogation on background data, information, or direct evidence received from victims and witnesses, physical evidence, and reconstruction of the crime scene. The plan, which should be written, should take into consideration the various means for testing the truthfulness of the suspect and gaining a psychological advantage over the suspect through the use of known facts and the proper use of time, place, and environment.

The Interrogation

No time limit should be placed on the duration of the interrogation, except that it should not be so long and under such conditions as to amount to duress. Questioning for many hours without food, sleep, or under glaring lights has been held to constitute duress and may invalidate the confession. Investigators who are not law enforcement officers have much more latitude in this area.

An interrogation should be conducted in complete privacy if possible. Witnesses to a confession may be called in to hear a reading of the statement and declare that it is the subject's statement, to witness the signing by the subject, and to affix their own signatures.

Attitude of the Investigator

Owing to the importance of an admission or confession, the investigator must become skilled in the art of interrogation. The investigator must master a variety of questioning techniques, learn to judge the psychological stress or weaknesses of others, and learn to take advantage of his or her own particular abilities in questioning any suspect or reluctant witness.

Types of Approaches

The Direct Approach

This is normally applied where guilt is reasonably certain—that is, "Why did you steal the money?"

The Indirect Approach

This is applied in interrogating a person who has knowledge of the crime (when you do not have enough evidence to point the finger)—that is, "Do you know who was involved in stealing the money?"

The Emotional Approach

This is a method designed to play upon the emotions of a person—that is, "You know that Mr. Smith has suffered severely from the theft of the money from the company. Is there anything you can tell me about who may have been involved?"

Subterfuge

This approach is applied to induce guilty persons to confess when all other approaches have failed, for example, a hypothetical story, a signed false statement, the cold shoulder, playing one suspect against another, and displaying contrasting personalities (good cop/bad cop).

Persons interviewed may later be interrogated. An interrogation is not confined to individuals suspected of criminal acts but may include persons who may have been accessories or may have knowledge of the crime which they are reluctant to admit. When information that will have value as evidence develops during an interview or interrogation, it must be recorded in a written, signed, and witnessed statement, or in a tape-recorded statement.

Reading Body Language

An estimated 70% of communication occurs on the nonverbal level. The nonverbal physical actions of the lying suspect may be characterized as follows.

Gross Body Movement

Examples are posture changes, movement of the chair away from the interrogator, and an indication of being about to stand up or perhaps leave the room.

Grooming Gestures

This includes rubbing the hands together; stroking the back of the neck; touching the nose, earlobes, or lips; picking or biting fingernails; shuffling, tapping, swinging, or arching the feet; rearranging clothing or jewelry; dusting; picking lint or pulling threads on clothing; adjusting or cleaning glasses; and straightening or stroking hair.

Supportive Gestures

Gestures such as placing hands over eyes or mouth when speaking, crossing arms or legs, holding forehead with hands, and placing hands under or between legs are characterized as supportive gestures.

Summary of Body Language Skills

The investigator should vary his or her expression to fit changes in the emotions expressed by the interviewee. Make polite and friendly use of the social smile, but do not overdo it. Use facial expressions to show interest as a listener and to be interesting as a speaker. Avoid undue use of facial expressions—especially a blank stare, which may be seen as showing hostility or lack of interest. Avoid fixed, frozen expressions that do not vary with changes in the situation. Avoid weak expressions that are badly timed and appear insincere. Failure to use expressions to accompany your own speech or to reflect what the speaker is saying may also convey lack of interest.

Eye Contact

The general rule is to maintain eye contact broken up by definite looks away. Look more while listening, less while talking. Look away when taking up the conversation, look back when handing it back. Maintain eye contact with serious expressions when trying to gain control of a situation. Avoiding eye contact, at one extreme, may convey nervousness and lack of confidence. Staring, on the other extreme, may convey hostility and intrusiveness.

Distance

Keep an appropriate distance, and adjust to cues to compensate when too close or too far away. Too much eye contact, leaning forward, and close proximity can give an intrusive or domineering impression. Too much distance, too little eye contact, or turning away can convey a cold impression.

Touch

A brief touch on the hand, arm, shoulder, or other acceptable area of the person's body can convey warmth and emotional support or can be used to draw attention to an important point that you are making. Sudden and uninvited touching can be seen as too intimate. Too many touches to control direction and attention can make you appear domineering.

Use of Voice

Aim for moderate volume, a resonant tone, varied pitch, and varied pace. High volume, a booming tone, and an overvaried or low pitch make you seem domineering. Low volume, a thin tone, and unvarying pitch and pace, especially a slow pace, convey a submissive, depressed attitude. Stuttering and some other speech disturbances convey anxiety.

Posture

For an attentive posture, lean forward with a straight spine and arms open, and turn toward the speaker. For a relaxed posture, lean back with your head up and let your limbs take a symmetrical position. Avoid slumped shoulders, bowed head, folded arms, and deflated chest. Do not turn your body away. These cues convey submissiveness, depression, and lack of interest.

Gesture

Use gestures of emphasis to make your speech livelier and easier to follow. Use gestures that clarify meaning (such as pointing) and that convey meaning of their own (such as nodding to show agreement). Do not overuse gestures when trying to secure a speaking turn, as this appears aggressive. Fidgeting and hand wringing convey anxiety. Foot tapping conveys irritation.

Appearance

To create a positive impression, dress to conform to the situation you expect to meet. Looking attractive is an advantage in almost any situation. The following points are important to remember about the use of body language:

- Posture—how you hold your body can reveal feelings about events or people and your degree of interest.
- Eye contact—most of us respond unconsciously to the eye signals of others, but with greater awareness we can learn to control situations more effectively and access moods and motives of others more reliably through eye contact.
- Reading of facial expressions—faces convey our most expressive body language. Reading faces tells us how we are getting along. Spontaneous smiles and frowns are especially informative, but just as sincere words can be selected, so can sincere facial expressions.
- Language of touch—how, when, and where we touch others can make or break relationships. If the message conveyed is appropriate, most people will respond positively to being touched.
- Making conversation—the art of conversation involves intricate skills. Showing interest, starting and ending conversations, taking your turn or interrupting, bring all our resources into play.
- Detecting insincerity—research has revealed principles for detecting lies and deception. Facial expressions may be the least revealing; the rest of the body may reveal signs of insincerity, as do some speech patterns, tone of voice, and even reduction in blinking.

Postures of Agreement and Disagreement

When people disagree with what is being said, they tend to have "closed" postures, holding head and trunk straight and folding the arms. If they are seated, they are likely to cross their legs above the knee. A more neutral attitude is conveyed by folding your hands on your lap and crossing your legs at the knee. When people agree, they are more likely to have "open" postures—leaning the head and trunk to one side and leaving their legs uncrossed.

An interested listener leans forward with legs drawn back. When interest fades, the head begins to lean and requires support by a hand. When completely bored, people let their heads drop, and the body has a backward lean with legs stretched out. People who are concerned about what their bodies might be signaling try to lean forward.

Posture provides a system by which conflicts can be avoided through signaling acceptance of another's dominance. If you do not want to challenge someone's authority or do not want to reveal a challenge before the time is right, avoid expansive arm gestures and turn both head and body in a show of attention, rather than the head alone. However, when you need to assert authority, hands on hips and attention that is confined to turning the head will demonstrate that you are in charge.

Even in one-to-one conversations or in some small groups, you sometimes need to penetrate the polite reactions of the listeners to be an effective speaker. Unconscious shifts in the positions of bodies and limbs can be early warning signals that you need to find something more interesting to say or you need to overcome objections.

Eye Contact

Eyes are usually thought of as receivers of information. We use our eyes to see the world around us, but they also transmit signals that play a vital role in everyday social interaction. How we look at other people, meet their gaze, and look away can make the difference between an effective encounter or one that leads to embarrassment or even rejection. Looking into the eyes of another is such a powerful act of communication that it must be carefully controlled.

As soon as the conversation begins, eye contact will usually be broken as the speaker looks away. Usually, the person who is listening will look more than the person who is talking. To show responsiveness and interest as a listener, you need to look at the other person's face for roughly three-fourths of the time, in glances lasting from 1 to 7 seconds. On other occasions, you might be faced with a person who will not let you get a word in edgewise. The speaker avoids your eyes at the very moment you want to signal that you are going to say something. There is a way to remedy this. First, switch off the support that you give by looking at the speaker. Look to one side, but in such a way that you can tell when you are looked at.

Looking away during the conversation can be self-revealing. If you ask someone a question, he or she will meet your eyes and then look away. Some will look away to the left, others to the right. It seems to depend on the anatomy of the brain. Those who look away to the left are likely to be more artistic or religious, and those who look to the right are more scientific minded. In most people, the left hemisphere of the brain deals with verbal questions (such as how to spell a word), and such questions prompt them to look right. The right half of the brain deals with spatial questions (such as how to get somewhere), and these are associated with looking to the left.

Pupil Signals

We find it difficult not to look at people who arouse our emotions. When the person is a stranger, we usually look less often and more briefly in an effort to mask our real feelings. Along with any emotional response comes a widening of the pupils of the eyes, even though the light falling on them remains constant. This is an involuntary reflex, originally an evolutionary adaptation to let more light into the eye, so more information is available to the eyes in an emergency, but it also acts as a mood signal. The sight of dilated pupils unconsciously triggers an emotional response and a corresponding pupil-enlargement response in the person being looked at.

Reading Facial Expressions

Usually, people's facial expressions seem to be better guides than their words about what they are feeling. It is possible to read emotions and attitudes from people's faces. Smiles and frowns are often spontaneous expressions of happiness and anger. Universally, people express and recognize four basic emotions. There are two other emotions—fear and surprise—distinguished by everyone except remote populations in New Guinea. Also, three independently expressive regions of the face—the eyebrows, the eyes, and the lower face—are used. The following six facial expressions will help you determine another person's emotions:

- Happiness—appears in a smiling mouth and wrinkles around the eyes.
- Sadness—raised brows, lowered eyelids, and a downturned mouth.
- Anger—gives the eyes a penetrating stare and causes the lids to tense. The lips of the angry mouth are pressed together or opened and pushed forward.
- Disgust—shows itself in a wrinkled nose and raised upper lip. The lower eyelids are pushed up, and the brows are lowered.
- Surprise—the brows are raised, the eyes are wide open, and the jaw drops, opening the mouth.
- Fear—raises and draws together the brows. The eyes are open and tense, and the lower lids are raised. The mouth is open, and lips may be drawn back tightly.

Detecting Insincerity

The ability to deceive others is thought to be a characteristic genetically selected through human evolution. There are many occasions in everyday social encounters when people, for one reason or another, want to avoid expressing their true feelings. The ability to do this varies, and success breeds success. Those who lie effectively will tend to lie more often, perfecting their deception skills in the process. Those who fail are deterred from future attempts and get less practice.

The way in which deceit oozes from our bodies is referred to as nonverbal leakage, a series of body language cues that indicate insincerity. Controlled observation has revealed just what these cues are. One of the most reliable is the way we speak. People who are deceptive make fewer factual statements, preferring instead more general sweeping remarks. They frequently leave gaps in the conversation to avoid mistakenly saying something that would give them away. They speak with a higher pitch and at a slower rate when lying. They hesitate more and are more likely to stutter or to make other speech errors.

A more difficult cue is facial expression. People are better at controlling this than any other aspect of their body language. In general, people smile less when lying, and they are slower to respond to what you are saying with facial expressions and other body language. The eyes, in particular, are hard to control. Pupil dilation and reduced blinking are among the most consistently observed nonverbal leakages.

Tip-Off Movement of the Body

The hands are especially reliable cues for detecting deceit. A noticeable mannerism of deceptive people is a decrease in simple hand movements. To curtail the messages of the hands, they keep them still or out of sight. Fewer head movements are also very common. When the hands are allowed to move, they display an above-average frequency of auto-contact behaviors. These self-touching movements are strongly related to high levels of arousal and nervousness, which is essentially what lie detectors measure. In everyday encounters, you need to be aware of people's hands as they touch their noses, stroke their chins, or brush their hands across their mouths.

Postural cues are also important. Liars tend to make more postural shifts than non-liars. Information about nonverbal leakage should help you detect deception and insincerity more easily. The question is, what should you do about it? It all depends on the situation and the motive the person has for deceiving you.

Taking Statements

A witness is anyone who has some particular knowledge of a given situation or occurrence. A witness is not necessarily an eyewitness. The three purposes for taking statements from witnesses are preservation of the recollection of an occurrence; to aid in the possible settlement of a matter without proceeding to trial; and impeachment of an untruthful witness in the event of a deposition, court hearing, or actual trial. The three different types of statements are the signed, handwritten, or printed statement; the in-person or telephone recorded statement; and the typed legal declaration under penalty of perjury.

One major problem with the phone interview or recorded statement is that you cannot see whom you are interviewing. Often, if your client is an attorney or an insurance company representative, he or she will rely on you to provide a detailed description of your impression of the witness, including appearance, attitude, demeanor, attentiveness, quickness of response, and general body language.

The most common form of statement you will use will be the in-person or telephone-recorded statement regarding a car accident or personal injury claim. Most personal injury (plaintiff) attorneys require that investigators have the witness write the statement in his or her own hand. This is done to protect the investigator from being deposed by opposing counsel. However, it is preferable that the investigator write the statement to ensure that it is accurate and legible and then have the witness read and sign it.

The most common method of beginning a statement is to identify and qualify the witness. This means that you give your client the witness's name, address, phone number, place of employment, date of birth, and social security number. Next, you state the purpose of the statement by identifying the accident or incident. Ask for a detailed description of the location, including all landmarks, points of interest, and individuals or vehicles present. Based upon the information presented by the witness, draft the main body of the statement showing the sequence of events (as a witness recalls, whether they are right or wrong), up until the time the witness departs the area.

Remember, once you submit the signed statement to your client, it may be read or reviewed by insurance companies, attorneys, or judges. It is therefore incumbent upon you to make it as clear and descriptive as possible. In other words, if the person reading the statement has never been to the area in question, he or she should thoroughly understand the condition at the accident site, including the locations of all individuals both before and after the incident, and who said what to whom.

The ending of the statement is also important, both in your discussion with the witness and in the documented statement. Once the witness has indicated that he or she has given all of the facts that he or she can remember, you can conclude in the following manner. If the witness is friendly and cooperative, simply show him or her the statement, and ask him or her to read and sign each page (one at a time). Once finished, ask the witness if there is anything you might have left out or anything he or she wishes to add. If the witness indicates the statement is adequate, simply add the final two sentences required by law: (1) "This statement is free and voluntary,"

MCMAHON & ASSOCIATES

Witness Interview Protocol

1. Introduction and identification of interviewing Investigator (show and explain ID, leave a business card).
2. Go over the "Witness Interview" Statement of interviewee's rights with the interviewee.
3. Ask permission to record the interview.
4. With recorder on, state date and time of interview, name of interviewer and interviewee, reiterate purpose of interview, and produce affidavit.
5. Fill out of witness data sheet recording verbal answers to data and personal information questions.
6. With recorder on, ask the following while the interviewee fills out the affidavit:
   A. Do you understand the purpose of this interview?
   B. Have you been promised any kind of reward whether it be cash or any other promise of favor in exchange for the information you are about to give?
   C. Have any threats or insinuation of negative action been made to entice you into giving the information you are about to give?
   D. Have any promises of favor or threats of negative action been made by others in an attempt to have you alter the truth of your Statements with us here today?
   E. You are about to give the following truthful information of your own free will?
   F. Have any promises of favor or threats of negative action been made against you by persons or parties opposed to you talking with us today?
   G. Do you understand that both parties in this situation may, under certain circumstances, be privileged to the information you are providing today?
7. Q & A session
8. With recorder on, ask: Is there any information you feel that is pertinent to this case that I have not asked you? Is there any information that you have provided today that you wish to correct or retract?

Signed: ______________________________ Date: ____________________
Witness

Figure 4.1 Witness interview protocol.

and (2) "No threats or promises have been made in connection with this statement" (Figures 4.1 and 4.2). You may want to have the witness sign an Acknowledgment of Interview (Figures 4.3 and 4.4).

Admissions, Confessions, and Written Statements

Obtaining written statements can serve four specific purposes:

- To provide a written record for the case file
- To be used at the trial to refresh recollection, impeach witnesses, and monitor testimony
- To discourage a witness from wrongfully changing his or her testimony at trial

MCMAHON & ASSOCIATES

Witness Interview

If you are in receipt of this document, you have been asked to participate in an interview concerning a situation to which you have direct knowledge.

The purpose of this interview is for us to ascertain the truth of a particular situation. As they say in the courts, we want the truth, the whole truth and nothing but the truth. We represent our client in this matter and wish to gather as much information as possible relevant to the situation so that our client and any legal representatives they may have, will be able to determine the viability of their claim.

As an interviewee, you should be made aware of the following:

1. We make no promise of reward of any kind whether it be cash, property, tangible items, or promise of favors in return for the Statement(s) you are about to make.
2. You are not required to talk to us. However, as you have been identified as having specific information relevant to this case, you may be subpoenaed to testify under oath in court. (One of the purposes of interviews such as ours is to find the truth in a matter so that court may not be necessary).
3. You have the right, if you feel uncomfortable speaking with us, to bring someone to the interview with you. It can be a friend or relative, your own legal representative, or even a tape recorder or video camera of your own so that you have direct record of what it is discussed.
4. The information gathered here today will be kept privileged amongst the parties involved in this matter. This includes our client and their legal representatives as well as the matter's opposition and their legal representatives. No part whatsoever of your Statements will be made publicly associated with you without your express permission.
5. Your photo (if one is taken) will not be used for any purposes other than to identify you to our client. Your photo will not be published or used to identify you to anyone not privileged to this information without your express consent.

Investigator:______________________________
(print)

______________________________ Date:___/___/___
(signed)

Figure 4.2 Witness interview form.

- To assist the attorneys in planning their presentation by reducing the elements of surprise that unforeseen testimony would produce

Admissions

An admission is a self-incriminating statement by the subject falling short of an acknowledgment of guilt. It is an acknowledgment of a fact or circumstance from which guilt may be inferred. A simple statement that the subject was present at the scene of the crime (or event) may be an admission.

Confessions

A confession is a direct acknowledgment of the truth of the guilty facts as charged or of some essential part of the commission of the criminal act. To be admissible in court, a confession must be voluntary and trustworthy.

MCMAHON & ASSOCIATES

Witness Acknowledgement

I ______________________ certify by signature below that the information I am providing is, to the best of my knowledge, complete, truthful, and unbiased. By my signature below I further affirm the following that:

1. I understand the purpose of this interview.
2. I have not been promised any kind of reward whether it be cash, tangible items, or any other promise of favor in exchange for the information I am about to give.
3. No threats or insinuations of negative action have been made to entice me into giving the information I am about to give.
4. No promise of favor nor threats of negative action have been made by others to have me alter my statements.
5. I am about to give the following truthful information of my own free will.
6. I have given permission for this session to be tape-recorded.
7. I have read the written notes taken by the interviewer and acknowledge that they are an accurate depiction of the answers I have given.
8. I have given my permission to be photographed for the purposes of identification by the client.

Agent: ______________________ Signature: ______________________ Date: __________

Interviewee: ______________________ Signature: ______________________ Date: __________

Witness: ______________________ Signature: ______________________ Date: __________

Page # ____

Figure 4.3 Witness acknowledgment form.

Examples of circumstances that would render a confession inadmissible are threats of bodily harm, illegal detainment, deprivation of necessities or necessary privileges, and physical oppression.

Furthermore, the investigator should be able to show that the confession was voluntary, as evidenced by one of the following:

- The statement was not obtained by urging or by request but was a spontaneous or self-induced utterance.
- The statement was obtained without coercion and not during an official investigation or while being detained.

Depositions

A deposition is testimony of a witness reduced to writing under oath or affirmation, before a person empowered to administer oaths, in answer to questions submitted by the party desiring the deposition and the opposing party.

MCMAHON & ASSOCIATES

Witness Interviews: Cover Sheet

Case Number: **Report Date:**

Re:

	Date:	Page #	Interviewee	By:
1				
2				
3				
4				
5				
6				
7				
8				
9				
10				
11				
12				
13				
14				
15				
16				
17				
18				
19				
20				
21				
22				
23				
24				
25				

Figure 4.4 Witness interviews cover sheet.

A deposition is ordinarily used to take the testimony of a witness who may be unavailable at trial (criminal or civil). A deposition is ordinarily taken by an attorney, not an investigator.

Written Statements

Whenever possible, important statements of witnesses and suspects should be reduced to writing. Written statements should be taken from subjects and suspects, recalcitrant and reluctant witnesses, key witnesses, any witness who gives an indication of a tendency to change his or her mind, and witnesses who will not be available at legal proceedings.

Contents of Statements

The investigator should consider first what information the witness may possess and could be expected to give at testimony and, second, what information is needed to support the case. The common grounds of these two considerations should be the substance of the statement given by witnesses.

The statement of a suspect should substantiate the elements of the charge or contain any information relevant to the issues of the case. In addition, it should include any details of extraordinary circumstances or explanations offered by the suspect.

Finally, the investigator should apply the criteria used to judge a report of investigation. The purposes of such a report are as follows:

- To provide a permanent record of information
- To present clear, direct, complete, and accurate information
- To present information that can form the basis of additional investigation
- To present information that can form the basis of charges or specifications

Methods of Taking Statements

The following methods may be used when taking statements:

- The subject may write his or her own statement without guidance. A statement of this nature, which is sufficiently complete, is usually a desirable form.
- The subject may dictate to a stenographer without guidance.
- The investigator may give the subject a list of essential points to be covered in the statement and suggest that the subject include these matters and add whatever other pertinent information that he or she may wish.
- The subject may deliver his or her statement orally to the investigator, who writes the statement.
- The subject may deliver the statement orally to the investigator or stenographer in response to questions put to him or her by the investigator. The answers are recorded verbatim.
- The investigator may assist the subject, indicating which statements will express the subject's intended meaning. Great caution must be exercised by the investigator to protect him- or herself from a charge of influencing the subject. Tape recording the statement would be useful.
- The investigator may prepare the statement by writing the version of the information provided by the subject. The investigator must use the expressions employed by the subject and submit the statement to the subject for corrections and changes.

Form of Statement

Identifying Data The first paragraph of a statement should contain the date, place, identification of the maker, name of the person to whom the statement is made, plus a declaration by the maker that the statement is made voluntarily.

The Body The body of the statement can be given in narrative form. It is of great importance, particularly in a confession, that the statement include all the elements of the crime and the facts associating the suspect to these elements. The words of the subject should be used, but the scope of the confession should be guided by the investigator. The investigator may write the statement him- or herself to ensure inclusion of all necessary details. The subject should then be requested to read the statement and initial each page at the bottom. Each page should be numbered by writing in the lower-right corner (i.e., "page ___ of ___ pages").

Conclusion The concluding paragraph should state that the subject has read the document of so many pages and has signed it. The subject should then be requested to initial any corrections made on the statement.

Witness to a Confession

The presence of witnesses will provide a defense against claims that duress in the form of threats and promises was employed by the investigator. After the investigator has prepared the statement for signature, witnesses may be introduced so that they can testify to the following:

- The subject read and revised the entire statement with the investigator.
- The subject objected to certain words, phrases, or statements.
- The subject corrected certain words and phrases and initialed the corrections.
- The subject evidently understood the contents of the statement.
- The subject was in his or her right senses, knew what he or she was doing, and acted voluntarily.
- The subject acknowledged the statement to be true and correct.

Each person witnessing the signature should sign as a witness. The signature should indicate the witness' name and address. If the witness is a member of a law enforcement agency, it should be accompanied by his or her grade, title, and assignment.

Admissibility of Confessions

A confession that was obtained under duress or by compulsion or without the presence of constitutional safeguards is inadmissible in court. The investigator who obtains a confession through the employment of illegal practices renders inadmissible not only the suspect's statements but very likely the evidence that might be developed subsequently from the leads contained in the statement (the fruit of the poisonous tree). Great caution and sound judgment must be exercised in obtaining a confession to avoid casting a shadow on its legality. The investigator should have a thorough knowledge of the court requirements for admissibility and of the procedures, safeguards, and standards of conduct.

The test for admissibility employed by the federal and state courts is that a confession must be trustworthy and voluntary.

Forms of Duress

Coercion Coercion is the direct application of illegal physical methods. This refers to beatings or forms of assault, such as hitting with a rubber hose, punching, forms of torture, and so on.

Duress The imposition of restrictions on physical behavior is considered duress. This includes prolonged (6 or more hours) detention in a dark room, deprivation of food or sleep, and imposing conditions of excessive physical discomfort and continuous interrogation over extraordinarily long periods of time.

Psychological Constraint The free action of the will may be unlawfully restrained by threats or other methods of instilling fear. Suggesting the prospect of harm to the suspect, his or her relatives, or his or her property can be interpreted as psychological abuse, even though the suggestions are not in the form of explicit threats.

5 Legal Investigations

The Legal Investigator

Anthony Golec, in his bible for legal investigators, *Techniques of Legal Investigation* (Charles C. Thomas, Springfield, Illinois, 1995) defines a legal investigator as "the trained professional who searches out the facts to which the attorney can apply the law." He goes on to describe the purpose and functions of the legal investigator as follows:

- To interview prospective witnesses and prospective parties to the litigation
- To find and interview prospective experts in the technical areas of the litigation
- To search for pertinent evidence, be it physical, testimonial, or documentary
- To assemble a complete factual picture of all the events surrounding the events under litigation

I became a Certified Legal Investigator in 1997, which is when I decided to switch my focus to conducting criminal and civil investigations. As a former federal probation officer for 12 years, I felt very comfortable working in the federal court system. I had also become acquainted with many high-caliber criminal defense attorneys, such as Roy Black, Joel Hirschorn, and former federal prosecutor Michael Pasano. I used that knowledge to market to the federal defense bar and establish a client base of attorneys doing federal criminal defense. Included in those cases is court-appointed criminal defense work, which I do for two long-standing clients: Albert Levin and Allen Kaufman. This means that I am paid for my work at a lower rate (usually $60 per hour) because the defendants are indigent and their attorney is appointed by the court in instances where the Federal Public Defender's office has a conflict. Levin and Kaufman are both on the CJA panel for the Southern District of Florida, where I live and work. Working CJA cases is something that I thoroughly enjoy and has been very helpful during the economic downturn.

In the 12 years that I have been working the federal cases I have noticed a disturbing trend. The goals and objectives of the government (prosecutors and agents) appear to have changed from the focus of getting the criminal at the top and bringing down the organization to one of prosecuting anyone who is in any way connected to anybody involved in the case. In essence, a numbers game. The prosecution is giving significant "plea deals" to the main conspirators in the case (the whales) in return for testimony about any and all of their minions who took part in the criminal conspiracy (the guppies). When I entered law enforcement in 1973, the deals were offered to the lower-level criminal in return for his or her testimony against the ringleaders. When and why has that central concept in criminal prosecution been abandoned?

Furthermore, the government appears to take the "battle" between the two sides, prosecution and defense, a lot more personally. There appears to be much more hostility from the government against the defense lawyers and the members of their team, including the criminal defense investigator. This is a trend I would like to see reversed. Both are doing their job to the best of their ability. It should not be personal.

In order to become a legal investigator, knowledge of the U.S. Constitution and the court systems is required. All the necessary information to accomplish that task is beyond the scope of this one chapter. However, an overview from which one sees the perspective needed in order to become a legal investigator is provided here.

Structure of the U.S. Constitution

The U.S. Constitution is divided into seven parts, or articles.

Article I

The first article sets up the structure and function of the U.S. Congress, which is comprised of two houses, the Senate and the House of Representatives.

Article II

The second article sets up the executive branch of government. It provides that the executive powers of the United States shall be vested in the President.

Article III

The third article vests the judicial power of the United States in the Supreme Court and in such lower courts as Congress sees fit to establish.

Article IV

The fourth article spells out some of the duties the states owe to each other, including the duties extending full faith and credit to the laws of sister states and granting equal privileges and immunities to citizens of other states and of interstate extradition.

Article V

This article defines two procedures for amending the Constitution:

1. The Constitution may be amended when three-fourths of both houses shall propose amendments, and these are ratified by three-fourths of the states or by state conventions in three-fourths of the states.
2. The Constitution may be amended by application of the legislators of two-thirds of the states. Congress will call a convention for proposing amendments that will be valid when ratified by the legislators of three-fourths of the states.

Article VI

This article contains the "supremacy" clause that provides that the Constitution, laws, and treaties of the United States shall be the supreme law of the land, and that state judges are to be bound by this law regardless of their state constitution and laws to the contrary.

Article VII

This historical article provides that the U.S. Constitution will become effective when ratified by nine states and will be operative for those states that ratify it.

Limitations on State Powers

The Constitution prohibits the states from entering into treaties, alliances, or confederations; coining money; passing a bill that inflicts punishment without a trial; and enacting *ex post facto* laws.

Powers Retained by the State

Under the case *District of Columbia v. Brooke* (214 US 138), states have passed laws defining crimes, regulating traffic, and providing for criminal procedural rules.

The Bill of Rights

The Bill of Rights, or the first ten amendments to the U.S. Constitution, was not intended to establish any new principles of government but simply to include certain guarantees the colonists wanted to maintain. The specific provisions of the Bill of Rights provide a broad framework that would mean little without court interpretation.

The First Amendment

The First Amendment prohibits Congress from making any law establishing a religion or prohibiting freedom of religion. It also provides freedom of speech, freedom of the press, and the right of the people to assemble and petition the government for redress of grievances.

The Second Amendment

The Second Amendment provides that the right of the people to keep and bear arms shall not be infringed.

The Third Amendment

The Third Amendment provides that no soldier during peace time shall be quartered in any house without the consent of the owner.

The Fourth Amendment

The Fourth Amendment provides against unreasonable searches and seizures.

The Fifth Amendment

The Fifth Amendment provides safeguards to persons accused of crimes. It provides that a person cannot be held for a capital crime without a Grand Jury indictment; that no person shall be tried twice for the same offense; that no person shall be compelled in any criminal case to be a witness against him- or herself; that no person shall be deprived of life, liberty, or property without due process of law; and that no person shall be deprived of his or her property for public use without just compensation.

The Sixth Amendment

The Sixth Amendment provides for speedy and public trial by an impartial jury of the state in which the crime was committed, the right to confront witnesses, the right to be informed of the nature of the charges, the right to have compulsory process, and the right to have an attorney represent you.

The Seventh Amendment

The Seventh Amendment is a safeguard of property rights. It provides for the right to a jury trial in property controversies exceeding a specified amount.

The Eighth Amendment

The Eighth Amendment restricts both the legislative and judicial branches of government and guarantees certain rights to individuals including guarantees against excessive bail, excessive fines, and cruel and unusual punishment.

The Ninth Amendment

The Ninth Amendment provides that certain rights contained in the Constitution do not deny others retained by the people.

The Tenth Amendment

The Tenth Amendment states that "powers not delegated by the Constitution nor prohibited by the states are reserved by the people."

Due Process of Law

Included in the Bill of Rights is the provision that "no person shall be deprived of life, liberty, or property without due process of law." This provision as it appears in the Fifth Amendment is a restriction only upon the federal government. It was not until 1868 that a federal constitutional provision concerning due process applied to the states. In that year, the Fourteenth Amendment was ratified. That amendment stated, in part, "Nor shall any state deprive any person of life, liberty, or property without due process of law."

In the early decisions of the Supreme Court, the judges decided that certain rights, such as free speech, were fundamental and must "be protected against abuse by state officials." In applying the "fundamental rights" theory, these judges justified making these rights applicable to the states by way of the Fourteenth Amendment's due process clause. These rights, such as freedom of speech, were so fundamental that a state in violation of these rights failed to comply with the demands of the Fourteenth Amendment.

In 1925, the Supreme Court in *Gitlow v. New York* (268 US 652) expressed the opinion that the rights protected by the First Amendment are fundamental personal rights protected by the due process clause of the Fourteenth Amendment.

Habeas Corpus

The Writ of Habeas Corpus (Latin for "you shall have the body") is used to question the legality of the detention of a prisoner. Its sole function is to release petitioners from unlawful imprisonment. When a defendant is charged with violating state statute in a felony case, after a preliminary hearing in a lower court, the defendant is tried in an intermediate court, often called a circuit court. If convicted, he or she may appeal to a State Court of Appeals and then to the supreme court of the state. Finally, on constitutional questions, he or she may appeal to the U.S. Supreme Court. This may be done by the appeals process through state and federal courts or by a Writ of Habeas Corpus. This writ sets up a hearing on the constitutional issues of a defendant. Habeas corpus proceedings in federal court determine the issues of whether the defendant was provided with his or her fair full constitutional rights and safeguards in state proceedings.

Criminal and Civil Procedure

Types of Law

There are two types of law: public law and private law.

1. Public law

   This type of law concerns the structures, power, and operations of a government; the rights and duties of citizens in relation to government; and the relationships among nations. It can be subdivided into four sections:

   a. Constitutional law

      The fundamental law of a nation is derived from the Constitution, which records the body of rules in accordance with which the powers of government are carried out. Constitutions may be either written or unwritten; that of the United States is written, and that of the United Kingdom is unwritten. In some nations, courts have the power of judicial review, whereby they declare unconstitutional, and therefore void, laws that go against the provisions or arrangements of the constitution.

b. Administrative law

Administrative law includes laws governing the organization and operation of agencies of the executive branch of government, the substantive and procedural rules that these agencies create and apply pursuant to their regulatory and other administrative functions, and court decisions involving public agencies and private citizens.

c. Criminal law

Criminal law consists of laws that impose obligations to do or to refrain from doing certain things, the infraction of which is considered to be an offense against the victim as well as society. Most laws are backed by sanctions (punishments) that are applied in the event of conviction. Major breaches of criminal law, usually defined as punishable by imprisonment for more than one year are called *felonies*; less serious crimes, called *misdemeanors*, are punishable by imprisonment for up to and including 1 year or by fines or both.

d. International law

International law concerns the relationships among nations, including the use of the high seas, international trade, boundary disputes, warfare methods, and so on.

2. Private law

Unlike public law, private law does not involve governments directly but rather indirectly as a mediator between disputing parties; private law provides rules to be applied when one person claims that another has injured his or her person, property, or reputation, or has failed to carry out a valid legal obligation. Private law is subdivided into six main categories: tort law, property law, contract/business law, corporation law, inheritance law (probate or wills), and family law. These will be discussed later in this book.

Sources of Law

Laws can also be subdivided on the basis of the sources from which they derive. Some of the major sources are constitutions and administrative rules, legislative statutes, judicial precedents (also known as case law), and customary practice.

Statutes are now outnumbered by the numerous administrative rules and regulations that have accompanied the growth of administrative government in modern times. Judicial precedents are recognized as valid law that later courts must follow in common law but not in civil law systems. Judicial precedents are prior cases decided by the courts.

Customary practice is a minor source of law in the legal systems of advanced nations but is the primary, if not only, source in primitive legal systems.

Civil Procedures

Each of the state and federal judicial systems has rules of civil procedure that govern the conduct of most noncriminal judicial proceedings. Procedural law exists so that substantive law can be implemented. The principal objective of procedural law is to give the parties to a dispute an equal and fair opportunity to present their cases to a non-prejudicial and convenient tribunal. If procedural rules are correctly drafted and implemented, both parties to the dispute should feel that they have been fairly treated. It should be understood that the federal government and each state have established procedural rules for their court systems.

Civil Trials

A trial is a legal procedure available to parties who have been either unwilling or unable to resolve their differences through negotiations, settlement offers, or mediation attempts. Trials involve the staging of a confrontation between the plaintiff and defendant as contradicting witnesses, and arguments collide in the courtroom in accordance with procedural and evidentiary rules. The trial process may, as a result of appeals, take many years, but it will result in either a dismissal of the complaint or a judgment.

In some cases, parties with a right to present their evidence to a jury prefer instead to try their case before a judge. This is called a bench trial. The right to a federal jury trial is provided by the Seventh Amendment to parties involved in a common law civil action. The right to a civil jury trial in the state judicial system is determined by state law. The judge is responsible for making sure the following occur:

- The jury is properly selected in a jury trial.
- Due process requirements for a fair trial are satisfied.
- Proper rulings are made with respect to admissibility of evidence.
- The rules of procedure are followed by the parties.
- The judgment is awarded in accordance with the law.

Criminal Procedure

Criminal procedure is that area of the law that deals with the administration of criminal justice, from the initial investigation of a crime and arrest of a suspect, through trial, sentence, and release. The goal of criminal justice is to protect society from antisocial activity without sacrificing individual rights, justice, and fair play. The procedures used to apprehend and prosecute alleged criminal offenders must comply with the requirements of law. One objective of using the adversary system, involving prosecutors and defense attorneys, is to ensure that procedural justice is afforded the defendant. The judge umpires the dispute between the litigants and tries to ensure that both parties receive a fair trial—one that meets the requirements of substantive and procedural law. The judge or jury determines the guilt or innocence of the accused by properly evaluating the facts presented in open court.

State and federal courts protect the accused from lengthy imprisonment prior to trial, prevent long delays that could impair the defense of the accused person through the loss of evidence, and prevent or minimize public suspicion and anxiety connected with the accused, who is yet untried. The right to a speedy trial starts when the prosecution begins, either by indictment or by the actual arrest. How much time must elapse to result in an unconstitutional delay varies with the circumstances. The accused has the burden of showing that the delay was the fault of the state and resulted in prejudice.

Basic Components of a Criminal Offense

A criminal offense includes the following components: the wrongful act, the guilty mind, concurrence, and causation. For a conviction, proof of each element is required beyond a reasonable doubt.

The Wrongful Act

The wrongful act, or *actus reus*, is an unjustified action against someone's person or property. There are special rules that govern the wrongful act. For instance, the law recognizes the existence of a legal duty, whereby the failure to act is equivalent to a criminal act. The duty to act can be imposed by statute (i.e., filing income tax returns), by contract (such as between parents and a daycare center), by one's status (parent/child or husband/wife), or because one has assumed a responsibility (taking care of a disabled person).

Another exception to the requirement of a physical act is recognized in possession offenses in which the law treats the fact of possession as the equivalent of a wrongful act. Possession can be actual, as when the accused is found with the contraband on his or her person, or constructive, as when the contraband is not on the suspect's person but is under his or her control.

Criminal State of Mind

The second requirement of a criminal offense is that the alleged criminal offender possess a criminal state of mind (*mens rea*) at the time of the commission of the wrongful act. This is called a concurrence of a wrongful act with a wrongful state of mind. Concurrence is required, because some people who commit wrongful acts do not have a wrongful state of mind. A specific intent crime requires proof of the commission of an *actus reus* plus a specified level of knowledge or additional intent, such as the intent to commit a felony. Criminal negligence results from unconscious risk creation.

Causation

There are some criminal offenses that require proof that the defendant's conduct caused a given result. The prosecution must establish causation beyond a reasonable doubt when it is an element of a crime. A key to establishing causation is the legal concept of "proximate cause." Criminal liability attaches only to conduct that is determined to be the proximate or legal cause of the harmful result. This includes both direct and indirect causation. The legal cause is often the direct cause of harm.

Proximate cause is a flexible concept. It permits fact finders to sort through various factual causes and determine who should be found legally responsible. In addition, the accused is responsible for only the reasonably foreseeable consequences that follow from his or her act. The law provides that an accused person is not responsible for consequences that follow the intervention of a new and independent causal force.

The Concept of Crime

Crime is a wrong against the public interest to which a governmental jurisdiction has attached a penalty. It is an act that has been committed or omitted in violation of a public law either prohibiting or commanding it. The law may prohibit the commission of overt acts, such as robbery, rape, burglary, speeding, or disorderly conduct. It may also require that acts be done. Thus, an individual's failure to act may constitute a violation of criminal law (i.e., failure to file a tax return).

Crime is classified by grades, generally in accordance with the degree of penalty attached to it. The three usual classifications of crime are treason, felony, and misdemeanor. Treason consists of waging war or giving aid and comfort to the enemy. A felony is a crime that carries a penalty of death or imprisonment for more than 1 year in a state prison. A misdemeanor is a crime that carries a penalty of less than 1 year to be served in a city or county jail.

The Effective Limits of Criminal Law

The concept of security of the person and the right of enjoyment of personal property appears to be the fundamental basis of criminal law. Crimes of aggression, such as murder, assault, rape, burglary, and theft of person or property, are considered *mala in se*—immoral or wrong by their very nature.

A second category of crime can be described as regulatory, which is designed to provide a degree of conformity for the purposes of safety, efficiency, and convenience (i.e., traffic laws). These crimes are *mala prohibita*—bad only because the legislature has prohibited them.

A third category of crime promotes honesty and morality. These laws prohibit such acts as sale of impure food and drugs, pollution of the environment, obtaining property under false pretense, and so on. These crimes are classified as protective crimes.

A fourth category of crime regulates personal morality. These are referred to as *vice crimes* and include adultery, sodomy, prostitution, pornography, and so on.

The final category of crime involves the use and sale of narcotics and alcohol. The addict and alcoholic are psychologically and physically dependent and, unlike vice criminals, can seldom voluntarily terminate their continuous offenses.

The Authority to Arrest

The general requirements (elements) of an arrest by a police officer are as follows:

- There must be intent on the part of the officer to make an arrest, intent to deprive a person of his liberty, and intent to restrain him or her physically if he or she does not peacefully submit.
- The officer must inform the individual of his or her intention to place the person under arrest and the reason or cause for the arrest.
- The officer must identify the authority under which he or she acts. If the officer is clearly uniformed, this requirement is normally met.
- The individual must be placed under the officer's actual control. If the officer communicates his or her intention, authority, and reason for the arrest, and the individual submits to the officer and obeys his or her commands, an arrest is made.

Investigative Detention Short of Arrest—Stop and Frisk

In 1968, the issue of a police officer detaining (stopping) and conducting a cursory search (frisking) was raised before the U.S. Supreme Court in *Terry v. Ohio*. In this case, the facts clearly indicated the good faith and reasonable judgment of the police officer and substantial motivation for his actions.

Searches

The Fourth Amendment prohibits unreasonable searches. Until 1914, the court had no authority to exclude evidence obtained from an illegal search from being admitted into evidence. In the U.S. Supreme Court case *Weeks v. United States*, the court created the exclusionary rule. It provides that evidence obtained as a result of an unreasonable search is inadmissible in any federal criminal prosecution. In 1961 in *Mapp v. Ohio*, the Supreme Court held that all evidence in violation of the Constitution is inadmissible in a state court.

Interrogating the Accused

Historically, the primary test for the establishment of validity of a confession admitted into evidence at a criminal trial was whether the confession was voluntary and trustworthy. Voluntary meant that no physical force was used to obtain the confession. Trustworthy meant that the circumstances under which the confession was obtained were unlikely to induce an innocent person to confess.

In 1943 in *McNabb v. United States*, the Supreme Court expanded the voluntary-trustworthy test for federal cases and established an additional test requiring civilized interrogation standards.

In 1957 in *Mallory v. United States*, the court held that before a confession may be admitted into evidence, it must be voluntary, trustworthy, obtained under civilized standards of interrogation, and not obtained during any unnecessary delay between time of arrest and taking the accused before a magistrate. (These rules applied only to federal cases.)

In 1964, the Supreme Court in *Escobedo v. Illinois* held inadmissible a confession obtained after police failed to advise a prisoner of his absolute constitutional right to remain silent and refused to honor his request to consult with his attorney.

In 1966 in *Miranda v. Arizona*, the court extended the Escobedo doctrine further and established a series of procedural requirements that must be met before any interrogation of an arrestee could occur.

The Trial

Preliminary Proceedings in the Trial Court

Pleas

The defendant may enter a plea of guilty, not guilty, *nolo contendere*, stand mute, or make a motion to invalidate the indictment or information. After entry of the plea, the defendant may be asked to choose to be tried by jury or by judge without a jury. The court will then docket the case for trial. In approximately one half of the states and in federal courts, the defendant may enter a plea of *nolo contendere*. By entry of this plea, the defendant indicates that even though not guilty, a decision has been made not to contest the charges. The defendant may choose to stand mute or not enter a plea. When this occurs, the judge will enter a plea of not guilty and proceed accordingly.

Motion to Suppress State's Evidence

A motion to suppress the state's evidence may be filed prior to the time of trial and frequently is filed during arraignment (the formal reading of charges) or shortly thereafter.

The motion alleges that the evidence the state plans to use at trial was obtained unlawfully through violation of the defendant's rights. Normally, this motion is filed in an attempt to exclude evidence obtained as a result of a search or wiretap, or to challenge the validity of a confession.

Motion for a Bill of Particulars

To be technically correct, the indictment or information must contain a statement of the act constituting the offense. The accusations must be certain and direct concerning the particular circumstances of the offenses charged. It is possible for the accusation to meet these requirements and yet be drawn in such a way that the major issue is not clearly defined. Under such circumstances, a defendant may file a Motion for a Bill of Particulars. A Bill of Particulars is a supplementary document prepared by the prosecution which presents more elaborate details of the charges.

Motion for Discovery of Evidence

A Motion for Discovery is a procedure by which the defendant is permitted to examine certain evidence possessed by the prosecutor prior to trial. Because of the defendant's privilege against self-incrimination, the prosecutor does not have a similar right of discovery. However, the prosecution may be entitled to notice of the defendant's intention to use an alibi or insanity as a defense and may obtain the names of witnesses to be used for this purpose.

Motion for a Change of Venue or Judge

If it can be established that a fair and impartial trial cannot be obtained in the county where the crime was committed, the defendant is entitled to have the trial moved to another county. This is accomplished by filing a Motion for Change of Venue. A Motion for Change of Judge, or a recusation, may be used to request the assignment of another judge to try the case, based upon grounds of bias and prejudice or other disqualifying circumstances.

Motion for Continuance

The court may grant a continuance, at its own discretion, when valid reasons are presented by the defendant, some of which are unavailability of important witnesses, illness of the defendant, need for more time to prepare the case adequately, or recent discharge of the defendant's attorney.

The Motion for Continuance is the most frequently filed motion by the defense.

Pretrial proceedings should be concerned with assuring the defendant's constitutional rights and correcting any defects in previous proceedings, thereby avoiding a reversal of the case on appeal and the expense of a retrial.

The Guilty Plea

In felony cases and in some serious misdemeanor cases, the plea occurs after an initial appearance and a preliminary exam, normally at the time of arraignment before the trial court. The acceptance of the plea by the court is usually a brief ritual at which the judge learns from the defendant whether he or she is fully aware of the charges pending against him or her; the extent of the punishment that may be assessed upon conviction; and the defenses available to the charges. The judge is also responsible for determining whether the plea is entered freely, intelligently, and voluntarily. The court is not required to accept a guilty plea if it feels injustice will result.

Limited resources of prosecutor's offices and the court and the desirability of avoiding the time-consuming and expensive process of trial by jury have led to the universal practice of plea bargaining. Plea bargaining consists of negotiations between the prosecutor, the accused, and the defense attorney to exchange prosecutorial concessions for a plea of guilty. Prosecutors may make a broad array of promises in exchange for these pleas. The promises may include such actions as follows:

- Recommendation of a specific sentence
- Reduction of charges
- Dismissal of other pending charges
- Agreement not to charge the defendant with additional offenses for which adequate evidence is available
- Recommendation for probation
- Similar recommendations

The courts generally recognize that the practices engaged in during plea bargaining, under proper conditions, constitute lawful exercise of prosecutorial discretion. The sentencing practices of the courts seem to reinforce plea bargaining and generally encourage the entry of guilty pleas.

Jury Trial and Jury Selection

After the arraignment and necessary hearings on motions, the case is docketed for a specific trial date. When the case is called for trial, the first action is selection of the jury. In all jurisdictions, the jury is viewed as the instrument for determining the facts. It is given broad discretion in exercising its decision-making powers. It is allowed to deliberate in secret and reach a decision that it is not required to justify. Traditionally, the jury in a felony case consists of 12 jurors who must reach a unanimous decision concerning the defendant's guilt or innocence. However, in a 1970 case, the Supreme Court in *Williams v. Florida* held that there was no constitutional requirement to seat 12 jurors, and that a state could establish a procedure requiring a different number.

Selecting the Jury Panel

State statutes or court rules will normally specify the procedure for selecting the jury panel (venire). Designated officials (i.e., jury commissioners, sheriffs, clerks of the court, etc.) will compile a list of prospective jurors within the court's jurisdiction. This list will normally be taken from voter's registration lists or the tax rolls. For normal operations, the court may specify that 50 prospective jurors (venire persons) be called. The clerk randomly draws the prescribed number of names and prepares court summons ordering the prospective jurors to appear for jury duty. In selecting a jury panel, the Supreme Court has made it clear that the Constitution bars conscious discrimination in jury selection by reasons of race, national origin, religion, sex, or economic status.

Qualifying the Jury Panel

The prospective jurors report at the time and place designated in the summons. The judge usually meets with the panel and explains the operation of the court system and the responsibility and function of the jurors. The judge also explains that under law, certain individuals are not qualified for service as jurors. Such exclusions may include the following:

- A person who cannot read, write, or understand the English language
- A person with unsoundness of mind or a physical defect such as deafness or blindness
- An individual convicted of a felony

The judge explains that certain venire persons, because of special conditions, may not be required to serve as jurors, even though they possess proper qualifications. Individuals who fall under these special conditions may exercise an exemption and choose not to serve as jurors. Some examples are physicians, clergymen, news media personnel, college students, and women with small children.

The judge instructs the clerk to draw the jury. The clerk draws 12 (or 6) names from the receptacle containing the names of qualified venire persons. Those selected are seated in the jury box. Through a process known as *voir dire* examination, the individual jurors are questioned to establish their qualifications for service in the particular case. Before such qualification begins, the jurors are placed under oath to answer truthfully all questions concerning their qualifications. The *voir dire* begins when the judge, the prosecutor, or the defense attorney introduces the parties in the case and makes general inquiries relating to a juror's qualifications. After completing general opening questions, counsel may ask specific questions relating to qualifications. If during questioning a prospective juror indicates that he or she has knowledge, attitudes, opinions, or relationships that clearly indicate a bias or prejudice toward either party, counsel may challenge the juror for cause. In some cases, grounds for challenge for cause are established by statute. Counsel directs challenge for cause to the judge. The judge then makes a ruling concerning the challenge. The judge may question the juror further if there is insufficient information upon which to base a decision. If the judge finds sufficient evidence to warrant dismissal, the juror will be dismissed, and the clerk will draw another juror. All that is required is that the juror must have no fixed opinion that will prevent him or her from rendering a fair and impartial verdict based upon the evidence admitted in the trial and the law presented by the judge.

After 12 (or 6) jurors have been tentatively accepted, counsel may then exercise peremptory challenges. Using a peremptory challenge, counsel may excuse a juror without stating a cause. The number of peremptory challenges available to each side is regulated by statute or court rule. Each time a peremptory challenge is exercised, the clerk draws a new juror who is then subjected to questioning to determine whether a challenge for cause applies to him or her. The process continues until all challenges are exhausted or waived. The 12 (or 6) individuals remaining constitute the jury for the case. Some states permit the selection of alternate jurors. If one of the principal jurors becomes ill or a personal emergency arises, the juror may be released and an alternate juror substituted. When the principal and alternate jurors are selected, the jury panel is sworn in.

The Trial

Although a relatively small percentage of total criminal cases are adjudicated by juries, the right to a trial should be recognized as a significant constitutional guarantee. The Sixth Amendment provides that the defendant in a criminal prosecution has a right to a public trial. Furthermore, the defendant has a constitutional right to be present in the courtroom during every stage of the proceedings from arraignment through sentencing, and to confront witnesses against him.

Opening Statements

After the jury has been impaneled, the indictment is usually read. The prosecution then makes an opening statement. The purpose of this statement is to inform the jury of the general nature of the case, the facts as the prosecution views them, and the significance of witnesses and physical evidence that will be presented to prove the alleged facts. The opening statement must be restricted to the specifics of the case being tried. After the prosecutor's opening statement is concluded, the defense attorney may make an opening statement or request permission to defer or reserve the statement until the prosecution's case has been concluded. If the defendant chooses, the opening statement may be waived.

The State's Case

After the opening statement, the prosecution must present its proof by calling its witnesses. The Sixth Amendment provides that "in all criminal prosecutions, the accused shall enjoy the right to be confronted with witnesses against them." All courts agree that the defendant's rights to confrontation and cross-examination of the witnesses are essential, fundamental requirements of a fair trial and due process.

If physical evidence is to be introduced, there must be a witness to identify it, testify to its relevance, establish that it is in approximately the same condition as it was at the time it was obtained (or adequately explain why it is not), show that there was no opportunity for anyone to tamper with it (chain of custody), and state that it was not obtained in violation of the defendant's constitutional rights (if challenged by the defense). Physical evidence is introduced during the course of the regular testimony subject to approval of the judge for admissibility.

The prosecutor begins the presentation of evidence by direct examination of the first witness. (See Figure 5.1 for a sample Witness Evaluation form.) In response to the prosecutor's questions, the witness relates information about the case. Upon completion of direct examination, the defense may conduct a cross-examination of the witness. With this, defense counsel attempts to clarify or enlarge upon testimony of the witness and, on occasion, to impeach credibility of the witness by attempting to discover any bias, prejudice, or interests in the defendant's conviction.

Upon completion of cross-examination, the prosecutor may conduct a redirect examination limited to those matters discussed during cross-examination. Additional examination may be conducted by the attorneys, but this examination is generally limited in nature and scope to those matters related during the preceding examination. After the testimony of the first witness,

WITNESS EVALUATION

Name:

Home Address: Home Phone:

Employer:

Work Address: Work Phone:

Occupation:

DOB: SSN: CDL:

Close Relative: Address: Phone:

Marital Status: SPOUSE:

Educational Background:

Military Experience: Branch________; Rank________; Type Discharge__________
Court Martials____________; Time Period in Service___

Criminal History:

Driving History:

Drug/Prescription Medication/Alcohol History:

Attitude Regarding Case:

Relationship to Case:

Personal Appearance: Ht:_____Wt_____Hair_____Eyes_____Glasses______
Scars/Marks/Tatoos_____________________________

General Impression:

Interviewer: Date:

Figure 5.1 Witness evaluation form.

the prosecutor calls subsequent witnesses, who undergo the same process. When the testimony of the State's final witness is concluded, the prosecutor announces that the State rests its case.

Motion for Judgment of Acquittal

At the close of the State's case, the defendant may enter a motion for a judgment of acquittal. Such a motion challenges the sufficiency of the evidence to sustain a conviction and asks the court to rule, as a matter of law, that the State has not met its burden of proof. If the State has clearly failed to meet its burden, the judge may grant the motion and acquit the defendant. If the possibility of conviction exists, the motion is overruled.

The Defense's Case

The defense attorney presents his or her case following the same format as that of the prosecution. In most instances, the only investigation conducted by the defense will be the work of the criminal defense investigator hired by the defendant, or the attorney, or appointed by the court in cases of indigence. The defense will call witnesses and conduct direct examination followed by cross-examination by the prosecutor. The defendant may waive presentation of witnesses and submit the case based only on the State's evidence. If the defendant presents witnesses, the defendant is not required to testify. If the defendant refuses to take the witness stand, neither the prosecutor nor the judge is permitted to call this lack of testimony to the attention of the jury. To do so would constitute reversible error by the judge. However, once the stand is taken, the defendant is subject to the same cross-examination as other witnesses, including disclosure of prior criminal convictions, for the purpose of attacking personal credibility. Upon completion of testimony of the final witness for the defense, the defense rests its case.

Rebuttal and Surrebuttal

After the defense rests its case, the prosecutor is given the opportunity to call additional witnesses for the special purpose of refuting or rebutting the evidence presented by defense witnesses. If the prosecution calls rebuttal witnesses, the defense may conduct surrebuttal and disprove points raised or established during rebuttal.

After receipt of all the evidence, the defense may again enter a motion for acquittal that challenges the sufficiency of the evidence and requests the court to rule as a matter of law that the State has not met its burden of proof.

Instructions to the Jury

The judge is responsible for instructing the jury clearly, fully, and accurately on all issues that were raised during the trial. The instructions traditionally include a definition of the crime with which the defendant is charged, the State's burden of proof, the presumption of the defendant's innocence, instructions relating to specific evidence in the case, and procedures for electing a foreman and returning a verdict.

During the progress of the trial, usually in chambers, the judge will give both attorneys the opportunity to submit suggested or requested instructions. In the absence of specific request, the judge may use a standard form or pattern instructions that apply to all cases of a specific type, or, if there are special circumstances in the case, the judge may require one of the counsel to draft a suggested instruction on the point in question.

Prior to the formal instruction to the jury, the judge prepares the set of instructions to be given. Both counsels review them. If there is a disagreement, there may be a conference between the judge and the attorneys. Subsequently, the judge prepares the final instructions and both counsels are given an opportunity to record any objections to them for possible appeal.

In some jurisdictions, along with giving the instructions, the judge may summarize the evidence, analyze it generally, and emphasize what are considered to be significant aspects.

Closing Arguments

After instructions to the jury, the prosecutor and defense attorney present closing arguments. The primary purpose of the closing arguments is to give counsel an opportunity to summarize the evidence, comment upon it in relation to theories on the case, and attempt to persuade the jury to accept particular inferences and deductions.

The attorneys are generally given liberal freedom in their range of discussion, use of illustrations, and employment of persuasion, as long as they confine themselves to discussion of evidence presented and normal deductions arising therefrom.

Jury Deliberations

Following the closing arguments, the jury retires to the jury room for deliberations in an effort to arrive at a verdict. Many jurisdictions do not permit the jury to separate once deliberations begin. This restriction may require that the jury stay overnight (or longer) in a hotel (sequestered).

If the jury reports back to the court that it is unable to reach a verdict after considering all the circumstances involved, the judge may send the jury back to the jury room for further deliberations and encourage the jury to reach a verdict. When the jury has arrived at a verdict or finds itself hopelessly deadlocked, the jury returns to the courtroom. If a verdict has been obtained, it is received and announced. If a verdict has not been obtained and all reasonable methods of obtaining it have been exhausted (hung jury), the judge dismisses the jury and declares a mistrial. After the jury has returned a verdict, counsel may request that the jury be polled. The judge or the clerk then asks each juror individually whether the verdict announced is the individual's verdict. This process is designed to determine whether each juror is acting freely, according to conscience, or is the subject of group domination by fellow jurors. If the poll discloses it was not a unanimous verdict, the judge may direct the jury to return for further deliberations or be dismissed and declare a mistrial.

If the verdict is not guilty, the defendant is discharged and the case permanently terminated, except in two states (Connecticut and Wisconsin) that permit the State to appeal a not guilty verdict. If the verdict is guilty, the judge will set a sentencing date and remand the defendant to jail or permit a release on bail. If a mistrial is declared, the parties are in the same position as if no trial had occurred, and proceedings may be reinstated against the defendant.

Motion for a New Trial

After receipt of a guilty verdict, in most jurisdictions the accused may file a motion for a new trial with the judge of the trial court within a specified time period (usually 10 to 30 days). The motion requests that the judge set aside the verdict and grant a new trial, because during the trial the defendant was deprived of a substantive right or the conduct or circumstances of the trial resulted in a prejudicial verdict. The grounds for a new trial may include the following:

- The trial was held in the defendant's absence.
- The jury received (and probably considered) evidence other than that properly presented in court.
- The jury was guilty of misconduct (a juror was intoxicated, a juror communicated with a third party, etc.).
- The court erred in a decision on a question of law during the trial (admission of tainted evidence, overruling a proper objection, etc.).
- The court gave an improper instruction to the jury.

Before a new trial can be granted, the defendant must establish that the error caused (or had a potential for causing) substantial prejudice, especially in cases where the defendant's guilt is clear and convincing. On occasion, a new trial may be granted because of newly discovered evidence of a substantial nature.

Sentencing

After a guilty verdict, the court sets a sentencing date for pronouncing formal sentence. At the appointed time, the prosecutor, the defense attorney, and the defendant are present in open court before the judge. Unless there is good cause shown, the court pronounces sentence.

The Sentencing Decision Sentencing alternatives available to the judge, depending on jurisdiction, may include the payment of a fine, probation, imprisonment, confinement in a nonpenal facility, a combination of the above, or death.

Depending on the nature of the case, the court may order the defendant to make restitution to the victim or forfeit the property used in the commission of the crime. If the crime involves addiction to drugs or alcohol or involves insanity or sexual psychopathy, the court may order the defendant to be confined in a specific treatment facility.

Probation Probation is a privilege the court may extend to selected offenders which permits them to avoid incarceration by conforming to prescribed conditions of good conduct during the probationary period. In granting probation, the judge may present a number of conditions that the probationer must meet. If the probationer fails to comply with the conditions of probation, he or she is subject to revocation followed by imprisonment.

Incarceration If the judge decides against probation in a case, the alternative is incarceration. Depending on the law of a particular jurisdiction, the judge may have two other decisions to make:

- Location of incarceration—work camp, reformatory, or prison.
- Length of sentence—the penalty for a particular offense is established by statute. The statute may provide for a minimum or a maximum sentence. Some states provide for an intermediate, which is a sentence that is not stated in a specific number of years. When the defendant is convicted of more than one offense during the same term or court, or the defendant is already serving a prison sentence, judges have the option of imposing either concurrent or consecutive sentences.
- Consecutive sentences—time served does not apply to the second sentence until the first sentence is completed.
- Concurrent sentences—the term served by the defendant applies to both sentences at the same time.

Appeals

The primary function of a defendant's appeal is to review alleged errors of law and defects in the trial process. Rearguing the facts of the case is not permitted in an appeal. On rare occasions, appellate courts will reverse a conviction based upon insufficient evidence. Appeals are based on the written record—in order to raise procedural defects as grounds for reversal, the court normally requires that objections must be raised at the time of the alleged defect and at subsequent opportunities, such as at a motion for a new trial. Before appellate courts will reverse a decision, the court must find the error to have substantially affected the defendant's rights and to have had the potential of affecting the results of the trial. The court may find that a procedural error was committed but conclude that it was harmless and affirm the conviction.

The Appeal Process

After notice of appeal, the defendant must file a petition with the appellate court specifying those errors and issues upon which appeal is based. The transcript containing pertinent court documents and relevant portions of trial testimony or ruling will be submitted with the petition. Supporting data in the form of a brief are also submitted. The brief should contain such items as an abstract of the case, presenting the questions involved and manner in which they are raised (objections and how they come about). A copy of the defendant's brief must be served on the official representing the State in appellate court. The prosecutor or Attorney General may file an answering brief opposing the arguments presented by the defendant. The appellate court may make a decision based upon briefs, or the court may request that the attorneys involved present oral arguments to a formal session of the court. After oral arguments, the case is submitted to members of the court for disposition. The decision of the court will be subsequently announced in a written opinion. The court will

- Affirm the lower court decision
- Reverse trial court; order a new trial
- Reverse based on insufficient evidence or other cause; defendant released

Writ of Certiorari

Petition for a Writ of Certiorari specifies the nature of the case, errors alleged, and previous court's disposition of a case. It is a petition for a review of a case by the U.S. Supreme Court.

Executive Review

Governors of individual states and the President of the United States possess the power to pardon an individual convicted of a crime, to commute the sentence to one less severe, or to grant a reprieve that orders a delay in execution of a sentence. These powers are vested exclusively in the chief executive and may be exercised at discretion.

Legal Investigations

Within the field of legal investigation there are several specialties, including criminal investigations and civil investigations. See the Law Firm Case Assignment form shown in Figure 5.2.

Criminal Investigations

Criminal investigations are those of serious crimes which may lead to arrest and conviction of a subject. Burglary, theft, homicide, fraud, auto accidents, arson, kidnapping, and so forth, are examples of activities where violations of laws have taken place.

McMahon & Associates Detective Division
1451 W. Cypress Creek Road, Suite 300
Ft. Lauderdale, FL 33309

Law Firm Case Assignment Form

Date ____________ Due Date ____________ Attorney/Contact ____________

Law Firm ____________ Phone ____________

Address ____________ Fax ____________

City, State, Zip ____________ E-mail ____________

Your Case Caption ____________

Your Client ____________

Court Case Gen. No. ____________ Your File No. ____________

Date of Incident ____________

Location of Occurrence ____________

Services Requested
(Please check all that apply)

☐ Activity Checks/Canvas			☐ Serve Legal Documents
☐ Asset Search	☐ Disability	☐ Misc ________	☐ Sexual Harassment
☐ Background Check	☐ Domestic/Custody	☐ Missing Persons	☐ Skiptrace
☐ Contract Matter	☐ Eavesdropping Sweep	☐ Obtain Records/Reports	☐ Surveillance
☐ Coverage Matter	☐ Employment Matter	☐ Personal Injury	☐ Traffic Collision
☐ Criminal Defense	☐ Interview Witnesses	☐ Photographs	☐ Video
☐ Death Investigation	☐ Malpractice ________	☐ Product Liability	☐ Worker Compensation

Subject/Search Request
(Complete if applicable)

Last Name/Company ____________ First Name ____________ Middle Initial ______

DOB ____________ SSN ____________ DLN ____________ State ____________

Address ____________

Telephone ____________ Spouse ____________ Minor Children Y / N

Employment ____________ Occupation ____________

Address ____________

Telephone ____________ Vehicles ____________

Physical Description: M / F Race ____ Height ____ Weight ____ Hair ____ Eyes ____ Glasses? Y / N Beard? Y / N Moustache? Y / N

Distinguishing Characteristics (Scar, Tattoos, Birth Mark, etc.) ____________

Injury Description ____________

Represented? Y / N **Please use reverse side for comments, instructions, detailed information or additional names or parties to this matter.**

Figure 5.2 Law Firm Case Assignment form.

Civil Investigations

Civil investigations are investigations pertaining to lawsuits in which questions of money or property must be settled. Violations of the law are usually not involved. Divorce, bankruptcy, and lawsuits of various types are examples of civil matters that require investigation.

Civil Actions

An attorney or client may hire an investigator to prove that either one of the parties to the suit is liable. There are two terms an investigator must know—plaintiff and defendant.

Plaintiff The plaintiff is the party who brings legal action; one who accuses another person of wrongdoing.

Defendant The accused, or the one who must defend him- or herself against charges brought by the plaintiff is the defendant. Although he or she may be accused of wrongdoing, the defendant is assumed innocent until proven guilty by the plaintiff and the plaintiff's attorney.

Role of the Legal Investigator

In essence, the role of the legal investigator is to assist the attorney in whatever task is deemed necessary to best defend the client. Whether you are working directly for the attorney or for the plaintiff or defendant, your job is to help the attorney win the case. In most instances, this will involve locating and interviewing potential witnesses, both for and against your side; reviewing the evidence of both sides, and finding additional evidence that either helps your case or refutes the evidence in favor of the other side; conducting background investigations on all potential witnesses and parties in the case; and in criminal investigations, supplying examination diagrams and photographs of the crime scene. An outstanding investigator is proficient in his or her ability to analyze a situation and achieve the results necessary for his or her side to win the case. I define winning as achieving the best results possible for the client. That does not always mean that the client actually wins the case.

Evidence

Evidence may be defined as anything that is legally seized and submitted to a court of law for consideration in determining the truth of the matter. Throughout the investigative process, the investigator will be seeking evidence to identify and connect the suspect to the commission of the crime, as well as any documentation tending to expose a possible motive. Evidence, regardless of form or type (business records, photographs, sketches, incendiary devices, etc.) must be identified, collected, and correctly packaged throughout the case-building process.

Direct Evidence

Direct evidence is evidence with such individualized or identifying characteristics that it tends to prove the fact without the support or corroboration of evidence of any other fact. This evidence can be positively identified as having come from a specific source or person if sufficient identifying characteristics or microscopic or accidental markings are present (i.e., fingerprints, palm prints, teeth, certain ballistic materials).

Circumstantial Evidence

Circumstantial evidence has class characteristics only. This evidence, no matter how thoroughly examined, can be placed into a class, but a positive source cannot be identified (i.e., soil, blood, hair, flammable vapors). Circumstantial evidence tends to prove the fact only with the intervention of evidence of other facts. It is evidence that falls into the logical progression of events and from which inferences can be drawn.

For example, evidence that substantiates a motive for arson includes the following:

- Lack of inventory, empty shelves, and so on, in a commercial retail business
- Business books and records that when audited identify an arson-for-profit insurance fraud scheme
- Files and office cabinets left open to expose records to the ravages of the fire
- Accelerant residue on the charred remains of a homicide victim showing that the fire was set to conceal a murder

Chain of Evidence

The term *chain of evidence* refers to the chain of custody (possession) of an item of evidence from the point in time that it was first discovered until the time that it was offered as an exhibit in court. Any break in the chain of custody will prohibit the use of the item as evidence in any court presentation. Each time a piece of evidence passes from one person to another, the identities of the individuals involved must be documented. Legal investigators might use a form similar to that shown in Figure 5.3 if the proper procedures were not followed.

In order to account properly for evidence from the time it is found to the time it is produced in court, an investigator must adhere to strict guidelines during each stage of the evidential procedure. The stages are as follows:

- Discovery—the date, place, and time of the discovery must be documented in your detailed notes.
- Collection and identification—photograph the evidence where it is found, mark the evidence carefully with an identifying mark, and then remove the evidence from the scene.
- Packaging—place the evidence in an airtight bag or cardboard box marked with the date, place, and time of the discovery along with some identifying information about the collector. When possible, it should be packaged in front of witnesses.

MALPRACTICE DATA SHEET

FILE#: ____________________ DATE: ____________ TYPE: ____________

CLIENT: ____________________ ATTORNEY: ____________________

CLIENT TELE: ____________________ ATTNY. TELE.: ____________________

CLIENT ADDRESS: ____________________

PLAINTIFF: ____________________

ADDRESS: ____________________ TELE: ____________

DOB: ____________ SS#: ____________ MARITAL STATUS: ____________

OCCUPATION : ____________________

DATE OF INCIDENT: ____________________ LOCATION: ____________

GENERAL SUMMARY OF SITUATION:

____

____

____

____

____

Figure 5.3 Malpractice data sheet.

- Vouchering and transmittal—a form on which the investigator lists all of the physical evidence collected, who examined it, and where the evidence has been up until presentation to the court.
- Laboratory analysis.
- Court presentation.

The investigator must decide which items will be removed from the scene for transport to the laboratory and which should be photographed and remain at the scene. The size of the samples to be taken and the areas within the scene from which they are removed are important issues that must be considered.

Documenting the Crime Scene

- Visual inspection—i.e., read the observable burn patterns.
- Note taking—keep a written record of observations and impressions at the scene.
- Give observations in chronological order.
- Avoid indiscernible codes and cryptic observations.
- Be clear and concise.
- Make decisions as to what is really important. Be sure to include the following:
    - Time of investigator's arrival
    - Exact address
    - Weather conditions
    - Identity of persons present
    - Statements made, verbatim if possible
    - Odors at the scene
    - Extent of damage and description of location
    - Anything unusual

- Keep your original handwritten notes in the case file. Do not destroy! If recorded on a cassette tape, keep the original tape.
- Photography—photograph the scene thoroughly. Long, wide shots of the area followed by close-ups for detail are preferable. Use color and black and white if possible (especially where there is evidence of blood and a color photograph is inadmissible). Sequences should be chronological entering the building and from room to room. Indicate in your notes the number of each frame and the subject of the picture. Mark the back of each developed photograph with date, location, name of photographer, and type of camera used.
- Sketches—thorough and accurate drafting of a crime scene sketch is the next essential step in documentation. The purpose is to provide orientation, showing the relationship of objects to each other. Give the overall view of the scene, eliminating clutter and items not important to the scene. Clarify issues and refresh the memory of witnesses during interviews; avoid unnecessary and legally prohibited return trips to the scene.

Conducting Legal Investigations

In the 21 years that I have worked as a private investigator, I can tell you that all my legal investigations involve two elements:

- Search for evidence
- Search for facts

The first step in the process upon obtaining a new case is sitting down with my attorney client and determining the theory of the case. In other words, what defense are they planning in a criminal case or what facts are required to prove or disprove the assertions in a civil case. Once that is established, my job is to find the evidence and the facts of the case that either support or disprove the underlying assertions. Sounds simple in theory, but trust me, it is never that easy.

Next, I review all of the information available. In a criminal case, that means reading all the federal agent and/or police reports, reading transcripts of interviews, and listening to wiretaps and any other oral or video tape-recorded statements of suspects and witnesses. I need to dissect and understand each piece of evidence that the prosecution may be presenting to the judge or jury.

Then I conduct interviews, starting with the defendant. I attempt to understand all of the facts and how they relate to my client's theory of the defense and then go about looking for evidence and facts that support or disprove the evidence to be presented. A common misconception by most laypeople is that a trial is a search for truth. A trial is a presentation of evidence through witnesses. Truth is not the objective. Winning and losing is what it is all about. All the rest is just semantics.

Following my interviews, I meet with the client and explain everything I have found. I write reports about what was done and catalog the evidence for presentation at trial. Following that meeting, additional follow-up work and interviews may be required. I may be asked to conduct background investigations on witnesses to be presented by the other side.

Finally, I get ready for trial by preparing witnesses that I have found, making arrangements for them to appear in court, and preparing the evidence I obtained for presentation by my client. Sometimes I am called to testify, but that is rare. Once trial starts, I await emergency requests by my clients for investigation of some new element that has developed during the trial. It is always an anxious and stress-filled experience to actively work an investigation that goes to trial.

I have worked on many criminal and civil cases. I have been fortunate to have worked with many skilled attorneys and to have experienced firsthand the thrill of victory when the jury returns with a not guilty verdict or a large monetary judgment for the client. I also experienced the disappointment when juries find clients guilty in cases where we felt strongly that the State had not proven guilt. It is a very humbling and frustrating job on those occasions. However, like most jobs, you have good days and bad days. I can definitely say that working as a legal investigator is never dull.

Case Study: *United States v. Nancy Walter*

Robert Gordon lived a life full of deceit and deception. Gordon wasn't his given name. He changed it from Kerner after he was convicted in a town on Long Island, New York, in 1966 for selling stolen seafood. He had the case subsequently expunged from the public record. With his new identity, Gordon moved to Florida and created a plastic card company that made him a very rich man. He was able to become rich by adopting an unusual business strategy—he never paid federal income taxes. For years, he failed to file returns on the millions of dollars in income his company generated. Neither did his 120 employees, whom he handpicked to work for him. Nancy Walter was his former mother-in-law. Her daughter helped Gordon set up the company in their garage.

In this case, the government entered into an agreement with Gordon to testify against his employees in return for a sweetheart deal—very little time to be served in Club Fed, plus he gets to keep his millions and doesn't have to pay the taxes he never filed. The reason for the deal? The government could get numerous convictions (the employees) rather than the one most responsible. I call this giving the deal to the whale to get the minnows. I thought the system was supposed to use the lower echelon criminals to testify against the kingpins—apparently not here in South Florida.

Nancy Walter had never worked a day in her life before she went to work for Robert Gordon. Her husband was a salesman for their daughter and Gordon's company until his premature death. Gordon promised to take care of her financially at the funeral. He gave her his salary and commissions on sales for several years until employees at the company complained. He then offered to let her work the clients, or the money would stop. He had already divorced her daughter and remarried. She reluctantly agreed, having no other means to support herself and her high-school-aged daughter. She told him she knew nothing about business. He told her not to worry, that he would take care of everything. It was the same thing he told most of the other employees of the $8 million company. Most were kids, primarily female, hired right out of high school. (Bobby liked his woman in their teens. He would later marry his 17-year-old adopted daughter.) The rest were friends or relatives of employees of Gordon. This was a group that was easily controlled by him. It was a group that had little business experience. And, it was a group that believed Gordon when he told them that the company accountant would take care of filing their taxes. They believed him. As always, he lied. No one filed their taxes. They were subsequently charged with income tax evasion—all but Gordon. Gordon was charged with other lesser charges and never paid the IRS the monies owed. The rest of his employees became financially ensnared for the rest of their lives based upon their reliance on the word of Gordon. This same person testified against them at trial and told the jury that he instructed each of them to pay their taxes. In the course of my investigation into Walter and other cases involving Continental Plastic Card Company, I interviewed most of the employees. No one remembered ever being told anything by Gordon other than he was taking care of their taxes. Should they have known better? Of course, some even had questions and spoke to accountants and filed taxes on their own. Most others did not. As a result, most ended up serving more time in prison than did Gordon. Was this fair? No one ever said that justice is meted out in a courtroom. This is the system. In order to be an effective professional investigator, you need to understand the system and how it works in order to overcome the inequities. That is what good criminal defense investigators do best—overcome the inequities. Especially in federal court, where proceedings are referred to as "trial by ambush." There is very little pretrial discovery in the federal system. You get the evidence as it is being presented at trial.

Case Study: *United States v. Pedro Huezo*

U.S. vs. Pedro Huezo–Mortgage Fraud Cases–Straw Buyers
United States v. Mayra Rodriguez, et al., Case No. 09-20628-CR-Graham.

On July 23, 2009, 19 defendants were charged in a 20-count indictment for their participation in a mortgage fraud scheme that resulted in approximately $21 million in fraudulent loans.

Charged in the indictment were defendants Mayra Rodriguez, 31, Lucia Peluffo, 29, Nelson Bermudez, 36, Yamile Segurola, 24, all of Miami; Carlos Rodriguez, 29, of Homestead; Mayelin Salas, 36, of Miami Springs; Nelida Rodriguez, 48, of Opa Locka; Sonya Balmaseda, 35, of Hialeah; Jorge Egeraige, 38, of Hialeah; Jaime Rojas, 39, of North Miami Beach; Alejandro Rabelo, 49, of Miami Beach; Pedro Huezo, 58, of Opa Locka; and Jose Arriete, 53, Gerard Wenzel, 50, Elias Fleites, 55, Marcelo Fernandez, 41, Lucy Segurola, 51, Ricardo Segurola, 51, and Jorge Lugo, 46, all of Miami.

According to the indictment, defendants Mayra Rodriguez, Mayelin Salas, Nelida Rodriguez, Yamile Segurola, and Lucia Peluffo were employed at companies owned by Magile Cruz. (Maggie Cruz previously pled guilty and was sentenced in January 2009 to 120 months' imprisonment for her participation in this scheme.) Cruz's companies included Star Lending Mortgage, State Mortgage Lending, Sherley Title Services, Doral Title Services, and Professional Title Express, all in Miami-Dade county. Star Lending Mortgage was a mortgage brokerage firm and State Mortgage Lending was a mortgage lender, both licensed in the State of Florida. Sherley Title Services, Doral Title Services, and Professional Title Express were title agencies but were not licensed by the State of Florida.

More specifically, the indictment alleges that from 2005 through 2007, Cruz, through her companies, would identify residential properties that were for sale. Thereafter, Cruz and defendants Mayra Rodriguez, Yamile Segurola, and Lucia Peluffo would prepare mortgage loan applications on behalf of complicit straw borrowers. These applications included false employment verifications, pay stubs, income and funds on deposit, and IRS Forms W-2. Defendant Nelson Bermudez, an employee of Wachovia Bank during the fraud, assisted the fraud by creating false verifications of deposit for the purported Wachovia accounts of straw borrowers. Defendants Carlos Rodriguez, Mayelin Salas, and others recruited and paid individuals to pose as buyers and borrowers in the transactions. Defendants Sonya Balmaseda, Jorge Egeraige, Ricardo Segurola, Lucy Segurola, Marcelo Fernandez, Pedro Huezo, Jose Arriete, Gerard Wenzel, Alejandro Rabelo, Elias Fleites, Jorge Lugo, and Jaime Rojas all acted as straw borrowers.

The indictment describes three methods used by the defendants to execute their scheme. First, the defendants created and submitted to the lending institutions false duplicate HUD-Settlement Statement Forms, which grossly inflated the true purchase price of the properties. At other times, the defendants adopted a shotgun approach to mortgage fraud, through which they obtained near-simultaneous loans for the same piece of property from multiple lenders. Finally, the defendants concocted entirely false real estate sales by stealing the identities of unwitting home owners, forging the sales documents in their names, and using complicit straw purchasers to obtain mortgages, all without the real property owners' knowledge or consent.

Once the mortgage applications were approved, the lenders wired the loan proceeds to the defendant's title companies for closing. At closing, Cruz, Mayra Rodriguez, and Yamile Segurola would keep the difference between the inflated mortgage loan proceeds and the actual selling price of the property. Moreover, to perpetuate the scheme and avoid detection, the defendants often filed change of address forms with the Postal Service to prevent unwitting home owners from discovering that their property had been sold without their knowledge or consent. The defendants would redirect the mail to post office boxes opened and controlled by Cruz and Nelida Rodriguez. In addition, to keep the fraud afloat and undetected, the defendants would make payments on the loans until the properties could be resold, often to another straw borrower, repeating the cycle of fraud. When Cruz failed to make payments on the loans, some properties went into foreclosure, resulting in substantial losses to the lending institutions.

The indictment charges the defendants with conspiracy to commit mail fraud and wire fraud, and substantive mail fraud and wire fraud.

I was appointed to work on this case by my friend and client, Allen Kaufman. The defendant we were representing was Pedro Huezo. Pedro was described by the government as a stray buyer—a person whose name, social security number, and credit information are used to obtain a mortgage or refinance on a property in which they will never live or make payments on. There were several problems with the government's case:

1. Pedro lived in the house in which the loan application was made.
2. Pedro had previously obtained bankruptcy protection and had poor credit.
3. Pedro never signed any of the loan documents—his signature was forged.
4. The prosecution admitted that he did not sign the loan documents.

The government in this case went into the Federal Prison System and persuaded Maggie Cruz, the mastermind of a multimillion dollar mortgage fraud scheme, who was serving 10 years for her role in the scheme, to testify against *all* the people who worked for *her* in this scheme. There were over 20 defendants in this case. Fortunately Pedro was in the second trial. Allen, with my help and evidence that I obtained, was able to show the jury that Pedro had nothing to do with this scheme.

Verdict: Not Guilty.

Ex-Parte Motion for Investigative Costs

COMES NOW, the defendant, ___, by and through the undersigned counsel and files his Ex-Parte Motion For Investigative Costs and in support thereof states as follows:

1. The defendant was arraigned on ___. A jury trial has been set for __.
2. This is a ___ defendant case. The indictment sets forth ___ counts. The defendant is charged in Count ___ of the Indictment with ___. Count ___ charges the defendant. These counts carry a maximum penalty of ___ years imprisonment and a minimum of 5 years imprisonment.
3. The history of the case dates back to 20__. The government's discovery submission contains thousands of pages of documents. There are bank records from various banks, photo lineups, DMV records, phone records, video recordings, police reports and over ___ documents.
4. The defendant requests this Court's authorization to obtain an investigator to assist in the preparation of the defense, including investi-

gating the facts of the case and interviewing and taking statements from prospective defense and government witnesses.

The investigator will also perform background investigations of witnesses.

5. The defendant requires the services of an investigator to assist in completing a background check of the informants and cooperating co-defendants, locating and interviewing adverse character witnesses, obtaining physical evidence from both the federal government and local police departments, reviewing records, transcripts, documents and reports as well as assisting counsel with the organizational preparation necessary for trial.
6. Services of a competent independent investigator are necessary and essential in order to conduct an adequate investigation and thereby safeguard the defendant's Fifth and Sixth Amendment Rights to receive a fair hearing, to present witness on his own behalf, to effective assistance of counsel and to preserve meaningful cross-examination and confrontation of government witnesses. Since the government conducted a lengthy investigation prior to filing the indictment in this case, defendant cannot perceive any prejudice to the government by the granting of this motion to afford this defendant at least some opportunity to contest the government's findings.
7. In *UNITED STATES v. SAILER,* 552 F.2D 213 (5th Cir.), cert denied, 431 U.S. 959 (1977), the Court recognized that investigative services are necessary in appropriate cases to aid in preparation of an indigent defendant's defense. It has been held that allowance of investigative expenses for indigent defendants is required when necessary to the proper preparation of the defense. A denial of government funds for such purpose may violate defendant's right to the effective assistance of counsel and to due process of law. *MAYSON v. ARIZONA,* 504 F. 2d 1345 (10th Cir. 1974).
8. Counsel submits that it is anomalous for the Court to appoint counsel to represent an indigent defendant and not provide that counsel with the necessary means to provide effective assistance, especially where such means are provided for by law under Title 18, U.S.C. § 3006 (1) and (3). The District of Columbia Court of Appeals has held that an attorney's failure to properly investigate violated the defendant's Sixth Amendment right to effective assistance of counsel. *HARRIS v. UNITED STATES,* 30 Cr.L.Rptr.2368 (D.C.Cir.). January 21, 1983). See also, *SULLIVAN v. FAIRMAN,* 819 F.2d 1382, 1291-93 (7th Cir.1987) (ineffective assistance when counsel failed to contact five witnesses whose names, addresses, and telephone numbers were in police reports that counsel possessed and whose testimony directly contradicted that of government's principal witness).
9. Defendant submits that the allegations contained in his motion clearly reveal the necessity for the use of investigative services in this

case to aid in the proper preparation of his trial. Therefore, defendant's motion should be granted upon the authorities set forth above and pursuant to Title 18, U.S.C. § 3006 (1) and (3). The defendant is requesting the CJA rates of $60.00 per hour for the investigator. Should the Court have any question, regarding the absolute necessity for excess funds to obtain adequate investigative services, it should set this matter for an *ex parte, in camera* hearing to enable counsel to further explain the need for investigative funds.

WHEREFORE, based upon the above and foregoing, the defendant respectfully requests that this Court authorize the initial expenditure of up $60.00 per hour up to $2,400.00, exclusive of costs, for the services of an investigator to aid the defendant in the preparation of his defense.

Fraud Investigation 6

Financial crime has grown at an astronomical rate in the past 10 years. It seems that we cannot pick up a newspaper, listen to a radio, or watch television without learning about some crime that has been alleged or committed. This type of crime is page one news. It seems to be everywhere. Let's recall one of the major headlines and sensational stories of 2002:

> August 21, 2002—A former Enron finance executive told a federal judge here today that he had paid large kickbacks to the company's former chief financial officer, Andrew S. Fastow, out of money he received for managing a partnership that was used to help the company hide debt and increase profits.

In 2008 Bernard Madoff was charged in what is described as the largest Ponzi scheme of all time. The following is an excerpt about the discovery of this fraud:

> Madoff was arrested by the Federal Bureau of Investigation (FBI) on December 11, 2008 on criminal charges of securities fraud. The previous day, he had told his sons that his business was "a giant Ponzi scheme." They called a friend for advice, Martin Flumenbaum, a lawyer, who called federal prosecutors and the SEC on their behalf. FBI Agent Theodore Cacioppi made a house call. "We are here to find out if there is an innocent explanation," Cacioppi said quietly. The 70-year-old financier paused, "There is no innocent explanation." He had "paid investors with money that was not there" The *New York Times* has reported that Madoff's lawyer, Ira Sorkin, has confirmed in a court filing that Madoff confessed.
>
> The criminal complaint alleges that investors lost $50 billion through the scheme, though *The Wall Street Journal* reports "that figure includes the alleged false profits that Mr. Madoff's firm reported to its customers for decades. It's unclear exactly how much investors deposited into the firm." He was charged with a single count of securities fraud. He faces up to 20 years in prison and a fine of $5 million if convicted. Apart from "Bernard L. Madoff" and "Bernard L. Madoff Investment Securities LLC (BMIS)," the order to freeze all activities also forbids acting and trading from the companies Madoff Securities International Ltd. ("Madoff International") and Madoff Ltd.
>
> Madoff was released on the same day of his arrest after posting $10 million bail.

A new approach is called for in light of the evolution of economic and white-collar crime in America—a financial investigative approach. The growth of money-motivated crimes mandates the need for financial investigations. The future success of law enforcement is contingent upon its ability to conduct financial investigations in conjunction with general criminal investigations. The major goal of a financial investigator is to identify and document specific events involving the movement of money during the course of a crime. Suppose an accountant is suspected of embezzling money from his employer. A financial investigator would determine what account the accountant is taking the money from, how he took it, when he took it, and where he put it. If the investigator is able to identify these events and link them together, he will have the basis of proof indicating the commission of a crime. If the events cannot be identified and linked together, the investigation may support the determination to discontinue further inquiry into the matter. This does not mean that a crime was not committed. It merely means the financial investigator cannot put all the elements together.

Financial investigations, by their nature, are records-intensive; specifically, records pointing to the movement of money are required. Bank account information (checking and savings account records), motor vehicle registration (title, place of purchase, and lien-holder records), and real estate files (mortgages and deed records) are documents of record commonly found in this type of investigation. In addition, utility bills, divorce decrees, and credit card receipts can play important roles in financial investigations. Any record that pertains to the paper trail of events is important to a financial investigation.

The investigation of fraud is a logical inquiry that requires some training but is not as difficult as one might imagine. Common sense is the most important tool for any investigator. In order to accomplish a professional and thorough investigation, an investigator must have a focused sense of direction, patience, and determination to properly gather all the evidence needed.

Fraud is defined as a false representation or the concealment of a material fact with the intent and result that it be acted upon by another to his or her loss or detriment. Fraud is making a false statement of a past or existing fact with knowledge of its falsity or with reckless indifference as to its truth with the intent to cause another to rely upon it, resulting in his or her injury:

- Knowledge—the maker of a statement knows it is false.
- Intent—the statement is made with the intent to gain a benefit.
- Reliance—the other party relies upon the false statements.
- Injury—the victim suffers a financial loss owing to reliance on the false statements.

Three main reasons for fraud investigations are to recover funds, to prevent repetition and deter others, and to clear innocent people.

Three important rules of fraud investigators are as follows:

- Whenever possible, inquiries should be concentrated around the central issue or hub of the fraud.
- Investigators should not seek the most complex solution to the case. The rule is to examine the most obvious answer and only when that has been eliminated go on to more complicated solutions.
- If concealment is difficult to unravel, investigators should "follow the money"—determine who benefited at the end of the fraud and work backwards.

It is not possible to provide a planned outline applicable to all investigations of fraud. However, these are the steps that would generally be followed:

- Selection of statutory violations—that is, which laws have been broken. Carefully identify the elements of proof for each statute and the method required to obtain the evidence desired (documents, witnesses, and so on).
- Identification of the documentation required to prove fraud. The best evidence rules require that original documents be submitted when available.
- Identification of witnesses who can authenticate records and who can define the subject's actions that constitute fraud.
- Identification of the appropriate investigative techniques to be used to obtain the desired evidence (witness interviews, use of technical investigative devices, etc.).
- Determination of the desired outcome for the client early in the investigation. Is criminal prosecution the goal, or is the client looking for identification of the subject, restitution if funds are found, and termination from the company in the case of corporate fraud by an employee?

Corporate Fraud

Fraud is a deliberate deception practiced on another to serve an unfair or unlawful gain. A survey by *Fortune* magazine revealed that a total of 117 of the largest and most prestigious corporations in the United States committed at least one federal criminal offense since 1970. The social cost of white-collar crime has been estimated to be between $400 million and $40 billion per year. Following are descriptions of three of these white-collar crimes:

- *Embezzlement* is the fraudulent appropriation of property by a person to whom it has been entrusted or into whose hands it has lawfully come.
- *Corporate fraud* is any fraud perpetrated by, for, or against a business corporation.
- *Financial fraud* is a material misrepresentation of a financial fact intended to deceive another to his or her economic detriment.

Financial Fraud Audit

Financial investigations are built on paper, although paper-based records are quickly being replaced by computer-based documentation. Thorough analysis of all financial transactions will reveal the fraud.

In order to determine whether a fraud has been committed, the amount of money taken, and the mechanism for the fraud to have occurred, an audit must be conducted. There is a fixed and orderly routine followed in a typical financial audit—that is, a set of predesigned tasks, procedures, and tests for the verification of business transactions and evaluation of the adequacy of the account system to reflect fairly, accurately, and consistently the financial condition of a business at a point in time. In essence, the auditor takes a snapshot of the business, and that picture should represent the reality of the company's financial situation at that time.

The financial auditor's purpose is to dissect and rebuild a structure by using infinite details. Auditors begin where a loss of something of value or a suspicion of property loss exists. Fraud auditing is unlike financial auditing in that it proceeds from a theory based more on investigative notions than on financial auditing notions.

The usual method of employee theft, fraud, and embezzlement executed within the accounting system involves the creation of a fake debit that, in turn, will be offset by a credit to an asset account or expense account, fake debits and phony credit memos, phony invoices, phony employees, phony expense vouchers, and so on. In frauds within the system, there is usually evidence of altered, forged, fabricated, or missing documents. In frauds outside the system, transactions may have bypassed the accounting system completely.

Corporate Fraud Investigations

An accounting system consists of records that provide detailed information of business transactions (journals), and summary information of account balances (ledgers). The most commonly used journals are for recording cash receipts and disbursements. Other journals used include those in which sales and purchases are recorded. Ledgers can be subclassified into general ledgers, which reflect current balances in asset, liability, revenue, and expense accounts in a summary form (i.e., total debits and credits posted), and subsidiary ledgers, which reflect the specific details of transactions between the firm and its customers and suppliers. These subsidiary ledgers are kept on the basis of individual customer or vendor name or account number. All books and records should be handled with care.

Audit Trail

The audit trail is made up of paper documents that support each step in a regular business transaction (purchase, sale of goods, etc.), from requisition to purchase to receipt of goods and payment, or from billing a customer to receipt of his of her payment on account and deposit in the bank. An effective audit trail is one that provides an auditor with an opportunity to trace any given transaction backward or forward from an original source of the transaction to a final total.

Analysis of the suspect's financial transactions, what he or she received, and where and how the money was spent will reveal if there is money remaining and where it is located.

Corporate Fraud Detection

Fraud uncovered during internal audits tends to involve lower-level officials of the company. Fraud by senior management is more difficult to find and document. Corporate fraud requires M.O.M.M.:

- Motivation
- Opportunity
- Methods
- Means

The fraud audit purpose is to determine the state of mind or mental disposition of employees toward fraudulent behavior. Fraud is committed by people, not by computers or accounting systems.

Detection Techniques

The primary rule in all fraud investigation is to follow the assets. There are 10 basic rules in fraud investigations:

- Never overlook the obvious!
- Look for deviations. Never start out looking for the most complex solution.
- Always concentrate on the weakest, most simple point in the fraud. Most frauds have three elements:

    - Act of theft
    - Concealment
    - Conversion
- If accounts have been manipulated or records destroyed, the person whose guilt would otherwise have been most obvious should be treated as the prime suspect.
- If, after an investigation of all available facts, guilt appears to point toward a particular person, chances are that person is the responsible party.
- Fraud detection is, or should be, a continuous management function. Fraud detection and prevention should not be an occasional exercise but rather a routine aspect of business.
- It is not necessary to detect all frauds at any one time. A deterrent is established with each case detected and investigated.
- To detect fraud, resources must be specifically allocated to that task.
- Detecting fraud is hard work. It is paper intensive.
- The reason fraud escapes detection is usually because nobody is made accountable for the task. An auditor is a watchdog, not a bloodhound. Police investigate fraud; they seldom detect it.

Individual Net Worth Investigations

An individual net worth investigation is simply the difference between what the person owns and what he or she owes at a given point in time. The net worth format is useful when a suspect systematically acquires assets, such as money, stocks, bonds, certificates of deposit, real estate, cash-value life insurance, and luxury items (jewelry, furs, automobiles, and antiques), and the suspect systematically reduces his or her liabilities, such as loans and mortgages. A typical net worth computation encompasses 4 complete years of financial records, preferably the years prior to and including the suspected fraud time frame.

Bank records and business financial records are the most important sources available for net worth analysis. However, traditional investigative techniques should also be used to develop additional information. These techniques include physical surveillance to document lifestyle, spending habits, and possible criminal activity—that is, drug use, prostitution, gambling, and so on. Additionally, searching through the suspect's garbage (dumpster diving) may reveal a wide range of useful information, including bank accounts and other indications of where the money may be located.

Economic Crime Schemes

These schemes are devised to obtain fees in advance for services the promoter has no intention of providing. They may be practiced in any type of financial dealings, but they usually occur when an offender claims to have the means of obtaining buyers for one's business, property, securities, or other assets, or to have access to sources of loan financing.

Advance Fee Scheme

Advance fee schemes are devised to obtain fees in advance for services the promoter has no intention of providing. They may appear in any type of financial dealings. In such cases, the advance fee artist claims to have access to sources of loan financing. He may also claim to have the means of obtaining buyers for one's business, property, securities, or other assets. An example of a lead-in to this type of scheme is the ad that appears below, which is typical of those that appear in major newspapers around the country:

$$$ MONEY $$$
BUSINESS LOANS
PRIVATE FUNDING
OVERSEAS SOURCES
$100K TO $2 MILLION
CALL 1-800-999-4761

There are three basic targets of the advance fee scheme. The most common is where someone has a "dream"—an idea that will benefit him, her, or us economically. Unfortunately, such people seldom have the required skill or financing to realize the "dream," and no bank will fund the loan. The second variation involves people who need money desperately and cannot get it anywhere else. The third variation is where someone just needs to unload property, securities, or assets in a short period of time and cannot do so.

This scheme is prevalent in the United States, Canada, and Europe. A loosely knit group of such scam artists exists around the globe. The individual needing capital is frequently "ripped off" by the first con artist and then referred to another who supposedly can help in the funding. The victim is then ripped off a second time.

The granddaddy of all economic crime schemes was the advance fee scheme. While a federal probation officer in Fort Lauderdale, Florida, I supervised Phillip Morell Wilson, who is credited with being one of the founding fathers of the advance fee scheme. He created a bank, The Bank of Sark, on the island of Guernsey, off the English coast. He created a phony set of books showing millions of dollars in assets, and he then issued letters of credit from his created bank to a host of South Florida con men. The deal was so complicated that he was offered a reduced sentence to help federal prosecutors unravel the scheme and testify against his coconspirators. This incident was given much attention in *The Fountain Pen Conspiracy* (Jonathan Kwitney, Knopf, New York, 1973, out of print), considered by many fraud investigators to be the bible on economic crime.

Pyramid Scheme

The pyramid scheme is an investment fraud in which an individual is offered a distributorship or franchise to market a particular product. The investment contract also authorizes one to sell additional franchises. The promoter of a pyramid scheme represents to the buyer that the marketing of the product will result in profits; however, he emphasizes the potentially quicker return on investment by the sale of franchises. Attempts to sell the product usually fail, because the actual product is overpriced, and there have been no real efforts by the promoters to market the product.

Ponzi Scheme

This is basically an investment fraud that has become the fraud crime of the decade that started in 2000. The Ponzi operator solicits investors in a business venture, promising extremely high return on dividends in a short period of time. The dividends are never paid. The Ponzi operator never actually invests the money in anything. The Ponzi operator actually does pay dividends to the investor, but in reality, he is simply returning some of the investor's original money. The return, paid promptly and cheerfully, is used to induce the investor to put up additional funds. In some cases, the phony dividend is used to encourage the investor to solicit friends and associates to invest in the scheme. The Ponzi operator, when sufficient funds have been accumulated, concludes the scheme by fleeing with all of the investor's funds.

This type of scheme was named after the notorious Charles Ponzi, a swindler who was active in the 1920s. In December 1919, with capital of $150, he began to borrow money based on promissory notes that he issued. He spread a false tale that he was buying and selling international postal coupons in foreign countries and selling them at 100% profit, as a result of the exchange rate differential between countries after World War I. Charles Ponzi promised to pay $150 for every $100 loaned to him within 90 days. Within 8 months, he took in $9.5 million dollars, for which he issued promissory notes for $14.3 million. By July 1, 1920, Ponzi was taking in $1 million per week. Because of an investigation by the government, Ponzi ceased his sales on July 16, 1920.

See *Cunningham v. Brown*, 265 U.S. 1 (1924; opinion by Chief Justice Taft) regarding the bankruptcy estate of one Charles Ponzi.

Ponzi schemes have been in the news with increasing frequency in the past few years. First we had the case of Bernard Madoff. Madoff was an icon in the financial industry as a result of his illustrious background. He was the former chairman of the NASDAQ stock exchange. He founded the Wall Street firm Bernard L. Madoff Investment Securities LLC in 1960 and was its chairman until December 11, 2008, when he was charged with perpetrating what may be the largest investor fraud ever committed by a single person.

Then we had the case of Scott Rothstein. He may not be as familiar a figure to those of you outside the state of Florida, but he was very big in the South Florida news world.

> "All Ponzi schemes do the same thing: They explode at the end," says convicted con man Scott Rothstein. While his $1.2 billion Ponzi scheme blew up in 2009, the debris is still falling to earth. In an attempt to get his 50-year sentence reduced, Rothstein is naming accomplices and detailing exactly how his scheme worked. The now-disbarred South Florida lawyer is in protective custody while he cooperates with government investigators. And he's testifying in civil lawsuits, brought by investors and the court-appointed trustee of his bankrupt law firm, to recover money from banks and hedge funds that allegedly aided the fraud. Over two weeks of depositions in December, Rothstein implicated lawyers, hedge funds managers, bankers, police officers, and his uncle. In a related trial where Rothstein didn't testify, an investor group sued Toronto-Dominion Bank, saying it led Rothstein victims to believe their money was safe as he depleted accounts. On Jan. 18 a jury ordered the bank to pay the group $67 million.
>
> For four years, Rothstein persuaded investors—mostly hedge funds and wealthy families in New York, Florida, and Texas—to buy stakes in what he said were payouts from settlements of sexual-harassment and workplace discrimination lawsuits. The suits weren't real: He'd fabricate the cases from scratch, using forged documents and elaborate ruses, such as having an accomplice pose as a bank officer. The scheme fell apart just after Halloween in 2009 when he couldn't lure enough new investors to pay earlier ones. After fleeing to Morocco, Rothstein returned to the U.S. Two years ago he pleaded guilty to five federal counts of racketeering, money laundering, and wire fraud.

Most recently we had Nevin Shapiro, who became a big story in 2011 when he attempted to bring down the University of Miami football program as a result of his interaction with the university as a "Booster" from 2002 until his 20-year sentence in federal prison in 2011 following a massive $200 million Ponzi scheme.

> Federal prosecutors say Shapiro used his wealth and prominent connections to bolster an image of a successful grocery broker selling stakes in lucrative import deals. In reality, prosecutors claim, the 41-year-old's business existed mostly on paper for the past five years. They claim the scam cost roughly 60 investors at least $80 million. Shapiro allegedly pocketed about $35 million—enough to finance a voracious gambling habit, a $6 million Miami Beach mansion, and the personal bodyguards that were often spotted with Shapiro, according to court documents and interviews with people who know him. Days after his arrest in New Jersey, a portrait is emerging of a man who pursued high-profile friends while trying to establish himself as a power broker in South Florida's sports circles. He spent $400,000 on Miami Heat floor seats, has a student-athlete lounge named after him at the University of Miami, and talked of starting his own sports management firm.

Finally we have R. Allen Stanford from the Stanford Financial Group, Houston. Federal authorities allege Stanford and coconspirators ran a $7 billion Ponzi scheme that defrauded some 30,000 investors globally until his companies were seized in February 2009. Stanford portrayed himself as a financier, sports promoter, and philanthropist, setting up many of his operations in the Caribbean.

> HOUSTON—A federal jury on Tuesday convicted R. Allen Stanford, a Texas financier, on 13 out of 14 counts of fraud in connection with a worldwide scheme that lasted more than two decades and involved more than $7 billion in investments. The jury decision followed a six-week trial and came three years after Mr. Stanford was accused of defrauding nearly 30,000 investors in 113 countries in a Ponzi scheme involving $7 billion in fraudulent high-interest certificates of deposit at the Stanford International Bank, which was based on the Caribbean island of Antigua. Prosecutors argued that Mr. Stanford had lied for more than two decades, promoting safe investments for money that he channeled into a luxurious lifestyle, a secret Swiss bank account and business deals that consistently lost money.

Planned Bankruptcy Scheme

A planned bankruptcy scheme is a merchandising swindle based upon the abuse of credit, which has been legitimately or fraudulently established. The scheme consists of over-purchasing inventory on credit, sale, or other disposition of merchandise obtained, concealment of the proceeds, nonpayment of creditors, and filing of a bankruptcy petition, either voluntarily or involuntarily. This scheme is referred to as a planned bankruptcy, or in more common terms, a "bust out," because getting out is the ultimate goal of those operating the scheme. Planned bankruptcies can be extremely lucrative, and organized crime has been particularly active in this type of fraud.

Chain Referral Scheme

This involves the sales of grossly overpriced products through false representations that the cost will be recovered by commissions the promoter will pay on sales made to the purchaser's friends.

Merchandising Schemes

While many economic crimes are hidden and difficult to detect, some of the more visible and blatant offenses are committed by retail stores. These frauds are based on twisting the truth for increased profits.

Bait and Switch

This is advertising a product with no intent to sell it as advertised. These ads are designed to bait or lure customers into the store. Once the consumer is in the store, the advertised product is criticized by the salesperson, who then tries to switch the customer to a higher-priced variation of the same product.

Phony Sales

Types of phony sales include going out of business sales, fire sales, liquidation sales, and so on.

Deceptive Sales Contest

Using this technique, a dishonest business through direct mail, TV, or newspaper advertising promotes a contest in which the victim is led to believe that the chance of winning a valuable prize is much greater than it actually is.

Short Weighting

Short weighting occurs when the producer at the packaging stage of production fills containers of the product to 9/10 capacity and then charges retailers or consumers for the full capacity.

Home Improvement, Debt Consolidation, and Mortgage Loans

Home owners already heavily burdened with debt are the victims. An individual whose home is in need of repair, whose debts need to be consolidated, or who needs a mortgage loan, is offered a loan sufficient to pay off all debts or finance home improvements. The one monthly payment, the victim is told, will be less, or at least no larger than the combined payments that are currently being made. The large amount of the loan offer stems from the promoter's intention to quickly sell the note at a discount to a finance or mortgage loan company. To do so profitably, the promoter knows that the amount must sufficiently exceed the cost of the home improvement work so as to offset the discount. In this type of scheme, the promoters rely on the confusing terms of the signed documents and numerous put-off tactics to delay serious consequences when home improvement work falls in arrears, is poorly done, or is not done at all.

Credit Card Fraud

Several distinct crimes are included under the classification of credit card fraud. An individual may falsely acquire a credit card by misrepresentation made on the application. Once the card is obtained, the individual uses the card to defraud merchants and other providers of service. Finally, professional credit card rings often deal in counterfeit, lost, stolen, or mis-delivered credit cards. They generally know how long they may use an invalid credit card without detection, and they also know the dollar amounts they may charge before detection is likely.

White-Collar Crime

The essential characteristic of a crime is that it is behavior prohibited by the state as an injury to the state, and against which the state may react by punishment. White-collar crime is described as the intent to commit a wrongful act or to achieve a purpose not consistent with law or public policy. It is the disguise of purpose through falsehoods and misrepresentations employed to accomplish the scheme, and concealment of a crime. These illegal acts characterized by deceit, concealment, and violation of trust are not dependent upon application or threat of physical force or violence. Such crimes are committed to obtain money, property, or services, or to secure personal or business advantage. White-collar crimes are deliberate and organized. Businessmen are organized formally for the control of legislation, selection of administrators, and restriction of appropriations for the enforcement of laws, which may adversely affect them.

The Watergate scandal in 1972 and the prosecution that followed clearly marked a high point in public awareness and concern for crimes of the rich and powerful. Illegalities perpetrated by individuals and businesses make innocent victims of the public through the use of cover-ups, deception, and violation of trust and power. Computers and other forms of high-tech record keeping have been viewed as a vehicle to wealth and have made white-collar crime a major public problem.

Corporate Crime

One frequent objection to the criminological study and call for greater legal control of corporate crime is the argument that these crimes are not as serious as other forms of crime, particularly street crimes. Even though the great economic cost of corporate crime is recognized, it is argued that these crimes are nonviolent and are therefore less important. The notion that these crimes are nonviolent or less serious is then used to justify their exclusion from greater legal controls. The most controversial issue in the study of corporate crime is whether it really is a crime. White-collar crime is real crime, but it is not treated as such by the criminal justice system.

Cost of Corporate Crime

Except in cases of fraud, the victim of ordinary crime knows that he or she has been victimized. The victims of corporate crime, on the other hand, are unaware that they have been victimized. Government experts estimate that violations of antitrust, tax fraud, bribery, pollution, and other federal laws by the nation's largest corporations cost the economy billions of dollars. A U.S. senator estimated that faulty goods, monopolistic practices, and other violations cost consumers between $174 and $231 million per year.

Difficulties in the Use of Criminal Sanctions

Some actions of corporate executives are more likely to be regarded as criminal in nature—that is, bribery of officials, price fixing, and manufacture and shipment of harmful products.

The use of criminal sanction against corporate officers is limited by the fact that they project certain profiles and are unlikely to be judged harshly except where they are responsible, for their faults are undeniable. The argument is often presented that corporate executives should not be subject to criminal sanctions for violating legal regulations, because they are responsible for advances in the industry that have raised living standards and the caliber of life in our society.

Difficulties involved in investigations leading to criminal prosecution have been and remain biased in favor of the corporate offender. The study of white-collar crime has attempted to do two things:

- To present evidence that persons of the upper class commit many crimes to get there, and these crimes should be included within the general scope of theories of criminal behavior

- To develop theories that may explain all criminal behavior—white collar and other

The first of these objectives has been realized in that a large number of corporations have been found to have violated laws with great frequency. The theory that crime is due to personal and social pathologies does not apply to white-collar crimes. Therefore, such pathologies are not essential factors in crimes in general.

The Racketeer Influenced and Corrupt Organizations (RICO) Act

The RICO Act of 1970 was initially designed to flush out crime and white-collar criminals who have no connection to organized crime. State and federal RICO laws provide remedies to organizations that have been victimized by fraud. Under the RICO Act, victimized organizations can sue for three times their losses plus attorneys' fees and costs.

Management Fraud

Management fraud goes beyond the narrow legal definition of embezzlement, fraud, or theft. It is made up of all forms of deception practiced by managers to benefit themselves to the detriment of the enterprise. It is usually covered up by its victims to avoid the adverse effects of publicity.

Environment of Corporation

Management should clearly set forth in written policies its commitment to fair dealing, its position on conflicts of interest, its requirement that only honest employees be hired, its insistence on strong internal controls that are well policed, and its resolve to prosecute the guilty. Management negligence or refusal to be realistic can generate a climate that may fuel the incidence of fraud.

Federal and State Fraud Statutes

Following are the five federal fraud statutes:

- False statements (18 USC 1001)
- False claims (18 USC 287)
- Mail fraud (18 USC 1341)
- Conspiracy (18 USC 371)
- Wire fraud (18 USC 1343)

In the state of Florida, there are four fraud statutes:

- Computer-related fraud (FS 815)
- Fraudulent practices and credit card fraud (FS 817)
- Forgery and counterfeiting (FS 831)
- Worthless checks/drafts (FS 832)

Types of Violations

In studies of corporations, the violations made by corporations showed great range and varied characteristics. The following six main types of corporate illegal behavior were found:

- Administrative violations involve noncompliance with the requirements of an agency.
- Environmental violations include incidents of air and water pollution.
- Financial violations include illegal payments or failure to disclose such violations.
- Labor violations fall into four major types: discrimination against race, religion, national origin, and sex.
- Manufacturing violations involve three government agencies: the Consumer Product Safety Commission, the National Highway Traffic Safety Administration, and the Food and Drug Administration.
- Unfair trade practices involve various abuses of competition (monopolization, misrepresentation, price discrimination, credit violations, and other abuses that restrain trade and prevent fair competition).

Business crime is an illegal act, punishable by a criminal sanction, committed by an individual or corporation in the course of a legitimate occupation or pursuit in the industrial or commercial sector for the purpose of obtaining money or property, avoiding the payment of money or the loss of property, or obtaining business or personal advantage. A corporate crime is an act committed by corporations that is punished by the state. Corporations, unlike individuals, cannot be jailed, only fined. White-collar crimes involve monetary offense not ordinarily associated with criminality until recent years.

Objectives for Investigation into Suspected Fraud

1. First and foremost, protect the innocent, establish facts, and resolve the matter.
2. Determine the basic circumstances and stop the loss.
3. Establish essential elements of the crime to support a successful prosecution.

4. Identify, gather, and protect the evidence.
5. Identify and interview witnesses.
6. Identify patterns of action and behavior.
7. Determine probable motives that will identify potential suspects.
8. Provide accurate and objective facts upon which judgments concerning discipline, termination, or prosecution may be based.
9. Account for and recover assets.
10. Identify weaknesses in control, and counter them by revising existing procedures or recommending new ones and by applying security equipment where justified.

Steps in the Investigation Process

The first step in the investigation process is to establish that a loss has occurred. The process should determine that the asset was accountable for at some point and then definitely missing at another. Once the time frame has been bracketed, it is relatively simple to determine which employees could have been involved in the loss.

Most frauds are discovered by accident, rather than by audit or accounting system design. Fraud detection is more of an art form than a science. It requires creative thinking as well as science, persistence, and self-confidence. Each fraud is unique.

The police should be informed if the loss is substantial, the evidence is strong, and the employee either appears to be untruthful or makes an admission or confession. Once charges are filed, the company should not withdraw its complaint without receiving a recommendation from the prosecutor. Charges should not be dropped in lieu of restitution, for the company will lose the confidence of the police, the prosecutor, and the court in future cases.

The second step is to establish the facts. Get as much information as possible from informants. Interview all who may have been involved in the control of the asset or given access to the asset during the bracketed period. Gather documents, organize data, examine documents for forgery, and look for "out of balance" conditions. Do not stop at the documents themselves, look behind them to the facts they are supposed to establish, and look for relationships—things that do not make sense.

The third step, interviewing, is a significant part of the investigative process. An interviewer should speak calmly and avoid an accusatory attitude. He or she should show compassion and interrupt the suspect only to clarify points. If the suspect elects to be silent, the interviewer should not threaten or intimidate; however, an employee should not be allowed to return to the work area, because valuable evidence may be lost.

Once serious wrongdoing is suspected and the evidence obtained, the suspect will have to be confronted and interrogated. However, suspected employees have certain common law and statutory rights. If these rights are infringed upon, whether or not the employee is guilty, he or she may have the right to sue the interrogator and the company. An accused employee can file a civil action if the employer made defamatory statements. Libel is a written defamation. Slander is an oral defamation.

An employer can be sued for false arrest or false imprisonment when he or she unreasonably restrains an employee's freedom of mobility. The restraint need not be physical touching or locking a person in a room. Intimidating employees or telling them they cannot leave the room or the city has been held to constitute false imprisonment.

Steps in Conducting Fraud Investigation

- Develop a theory of the fraud after initial analysis.
- Determine what information or evidence (records, financial statements, interview of witnesses, etc.) is likely to unravel the scheme and identify the perpetrator.
- Analyze the information or evidence, conduct interviews, and identify the culprit.
- Interrogate the perpetrator, obtain a confession, and locate and recover the stolen assets.
- Determine if the evidence is sufficient to bring charges, either criminal or civil.
- Complete the investigation.
- Safeguard the evidence.
- Prepare reports linking evidence and witnesses.
- Analyze defenses and weaknesses in the case.

Interrogation

A trained and experienced investigator can tell whether the person he or she is interrogating is lying or telling the truth.

Unusual or specific indicators in response to hot questions may suggest that the subject is less than truthful. These may include dry mouth and lips that result in a clicking sound when speaking; avoiding eye contact or staring at the interviewer, then dropping the eyes down and away to the side as the question is answered; an unusual high pitch to the voice or rapid speech patterns; and restlessness and shifting in the chair, crossing both the arms and legs with elbows kept tucked into the side. Also watch for abnormal eye blink rate, biting the lips or tongue, tightly squeezing the lips together, looking at or playing with fingernails, crying at inappropriate times, claiming memory failure or having a remarkably keen memory, and smiling at inappropriate times or phony oversmiling.

Other key nonverbal signals include rounding the shoulders with the elbows at the knees, dropping the head to look downward at the floor, and deep sighing that may indicate an admission is forthcoming. An experienced investigator will be aware of these signals and press the line of questioning accordingly.

Compounding a Felony

The laws in the United States provide that the right to punish or to forgive a criminal is reserved for the state. Defrauded employers who have been the victims of fraud cannot take those rights upon themselves. Agreeing to a consideration, not to prosecute, is itself a crime. It is called compounding a felony and can result in legal punishment for the employer, investigator, or both.

Controlling Crime/Accountability for Asset Protection

Protection and preservation of a firm's assets (human, capital, technological, and informational) from the foreseeable consequences of acts of public enemy (property theft, fraud, embezzlement, sabotage, information piracy, and commercial corruption) and human errors and omissions (employee negligence) are the responsibility of firm officers, directors, and agents by a host of federal, state, and local laws.

Proving Corporate Fraud

A fraud audit is the result of two events: the finding of accounting discrepancies, and allegation by some person that a fraud has been committed. When fraud is found, an investigator is needed. Where a discrepancy is found, an auditor is needed. The two principal types of auditors are internal and external.

Reasons for Leniency in Corporate Frauds

The reasons for leniency in corporate fraud situations are the wealth and prestige of the businessmen involved, their influence over the media, the trend toward more lenient punishment for all offenders, the complexity and invisibility of many business crimes, and the existence of regulatory agencies and inspectors who seek compliance with the law rather than punishment of violators.

Financial Investigative Skills

When a financial investigator embarks upon a fraud audit, he or she brings a unique set of skills to the task. The investigator has drawn on different aspects of many professions to blend information in ways, shapes, and forms never imagined by his or her predecessors. Financial investigators need to be part police officer, part investigator, part accountant, part sociologist, part computer expert, and part attorney in order to combat and resolve the many crimes he or she detects. The ability to understand the interdependence between financial events and criminal activity is the essence of a successful financial investigator.

The financial investigator

- Knows the statutes that define crimes uncovered during investigations
- Understands concepts relating to the collection and admissibility of evidence
- Can locate and interpret records that contain financial information
- Has the ability to trace the movement of money through a corporation or financial institution
- Has knowledge of accounting and auditing techniques
- Can conduct financial interviews, record findings, and summarize them in report form

The beginning financial investigator has to have a thorough knowledge of the types of business organizations and normal business records.

What Is Involved in the Financial Investigative Approach?

The major goal of a financial investigator is to identify and document specific events involving the movement of money during the course of a crime. Suppose an accountant is suspected of embezzling money from his employer. A financial investigator would determine what account (or accounts) he is taking the money from, how he took it, when he took it, and where he put it. If the investigator is able to identify these events and link them together, he or she will have the basis of proof indicating the commission of a crime. If the events cannot be identified and linked together, the investigation may support the determination to discontinue further inquiry into the matter. This does not mean that a crime was not committed. It merely means the financial investigator cannot put all the elements together.

Financial investigations are records-intensive; specifically, records pointing to the movement of money are examined. Bank account information (checking and savings account records), motor vehicle registration (title, place of purchase, and lien-holder records), and real estate files (records showing mortgages and deed records) are documents of record commonly found in this type of investigation. However, records such as utility bills, divorce decrees, and credit card receipts can play important roles in financial investigations. Any record that pertains to or shows the paper trail of events is important to a financial investigation.

Crimes with a Financial Aspect

Now that you have a general understanding of what is involved in the financial investigative approach, we will identify some criminal activities where the application of the approach would be appropriate. The list below presents some important terms the financial investigator should know; they are activities related to the field of finance:

- Blackmail—a demand for money or other considerations made under threat to do bodily harm, to injure property, to accuse of a crime, or to expose disgraceful defects
- Bribery—occurs when money, goods, services, information, or anything else of value is offered with the intent to influence the actions, opinions, or decisions of the taker
- Counterfeiting—occurs when someone copies or imitates an item without having been authorized to do so and passes the copy off for the original or genuine article
- Insider trading—occurs when a person uses "inside" or advance information to trade in shares of publicly held corporations
- Kickback—when a person who sells an item pays back a portion of the purchase price to the buyer or public official
- Money laundering—the investment or transfer of money from racketeering, drug transactions, and other illegal sources into legitimate channels so that its original source cannot be traced

Corporate Accounting Systems/Records

An accounting system consists of records that provide detailed information concerning business transactions, called journals, and summary information of account balances, called ledgers.

Financial information is taken from source documents and entered into the accounting system through the journals of a business. Journals are called the "books of original entry." Maintained in journals, in chronological order, are the details of each financial transaction entered into by a business. Special types of journals are devoted to particular kinds of business transactions. Examples of some types of journals are as follows:

- Cash receipts journal—records the dates, sources, and amounts of money received into a business

- Cash disbursements journal—records the dates, sources, amounts, and recipients of payments made by a business
- Sales journal (accounts receivable journal)—lists sales invoices by date or in numerical order for sales made on credit
- Purchase journal (accounts payable journal)—records all acquisitions of merchandise or services purchased on credit by a business

Journalizing entries (recording each business transaction from a source document into the journals) continues throughout the accounting period. Because of this, financial information contained within the journals grows during the accounting period, particularly in businesses that engage in a high volume of transactions. It would be difficult for a business owner, accountant, or financial investigator to analyze a journal full of financial transactions entered in chronological order, particularly when he or she is searching for specific account information (i.e., "all the rent expense payments" or "all the sales to a particular customer").

An accounting device called a ledger is used to summarize journal entries by specific accounts. The summary of account information contained in ledgers is used to prepare a business balance sheet and income statement.

Ledger

A ledger is established to accumulate all the transactions affecting a specific account during the accounting period. For example, all transactions affecting the "cash account," a business' receipt of cash (debit) and payouts of cash (credit) recorded in the journal, would be summarized in the ledger account entitled "cash." At the end of the accounting period, the balance of the ledger account (the mathematical difference between the total debit entries and total credit entries) is used as the basis for balance sheet and income statement reports.

Fraud Audit

The purpose of the fraud audit is to determine who is committing the fraud. In the audit, or investigation, employees must be evaluated to determine their state of mind or mental disposition toward fraudulent behavior. Fraud is committed by persons, not by computers or accounting systems.

Fraud Detection Techniques

The primary rule in all fraud investigations is to "follow the assets," or "follow the money." There is a tendency among some fraud investigators to look for complex schemes when in fact most are not complex at all. The fraud investigator should bear in mind two terms that are frequently used in court:

- The Principle of Occam's Razor—The court should not rely on allegations of complex schemes but should focus on the simplest answer, which is almost always how things work out.
- Qui Bono—Who benefits from the action?

Reasons for Fraud Investigations

There are three main reasons for fraud investigations:

1. To recover funds
2. To prevent repetition and deter others
3. To clear innocent people

Following is a summary of some of the most important rules in fraud investigation:

1. Whenever possible, inquiries should be concentrated around the central issue, or hub, of the fraud.
2. First examine the most seemingly obvious answer, and only when the most obvious answer has been eliminated, go on to more complicated solutions.
3. If concealment is difficult to unravel, the investigator should "follow the money." Determine who benefited at the end of the fraud and work backward.

The financial investigator may spend a great deal of his or her time involved with corporate fraud. For this reason, it is best to have an idea of the types of fraud committed by or against corporations.

Steps in the Fraud Investigation

- Develop a theory of the fraud after initial analysis.
- Determine what information and evidence (records, financial statements, interviews of witnesses, etc.) are likely to unravel the scheme and assist in identifying the perpetrator.
- Analyze the information and evidence, conduct interviews, and identify the culprit.
- Interrogate the perpetrator, obtain a confession, and locate and recover the stolen assets.
- Determine if the evidence is sufficient to bring criminal or civil charges.
- Complete the investigation.
- Safeguard the evidence.

- Prepare reports linking evidence and witnesses.
- Analyze defenses and weaknesses in the case.

Boiler Rooms—Telemarketing Fraud

The average boiler room is an organization of salespeople who fraudulently offer a product or service to the public over the telephone.

Every business day, in dozens of offices around the United States and Canada, telephone salespeople hunker over desks, speaking to strangers over the telephone, offering these strangers opportunities to invest in commodities, securities, investments, business opportunities, charities, and moneymaking programs. They solicit these people to invest in fraudulent schemes. These salespeople are not registered commodities or securities brokers. They are telemarketers who work for "boiler rooms." At any one time, hundreds of these operations are taking place, in South Florida, Las Vegas, and the Newport Beach, California, areas, for example. They are tremendous headaches to law enforcement and regulatory agents. There are licensed, legitimate securities and commodities brokers out there. Many honest telemarketing operations exist. The boiler room operators cause serious damage to the image of the legitimate telemarketing industry.

To the casual observer, boiler room operators and telemarketers appear to be average businessmen or businesswomen. They may be dressed in suits, wearing neckties, and carrying briefcases, or they may look somewhat Bohemian. They are no trouble for their neighbors and seldom come under suspicion.

What Boiler Rooms Sell

Boiler room operators do not sell only one product. Today they may be selling business franchises; tomorrow they may sell fraudulent commodities.

Several years ago, former Deputy Comptroller Larry Fuchs of the Florida Comptroller's Office testified before a Senate subcommittee that boiler rooms don't specialize in a single product. Their product is the "fraud du jour" (i.e., whatever fraud is a moneymaker at the time). That is the determination of the telemarketing fraud scheme that is chosen. The types of boiler rooms are limited only by the imagination of the operators. These include frauds in such offerings as:

- Advance fees for loans
- Business opportunities
- Commodities
- Employment

- Investments in coins, gems, greyhounds, oil and gas, ostriches, precious metals, private pager systems, 900 lines, securities, wireless cable systems, and so forth
- Lotteries
- Time shares re-sales
- Vending machines

Boiler rooms were first noted in Florida in the 1920s when the telephone was recognized as an inexpensive marketing tool. It was first used to sell Florida land, with much of the land being nonexistent or of poor quality. No longer did a salesperson have to travel and speak for hours with potential investors, and in cases where fraud was present, the phone was an especially useful tool. The investor never got to meet the salesperson and thus could not identify the salesperson in court.

As is true today, these boiler rooms required owners, managers, and phone workers. Telemarketing fraud has continued in Florida for over seven decades. At least three generations of boiler room workers have plied their trade in Florida. Phone workers advanced to managerial positions with the growth in the industry. Frequently, they branched off and became owners, working the same scams the companies they previously worked for offered.

Telemarketing scams have branched out of California, Nevada, New York, and Texas. Any student interested in telemarketing fraud should read the book *Fleeced! Telemarketing Rip-Offs and How to Avoid Them*, by Fred Schulte (Prometheus Books, Amherst, New York, 1995). It is a classic work on the subject.

Training

The boiler room telemarketer has to have an organized presentation for the customer. These presentations are called "scripts" or "pitch sheets" in the industry. Con men, through trial and error, designed sales presentations for salespeople to use decades ago. Today's con men are well versed in approaches to convince the public to invest in their product or service. A whole industry of professional writers has entered the picture and does nothing but prepare professional sales pitches covering the gamut of aspects of telephone solicitation. There are pitch sheets for initially approaching the target, scripts for presenting the program, scripts for overcoming objections, scripts for closing, and scripts for getting the client to invest again.

The following is a brief presentation of a script that netted over $25,000 per month for an Orange County, California, precious metals boiler room. This company was investigated, and prosecution began in 1995.

Salesperson: This is (name) account executive calling from California Prime Metals, Inc. How are you today? (customer name), I spoke to you last week and wanted to give you a call to see if you read our information packet over and had any questions that I could answer for you at this time. OK (customer name), I'd like to ask you a question. Did you make money in silver in 1990 or 1995?

(If customer says no) Well, that's not going to happen to you again.

(If customer says yes) Then I am sure you can appreciate the timing of this call.

Salesperson: Investors who responded to a similar call only 2 years ago in September and invested \$25,000 picked up profits over \$43,000 in less than 3 months. Making money in any investment simply requires buying before the public stampedes the market. You've seen that, haven't you?

Customer: Yes.

Salesperson: Then making money is important to you, isn't it?

Customer: Yes.

Salesperson: Are you financially in a position to react to an intelligent investment opportunity at this time? (and so on)

The conversation is staged and rehearsed to perfection, and the customer is kept on the phone. Bits and pieces of information about the customer's personal and financial status are gathered to build a profile of the victim. Boiler room owners do not always pay to obtain scripts. Once a company has paid for professional scripts, it is not unusual for a telemarketer leaving a "room" to sneak out a copy of the script and present it to other boiler room owners to open their own operations.

Obtaining Customers

There are three methods of selecting potential customers:

1. Cold calling—This involves dialing names at random from a phone book. It is the least effective method. Many people called will have low incomes and not be even remotely qualified to be the victim of the scam. This costs the "boiler room" operators money. They have to pay for the calls.
2. Mail-in cards—Many magazines have little postcards attached to pages. The card asks the reader if there is some area he or she would be interested in investing in, or lists various types of business opportunities. The interested person has only to check certain blocks and mail the card. The address is already on the postcard. The card may have been placed in the magazine by either the boiler room or a lead company. If the former, the card goes directly to the boiler room. If the latter, the card goes to the company that specialized in selling leads to both legitimate and boiler room operations.

3. Lead companies—These are companies that specialize in selling "leads," both to boiler rooms and to legitimate commodities and securities companies. Some individuals interested in different types of investments and services are furnished "deck-packs," packages of cards detailing all types of investment opportunities. Some cards in the deck-pack are placed there before the telemarketer, and they pay for this service. Lead companies may sell these leads to the boiler room operators at rates from fifty cents to a dollar a piece. Another source of leads for telemarketers are the brokers. Although leads are closely guarded, brokers sometimes steal some and take them to their new employers. The boiler room operators pay far less for these leads than those bought from a lead company.

What Goes on in a Boiler Room?

Typically, personnel start arriving at the boiler room between 9:00 and 9:30 a.m. for the first shift. People do not like to be bothered by telemarketers, and it is found best not to make calls until around 10:00 a.m. In a large operation, a second shift will come in around 7:00 p.m.—telemarketers who target the west coast.

Managers hand out groups of "lead cards" to the telemarketers, along with C&Ds (cease and desist orders that were served on the company, barring the boiler room from doing business in a particular state). Some states issued D&Rs (desist and refrain orders). These tell the salespeople that there are certain states in which they cannot sell. Usually, the secretary will post a typewritten list of those states where calls cannot be made. The secretary will bring in handfuls of messages from clients and hand them to the individual telemarketers.

Trainees (called "green peas") will go to a training room where an experienced boiler room manager will train them on the use of scripts. The manager will also advise them of what states they cannot solicit in. As part of the training, the trainer will listen to the trainees to determine if they are qualified to use the phone. Qualifiers will call individuals from the lead cards. The purpose is to cut out potential clients who do not have the money to invest or may be "stokes." A stoke is a potential investor who is talkative on the phone but who does not necessarily want to buy. The main job of the qualifier is to make the operation sound professional, asking questions about whether an individual is interested in investing, the particular range of annual income, and if he or she would be interested in reviewing solicitation material. On average, it takes 2 or 3 days before the material is received by the client and, supposedly, read.

The regular telemarketers (also known in the industry as "yaks") start working the phones, talking to people who have received the solicitation material. Seldom will they use their own names. They will use a phone name. Their preference is for a "mooch," a customer who has the attractive dual qualities of being financially well off and easily persuaded. Most of them carry a private notebook in which they maintain a list of "laydowns"—clients whom they have sold to in the past and who buy without fail.

Floor managers (sometimes known as "hawks") move among the booths, occasionally plugging in a jack to eavesdrop on a telemarketer's conversations with a client. If the broker is having problems with a client, the manager may take over to make the sale. There are well-trained brokers called "closers" whose job it is to finish most sales if the regular phone workers cannot.

When a sale is finalized, the client/victim is told that the terms of the sale will be tape-recorded for the customer's protection—a method to convince the client that everything is aboveboard.

Detection

With so many boiler rooms in operation, the only way investigators can know about an operation is through an inquiry. These can come from several sources:

1. An individual who has been solicited, calling to check on the authenticity of the company
2. A disgruntled ex-employee with an ax to grind—he or she possibly was denied a commission check
3. A call from the local Better Business Bureau or the chamber of commerce inquiring about a company wanting membership
4. Calls from bank security officers, because the bank is getting too many charge backs
5. A complaint from a dissatisfied customer

Investigation

Customers at some point realize that they have been swindled. When they call, the company salesperson is always out of the office on important business, is on vacation, or has been fired. Often the client is told that a refund check has been mailed. It never reaches the client. Eventually, the customer talks to a manager who keeps stalling him. The point comes when the client can no longer take it and attempts to contact the appropriate authorities in the state where the boiler room is located—a sometimes frustrating experience. There are several possible steps that can be taken once a formal investigation is begun. Because of circumstances, some steps have to be skipped.

Steps in Investigation of Telemarketing

1. Route the complaint to the correct agency. If it appears to be straight grand theft, the police department or sheriff's office in the jurisdiction where the boiler room is located should be notified. If some regulatory agency should be involved, route the complaint to that agency. Complaints about a commodities company should be referred to the Commodities Futures Trading Commission. Complaints concerning securities should go to the Securities and Exchange Commission, or the state agency that regulates the sale of securities. In Florida, the State Comptroller's Office handles both securities and the sale of investments. The Federal Bureau of Investigation and the Postal Inspection Service have their own internal arrangements for routing complaints.
2. Obtain an affidavit and copies of all supporting documents from the complainant. (Note that whether the cause goes criminal or civil, the chain of custody must be maintained. The complainant must be able to produce original documents before the court. If original documents are sent, immediately return them with a cover letter instructing the complainant to keep the original documents—preferably, they should be sent back by registered mail.) Whether the complaint is handled by a police agency or some regulatory agency, it is necessary to get detailed information from the complainant in the form of an affidavit. The affidavit plus copies of documents from the complainant are necessary to establish probable cause for subsequent action. Gathering this information may require that the investigating agency send a draft copy of the affidavit by some courier service for overnight delivery and provide for the complainant to return the affidavit with documents the same way. Time is of the essence, especially where a massive fraud appears to be operating.
3. Coordinate with the various police and regulatory agencies in the area to determine if other complainants exist. The more complaints supported by affidavits, the better.
4. Immediately gather all possible data to file for a search warrant or to file for some sort of civil action with the local court. In either case, several steps are necessary in preparing for either type of action.
5. Take the following minimum steps:
    a. Determine the exact location of the boiler room.
    b. Contact the leasing agent for the floor plan of that section of the building that contains the boiler room, and try to get a copy of the leasing contract.
    c. Obtain copies of corporate filings and occupational licensing information.

   d. Check with the chamber of commerce or Better Business Bureau to determine if those agencies have any identifying data on the principals.
   e. Search all available intelligence databases for identification of the principals and any possible background information.
   f. Obtain from the complainant information about where checks were deposited to identify bank and account numbers.
   g. Coordinate with other agencies that may have an interest in the case.
6. Maintain total secrecy about planned action, and where applicable, apply as soon as possible for a search warrant. Boiler rooms will cease doing business and move to another location if there is even the slightest hint that police authorities are about to move in. If they do, all the business records will be gone. These business records "make the case" in almost every boiler room case.

Note: Steps 5 and 6 may take place simultaneously.

7. File for temporary and permanent injunctions, appointment of a receiver, and a freeze of assets, if a civil case is filed by a regulatory agency. A motion for an *en camera* hearing before the court will frequently be requested—that is, a hearing without the defendant present. If the defendant learns about it, those records will be gone.
8. Note that in areas with large numbers of boiler rooms, law enforcement and regulatory agencies are well versed in serving search warrants. The steps are as follows:
   a. Investigators meet at a predetermined time near the target building, out of sight of any occupants.
   b. Uniformed police officers move to cover all entrances to the building with their vehicles.
   c. Police officers are stationed at each door and positioned so that they can observe all windows.
   d. A uniformed officer and a detective gain entry and identify themselves. They request that the highest ranking person on the premises come forward. In some cases, a battering ram may be necessary.
   e. Nonsworn investigators do not enter until the premises have been secured.
   f. The search warrant is read to the highest ranking person present, and a copy is presented to that person. If no one is present, a copy of the search warrant is left in the main office.

g. The room is searched, along with suspicious individuals, for weapons. Only law enforcement personnel are allowed to answer the phone.

   While serving a search warrant, a detective answered the phone. The customer on the other end said, "Who is this?" The detective replied, "Detective Wilson, and we are serving a search warrant here!" The customer replied, "Okay, I'll call back tomorrow."
h. Once the room is secured, nonsworn investigators enter and assist in the servicing of the search warrant.
i. Each individual on the premises is photographed, and a copy of his or her driver's license is made. The individual is interviewed by a detective or a financial investigator assigned to the search team. Each must provide information for a questionnaire. They must provide the following information: name, home address, home phone number, position title, name of supervisor, length of time employed, phone names used, and prior employment.
j. The police run an NCIC/FCIC (National Crime Information Center/Federal Crime Information Center) report on all those present. Those who have outstanding warrants are taken into custody. The rest of the people in the office are then released and permitted to take only personal possessions.
k. Investigators then move about the premises. A white piece of paper is placed on each table or booth with a number on it.
l. Police officers then videotape every inch of the premises.
m. Sworn law enforcement officers, frequently under the direction of financial investigators, then start a search of each desk and cabinet on the premises. Normal items taken include pitch sheets, lead cards, employment records, bank account information, deposit slips, computers and computer printouts, telephone records, client files, and anything else that may be necessary to complete a report of investigation. Note that the secretary's desk will, most of the time, have a sheet of paper listing each broker and the phone names used. The bookkeeper will frequently have a list of brokers and the commissions received on specific customers. The walls of the phone workers' booths will usually have items posted identifying phone names being used, memos of calls from the latest customers, and a list of states they are not allowed to call.
n. Each item taken is listed on an inventory sheet, along with the location from which it was taken and a brief description of the item.

o. Upon completion of the inventory, items are placed in boxes or plastic bags and sealed with red tape marked "EVIDENCE."

9. Consider the steps for an injunctive action. Departmental attorneys for the regulatory agency review the affidavits and documents provided by the financial investigators. If they feel that sufficient probable cause exists for an injunctive action, they will prepare the necessary paperwork for the request.

   An appointment is made to present the case to a judge. In most cases, every effort will be made to keep the pending action secret. Preliminary work involves investigators locating each bank where a freeze order will have to be served. A locksmith is contracted to arrive at the boiler room location at the same time as the attorneys.

   At the court hearing, departmental attorneys must convince the judge that irreparable harm may befall investors if the defendant has a chance to be at the hearing. This is usually where the possibility of immediate "bleeding" of bank accounts is brought up. At this point the judge makes a decision—one that will affect the lives of many investors. If the judge decides the defendant has a right to be heard, the judge will not issue the necessary order. The defendant will be notified, and the normal pattern is that the bank accounts will be immediately drained. Usually, the judge will issue a temporary restraining order, and an order appointing a temporary receiver. A hearing date will be set, at which time the defendant will get a chance to tell his or her side of the story.

   If the judge decides to issue a temporary injunction, appoints a temporary receiver, and grants a freeze of assets, several things happen at the same time:

   a. Certified copies of the freeze order are handed to the investigator who immediately goes to the assigned banks and serves them on the banks. At this point, no individual from the company may touch the money in the accounts.
   b. Department attorneys will proceed to the boiler room location and immediately give a copy of the temporary injunction to the ranking person on the premises.
   c. The temporary receiver will immediately take charge and inform all personnel that, for the moment, he or she is in charge of the company. Except for those personnel that the receiver wants to keep to assist in the receivership, the rest are identified and sent home.
   d. The locksmith then changes all the locks, and the new keys are handed to the receiver.

10. Analyze the records. Financial investigators immediately begin to analyze the business records of the company, whether seized in a search warrant or obtained in an injunctive proceeding. Particular attention is paid to the bank accounts. The objective is to determine from the corporation's business records the financial state of the company and whether it was doing what it said it would be doing with money received from clients. This process of analyzing business records is known as forensic accounting.
11. Determine steps to take when there are no records. In more than 50% of cases worked, the corporation will be long gone, and bank accounts bled, before any investigative agency comes down on them. Under these circumstances, financial investigators will have only bank documents and other documents of public record to work by. The task is to reconstruct the company and its operation, working backwards with whatever documents are available. Bank records are the most helpful tool for the forensic accountant. For these records, most of how a company functioned can be recreated. The main goal when reviewing financial records is to discover where the money came from and where it went. The name of this process is the "analytic cash flow." It is part of forensic accounting. Incidental to this, the financial investigator is almost always able to discover and identify principals, sales personnel, and office help. The process will also reveal how long personnel were with the company, salaries and commissions, and what other companies they dealt with. Nearly every investor can be identified through this procedure.
12. Gather other information. Once investors are identified, they can be contacted and questioned about what they were told by company representatives. If they wish to complain, they send in affidavits and supporting documents that help build a case.
13. Consolidate information. The financial investigator takes all the information he or she has garnered from all available sources and analyzes the data in order to gain an overall picture of what transpired.
14. Generate a report of investigation. The financial investigator incorporates everything into a report of investigation to be used by civil or criminal prosecutors. In the report, the investigator will do the following:
    a. Identify all known principals, salespersons, and others who worked for the company.
    b. Cite all laws that were violated based on an analysis of complaints received, including certificates of non-registration where state laws pertaining to licensing requirements exist.
    c. Identify the criminal action allegedly committed by each proposed defendant.

d. Provide an analysis of all pertinent documentation used in the solicitation of victims.
e. Include a witness list for later use by prosecutors or civil attorneys.
f. Provide a summary of the entire case.

The report of investigation is referred to attorneys for whatever agency is involved. There it is reviewed. If it appears that the evidence of guilt is overwhelming, the report is referred either to the local prosecutor's office or to federal prosecutors. If it does not present an overwhelming picture of guilt, a civil case may be filed.

When a case has been thoroughly investigated, the guilt is usually clearly established. If the job is done thoroughly, especially the analytic cash flow, the defendant almost always pleads out.

Secondary Rip-Offs

The boiler room con men are not content with hitting a victim just once. Secondary "rip-offs" are quite common. With the secondary rip-off, customer lists of a boiler room are recycled. The boiler room that did the initial swindle may save the customer list for a year or two and then contact the victims with the new scheme. Most of the time the customer lists are sold to another group of swindlers.

These con artists then contact victims and state that the company they did business with either went out of business without delivering the investment or service promised or sent the victims merchandise of inferior quality. The task of this new company is to make the customer "whole." The basic scheme is that the customer must send in a sum of money to get the situation corrected.

Steps in the Investigative Process when Internal Fraud Is Involved

1. Establish that a loss has occurred and an asset was lost. The process should determine that the asset was accountable at some point and then definitely missing at another. Once the time frame has been bracketed, it is relatively simple to determine which manager or employee could have been involved in the loss.
2. Establish the facts. Get as much information as possible from informants (if there are any). Gather documents, examine documents for forgery, and organize data.
3. Conduct interviews. Interviewing is a significant part of the investigative process. Interview all who may have been involved in the control of the asset or who had access to the asset during the bracketed period. Interviewers should speak calmly and avoid accusatory attitudes. They should show compassion and interrupt the subject only

to clarify points. If the suspect is identified and elects to be silent, the interviewer should not threaten or intimidate; however, an employee should not be allowed to return to the work area, because valuable evidence may be lost. While conducting interviews, the interviewer should be aware and take note of the interviewee's body language.

How to Conduct a Criminal Fraud Defense Investigation

The formal portion of this chapter concludes, after a brief background description, with an excerpt from an article written by Mark J. Murnan, wherein he outlines how to conduct a criminal fraud defense investigation. He does an outstanding job describing the required steps.

Some Background

In the high-flying 1990s, when tech stocks and companies were increasingly multiplying, "investors" (a loose definition for anyone with cash, equity, or a credit card who had a phone or an Internet connection) were pouring money into any venture that cleverly named itself "something.com." In the course of going public, hundreds of these companies made instant, paper millionaires of those lucky ones who had "gotten in early." Their successes were paraded across lifestyle magazines that featured lavish examples of conspicuous consumption, and the speculation-home market gobbled up every available lot within sight of the ocean, gulf, intra-coastal area, or even canal in the state of Florida.

Occasionally, the business magazines would report the other side of the story—the thousands of companies that folded or reorganized, taking billions of dollars of their investors' money with them into the black hole of insolvency. And of course, even though the majority of these companies failed due to legitimate business reasons (mismanagement, lack of capital, failed technology), a significant number failed for illegitimate reasons—they were never meant to succeed, because they were out-and-out frauds.

Unlike crimes of violence or ordinary theft, which are typically straightforward and center around physical evidence and alibis, fraud is designed to be obscure, and the paper trail that is left must be interpreted by knowledgeable investigators. Depending on the scale of the fraud, witnesses could number from the dozens to the hundreds, the amounts could be in the tens of thousands to the hundreds of millions, and the "crime scene" could be in several locations or even states. The sheer size and scope of the fraud is the biggest inhibitor to the defense investigator, who is called in only after the state or government has filed charges and had months or even years to conduct an investigation. There is a lot to catch up with and not much time.

"Eating the Elephant": Defense Investigations for Complex Fraud Cases

Mark J. Murnan

If you're anything like me, phrases like "wire fraud" and "money laundering" glaze your eyes over like a fresh Krispy Kreme donut. Perhaps you've seen the cases come into the office: rented delivery vehicles disgorging boxes of discovery like a relief plane unloading CARE packages in a starving third-world nation, but no one wants *these* packages; they're for the "white collar" guy. Then it happened. I was assigned a complex fraud case involving a WCC—"white collar crime" or "white collar criminal."

"No," I protested, "it can't be! We didn't get any boxes!" The attorney pointed grimly to a stack of CD-ROMS on his desk.

It was at this point that I discovered the need for a methodology to organize, investigate, and defend complex fraud cases.

There is a secret to eating the elephant: you eat it one bite at a time. And in conducting a defense investigation of a complex case, it's really the same principle: you tackle it one component at a time. This also helped me understand a basic secret of complex cases: **you're not handling *one* investigation, you're handling *dozens* of investigations under one case.**

You'll be doing background investigations, locates, asset checks, criminal histories, and interviews of cooperative and hostile witnesses. In other words, every aspect of your investigative expertise will be called on during the defense of a complex fraud case.

Component One: Case Review and Analysis

This is where the defense investigation begins: reviewing the charging document and complaint (if any). Because many of these cases are prosecuted in federal court, I will use that venue as the example. Cases filed in state court will follow a similar course.

Whether the case involves a phony real estate loan, fraudulent insurance investments, or a long-term "boiler-room" operation is not relevant to our discussion here. We want to focus on those big boxes, or CD-ROMs that constitute the prosecution's case. Regardless of the nature of the charges, the basic story will be contained in the charging document, and this document will provide us with a basic framework for beginning the investigation.

Dates of the alleged fraud will be included in the indictment, along with names of the defendants. Typically, more than one person is involved in larger schemes, and several codefendants may have been indicted; however, you may have a single defendant, with several unnamed coconspirators referred to in the indictment. Also included will be names or initials of alleged victims of the fraud, dates of specific overt acts, and amounts alleged to have been misappropriated by the defendants. The elements of the crime will be specifically mentioned by name and statute. It is crucial to have a clear understanding of what constitutes criminal intent in these cases, as well as the elements of a conspiracy if one is alleged.

Author's note: Once the charging document has been carefully reviewed, it is time to begin the arduous task of sorting the discovery. Several methods have been suggested for this task, including the following, taken from *Uncovering Reasonable Doubt: The Component Method* (Brandon Perron, Morris Publishing, Rearney, NE, 1998):

- Chronologically
- Alphabetically
- By location
- By topic
- By continuum or magnitude scale (how the item fits into the overall picture)

My experience is that documents are never introduced in court unless established through a witness. Therefore, I suggest that each document be collected and maintained alphabetically according to the witness—the author, originator, or subject of the document. For instance, a contract should be filed by the name of the individual alleged to have signed the contract, and perhaps another copy of the contract filed by the name of the company representative alleged to have filled out the contract. Either of these parties could be called to testify to the document's authenticity. By organizing the data alphabetically by witness, you begin to put faces to the papers and to develop an idea of how the government's case will be structured.

Timelines

The importance of establishing a timeline of events cannot be overstated in complex cases. Fortunately, the government has already established the basic time frame within the indictment; however, the defense investigation will typically extend both before and after the allegations in order to "frame out" the circumstances in which the alleged activity occurred. If a company was formed by the defendant, employees may be called and interviewed to determine if they have been contacted by the government (believe me, they have) and what they may say if called to testify. It is important to know when they were hired, who was already at the company, and who may have come in subsequent to their hiring.

Author's note: The documents will assist in constructing the timeline. Checks, purchase orders, phone bills, company invoices, contracts, and employee applications will assist in filling out the sequence of events so you and the attorney can begin to see what the government has chosen to focus on, or, typically, what it has chosen to overlook. Remember, law enforcement has been working on the case for months or years, but their investigation is summarized (albeit not completely) in the discovery.

Component Two: The Client Interview

I will say this up front: I have rarely had a WCC admit he or she had done *anything* wrong in the initial interview.

What I *have* gotten are some extremely fascinating interpretations of actions and events, with the most novel explanations of self-justification imaginable. "My partners took advantage of me." "I had *no idea* he was keeping all the money for himself." Here is my personal favorite: "We were *on the verge* of [going public, getting the financing, blah, blah, blah] before the government shut us down!"

Author's note: Client interviews with WCCs are typically ongoing, with hours spent reviewing documents, witness statements, and audio- and videotapes. If the client is fortunate enough to be on bond and available for office conferences, he or she can be a valuable asset in assisting with the organization of the files. Otherwise, it will be necessary to break the case down piecemeal, and review key aspects with the client at the detention facility. Most of the interviews with the client after the initial series of contacts may be conducted by the attorney, without the investigator having to be present; many attorneys, however, feel it is important to have a third party present to witness and note the client's responses and requests at certain times in the litigation.

During the initial interviews with the WCC, cover the usual bases—personal information, prior criminal history, work/employment history, assets owned, and medical treatment, including drug- and alcohol-related treatments. Make sure you have several medical releases available for the client to sign, and get names and addresses of treating physicians and hospitals. Begin to flesh out the client's story—is he or she claiming that none of the allegations occurred (the "ostrich" defense)? That he or she was unaware of the misfeasance of the partner (the "see-no-evil" defense)? That the business was totally legitimate, and that the government has conspired against him or her (the "bogeyman" defense)? More than any other type of defendant, it has been my experience that the WCC has almost a pathological need to legitimize his or her behavior.

Author's note: Because of the scope of discussions necessary in these cases, Component Two (like Component One) should be considered ongoing, continuing all the way through trial or plea and sentencing.

Component Three: Crime Scene Examination

Fraud cases take place in every imaginable venue—a home office, a place of business, over the phone, or online. Pinpointing a specific location is sometimes less important than determining *what was said or done* at the location. There are, however, crucial locations that need to be identified and visited, if possible. If the fraud is alleged to have occurred at a company office, that site should be inspected and photographs taken, if possible. Often this isn't possible, because the company has gone out of business either voluntarily or by judicial order, and the location has been leased out to another company. You should still plan a field trip to the location. Talk to building personnel there, and see if anyone was contacted by law enforcement (believe me, they have) and what they said or were told. Check with city utilities; who arranged for the water and trash pick up? The government has typically obtained phone records for the location and provided them in discovery (especially if the indictment includes allegations of wire fraud), but if not, go ahead and get them under subpoena. Was furniture leased or rented? Get those records as well. Determine, with the help of the client and witnesses, who sat where. Was there a receptionist? Who sat in the office adjacent to the defendant? Can you account for every employee affiliated with the company during its existence? *The most damaging witnesses to the defense are former coworkers who decide to cooperate with the prosecution, usually to avoid indictment themselves.*

Component Four: Witness Background Investigations

Remember our earlier statement about complex cases—you really are not handling *one* investigation, you are handling *dozens* of investigations under one case. It is very easy to get bogged down at this point in your investigation, as you have literally dozens of people who need to be checked out to some degree.

Begin to *organize* and then to *prioritize*. Take your list of names, and develop folders for each individual, whether victim, employee, associate, or known witness. Label each folder so you have an alphabetical listing of witnesses you can easily locate. Begin to assemble whatever documents you have in each folder by witness. As you continue, it will become clearer to you who the priority people will be. Typically, these will be victims of the fraud, those who made concerted efforts to get their monies back, and the discovery will contain numerous references to them—phone messages, tape-recorded telephone calls or personal meetings, letters, or e-mails. Coworkers or vendors who may be cooperating with the prosecution will also become evident in the discovery, through correspondence, taped statements, or telephone calls. Later, as these individuals are contacted, they may direct you to other people who are farther out on the concentric circle of involvement, who may also have been contacted (or ignored) by the prosecution, and who may have additional (possibly exculpatory) information.

This process requires tremendous focus and discipline on the part of the investigator. There are no shortcuts here. Each individual needs to have some form of background check completed, but the prioritization of each witness can alleviate much of the mundane process.

Author's note: For instance, a detailed investigation needs to be completed on the primary victims of the fraud, including a civil and criminal history in their home jurisdictions and, perhaps, contact needs to be made with their employers or neighbors to determine their reputation for truthfulness. The majority of the witnesses will be more peripheral, however—vendors and office staff who had limited contact with the defendant or his or her employees or associates, those who delivered a service to the company's location, or the salesperson who sold a car or a boat to the defendant when he walked in off the street. The process of prioritizing should include several hours with the attorney, who can direct your efforts and save considerable time in the next step.

As you begin to assimilate all the documents into individual folders, you will notice that many of the witnesses are out of town or even out of state. Some will have moved in the months or years since the investigation began. Current addresses and phone numbers will need to be developed for each priority witness. This is done through the usual sources, including databases and courthouse research. Criminal and civil histories can be obtained in outside jurisdictions through the help of other investigators, either in the local public defender offices, or through affiliations with investigative associations, such as National Defense Investigators Association (NDIA), National Association of Legal Investigators (NALI), or a statewide organization. On these occasions, "it pays to be a member." If I receive a request for assistance from an investigator in another jurisdiction, that request moves to the top of my to-do list, because I have been around long enough to know that someday I am going to need their help!

Component Five: Witness Interviews

As you develop information about your witnesses, you are now ready to begin contacting them. In large, complex cases, the sheer number of witnesses makes personal interviews difficult, but many will have to be done that way. The majority will have to be contacted by phone. It is important to *know what you need from each witness.* Have a list of questions ready before each attempt to contact is made—questions you developed through discussions with the attorney. Review the witness' folder, and determine what part he or she had in the case. Keep the questions in the folder, so if the witness returns a telephone call, you can grab the file and fire away with your questions. If he or she is a major player, consider taking the attorney along for the interview. If you need to travel out of state, make sure you have a clear understanding of what the attorney is looking for, and double check with him or her before you leave town, and again from the road before you make contact with the witness.

It used to concern me that witnesses would not talk to me, especially government witnesses, or victims. Time and experience have taught me that the opposite is generally true. People love to talk, and they are often not discriminating in whom they talk to.

Author's note: Years after I discovered this phenomenon, it occurred to me that this was probably the reason they became victims of the fraud in the first place.

It should be carefully stressed here that contact with known government or potentially hostile witnesses should be carefully documented by the investigator, and a strict protocol for identification should be established before interviews are commenced. My former partner was accused by an unscrupulous (and later demoted) FBI agent of threatening or intimidating a government witness. Although the allegations were false and were later dismissed, it cost my partner some of his hair (already in short supply) and an increase in his tobacco intake.

Because of incidents like this, make sure you have the identification procedure worked out in advance. Know how you are going to introduce yourself to the witness, what you are going to say about who you work for and who you represent, and have a business card ready to give to the witness immediately. If you have some type of government identification, consider leaving it in the car, especially if you have one of those oversized badges issued by the federal defender. Nothing says "I'm a cop" more than a large gold shield, even if it says *Federal Public Defender* on it. Because misrepresentation is the most common allegation made against defense investigators, I have come to the conclusion that a plain white business card with my name on it is the surest safeguard against possible indictment. Now that I am in the private sector, I have even gone to the expense of having a graphic artist design a card for me that cannot possibly be confused for an official government agency. If you are not in that market, consider a card without your agency or state logo. And by all means, list any credentials you obtained, such as the Certified Legal Investigator (CLI) or Certified Criminal Defense Investigator (CCDI) designation. (Contact NALI and the CDITC for information on the process of becoming certified.) Government agents do not identify themselves as *Board*

Certified Criminal Defense Investigators. Sometimes, if the witness agrees to talk to me, I will even have him or her initial another business card, which I then tape to the witness' folder.

Author's note: The biggest problem you will encounter, however, is not a witness who won't talk to you. It will be the witness who won't shut-up. I once had to contact the victim of a loan origination scam, a retired colonel who sent a $300,000 cashier's check to Las Vegas, Nevada, in the care of an unscrupulous real estate agent and a developer, to be handed over to our client, a man he had never met, and who had four prior fraud convictions. I went to the colonel's door at 7:00 p.m., fully expecting to be thrown out or otherwise dismissed. I was certain I would be home for dinner by 7:30 p.m. At 10:00 p.m., I left his home after 3 hours of the most interesting conversation I had in months. While he was initially recalcitrant, and claimed he had nothing to say about the case, I asked him instead about his military service. He gradually opened up, and we shared some war stories about our experiences, and he told me about his civilian career. He was a remarkable man, and I asked him frankly how a man of his caliber got mixed up with a "tuna head" (my own words) like our client. He smiled, and gave a thoughtful answer that I later shared with the attorney. The rest of the conversation yielded some additional information, but most of it was just pleasant "guy talk." While that is an extreme example, it is representative of a witness's desire to talk, even against their own interests.

If people really knew what talking to an investigator would eventually entail, nobody would talk to us. But because people love to talk, all an investigator really needs to do is give them an opportunity to do so.

Component Six: Reports and Testifying

It is vitally important to take careful notes during an interview, because you are dealing with people who have information about a series of different and sometimes unrelated events. Sometimes it is not possible to take notes during the interview for any number of reasons. Immediately afterward, you must record your recollections on paper, even if it means sitting in your car in the witness' front yard or sitting a block away, after the interview.

Author's note: Dictated reports must be reviewed after they are typed, to compare with the investigator's notes to see if anything was missed during the dictation. This happens frequently, and it is the investigator's responsibility to ensure that the information is added to the finished report.

Because of the months involved in the defense of a complex WCC case, a "final report" is unrealistic. Instead, reports and memorandums must be completed on a weekly, and sometimes daily, basis. Witness interviews are seldom one-time events. Some witnesses, even government witnesses, may be contacted and interviewed several times during the investigation, just as they were by the government agents. Therefore, it is crucial to maintain open lines of communication with the witnesses, if at all possible, and to update the initial interview with any new information developed. Maintain all interviews in the folder assigned to that witness, chronologically, from most recent on top to original contact at the bottom. This will ensure that you have the latest address and contact information immediately available.

All notes taken by the investigator relating to the witness should also be maintained in the witness folders, on the other side of the file. Attach all sheets of paper to the file with a fastener; do not let them sit in the file unattached.

As the trial date approaches, hours will be spent with the attorney preparing exhibits and coordinating defense witnesses. Make sure some of that time is spent reviewing your own possible testimony. As part of the defense team, your contribution does not end when the jurors are picked. Witness coordination and testifying are also part of the investigation. Scheduling appearances, making sure your witnesses know where the courthouse and courtroom are, and being prepared to take the stand yourself are all crucial aspects of a properly defended case. After the verdict is reached, whatever the outcome, your duties will include maintenance of the investigative files for possible appellate issues or to memorialize the acquittal, because the best part of a WCC case is that sometimes the defense wins.

A Final Word

Remember our premise—you really are not handling one investigation, you are handling dozens of investigations under one case. The time you devote to complex cases will raise your level of competence and confidence, the investigator's best offensive weapon.

So, the next time the delivery truck pulls up in front of your office, boxes start accumulating in the lobby, and everyone else in the office is starting to look for the exit, put a smile on your face and announce in a loud voice, "Boys and girls, *dinner is served*!"

Case Studies

Internal Fraud Investigation

Uncovering a Classic Bribery Corruption Scheme

In April 2004, my firm, McMahon & Associates Detective Division, was retained by a prominent Miami, Florida, law firm representing a local community blood bank, a not-for-profit corporation. The blood bank was operating in several locations throughout South Florida. At the time of the initial meeting, the attorney had received correspondence from two vendor delivery companies regarding outstanding invoices of approximately $1,000,000 due them from the blood bank. The objective of the investigation was outlined as follows:

- To determine how invoices of approximately $1 million could be owed to outside delivery companies when the blood bank has its own delivery fleet of drivers.
- To stall or prevent litigation from being filed by two vendor companies while the investigation unravels the possible fraud.
- To identify if there is fraud, determine what happened and which, if any, employees are involved.

Following the meeting with the attorney, we met with the blood bank's chief executive officer (CEO) and the vice president (VP)/and director of human resources (HR). We obtained an overview of the operation of the company and the various departments connected to the delivery process, including a listing of employees assigned and the supervisors responsible for oversight. The VP/HR director was assigned by the CEO to be the main contact for my team.

Upon review of the information received and the objectives required, we established the following plan for the investigation:

- Phase One—Conduct background checks of employees assigned to the delivery department and due diligence investigations of the two vendor companies.
- Phase Two—Audit the financial records involving the invoices submitted by both vendor delivery companies, review all contracts and policies and procedures regarding the delivery process, and identify key employees involved.
- Phase Three—Conduct interviews of employees and other persons having information regarding the delivery process, including drivers from the two vendor companies.
- Phase Four—Identify the procedures and policies that were in place to determine how the problem became so out of control, and develop a plan of new procedures and policies that will prevent a problem from developing again in the future.

One of the first observations that became apparent was that the blood bank had opened two new offices in the past 2 years. The first was a new headquarters opened in Palm Beach County. The second was a new building recently opened in Broward County. The CEO, chief financial officer (CFO), and other officers of the blood bank were primarily focused on the building and opening of these two new facilities during the time frame involved.

The primary function of the blood bank is to collect blood from various locations and act as a resource for hospitals in the community that need the blood. In the event that the blood bank does not have enough blood from contributions, they purchase blood from other sources. The blood bank is then contacted by medical facilities that order the units of blood to be delivered to their facilities, and hence the need for drivers. The blood bank charges the medical facility for the blood and blood products and also for delivery. There is an extra charge for rush and after-hour deliveries.

At the time we started our investigation, a new transportation manager had recently been hired by the blood bank. He was assigned to oversee all deliveries, review existing policies and procedures, and return the primary responsibility for delivery to the drivers employed by the company, as opposed to outside vendors. In view of the fact that he was hired after all the problems were identified, he was enlisted to help us conduct our investigation. Our first request to him was to identify the policies and procedures in place and why they did not work. We requested that he write a memo addressing the following:

1. Describe the conditions that were in place when you started at the blood bank regarding deliveries and the use of outside vendors, including the percent of deliveries made by in-house personnel as opposed to vendors, as well as location of delivery drivers.
2. Describe the procedures in place upon your arrival for authorization of outside delivery vendors. Who was authorized to make the calls? Who approved use of the vendor?
3. Report which employees provided information about kickbacks by vendors. What were the circumstances surrounding those reportings?
4. Provide your analysis of the services and pricing and invoicing methods of Delivery Company Two (Dade County company).
5. Provide your analysis of the services and pricing and invoicing methods of Delivery Company One (Palm Beach company).
6. Describe how their billing differs from your understanding of the accepted industry standard for delivery companies.
7. Reveal what transpired when you spoke with both vendor companies after your arrival at the blood bank.
8. Conclude by discussing your background in the delivery industry.

The transportation manager reported the following:

> I am going to cover the issues you wanted in the same sequence that you asked them. I hope that you will find them thorough. (Keep in mind I have only been here less than a month, and I may not have all of the answers.)
>
> 1. The conditions which I found regarding deliveries when I started were by industry standards not managed properly.
>   a. Any blood bank employee could call a vendor/courier and request a pickup or delivery without prior approval from the operations supervisor/manager on duty.
>   b. The percentages of deliveries made internally and externally were not being recorded properly, so there is no measurement of percentages that I would deem accurate.
> 2. Anyone had the ability to call couriers. The approval for billing was handled by the VP of General Services, who is no longer with the company.
> 3. The employee that I know about who came forward with kickback information was Source One. He gave the envelope with the $50 to his supervisor. I know of no other employees—you may want to ask the director of Human Resources.
> 4. The service provided by the courier services was impeccable—they would actually loiter on the properties to wait for calls. I sent them a memo requesting that they not loiter on the property due to insurance reasons.
>   a. The pricing was another issue. There were no set discounts from the base tariffs, which is unheard of in the transportation industry.
>   b. There were multiple pickups from one location to another location billed individually.
>   c. There were multiple pickups that should have been rated stop to stop and were billed from origin to destination.
>   d. The invoices read as a call log and provide no POD (proof of delivery, the bible of the transportation industry). Without this POD, we are not obligated to pay the invoice.
>   e. The billing does not seem to ever have been audited for accuracy.
>
> The above pertains to both couriers.
>
> 5. See above.
> 6. See above.
> 7. Company Two was really excited about the opportunity to work together and wanted to ensure we would keep our relationship strong. He mentioned that he could not give me any pricing—he was going out of town and would have to get back to me. I have this on file if you would like to review. He also stated that if we were willing to sign an annual contract, they would be willing to renegotiate pricing. He also stated that he had discussed the possibility of utilizing

their drivers with the VP Director of General Services at a daily rate of $150 with no company liabilities.

Company One was in the process of moving and said she would be out to meet with me and also wanted to make sure we kept using their service. She came bearing the $100 ABC card and an immediate discount stating that we would not pay after-hours or weekend rates. She also mentioned wanting to be contracted to have additional discounts applied.

8. *Conclusion*: I have been involved actively in the transportation industry for 17 years. I have been in management for 15 of those years. I have extensive experience in managing fleets, warehouses, and budgets.

The Investigation

The first phase involved conducting background checks on the blood bank employees and due diligence investigations on the two vendor companies. The background checks revealed criminal histories for both the delivery supervisor and one of the lead drivers, who was recommended by the delivery supervisor. The due diligence check revealed that Company One (Palm Beach company) was a sole proprietorship (operating as a fictitious name filing) formed the year before it was hired by the blood bank. Also noted was that the reported income for Company One for that year according to Dun & Bradstreet was $35,000.

The second phase involved the audit of invoices and analysis of bills and receipts submitted with them. Each month was broken down by day and put in an Excel spreadsheet format. The bills were also analyzed by month and totaled (see monthly breakdown for the two companies). It quickly became apparent that there was overbilling, as the analysis of Company Two below reveals:

- February 2004—117 tickets missing on invoiced items.
- March 2004—92 tickets missing on invoiced items; no tickets found for March 1 and March 2.
- April 2004—27 tickets missing for invoiced items.

Additional information:

- Over 90% of the tickets did not have both the pickup and delivery times reported.
- Over 50% had no time reported (thus making it impossible to determine if it was an after-hours delivery).
- Many drivers made multiple deliveries on each day, yet all deliveries were billed as if they were single destination deliveries.

- Many drivers went to the same locations repeatedly during the same day, yet the deliveries were billed as single-destination deliveries.

Because the records were provided in such a disorganized and haphazard fashion, it took over 40 hours to reconcile each month's invoices. The tickets were cut and written so poorly that in many instances it was difficult or impossible to read all the information on the ticket, and in over 90% of the tickets all of the required information was not completed.

The audit also revealed that in April 2004 two pints of blood were picked up at the Palm Beach location and delivered by Company Two to Jackson Hospital in Miami, Florida. They were billed as two separate deliveries and charged door-to-door at a rate of $138.40 per delivery. That same company picked up 4 pints of blood at the Palm Beach location and delivered them to Fort Pierce (Indian River County), Okeechobee (Palm Beach County), Plantation (Broward County), and Aventura (Dade County). They also were treated as four separate pickups and deliveries by the Dade County vendor, instead of using the nearby Palm Beach vendor. The cost of delivery was $125 for each pint. It should have been billed stop-to-stop.

In conclusion, as referenced above, review of the records failed to disclose time of delivery and person who received the delivery, which makes verification of the delivery impossible. It also creates a problem when determining if the charge was made for a "rush" or an "after-hours" delivery, for which the vendors charged an additional cost. It also created a problem for the blood bank billing, as most times they were not passing on the surcharge to the hospitals. Finally, the analysis revealed that over 20 different employees, ranging from delivery drivers to blood bank vice presidents, called for contract vendors to make pickups and deliveries.

The third phase involved interviews of the employees. After interviewing some of the supervisory personnel and clearly identifying that there was no central system for using the outside vendors as opposed to delivery employees, we focused on the blood bank drivers. On May 18, 2004, we interviewed Source One, who received a card with $50 from the driver of Company One in April 2004. He stated that he was a lead driver assigned to work the weekend shift. He had the responsibility for assigning all deliveries in the Palm Beach location. Sometime in 2002 he noticed that more and more deliveries were assigned to the vendors. He was told that the VP of General Services believed that it was less costly to use the vendors, as the blood bank had to pay for the benefits of the employees. This resulted in that VP terminating all the part-time drivers and requiring more vendors. He was given the card with the money by the driver as a thank you for using them so frequently.

Source One also suspected that other blood bank drivers were receiving gratuities from other vendor drivers. He also stated that Company Two drivers were receiving so much weekend work that their company was paying for them to stay at a Days Inn in Palm Beach, close to the blood bank office. They would then hang out in the blood bank parking lot awaiting assignments for deliveries. Furthermore, he stated that the delivery supervisor would report to the office on weekends, while he was off duty, to ensure that assignments were being channeled to the vendor companies, particularly Company Two (Dade County). On one occasion, the supervisor even ordered a driver to return to the blood bank office in the middle of a delivery to give the blood units to a vendor driver.

On two occasions, we interviewed Source Two. On the first occasion, he was not truthful and denied any wrongdoing. On May 21, he was reinterviewed and presented with evidence of accepting gratuities. He admitted that he received cash ranging from $20 to $50 on a regular basis. He stated that he believes that he received between $500 and $1000 in total. The first occurrence was the previous year while the driver supervisor, his high school classmate, was on vacation. The supervisor recommended him for the job. Upon his return, he told the supervisor about the cash, and from that time on they shared the proceeds.

Source Two also reported that he was given packages (envelopes) to be delivered to the VP of General Services. He never opened the thick envelopes, but on several occasions after the delivery, the VP came out and gave him "gift cards" for himself and to share with the other drivers. He stated that one vendor company provided cash to the drivers and the other gave gift cards in various denominations to such stores as Starbucks, Home Depot, and ABC Liquors. At the conclusion of the interview, Source Two signed a written statement.

On two occasions, we interviewed the delivery supervisor. After initially lying to us, he was forthcoming when confronted with evidence of wrongdoing. He stated that he was instructed by the VP of General Services to use the vendor companies more than the blood bank drivers. He was further instructed to use the Miami company more than the Palm Beach vendor. He admitted that he received cash and gift cards from the drivers of both vendor companies. He also acknowledged that he received cash from the owner of Company One. He stated that he knew that the VP of General Services received packages with gift cards from Vendor Two, because he would receive some of them from him to distribute to the drivers. He admitted working after hours and weekends to make sure that the assignments were given to the vendors instead of being handled by the employees. He signed a handwritten statement after the interview was completed.

On June 7, 2004, we interviewed the former VP of General Services. He was reluctant to speak with us, and the interview was conducted on his front porch. He had heard about our investigation, as well as the allegations. He denied any improper activity. He denied receiving anything other than occasional "gifts" from the vendor companies. He confirmed that his former employee, with whom he had a romantic relationship, was an employee at Company Two, but that had no bearing on the blood bank workload provided to that vendor. He admitted that he terminated the part-time drivers because he believed that employees cost more than using vendors. He was unaware as to the amount of the billings and monies owed to the vendors as he left the company in early 2004. He was astounded when told of the $125 delivery costs for single blood units. He instead blamed all the problems with delivery and other facets of the business on the CEO and upper management, who he alleged did not provide proper oversight and were too busy with their new buildings. He further stated that he brought his allegation to the board of directors. He resigned after he was confronted by the CEO about the allegations he brought about the CEO to the board.

Upon completion of the first three phases, we provided our findings to the attorney and the CEO. The following is a summary prepared for the attorney for use in meeting with the attorneys representing both vendor companies.

Summary of Investigation of Invoices for Blood Delivery Findings

- The blood bank's distribution supervisor received envelopes from both companies containing money and gift certificates on a regular basis.
- He came in after hours and on his days off to make sure the delivery staff was giving deliveries to Company Two, and he prevented staff from using blood bank drivers. He prevented some drivers from taking deliveries.
- On some occasions, when in-house drivers were making rush deliveries, even if they were halfway to their destination, he called them back to the Palm Beach facility, where he then gave the units to a courier.
- Source Two delivered envelopes from both couriers to the VP of General Services. He opened one of the envelopes and found numerous gift certificates.
- The VP of General Services fired all part-time drivers after Company Two started handling deliveries.
- The VP designed the system so that the remaining in-house drivers would be busy handling the daily routes so that all regular and rush deliveries had to be done by outside couriers.
- A driver received an envelope from a driver for one of the courier companies marked "April" (as if to imply that envelopes were delivered monthly). The envelope contained $50 and a thank you note.
- We examined some of the invoices for which Company Two was demanding payment and found them to contain inaccuracies and inflated prices.

- We never received a pricing sheet from Company Two reflecting that any Palm Beach to Miami delivery would cost $156.
- Our internal log does not reflect any of the deliveries that Company Two invoiced for March 31, 2004.
- That invoice shows six deliveries, all picked up at the same time, all going to the same place, and all billed at $156 each.
- All six of those deliveries plus 14 others at the same time are noted to have been called in by __. The only person in blood bank distribution with a similar name is the delivery supervisor, and he was not on duty when those jobs, all of which are billed as after-hours rushes, are shown to have been called in. He will state that he did not make any of the calls.
- Company Two provided no backup to show that the deliveries were actually made.
- It appears from what we have learned so far that the delivery supervisor and VP of General Services were steering increasing amounts of work to Company Two, ignoring inflated and inaccurate invoicing, failing to obtain fair terms for the blood bank, with the expectation of receiving monetary and material rewards from Company Two or its drivers.
- The result was that invoices from Company Two increased threefold beginning in November 2003 and continued to increase through April 2004 when we terminated our relationship.
- We do not believe it is fair for the blood bank to pay for an increase where the invoices are clearly inaccurate and where its staff was corrupted by promises of rewards to increase payments to Company Two.

Conclusion

Based upon our investigation and the evidence obtained, the attorney was able to successfully reach agreements with both vendor companies that substantially reduced the liability of the blood bank and resulted in no legal actions being filed by either side. Working closely with the new transportation manager, we helped him develop policies, procedures, and a method of accountability that would allow for the successful flow of work in the delivery department.

It was the decision of the CEO, in consultation with the company attorney, that no criminal charges would be brought against any current or former employees. All persons involved in the fraud were terminated from the company. Both vendor companies were no longer used. The investigation saved this not-for-profit company hundreds of thousands of dollars.

United States v. Roby Dudley

One of the many criminal defense fraud cases that I have worked on involved Roby Dudley. Roby worked for Best Marketing as a salesman in this advertising specialty "boiler room." A boiler room is a telemarketing company. An advertising specialty room sells advertising products, such as pens, pencils, and key chains with your company name and logo at grossly inflated prices. What was very different about this company was that they targeted small businesses—not senior citizens. They would call the business, offering "guaranteed prizes" along with purchases. The prizes ranged from a truck or car to jewelry to a portable boom box. Obviously, most of the "customers" received the least expensive item as their prize.

As the owner of a small business, I know that the prices they were charging for these items were way above what I would pay my local Office Depot for similar products. I had to assume that these "victims" were also aware that they were being overcharged but were placing orders for the prizes. Where is the crime in that?

During the course of my investigation for Dudley's attorney, Albert Levin (for whom I have worked many federal fraud cases), I obtained the list of customers of the business and the designation of prize awarded. I also conducted extensive interviews with Roby, who swore that he did nothing illegal and that prizes were awarded in every case. Not as randomly as it was suggested to the customers, but in fact, one car or truck was given out each year on a random basis. That premise became the focus of our defense.

I was able to identify and contact three individuals who actually received cars or trucks. Two of the three were single-sale, no-repeat, long-term customers. I also spoke with other customers who knew that they (or actually their companies) were being overcharged for the advertising items, but they liked the prizes, either for themselves or for their wives, girlfriends, or significant others. Basically, you have the company paying a legitimate business expense and the buyer getting a "reward." Where's the crime?

As a criminal defense investigator, I often coordinate witness testimony for the attorneys. In the Dudley case, I scheduled the witnesses' travel and transportation to the federal courthouse in Miami. As the trial was taking place in South Florida, and most of our witnesses were from the winter-stricken Midwest, many were happy to travel here to testify at our expense. One of the three car/truck winners also happened to be an auxiliary policeman. The jury paid very close attention to his testimony. Needless to say, he had no problem with Best Marketing and did not feel that they had committed any fraud against him.

As a result of Albert's brilliant courtroom presentation, fueled by my thorough investigation, Roby was acquitted of all charges. It is very seldom that "not guilty" verdicts are obtained in federal court. However, in this instance the government agents, which were the FBI, failed to adequately investigate and prove the facts of their case, resulting in them making unsubstantiated charges that none of the customers received awards of significant value. We were able to demonstrate that the facts proved otherwise.

Appendix 6.1: Sample Activity Reports

Fraud Investigation Activity Report

Privileged and Confidential

July 26, 20__

2:30 p.m. Investigator McMahon met in the office of Weisberg and Kainen with Weisberg, and his clients, __. We reviewed the circumstances regarding the fraud committed against their business, __ Pharmacy by their accountant, __. It was decided that __ and this investigator would proceed to __'s office to obtain documents still in his possession that belong to the __ Pharmacy.

4:00 p.m. Investigator McMahon and __ arrived at __, Miami; the office of __ Associates Accountants, Inc. __ was not present, so we met with __. He agreed to provide copies of __ Pharmacy documents contained in the files maintained in their office. He was in the process of doing that when __ arrived. He agreed to release all file material in his office possession to __. He also agreed to provide __ with the keys to his residence at __, Miami, on Monday, August 1. He will be moving all his possessions out of the residence over the weekend. He stated that he would be moved out of his office by August 15 and would provide the keys to the office to the client on that date. Investigator McMahon conducted an inspection of the premises and observed no diplomas or certificates on the walls regarding __ or any other employee. He observed numerous documents from the Internal Revenue Service (IRS) and the Florida Department of Revenue addressed to __ Pharmacy regarding delinquencies and liens that they were placing against the Pharmacy as a result of failure to make payments.

5:45 p.m. Investigator McMahon dropped off the client at the Pharmacy.

July 27, 20__

9:00 a.m. Investigator McMahon conducted numerous online database searches on __ and his associates. Numerous reports and documents were reviewed and copied for the file, including Division of Corporation records, Miami-Dade official records and property records, and Miami-Dade civil and criminal court records.

July 28, 20__

Investigator McMahon briefed the client on the findings to date. He informed the investigator that in addition to __, that __ was also married to __ and either a Marta or Maria.

July 29, 20__

Investigator McMahon reviewed property and other documents and organized the file.

August 2, 20__

9:30 a.m. Investigator McMahon conducted additional database searches on __ (née __) __, Marta __, and Maria (née __) __. It was determined that Beatrix was married to a different _. Additionally, Investigator McMahon conducted searches for businesses and properties in the names of his ex-wives and current girlfriend. Investigator McMahon also spoke with the client regarding interviews to be conducted tomorrow morning at the __ Pharmacy.

August 3, 20__

10:25 a.m. Investigator McMahon and __ (Spanish translator) arrived at the Pharmacy. Interviews were conducted with __, __, __, and __. It was decided that an interview of Notary Nancy _ was unnecessary. Affidavits will be prepared for all of the witnesses for their review and signature documenting that the signing of the Quit-Claim Deeds by __ on July 22 at the Pharmacy were voluntary. Subsequent to the interviews, Investigator McMahon met with the client and discussed and reviewed documents obtained by Investigator McMahon during the past week. It was decided to obtain copies of records from __'s divorce from both __, who works in the same shopping center as the Pharmacy, and __.

1:15 p.m. Investigator McMahon departed from the Pharmacy.

5:30 p.m. Investigator McMahon conducted additional database searches in an effort to identify the current girlfriend. A comprehensive report was obtained.

August 9, 20__

10:30 a.m. Investigator McMahon prepared affidavits of the witnesses of the __ meeting to sign. Investigator L. Garcia obtained copies of the divorce records between __. He ordered the __ divorce file from the records center.

August 10, 20__

2:30 p.m. Investigator McMahon arrived at __ Pharmacy, where he met with Interpreter Doucet. They reviewed the affidavits with the witnesses in order to obtain their signatures.

August 12, 20__

11:00 a.m. Investigator Garcia reviewed the voluminous divorce files of __ and __. Copies of pertinent filings were obtained.

August 14, 20__

2:30 p.m. Investigator McMahon reviewed the __ divorce files. Pertinent pages were faxed to the client.

August 16, 20__

Investigator McMahon organized the __ files and created a file with all the significant documents involving __.

Divorce and Property Timeline

July 30, 1994 Married __
August 1999 Separation from __
November 19, 1999 Separation and property settlement agreement
- 1999 BMW: __
- 1998 Honda: __
- Property:
    - Home: NW 11 Terrace, Miami
    - Office: Le Jeune Road, Miami
    - Quit-Claims to ______ for $65,000
    - Tax Services, Inc.: owned by husband
        - __ Investments 50% Partnership ____ and ____ (ex-wife's family) Partnership owns rental property at W. Flagler Street, Miami.
- Financial affidavit (husband):
    - Monthly income: $6977.17
    - Monthly expenses: $6925.55
    - Monthly income – monthly expenses = $51.62

Other assets:

Property	*Current Value*	*Mortgage*
NW 11 Terrace, Miami	$144,990	$132,643
____ Accounting	$25,000	
	$280,000	$243,767

Investments:

Property	*Current Value*	*Mortgage*
W. Flagler	$443,170	$475,000

August 12, 2001 Married __
November 23, 2001 Separated
Property:
NW 174 Lane, Miami
NW 11 Terrace, Miami
Business holdings:
__ Accounting Tax Services, Inc.
__ Investments

September 19, 2002 Marital settlement agreement
All property and businesses remain with husband.

October 10, 2002 Final judgment of divorce

Computer Crime

7

The Internet is the new frontier for most professional investigators. Computers are not simply useful tools to make the job of an investigator easier; they are also a necessity for remaining in business. Those who do not operate on the World Wide Web will soon become as extinct as the dinosaur.

In the United States, all financial institutions report incidents of frauds committed against them to the Securities and Exchange Commission (SEC). The amount of computer fraud as a product of the increasing use of computers will grow unless computer security can eliminate traditional frauds by employees.

Computer Crimes

A computer crime is defined as an illegal act in which knowledge of computer technology is used to commit the offense. According to the Federal Bureau of Investigation (FBI), 21 states have enacted laws dealing with computer crime, but there is little consistency from state to state, and several have failed to deal with hackers who enter the systems for fun rather than profit. Computer manipulation crimes involve changing data to create records in a system for the specific advancement of another crime. Virtually all embezzlement in financial institutions requires creation of false accounts or modification of data in existing accounts. The perpetrator does not need to know computer programming but must have a good sense of how to operate the system.

The FBI categorizes computer crime into five groups, and not all involve financial transactions. Computer thieves can also steal goods and services, college degrees, and titles to properties, as well as negotiable securities. The five categories of computer crimes are system deceit/unauthorized transactions, system alteration, physical destruction, theft of information, and time theft—that is, unauthorized use of the computer.

It is estimated that 85% of computer fraud cases are never reported because of embarrassment, loss of public confidence, false arrest concerns, and overall difficulty of prosecution.

Institutions are heavily dependent on automated systems and electronic transfers of funds for various business activities. They are exposed to the possibility of significant fraud in the computer area, because computer records are in electronic form, and computer processing of accounts and transaction data may be performed by a group of persons outside the financial institution. Additionally, transactions may be initiated from remote facilities by various employees, customers, and external parties.

The following are necessary to maintain the security of a computer system and electronic transactions:

- Adequate physical security to prevent accidental or intentional damage to the computer system and related equipment
- Software and data file security to ensure that computer programs and data files are not altered accidentally or deliberately
- Techniques for maintaining transaction data controls and for analyzing the reasonableness of transactions so as to detect and report possible crime attempts
- Use of customer identification methods to restrict unauthorized individuals from initiating transactions to customer accounts
- Secure communications networks to prevent unauthorized interception of or alteration of electronic data
- Adequate internal controls to prevent, detect, and correct computer crime and other concerns

Computer Fraud

Any incident involving computer technology in which there is a victim who suffered (or could have suffered) a loss and a perpetrator who intentionally made (or could have made) a gain is defined as computer fraud.

An indicator of possible problems is present in some, or all, of the following elements of a vulnerable computer system (five tip-offs of computer-related fraud):

- The computer generates negotiable instruments or is used to transfer credit, process loans, or obtain credit ratings.
- Employee relations are poor; dismissed data-processing personnel remain on the job until their termination dates; or a computer programmer is overqualified for the job, with the possible result that bottled-up creativity will seek undesirable outlets.
- Separation of key personnel is inadequate, in terms of either responsibility or physical access.
- After-hours data-processing operations are loosely supervised.
- Auditors have little expertise or background in computer operations.

Indicators that require follow-up investigation include situations in which the following occur:

- Computer reports or copies of pertinent forms are inside the trash bins.
- Auditors are not involved in the development of application programs, resulting in the absence of built-in checks and balances.
- The industry is depressed, yet computer-generated data indicate record sales for the company.
- Frequent violations are reported of the rule that requires that at least two people should be present when data-processing equipment is operated.
- Computer operations, including storage of output data, can be viewed by the general public.
- System components are near open windows, next to outside walls, or in front of open doors (easily accessible).
- The personnel department submits candidates for data-processing positions with only routine screening. The chief weakness of computer systems is people.
- Data preparation equipment is easily available and loosely controlled.
- Access to computer facilities is not limited to those with a need to be there.
- Transactions are rejected by the system, because they did not pass one or more control points or were put aside, ignored, or deliberately overridden.
- Increase is noted in employee complaints about overwithholding by the computer or about inaccuracies in the year-end earning statements.
- There is a surge in customer complaints about delays in crediting their accounts.
- Key forms, such as purchase orders, invoices, and checks, are not numbered sequentially.
- Continuous-form checks are not stored securely.
- The bill for use of computer time is much larger than the computer time logs seem to indicate it should be.
- Access to central processors is attempted from a remote terminal whose exclusive user is on vacation.
- Payments are sent to new suppliers, but they are not listed in company directories.

The Computer Crime Investigator

The computer crime investigator is a specialist in criminal investigation, data processing, auditing, and accounting. His or her knowledge of data processing should include computer operations, systems design and analysis, programming, and project management.

A primary element in a computer crime investigation course is the manner in which it is structured and whether it contains all the vital areas of required knowledge. A computer crime investigation curriculum should include the following:

- The types of threats and vulnerabilities to which a computer is susceptible
- Data-processing concepts relative to software (programming) and hardware (the equipment)

Investigative Methodology

Investigative methodology includes investigative procedures, forensic techniques, review of technical data systems, investigation planning, interview and interrogation techniques, information gathering and analysis, and case presentation techniques.

The Investigative Process

Most computer frauds are complex, hidden, and extensive. The detection of wrongdoing is usually first noticed by the internal auditor. The investigator must then establish essential elements of the crime to support successful prosecution; identify, gather, and protect evidence; identify and move closer to suspects; identify patterns of action and behavior; determine probable motives, which will often identify potential suspects; provide accurate and objective facts upon which judgments concerning discipline, termination, or prosecution may be based; and identify weaknesses in control and counter them by revising existing procedures or recommending new ones, and by applying security equipment, where justified.

The first step in the investigation of computer fraud is to establish that a loss of asset occurred; the process should determine that an asset was accountable for at some point and definitely missing at another point. The second step is to establish the facts. Get as much information as possible from everyone involved. Interview anyone who may have had control or access to the asset during the established time frame. Finally, gather evidence, organize data, examine documents for forgeries, and look for "out of balance" conditions.

Areas of Computer Abuse

The following are the most likely areas where computer abuse will occur.

Payroll

Fictitious personnel can be created.

Inventory

Fictitious accounts can be created and records falsified to show bills were paid, while inventory was delivered to fictitious persons and locations.

Accounts Receivable

This information can be mismanaged by a loss of computer records of monies owed to the firm.

Disbursements

Through manipulation of data, a company may be tricked into paying for goods and services that were never received.

Operations Information

This data can be very valuable to a firm's competitors, especially in the areas of growth plans and new designs.

Telecommunication Crimes

Telecommunication crimes involve illegal access to or use of computer systems over telephone lines. A hacking program tries to find valid access codes for a computer system by continually calling the system with randomly generated codes. Use of a hacking program constitutes unauthorized access to a system, and access codes generated by a hacking program are stolen property. Misuse of telephone systems also falls into the telecommunications crime group. *Phone phreaking* and *BBSing* are terms used to describe telephone frauds in which stolen or false telephone access cards are used to pay for long distance telephone calls.

Computer Manipulation Crimes

These types of crimes involve changing data or creating records in a system for the specific advancement of another crime, usually theft. Virtually all embezzlements in financial institutions require the creation of false accounts or modification of data in existing accounts to perform the act.

Hardware and Software Thefts

These thefts characterize the illegal use of a computer. Software piracy involves the duplication of programs without authorization or payment. Virtually millions of dollars are lost by software developers to this type of crime each year, even though vendors are now attempting to safeguard their programs through the use of copyright protection devices.

Computer Losses

In an American Bar Association survey of 283 large companies, 48% admitted they had suffered from computer crime; 72 of them assessed their losses at between $145 and $730 million. The U.S. Chamber of Commerce estimates that computer crime losses total around $100 million per year; other estimates are closer to $500 million per year. The average computer crime loss is $500,000.

Methods of Attack

There are many ways to compromise a computer. Some are complicated technical attacks, while others can be accomplished with only a basic understanding of computer operations. The following are the most common methods of attack.

Data Diddling

This is the simplest, safest, and most common method used by insiders. It involves putting false information into the computer. The data are changed before or during input from a computer, such as fraudulent payroll information.

Trojan Horse

The computer criminal can alter the computer circuitry or a computer program by adding instructions unknown to the owner. As a result, the computer performs unauthorized functions (e.g., it deletes accounts payable or receivable).

Salami Slicing Techniques

Typically, this involves a money crime. It is an automated form of stealing small amounts of assets from a large number of sources.

Trap Doors

In the development of large application programs and computer operating systems, programmers often develop debugging aids that provide breaks in a code. These programs are made deliberately to change or alter existing programs legitimately. These programs, called trap doors, provide computer abusers with the ability to alter data without detection.

Logic Bombs

These are illegal instructions that operate at a specific time or periodically after being given to a computer. They are often dependent upon date, time, or another operation for execution.

Trashing (Dumpster Diving)

This practice, also known as scavenging, is the surreptitious obtainment of information from discarded printouts, manuals, tapes, and disks. It often involves searching through trash bins for discarded computer listings or carbon sheets from multi-copy forms.

Piggybacking and Impersonation

Physical piggybacking is a method for gaining access to controlled access areas through the use of stolen or fraudulent cards. Electronic piggybacking involves gaining access to secured data through the use of someone else's password or identification sign-on. Compromise of the security system takes place when the computer verifies the sign-on but not the person. Impersonation is simply the process of one person assuming the identity of another, either physically or electronically.

Although most of the attention regarding the misuse of computers is given to criminal aspects of computer abuses, it is likely that civil actions will have an equally important effect on long-term security problems. The issue of computer crimes draws attention to the civil and liability issues in computing environments. In the future, there may be more individual and class action suits against businesses and employers. All of these give rise to a bright future for the investigator who specializes in computer-related investigations. This area is the fastest-growing area of need for the investigative industry. Not only is there a need for detection of events that occurred on the computer; there is also a need for an analysis of computer operations to safeguard the business community from outside abuse, misuse, and hacking. Systems security is now a need in all business communities that conduct business through a computer.

Institutional Vulnerability

Institutions are heavily dependent on automated systems and electronic transfers of funds for various business activities. They are exposed to the possibility of significant fraud in the computer area because of the following:

- Computer records are in electronic form.
- Transactions may be initiated from remote facilities by various employees, customers, and external parties.
- Computer processing of accounts and transaction data may be performed by a group of persons outside the financial institution.

Design and Personnel Rules for Security

Certain commonsense steps can greatly reduce the possibility of computer crimes:

- Locate the computer operations facility so that it cannot be viewed by the general public.
- Ensure that computer system components are not easily accessible and are not located next to outside walls, in front of open doors, or near windows.
- Use key forms with the system, such as purchase orders, invoices, and checks, and make sure they are always numbered sequentially.
- Have auditors present when application programs are developed so that checks and balances are automatically built into the design.
- Ensure that continuous-form checks are securely stored.
- Establish strong rules about who is allowed access to computer facilities.
- Establish strong controls about data preparation equipment, and establish from the start who will have access to it.
- Provide for extensive background screening of individuals who will do data processing.
- Require that at least two persons be present when data-processing equipment is operated.
- Ensure that access to central processors is denied when exclusive users of remote terminals are on sick leave or vacation.
- Ensure that computer reports or carbon copies of pertinent forms are shredded or otherwise destroyed with a witness present.

Computer System and Electronic Transactions Security

Maintaining the security of a computer system and electronic transactions involves the following:

1. Adequate physical security to prevent accidental or intentional damage to the computer system and related equipment
2. Security of software and data files to ensure that computer programs and data files are not altered, accidentally or deliberately

3. Established techniques for maintaining transaction data controls and for analyzing the reasonableness of transactions to detect and report possible crime attempts
4. Use of customer identification methods (passwords, encryption, etc.) to restrict unauthorized individuals from initiating transactions to customer accounts
5. Maintenance of a secure communications network to prevent unauthorized interception or alteration of electronic data
6. Insurance of adequate internal controls to prevent, detect, and correct computer crime and other concerns

Tip-Offs to Possible Computer Fraud

An indicator of possible problems is present in some, or all, of the following elements of a vulnerable computer system (five tip-offs of computer-related fraud):

- The computer generates negotiable instruments or is used to transfer credit, process loans, or obtain credit ratings.
- Employee relations are poor; dismissed data-processing personnel remain on the job until their termination date; or a computer programmer is overqualified for the job, with the possible result that bottled-up creativity will seek undesirable outlets.
- Separation of key personnel is inadequate, in terms of either responsibility or physical access.
- After-hours data processing operations are loosely supervised.
- Auditors have little expertise or background in computer operations.

Areas of Computer Abuse

- Payroll—Fictitious personnel can be created.
- Inventory—Fictitious accounts can be created. Records can be falsified to show that bills were paid, while inventory was delivered to fictitious persons and locations.
- Accounts receivable—There can be a loss of computer records of monies owed to the firm.
- Disbursements—Through manipulation of data, a company may be tricked into paying for goods and services never received.
- Operations information—This data can be very valuable to a firm's competitors, especially in the areas of growth plans and new designs.

Guidelines for Conducting an Investigation (Insider Suspect)

1. Opportunities:
    a. Familiarity with operations
    b. Position of trust
    c. Close association with suppliers and other key people
2. Situational pressures—financial:
    a. High personal debt
    b. Severe illness in family
    c. Inadequate income or living beyond means
    d. Extensive stock market manipulation
    e. Loan shark involvement
    f. Excessive gambling
    g. Excessive use of alcohol or drugs
    h. Heavy expenses incurred from extramarital involvement
    i. Undue family, peer, company, or community expectations
3. Situational pressures—revenge:
    a. Perceived inequities (e.g., low pay or poor job assignments)
    b. Resentment of superiors
    c. Frustration, usually with the job
4. Undesirable personality traits:
    a. Low self-esteem
    b. Lack of personal honesty
    c. No well-defined code of personal ethics
    d. A wheeler-dealer (i.e., someone who gives feelings of power, influence, social status, and excitement associated with rapid financial transactions involving large sums of money)
    e. Arrogant or egocentric
    f. Neurotic, manic depressive, or emotionally unstable
    g. Psychopathic
    h. Personally challenged to subvert a system of controls

Conduct Thorough Background Investigations

In addition to evaluating suspects in terms of opportunities and situational pressures (financial or personal), the investigator should construct a personal biography on all known suspects. The biography should include the following:

1. Criminal history
2. Review of personnel file for such things as a record of excessive absences, counseling, reprimands, and other disciplinary actions
3. List of associates

4. References (if not verified, do so during the investigation)
5. Documented comments from former employers

Appendix 7.1: Investigation of Computer Fraud

When investigating what appears to be an inside computer crime, the factors listed previously, in "Guidelines for Conducting an Investigation (Insider Suspect)" should be taken into account.

Investigators should also construct a personal biography of suspects composed of three factors: criminal history, list of associates, and references.

Appendix 7.2: Computer Crime

Profiling the Computer Criminal

Profiles on computer criminals should include the following:

- Tools or devices used
- Computer or other skills demonstrated in the crime
- Orientation as to politics, religion, or interest in pop culture, which forms a subtext of the crime (i.e., reference to religion, gangs, political movement, etc.)
- Files may provide a clue as to information a suspect is looking at and how that information would be used (Who would benefit from having that information?)
- Evidence as to the criminal's personality and way of thinking (Is suspect well organized or impulsive? Was the crime planned in advance with meticulous detail or was it a random, haphazard event?)
- Occurrence of crimes in any logical pattern (day, date, time of day) or random times and days
- Unusual qualities in the method of attack on software or hardware or the altering of information on the computer

Investigative Procedures on Malicious E-Mail

- Preserve the evidence.
- Trace the e-mail's path through your system with the help of the network administrator. Be on the lookout for any bypasses of e-mail security.
- Obtain complete e-mail records of individuals involved for the preceding 30 days.
- Review all personnel files.

- Interview the individuals involved. Get their version on the record. Who had access to their computers? Why?
- Interview coworkers, witnesses, supervisors, and so on.
- Follow the audit trail.
- Inspect the computers involved for signs of tampering, unauthorized access, and so on.
- Compare stories, events, and evidence against all other records, access logs, terminal logs, and so on.

Indications of Suspicious Behavior by Employees

- People who never take a vacation
- Workers with excessive overtime, living at the job, and who are always around the job site
- Employees with a criminal record, history of substance abuse, or gambling problems
- Employees with constant financial problems
- Workers with extreme political views or radical lifestyles

Examine the elements of the crime, and analyze what is necessary to commit the crime, such as knowledge of software used, knowledge of how to create a logic bomb—an accomplice in accounts payable, a mail drop to receive the checks, dummy businesses to act as vendors, fake IDs to open bank accounts, and bank accounts to negotiate the checks.

Analysis of these elements gives the investigator new avenues to explore and leads to follow (e.g., an accomplice within the company). Physical evidence of penetration of computer security includes broken glass, cut wire fences, picked locks, cut locks, jimmied doors, disabled security cameras, changed locks, security guards unable to access the computer area, holes cut in walls or doors, and disabled alarm systems.

In cases of embezzlement, you need to analyze the flow of data and documents through the financial processing system (FPS). Determine the following:

- What steps are required to issue a check?
- Where are the checks printed? Who has access to that area?
- What steps are necessary to have someone added to the payroll?
- Is it possible to change information within the FPS programs? How?
- Is there an FPS paper or audit trail? How does it work?

Conducting Internal Investigations

The Risk Matrix

The risk matrix includes opportunity factors as well as means, motive, and high risk factors. Included in opportunity factors are events that occurred on the suspect's shift, or just before or after; whether the suspect is knowledgeable about the work involved; whether the suspect had the necessary skills to commit the event; whether there is a relationship between the suspect's actions and the event; and whether the suspect has an alibi.

Included in the means factors are whether or not the suspect had access to the area, whether or not the suspect possessed access materials to the area, and whether or not the suspect had the ability to bypass security to obtain access to the area. Motive factors include the suspect having high risk factors, the suspect having resentment against the company, and the suspect having political grievances. High risk factors include family problems, financial problems, a lifestyle beyond salary means, coworkers suspicious of the suspect, the suspect acting defensive during interviews, substance abuse or gambling problems, and other suspicious lifestyle factors (extramarital affair, cult activity, etc.). Anyone who exhibits characteristics within the risk matrix should undergo the following investigation:

- Review personnel records.
- Interview previous coworkers and supervisors.
- Review the suspect's work product.
- Conduct an extensive background check of the suspect.
- Interview current associates.
- Make asset searches.
- Provide surveillance of the suspect after work.
- Interrogate the suspect once incriminating evidence is found.

Conducting External Investigations

The investigator should cooperate with police or any other investigative agency; preserve evidence and the crime scene; obtain the dollar loss and provide documentation; obtain intelligence information; identify and interview witnesses and suspects; and question vendors, suppliers, and visitors.

Report Writing

Your report should include a summary of the incident, a description of the evidence establishing a *corpus delicti* (body of the crime), a description of how the crime was committed and the suspect's motive, the financial impact of the crime, and a review of the evidence identifying those responsible.

If the crime was committed by an employee of the company, your report should provide the employee's history with the company, any previous disciplinary problems, criminal history, family background, amount of gain from the crime, and the suspect's financial resources.

If the crime involved a vendor, supplier, or contract worker, your report should provide a history of the relationship with the company, the compensation received, background on the suspect, criminal history, profit from the crime, and the insurance coverage and financial stability of the employer.

If the crime was committed by another company, your report should provide a background of the other company and its officers, a criminal background check of the officers, profit from the crime, and the applicable insurance.

If the crime was committed as part of an ongoing criminal enterprise (Racketeer Influenced and Corrupt Organizations [RICO] Act), your report should provide a pattern of criminal activity, the types of crimes involved in the pattern, and the evidence proving the crimes.

Appendix 7.3: The Internet and the World Wide Web

The Internet is a worldwide network of computers that allows a multitude of types of computers to communicate with each other. Information may be sent or received. The Web is part of the Internet and may be accessed to use text, graphics, sounds, and animation; for commercialization purposes, there are unlimited "pages" or Web sites, and the Web provides hypertext on links.

E-mail is noted for its ease of use, speed, and its multiple addressing capability. It is an inexpensive method of communication.

Search engines are convenient methods of finding information; they are home page locators that provide various searching methods when you register with the search engines. There are over 40,000 newsgroups. One well-known newsgroup is Usenet, also called net news. E-mail messages may be posted to newsgroups such as Alt.private.investigator.

The Universal Resource Locator (URL) provides information page addresses. Users need only to type in an address or click to link. This is the most common hypertext transfer protocol that directs users to home pages.

There are numerous search tools with broad-based search engines containing subject directories, meta search engines, and specialized search tools. The top search engines include Google, Yahoo, Hotbot, AltaVista, Excite, e-infoseek, Lycos, and WebCrawler. There are also subject directory engines like Yahoo and Virtual Reference Desk.

To structure a search, review search engine techniques. Read the FAQ section of the search engine, and focus the search using primary and secondary words.

Meta search engines are useful for searching several engines at the same time. Remember to keep search terms simple. Metacrawler, dogpile, and Inference Find may also be used.

If you cannot find the results you are seeking, reconsider search terminology, check the spelling and truncation, use specialized search engines, post your inquiry to discussion groups or listserves, and contact your local librarian.

For professional investigators who work in the corporate world, I highly recommend that you obtain a copy of *The Art of Deception: Controlling the Human Element of Security*, by Kevin D. Mitnick, William L. Simon, and Steve Wozniak (Wiley, New York, 2003). Mitnick is the legendary hacker who was sent to federal prison for his exploits. Released in 2000, he is now a security consultant to Fortune 500 companies that wish to avoid hackers getting into their computer systems. Chapter 16 in his book is entitled "Recommended Corporate Information Security Policies." He states that if these policies were in effect, he would not have been able to hack into the systems he did. This should be considered the bible for those wishing to avoid cyber desperadoes.

Computer Forensics

The Online Security Primer for Recovering Electronic Digital Evidence

How Hard Drives Work

A hard drive (such as the "C" drive) contains hard round flat disks (known as platters) coated on both sides with a magnetic material designed to store information as binary numbers (magnetic patterns of 0's and 1's). The platters are mounted on a spindle that rotates at high speed, generally 5,000 to 10,000 rpm.

Electromagnetic read/write devices, known as "heads," mounted on sliders and connected to an actuator arm, are positioned over the surface of the disk. A logic board controls the motion of the heads, the process for reading and writing data, and the protocol for communicating with the rest of the computer.

Conceptually, the inside of a hard drive is similar to the inside of an old jukebox, with the record being the platter, the jukebox tone arm being the hard drive's actuator arm, and the needle being the read/write heads.

How Data Is Stored

The surface of each platter can hold tens of billions of individual bits of data. Groups of bits, of either a 0 or 1, could be eight, sixteen, or thirty-two bits in length. These bits form a "byte," representing an alphabetical character or numerical number. Most desktop and server hard drives are 3.5 inches in diameter and notebook PCs have 2.5-inch and 1.8-inch drives. A large capacity drive, measured in gigabytes (GB), can store hundreds of billions of individual bits of data and is commonly available for under $200.

Each platter has two surfaces capable of holding data (the top and bottom), and each surface has a read/write head. Thus on a hard drive with three platters, there are a total of six "surfaces" with information being read by six heads.

The recording surface of each platter is divided into concentric tracks (circles), and the vertical area of similar tracks on multiple platters is referred to as a "cylinder." These tracks are further subdivided into sectors and clusters, which are groups of sectors. The logical organization of information on the platter is similar to slices of a pie. Data is stored in all sectors of each track, except parts of the outside track, which is generally reserved for the file allocation table (FAT) directory. The FAT contains the file names and the locations of active files on the disk. The file allocation table tells the computer's operating system which sectors (the "geographic location") contain data. A sector typically will hold 512 bytes of data (about the length of this sentence), plus "address" information used by the drive controller circuitry. There can be over 40 million sectors on a 20-GB hard drive. "Formatting" a hard drive is the process by which the disk surface is organized into tracks and sectors.

Sectors are also grouped sequentially into clusters, and generally there are 32 sectors per cluster. More often than not, data is stored sequentially in sectors within the clusters.

Reading and Writing Digital Data

When a user clicks on a file to open it, the application being used passes the file name to the computer operating system, which consults the FAT to determine the address (platter track and sector) where the first portion of the file is located. The operating system transmits this information to the disk controller, which positions the heads on the actuator arm over the correct physical location. The initial cluster will contain the address of subsequent sectors from which the controller must retrieve data. The controller retrieves the packets of data and reassembles them in the correct order before sending the "file" to the central processing unit (CPU) for display on the screen.

Disk systems, unlike tape, do not store records together physically. With tape, each time a change is made to a block of data, such as an insertion in a text file, the entire block of "data" is rewritten onto the tape with the new data incorporated. When a similar change is made to text stored on disk, the **original** file usually remains intact. The disk controller checks the file allocation table for the location of an unallocated cluster (a group of sectors available to store data), and inserts the data there.

Thus the various parts of a file, such as this article, can be scattered randomly among hundreds of sectors and clusters on various tracks. [Hence the term, random access device, meaning a drive that can retrieve or store data in any order to any location on the disk. Sequential access devices, such as backup tapes, store data in sequential order, and are unable to retrieve data as quickly.]

Allocated clusters contain data that is "active" according to the file allocation table.

Unallocated clusters may contain data, but in storage space that the computer is no longer using for active files (see Deleted Files below). Thus, although unallocated clusters frequently contain "residual" data, this space will be randomly used (overwritten) to store new active data.

Why Is Deleted Not Always Deleted?

When a user deletes a file, the operating system only deletes the first letter of the file name from the file allocation table, and reports the sectors containing the "deleted" data as "empty," or available for the storage of new data. However the old data remains unchanged and "intact" until new data is stored in the specific sector and cluster containing the "residual" data. It is during this process of "overwriting" new data into the sectors containing the old data that the residual data is truly deleted. However, since data is randomly stored into the millions of potentially available sectors, it is unusual for all sectors containing a file to be overwritten with new data. This provides the opportunity for portions of deleted files to be recovered from "unallocated" clusters long after the user has deleted the file from the computer.

The Process for Recovering Electronic Evidence

There are two primary steps for recovering electronic data. The first is the "acquisition" of the target media, and the second is a forensic byte-by-byte analysis of the data. Utilizing special computer forensic tools, the target media is acquired through a noninvasive procedure by making a complete sector-by-sector bit-stream mirror image.

During the imaging process, it is critical that the mirror image of the target drive be acquired in a DOS environment. Turning on the computer and booting into the operating system (usually Windows) will subtly modify the file system and destroy some potentially recoverable evidence.

The resulting image becomes the "evidence file," which is mounted as a read-only or "virtual" file, on which the forensic examiner will perform an analysis of the data. The forensics software used by Online Security will create an evidence file that will be continually verified by a Cyclical Redundancy Checksum ("CRC") algorithm for every 64 sectors (block) of data and by a MD5 128 bit encryption hash file for the entire image. Both steps verify the integrity of the evidence file, and confirm the image remains unaltered and forensically intact, and that critical date and time stamps remain unchanged. (Under MD5 hash encryption, changing one bit of one byte of data will result in a notice stating that the evidence file data has been changed and that the evidence is no longer forensically intact.)

Searching Digital Evidence

Specialized forensic software provides several methodologies for searching the evidence file. Multiple pieces of evidence, for example two hard drives, a floppy and a multiple session CD-ROM, can be searched, sorted, and analyzed simultaneously.

A Windows Explorer view displays the files and folders of the target hard drive in an easy to browse format. Each file is displayed in a spreadsheet format where the files can be sorted and filtered under numerous fields. The examiner can designate which files to include in this view, such as files from a single folder or a single volume. A preview pane displays the highlighted files allowing the examiner to easily scroll through individual files. A hex/text viewer shows the contents of any file, with the file slack—portions of unallocated clusters—shown in red. Search hits are highlighted automatically.

Forensic search utilities are used to search for keywords in order to locate relevant documents. These searches will locate any "bytes" of data matching the search term.

The development of effective search terms is a critical component of recovering digital evidence and will be a major factor in the success of the forensic investigation. As an example, searching for the word "info" may locate tens of thousands of hits where the letters "info" were used in a file or line of code. Redefining the search for "info@OnlineSecurity.com" will help narrow the number of responses. Reviewing the hits from the word keyword searches consumes a major portion of the time resources necessary for searching digital evidence. Narrowing the search to terms or phrases that are unique to the specific case situation will enhance the results and reduce the cost.

Forensic software will also locate drafts of documents, back-up files (.bak, .wbk), temporary files (.tmp), cache files, autosaves, registry data, and residual data. Advance searches can be conducted for "general formats" such as telephone numbers, network ID, logon records, or Internet protocol addresses (IP numbers), even when the specific number is not known.

Time and date stamps, access logs, and recycle bin activity are often a critical focus of the investigation and can be recovered. Files (but not residual data) can be sorted by creation date, last accessed, or last saved. Swap files and file slack, which are locations on the disk where deleted residual data often resides, can be recovered. Print spooler files, with their original time stamps, can be recovered and reviewed. Files that were recently accessed can be determined and a list of all Internet sites (URL's) accessed, and the time and date of access, can be compiled. Also, a forensic picture gallery automatically identifies all graphic files and displays them as thumbnails that can easily be copied onto a CD-ROM or thumb drive.

Forensic investigators will also be able to identify any attempts to hide a file by merely changing its name. Each file's extension (i.e., .jpg, .gif, .doc) is matched against the file's actual "signature" to determine if an attempt has been made to "hide" the file. If a file was created in Word (.doc) and the extension was changed to .jpg, the forensic examiner is able to identify and flag that file.

Advantages of Digital Evidence

In addition to the advantages of recovering deleted files, digital evidence contains a wealth of critical data and "embedded" information for both intact files as well as deleted files. For example, forensic software can view the contents of a PowerPoint file to reveal (depending on how it was configured by the user) information such as: the creation date and original author; dates the file was last accessed, modified, and printed; when the file was last saved and by whom; the number of times the file was edited, for how long, and by whom; the number of revisions; client name, id and matter number; hidden key words and comments that identify who edited or collaborated on the file; and the original file location.

WordPerfect allows the user to open a saved file and "undo" the last 20 or so entries, charting the latest changes that have been made to the document. Word has a tracking device that can be secured with a password that can invisibly track **ALL** changes made on a document allowing a subsequent user with a password to review every keystroke and peruse every comment made to the document.

Searches also could reveal embedded information in e-mail headers including routing details and a list of associated file attachments. Palms and other digital assistants leave a log of when they were last synched with the desktop, and what information was downloaded. WinFax keeps a log file of all electronic faxes sent, sometimes for years after the original document was lost or destroyed.

Effective Strategies for Electronic Discovery

Prior to conducting on-site electronic discovery, preliminary information pertaining to the target machine and operating systems must be determined. Each computer system (platform) is different, and poses different types of technological issues for the effective and non-invasive imaging of the drive. Determining in advance whether the computer is a desktop or notebook, the size and type of the hard drive, the manufacturer and year of manufacture, the operating system, and the type of browser and e-mail package being used (Netscape mail, Outlook, AOL, etc.) is critical and will eliminate the potential for numerous technological glitches in the field. Each computer may require a different type of interface and adaptor. Additionally, determining the system architecture of the opponents' premises will assist the forensic investigative team in verifying that all applicable systems and source media are identified and imaged.

In addition to the "traditional" locations of electronic evidence, such as computer hard drives, off-site servers, mirror sites, backup tapes, and removable media such as diskettes, etc., critical evidence may exist in a number of other locations. Some fax machines contain exact duplicates of the last several hundred pages of documents transmitted and received. Digital telephone systems may contain computer logs of all calls made and received, and often store voice mail messages in digital form on hard drives (.wav files).

Network audit programs (if properly configured) can contain a history of all files accessed, downloaded, or printed. Network firewalls monitor all web sites visited, external (outside of the Network) communication and information transmitted or received from the Internet.

Steps to Preserve (or Destroy) Electronic Evidence

Preservation of electronic evidence is critical. Depending on numerous factors, electronic evidence can be very perishable, or can last for years. The key to the success of electronic discovery and forensic investigations is to gain access to (or preserve the integrity of) the target media as quickly as possible. Relevant target media includes not only PC hard drives, but other types of storage media including tape backups and archives, floppy diskettes, PDAs (personal digital assistants such as Palms), and other removable electronic media.

Recently we have observed an increase in the types of actions that can impact the integrity and availability of electronic evidence including: (1) the use of data compression, disk de-fragmentation, and optimization programs; (2) the downloading or transfer of large files (such as .jpg pictures) which rapidly overwrite data in unused clusters; (3) the use of programs that overwrite sectors with a string of 0's, such as Norton Utilities' Wipe-Info; (4) the reuse of back-up tapes; (5) installing new software applications; (6), low level formats, operating system formats, partitioning formats, etc.; (7) deleting of temporary Internet files, browser history, and cookies; and (8) changing of the time clock on the computer. All of the steps taken above will destroy potentially recoverable evidence, and a number of the steps above could wipe the drive clean. Any of the steps above could alter, delete, or modify recoverable evidence.

Summary

During the last several years, there have been exponential advances in technology and with the advent of the Internet computers have become pervasive in everyday life. As a result, digital data in some form or another will be critical to most types of civil litigation and criminal proceedings.

The tools for conducting forensic investigations have also rapidly evolved, expediting the ability for securing evidentiary images, guaranteeing the integrity of digital evidence, and reducing the time and resources necessary for conducting a comprehensive investigation of electronic media.

There is a rapidly emerging trend to use computer forensics for a broad range of civil litigation matters involving intellectual property rights, trademark infringement, misuse and theft of trade secrets, patent and copyright violations, as well as more traditional matters such as employment law litigation and criminal fraud.

Criminal Investigation 8

The Investigative Function

A criminal investigation is the systematic process of identifying, collecting, preserving, and evaluating information for the purpose of bringing a criminal offender to justice. Successful investigations are based upon a systematic plan that proceeds in an orderly and logical manner. Without such a plan, relevant and highly significant evidence may be overlooked and improperly or inefficiently gathered, and incorrect conclusions may be drawn. Each piece of information relating to a crime is subject to use. Examples include the testimony of an eyewitness, fingerprints left at the crime scene, or a forged traveler's check.

Basic Elements of the Investigative Process

The basic elements of the investigative process include recognition, collection, preservation, and evaluation of information.

Recognition

Information relating to a crime must be recognized as such by the investigator. Examples include drops of blood at an assault scene, a neighbor who viewed a burglary, and the bank records of a drug dealer.

Collection

Relevant information must also be collected by the investigator. Examples include scraping the dry blood, interviewing the neighbor, and reviewing the dealer's bank records.

Preservation

The information must be preserved to ensure its physical and legal integrity. Examples include sealing the blood scrapings in an evidence bag, obtaining a sworn statement from the neighbor, and obtaining copies of the dealer's bank records.

Evaluation

The information must be evaluated by the investigator to determine its worth. Examples include recognition that blood of a common type is of little value, the ability of the neighbor to pick the offender from a lineup, and bank records that clearly indicate deposits of money far in excess of the suspect's salary.

Role of the Criminal Investigator

The criminal investigator carries out the investigative function and will perform five different tasks. See Figure 8.1 for a sample investigation checklist.

Determine That a Crime Has Been Committed

Conduct that does not violate any statute is not a crime. Crimes are defined by written penal codes, and conduct that does not fall within the definition may not be illegal. Agency jurisdiction may be limited. The investigator needs to conduct a preliminary investigation to determine in which jurisdiction the violation has occurred. There is also the possibility of a false report. For a variety of reasons, a person may falsely report that a crime has occurred. The legal concept of *corpus delicti* (body of the crime) establishing the existence of a crime is important, because the prosecution is required to prove the existence of a criminal act.

Identify the Offender

The primary task of the investigator is to identify who committed the crime. The true name of the offender is not required. The identity concept means individualizing a particular person as the offender, not necessarily determining the suspect's true name. Specific identification may not be possible until arrest and fingerprinting. Identification of the offender must be assured in an arrest warrant. The law requires that an arrest warrant contain the name of the accused or, if unknown, some description by which the accused can be identified with reasonable certainty.

Locate and Apprehend the Accused

The U.S. Constitution requires the presence of the accused. A criminal suspect has the right to be present at his or her own criminal trial (*Illinois v. Allen*, 397 U.S. 337). Most offenders are not actively hiding or avoiding

DEATH INVESTIGATIONS CHECK LIST

THE INVESTIGATION:
The primary issues to be investigated are identification of the subject, and the circumstances surrounding, and causing the death, providing the death itself has been established.

A point to be kept in mind is motive. Obviously there is a beneficiary to the policy of insurance and therefore a financial motive for fraud could always exists.

SUBJECT IDENTIFICATION & BENEFICIARY IDENTIFICATION:
By the time the investigator is instructed the subject body has been buried, cremated, or otherwise disposed of, and is not available to view or examine.
Identification is therefore based on identifying details (primarily the full name) and/or photographs.
The investigator throughout the course of the investigation should attempt to examine and copy all available documents containing full name, identity card number, passport details, date of birth, place of birth, previous name/s, marital status and spouses details, permanent address, previous address. I recommend throughout the investigation to have a camera with color film, and to always photograph any document containing the subjects picture.

Additionally during interviews ask for a detailed description of the subject, or a photograph which is usually available from relatives, and friends.

The beneficiary must also be identified based on documentation, and (Beneficiaries Relationship to the Deceased).

Beneficiaries Relationship to the Deceased - Prove based on document - if widow/widower then photograph the I.D. Card where states husband/wife, or marriage certificate, or other document to prove relationship as stated in policy of insurance.

DOCUMENTATION:
Documentation is important in a death investigation, however it should always confirm information obtained from other sources. This is important as in many foreign countries original or certified copies can be purchased due to corruption. Originals are sought after whenever possible. When not possible certified (signed and/or stamped) copies, notarized by a public notary or certified by an attorney as "identical to the original". Wherever possible notarizations, certifications, and/or translations should be effected at the American Embassy.

Figure 8.1a Death investigations checklist. (continued)

the police. The majority rely on the possibility of not being identified as the offender.

Success in locating fugitives typically depends upon assistance from relatives and associates. Many fugitives are apprehended while committing another criminal act.

Documents of any type should always be put into a plastic sleeve, or envelop for protection. Never write on them, mark them, or alter them in any manner. This includes photographs.

On receiving any type of document and/or document certification always note the full name, position, department, and other relative details of the provider. If documents are not received from the source always go to the issuing authority to confirm the documents authenticity. When photographing always make note of the subject, location, date, and time.

DOCUMENTS:
This is by no means an complete listing of documents. Further depending on the country, circumstances surrounding the death, and other factors some documents will not be available. As an example in Syria, and most Arabian countries the profession of private investigation is illegal, and only police are permitted to investigate. It is therefore understood that an operative in Syria would not legally be in a position to obtain a police report.

- ☐ Death Certificate
- ☐ Hospital Records
- ☐ Medical Examiner Reports
- ☐ Police Reports
- ☐ Cemetery – Forms, Documents, Burial Register. In addition photographs of the cemetery, the burial site, and any inscriptions on the subject tomb stone.
- ☐ Funeral Home – Forms, Documents, Register, Other.
- ☐ Newspaper Articles and/or Obituaries
- ☐ Ambulance Forms, Reports, Bills, Payment Receipts

INTERVIEWS:
Interviews and statements are a primary source of information. Often a family member, friend, neighbor, or business associate will divulge information pertinent to the investigation not apparent in any documentation.

Topics which should be covered during all interviews would include the subjects identifying details, circumstances surrounding the death, cause of death, health, marital and family status, civil and criminal court status, and financial status.

Sources to interview should include:

- ☐ Individual/s who identified the body. In addition to the mentioned topics areas to cover should include when, where and how was the body identified, and who was present at the time.

Figure 8.1b (continued) Death investigations checklist. (continued)

Present Evidence of Guilt

Assuming an offender can be identified and arrested, evidence of guilt must be provided at trial. The responsibility for collecting such evidence rests with the investigator. Two basic legal principles greatly affect this task.

- ☐ Physician who pronounced the death.
- ☐ Relatives
- ☐ Friends
- ☐ Neighbors
- ☐ Business Associates
- ☐ Previous husbands or Wives
- ☐ Cemetery Care Taker/s
- ☐ Funeral Home Employee/s

Figure 8.1c (continued) Death investigations checklist.

Legally Admissible Evidence

Information that may logically prove a person guilty of the crime is not necessarily admissible in court.

Proof beyond a Reasonable Doubt

The prosecution must produce evidence that leads to no other reasonable conclusion than that the accused committed the crime as charged. Evidence sufficient to arrest a suspect may be insufficient to convict.

Recover Property That Is Wrongfully Held

In many cases, an investigator has the responsibility for recovering stolen property. More than 90% of all serious crime involves the taking of property from its rightful owner. An object that may not lawfully be possessed is called contraband. The investigative mission may also include suppression and collection of such items.

Reasons for Investigating Crime

The investigative process has four social goals:

1. Future deterrence—Identification and punishment of a criminal offender will deter him or her from misconduct in the future.
2. Deterrence of others—Identification and punishment of an offender may deter others from engaging in similar undesirable activities.
3. Community safety—The investigative process promotes public safety by identifying and bringing to court those persons who pose serious threats to the safety of the community because of violent or other antisocial behavior.
4. Protection of the innocent—Accurate investigations help ensure that only criminal conduct is punished and that innocent parties will not be subject to prosecution.

Limitations on Solving Cases

Not all crimes can be solved. Factors over which investigators have little control will greatly affect the solvability of a crime. These factors include the following.

Unknown Crime

The commission of some crimes may never be known to police (e.g., the murder and disposal of a derelict).

Unreported Crime

Some crimes are never reported to the police even though someone knows they occurred. This failure to report may be due to personal embarrassment of the victim, the pettiness of the offense, or skepticism concerning the ability of the police to solve the crime.

Lack of Ability to Solve a Crime

Clearance-by-arrest figures indicate that crimes that lack witnesses or in which the property taken cannot be identified have low solution rates. In crimes against persons, investigators arrest a suspect in almost one half of the cases. In property-based crimes, less than 20% of the cases are cleared by arrest.

Petty Offenses

Other crimes remain unsolved because they are too petty to justify the expense of police resources to identify the offender.

Investigative Theory and Methods

Crime and Information Theory

Every crime generates information signals. Systematic interpretation of these signals can help solve crimes. Types of information include sensory forms, written forms, and physical forms:

- Sensory forms—the outward signs of a criminal event that can be perceived by the five senses
- Written forms—any written material produced by a criminal act
- Physical forms—a physical object that proves, upon evaluation, to be a clue in the investigation

Some information generated by criminal activities may be time critical, meaning that failure to retrieve the information at the right time will cause it to be lost forever.

Types of Evidence

All criminal evidence fits into one of the following categories.

Testimonial Evidence

This is the most common form of evidence. It is usually obtained by interviewing and interrogation. Events that witnesses see, smell, and hear are described to the investigator.

Documentary Evidence

This type of evidence is in the form of writings and includes official records. Documents differ from other real-type evidence in that the contents speak for themselves when read by the investigator.

Physical Evidence

This includes objects that must be evaluated to determine their relevance to the investigation. Physical evidence is obtained through searches at the crime scene and through follow-up procedures, such as during searches authorized by search warrants.

Uses of Evidence

The above forms of evidence can be used to prove facts in dispute in one of two ways. As direct proof, evidence can be used to prove the facts without any inference or presumption. The sole determination the investigator must make is whether the evidence is true. The two most common types of direct proof are eyewitness testimony (a witness testifies about what he or she observed) and confession (the suspect admits what he or she did).

Circumstantial evidence can be used to prove a fact in dispute by proving one fact that gives rise to an inference or presumption about the existence of another fact. Examples of circumstantial evidence include motive, the reason a crime was committed (e.g., revenge, hate, or a jilted lover), and opportunity, being in a position to commit the crime.

Other examples of circumstantial evidence include declarations and acts indicative of guilt, including actions on the part of an individual which raise an inference of guilt; preparation for the commission of a crime (i.e., acts prior to the crime which are necessary for its commission); possession of fruits or evidence of crime which raises a presumption that the suspect was connected with the crime; *modus operandi* (MO), a suspect's pattern or method of operation (because human beings are basically creatures of habit, it is assumed that a successful criminal will perform his or her act in essentially the same manner each time he or she commits it); associative evidence, the physical evidence that links a suspect to a crime scene; and criminal potentiality, the possession of the knowledge, skills, tools, or facilities that could be easily adapted to criminal use.

Development of a Set of Suspects

Elimination of Nonsuspects

At the start of a criminal investigation, the suspect of the crime could be anyone. As witnesses are interviewed, physical evidence is collected and analyzed, and other investigative leads are pursued, the number of potential suspects is reduced by eliminating nonsuspects until the focus is upon a single individual. This process is similar to a mathematical set theory.

Methods of Investigation

A criminal investigator collects facts to accomplish a threefold aim: to identify the guilty party, to locate the guilty party, and to provide evidence of his or her guilt. The tools of the investigator are referred to as the three Is, namely, information, interrogation, and instrumentation. By applying the three Is, the investigator gathers the facts necessary to establish the guilt or innocence of the accused in a criminal trial.

Many crimes are not solvable because there is insufficient evidence. The absence of eyewitnesses, identifiable motives, and physical clues will preclude a solution unless the criminal confesses. Often, the *corpus delicti*, or the fact that the crime was committed, cannot be established, and even a confession is of little value.

To the general public, the phrase "solving the crime" describes the process of discovering the identity of the suspect and apprehending the suspect. These are only two of the objectives of an investigation, and accomplishing these alone would leave the investigator far short of his or her ultimate goal of presenting sufficient evidence in court to obtain a conviction.

Information

Information describes the knowledge obtained by the investigator from other people. There are basically two kinds of information. The first type is obtained from regular sources such as public-spirited citizens, company records, and the files of other agencies. The second type, which is of particular interest to the criminal investigator, is the knowledge gathered from cultivated sources, such as paid informants, bartenders, cab drivers, former criminals, or friends. Of the three Is, information is the most important, because it usually reveals who committed the crime.

Professional crime is usually motivated by economic gain. Larceny, robbery, and burglary share this motive. Assault and homicide are often incidental to crimes of greed or are the products of disputes over divisions of spoils or rights. The crime of greed, when perpetrated by the professional, is most frequently solved by information.

Interrogation

Interrogation is the skillful questioning of witnesses as well as suspects. The success of an interrogation depends on the intelligent selection of informative sources. The effectiveness of interrogation varies with the craft, logic, and psychological insight with which the investigator questions a person in possession of information relevant to the case. The term "interview" means the simple questioning of a person who has no reason to withhold information and is expected to cooperate with the investigator. The term "interrogation" means the questioning of a suspect or other person who may normally be expected to withhold information concerning the subject under investigation.

The novice investigator often overlooks the most obvious approach to the solution of a crime by asking the suspect if he or she committed the offense. The guilty person is in possession of most of the information necessary for a successful prosecution, and if he or she is questioned intelligently, he or she can usually be induced to talk. A confession, which includes details that could not be known by an innocent party, is a convincing form of proof. If the accused can be induced to talk, the chances of a successful prosecution are usually great.

In the absence of eyewitnesses or an admission by the accused, it is rare that the available circumstantial evidence is strong enough to support a conviction. The physical evidence may place the suspect at the scene or associate the subject with the weapon but will contribute little to proving malice, motive, intent, the criminality of the act, or matters relating to the state of mind of the suspect.

The investigator should look upon a suspect or a reluctant witness as a person who will provide the desired information if he or she is questioned with sufficient skill and patience. To acquire the necessary proficiency in interrogation usually takes several years.

Instrumentation

Instrumentation includes the application of instruments and methods of the physical sciences to the detection of crime. Physics offers aids such as microscopes, photography, and optical methods of analysis. Chemistry, biology, and pathology are particularly important in crimes of physical violence. The sciences that apply to crime detection are called criminalistics. Their usefulness is usually associated with physical evidence.

Instrumentation also includes all the technical methods by which the fugitive is traced and the investigation advanced. Fingerprint systems, *modus operandi* files, lie detectors, communication systems, surveillance equipment, searching apparatus, and other investigative tools are included in the category of instrumentation. Instrumentation is most effective in cases where physical evidence is abundant.

Phases of the Investigation

The objectives of the investigation are divided into three phases. The criminal is identified, he or she is then traced and located, and the facts proving his or her guilt are gathered for court presentation.

Identifying the Criminal

The criminal is identified in one or more of the following ways: confession, eyewitness testimony, or circumstantial evidence. Confession is an excellent means of identifying the criminal. However, it must be supported or corroborated by other evidence.

Eyewitnesses

The ideal identification is made by several objective persons who are familiar with the appearance of the accused and who personally witnessed the commission of the crime. When the witness and the accused are strangers, the validity of the identification depends on the ability of the witness to observe and remember the specifics of the accused's appearance and can be affected by lapse of time between the criminal event and the identification.

Circumstantial Evidence

Identification may be established indirectly by proving facts or circumstances from which, either alone or in connection with additional facts, the identity of the perpetrator can be inferred. Evidence of this nature usually falls into one of the following classes: motive, opportunity, or associative evidence.

Tracing and Locating the Criminal

The question of the criminal's whereabouts is usually solved once he or she has been identified. Usually, the criminal is not hiding, he or she is simply unknown. The amateur usually commits a crime because of an exceptional opportunity. It is to his or her advantage to maintain normal hangouts and schedule, because flight might betray his or her guilt. However, in many cases, it is necessary to trace a fugitive who is hiding. Tips, interviews, and information obtained through interrogation will be the most useful means of tracing the fugitive.

Proving Guilt

When the criminal has been identified and is in custody, the investigation is still not complete. It has entered the most difficult phase—that is, gathering the facts to prove the guilt of the accused beyond a reasonable doubt. The fact that the accused may have confessed is not sufficient.

The final test of a criminal investigation is the presentation of evidence in court. The defendant must be identified and associated with the crime scene; competent and credible witnesses must be available; the physical evidence must be appropriately identified, its chain of custody established, and its connection with the case shown; and all this must be presented in an orderly and logical fashion. The complete process of proof must establish the elements of the offense.

Corpus Delicti

Early in the criminal trial, the prosecution must prove the *corpus delicti*, the fact that a crime was committed. The *corpus delicti* is proved by showing that there exists a certain state of facts that forms the basis of the criminal act charged, and by proving the existence of a criminal event that caused the state of facts to exist. The state of facts should be established by direct and positive proof, but circumstantial evidence will suffice.

Elements of the Offense

By adding certain facts to the *corpus delicti* concerning the accused, such as his or her identity, we have the elements of the offense and the necessary sufficient conditions that must be fulfilled before the guilt of the accused has been proven. The three elements of the offense include the form, the accused and the acts alleged, and the intent.

1. Form—To acquire knowledge of the elements of criminal offenses, the investigator must study the penal law of the jurisdiction under which he or she is operating. The elements of an offense will consist of the fact that the accused did or admitted doing the acts as alleged. The circumstances are as specified.
2. The accused and the acts alleged (the first general element)—The identity of the accused must be established and his or her connection with the acts clearly shown. A close causal connection must be established between the accused and the offense. It must be shown that the objective in acting could not have been accomplished without violating the law.
3. Intent—The investigation must be designed to develop facts that give evidence of the frame of mind of the accused. Intent is an essential element. Some crimes include the additional element of malice—that is, the intent to do injury to another. This is the mental state of the accused when performing the act. Motive, or that which induces the criminal to act, must be distinguished from intent. Motive may be the desire, while intent is the accomplishment. Motive need not be shown, but intent must always be proved. To establish the motive of revenge, hate, or jealousy, the investigator should look into the history of the victim.

Informants

An informant is a person who gives information to the investigator. He or she may do this openly and even offer to be a witness, or he or she may inform surreptitiously and request to remain anonymous.

A confidential informant is a person who provides an investigator with confidential information concerning a past or projected crime and does not wish to be known as the source of information. The investigator must take special precautions to protect the identity of such an informant, because his or her value as a source is lost on disclosure.

An informant may volunteer information for any number of reasons, such as vanity, civic-mindedness, fear, repentance, avoidance of punishment, gratitude or gain, competition, revenge, jealousy, and money or other material gain.

Protecting the Informant

The investigator should compromise neither him- or herself nor his or her informant in pursuit of information. He or she should make no unethical promises or deals and should not undertake commitments he or she cannot fulfill. The investigator should safeguard the identity of the informant, first as a matter of ethical practice, and second because of the danger of undermining the competence of the source. The identity of an informant should not be disclosed unless absolutely necessary and then only to the proper authorities. To avoid discovery of the identity of the confidential informer, great care must be exercised when a meeting or communication is planned.

Treatment of the Informant

To aid the investigator, some general rules are provided. The informant should be treated fairly and with consideration regardless of character, education, or occupation.

The investigator should be fair in the fulfillment of all ethical promises he or she has made. Any other policy implemented results in distrust and loss of the informant. The informant should not be permitted to take charge of any phase of the investigation. The investigator should always be in control of the investigation.

Communicating with the Informant

In order to avoid revealing the status of the informant, the following points should be observed. Meetings should be held at a place other than the investigator's office. The proper name of the informant should not be used in any contacts. Designation by code may be used, and the investigator's organization should not be identified in any communication with the informant. Confidentiality on behalf of the investigator and the client is a requirement in many states.

Evaluating the Informant

The investigator should continually evaluate his informants and form an estimate of reliability. The information received should be tested for consistency by checking against information obtained from other persons. The motives and interests of the informer should be considered in the evaluation.

Rules of Evidence

The success or failure of a criminal prosecution usually depends upon the evidence presented to the court. Evidence is all the means by which an alleged fact, the truth of which is submitted to scrutiny, is established or disproved. The purpose of evidence is discovery of the truth of the charge. The laws of evidence are the rules governing its admissibility.

Classification

Evidence may be divided into three major classifications. Direct evidence directly establishes the main fact. Circumstantial evidence establishes a fact or circumstances from which another fact may be inferred regarding the issue. Where direct evidence is the immediate experience on the part of the witness, the essence of circumstantial evidence is inference. Real evidence includes tangible objects introduced at trial to prove a fact. The evidence speaks for itself. It usually requires no explanation, merely identification.

Admissibility

In order to be admissible, evidence must be material and relevant. The rules of evidence are concerned with admissibility of facts and pertinent material, and not with their weight. The weight of the evidence is a question for the judge or jury to determine.

If the fact the evidence tends to prove is part of an issue in the case, the evidence is material. Evidence that proves something that is not part of the issue is immaterial. To be material, the evidence must significantly affect an issue of the case. Evidence that tends to prove the truth of a fact at issue is called relevant.

Competency of a Witness

A competent witness is eligible to testify. The mental and moral competency of a witness over 13 years of age is presumed. Mental competency refers to the ability to see, recall, and relate. Moral competency implies an understanding of the truth and consequences of a falsehood. A record of convictions of crimes is unrelated to competency but may affect credibility.

Impeachment of a Witness

Impeachment is the discrediting of a witness. A witness may be disqualified by showing lack of mental ability, insufficient maturity, previous convictions of crimes, or a reputation for untruthfulness.

Judicial Notice

Certain types of facts do not need to be proved by the formal presentation of evidence because the court is authorized to recognize their existence without such proof. This recognition is called judicial notice. The general rule prescribes that the court will not require proof of matters of general or common knowledge.

Burden of Proof

No person is required to prove his or her innocence. The burden of proof for a conviction rests solely with the prosecution. In criminal cases, the prosecution has the burden of proving the accused guilty beyond a reasonable doubt. However, the accused must prove his or her allegations when making claims regarding alibis, witnesses, self-defense, and insanity.

Presumption

A presumption is a justifiable inference of the existence of one fact from the existence of some other fact founded upon their previous connection. Presumptions generally serve the purpose of shifting the burden to the other party to establish contradictory facts. Conclusive presumptions are considered final, unanswerable, and not to be overcome by contradictory evidence. Rebuttable presumptions can be overcome by proof of their falsity.

Rules of Exclusion

Much of the body of the rules of evidence concerns the rules of exclusion. These are the conditions under which evidence will not be received. They are often extremely technical in nature. The rules of exclusion are primarily to control the presentation of evidence in a trial before a jury. The function of the rules is to limit the evidence a witness may present to those things of which he or she has a direct, sensory knowledge. The witness may relate what he or she saw, felt, touched, heard, and smelled.

All direct evidence and circumstantial evidence, if material and relevant, are admissible except for opinion evidence, evidence concerning character and reputation, hearsay evidence, privileged communications, and secondary evidence.

Opinion Evidence

The general rule is that opinion evidence is not admissible in a trial. A witness may testify only to facts, not to their effect or result, or to his or her conclusions or opinions based on the facts. The witness can bring before the court only those facts that he or she has observed through the five senses.

Exceptions to the Opinion Rule

Several exceptions are attached to the opinion rule. The following exceptions are recognized:

- Certain simple judgments based immediately on sensory observation are a matter of common practice in the mind of the average person and may be given greater reliability than the word "opinion" ordinarily describes.
- The court recognizes that the opinions of certain specialists in regard to their specialties should be treated with greater consideration than mere opinion. The lay witness may express an opinion on matters of common observation. These opinions are permitted only concerning subjects of which the average person has considerable experience and knowledge.
- Expert testimony is given by a person skilled in some art, trade, or science to the extent that he or she possesses information that is not common knowledge. The testimony of an expert can be admitted to matters of a technical nature that require interpretation for the purpose of assisting the judge and jury in arriving at a correct conclusion. Expert testimony is not proof but is evidence that can be accorded its own credibility and weight by each member of the court.

Evidence Concerning Character and Reputation

As a general rule, testimony concerning a person's character and reputation cannot be introduced for the purpose of raising an inference of guilt. The usual exceptions to this rule are when the defendant introduces evidence of his or her own good character and reputation to show the probability of innocence. When such testimony has been introduced, the door is open for the prosecutor to introduce evidence concerning those specific areas of character treated in the defendant's testimony. Previous acts of crimes of the accused may be introduced as evidence if they tend to show that the defendant actually committed the crime for which he or she is being tried. Some examples are *modus operandi*, previous acts, identifying evidence, guilty knowledge, or intent.

Hearsay Evidence

Hearsay evidence comes not from the personal knowledge of the witness, but from repetition of what the witness has heard others say. Hearsay applies to oral statements as well as written matter.

Hearsay evidence is excluded because the author of the statement is not present and under oath, and there is no opportunity for cross-examination afforded to the defense.

Exceptions to the Hearsay Rule

There are numerous exceptions to the rule of exclusion of hearsay, including confessions, conversations in the defendant's presence, dying declarations, spontaneous exclamations—utterances concerning the circumstances of a startling event made by an individual in a condition of excitement, shock, or surprise which lead to the inference that the exclamations were spontaneous and not the product of deliberation or design (such a statement is admissible when made by anyone who heard it)—documentary evidence, and matters of pedigree (family tree).

Privileged Communications

Information obtained in the course of certain confidential relationships will ordinarily not be received into evidence. The court considers such information to be privileged. State secrets, police secrets, and personal privileged communications (i.e., attorney-client, clergyman-penitent, and doctor-patient) are examples of privileged communications.

Entrapment

In obtaining evidence of a crime, the investigator must not permit his or her enthusiasm to involve him or her in a situation in which the investigator becomes the cause of the commission of a crime. The term "entrapment" is given to an act of a government agent inducing a person to commit a crime not previously contemplated by that person, for the purpose of instituting a criminal prosecution against him- or herself.

Physical Evidence

Physical evidence may be defined as articles and material found in connection with an investigation which aid in establishing the identity of the suspect and the circumstances under which the crime was committed or which assist in the discovery of the facts.

Care of Evidence

A few simple rules can guide the investigator in the protection of evidence from the time of its initial discovery at the crime scene until its final appearance in court. A violation of these rules may lead to a partial loss of the value of the evidence and, in some instances, to loss of the case.

Physical evidence can serve several investigative purposes. *Corpus delicti* evidence consists of objects or substances that are an essential part of the body of the crime or tend to establish the fact that a crime has been committed. Associative evidence links the suspects to the crime scene or to the events. Identity evidence is associative evidence that directly establishes the identity of the suspects (i.e., fingerprints or blood).

Before an object can become evidence, it must be recognized by the investigator as having significance with relation to the offense. The ability to recognize and gather valuable physical evidence must be supplemented by knowledge of the correct procedure for caring for evidence from the time of its initial discovery until its ultimate appearance at the trial. In order to introduce physical evidence in a trial, three important factors must be considered: the articles must be properly identified, continuity for chain of custody must be proven, and competency must be proven (i.e., the evidence is material and relevant).

Procedure for Gathering Evidence

A systematic procedure for gathering evidence consists of the following steps: protection, collection, identification, preservation, transmission, and disposition.

Chain of Custody

The number of people who handle evidence between the time of commission of an offense and the ultimate disposition of the case should be kept to a minimum. Each transfer of evidence should have a receipt. It is the responsibility of each transferee to ensure that the evidence is accounted for during the time it is in his or her possession, that it is properly protected, and that there is a record of the names of the people from whom he or she received it and to whom it was delivered, together with the time and date of such receipt and delivery.

Protection The protection of physical evidence serves two major purposes. First, certain types of evidence, such as fingerprints, are so fragile in nature that a slight act of carelessness in handling them can destroy their value as clues and remove the possibility of obtaining information from them which would further the investigation. Second, it is necessary that the evidence presented in court be in a condition similar to that in which it was left at the time of the offense. Hence, evidence should be protected from accidental or intentional change during the period of its ultimate disposition at the conclusion of the investigation.

The exercise of a reasonable degree of care will minimize the possibility of alteration from natural causes, negligence and accident, and intentional damage and theft. When physical evidence is not obtained at the scene but is obtained from some other source, such as from an informant or from the possessions of a suspect, the investigator should take the necessary measures to protect it from any extraneous contact. Some risk of damage is incurred in the process of transporting the evidence. Much of the physical evidence collected in a typical criminal case is not found at the scene. Evidence is often delivered to the investigator by a victim or is found in the course of a search of a suspect's possessions. The investigator should improvise methods of collecting evidence until he or she has the proper equipment. Articles that can be removed and conveniently packaged should be placed in clean containers, such as envelopes, pill boxes, large cardboard boxes, and glass containers. Ordinarily, there are two phases of the packing of evidence. The first is the transportation of the evidence from the crime scene (or place where it was obtained) to the office. Second, if the evidence is to be submitted for laboratory examination, it must be appropriately prepared for shipping.

Adequate facilities for storing evidence should be maintained by an investigative agency. Each instance of deposit and removal of evidence should be recorded by inked entries indicating date the evidence was received; file number of the case; title of case; person or place from whom or at which the evidence was received; person who received the evidence; a complete description of the items, including size, color, serial number, or other identifying data; disposition, including the name of the person to whom the evidence was delivered or an indication of any disposition other than delivery to a person; and identification by signature of the investigator in control of the evidence.

Preservation In taking measures against deterioration of evidence, the factors of time and temperature should be given special consideration. Certain types of perishable evidence require special preservatives to maintain their evidentiary value.

Collection Most of the errors committed in connection with evidence take place in the collection of samples. Insufficient quantity of a sample and failure to supply standards of comparisons and controls are the most common errors. Take an adequate sampling, use standard or known samples (in cases of foreign substances or materials with stained backgrounds, two different samples should be collected—one bearing the stain trace and the other free from stain), and maintain the integrity of the sample (an evidence sample should not come into contact with another sample or with any contaminating matter). The simplest division of the types of evidence is into two categories—portable and fixed.

Identification Evidence should be properly marked and labeled for identification as it is collected. The importance of this procedure becomes apparent when considering the fact that the investigator may be called to the witness stand many months after the commission of the offense to identify an object as evidence which he or she collected at the time of the offense.

Marking solid objects of 1 cubic inch or greater should be done with the initials of the investigator who receives or finds the evidence. The identification should not be placed in an area where inventory traces exist. Whenever practical, articles of evidence should be enclosed in separate containers and sealed so that they cannot be opened without breaking the seal. The investigator's initials (or name) and the date of sealing should be marked on the seal with ink. After the article of evidence is marked and placed in a sealed container, a label should be attached bearing the following information: case number, date and time of finding the article, name and description of the article, location and time of discovery, signature of the investigator who made the discovery, and names of witnesses to the discovery.

Role of the Police

The police are government agents charged with maintaining order and protecting persons from unlawful acts. In most modern democratic nations, the police provide a variety of services to the public, including law enforcement (detection of crime and apprehension of criminals); crime prevention (preventive patrol); and maintenance of order, resolution of disputes, among other tasks. In the United States, the police force is the largest and most visible component of the criminal justice system.

Role in Society

The role of the police involves law enforcement, maintenance of order, and community service. The police are given a great deal of authority to enforce the law. They can arrest, search, detain, and use force—all actions that disrupt personal freedom—yet democracy requires the police to maintain order to make a free society possible. Thus, police officers must act within the confines of the U.S. Constitution and case law while enforcing the laws and satisfying a public that expects protection.

Selection and Training

In selecting police officers, police agencies use a number of criteria to pick the best-qualified people. These include a written exam, a background investigation, an oral interview, and a medical exam. More recently, psychological testing has been used to eliminate undesirable candidates.

Virtually all departments have minimum requirements for age, height, weight, and visual acuity. Standards vary for each of these categories. Most departments require a high school diploma as a minimal level of education. The formal training of a police recruit primarily involves the technical aspects of police work and includes the details of criminal law procedures, internal departmental rules, and care and use of firearms.

Operations

The range of police activities is quite broad. It involves patrol, detective work, traffic control, vice, crime prevention, and special tactical forces.

Patrol

Often called the backbone of police work, the patrol function has three basic components: to assist/answer calls for assistance, to maintain a police presence, and to probe suspicious circumstances.

Detectives

Primarily concerned with law enforcement activities after a crime has been reported, detectives are involved in an investigative function, relying on criminal history files, laboratory technicians, and forensic scientists for help in apprehending a criminal.

Specialized Operations

These are units set up to deal with particular types of problems. The traffic control function includes accident investigation, traffic direction, and enforcement. Enforcement of vice laws (i.e., prostitution, gambling, or narcotics) is an area that involves undercover work and the use of informants. Juvenile divisions process youth arrests, prepare and present court cases in which juveniles are involved, and often divert juvenile offenders out of the system. The special weapons and tactics (SWAT) units are trained in marksmanship and are equipped with weapons and specialized equipment useful in dealing with snipers, barricaded people, and hostage takers.

Government Agencies

The U.S. police establishment operates at several levels. A number of federal law enforcement units exist in different U.S. governmental agencies. The Federal Bureau of Investigation (FBI) is the largest. Other prominent federal units include the Drug Enforcement Agency (DEA), Immigration and Naturalization Service (INS), Secret Service, Internal Revenue Service (IRS), Customs Service, and Bureau of Alcohol, Tobacco, Firearms, and Explosives (ATF). Along with the FBI, these make up the seven most important federal agencies.

All states except one (Hawaii) have state-level police units with sworn personnel engaging in law enforcement functions. These are classified as state police (23 states) and state highway patrol (26 states). Highway patrols direct their efforts to highways, motor vehicles, and traffic safety functions. The state police authority includes jurisdiction over many criminal activities as well as traffic services.

Virtually all of the nation's 3000 counties have their own police forces, most directed by an elected sheriff. Municipal departments constitute the largest number of police agencies in the country. Nearly three-fourths of all of the 650,000 full-time police employees work for municipal agencies.

The London Metro Police Department, with its headquarters at Scotland Yard, is the largest agency in Great Britain. The Royal Canadian Mounted Police (RCMP), which is mandated to enforce Canadian federal laws, is the counterpart of the FBI in Canada. The United States is a member of the International Criminal Police Organization (INTERPOL), which exchanges information among its police members about criminals who operate in more than one country, whose crimes affect other countries, or who have fled from one country to another to escape prosecution.

Nuts and Bolts

There are several keys to a successful criminal investigation. The following are offered as guides:

- Take the time to read and understand the statutes charged in the crime. You cannot defend someone if you do not understand the crimes he or she is accused of committing.
- Create a timeline—that is, a list of events in chronological order. Timelines have been shown to be successful in many major criminal cases.

- Interview the defendant. For the investigator to fully understand the case, he or she must interview the defendant. How else will the investigator know who, what, when, and where events occurred?
- Conduct background investigations on all individuals involved in the investigation. You never know what may turn up about someone.
- Find experts that can help your client. Your expert may be able to shed a different light on the examination of evidence that the prosecution expert overlooked.

Conducting a Criminal Investigation

An investigator should follow these steps when conducting a criminal investigation:

- Interview the attorney and the client.
- Obtain evidence. Check police reports, ambulance/medical/hospital records, court transcripts from all proceedings, complaints/indictments, and the physical evidence, and check and review statements of prosecution witnesses for inconsistencies.
- Visit and dissect crime scene and interview witnesses:
  - Police, medical, or hospital personnel
  - Factual witnesses
  - Circumstantial witnesses
  - Alibi witnesses
  - Character witnesses
  - Expert witnesses—for both sides, if possible
- Examine and analyze the evidence.
- Understand the defense theory—what is the defense attorney attempting to establish or disprove?

Investigator's Pretrial Responsibility

Civil or Criminal Trial

Law firms have different methods of preparing for trial. Some have in-house investigators who assist in the entire process, some use paralegals and secretaries. We focus here on hired/subcontract investigators.

The File

Read every paper in the file(s), line by line, word by word.

- Always know the documents that are in your file.
- Organize documents where you can have easy access to them. Have multiple copies available to distribute to all parties and the court.
- Prepare witnesses and experts for their testimony.
- Prepare exhibits for presentation by the witnesses.
- Obtain equipment for showing videos or overheads.
- Write and serve subpoenas.
- Research backgrounds on witnesses (ours and theirs).
- Find sources of information for use on cross-examination of their witnesses.

The best way an investigator can be trained to do trial work is to attend a trial and watch how it works. By doing this the investigator will learn to anticipate what will be needed, such as how many copies of documents, what exhibits when, when a video is going to be played, and last-minute corrections or additions as attorneys respond to daily events. The only way an investigator can anticipate what an attorney needs is to have trial experience.

The Trial Notebook

A trial notebook should be prepared by the investigator to lead the attorney through the entire case, starting with pretrial pleadings, motions, order of proof, exhibit list, witness list, summary of witness direct examination, copies of depositions and interview statements, and copies of each exhibit the witness will introduce. Photographic exhibits can be placed on PowerPoint and shown after they have been introduced.

Witness List

Many attorneys list every witness who has ever had anything to do with the case. Sometimes this is done to increase the workload and preparation time of the opposing counsel, and sometimes it is because they wait until the eve of trial to determine the best witnesses to make their case.

Exhibit List

Don't list every document and every item that has been reviewed during the course of your investigation. **List what is important to proving your case.** Go through the documents; know what is in the file. Pick out those documents, photographs, and materials that are the most significant and list them.

Order of Proof

The order of proof is the attorney's roadmap to the trial of the case. It lists the witnesses in the order they will testify, in addition to a listing of the exhibits that each one will be admitting. The order is fluid, subject to changes as needed.

Subpoenas

Subpoenas should be issued and served at least one month before trial. I prefer to serve the subpoenas myself so that I can prepare the witness for his or her testimony and help with any scheduling or transportation problems.

Organization of the File

In order to find what you need in a file, it needs to be organized. The larger the file is, the more the need for organization. Color coding is helpful, blue folders for witnesses, red folders for exhibits, all numbered and ready to be admitted into evidence. Make sure that documents are copied and there are enough copies for all parties. Videos should be organized and ready to play.

Investigator Trial Witness Responsibilities

Make sure that all trial witnesses are issued subpoenas at least 30 days prior to the trial. If you do not personally serve the subpoenas, make sure that the witnesses are instructed to contact you several days prior to the trial so that you can review their testimony or schedule a meeting to do so if necessary. Discuss any possible scheduling conflicts; they may be on vacation the week they are scheduled to testify, etc. Assist with any transportation problems. If the witness is from out of town, make arrangements for lodging and transportation to the courthouse. Respect the witnesses' time, and they will respect your efforts.

Make sure that you and the trial attorneys are on the same page. Have a strategy meeting prior to the start of the trial and discuss how everything should proceed and outline everyone's responsibilities. Try to meet either every morning before trial or every evening after trial to ensure that everything is covered for the following day.

A well-organized and prepared attorney and investigative team are more likely to prevail in the outcome of the trial.

Rules for Approaching Adverse Witnesses

In most criminal cases the list of adverse witnesses is much longer than the list of friendly witnesses. Most lawyers don't recommend interviewing adverse witnesses. I disagree. I attempt to interview every potential witness in a case, criminal or civil. There are some rules that should be followed:

1. Try to get an appointment. You will never get a statement if you don't make contact with a witness.
2. Go in person. It is sometimes better to knock on the witness's door rather than arrange an appointment by phone. Over the phone it is easy to say no. It is more difficult when you are standing in front of the person, possibly having come a long way to speak to him or her.
3. Be prepared. Know what you need to ask the witness.
4. Be honest and polite. Tell the witness who you are and who you are representing. Try to put the witness in your client's position so as to better understand the need for his or her cooperation.
5. Avoid promising anything. Do not promise that if he or she cooperates and speaks with you that he or she will not be required to testify. If the witness has valuable information, he or she must testify.
6. Pick the right timing. Assume that once one witness has been interviewed the word will spread to all the other witnesses, so it is best to try to interview everyone as soon as possible after the first adverse witness interview.
7. Know your most important witness. A brief background investigation should be conducted on *all* witnesses. Criminal checks are mandatory. Knowing some facts about the witness's background will also help you determine his or her credibility and veracity.
8. Start with the questions that are easiest to answer. Once you get the witness talking it is easier to get into the more complex and difficult questions.
9. Give the witness the opportunity to give you additional leads. For example, "Is there anyone else you think I should speak to?" "Is there anything else the lawyer should know?"
10. Keep the door open for additional follow-up. You may have forgotten to ask an important question or need to clarify a point. Make sure you obtain phone numbers as well as permission for additional follow-up. However, expect that you may have only one opportunity to speak to the witness. Usually the attorney representing the other side will instruct the witness to not have any additional contact with you. With a transient witness, try to identify a contact person who will know the witness's location or be able to get him or her a message from you. Try to interview the witness in a place where there

are few distractions. Ask to move to a different location if there are problems or distractions from friends or family. Provide them with your business card so that they know who you are and have a way to contact you if necessary.

Investigating Your Witnesses

Virtually everyone who testifies in a case, be it civil, criminal, or other has certain biases or points of view that may slant his or her testimony. A well-conducted background check can lead to questions that will help you identify those concerns, such as

- Does the witness have something personal against your client?
- Is the witness prejudiced against your client?
- Does the witness have a background that will have a positive or negative reaction to the police or prosecution resulting in bias against your client (i.e., defendant in criminal case)?
- Does the witness have credibility problems, such as convictions for acts of dishonesty, drug dealing, or acts of moral turpitude?
- Does the witness have a motive to lie?
- Has the witness been promised anything of value by the other side?
- Is the witness competent?

The arresting officers in a criminal case may have a history that suggests that their testimony or even the entire investigation may be suspect. For example, in the O.J. Simpson case, the testimony of Detective Mark Fuhrman was undermined when it was learned that he had a racist attitude and lied about using the "n word." It was his background check that revealed that information and led to interview of that source.

Background investigations must be conducted on any individual whom either attorney intends to call as a witness or may be identified as a suspect in the case. The fact that the suspect may have a history of committing such crimes, have a credibility problem, and/or have a motive for committing the crime are all facts that can be discovered by a well-conducted background investigation.

The prosecutor and/or opposing attorney's reputation is also a factor to be considered.

Does the prosecutor have a reputation for fairness?
Have they ever been reprimanded by the Bar Association?
Are they likely to be prepared?
Are there any secrets in their background?

In many cases, the victim's background and reputation must be investigated. In sex cases this is especially important but deemed politically incorrect. In these cases the victim is usually the most critical witness. The ability of the investigator to uncover that the victim has a terrible reputation may be the key to the defendant's freedom. The ability to prove the victim has a history of violence may help validate a self-defense claim.

The Art of the Background Investigation

Conducting a thorough background investigation is a true art. Developing facts from interviews, searching through reams of public records, developing rapport with reluctant witnesses, and deciding what material is relevant are acquired skills. To develop those skills, the investigator must have the ability to look beyond the data to identify the important information needed for the investigation, develop excellent communication skills, and be organized and thorough. The investigator must recognize which facts or data have relevance in the pending investigation. The art is to recognize the difference between data and information—seeing the "big picture."

Because much of the background information may come from witnesses, the investigator must have effective interviewing skills. The most important communication skill is the art of listening, not only to what the person is saying but how it is said. The investigator must have empathy to relate to the speaker and an ability to determine what motivates the witness to provide the investigator with the information. The ability to ask questions that both elicit details and encourage further information is another important skill.

The objective of the background phase of the investigation is to develop information about the victim, witnesses, and possible suspects. The focus must remain on how the background of the witness might mitigate his or her testimony. The second task is to list what is being investigated, why, and how—categorize the witnesses and prioritize their importance. Set up a file for each person or entity investigated, compiling a list of what is known and what information needs to be obtained.

Civil court records should not be overlooked as they are a tremendous source of information. These records show a history of misconduct, hidden motives of witnesses, and other reasons to be biased. Expert witnesses have been sued for malpractice. Law enforcement officers have been sued for misconduct. Paid informants may have civil judgments pending.

Additional background data can be obtained from nongovernment public records such as newspapers, the Internet (Google searches), telephone directories, public library sources, industry journals, and other resource materials. This information may be extremely helpful in discrediting a professional, paid expert, as they sometimes tend to puff up their credentials.

Another source for records is private documents that can only be secured by subpoena, or in some cases with a signed release. These records include police reports, employment records, school records, income tax filings, medical records, telephone toll records, credit reports, bank records, and charge card records.

Another source for background information is people. Interview sources for information can include neighbors, landlords, coworkers, associates, teachers, codefendants, law enforcement, informants, reporters, and even "anonymous sources." Some of the information obtained may be factual and evidentiary. Other information may be hearsay, biased and questionable. If possible, witness interviews should be done in person. You can obtain more information and assess the person's credibility better in person. If a written statement is needed, it is easier to obtain it immediately after the interview. Many statements are lost after the witness has had time to reconsider. If an in-person interview is not possible, consider a recorded statement if the witness will allow it.

There are some states where one-party consent is all that is required. This means that it is legal for the investigator to record without the knowledge or permission of the witness. This should not be done without careful consideration and consultation with your attorney/client, as it may backfire if used in court, as an underhanded trick that "violates the witnesses' privacy."

After setting up files for each witness or company investigated, the next objective is to determine how each fits into the case, what their testimony might be, how it will impact the case, and what sources can confirm or discredit the accuracy of their testimony. For each witness a thorough criminal and civil check should be conducted to identify previous misconduct or evidence of motive for false testimony. In some cases the criminal or civil judgments should be obtained (certified copies), and possibly even transcripts of their testimony secured.

In conclusion, it is important that the investigator be unbiased and fair. The investigator is the seeker of objective facts, not an advocate for the defendant. If the witness understands that you are fair and impartial, he or she will be more willing to speak to you. The unbiased approach will prove more valuable in the long run because it is more likely to provide the attorney with all of the information that needs to be considered for a successful resolution of the case.

Court Preparation

Your preparation for court begins the day you receive information to start your case. You must gather information with the objective that it will be ready for use in court if needed. You need to be able to present the facts of the case in court in a complete and convincing manner. Once the case is complete, you should consolidate the information and provide it to your client or the attorney handling the case.

The following information should be prepared for each file:

- The date and approximate time the original information was received
- The names and addresses of all witnesses
- A brief summation as to what is contained in the file
- All statements given by the witnesses
- Copies of all witness statements
- Diagrams, charts, and any pictures taken
- Copies of police reports
- Copy of the investigative file
- Any videotapes that were taken—provide copies
- Any audiotapes that were obtained—provide copies
- A timeline or chronological sequence of events for the event
- Activity report—sequence of events of your investigation, any and all observations, a list of each witness and what he or she can testify
- A summation of what needs to be done; approximate date when case will be completed

Obtaining Evidence in a Criminal Case

When conducting a criminal investigation that will be presented to a prosecuting attorney for criminal filing, it is important to have your case organized in an easy-to-follow manner, for example in a three-ring binder with tabs. It is helpful to have a condensed summary of your case at the beginning, in addition to your full report. List all witnesses, giving a synopsis of their statements. Make sure that you are familiar with the statutes that govern the crimes that you are trying to prove, and that your evidence is sufficient to overcome the "beyond a reasonable doubt" threshold.

Burden of Proof

Criminal cases require the highest burden of proof for conviction than any other proceeding in the American legal system. If you conduct your investigation with that in mind, any investigation that ends up in civil court will be very strong. Burden of proof includes:

- Reasonable suspicion
- Probable cause
- Preponderance of the evidence
- Clear and convincing evidence
- Beyond a reasonable doubt

Generally, courts have found that probable cause exists when the facts and circumstances known to the investigator, and of which he or she has reasonable trustworthy information, are sufficient in and of themselves to cause a peace officer of reasonable prudence and caution to believe that the person charged has committed or is committing an offense.

Most civil cases (personal injury, contract disputes, etc.) require a burden of proof of preponderance of the evidence. Proof by preponderance of the evidence means that taking the evidence as a whole, the fact or cause sought to be proven is more probable than not. This burden is sometimes compared to putting the evidence presented by both parties on either side of a scale—whichever way the scale tips, however slightly, determines which side wins.

To prove a matter by clear and convincing evidence means to demonstrate that the existence of a disputed fact is highly probable—that is, much more probable than its non-existence. Legal commentators have often said that this means that the proponent has proven his or her case with a 75% certainty.

The constitutional standard for testing the sufficiency of the evidence requires that a conviction be based upon proof sufficient for the trier of the fact, viewing the evidence in the light most favorable to the prosecution, to find essential elements of the offense beyond a reasonable doubt.

Reasonable doubt means a doubt for which you can give a good reason, or a doubt that makes sense in light of common, ordinary experiences. Only the elements of the offense need to be proven beyond a reasonable doubt. Reasonable doubt is **not** proof beyond **all** possible doubt or proof to an absolute certainty, or even beyond a shadow of a doubt. The evidence must, however, negate any reasonable hypothesis of innocence. Legal scholars have often compared this as proof over 90%.

Brady Material

In *Brady v. Maryland* (1963) the U.S. Supreme Court held that prosecutors are required to disclose to a defendant or his or her attorney, upon request, any evidence favorable to the defendant which is either exculpatory or impeaching and is material to the defendant's guilt or punishment. Exculpatory evidence is evidence that is favorable to the defendant and material to his or her guilt. The *Brady* rule includes evidence that impeaches the testimony or credibility of that witness when the reliability of that witness may determine guilt or innocence.

Prosecutors will be held to the same standard concerning any information provided or withheld by an investigator as with the police, as to whether they believe it is exculpatory or not. The decision as to whether a piece of evidence falls under the *Brady* rule should be left to the prosecutor, and not the investigator submitting the case for prosecution. This legal issue is complex and should be left to the attorneys. You would not want to lose the case on a technicality.

Prosecutor Has Ultimate Authority

In practically every jurisdiction in the country, the prosecutor has charge and control of every prosecution pending in his or her district, and determines who, when, and how he or she will prosecute. The prosecutor does not take this authority lightly. For that reason the law has left the prosecution decision in the hands of the prosecutor. Do not be discouraged if the prosecutor decides to decline prosecution of the cases you bring to them. They may be able to guide you to obtain the additional evidence necessary to bring the case, or they can certainly recommend if there is enough evidence for your client to file a successful civil suit.

Case Studies

Anatomy of a Federal Case: *U.S. v. Albert Takhalov*

Feds charge 17 in Miami Beach 'B-girls' scam

Curt Anderson
The Associated Press

MIAMI—Seventeen people have been charged in an alleged scheme to defraud out-of-town visitors by using so-called "B-Girls" to lure them to shady South Beach private clubs where they are charged exorbitant prices for liquor, champagne and other alcoholic beverages, federal prosecutors said Wednesday.

The "B-Girls"—short for "Bar Girls"—troll legitimate Miami Beach nightspots for businessmen and tourists who appear wealthy based on such accessories as expensive watches and nice shoes, according to an FBI affidavit. The women, most of them brought into the scheme from Eastern Europe and Russia, then invite the men to private clubs and begin pouring the booze, racking up huge charges on the victims' credit cards.

Sometimes the men are so drunk they don't realize what is happening and can't remember a thing the next morning, the FBI affidavit says.

"Some victims are so intoxicated by the drinks forced upon them by the B-Girls that they cannot stand and are not competent enough to sign credit card receipts," FBI agent Alexander V. Tiguy said in the affidavit. "Those victims are propped up by the B-Girls long enough to obtain signatures."

The clubs aren't open to the public and exist only for the fraud scheme, according to the FBI. Yet they have the requisite exotic-sounding South Beach names: Caviar Bar, Nowhere Bar, Steel Toast, Tangia Club, to name a few.

Prosecutors say at least 88 victims have been identified with total losses in the hundreds of thousands of dollars. Sometimes if they refused to pay, the scam operators would call local police under a Florida law that requires bar and restaurant patrons to pay a disputed bill first and take it up later with the credit card company.

The operators also sometimes took pictures of the victims with bottles of alcohol to use as proof of the purchase, which sometimes ran $6,000 a pop or more, and one victim lost $43,000. The FBI affidavit says the "B-Girls" kept 20 percent of the business they brought in, with the owners getting 10 percent.

All 17 suspects, a mix of club operators and "B-Girls" mostly from Latvia and Estonia, face charges of wire fraud conspiracy, which carries a 20-year maximum prison sentence. The women and some of the operators made initial court appearances Wednesday despite a delay caused by an unavailable Russian translator.

The Investigation

1. INTERVIEW the Defendant and determine the facts based upon his/her statements;
2. REVIEW the DISCOVERY—the documents provided by the government (prosecutors) that outline their case. Included in this discovery are the FBI Reports (302's) which are the reports of the undercover informant (an "off duty" Miami Beach Police Sgt. Luis King) based upon his ongoing interviews with the assigned FBI agents. Each day he worked there were reports and sometimes audio and video of events at the clubs.
3. READ all the Reports of Interviews with King and all other reports generated by the FBI, Miami Beach police department (PD), and any other agencies involved in the investigation.
4. IDENTIFY and LOCATE all witnesses in the case:
   A. Prosecution
   B. Defense
5. CONDUCT background Investigations on all witnesses.
6. INTERVIEW all witnesses who may have pertinent information in the case.
7. Determine the validity and significance of each of the witnesses based upon the interviews. Assess the credibility of the witnesses.
8. Verify the facts presented by the witnesses for truth and accuracy.
9. IMPEACH the testimony of the government witnesses.
10. VERIFY the accuracy of the defense witnesses.
11. Meet with attorney and determine the defense's theory of the case.

Prepare for Trial: The Controversy

Russian Mob Eclipses Italian Mafia in South Florida, FBI Says

Jay Weaver
Miami Herald

When the feds busted a syndicate of Russian-speaking nightclub owners and their so-called Bar Girls, it seemed like just another titillating tale from South Beach.

But the April bust showed that the FBI is taking the Eastern European mob a lot more seriously these days than the Italian Mafia. La Cosa Nostra is no longer the bureau's Public Enemy No. 1 when it comes to organized crime in South Florida.

"Eurasian organized crime is our No. 1 priority," said FBI supervisory special agent Rick Brodsky of the Miami office.

In April, six reputed members of an Eastern European network—along with a Sunny Isles investor and 10 Bar Girls imported mostly from Latvia and Estonia—were charged with conspiring to seduce and fleece unsuspecting South Beach tourists by running up their credit card bills for booze at private clubs on Washington Avenue. The prosecution's case has moved so quickly that two of the "B-Girls" plan to plead guilty on Thursday in Miami federal court.

One defense lawyer quipped that they're about to become "G-Girls," as in guilty.

Sunny Isles Beach, where some of the reputed mobsters live, has so many immigrants from the former Soviet Union that it has earned the nickname "Little Moscow." The high-rise coastal cities of Hollywood and Hallandale Beach also are home to many Russian-speaking nationals.

The alleged B-Girl scam was hardly the first time the Eastern European mob struck South Florida. In February, 13 South Florida members and associates of an alleged Armenian crime organization were charged with extortion and other offenses as part of a series of indictments against more than 100 suspects from Miami to Los Angeles.

The main extortion charge accused ringleader Aram Khranyan, 41, of Sunny Isles Beach, and others of threatening "physical violence" against a man if he did not pay a $12,000 debt to a member of Khranyan's organization.

Despite the nationwide publicity, it didn't quite measure up to the B-Girl scam for sheer amusement.

Consider this tale: Brett Daniels, a professional magician, had just finished his February show at the Gulfstream Casino when he and a few colleagues headed down to South Beach.

At Mango's, a lively tourist spot on Ocean Drive, he met an attractive woman clad in a short leopard-skin dress and her sidekick, who wasn't as pretty. After showing them a few magic tricks, one of the girls told Daniels it was her birthday and proposed taking him to a private club a few blocks away to drink Russian vodka.

Four or five shots later—he can't remember exactly—Daniels found himself fighting over an incomprehensible $1,368 credit card tab with the owner of the Tangia club on Washington Avenue. "Pay your bill or you're going to jail," the bouncer told him.

What Daniels didn't know at the time was that he had been scammed by the Eastern European mob, according to the FBI.

At the helm of the alleged South Beach club racket: Alec Simchuk, 44, of Hallandale, who is now a fugitive. Simchuck and others in his network—including Albert Takhalov, 29, of Aventura—brought in longtime Sunny Isles real estate broker Isaac Feldman as an investor in Stars Lounge on Washington Avenue.

Feldman, who lost his bid for a city commission seat last year, plans to fight the charges, including conspiracy to commit wire fraud. His attorney, Myles Malman, said his client was a "minority investor" in the Stars Lounge, which was controlled by Simchuk and Takhalov.

"He was hardly ever there and he didn't supervise or control the women," said Malman, a former federal prosecutor. "He did not operate or run this club. The notion that the Russian mob is involved in this club is far-fetched and the ultimate stretch."

Malman then added: "My client lost everything."

That may be so, but for a while, Simchuk's organization ran up hundreds of thousands of dollars in bogus bills for booze, wine and champagne on the credit cards of bedazzled male tourists, prosecutors charge. All together, the B-Girls, who received 20 percent commissions for bringing in customers, ripped off about 90 patrons, mostly tourists or businessmen with telltale signs of wealth, such as expensive watches or shoes, authorities say.

One victim from Philadelphia, who was approached by two B-Girls at the swank Delano Hotel, complained he was taken for $43,000 at Caviar Beach on Washington Avenue. His American Express bill included dozens of charges for booze. Another victim was charged $5,000 for a bottle of champagne.

Authorities say the case is a sign of the mob from the former Soviet Union reaching deeper into South Florida to commit "any type of fraud you can think of," said Brodsky, in charge of the Miami FBI's organized crime squad. Their stocks in trade: credit card fraud, cybercrime, human trafficking, prostitution, drugs, extortion and arms smuggling. …

He held up Simchuk, the alleged leader in the B-Girl case, as a classic example. Simchuk, 44, is accused of smuggling sexy B-Girls from his Baltic State clubs back home to work in private, leased venues along Washington Avenue. Brodsky said Simchuk works for a "thief in law" in his homeland who acts like a "general," controls underworld enterprises, and resolves disputes, including using threats and violence.

A thief-in-law, known as a "Vor" in Russian, arose in Stalin's forced labor camps of political prisoners and criminals. The term now refers to a high-ranking member of a criminal syndicate from Russia or the former Soviet Union. "The challenge [to law enforcement] is the hierarchy is overseas and has greater access to political protection," Brodsky said.

According to court records, Simchuk and five other Eastern European men operated the alleged racket for a year at Caviar Bar, 643 Washington Ave.; Stars Lounge, 643 Washington Ave.; Nowhere Bar, 653 Washington Ave.; Steel Toast, 758 Washington Ave.; Tangia Club, 841 Washington Ave.; and Club Moreno, 1341 Washington Ave.

Today, Caviar, Stars and Tangia are not open for business. Steele Toast plans to reopen as an actual nightclub, Havana Nights, this weekend. Club

Moreno is a scooter shop. As for Nowhere Bar, it is still operating. General manager Vladislav Salaridze said his business never conducted illegal activity. "No, no, no, we are a legitimate business. We do bar mitzvahs, weddings, parties for celebrities and comedy shows," he said. "But we always were getting mixed up with Caviar [Bar] because we both have Russian owners."

According to court records, Simchuk and the others leased the private clubs, obtained credit-card merchant accounts, flew in B-Girls from Eastern Europe or the Baltic States with 90-day visas, rented apartments for them, and sent them out to hotels like the Delano, Clevelander and others along Ocean Drive to seduce male visitors into coming to their private clubs.

An FBI agent who led the investigation said they went "hunting" in pairs, worked between 10 p.m. and 5 a.m., lured "wealthy males" back to the clubs and ordered multiple bottles of booze without telling the victims the price.

"The clubs are not open to the public, and operate solely as a front for fraud," FBI agent Alexander V. Tiguy wrote in an April affidavit.

The goal was to jack up the bills, and squeeze the customers to sign off on their credit card slips—no easy task.

"Some victims are so intoxicated by the drinks forced upon them by the B-Girls that they cannot stand and are not competent enough to sign credit card receipts," Tiguy wrote in the affidavit. "Those victims are propped up by the B-Girls long enough to obtain signatures."

In most instances, the bartender or manager explained to the victims that they agreed to purchase the alcohol, that the bar had surveillance video of them, and demanded that they pay or the police would be called to arrest them.

On several occasions, the bouncer or Miami Beach police officers would inform the victim about the state's Innkeeper Law, which requires patrons disputing a charge to challenge the bill with their credit card company—or risk getting arrested.

At several of the clubs, an undercover Miami Beach police officer was working as the bouncer to obtain evidence for the investigation.

Daniels, the magician, said he felt like he had no choice but to pay his bill after he called police and club Tangia's bouncer told him he would be going to jail. The bouncer was an undercover cop, but he did not know that at the time.

"They had my driver's license and credit card," recalled Daniels, 50, who turned to the FBI. "I couldn't do anything."

The Conclusion

The case went to trial in October 2012. I am still trying to understand how my client, Albert Takhalov committed a crime. He was employed as a credit card merchant provider. He installed processing machines in the bars. There was never intent to defraud anyone. If there was fraud (I'm still trying to figure out who was defrauded), it was done by the employees, managers, and the bouncer, Luis King, who also happened to be the undercover Miami Beach Police Officer who was planted into this organization. He could have stopped this crime at any time, yet he and his superiors at the Miami Beach Police

Department and the FBI allowed it to continue for almost one year. He was the one who told the customers in the clubs that if they did not pay the bill they would be arrested. Isn't that extortion? Isn't that entrapment? I guess I'll find out when the jury returns with the verdict.

Reliance on Informants: *United States v. Bruce Bertman*

During my career in federal law enforcement, I noticed a disturbing trend that was increasing over the years at an alarming rate—the government use of and reliance on informants. As a federal probation officer, I was responsible for supervising persons in the Witness Protection Program. I also supervised probationers and parolees who were authorized to work as informants for law enforcement agencies. The violation rate for those two categories of offenders was nearly 80%, which was double the rate of violation for the balance of my caseload that was comprised of career criminals. This means that three out of every four of those "informants" were sent to prison for violating the conditions of their supervised release. What this indicated to me was that they believed that they had license to do whatever they wanted, and they would be protected by their "control" agents to whom they reported. Unfortunately, too many times they were correct.

In the early 1980s, I supervised Hilmer Sandini, a notorious con man and swindler who became a drug dealer. Sandini became an informant for the FBI and was working in an undercover capacity for many years. He was able to successfully "flip" his control agent, Dan Mitrione, and turn him into a drug dealer and possible murderer. Both were subsequently caught and convicted for their crimes after I brought reports of Sandini's ongoing criminal activities, as reported to me by local law enforcement agencies, to the attention of the federal judge in Alabama who placed him on probation at the request of the FBI. I was also involved in the supervision of Michael Burnett, aka Michael Raymond (formerly in the Witness Protection Program), who ended up becoming a serial murderer while he was working as an informant for the FBI. I would like to say that these two cases are an aberration in the system—but unfortunately, they are not.

In *U.S. v. Bruce Bertman et al.*, the centerpiece of the government's case was a sting operation run by two convicted felons named Robert Schlien and David Jones, and later code-named "Operation Bermuda Shorts." Schlien and Jones may be the most prolific fraudsters and con artists of all time. Here is their background.

Sky Scientific Inc. was formed as a private company in the early 1990s. It was reportedly mining gold and precious metals at various sites around the world. In 1994, the company mailed out 350,000 glossy promotional brochures to prospective investors claiming to have hundreds of millions of dollars worth of mineral reserves. In reality, there were no such reserves.

The Securities and Exchange Commission (SEC) found that Schlien received $2,606,729 as a result of the scheme. Jones received $4,546,500 from his participation in the scheme. Both were ordered to pay fines in those amounts. They were never prosecuted for these crimes, as well as numerous crimes committed prior to the Sky Scientific fraud. Instead, they entered into an agreement with the FBI to become government informants. They were allowed to set up an undercover sting operation to entice private companies to go public with them, providing the expertise to make it happen. This is like giving kids the keys to the candy store. Schlien and Jones called upon a few of their old cronies and soon had a thriving business going—enticing unsuspecting companies into going public with the promise of making them millions in return for a little kickback. Is that not the American Dream (minus the kickback of course)? Hey, what's a couple hundred thousand dollars when they were promising millions?

Enter Bruce Bertman, his company, A1 Internet.com, and a host of others who were ensnared (I call it entrapment) by Schlien and Jones into this dubious deal—all under the not-so-watchful eyes of their FBI control agents. It turns out that while they were working for the FBI, they continued their double-dealing fraudulent ways. This was all disclosed during the course of the Bertman trial and admitted to by Schlien under cross-examination by Bertman's attorney. It did not matter—the jury found them and others guilty in the many cases brought under "Operation Bermuda Shorts."

The criminal justice system is becoming derailed by the use and misuse of government informants. It is a common thread in many criminal cases in courtrooms all across the United States. This is a fact that legal investigators and criminal defense attorneys need to overcome if the system is to be saved. It is just one more of the many factors causing juries to convict innocent persons.

Component Method™ of Criminal Defense Investigation

The Component Method™ was developed by Brandon A. Perron, a board-certified criminal defense investigator, to provide public defender investigators and private investigators with a formula for conducting successful and comprehensive criminal defense assignments. In his book, *Uncovering Reasonable Doubt: The Component Method—A Comprehensive Guide for the Criminal Defense Investigator*, Perron writes that his method utilizes accepted and proven investigative procedures in an easy-to-follow format. Each component of the investigation process is designed to uncover leads and develop questions leading to the next component. The subsequent components support the investigator's efforts to track leads and answer questions developed in previous components. Utilization of the Component Method allows the criminal defense investigator to begin and end an investigation with the knowledge that an effective and professional investigation was completed.

The Component Method also performs well as a management tool. Senior investigators maintaining supervisory roles, as well as the responsibility for a significant caseload, are able to utilize the system to monitor the progress of subordinates. Historically, the problems associated with "passing the torch" of experience to entry-level criminal defense investigators have been significant. Adherence to a specific methodology allows the supervisor and field investigator to cultivate and pursue a team approach while still allowing for individual critical and creative thinking. The Component Method provides a general course of action while conducting comprehensive assignments. Utilizing this methodology provides an understanding between the supervisor and field investigator regarding expectations and the general course of inquiry.

The six components of criminal defense investigation defining the Component Method are investigative case review and analysis; the defendant interview; crime scene examination, diagrams, and photographs; victim/witness background investigations; witness interviews and statements; and the investigation report and testimony. The Component Method reinforces the investigator's role as the primary investigator in control of the course of the investigation. Utilization of resources such as forensic experts and specialists to support the primary investigator and his or her pursuit of the truth is also explored. In addition, the investigator's responsibility as a thinker and strategist is discussed on an intellectual as well as practical level. The Component Method maintains that the investigator must be an impartial and objective advocate of the truth. This requires discipline, integrity, and an unwavering sense of honor.

The Component Method is intended to be a guide to assist the criminal defense investigator in the course of his or her investigation. Utilizing the Component Method as a reference source for fundamental information, techniques, and skills will enable the criminal defense investigator to perform assigned tasks effectively and efficiently. The Component Method can be utilized as a preliminary or comprehensive plan. The individual components can be limited or expanded to conform to the specific needs of each case. Proper execution of the Component Method allows the criminal defense investigator to submit his or her final report with the confidence that a thorough investigation has been accomplished. The report of investigation documenting the criminal defense investigator's findings will allow defense counsel to develop a defense strategy based upon facts and not abstract theory or conjecture. Subsequently, defense counsel may request additional investigation based upon initial findings, investigative recommendations, or supplemental discovery.

Suggested Reading

Brandon A. Perron, *Uncovering Reasonable Doubt: The Component Method—A Comprehensive Guide for the Criminal Defense Investigator* (Morris, Kearney, Nebraska, 1998). This is a complete and definitive resource that can be purchased from the Criminal Defense Investigation Training Council on their Web site www.defenseinvestigator.com. Anyone interested in specializing in criminal defense investigation should become a member of the organization and undergo the recommended training.

Warren J. Sonne, *Criminal Investigation for the Professional Investigator* (CRC Press, Boca Raton, Florida). I highly recommend this book to any investigator who is interested in doing criminal defense work. Warren is a good friend and we share the same publisher, CRC Taylor & Francis. He is a retired New York City Police Department Detective who worked in the organized crime, terrorism, sex crimes, fraud, assaults, and homicide units. Upon leaving law enforcement Warren opened up two very successful PI agencies—the first in New York City and the latest in Stuart, Florida, where he currently resides. He is highly qualified to write a book on this topic, which shows both sides of how the investigations are conducted. Included are chapters on crime scenes, death investigations, homicide investigations, interrogations and confessions, robbery, burglary, narcotics, and sex crime investigations, arrest strategies, testifying, investigative tools, and the role of the criminal investigator. It is a must-have book for every professional investigator.

Appendix 8.1: The Grand Jury

An institution of legal and historical stature, the grand jury existed in England for some 700 years and was inherited during the early colonial period as a feature of the American legal system. Its repressive potential is disguised by a structure that would appear to be the opposite of arbitrary government action. The grand jury is composed of ordinary citizens who must grant their approval before another citizen can be prosecuted for a serious crime. The U.S. Supreme Court maintains that protection against arbitrary prosecution is the main function of the grand jury.

Grand jurors return indictments for criminal offenses and presentments, which differ from indictments in that the grand jurors can initiate the investigation and can offer any evidence they personally possess. Presentments signify noncriminal complaints, usually against public officials, but criminal charges can only be brought under an indictment prepared by the prosecutor.

After 1776, the grand jury was included in many state constitutions, and the Fifth Amendment assured that any serious federal criminal charge would be screened by a grand jury. The federal constitution's provisions were adopted because many colonists were fearful of creating a powerful central government that could arbitrarily use the criminal process against its political enemies. The grand jury never fully developed into a consistent neutral institution, carefully sifting the evidence and providing protection only for the innocent. It frequently reflects local or prevailing prejudices in its decision to indict or not to indict.

Grand juries at both state and federal levels operate best when dealing with routine matters. This is because a prosecutor has no interest in bringing weak cases before the grand jury. With strong cases, the jury's function will be to confirm a reasonable discretionary judgment.

The scope of state grand juries is much broader than that of the federal grand jury, because the former are authorized to investigate any criminal matter that violates the common law, including such offenses as murder, burglary, and robbery. Because the federal grand jury can indict only for federal offenses, it had a limited scope of operations until Congress recently passed more federal statutes.

It was generally thought that federal grand juries were empowered to investigate and indict only for statutory offenses. Today, they have much more latitude in conducting criminal investigations. Previously, they were not as accessible to pressure applied by lay citizens regarding the operation of the federal government. Today, the federal grand jury has become an instrument for prosecution by a centralized government administration.

The history of the grand jury shows that grand jurors will support indictments against the enemies of the government if the public from which they are drawn perceives the enemies the same way.

All kinds of evidence that cannot be used at trial are permitted into the grand jury (e.g., hearsay), but the absence of procedural protection is more extensive than that. The constitutional prohibition against double jeopardy bars the government from giving the defendant a second sentence for the same offense. This is not the case in the grand jury. None of the Miranda or other constitutional safeguards are afforded any grand jury witness, not even the prime suspect should he or she be called as a witness. The witness has an obligation to testify before the grand jury to answer all questions except those to which the witness makes a specific timely objection on Fifth Amendment grounds or on the basis of some other well-established privilege (i.e., attorney-client).

In this sense, the subpoena is similar to that issued to require a witness to testify at a criminal trial or similar to an arrest and the beginning of a police interrogation. The courts have also said that a witness or suspect must respond to questions to which he or she cannot invoke the Fifth Amendment, because the witness may be a source of evidence on other offenders.

In addition to the limits on a witness' Fifth Amendment rights, Fourth Amendment rights may not be respected in the grand jury. A witness may be forced to produce evidence even though the prosecutor offers no proof that it is linked to criminal activity. The witness can also be the subject of an unlawful invasion of privacy in which the police have broken into his house without a warrant and still be made to answer questions on the basis of what the police may have seen or taken.

In general, a witness is not afforded the legal rights provided to a defendant, because at that point the defendant is not being charged with a crime. Even a witness whom the prosecutor seeks to indict does not have the protections that must be afforded to defendants in interrogation by the prosecutor or the police outside the grand jury.

Attorneys are barred from the grand jury room because the proceedings are non-adversarial, and the witness is deemed to have the maximum protection that he or she needs because the witness can invoke his or her right not to give testimony that is incriminating. Other negative consequences result from the fact that contempt of grand jury proceedings is technically civil and not criminal. Thus, a witness does not have the right to a jury trial, because no criminal offense has been committed. Rather, the court is using "remedial" measures to deal with the obstruction of its process by the witness. Under civil contempt, the witness can secure his or her own release any time he or she chooses to testify. Because the imprisonment is not for a fixed and definite term, it is not a criminal sentence. Thus, a second refusal to testify becomes a new occasion for the application of the non-punitive measure, and the witness has the ability to avoid imprisonment by testifying.

A defendant cannot object to evidence seized in violation of the constitutional rights of another person. A defendant can object only to evidence seized in violation of his or her own constitutional rights. However, the Supreme Court, by the slimmest margin (5 to 4), held that a witness could not be convicted of contempt when the government refused to deny that its line of questioning was based on illegal wiretapping (*U.S. v. Gelbhart*, 408 U.S. 41).

Because the grand jury is designed for, and may even be limited to, investigations of criminal activity, it should primarily be an instrument used to look at past events in gathering evidence to prove a prior offense. It can also look at any current ongoing criminal schemes; it is not in theory or purpose supposed to be a data- or intelligence-gathering mechanism, especially if the government's only purpose is to monitor the activities of its lawful citizens.

Open and unlimited probing is possible because most rules of evidence that normally protect a defendant in a criminal trial, such as barring hearsay or irrelevant and prejudicial evidence, need not be observed in grand jury proceedings. The court's explanation for the lack of limitations on this probing is that the grand jury is engaged primarily in protecting the innocent, a notion belied by history.

Congress strengthened the statutory basis for potential harassment of witnesses by enacting portions of the Organized Crime Control Act (OCCA) of 1970 that regulates granting witnesses immunity from prosecution when giving grand jury testimony. The 1970 legislation established "use immunity," which provides much less protection to the individual. The prosecution is barred only from using the witness' testimony in later attempts to develop evidence to prove any offense the witness is charged with, but the witness may be prosecuted on offenses about which he or she can be compelled to testify. The Supreme Court has said that the use of immunity statutes does not violate the Constitution.

Death Investigation

9

DEAN A. BEERS, CLI

The cause of death investigation has multiple phases including scene investigation, body assessment, medical records, and the forensic autopsy. This is finalized in three documents: the death certificate, the investigator's report, and the autopsy report. "Autopsy" is from the Greek "autopsia," meaning "to see with one's own eyes." This chapter will allow the private investigator to view death and even non-death cases "with one's own eyes."

An Overview of Death Investigation*

First, not all death scenes—or any scene—are crime scenes. They are places where an event took place—an incident scene. At all death scenes there are actually at least two scenes: location(s) of the incident and the body itself. If a crime is suspected (and all suspicious death investigations should be treated as such), the incident will belong to the investigating law enforcement agency, and the body, together with all items on or about it, will belong to the medical examiner's office (including their appointed deputies—death investigators). The agencies will work independently of each other with overlapping goals. The death investigator has certain responsibilities and a duty to pursue those responsibilities. Of course there are legal and cooperative exceptions to these based on the greater good of the needs of all investigating agencies, particularly involving possible homicides. The body is exclusively under the custody and control of the death investigator. Until the death investigator arrives on scene, no other person can touch, move, or remove the body, or those items on or about the body. The assessment includes complete photography, documenting wounds and injuries, or lack thereof, rigor and livor mortis, body position and relationship to the scene, and condition of the body due to postmortem interval and environment. If the body has been moved, possibly to a remote area, there will be another incident scene at the place the death actually occurred.

Death and personal injury investigations are forensic specialties. So, what is "Forensics"? It truly depends on whom you ask—but here is an easy acronym:

* Adapted from *Reviewing and Comprehending Autopsy Reports,* Dean A. Beers, CLI (2010)—adapted to *Practical Methods for Legal Investigations: Concepts and Protocols in Civil and Criminal Cases* (CRC Press, Boca Raton, FL, 2011).

***F**acts **O**r **R**easonable **E**vidence **N**ecessitating **S**ystematic **I**nvestigative and **C**ritical **S**olutions specific to jurisprudence*

Forensics is simply the application of [*specialty—fill in the blank*] to the law. It is finding the evidence, analyzing the evidence, and reporting the evidence—evidentiary fact finders, a very important component of death investigations. Death is the cessation of life as determined by the absence of respiration, pulse, and brain activity. Although this may seem "obvious," it may not be—more than one person has been transported, and even placed on an autopsy table or in a coffin, and incorrectly presumed to be deceased. Often an incident involving death begins with a call to 911 with emergency services responding. Death may be first determined by a skilled and licensed medical practitioner, such as a registered nurse or paramedic. All deaths must be legally pronounced—or affirmed; pronouncement by telephone is insufficient and must be done in person. Paramedics may medically determine death, but cannot pronounce death—the legal determination of death after consultation with their supervising medical doctor. Pronouncement is only by a medical doctor, a doctor of osteopathy, or a deputized coroner or medical examiner.

What Is Death?

The obvious signs of death may include traumatic injury—from a fractured neck determined by palpitation, to visible brain avulsion. Other obvious signs include early to advanced decomposition and skeletal remains. Deaths fall into two primary categories—natural and other. Natural deaths, as later explained, have a medical history and/or diagnosis. Natural deaths are typically not the result of any contributory event. However, altitude and exertion are two examples of possible contributing events to a natural death. Other deaths may be the result of accident, homicide, or suicide, and even undetermined. There has been an outside contributory event causing the death. Can a death in "Other" be mistaken for "Natural"? Yes, and as an example may be seen in elder deaths and is a more advanced death investigation involving medical records and toxicology. The private investigator will be involved after the initial and official death investigation, usually in a criminal defense or civil plaintiff role, or possibly in the civil defense or insurance investigation role. To properly evaluate and conduct a death investigation in any of these roles, it is first important to understand the components presented in this chapter.

The conclusion of the official death investigation is the Cause and Manner of Death, including the Mechanism of Death.

- Cause of Death [COD] is the medical reason for death, the underlying disease or injury that is the specific and immediate medical reason for death.
  - The cause of death is determined from the investigative and forensic evidence—both direct and circumstantial.
  - This includes a review of the medical records, investigation, and if warranted, an autopsy.
- Manner of Death [MOD] is the classification of death based on how the cause of death was brought into play.* Commonly referred to as the "Type" of death, there are five possible choices:
  - Natural (i.e., disease, cardiac, etc.)
    - Death caused solely by disease, like heart disease, cancer, etc.
    - If natural death is hastened by injury or any other non-natural event, the manner of death will not be considered natural.
    - If the disease process is caused by a non-natural event (e.g., pneumonia due to long-term bed confinement as a result of a motor vehicle accident), the manner of death will not be considered natural.
  - Accident (fall, automobile, industrial, etc.)
  - Deaths other than natural, where there is no evidence of intent: an unintentional event or category of chain of events
  - Many forms of apparent Accident deaths may instead be Suicide or Homicide, or possibly Undetermined. These deaths should be particularly closely investigated due to possibly accidental death insurance double indemnity clauses.
  - Homicide (death is caused by another person)
    - Death resulting from intentional harm (explicit or implicit) of one person by another, or by grossly reckless behavior
  - In death investigation, homicide is the medical determination.

Note: This is a medical determination of homicide, not the legal determination. A motor vehicle collision resulting in the death of a person is ruled an accident, but a person may be legally charged under vehicular homicide statutes.

  - Suicide (death is caused by the decedent)
    - Death as a purposeful action set in motion (explicit or implicit) to end one's life.

* Basic Competencies in Forensic Pathology (College of American Pathologists, Washington, DC, 2006).

- Do not try determining the person's "final thoughts"—only his or her final actions.
- Suicide is a ruling that is to the exclusion of all other MODs and is presumptive to the decedent having not committed suicide. This manner is not used as a fallback when the other manners are inconclusive. For example, if not accident or homicide, it must therefore be suicide. This is the most common death investigation and such lack of conclusive evidence is best ruled undetermined.
- There are four elements to suicide:
    1. Intent to commit the act knowing that it may result in their death
    2. Knowledge of the instrument used and that it may cause death
    3. History of attempts, ideation, or documentation of evidence supporting suicide
    4. Evidence of contributing factors to the act

• Undetermined (facts and investigation are inconclusive)
• Manner assigned when there is insufficient evidence or information, especially about intent, to assign another manner. May be seen in
    - Sudden infant death syndrome (SIDS)—now referred to as sudden unexpected infant death syndrome (SUIDS)
    - Advanced stages of decomposition
    - Skeletal remains
    - Unknown identification and/or history

Medicolegal Death Investigations in Criminal Cases

Death investigation is not limited to death, as the components of death investigation apply to personal injury and injury causation investigations. Understanding death investigation leads to a better understanding of these, adds marketing value to the private investigator, and more importantly, adds value to the services and benefits to the client. This is simply because fractions of an inch, or an alteration in an event, or series of events, may be the only difference between a serious bodily injury and death. Death investigation is often a multi-faceted team approach. It does require often communicating with, reviewing reports and records of, and having contacts of these and other specialists and experts, detailed later in this chapter.

The Investigative Protocol*

The process of investigation is conducted and completed by following five basic steps: prepare, inquire, analyze, document, and report.† Depending on the investigation and other factors, these may all be within one assignment (i.e., scene investigation) or multiple assignments (multiple witness interviews).

Prepare

The importance of investigative preparation is so important, but unrealized, as to be often overlooked. Investigations are methodical, not spontaneous. Although it may be fun to jump in a car and head to destinations unknown for a vacation, that is not wise in an investigation. A map, compass, and itinerary are important, and so is some information about your destination and agenda. The investigative process follows the same concept.

Inquire

The inquire stage is where many investigators begin—which is the actual investigative process. Because private investigators are not first responders, who may not be able to prepare the investigative process, there is generally no excuse for jumping to this inquire stage. Often it is seen that the investigative process consists of inquire (investigate) and report—which is essentially a conducted versus completed investigation. There is a duty to the client to be complete, and in death investigations that is paramount. After all, the private investigator may be determining facts and information that differentiate between accident and suicide, or homicide and suicide, which not only carries an emotional difference to family members but also possibly a financial difference. Consider inheritance matters and double indemnity insurance for accidental deaths.

Analyze

It is important to organize your investigation into assignments and stages. These might include immediate, interim, and long-term assignments. After completing each stage of an assignment, analyze the case and progress to determine any new or different courses of action. This analysis is comparative of the provided information to the learned information in the investiga-

* Adapted from *Practical Methods for Legal Investigations: Concepts and Protocols in Civil and Criminal Cases*, Dean A. Beers, CLI (CRC Press, Boca Raton, FL, 2011).

† Ibid.

tive process—evidence analysis. This process will continue until disposition or completion.

Document

All evidence must be documented. At the same time, due to discovery and disclosure issues, and particularly in civil cases, documentation is done in the manner requested by the client.

Maintain a table (or tables) of supporting and conflicting information of the initial investigative process, your own investigative process, and evaluation leading to the truth. This is continuous as case progress information is indexed. Use of evidence logs, photograph logs, diagram details, witness information, time lines, etc., is very helpful.

Report

The final component, and due to its purpose one of the most important, is the report of investigative findings. As with the document stage, due to discovery and disclosure issues, and particularly in civil cases, the report to the client is done in the manner requested by the client. This may be verbally or in writing, and to include only what is requested. This is not unethical; it is part of the legal strategy. If practical and requested, confidential memorandums can be provided after a verbal report of any negative issues. The report will detail specific factual evidence and learned information.

What Is Death Investigation?

As introduced in this chapter, deaths fall within natural causes and other causes. The private investigator will often be consulted to look into death investigations, conducting and completing an investigation to determine if the reported and certified manner and cause of death are consistent with the reported evidence, as well as any new evidence determined during the resulting investigative process. Therefore, two investigations are taking place—a re-investigation of the initial official investigation, and the concurrent investigation for which the private investigator has been retained. The common death investigation types and ultimate question in the death investigation are

- Is it a homicide investigation?
- Is it an accident investigation?
- Is it a suicide investigation?
- Is it civil (defense or plaintiff) or criminal (defense or prosecution)?

The fact is that at the onset the answers are not known or should not be predetermined. To do so is to judge and not investigate. At the conclusion of the investigative process the conclusion may be the same as officially reported, which is acceptable, or it may be different which is also acceptable. Conclusions cannot be made without a thorough investigation and evaluation of the evidence.

Are All Deaths Autopsied, or What Determines an Autopsy?

The majority of deaths are natural deaths with a diagnosed medical condition (i.e., cancer, congenital defect) or cause of death determined by medical history (i.e., diabetes, cardiac history). These will not be typically autopsied forensically. Some jurisdictions require an autopsy for all homicide or suspected homicides, including government execution under a death penalty. Others have no requirements. Medical examiner systems typically have more stringent requirements in mandating autopsies in nearly all questionable, sudden, and unnatural deaths. Coroner systems, on the other hand, are often elected laypersons with no medical—sometimes even death investigation—background, and the value of an autopsy is not properly evaluated or understood. Autopsies are often neglected because the cause of death is "obvious." This is frequent in motor vehicle collisions and even some "suicides" that are "obvious." Following are two examples.

Joe Citizen, an 82-year-old male, is driving home from a wedding reception when he fails to obey a stop sign at a t-intersection and continues into an irrigation ditch. He experiences serious injuries and is pronounced dead at the scene. The coroner responds to the scene and after assessment and investigation determines that he died of multiple blunt force injuries due to impact with the opposing ditch bank at high speed, due to the loss of control of the vehicle. For our purposes, acknowledge that law enforcement will investigate the incident, and blood is drawn (most state laws require ethyl alcohol testing of all deceased persons of motor vehicle collisions), and it will be reported that he was not intoxicated. What considerations are there?

1. Natural, accident, or suicide (homicide could happen, but let's not complicate this)?
   a. Medical (natural) may include cardiac event, diabetic reaction, or stroke prior to and causing the loss of control or even death then causing loss of control. The latter would be natural, the former still accident, but now there is a known cause of loss of control.

b. Suicide may include previous suicidal ideation exacerbated by an event at the wedding reception and knowing the intersection caused the collision and his own death.

2. Mechanical? Although not determined at autopsy, perhaps the vehicle had a malfunction causing the incident, or a malfunction that could have prevented his death (i.e., airbag deployment). This may not change the death certificate, but it may impact the family emotionally and insurance benefits. This may also be cause for legal action, and the autopsy findings will demonstrate that the driver, by way of actions or medical history, did not contribute to the incident.

To the above scenario, let's add that Joe's wife was with him and also died as a result of the collision. They each had two children of previous marriages, both were preceded in death by their spouses and they remarried late in life. In addition to the above, of importance is who died first due to hereditary and insurance concerns. Scene investigation is important, and an autopsy may or may not answer the question. As an example, if Mr. Citizen had a cardiac event and died, causing the collision that consequently killed his wife—this impacts two things:

1. Mr. Citizen died first, of a cardiac event—his surviving wife (excluding any provisions of a will) inherits from him. Further, his double indemnity insurance clause does not apply due to the natural death.
2. Mrs. Citizen died second, due to injuries from the collision caused by her now deceased husband. Her inheritance—preceded by Mr. Citizen's—transfers to her biological children. Further, her double indemnity insurance clause does apply due to her death by accident.

As can be seen, death and motor vehicle collisions can be complicated by what is seemingly unimportant. The above scenarios could only be answered by autopsy—it cannot be assumed that Mr. Citizen did/did not have a cardiac event due only to his medical history. There are no surviving or outside witnesses.

Let's take a final look at our scenarios involving Mr. and Mrs. Citizen. They have survived the collision and were hospitalized with well-documented treatment and injuries. After 3 to 4 days one or both are deceased. This would still be a coroner's case, an autopsy would not be necessary as there is an abundance of medical treatment documentation. If either survived the collision and were discharged from the hospital to a rehabilitation center and then died of pneumonia (not uncommon), an autopsy would also be unnecessary. If they are released from the rehabilitation center to home with an expected death (also not uncommon), again an autopsy would be unnecessary. In each of these cases the death certificate may read: Manner—Accident; Cause—due to (i.e., pneumonia) complications consequential to a single vehicle motor vehicle collision. But pneumonia is natural, right? Yes, but it was onset by a non-natural event—the manner cannot be natural. Deaths specifically involving the young and elderly are a more advanced undertaking.

Key Concepts to Review and Analyze

Scene Investigation

There are at least two scenes to all death investigations: the body and the incident scene. If the body is transported or the underlying incident occurred at a place different than the death, there will be additional scenes. This is seen in homicides where the body is disposed of after the fatal incident. The duties of the medical examiner and considerations of the alternate private (equivocal) death investigations include

- Was there a proper assessment of the body and all evidence on or about the body?
- Was evidence of the underlying incident, fatal incident, and death collected and evaluated (and turned over in discovery)? This may be weapons, clothing, drugs and paraphernalia, medical chart (i.e., blood glucose log), etc.
- Was the scene or any evidence altered?
- Was any transient evidence overlooked, altered, or destroyed by the environment or scene investigation? Evidence must be documented before it is moved, inspected, analyzed, collected, or tested.
- Tunnel vision—determining the outcome of the investigation before completed—is a "fatal" error in death and personal injury investigation. There are many myths and "not as it seems" in death investigation. As an example, seemingly happy people do not commit suicide (i.e., if they have made that final decision and feel relief, they may appear "happy").
- Consider the objective and subjective information and evidence. Step away from the private investigator role and consider the perspective of the decedent and involved persons. What does the decedent, scene, and evidence tell you?
- Death is the product of multiple possibilities—people do unspeakable things to themselves and each other and go to great lengths to hide their own actions or intents. Consider all possibilities and then focus on what the evidence tells. Think beyond the "obvious."
- Evidence does not lie *but it can be misunderstood, misinterpreted, altered, and give false results.* People lie—the truth may not be in their favor or acceptable to them.

- Document lack of evidence (no suicide notes, no prior illness, no skid marks) and mitigating and supporting evidence. As an example, a bloodstain pattern on a shirt may reveal if, and how, the decedent was holding a firearm during a suicide. Negative evidence—contradictory—should be noted. If it is expected to be seen and is not (or the reverse), it must be explained.
- Determine and analyze the exact position of the body and all evidence, if any has been moved or manipulated (if so, why), and if any evidence was overlooked.
- Physicians and paramedics treat injuries, law enforcement investigates crime, families mourn, and attorneys litigate. Private investigators, particularly in death investigations, are evidentiary fact finders.
- Know the importance of medications found, including illicit drugs and paraphernalia, and other toxins (paints, glues, poisons, inhalants, over-the-counter self-medications).
- Anticipate the questions of the family, attorney, and trier-of-fact.

Evidence

Private investigation involves finding, reviewing, analyzing, documenting, and reporting evidence. Evidence is any factual information that tends to prove or disprove an assertion. Information is not necessarily factual and/or evidence. Information must be proven factual to be evidentiary. Key considerations of evidence include

- Evidence can be both insignificant or a key component of a case—review and analysis are important.
- Evidence can be easily destroyed, lost, overlooked, altered, and even contaminated. Look for indications of this.
- Verify the chain of evidence. The integrity of the evidence is unyielding. This includes ethics—information without integrity is not evidence, and only evidence is admissible and considered by the attorney and trier-of-fact.
- Consider if evidence may have been overlooked or discarded as being unrelated, insignificant, or unimportant. A shoe lying in the hallway, although belonging to the decedent, may be as important as if it belonged to her killer.
- Look in the overlooked and less obvious places. Evidence can be transient in itself, can be moved or hidden, or can be influenced by the environment.

Examples of Evidence

- Fingerprints, footprints, tire tracks, tool marks
- DNA (includes blood, semen, saliva found on breasts, thighs, neck, etc.)
- Bite marks, abrasions, or cuts by the perpetrator or victim
- Trace evidence (hairs, fibers, chemicals, ashes, gunshot residue)
- Physical evidence (vomit, feces, liquids and inhalants, drugs and paraphernalia, alcohol, weapons and ammunition, clothing, vehicle debris, suicide notes or other writings and documentation, pornography)
- Clothing (yields patterns of weapons used, blood, fibers, body fluids, gunshot residue, and other evidence that will not be found on the body. Can show gunshot distance that nude body at morgue will not show.)
- Witness statements—official and in the course of the death investigation
- Blood spatter and incident scene analysis
- Photographs and videos, measurements and diagrams
- The autopsy report, investigative report, toxicology report, and medical records

Decedent Investigation

Traumatic Injuries

Traumatic injuries are best defined as those that require urgent medical attention and are caused by the actions of the victim, another person, or environment within which the victim is (outdoors, indoors, vehicle, etc.). These can be divided into bodily injury, serious bodily injury, and fatal injuries. To understand each of these, it is necessary to know and understand the definition: *serious bodily injury (SBI) involves a substantial risk of death, unconsciousness, extreme physical pain, protracted and obvious disfigurement, or protracted loss or impairment of the function of a bodily member, organ, or mental faculty.* Bodily injury is less substantial than SBI, and a fatal injury is an SBI that has resulted in death. In some jurisdictions, such as Colorado, an injury involving a break or fracture is also classified as SBI, regardless of how minor or severe (i.e., finger or nose fracture).

Traumatic injuries may not be visible; however, there are usually indications of such injuries. Injuries are first classified as either sharp force or blunt force injuries. Sharp force injuries include incisions (cuts) and punctures (stabbing). Blunt force injuries include lacerations (tear), abrasions (bruise), and avulsions (removed area). Other injuries include thermal injuries (burns, including electrocution). Injuries may take the form of pattern injuries, often distinctly caused by an instrument (i.e., cord, knife, baton, etc.), or non-pattern injuries, often seen as circumstantial to the incident (abrasions are common non-pattern injuries). A perforating injury has an entry and exit, and a transecting injury is typically an incision or laceration resulting in the through-and-through separation of a limb, organ, or other body part—as little as a transected nerve or artery, to as large as a transected spleen or liver. Finally, there are external and internal injuries—those that are on the surface or under the surface. All organ injuries, save the skin (the largest organ of the body) are internal injuries. These injuries of themselves may not be the direct cause of death; however, a cluster of injuries, such as multiple blunt force traumas in a motor vehicle collision, may collectively be the cause of death.

Reviewing autopsy reports at the local coroner or medical examiner offices is an excellent resource for learning the different types of injuries, how inflicted, and how they may be contributory or non-contributory to death. Injuries, particularly pattern injuries or the location of injuries, may assist in determining where a person was positioned in a vehicle, if the person was restrained by a seatbelt, if a person was wearing a helmet, how the person was moving when crossing a street, and other helpful indicators in investigating a death or even personal injury case. A vehicle occupant injured by shards of glass, indicated by multiple "dicing" incisions of the skin caused by the shards of glass, will be injured on the side adjacent to the source—passenger or driver. A restrained person will have a pattern injury (or transfer of fibers) from the seatbelt that corresponds with the seated position—from right shoulder to left hip (passenger/side) or left shoulder to right hip (driver/side).

Clothing

The clothing of the decedent, or victim, is important evidence for a variety of reasons. These include corresponding injuries, trace evidence, and possibly aiding identification.

- Corresponding injuries—if the decedent is clothed and has a blunt force or sharp force injury, there will be a corresponding defect in the clothing if the instrument causing injury is capable of a laceration or incision. This may not include internal injuries. Incised or puncture wounds of the torso, including knife or gunshot wounds, will have a corresponding defect. This defect may have indicators of the type of weapon (single- or double-edged knife) or distance (gunshot powder pattern detectable using alternate light source).
- Evidence—there may be a transfer of hair, fibers, blood, or other material from the assailant to the victim or evidence that assists with identification of the weapon or instrument causing injury.
- Trace evidence—trace evidence is an oft-used phrase that typically refers to small or minute evidence that may link person to a crime or incident scene, victim to a crime or incident scene, instrument to the assailant and/or victim, and instrument to the crime or incident scene. Trace evidence may be hair, fibers, blood, tool marks, ballistics, fingerprints, and other forms of DNA (saliva, semen, etc.).

Trace evidence is based on Locard's Theory. Moreover, trace evidence is direct only in that it places two questioned items together. Additional direct and circumstantial evidence will complete the link and determine if the two questioned items were together at the time of the crime or incident.

- Person to scene—this can be determined by trace evidence found at the scene which is proven to have come from the person. Further investigation will determine if that person was at the scene at the time in question.
- Victim to scene—this can also be determined by trace evidence found at the scene that is proven to have come from the person. Further investigation will determine if that victim was at the scene at the time in question. This may also assist in determining chronology of a crime and multiple scenes.
- Instrument to scene—this can be determined by trace evidence found at the scene that is proven to have been caused or left by the instrument. Tool marks from a screwdriver to a door jamb is an example. Multiple scenes with the same tool mark link the scenes. Further investigation will determine if that instrument was used by a suspect or victim at the scene at the time in question.
- Instrument to person and/or victim—this can also be determined by trace evidence found at the scene, and also on the person or victim, and is proven to have come from the person(s) in question. Further investigation will determine if the person(s) was/were at the scene at the time in question.

Connecting the trace evidence to the person(s), scene(s), and instrument(s), together with additional direct and circumstantial evidence will develop a picture of the incident under investigation. Following this evidence may eliminate persons, scenes, and instruments from any involvement in the incident, as well.

Fatal Incident and Medical History

As has been noted, a fatal incident may be attributable to the medical history of the decedent. Careful and thorough investigation may reveal medical history that was neglected, such as failing to follow medical directives for therapy or medication (i.e., non-compliant diabetic), an acute event without any history (i.e., transient ischemic attack [TIA] or mini-stroke, without history), or a chronic history with unintended or unexpected consequences (i.e., acute cardiac event with known and treated/compliant history). Such medical conditions and events are common and may contribute to death or injury due to a consequential motor, bicycle or walking accident, fall, or other traumatic event.

Medical history is, in part, regulated by the Health Insurance Portability and Accountability Act *(HIPAA, not HIPPA, often improperly referred to as the Health Insurance Privacy and Portability Act)*, under the Code of Federal Regulations [CFR] 164.502 et seq. Generally, health records (protected health information [PHI]) can only be released for specific reasons. For our purposes, coroner and medical examiner offices are exempt and may be disclosed to without a release. Law enforcement is not always under the same exemption with limitations, and private sector investigators have no exemption so a HIPAA compliant release is required. Finally, these records cannot be disclosed or distributed to a third party. The coroner obtains records from the primary care physician (PCP) but cannot further disseminate them—not to the family, law enforcement, another physician, an insurance company, or the prosecutor's office—no redistribution or dissemination, period. Any person or entity, including the private investigator, must obtain the record from the custodian of the original record, under the authority of the properly drafted and executed release.

In all death or personal injury investigations, the following information must be determined from investigation and review of the reports and records:

1. Document when, where, and by whom decedent was last known to be alive.

   As previously noted, the body is a scene, with the location of death being a scene and the location of the underlying incident being a scene. This may encompass two scenes (body and incident/death scene) or multiple scenes (body, disposal site, scene of death, and scene of initial assault, as well as mode of transporting the body). All persons who had contact with the decedent or instruments recording the decedent's whereabouts are important. Additional direct and circumstantial evidence may assist in determining the time and location of the incident, events, and death, as well as those involved.
2. Who, when, and how the body was discovered.

   Persons reporting the incident and discovery of the body may be involved, know who is involved, or have no involvement or additional information. It is important to review all relevant records and reports and then interview these persons. All too often brief statements, oral and/or written, given by involved persons may be lacking in detail, partially true, or mostly to completely false—a proper interview will complete this information.
3. Medical incidents, complaints, injuries, and symptoms prior to death are important to a complete death investigation, particularly in determining if a natural event may have contributed to the incident or not. As previously detailed, it is important to obtain all relevant medical records, EMS records, medical history, current medications,

drug use, alcohol use, tobacco use, family medical history, and other information assisting with the investigation.

4. Social history is essentially the non-medical background of the person. Mental health is considered social history but may also be found under medical treatment (i.e., a psychiatrist is a MD) or similar (i.e., a psychologist is a PhD, counselor, or therapist). These are protected under HIPAA and may include medical history. Social history includes past suicidal ideation and attempts, alcohol and other drug use/abuse (prescription, over-the-counter, and illicit). Particular attention should be paid to proper dispensing and use of prescription medication—abuse is illegal but easily hidden. Other social history includes marital status, education history, employment history, and both familial and social relationships.

Time of Death

Determining the *exact* time of death (TOD) is really no mystery because it is often undetermined. This is because unless there is a recording (video or audio) or witness or the perpetrator confesses, there is only a *time frame of death* or *postmortem interval* (PMI). Postmortem interval is that time between death and discovery. All other determinations are approximate based upon all available direct and circumstantial evidence, as well as assessment of the body and information from the autopsy, if performed.

Law enforcement (and prosecutors) and criminal defense are often concerned with TOD/PMI—the former as an element of the crime and the latter to refute said element of the crime. (The TOD/PMI in criminal cases may implicate or exclude a suspect.) This determination may also be important in determining how a crime or incident occurred, insurance benefits, and hereditary issues. Determining TOD/PMI is not as easy as portrayed in television, movies, or even mystery novels. The TOD/PMI is based upon the totality of the evidence determined in the incident circumstances, scene investigation, physical signs, body assessment, and all other available data.

History of Decedent

Medical History

In all death investigations it is important, imperative, that medical records, including mental health records, be provided or obtained. The federal HIPAA law oversees the retention and dissemination of medical records, as well as state law and provider policy (these policies cannot be contrary to law). It is important to know and understand that HIPAA provides that the custodian of the record is the only disseminator of that record. The decedent's medical chart at his PCP's office is available only from that office. If his or her PCP provided that record to the medical examiner, prosecuting attorney, or insurance company, the PCP cannot provide that record to a third party. Rules of evidence, civil procedure, and criminal procedure may provide limited disclosure exceptions that will be advised by the attorney-client.

Additionally, it is important to know what records are typically maintained, what is provided upon request to specific entities, as well as what records are used in official investigations, such as by the medical examiner. Typically the history and physical (H&P) of the decedent, list of prescription medications, laboratory tests, and other items are the most requested and necessary. An expert in medical records analysis is recommended for complex medical issues. This may include a forensic pathologist, trauma surgeon or other medical specialist, operating nurse, or nurse practitioner.

Social History

As previously provided, social history of the decedent is important. This may overlap the medical history component—such as being a smoker and having lung cancer, or being hospitalized for mental health evaluation or personal safety.

Common social history includes

- Marital status and family members (this includes their personal relationships and statuses)
- Education and employment status and history
- Address history, particularly if recently moved or planning to move
- Mental health history, including family history (particularly in suicides)
- Use of alcohol and other drugs, including prescription and illicit drugs, or illicit prescription drug use (including medical marijuana and natural supplements)
- Use of tobacco or cessation programs
- Sexuality and preference—were there any latent sexual relationships or fetishes? This is particular to suicides and autoerotic deaths
- Historical or recent episodes of depression, suicidal ideation, or suicide attempts

The who, what, when, where, why, and how are important to answer the following:

- Who did they consume alcohol and/or use drugs with, or was it alone?
- What type of alcohol and/or drugs (including prescription or illicit) did they prefer and why? As an example, a common myth is that

vodka has no taste or smell and is therefore thought to best conceal chronic alcohol consumption.

- When did they most often consume alcohol and/or use drugs (time of day, day of week, particular events, etc.)?
- Where did they most often consume alcohol and/or use drugs? At home, at friends', at a local bar, or at other places?
- Why did they consume alcohol and/or use drugs? Were they celebrating, shy, sad, depressed, liked the activity, to relax, or to get some pep?
- How did they present their alcohol and/or drug use? Were they open or secretive? Also, how did they obtain their alcohol and/or drugs? This is particularly important if there was concealment of otherwise legitimate use (chronic alcoholism) or illicit use (illicit drug use or illegal alcohol consumption by a minor).

Forensic Autopsy*

For simplicity, all references will be to medical examiners and forensic pathologists, not on the difference between the medical examiner and coroner systems, or a hospital autopsy and forensic autopsy. For our purposes, the focus will be on the forensic autopsy conducted by a board-certified forensic pathologist and autopsy technician. In addition, there are exceptions to every protocol, and jurisdictional policies will differ. Two important things to consider are:

- The medical examiner's office is an independent, often law enforcement based, agency that is supposed to be neutral as to their findings; they conduct separate investigations. For this reason they are available to the criminal defense team, both parties to civil litigation, and are often overlooked by many.
- These investigations are often concurrent and cooperative investigations between the medical examiner's office and the law enforcement agency.

Mechanisms of Death and Injury Causation

The Mechanism of Death is the physical reason for a death (i.e., head trauma induced brain swelling that caused decreased brain function that caused the heart and/or lungs to stop functioning). In addition to determining the

* Adapted from "Reviewing and Comprehending Autopsy Reports," Dean A. Beers, CLI, 2010—adapted to *Practical Methods for Legal Investigations: Concepts and Protocols in Civil and Criminal Cases* (CRC Press, Boca Raton, FL, 2011).

Cause and Manner of Death, also the Mechanism of Death as applicable, autopsies and the final report can also clarify a cause of action for both civil and criminal cases. Factors and considerations in determining the mechanism of death and injury causation include alcohol and other drugs used by a surviving driver, exceeding therapeutic levels of prescriptions medications, non-compliant use of therapeutic medication, medical malpractice, and other often overlooked but actionable negligence. An example is a person with epilepsy who did not comply with the prescription directives that resulted in a seizure and a collision, thereby causing serious bodily injury or death to him and/or others.

Gunshot Wounds

A common gunshot wound autopsy is to the head and is ruled a suicide. With the recommended reports and records in hand, next consider the toxicology and condition of the organs. Drug abuse affects the heart and other organs and can support a reported history of illicit drug abuse. Although not directly associated with the act of suicide, it may be relevant to the history of suicidal ideation. Could the decedent have been too intoxicated to cause a self-inflicted gunshot wound and was instead "assisted" by an associate with a resulting finding of homicide? The ruling of suicide is based upon evidence supporting suicide and the absence of evidence supporting the possibility of an accident or homicide. If there was evidence suggesting the possibility of another finding, it should instead be ruled undetermined. The first question is: What factors contributed to suicidal ideation?

Let's consider a suicide due to a terminal disease process. In the investigation, prescription medications would be expected and toxicology levels must be considered. Next we look at the terminal disease process that affects the weight and condition of the affected organs. The forensic pathologist will consider the information of how the body was found and the type of wound. Was it contact, close contact, or greater distance; was the angle appropriate? At autopsy the weapon is also examined for blowback and to determine if there is a contact wound (i.e., appropriate muzzle imprint to the scalp). The specifics of the wound are also examined and reported—entrance, pathway, trajectory, exit, and evidence of the projectile. Notations are made of muzzle discharge tattooing, stellate wound of the scalp, and beveling of the skull at the entrance and exit sites. Measurements and trajectory information will be detailed in the report. This information is compared to the ancillary reports, records, and scene investigation to reach a conclusion. Similar examinations are considered in ligature strangulations, stabbings, motor vehicle accidents, etc. As detailed in this chapter, the expertise in analyzing each type of gunshot includes specific criteria—skin burns with tattooing or stippling, wounds with stellate and non-stellate patterns, angle and trajectory, etc. The analysis of the empirical wound data is the underlying knowledge necessary to knowing what criteria to expect and to confirm the existence of those criteria. The absence of an expected result (i.e., no stellate wound in a reported contact is contradicting) is cause to closely investigate the case.

Motor Vehicle Incidents

Not all motor vehicle "accidents" are such—they are collisions, which may have been accidental or deliberate (i.e., staged accident for insurance fraud gone bad). The dynamics of a motor vehicle collision on the vehicle, occupants, items in the vehicle, and the scene are complex and very dependent upon physics and the totality of the circumstances. For our purposes there are criteria to look for in the autopsy report. One area is the trauma to internal organs, such as being lacerated (tear due to blunt force impact—not an incision), macerated (multiple lacerations resulting in smaller pieces), or transected (perforating laceration resulting in divided organ or other body part), etc. Multiple occupants, surviving and deceased, will have different injuries dependent upon where they were in the vehicle relative to the point of impact and speed, and if they were restrained or hit by other objects. A common task is determining or verifying who was driving. Often complicating this is if any or all of the occupants were ejected or left the scene. Another consideration is multiple impacts, determined by the location and types of injuries, to the decedent as a result of a multivehicle collision. Which injury(ies), and corresponding impact, caused the death?

One of the most common injury classifications is summarized on the death certificate as "multiple blunt force injuries," which is detailed in the autopsy report. What elements help determine who the driver was, if the occupants were restrained, and other contributing factors? Was this an accident, was it staged, or was it suicide? A single decedent (or injured person) at the scene is not prima facie evidence of him or her being the driver; it may be presumptive. People have walked away from a scene, both deliberately and in a semi-conscious state. People have intentionally driven off of roadsides or into stationary and solid obstacles. A medical condition that may have preceded and contributed to the collision should be considered. With these, did the collision cause the death or was the death caused by the natural event? In one case, a person exited the interstate and then shot herself in the head with a small caliber pistol, which was ejected from her rolled vehicle. This appeared to be an accident but was determined at autopsy to be a suicide.* The time of death can be important for hereditary and insurance purposes of survivorship, also associated civil or criminal action.

* *The Pueblo Chieftain* (January 31, 2007).

The ruling of a natural death will include examination of the organs and toxicology. The ruling of a suicide will be primarily dependent on the investigation as a whole. As most motor vehicle–related deaths are ruled accident, the primary issues become the drivers and passengers, time of death and nature of the injuries. Sudden impact and associated forces cause the body to continue in its original direction of travel, or if stationary, with the direction of impact. Sudden deceleration can cause both internal and external injuries. Intra-abdominal injuries are secondary to blunt force trauma, such as organ shearing and detachment or organ crushing, and finally rupture of hollow organs due to pressure. Internal injuries, such as to long bones (arms and legs), can be determined by external examination, particularly compound and exposed fractures. External injuries to look for include abrasions and lacerations to exposed skin and similar injuries to clothed skin with corresponding damage to the clothing. Other external injuries, including the absence of, are dicing injuries from impacting the windshield or side window. This indicates possibly unrestrained occupants. For front seat occupants, left-side injuries indicate the driver and right-side injuries indicate the passenger. Additional pattern injuries include impressions from the seatbelt across the chest—left shoulder to right abdomen indicates driver, and right shoulder to left abdomen indicates passenger.

Evidence collected may include hair from the windshield or airbag fibers from the decedent's face and clothing. Shoe impressions from an occupant, which can be matched to the brake, clutch, or gas pedals are also indicative of both who was driving and what actions were taken approximate to and during impact. Other injuries will correspond to the type of collision, occupant position, and even expected injuries from certain types and models of vehicles.

Pedestrian Incidents

When a pedestrian (including a bicyclist) is struck and killed by a motorist, it is often classified as a motor vehicle-pedestrian accident. The assumption is often that the driver is at fault, but circumstances of the investigation might conclude otherwise. An example of a pedestrian at fault accident would be an intoxicated pedestrian, or a wheelchair-bound person crossing a major thoroughfare, outside of the crosswalk and without the aid of reflectors or street lighting. In another example a pedestrian is crossing a dark street and obeying all laws. He has an acute cardiac event and collapses and is struck by a vehicle turning the corner because the driver could not see him. Initially, is the death the result of the heart attack or impact of the vehicle? Let's assume the driver was intoxicated and the question becomes: Absent the subsequent impact by the vehicle, would the decedent have died at the scene? In all of these examples, the autopsy determines the events causing death and the underlying investigation determines fault/no fault. This is a classic example of how an incident may take on two separate but cooperative investigations of responsibility—a surviving driver (law enforcement) and the deceased pedestrian (medical examiner's office).

Of primary concern to the private investigator is the nature of the injuries. Common injuries include hyperextension of the torso, broken long bones, soft tissue and head injuries, abrasions and lacerations, and various injuries to the extremities. These will tell us if the decedent was facing to or away from the vehicle, walking or pedaling, crouching or lying down, etc. These injuries will also be able to tell us if the vehicle braked, accelerated, or decelerated prior to, at the time of, or after the impact. Although these deaths are predominantly ruled as accidents, criminal charges of vehicular homicide or a civil action for wrongful death can be very dependent on the autopsy findings.

Workplace Incidents

Accidents occurring in the workplace take on a new aspect of investigation, similar to aircraft and amusement park deaths. Every aspect of litigation could be involved, and as with all civil claims, contributing negligence is always a factor. The autopsy may determine the mechanism of death, such as a fan blade separating from the shaft and impaling the decedent. The investigation and autopsy reveal this death was an accident, but the incident and related causation (the blade and shaft separation) are not specifically addressed. Also consider a construction worker who falls and is impaled on a pile of metal debris or building material. Several questions, answerable at autopsy, come to mind. These include the possibility of a natural event, such as an acute cardiac event causing him to fall. Was he deceased before or after the fall? Was death caused by the impalement? The issue of appropriate harnessing, restraint, and material storage, although very relevant and part of the death investigation, may not be relevant at autopsy.

As with motor vehicle collisions, the nature of the injuries, also the sequence of events will assist with the autopsy and may also be answered at autopsy. The findings may bring to issue if this is a workers' compensation claim, and may indicate other insurance and survivor implications.

Wrongful Death

The issue of a wrongful death claim, including consequential to criminal homicide, can be dependent on many factors often addressed at autopsy. An example would be the O.J. Simpson and the Brown and Goldman families' civil wrongful death action after a criminal not guilty verdict. These include intoxication of the decedent, health history (acute event or chronic history), debilitating or restrictive factors (aforementioned epileptic driver who was non-compliant with medications), and activity at death such as leaving the danger zone or acting in self-defense (turning away from the attack or protecting their face or vital organs), surprise attack, mutual combat, etc. These types of deaths can be supported by a separate law enforcement investigation, and all autopsied deaths are supported by the autopsy findings. The nature of the injuries, contributing natural disease processes, levels of intoxication, proper restraint, etc., are all issues that should be noted for both support of the wrongful death claim, as the plaintiff, or comparative negligence, as both the plaintiff and defense. All wrongful death claims originate from the more specific event causing the underlying incident. It is important to look at the specifics of the autopsy and supporting investigation.

Negligence and Personal Injury

Most causes of death can be the foundation of a civil action claim, which is covered in more detail in the appropriate subcategories of this chapter. The most common, and obvious, purpose of the autopsy report is a wrongful death action. This is followed by being the foundation of negligence or personal injury actions. The latter should be conducted in the same manner as a death investigation, sans the death and benefit of an autopsy. If you are familiar with death investigation and autopsy protocol, a personal injury or negligence investigation will seem very familiar. Autopsy reports will have detailed and important information requiring further investigation and documentation to support your claim. As an example, if the decedent was the causing factor, such as being an intoxicated driver who paralyzed a pedestrian, but was killed in the resulting collision.

Drug and Alcohol Overdoses

Overdoses, dependent on circumstances and levels of intoxication, can be any manner of death, excluding natural. Examples include homicide (i.e., intentional poisoning of another), suicide (acetaminophen overdose), accident (acute ethanol poisoning), or undetermined. A common example of a natural death due to alcohol is cirrhosis of the liver, a natural disease process onset by alcoholism. An acute alcoholic event is not natural; it may be ruled accident or other manner due to the nature of the specific event causing death. These deaths can be combined with motor vehicle collisions, workplace accidents, and other injuries such as self-inflicted wounds and head injuries from a fall. Evidence found on the body (fresh needle marks, cone of foam at the nose and mouth which is often indicative of opiate overdose) and evidence found at the scene (syringes, illicit drug paraphernalia, prescription medication bottles, and receipts, etc.) are important and are often noted in the autopsy report.

The two important factors are the underlying investigation and toxicology results. With the autopsy report should be a reference to the therapeutic level, or non-fatal level of any positive results (marijuana is not quantified). One important consideration is the combination of alcohol and drugs, mixed over-the-counter and/or illicit drugs, and illicit drugs mixed with prescription or over-the-counter medications. Drug- and alcohol-related deaths may have non-fatal levels of individual drugs, which when combined become toxic, especially mixed narcotic drugs. This is often recorded on the death certificate as multi-drug toxicity, with the manner of death determined by the investigation and circumstances of death. The autopsy may also reveal if the person was deceased at the scene, was moved, or died while being transported to a hospital. The first concern is the time of death and the related circumstances. It is important to consult with a forensic toxicologist to formulate a timeline and effects of the drug(s) on the body during the perimortem period.

Determine the Cause and Manner of Death

The following is a fictional account based upon a somewhat nonfictional presentation. It is "Internet lore"—the story is fictional, but it was presented at a conference to demonstrate several key points. Over the years, all the names and dates have been changed. Their origin is not important to the story or your conclusion.

On March 23, 1994, the medical examiner viewed the body of Ronald Opus and concluded that he died from a shotgun wound to the head. Mr. Opus had jumped from the top of a ten-story building intending to commit suicide. He left a note to the effect indicating his despondency. As he fell past the ninth floor, his life was interrupted by a shotgun blast passing through a window, which killed him instantly.

Neither the shooter nor the deceased was aware that a safety net had been installed just below the eighth-floor level to protect some building workers and that Ronald Opus would not have been able to complete his suicide the way he had planned.

The room on the ninth floor, where the shotgun blast emanated, was occupied by an elderly man and his wife. They were arguing vigorously and he was threatening her with a shotgun! The man was so upset that when he pulled the trigger, he completely missed his wife, and the pellets went through the window, striking Mr. Opus.

When one intends to kill subject A but kills subject B in the attempt, one is guilty of the murder of subject B.

When confronted with the murder charge, the old man and his wife were both adamant, and both said that they thought the shotgun was not loaded. The old man said it was a long-standing habit to threaten his wife with the unloaded shotgun. He had no intention to murder her. Therefore the killing of Mr. Opus appeared to be an accident; that is, assuming the gun had been accidentally loaded.

The continuing investigation turned up a witness who saw the old couple's son loading the shotgun about 6 weeks prior to the fatal accident. It transpired that the old lady had cut off her son's financial support, and the son, knowing the propensity of his father to use the shotgun threateningly, loaded the gun with the expectation that his father would shoot his mother.

Because the loader of the gun was aware of this, he was guilty of the murder even though he didn't actually pull the trigger. The case now becomes one of murder on the part of the son for the death of Ronald Opus.

Now comes the exquisite twist.

Further investigation revealed that the son was, in fact, Ronald Opus. He had become increasingly despondent over the failure of his attempt to engineer his mother's murder. This led him to jump off the ten-story building on March 23, only to be killed by a shotgun blast passing through the ninth-story window.

- What is your conclusion based on this information?
- Articulate how you reached this conclusion.
- Is your decision based upon the medical definition or legal definition?
- What information would change to another Manner of Death?

It is said that the presenter, a forensic pathologist sharing this story at a large national conference of fellow professionals, offered this finding: The son, Ronald Opus, had actually murdered himself—suicide.

Following a methodical investigative protocol will uncover the information, facts, and evidence necessary to present to the interested party. Because of the impact to the families and judicial system, the findings of a death investigation are significant. As the conclusion of the death investigation is reliant upon understanding the cause and manner of death, knowing the definitions and elements at the onset of the investigative process is paramount. This story is similar to assisted suicide, in which the manner of death would appropriately be homicide, as the decedent did not put into play those actions causing their own death. Mentioned earlier in this chapter are these definitions and elements. After reviewing these and your own investigative process, consider your initial determination. Is there any change or further consideration?

- Accident (fall, automobile, industrial, etc.) is a death other than natural, where there is no evidence of intent: an unintentional event or category of chain of events. Many forms of apparent accidental deaths may instead be suicide or homicide, or possibly undetermined. These deaths should be particularly closely investigated due to possibly accidental death insurance double indemnity clauses.
- Homicide (death is caused by another person) is a death resulting from intentional harm (explicit or implicit) of one person by another, or by grossly reckless behavior. In death investigation, homicide is the medical determination.
- Suicide (death is caused by the decedent) is a death as a purposeful action set in motion (explicit or implicit) to end one's life. Suicide is a ruling that is to the exclusion of all other MODs and is presumptive to the decedent having not committed suicide. In reviewing the four elements to suicide, it is clear that this death cannot be ruled as a suicide. These are
  1. Intent to commit the act knowing that it may result in their death
  2. Knowledge of the instrument used and that it may cause death
  3. History of attempts, ideation, or documentation of evidence supporting suicide
  4. Evidence of contributing factors to the act

Stephen Cina, MD, a renowned forensic pathologist and consultant to this author, has offered the following opinion and explanation:

> It is important to remember that the Manner of Death determined by a medical examiner may be at odds with a legal definition. Medical Examiners must use a construct of Vital Statistics Departments to classify all deaths as Homicide, Suicide, Accident, Natural, or Undetermined in manner. By convention, most deaths involving drunk driving are classified as Accident, although the impaired driver may be charged with vehicular homicide if he kills someone. If the police shoot a person involved in a violent crime who is pointing a gun at them, the manner is ruled Homicide though no wrongdoing has taken place. In the case detailed below, Mr. Opus died of a shotgun wound to the head. This shotgun was willingly fired by a person other than Mr. Opus and the weapon's discharge resulted in death. For this reason, I would deem the manner of death Homicide in this case. Some would argue that Accident

is more appropriate in that the shooter did not know the weapon was loaded. I would not choose Suicide as there is no indication that Mr. Opus attempted to shoot himself.*

Of course this investigative process would be more than a story, so think of the story as a summary of the investigative process. The investigation would have had to determine several different factors to change the finding of homicide in this death. If you consider only the four rules of firearm safety, this will help determine accident from another manner. These are as follows:

1. *Always* keep the gun pointed in a safe direction.†
   This is the primary rule of gun safety. A safe direction means that the gun is pointed so that even if it were to go off it would not cause injury or damage. The key to this rule is to control where the muzzle or front end of the barrel is pointed at all times. Common sense dictates the safest direction, depending on different circumstances.
2. *Always* keep your finger off the trigger until ready to shoot.‡
   When holding a gun, rest your finger on the trigger guard or along the side of the gun. Until you are actually ready to fire, do not touch the trigger.
3. *Always* keep the gun unloaded until ready to use.§
   Whenever you pick up a gun, immediately engage the safety device if possible, and if the gun has a magazine, remove it before opening the action and looking into the chamber(s) which should be clear of ammunition. If you do not know how to open the action or inspect the chamber(s), leave the gun alone and get help from someone who does.
4. *Always* be sure of your target and what is beyond.
   This rule is intended to eliminate or minimize damage to non-targets when a firearm is intentionally discharged. Unintended damage may occur if a non-target is misidentified as a target, if the target is missed, or if the bullet hits something or someone other than the intended target.

The investigative process, as presented, has eliminated the natural category of death. It has also eliminated suicide—there was no intent by

* Stephen J. Cina, MD (www.AutopsyReview.net).
† National Rifle Association, Education and Training (http://www.nrahq.org/education/guide.asp).
‡ Ibid.
§ Ibid.

the victim to end his life because he did not have control of the firearm. Although he intended to commit suicide by the act of jumping from the building, his intent was interrupted by the act of another. As to that act, the investigative process has also eliminated accident—the shooter pointed a firearm he thought was unloaded at a potential victim, but he did not check the firearm himself and he was not certain of his target or beyond. He intentionally pulled the trigger and caused the firearm to discharge. Therefore, it is homicide. By legal definition, perhaps it was criminal involuntary manslaughter and civil negligent or wrongful death. He unintentionally caused the death of another person by an intentional act of his own negligence.

In Conclusion

During the course of this chapter, the investigator has been exposed to death investigation and the multiple disciplines and phases involved. This chapter has revealed how the private investigator will view death and even non-death cases "with one's own eyes." Death and personal injury investigations are forensic specialties. Death investigation is finding the evidence, analyzing the evidence, and reporting the evidence—evidentiary fact finders, a very important component of death investigations.

Deaths fall into two primary categories: natural and other. Natural deaths, as later explained, have a medical history and/or diagnosis. Other deaths may be the result of accident, homicide, or suicide, and can even be undetermined. There has been an outside contributory event causing the death. The private investigator will typically be involved in criminal defense or civil plaintiff cases, or possibly in the civil defense or insurance investigation role.

Death investigation is complex, and the investigator must anticipate the questions of the family, attorney, and trier-of-fact. Physicians and paramedics treat injuries, law enforcement investigates crime, families mourn, and attorneys litigate. Private investigators, particularly in death investigations, are evidentiary fact finders.

In death investigation you are speaking for the decedent—and the decedent has a lot to say. To summarize Voltaire, we owe respect to the family—to the dead we owe the truth.

Terrorism Investigations 10

DOUGLAS K. HAAS

Terrorism Defined

Terrorism is not a new phenomenon. Its use as a tactic dates back to AD 56 with a Zealot group fighting the Romans culminating with the Zealots' mass suicide at the fabled Fortress at Masada.

Its modern day adherents have taken on many forms, making it difficult to come up with a definition that suits all needs for governments and law enforcement entities. For the purpose of this chapter, two definitions will be used: one originated by the Federal Bureau of Investigation (FBI) as found in the U.S. Code of Federal Regulations and the other used by academicians who had studied terrorism years before it became national phenomena after the September 11, 2001, attacks on New York, Washington, and Pennsylvania.

Terrorism as defined by the FBI:

> The unlawful use or threatened use of force or violence by a group or individual based and operating entirely within the United States or Puerto Rico without foreign direction committed against persons or property to intimidate or coerce a government, the civilian population or any segment thereof in furtherance of political or social objectives.
>
> International terrorism involves violent acts or acts dangerous to human life that are a violation of the criminal laws of the United States or any state or that would be a criminal violation if committed within the jurisdiction of the United States or any State.
>
> These acts appear to be intended to intimidate or coerce a civilian population, influence the policy of a government by intimidating or coercion or affect the conduct of a government by assassination or kidnapping.
>
> International terrorist acts occur outside the United States or transcend national boundaries in terms of the means by which they are accomplished, the person they appear intended to coerce or intimidate, or the locale in which their perpetrators operate or seek asylum.

Common definition:

> Terrorism is the threat or use of force to bring about change. The change is political in nature. Terrorism is a **TACTIC** used to bring about that political change.

The first definition used by the FBI and some states is used in the belief that terrorists violate criminal statutes to foment their violent acts; therefore, they should be prosecuted under those statutes.

The second definition recognizes that terrorists, although violent, view their activities as political in nature and therefore justifiable in their viewpoint of warfare. One man's terrorist is another man's freedom fighter.

These are important distinctions if the investigator is dealing with a client who has been arrested for terrorist-related charges. Most people accused of terrorism do not view themselves as murderers or common criminals. They view themselves as soldiers and oftentimes martyrs to a cause.

Types of Terrorism

State-Sponsored Terrorism

State-sponsored terrorism includes terrorist acts generated by a host state against targets outside that state using surrogate terrorists or their own trained operatives. An example of this would be the Libyan president using his agents to bomb a Pan Am flight over the skies of Lockerbie, Scotland. Iran has been accused of sponsoring terrorism against Israel using surrogates such as Hezbollah.

Violent Global Jihadists

There are a number of Jihadist groups around the world. The primary one is al Qaida which was responsible for the 9/11 attacks on the United States. The problem in combating al Qaida is that it is a stateless organization that resides in several countries around the world. In some countries it is welcomed and in others it is not. Cells can be found in the Pacific region and the Middle East.

Their goal is to bring about the return of the Caliphate so Islam can rule the world.

Domestic Terrorists

Domestic terrorists are individuals or groups operating within the borders of the United States or Puerto Rico without the direction from a foreign nation. These groups are often referred to as extremist groups. The most common are

1. *ALF.* Animal Liberation Front
2. *ELF.* Earth Liberation Front

These two groups mostly target businesses, governmental facilities, research centers, and universities. They have made some threats against some scientists and college professors.

3. *White supremacist.* These groups are composed mostly of individuals who believe that white Anglo-Saxon descendants are superior. Historically they have targeted Negroes and people of the Jewish faith. They consider Jews to be evil and that they must be exterminated. Most of these organizations historically felt that they must live separate from Negroes but hold a special hatred for Jews and people of mixed races being married.

   Because of aggressive infiltration and prosecution by law enforcement, these groups splintered to smaller groups to prevent infiltration. Some cells are as small as two people and are encouraged to act on their own against those they consider to be the enemy. The appearance of a group called *Phineas Priests* is an example of this. These people are violently against the mixing of the races (miscegenation) and have been responsible for several attacks in the United States.

   Some American militia groups have also been accused of extremist activity.
4. *Anti-abortion.* These groups consist of people who are mostly peaceful. They advocate a stop to abortion on demand and will picket abortion clinics. Historically, there have been fringe members who feel it justifiable to bomb abortion clinics and even murder doctors. Law enforcement has had problems stopping these fringe elements because the bombers or shooters usually act alone or in concert with one or two others.
5. *Identity movements.* Caucasians (AKA white supremacists) and African Americans. The African American identity movement, sometimes called Black Nationalist, supports African superiority and a hatred for Jews. Their goals are similar to white supremacists except for their racial identity.
6. *Lone wolf problem.* Fringe followers who do not join groups but act alone on propaganda learned from larger groups.
7. *Some tax protesters*

Government Approach to Terrorism

The government has settled on two different approaches to combat the terrorism problem. Both models are hotly debated in the halls of government and have even been a topic in recent presidential races.

One method is to treat terrorism as a law enforcement problem utilizing criminal statutes to prosecute terrorists. This philosophy brings into play all the tools used by law enforcement reminiscent in our country's "war on drugs." Proponents of this philosophy believe that terrorists use criminal activity to carry out their missions; therefore, those activities (i.e., murder, bombing, extortion) expose them to criminal prosecution.

The other method is treating terrorism as a military problem, utilizing the nation's military to fight, capture, or kill terrorists, then turning detained individuals over to military holding facilities for the duration of the conflict or prosecuting them in military tribunals.

Neither system is perfect. From a private investigator's perspective, the law enforcement approach makes the investigator's job much easier. Once the terrorist is turned over to civil authorities by the military or is arrested by government agents, that terrorist is afforded all the rights and privileges of any other accused. The rules of evidence and protections guaranteed by the constitution apply. It affords the PI many more avenues of investigation which are not available in the military model.

In the military model, just gaining access to your client can be difficult. Security clearances have to be granted to the investigator and lawyer so that critical evidence can be reviewed. Visiting the client in a military holding facility is restricted, and clients detained in these facilities are often hostile to their defense team.

Today the private investigator will probably be involved in a criminal trial held in a U.S. Federal District Court. If the investigator decides to become part of the defense team in a terrorism case, he or she must prepare for certain realities.

Your presence in the case is not going to be viewed positively by the prosecution or law enforcement agents involved in the trial. The negative feeling concerning your involvement goes far beyond normal animosity between prosecution and defense team members. The memory of 9/11, violence, and anti-American activity are felt as a direct assault on the country. The prosecution team views themselves as the tip of the spear against terrorism, and your presence on the defense team is often viewed as traitorous. This is even more pronounced if the investigator is a former law enforcement officer or agent. The fact that a person is guaranteed certain rights does not mitigate the hard feelings caused by your presence.

If an investigator chooses to become part of a defense team, he or she can expect activities by the government that are foreign to them in other criminal trials. They can expect to have wiretaps put on their phones, and they will have their integrity tested.

Attempts to test the investigator's ethics can also be expected. This can include attempts by law enforcement to have a witness approach the investigator and offer to lie to the federal authorities on the client's behalf. Not properly handled by the investigator, this could lead to charges of obstruction of justice.

The investigator must understand that the government is not being mean spirited or has thrown out the rule book, the government just is not sure of your loyalties as a U.S. citizen. Your past history as a military veteran, a law enforcement officer, or a patriot is forgotten. All they see is that you are defending a person who has been accused of terrorism.

Government Tactics

The government is relying on an old standby strategy used in the war on drugs: the reverse sting. This method has been very successful in the past and will continue to be successful in the future. It is seen as a way to gather intelligence and allow the government to become proactive in terrorism investigations.

An informant or government agent lets it be known in a certain community that he or she has access to weapons or is willing to engage in certain terrorist activities. People will contact this individual and sign on for whatever activity is being offered. This has been successful in some Islamic extremist cases, where individuals from a mosque, who have been radicalized, reach out to someone who seems to have an answer for their grievances.

The informants and individuals will get involved in a conspiracy to perform certain terrorist activities. Unknown to the individuals, their activity is being monitored by the government. The major question for the government is how long they let the conspiracy unfold before they make an arrest. The question for them is do they have all the like-minded people in their sights or are there others who have just not come forward. These investigations can take several years to unfold and always produce big media headlines for the government.

From a defense standpoint, these cases present an abundance of opportunities for a good defense team to exploit. There are always mountains of electronic monitoring evidence as well as paper trail evidence to review. The initial informant is oftentimes an unsavory individual and questions of entrapment come into play. Entrapment is usually a key factor in a successful defense.

Entrapment

In criminal law entrapment is defined as conduct by law enforcement officials or their agent inducing a person to commit an offense that the person would otherwise have been unlikely to commit.

An investigator should note that there is no entrapment when a defendant is ready and willing to break the law and all the government agents are doing is providing an opportunity for the person to commit the crime.

From a civil libertarian point of view, use of the reverse sting strategy of law enforcement causes much concern. The initial meeting between the government operative and defendant is not always monitored by the informant's handlers or the initial conversations are not electronically captured. Investigators do not always know what verbal exchanges are made between the defendant and operative. This can cause a problem because the operative is often motivated by money and may say anything to obtain the cooperation of the defendant.

If the investigator can develop information that the operative *enticed* the defendant to commit a crime, it will go a long way in proving a case of entrapment.

Once the identity of the informant is disclosed, a private investigator should establish the operative's motive for cooperation. Is the cooperation motivated by money, lighter sentence for a crime, helping someone else, or patriotism? This goes a long way in establishing credibility.

Criminal Activity by Terrorist

A South American terrorist by the name of Carlos Maranguilla wrote a book titled *The Mini Manual for the Urban Guerilla*. It is a how-to manual on starting a revolution, as well as on raising money, choosing arms to use, and choosing who to kill. It was widely used by all extremist terrorist groups in the 1960s through the 1990s. Most left-wing communist leaning groups used the manual. White supremacist groups in America used a book titled *The Turner Diaries* as their how-to manual on how to start and fund a revolution in America. Both books promote criminal activity as a way of funding their activities. They promote bank robbery, armor car robbery, extortion, and kidnapping as funding sources.

A white supremacist group called Aryan Nations (The Brotherhood) used *The Turner Diaries* to outline their attempt to start a revolution in America. They robbed several armored cars, stealing well over $1 million, to fund their cause. It is little wonder that some law enforcement officials believe that the way to combat terrorism is through traditional law enforcement tactics.

One can hardly argue with that approach; however, terrorists have in recent years become motivated not by politics but by religion. They view their cause as a holy war. Most of their funding comes from donations. The law enforcement tactic comes into play after they have committed a terrorist act. This is one reason the government has focused so much effort on the reverse sting, because it is designed to stop the terrorist act before it is completed.

See the case study at the end of this chapter for a journalist's report on a trial in South Florida concerning the arrest of several men accused of terrorism.

ALF/ELF

This group is motivated by their feeling that the earth and its resources are being exploited by corporations. The ALF (Animal Liberation Front) is concerned with the testing and treatment of animals, especially in research. The ELF (Earth Liberation Front) concerns itself with the damage caused to the environment by pollution, development, and industry. The government has had trouble infiltrating these organizations because their operating cells are small, usually three people or less. They act on their own and report their activities on Web sites. They are responsible for bombings, arsons, and the "liberation" of animals from university research labs. The ALF has been responsible for breaking into testing facilities at universities and releasing test animals that have been infected with diseases. They have also harassed and threatened researchers and doctors. Most ELF activity has centered on arson and vandalism.

Islamic Terrorism

Terms defining this form of activity have not been finalized. Politics and political correctness have interfered with our national need to neatly pigeonhole definitions of the problem. Terrorists of the Islamic faith have decided to commit terrorist acts to bring about two different changes.

Extremist terrorists of the Sunni Sect of Muslims, belonging to a group called al Qaida, attacked New York City twice, the Pentagon, and a plane over Pennsylvania. They were Saudi Arabian nationals. Their goal is to force the United States to change its foreign policy with Israel and have the United States stay out of the Middle East. They want to set up a worldwide Caliphate to bring on the coming of the 12th Imam. They do not view themselves as criminals but as soldiers in a holy cause. They have spread around the globe.

The Shi'a Sect of Muslim has its own brand of terrorists. These groups are represented in groups such as Hezbollah and Hamas. They are sponsored by Iran and also Syria. Like the Sunni extremist they want the United States out of the region and the abolition of Israel. Their other goal is to rule the region. They are responsible for killing many Americans, but not on American soil.

Your Client

The private investigator must remember that he or she is there to represent the client. That said, the investigator has to take some things into consideration. If the client is being charged with a criminal offense, he or she is facing a lengthy prison sentence and possibly the death penalty.

You must remember that the client does not think he or she is a criminal but a soldier in a cause. In the case of an Islamic terrorist, who believes in Shariah Law, it is permissible to lie, cheat, steal, and even kill a nonbeliever. Lying to the investigator is not unheard of. The investigator must become well prepared by researching all available data concerning the client's beliefs and organizations. This will prepare the investigator in dealing with the client.

A private investigator working cases involving terrorism must utilize all the skills highlighted in this book. He or she must sharpen interview skills plus constantly be alert for any enticements that may land him or her in trouble with the government. The investigator must be well read and up to speed on the vast knowledge base that is available on terrorists and their causes as well as organizational fund raising and propagation of the extremist's message.

Suggested Reading

1. Prior to the events of 9/11 there was little academic study concerning terrorism. Prior to that event the world leader in research concerning terrorism was Jonah Alexander, professor at SUNY Ithaca in New York State. He published a journal called *Studies in Conflict and Terrorism*. Every investigator interested in becoming well read on the topic of terrorism should seek these volumes. Currently the journal is being published by Taylor & Francis and can be found online. It is strongly suggested that anything written by Jonah Alexander become part of the investigator's library.
2. *The Silent Brotherhood: Inside America's Racist Underground* by Kevin Flynn and Gary Gerhart (Free Press, New York, 1989). Insights into the mind-set of the white supremacist, it conveys the strategy of one of the most violent and active organizations of its kind.
3. *The Turner Diaries* by Andrew Macdonald, National Vanguard Press, 1978. This is the white supremacist bible on how to start a revolution in the United States. It is dated but still used by militant groups in the United States.
4. *Mini-Manual of the Urban Guerrilla* by Carlos Marighella. This is a book used by Central and South American extremist groups which teaches tactics on how to set up a terrorist organization—how to train, how to raise funds, and whom to target. It is still used today but is considered by some to be outdated. Its principles, however, are still being adhered to.

5. "Shariah: The threat to America. An Exercise Competitive Analysis," Report of Team II (shariahthethreat.org). This provides an analysis of the introduction of Shariah law into the West. It will give the investigator insights into the thinking of the client who is a Muslim.
6. *Triple Cross* by Peter Lance (William Morrow, New York, 2006). Presents insights into the use of informants and government shortsightedness in dealing with Islamic terrorists planning attacks on the U.S. homeland.
7. *The Looming Tower* by Lawrence Wright (Random House, New York, 2006). Provides insight into missed opportunities in preventing the 9/11 attacks. Serves as a resource on how the government prosecuted the war on terror.
8. *1000 Years for Revenge* by Peter Lance (HarperCollins, New York, 2003). Provides a historical perspective on Muslim terrorism.

Case Study: Terrorism Investigation

Have Terror, Will Travel: How Two FBI Mercenaries Cashed in on the Liberty City Seven Terrorism Case

Bob Norman
The New Times, November 22, 2007

One extorted $7,000 from a friend who raped his girlfriend and then, after accepting the money, beat her up and went to jail.

The other failed an FBI polygraph test while working on an undercover investigation, which one former FBI agent says should have disqualified him from ever working for the government again. Oh, and he was also once charged with roughing up a woman.

And these are supposed to be the good guys.

All of America has heard about the bizarre Liberty City Seven terrorism trial now winding down at the federal courthouse in Miami. It began with the arrest of seven members of an obscure religious sect in June of last year. At a nationally televised news conference, then-U.S. Attorney Alberto Gonzalez told the country that the dirt-poor black defendants were prepared to "wage a full ground war on the United States."

It made for a sensational sound bite—and a temporary diversion for the administration, a moment of seeming victory in the War on Terror, a fleeting quiet place in the growing public clamor about illegal wiretaps and the growing disaster in Iraq. But FBI brass was a bit more realistic. They cautioned that the ineffectual group was "more inspirational than operational." Today, that even seems a bit overstated. Forget about America; this was a ragtag group that couldn't wage a ground war on a jar of peppercorns.

The question at the heart of the farce: Was the group's leader, Narseal "Brother Naz" Batiste, really bent on destroying the Sears Tower in Chicago, or was he just trying to beat a couple of government informants posing as al Qaeda operatives out of $50,000?

Al-Saidi

The jury will try to answer that question (and if it chooses guilty, the defendants could be sentenced to 70 years in prison each). But what of those two informants? Who were these guys who posed as al Qaeda Jihadi, who acted as America's frontmen in a terror investigation that is now known around the world? What motivated them?

The answer to that question is painfully obvious, and it's the same thing that Batiste says was motivating him: cold cash.

Precious little has been revealed publicly about the informants. Even the jury has been deprived of crucial information about the two informants, thanks in large part to questionable decisions by U.S. District Judge Joan Lenard, who has squelched attempts by the defense to expose the informants' ignominious histories to the jury.

That has led to almost tangible frustration for the defense, including veteran Fort Lauderdale private investigator Rory McMahon, who was hired by Seven attorney Albert Levin to dig up information on the government operatives.

"If I was one of the lawyers, I'd be in jail for contempt right now," says McMahon, a former federal probation officer. "I would be ranting and raving. It's like the judge is saying, 'They're terrorists, so let's throw out the rulebook.'"

A look at what the jury doesn't know—much of which McMahon uncovered—paints a dubious picture of the government's frontmen, beginning with Abbasal-Saidi, a 22-year-old Yemeni operative at the heart of the case. By his own account in court, al-Saidi, who moved to Brooklyn with his family when he was 9 years old, began snitching on drug dealers to the New York Police Department when he was 16.

Although he told the jury that he became an informant to do "good," all narcs have ties to the drug world. Otherwise, they couldn't be narcs. And al-Saidi has been charged at least twice with marijuana possession and admitted on the stand that he smoked pot while participating in the Liberty City Seven investigation.

But al-Saidi didn't just inform on drug dealers he didn't like; he also got involved in terrorism investigations. While he was still a teenager, the NYPD put him up in an apartment and paid him $40 a day for the work.

In 2003, he moved to Bridgeport, Connecticut, with his family, where he met a red-haired teen named Stephanie, who would become his long-term girlfriend. They moved into an apartment together in Harlem, where a close friend and business partner of al-Saidi's raped her (which is why I'm not giving her last name). In a move that showed how eager al-Saidi could be to make money by subverting the justice system, he extorted the rapist. In exchange for $7,000 from the friend, he had Stephanie drop the rape charge.

In late 2004, they used the money to move to Miami Beach, where he promptly beat her up. The argument that led to the battery charge began when Stephanie happened upon al-Saidi's wedding picture. Unknown to her, he had married another woman during one of his frequent trips to Yemen (he now has a daughter). He was jailed on the battery charge on November 14 and, unable to make bail, was still sitting in jail five weeks later. Desperate, he called his old benefactor, the NYPD, which put him in touch with the FBI. Special Agent John Velazquez, who would work the Liberty City case, visited him in jail and helped secure his release.

Armed with a federal contact, al-Saidi first told the FBI about "Brother Naz" and his compatriots in September 2005. He met the group at a convenience store where he worked. Al-Saidi told the bureau that Batiste believed he was in al Qaeda and that he believed they might be terrorists. The FBI hired al-Saidi, gave him a recording device, and ultimately paid him some $40,000 for his "work."

Before the trial, al-Saidi flew from Yemen on the FBI's dime to testify. Once here, the FBI had to arrest him and bond him out of jail on a bench warrant for a traffic charge. The government paid his tickets.

"They helped me out," al-Saidi testified last month in his new government-purchased suit.

During his testimony, attorney Levin managed to get some of al-Saidi's unsavory past on the record. The lawyer managed to get in some questions about the $7,000 extortion in the rape case, prompting al-Saidi to admit it.

"I didn't receive not one dollar," al-Saidi testified on the stand. "[Stephanie] got that money, and two weeks later, I was here in Miami locked up because of her and she's gone with everything I had, including that money."

Not only did al-Saidi contradict himself about whose money it was but he also mentioned his battery arrest, which Lenard had barred the defense from bringing up. The following exchange ensued:

Levin: You were locked up because of her?

Al-Saidi: Yes, sir.

Levin: So you take no responsibility with regard to your arrest in connection with her?

Al-Saidi: I did take responsibility. And I did serve time. And I think, yes, I was wrong for standing there to argue with her...

Levin: So [Stephanie] received $7,000... so she would not show up to court, having been raped... in the apartment that you, sir, shared with her. Isn't that true, sir?

Prosecutor: Judge, I would object to the relevance of all of this.

Judge Lenard: Sustained.

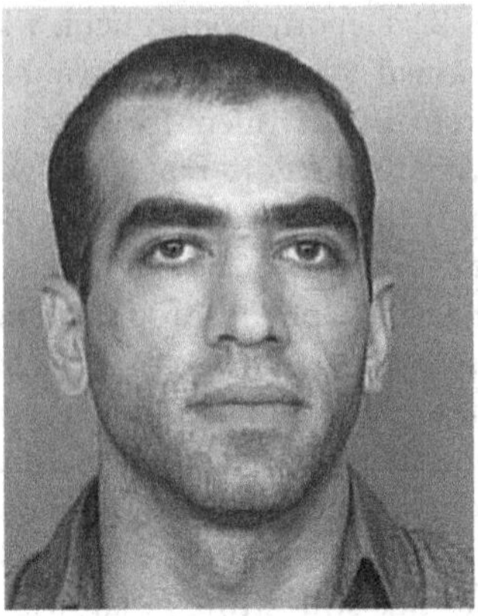

Assad

So it went. Lenard has seemed intent throughout the trial to keep the jury in the dark about the nature of the government informants. And it got worse. The most damning revelation about the second informant, a Lebanese immigrant named Elie Assad, was barred from the jury altogether.

Agents flew Assad, who sometimes uses the last name Montana for the character he idolizes from *Scarface*, to Miami from Mexico to pose as an al Qaeda operative. The feds ultimately paid the career informant $80,000 for his efforts, but former FBI agent James Wedick, who was hired as an expert witness by the defense, says Assad never should have been authorized to work on the case at all.

Why? Because Assad, who like al-Saidi has a domestic battery charge on his record, had failed a polygraph test administered by his FBI handlers while working on a previous case in Chicago. That seemingly crucial fact came out during a federal hearing on the case in July, when FBI agents admitted during the hearing that Assad had failed the lie detector test.

While the credibility of a confidential informant might seem relevant, Lenard barred any mention of the polygraph during the trial.

"What I found to be startling was the fact that the bureau had used an informant who had been found to be deceptive in a prior operation," says Wedick, who worked for the FBI in California for 35 years. "I'm just shocked, because it appears to me they violated attorney general's guidelines. The single most important factor when evaluating an informant's suitability is truthfulness."

Wedick says that once an informant is known to have lied, it "knocks him out of the park." And he suspects that the information was withheld when Assad was approved by FBI headquarters in Washington.

"If you fail a bureau polygraph as an agent, you lose security clearance; you're done," he says. "And they use Assad knowing him to be dishonest? You can't do it... I'm shocked that this issue hasn't developed into a full-blown donnybrook. We've got to live up to some standards, and if you use a guy that is a known liar, you've got rocks in your head."

And Wedick should know about FBI standards. He spent several years as head of the corruption unit in the Sacramento field office. When he retired, then-U.S. Attorney General John Ashcroft wrote a letter commending his career and noting that other agents should "emulate" his work.

But Judge Lenard didn't see any value in his expertise; she granted the prosecution's motion to bar Wedick from testifying. And she refused to allow any testimony about Assad's failed polygraph test.

Lenard, however, did allow the prosecution to call a neocon professor named Raymond Tanter to the stand. The former Reagan administration official and longtime right-wing think-tanker testified that the Liberty City defendants were dangerous terrorists who, in part because of their extreme poverty, had reached the "jihadization" stage.

Although Tanter never interviewed any of the defendants, he should know something about terrorists. After all, he has been busy promoting a terrorist organization called the MEK (Mujahedin-eKhalq) that is opposed to the Iranian government. As a founding member of the Iran Policy Committee, he has urged the Bush administration to remove the MEK from the terrorist list and back it for "regime change" in Iran.

For McMahon, Tanter personifies the political nature of the entire case. The case, he says, is a sham by the Bush administration and the FBI to fool the American public into believing they are "winning" the amorphous war on terror.

"The real sham here is being perpetrated by the government," he says.

That's his opinion. You have to wonder if Lenard has allowed the jury to hear enough of the truth about the two men who made the case to make a reasoned one of their own.

Liberty City Charade Ends with Injustice

Bob Norman
The New Times, May 14, 2009

Yesterday morning's headline on the top of the front page of the *Sun-Sentinel* was, "5 Guilty in Sears Tower Plot." This morning's lead headline is: "Desperation Turns Deadly Off Florida."

They are connected in a way, because both are about Haitians. The first is about the Liberty City defendants who have been entrapped and set up by lying informants and pressured feds and the second about ten Haitians drowning while trying to make it to America.

Patrick Abraham could have easily been on that boat. In his jail cell, the 26-year-old immigrant says he loves America and would never try to hurt it. But now he's a convicted Liberty City "terrorist" who will likely spend most of the rest of his life in prison.

That's one of the dirty little secrets about the Liberty City case. We always say the defendants are poor African-American men. More specifically, all but the leader of the group are poor *Haitian* men. And we all know about that terrible problem we have with Haitian terrorism in America, right?

Nobody seems to be in their corner as the government railroaded them into prison in one of the most absurd federal cases you'll ever see. You don't see Jesse Jackson or Al Sharpton stepping up to the plate on this one.

There never was any "Sears Tower Plot." Just a bunch of hot air.

Those five men never should have been found guilty. They were led along by two corrupt informants and an FBI unit that was hungry for a terrorism case to feed the Bush Justice Department, whether it was cooked up or not.

At the time of the arrest, since-disgraced former Attorney General Alberto Gonzales talked about the case as if he'd just personally saved the country from destruction. The FBI's John Pistole, however, conceded the group was more "aspirational than operational."

This is a case that during the past three years has gone from a joke to an injustice. And the failure of the press to expose it is astounding. I'm just about the only reporter in the country who dug into the pasts of the career informants who led the case for the FBI. The informants, one of whom extorted $7,000 from someone who raped his own girlfriend and the other who failed an FBI polygraph that should have disqualified him from the case, offered the group's leader, Narseal Batiste, money, big money, if he would pledge allegiance to al Qaeda and promise to commit terrorist acts. Batiste obviously said what he needed to say to get the money. He never acted on a thing.

And while we're on Batiste, it's important to say: If anyone could have possibly been found guilty in this farce, it was Batiste. He was the only one who did any talking. The others were just hanging around, silently.

The first two trials, because of these obvious problems, ended with hung juries, even though the government held all the cards and had an obviously sympathetic judge in Joan Lenard, who ruled in the prosecution's favor at nearly every point. She wouldn't let key evidence about the informants be heard by the juries or key witnesses for the defense take the stand. Basically, she obstructed the true narrative so that the truth was hidden behind the smoke and mirrors brought forth by the prosecution.

Private investigator Rory McMahon, who was working on behalf of Patrick Abraham, complained about the first trial in the *New Times*. To this day the former federal probation officer says it's the most ridiculous case he's ever seen. So what did Lenard do? Even though McMahon had broken no court rules, she conducted a mini-inquisition and then refused to authorize payment of $10,000 in work he'd done on Abraham's behalf for attorney Albert Levin.

That's right, in a trial that is supposed to be about preserving American ideals, a guy was basically fined $10,000 for exercising his basic right of free speech. And that's the great irony of this case: While supposedly trying to defend America, the government has violated the country's ideals and perpetrated a great injustice.

Even with the obviously biased Lenard at the helm, there were two hung juries. But Lenard and the U.S. Attorney's Office weren't going to be denied, no matter how many trials and how much money it cost taxpayers to prosecute this sham. In this last trial, it seems the fix was in.

First, one of the three black jurors on the jury came down ill. Why? Was it because he was getting browbeaten in deliberations? We don't know. But Lenard sent in an alternate, a Hispanic woman, and ordered the other jurors to "wipe your minds clean." Then one of the remaining two black jurors, Juror No. 4, said she too had become ill because of pressure exerted on her by other jurors. Obviously, she wouldn't go along with a guilty verdict and believed the defendants were innocent. She'd made up her mind. Other jurors complained that she didn't "trust the law."

Yeah, looking at this sham case, what right-minded person would?

Lenard should have found which way the juror had decided and then, if it indicated a hung jury, ordered a mistrial. Instead she gave a speech about the juror had abrogated her duty as an American and replaced her with somebody else.

Where was the *Miami Herald* and *Sun-Sentinel* in all this? AWOL, completely AWOL. Sure, Jay Weaver covered the play-by-play and offered up valuable details, but neither newspaper ever revealed the truth about the government's informants or properly exposed this charade. It was typical "balanced" he said-she said bullshit. Neither newspaper mentioned Lenard's extraordinary fining of McMahon for criticizing her in public. Instead both sat idly by and watched the train wreck unfold, occasionally offering a description or two about how it was progressing.

Insurance and Arson Investigation 11

Insurance

What Is Insurance?

Insurance is a service that combines the risks of individuals into a group using funds contributed by members of the group to pay for losses. The essence of the insurance concept is that it is a device that involves the accumulation of funds. It also involves a group of risks that each member of the group transfers to the entire group.

Purpose of Insurance

The fundamental purpose of insurance is to reduce the uncertainty caused by potential loss. This is accomplished by spreading the economic burden of losses among members of the group. Insurance does not prevent the loss from happening, but it relieves victims of the financial burden created by the loss.

What Do Insurers Do?

Insurers estimate the possible size of a loss, estimate the probability of a loss, spread the risk by pooling, accumulate funds to pay for losses, retain only what they can bear, reinsure what they cannot bear, and refuse to assume risks for inadequate premiums.

How Insurance Works

Risk Assumption

Insurance is created by an insurer who assumes financial risks transferred to the insurer by their insured members. Most insurance contracts are expressed in terms of money, although some indemnify those insured by providing services (e.g., a life insurance contract obligates the insurer to pay a specified amount upon the death of the insured).

A liability policy requires the insurer not only to pay money on behalf of the insured but also to provide the legal and investigative services needed when the event insured against occurs.

Health insurance policies require medical and hospital services for the insured when he or she is sick or injured. Whether the insurer meets its obligation with money or services, the burden the insurer assumes is financial.

Risk

Why is the insurer better able to assume a financial risk than the insured? The fundamental difference between the insurer and insured lies in predicting future events. You must predict what will happen to you as an individual, but the insurer makes predictions with regard to all insured clients as a part of large groups of risk. Therefore, the insurer can make more accurate predictions with regard to possible risks. The reason for this difference lies in the concept of pooling. By pooling its risks, the insurer is able to improve its predictions. This, in turn, results in smaller deviations from expectations. Pooling changes the nature of the risks and improves predictability.

An insurer assumes risks with the expectation of substituting average losses for actual losses, thereby reducing uncertainty for the insured. Because the funds that are used to pay for losses suffered by the insured are collected in advance, it is critical that the insurer be able to predict losses accurately. The premium fee for assuming risks is based on accurate predictions, and the predictions are based on probable estimates.

Probability

A person who says that there is a great or little chance that something will or will not happen is thinking in terms of probability. Probability is a measure of the chance of an occurrence. When there is no possibility of an occurrence, the probability is zero. When an occurrence is certain to take place, the probability is one. Probability may be expressed as a fraction or as a percentage. If there are two possible outcomes, each of which is probable, the probability is one out of two, or 50%. The numerator is the number of favorable or unfavorable happenings, while the denominator is the number of all possibilities.

Deductive and Inductive Reasoning

Estimates of probability may be made through deductive or inductive reasoning or a combination of both methods. The deductive approach involves determining all factors that can influence the outcome and using logical reasoning to arrive at an estimate of the actual outcome. When the number of possible outcomes is known, the probability of any one is one minus the sum of the probability of all others.

Sometimes it is impossible to calculate every factor that will determine an outcome. In that case, the deductive process will be unreliable. When this happens, probability estimates of outcomes must be made through the inductive process. The inductive process involves observing what has actually happened in the past and assuming (predicting) that the same will happen in the future if the same conditions prevail.

The Law of Large Numbers

The law of large numbers states that the greater the number of trials, the more nearly the experience will approximate the underlying true probability. If we flip a coin for an indefinite length of time, the distribution of heads and tails will approach 50% as the number of trials increases. In other words, actual results tend to equal expected (probable) results as the number of independent events increases.

Insurance companies are affected by the law of large numbers in two ways. In order for accurate estimates of the probability of an occurrence to be made, insurance companies must consider very large numbers of cases. After an estimate of probability is made, it can be used as the basis for predicting future experiences.

Investigators should be familiar with the term "credibility," which indicates the degree of reliability that can be placed on the use of past experience to predict what will happen in the future.

Adverse Selection

Adverse selection is the tendency of people who have a greater probability of loss than the average to seek insurance. It can result in much greater losses for the insurer, and insurers try to prevent this by screening applicants.

Ideal Requirements for Insurability

The ideal risks for the insurance company would be as follows. The potential loss would be significant, but the probability would not be high, making insurance economically feasible. The probability of loss would be predictable. There would be a large number of similar exposure units. Losses that occur would be fortuitous (a matter of chance). Losses would be definite in time and place. A catastrophe would not occur.

Reinsurance

Reinsurance is an agreement by which an insurance company transfers all or a portion of its risks under a contract to another insurance company. This protects the insurance company from all or part of the losses of its policyholders. In this process, the company transferring the risk is called the "ceding company," and the insurance company assuming the risk is the "reinsurer." When there is a claim on the policy, the reinsurer is liable to the ceding company, not the insured. The amount the reinsurer is willing to assume is called its retention.

The main reason for reinsurance is that the ceding company wants to protect itself against losses in individual cases beyond a specific sum. Reinsurance is significant to the buyer for three reasons. First, reinsurance spreads the risks and increases the financial stability of the insurers. Reinsurance reduces the costs of the buyer and seller by being able to place the policy through another company. It helps small insurance companies stay in business, thereby increasing competition in the industry. Without reinsurance, small companies would find it much more difficult to compete with large companies.

Insurance Contracts

The process of transferring a risk to an insurance company is commonly referred to as buying insurance. In effect, the insured buys a promise from the insurer. The written agreement between the two parties is called a policy or policy contract. The policy states in detail the legal rights and duties of the parties to the contract.

Basic Legal Principles

Indemnity

Indemnity is when the insurer agrees to pay for no more than the actual loss suffered by the insured. The purpose of the indemnity concept is to restore the insured to the same economic position that he or she had prior to the loss but not to improve that position.

Insurable Interest

If the occurrence of risks such as fire or auto collision will cause loss to a person or firm that is the subject of a risk, an insurable interest exists. Examples of insurable interests include ownership of property; the mortgage holder of property, building, or auto; a secured creditor; a tenant with a long-term lease; and your own life or the life of another (based on relationship or other financial consideration).

Subrogation

This is a contract right that gives the insurance company claim against third parties as a result of a loss for which the insurer paid. The actual cash value of a loss equals replacement cost less depreciation. When the insurer is considering accepting a risk, accurate information is critical to make a good decision. The person who makes the decision about insurability is called an underwriter, and the decision-making process is known as underwriting.

Warranties

Absolutely true statements made by the insured to the insurer about the risk are warranties. Based on warranties, the insurance company may make a favorable decision to insure the risk. Once the warranties are put into a contract, they have to be strictly true, not approximately true. This places the burden of absolute accuracy on the insured.

Representations

Representations are statements made by the insured for the purpose of inducing the insurer to enter into the contract. If the insured misrepresents a material fact, the insurer can void the contract or refuse to pay a later claim.

Concealment

Concealment occurs when an applicant for insurance fails to reveal material facts about the risk which only he or she knows. The insurer cannot be held to the contract if the insured concealed important and material information.

Waiver

Waiver is the intentional giving up of a known right. In order to waive a right, the person must first know and understand that he or she has the right and then must give it up intentionally.

Estoppels

Estoppels prevent a person from alleging or denying a fact when he or she has previously admitted the contrary. For example, an insurance company cannot waive a right and then assert it later. Once an agent waives the right to refuse coverage to the applicant, that company is estopped from denying liability for losses that occur while the contract is in force.

Requirements of Insurance Contracts

The relationship between the insurer and the insured is spelled out in the insurance policy. The policy is a contract between two parties. A contract is an agreement enforceable by civil law. If an agreement is to be considered a valid and enforceable contract, it must have a legal purpose. There must be an offer and acceptance, which are essential to the creation of an agreement. An agreement is reached when one party makes an offer and the other party accepts.

Another requirement is consideration. The premium payment that the insured makes and the insurer's promise to pay losses are the consideration of the contract.

The final essential element for a contract is that the parties must be competent. Examples of incompetent parties would be insane or intoxicated persons or someone under legal age.

A contract is therefore an agreement between two or more competent parties, supported by a consideration and having for its purpose a legal objective.

Components of the Insurance Contract

- A statement is a declaration that the insured makes to identify him- or herself. Statements also give information about the risk and the premium.
- A binder is a temporary contract to provide coverage until the policy is issued by the agent or company.
- The period of coverage is the period of time during which coverage applies.
- A named peril policy provides protection against loss caused by the perils listed.
- An all-risk policy provides protection against loss except loss caused by the excluded perils. The policy names the proximate cause (i.e., the actual cause of the loss). It also names exclusions. In order to know what the policy covers, you must know what it does not cover. This includes the excluded perils, excluded property, and excluded losses. Generally, whether the policy is all-risk or named peril, the coverage it provides cannot be determined without first examining the exclusions.
- Conditions describe the duties of the parties to the contract. Failure of one party to perform relieves the other party of its obligation.
- Riders and endorsements are two terms with the same meaning. Riders are used with life and health policies, and endorsements are used with property and liability policies. These articles make a change in the contract to which they are attached. They may increase or decrease the coverage, change the premium, make a correction, or make any number of other changes.

Negligence

Every form of personal, business, or professional activity is exposed to loss because of liability claims based on negligence. If a negligent act or omission interferes with the rights of any individual, the party responsible for the negligence is liable for the damages to the injured party. To meet the legal consequences of all these exposures, liability insurance has become essential.

During recent years, great losses from fraudulent claims have resulted from alleged injuries. An invasion of the legal rights of others is the legal basis for liability claims. Legal rights impose responsibilities and obligations, such as not invading privacy or property or not creating an unreasonable risk or actual harm to others.

The invasion of such legal rights is a legal wrong. A wrong may be criminal (public) and may be an injury involving the public at large and punishable by the government. A wrong may also be civil (private) and may be based upon the concept of a tort. This is a wrong independent of contract (e.g., assault, fraud, libel, and slander). It may also be based on a contract and may involve legal wrongs when implied warranties are involved or contract obligations are breached.

The government takes action with respect to crimes, but civil injuries are remedied by court action instituted by the injured party. In a civil suit, the remedy is usually the award of monetary damages to the injured party. Liability insurance focuses on civil wrongs and, in particular, on torts. Of greater importance to the investigator are torts based on negligence (intentional acts or omissions).

Requirements for Negligence Liability

Negligence is the failure to exercise the proper degree of care required by circumstances. Requirements for negligence liability include a legal duty, a wrong, a proximate relationship between the wrong and the injury, an injury or damage, and foreseeability. Four forms of negligence are contributory negligence, comparative negligence, presumed negligence, and imputed negligence.

Comparative Negligence

Anyone who was so negligent in an act as to contribute to his or her own injuries or damage cannot recover losses from another party for these injuries. Comparative negligence modifies the common law doctrine of contributory negligence, because only a very slight degree of negligence on the part of the injured person would bar recovery. A majority of the states have now passed statutes stating that contributory negligence shall not bar recovery for damages. However, damages will be reduced by the court in proportion to the amount of negligence attributed to the person injured.

Presumed Negligence

In order to establish a case, the claimant must show a failure to exercise reasonable care. This is known as presumed negligence. The burden of proof is on the claimant. In certain cases, presumed negligence may be assumed from the facts. The legal doctrine that applies, *res ipsa loquitur* (the thing speaks for itself), establishes a prima facie case of negligence. This doctrine operates when an accident causes an injury if the instrument would not normally cause injury without negligence, especially if inspection and use of the instrument is within exclusive control of the party to be held liable, or if the party to be held liable has superior knowledge of the cause of the accident, and the injured party is unable to prove negligence. In the case of presumed negligence, there cannot be contributory negligence, and the accident must be of such a nature that injury would not ordinarily occur without negligence.

Imputed Negligence

Not only is a person responsible for his or her own acts, but he or she may be held liable for the acts of others (e.g., employers and supervisors, landlords, parents, and auto owners). This is called imputed negligence. Vicarious liability includes those liability situations when the responsible person is not present.

Insurance Adjusting

Loss Payment

The basic function of insurance adjusting is loss payment. There are five types of insurance adjusters. Agents settle small losses and help in many other losses depending on the type of insurance. Staff adjusters are full-time salaried employees of the insurer and are active in fields such as automobile losses. Independent adjusters represent various insurers on some losses. Adjustment bureaus regularly represent many insurers and are especially useful in situations involving fire, wind, and storm damages. Public adjusters are hired by the insured to settle difficult claims.

Liability Insurance Clauses

The adjustment of liability claims differs from the adjustment of direct damage claims in that the claimant is not the insured. A liability claim carries with it a basic element of conflict with respect to the claim, because one person has caused someone else either property damages or personal injury. The extent of a claim for damage to property is measured by the amount of loss to the property owner. Most persons insure their homes, autos, or other property before insuring their life and health.

Types of Insurance

Individual Health Insurance

Health insurance applies to those forms of insurance that provide protection against the financial impact of illness or injury. Health insurance has as its purpose the payment of benefits for loss of income and expenses arising from illness and injury. Not only is loss of time from the productive enterprise a source of loss to the insured, but the cost of care and necessary medical attention adds to the amount of the loss.

Health insurance provides protection against loss of time or earning power and added medical expense. Health insurance losses fall into two major categories: cost of medical care and loss of income.

An exception in a health insurance policy is a provision where coverage for a specified hazard is eliminated.

Fire Insurance

The purpose of fire insurance is to indemnify a named insured in the event that certain described property is destroyed by the peril of fire. The basic parts of the standard fire policy are the declaration statement as to the parties, period, property, perils, and premiums of the contract. The insuring agreement (the heart of the contract) includes exceptions and termination, property and location, personal nature, actual cash value, perils insured against (proximate losses caused by hostile fires and lightning), and assignments. The conditions and exclusions explain the control terms as to concealment or fraud, excluded property and peril suspension, added provisions and cancellations, and loss provisions (including mortgage, interest, the pro rata liability clause notice, and proof of loss, appraisal, repair, and subrogation rights).

Insurable Interest

The element of insurable interest makes a fire contract a contract of indemnity. When the nature of an interest or a liability in regard to property is such that the insured would suffer financially if a loss occurs, then insurable interest exists.

Perils Insured Against

The standard fire contract is a named perils or specified perils contract. It covers only the listed perils in the contract. The perils are "fire, lightning, and by removal from the premises articles endangered by the perils insured against in this policy." The courts have defined fire as "oxidation which is so rapid as to produce either a flame or a glow. Fire is always caused by combustion, but combustion does not always cause fire."

Excluded Perils

Excluded perils include hostile or war-like actions; insurrections, rebellion, revolution, civil war, or action by government authority in defense of such occurrences; theft; and neglect to prevent further damage by the insured.

Direct Loss

The insuring agreement specifies that to be covered under a policy, a loss must be a direct loss. This has been interpreted by the court to mean that fire must be the immediate or proximate cause of the loss as opposed to the remote cause.

Examples of losses included in the direct or proximate categories are loss or damage caused by smoke or heat from a hostile fire, damage by water or other materials used to extinguish the fire, damage caused by the firefighters, and unavoidable exposure at or following the fire. The proximate cause is held to be the efficient cause—that is, the cause that sets intervening agencies into motion.

Assignment

The transfer of the legal right of interest in an insurance contract to another person is called "assignment." Under the terms of the fire insurance contract, an assignment is valid only with the written consent of the insurer.

Misrepresentation

The entire policy will be void if either before or after a loss the insured willfully conceals or misrepresents any material facts or circumstances concerning the fire insurance, the property insured, or its interest, or in the case of any fraud by the insured. False statements, concealment of salvage, falsification of records, false testimony given under oath, and false written proofs of loss are also fraud and will void the policy. Certain types of property are excluded from coverage of the policy, such as accounts, bills, currency, deeds, evidence of death, money, or securities, unless specified in writing in the policy.

General Liability Insurance

There are two basic types of general liability insurance: bodily injury, sickness, or disease, and property damage (the physical injury or destruction of tangible property).

The insured's duties in the event of occurrence, claim, or suit are a combination of the three requirements for notice of accident (in writing, as soon as possible, explaining the circumstances), assistance, and the cooperation of the insured (for settlement, in hearings and trials, etc.).

The treatment of a patient by a medical practitioner (i.e., surgeon, physician, or dentist) with a lack of care or professional skill and with injurious results constitutes malpractice. Liability for personal injury in such instances is known as professional malpractice liability. Professional liability insurance has been extended into fields to cover losses where monetary damages (as opposed to bodily injury) are a consequence of the negligent professional services of the insured. Architects, accountants, attorneys, insurance brokers, real estate agents, stock brokers, consultants, private investigators, and many others can be held liable for their professional errors or mistakes.

Employer's Liability and Worker's Compensation

Worker's Compensation is a combination of social and private insurance. Worker's Compensation laws in all states require employers to provide certain benefits for occupational injuries and diseases. The statutory requirements in most states can be fulfilled by the employer purchasing Worker's Compensation insurance from a private insurer or by qualifying as a self-insurer.

Occupational disability because of work injuries is a peril of great importance to business and society. The solution to the financial burden of disability because of employment is a dual one: Many of the state government's requirements for Worker's Compensation insurance are met by insurance contracts purchased from private insurers.

The theory behind Worker's Compensation legislation completely disregards the old idea of liability based on negligence. Rather, the theory is based upon the idea that the cost of occupational injuries and many diseases will be charged to the employer regardless of liability and then passed on to the consumer as part of the cost of doing business.

Worker's Compensation laws make the employer responsible for indemnity to the disabled employee without regard to the matter of fault or negligence. The amount of indemnity to apply in particular cases is predetermined by law, although it does not equal the full income the employee would have received. The laws relate payments to injuries and sickness; if these are fatal, death benefits are provided for the employee's dependents. Medical expenses, income, and rehabilitation benefits are included.

Based upon employee's rights, there are two types of Worker's Compensation laws: compulsory and elective. Almost all states (except three) are compulsory, which means that all employers to whom the laws apply are required to pay for work injuries or diseases as specified under the compensation statutes.

Compensation is provided for all injuries and many diseases arising out of and occurring in the course of employment. No benefits under compensation acts are allowed when it is proved that the injury was caused by the willful acts of the employee or by intoxication while on duty. Willful misconduct can be defined as any act or service performed by an employee who willfully disobeys all the safety rules of which he or she has full knowledge.

Occupational disability includes both injury and disease. Occupational diseases are defined as diseases peculiar to the occupation in which the employee is engaged and caused in excess of the ordinary hazards of employment. In the case of occupational disease, there must be a cause-and-effect relationship between the occupation and the disease as well as frequency and regularity of the occurrence of the disease in a particular occupation. The basic types of benefits include medical expenses, income benefits, death benefits, and rehabilitation benefits.

Financing of Benefits

The employer has the direct responsibility for paying benefits to qualified workers in accordance with Worker's Compensation laws. Insurance may be provided either through a state fund or by private insurers authorized by the particular state to conduct the business of Worker's Compensation. More than two million persons per year are hurt at work in the United States, according to the National Safety Council, which estimates annual compensation payments and production losses at $16 billion, including 240 million workdays in time lost annually.

In the majority of states, funding is regulated by the state but accomplished through nonstate insurance or self-insurance means. Regulation of the law is under the Division of Worker's Compensation of the Department of Labor and Employment Security. In the state of Florida, Statute 440.9 states that every employer shall be liable for and shall secure the payment to his or her employee of the compensation payable. Compensation shall be payable regardless of fault or cause for injury. The liability of an employer shall be exclusive and in place of all other liability of such employer to any third party and to the employee or legal representative thereof, and to anyone otherwise entitled to recover damages from such employer on account of injury or death.

Employer and Employees

The law describes an employer as one who must secure benefits for an employee at any level, including the state, political subdivision, public, and quasi-public corporation. Employment includes private employment with three or more employees and all other jobs without regard to the number of employees. An employee is defined as a person engaged in any employment under any appointment or contract of hire, including aliens and minors. The term "employee" does not include independent contractors, casual laborers, and volunteers.

Injuries Covered

Benefits are payable to any employee who suffers an injury. Injury is defined to be personal injury or death by accident arising out of and in the course of employment and such diseases or infection that result from such injury. Accident means any unexpected or unusual event or result that happens suddenly. It does not include mental or nervous injury owing to fright or excitement, or disability or death due to the accidental aggravation of a venereal disease or of a disease owing to the habitual use of alcohol or drugs. Occupational diseases are treated as injury by accident. An employee is not entitled to compensation if the injury is caused by the employee's intoxication or wrongful use of drugs or willful intention to injure or kill one's self or another.

Benefits

Benefits may include payment of medical expenses, compensation for disability, and death benefits. The obligation of the employer is to furnish any required medical treatment, care, and attendance under a qualified physician, nurse, or hospital. There is no dollar limitation upon this obligation. Disability means incapacity because of the injury to earn, in the same or any other employment, the wages that the employee was receiving at the time of the injury. Compensation is for such wage loss or difference. The measure used to determine disability benefits is the average weekly wage of the employee at the time of the injury.

The Occupational Safety and Health Act (OSHA)

Job safety for employees became the top Worker's Compensation issue with the passage of OSHA in 1970. The federal law took considerable control of work safety regulations from the state and mandated that the state must put into effect rules at least as strict as the federal standards in order to maintain jurisdiction for work safety conditions of its employees. The penalties that can be imposed (fines of $10,000 or more) and the investigative role of OSHA are extensive, including inspections by 1400 officers across the United States.

Automobile Insurance Coverage

Basic coverage for automobile insurance usually includes liability, medical payments, uninsured motorist coverage, and physical damage protection. Basic policy forms are standardized for insuring individuals and businesses. Automobiles are classified as private passenger, commercial, public, dealers, or miscellaneous.

Three viewpoints are relevant in determining the need for auto insurance. These include society, automobile motorists, and the injured victim of an auto accident. More than 87% of all traffic accidents are reported to involve improper driving. In fatal accidents, speeding is a factor in 33%, and intoxicated drivers are a factor in about 50%. Approximately 50% of all states have compulsory laws requiring insurance. All owners of cars are required to produce an insurance policy before registration and plates will be issued. In essence, this makes financial responsibility mandatory in order to own and use a car.

The basic parts of the personal auto policy (PAP) illustrate the readable contract trend with personalizing and simplifying the format. This includes declarations and contains basic data about insurance, automobiles, types of coverage, and the insuring agreement and definitions. Following are the six major parts of basic insurance policy coverage.

- *Part A: Liability*—This is the most important coverage and includes bodily injury and property damage in a single limit of liability; defense and supplementary payments for defense investigation and bonds; covered persons insured, which are carefully defined; and policy limits and other insurance conditions that are explained.
- *Part B: Medical payments*—This covers the cost of medical services for the named insured, relatives, and anyone else in the insured's car. This does not apply to pedestrians or occupants of buildings or other vehicles into which an insured vehicle may crash. This coverage is quite broad for all reasonable medical expenses, including surgical, dental, ambulance, hospital, nursing, as well as funeral expenses.
- *Part C: Uninsured motorists*—By definition, an uninsured automobile is not covered for bodily injury, liability, policy, or bond at the time of the accident. It also includes other cars for which no insurance applies, such as stolen or improperly registered autos. The insurance applies whether or not the injury caused by the uninsured motorist results from an occupied automobile. Many unowned autos are

operated by the named insured; therefore, only the named insured and relatives are covered.

- *Part D: Damage to your own auto*—This is physical damage coverage for your own car. Collision losses may be excluded if the collision peril is not shown in the declaration section as covered. Towing and labor costs may be included. The importance of physical damage insurance is related to the value of the car and to the need and ability of the owner to repair or replace the car if damaged.
  - *Collision coverage*—This reimburses you for damage to your car sustained by reason of a collision with another car or with any other object, movable or fixed. Collision is one of the most common situations in which subrogation may apply. When you collect your damages from the insurer, they take your right and sue the responsible party to recover the payment made to you. Collision insurance is a common illustration of the use of the deductible to avoid the high costs and administrative expenses of frequent small collisions and losses. The normal collision deductible provides there shall be no liability on the part of the insurer unless the loss exceeds the named amount (usually $50, $100, $250, up to $1000).
  - *Comprehensive coverage*—Comprehensive physical damage is virtually an all-risk physical damage coverage. Protection is provided for direct and accidental loss or damage to your car and its normal equipment. Basically, it is used to pay for a loss caused by something other than collision to the insured auto. Among the perils covered are fire, theft, larceny, wind, storm, earthquake, flood, vandalism, and so forth.
- *Part E: Conditions in order to collect under the contract*—These are the conditions that the insured must fulfill following an accident or loss. Failure to fulfill these conditions could result in the insurer not having to pay the loss. When an accident occurs, you must provide (written) notice to the insurer as soon as possible. You should give the insurer notice as to whether you were liable. You must comply with state requirements for reporting accidents. You should make a duplicate copy on any written reports and provide it to your insurer. You must provide assistance and cooperation to the insurer in the settlement or adjustment of a suit.
- *Part F: General provisions*—Cancellation provisions require the insurer to give the policyholder 10 days notice in writing, with a proportional return of the unearned premium to the end of the policy.

Assigned Risk

In addition to the basic financial responsibility law or the compulsory auto liability insurance law, assigned risk plans have been developed to meet the problems of rejected risks. Provisions have been made by the state for taking care of higher risk drivers by distributing individual rejected risks among all insurers. Assigned risks are rotated among the different insurers in proportion to the business that each insurer writes in the state.

No-Fault Insurance Plans

The fundamental basis for a no-fault system is that it abolishes tort liability in car accidents, with drivers or owners accepting responsibility for some or all of the losses sustained by pedestrians or by occupants of their own vehicle in return for immunity from liability for those losses. The need for establishing fault before loss payments are made is eliminated by such plans. The insured motorist has the right to collect directly from his own insurer. Vehicle damage liability does not come under most no-fault (more correctly called "payment without fault") laws.

Uninsured Motorist

Uninsured motorist (UM) coverage is a form of insurance to pay compensatory damages for bodily injuries under one's own policy for amounts that would otherwise have been recovered from the liability insurance of another—either an uninsured motorist or an underinsured motorist, one who carries liability limits that are lower than the insured's damage. Determination of damages may be decided through an agreement between the insured and the UM insurer, or by arbitration proceedings between the insured and the UM insurer. If the UM insurer refuses to arbitrate, then coverage will be determined by joint suit against the other party and the UM insurer.

The law permits the insurer to limit UM coverage in several ways. Ordinarily under some states' laws, the coverage provided for two or more vehicles may be added together to determine the limit of coverage available to an injured person in any one accident. This practice is called stacking. However, the company is permitted to issue an endorsement that provides that limits may not be stacked. In other words, two or more coverages may not be added together. If the insured agrees to this limitation and signs the endorsement, the company must issue the policy at a reduced premium.

The coverage available to a person injured while occupying a motor vehicle is the same as the coverage available to that motor vehicle.

An injured person is entitled to the highest limits of UM coverage that apply to any vehicle for which that person is a named insured or family member of an insured if that injured person is occupying a motor vehicle that he or she does not own or is not owned by a member of his or her family who resides in the same household. This coverage is in excess of coverage on the vehicle the injured person is occupying. Coverage applies to the named insured and family members in their own vehicles, any other vehicle, and as pedestrians. Other persons are covered only while occupying the named insured's vehicle. Under UM coverage, the injury must be caused by a vehicle that is not covered by liability insurance or liability insurance with a limit that is lower than the insured's damages. Additionally, coverage applies if the other party's liability insurer is broke or if the other vehicle is a hit-and-run and cannot be identified. Limits of coverage are offered the same way as auto liability coverage.

Automobile Insurance Claims

If someone commits a tort, negligence, liability, fraud, and so forth, he or she can be held responsible for damages in a court of law. There are three types of damages in auto accidents:

- Special damages are the out-of-pocket losses incurred by the insured party. They usually include such items as medical bills, lost wages, and property damage, as well as funeral expenses.
- General damages refer to real losses that cannot be measured and where no bill or receipt or loss of money can be demonstrated. Concepts of pain and suffering and loss of use come under this heading. The accident victim is compensated for the pain and suffering that he or she experienced or will continue to experience from the accident. Loss of use attempts to compensate for the loss of a body part or function.
- Punitive damages are designed to punish wrongdoers who intentionally engage in misconduct. Sometimes punitive damages are also awarded for gross negligence, which is negligence so horrible that it deserves punishment.

Plaintiffs usually hire attorneys on a contingency basis, which means they will pay the attorney a percentage of the amount of money the attorney collects on their behalf. There are costs such as paying court reporters for depositions and court filing fees. Clients are responsible for these costs regardless of who wins the lawsuit. Another expense is medical treatment and doctor testimony.

Liability Coverage Driving outside the standard of care required of operators of automobiles is considered careless driving. Negligence requires more than mere speeding. In order for negligence to arise, there must be some form of actual harm or damages that result directly from bad driving. If your negligent driving causes death or injury to another, you must pay monetary damages that result from the accident.

Medical Payments Two classes of people are entitled to receive benefits: the insured and family members of the insured in the same household, and any passenger injured in the covered auto.

Collision and Comprehensive Collision protection is subject to a deductible. Vehicles that are damaged or stolen may be covered in one of two ways to be decided by the insurance company. The insurance company may pay the amount necessary to repair the vehicle or replace the property lost, or it may pay the cash value of the stolen or damaged property (i.e., totaling the car). Collision coverage is not dependent on fault.

Your collision policy will pay benefits for vehicles you do not own.

Figure 11.1 is an example of an incident report for an auto accident.

Government Regulation of Insurance

Insurance has characteristics that set it apart from tangible goods industries and account for the special interest in government regulation. Insurance is a commodity that people pay for in advance, with benefits that are reaped in the future, often by someone entirely different than the insured. Insurance is affected by a complex agreement that few laypeople understand and by which the insurer could achieve a great and unfair advantage if inclined to do so.

Insurance costs are unknown at the time the premium is agreed to, and there exists a temptation for unregulated insurers to charge too little or too much. Charging too little results in removing the security that the insured thought was being purchased; charging too much results in unwarranted profits to the insurer. Insurance is regulated to control abuses in the industry. The insurer is the manager of the policyholder's funds. The management of other people's money, particularly by one of the largest industries in the nation, requires regulation because of the temptation to illegally use these funds.

As in any business, abuses of power and violations of public trust occur in the insurance industry. These include failure by the insurer to live up to contract provisions, drawing up contracts that are misleading and appear to offer benefits they really do not cover, refusal to pay legitimate claims, improper investment of policyholder's funds, false advertising, and many others. Some state insurance departments maintain offices to handle customer complaints against insurers and their agents and to effect settlement of disputes without formal court action. Most insured clients do not find it practical to sue under insurance contracts unless the sums involved are relatively large. Abuses in

MCMAHON & ASSOCIATES

INCIDENT REPORT – AUTO ACCIDENT pt.1 of 3: The Accident

Day:________ Date:___/___/___ Time:______am/pm Re Case #:________________

Occurred on road:________________ Lane: N S E W At intersection:________________

At block #:________ At Mile:______ At Exit #:______ Other identifier: Posted speed:____

At or near Address:

City: County: St: Zip: -

Total numbers: # Vehicles:______ # Injuries:______ # Deaths:______

Total $$ vehicle loss:____________ Total $$ external property damage:____________

Basic description of accident:

Miscellaneous Factors as Verified/Investigated from Official Reports:

Weather	Temp	Road Condition	Road Constr.	Road Defects	Main Causal Event		Causal Factors
o Clear	o Hot	o Dry	o Dirt	o None	o Blowout	o Main initial causal event was collision with fixed object or other object listed below.	o None
o Rain	o Cold	o Wet	o Gravel	o Pot holes	o Fire		o DUI
o Fog	o	o Standing Water	o Asphalt	o Bumps	o Explosion		o Police pursuit
o High Wind		o Running Water	o Tar & gravel	o Debris	o Aircraft		o Faulty traffic signal
o Storm		o Icy	o Concrete	o Construction	o Driver Error		o Driver disregard signal
o Snow		o Oil	o Other	o Bad Shoulder	o Jacknife		o Road defects
o Sleet		o Other		o Other			o Animal/Obstacle
Road Character		**Traffic Flow**	**Signals/Signs**	**Light/Visibility**	**Collisions**		o Pedestrian
o Straight		o One way	o None	o Daylight	o Pedestrian	o Utility Pole	o Driver lost control
o Curve		o Two way – no divider	o Light/Signal	o Dusk/Dawn	o Train	o Culvert	o Driver fell asleep
On:		o Two way – divided	o Stop or yield sign	o Dark w/lights	o Animal	o Ditch	o Driver illness
o Level		o Two way – barrier	o RR crossing	o Dark, no lights	o Parkd Vhcl	o Mailbox	o Driverless vehicle
o Grade			o Warning: ________		o Bridg Pilon	o Fence	o Violation listed below
o Hill Crest			o No Passing		o Guardrail	o Tree	o Weather
o Bridge			o Construction		o Sign		o Vehicle failure
					o Other:		o Other

V#	Driver	Citation	DUI	#Psngr	#Injrd	#DOA	File
							o
							o
							o
							o
							o
							o

Responding Personnel

Official:	Name:	Phone:	Case/File #:	Intvw	File
Fire Dept				___/___/___	o
"Police"				___/___/___	o
EMS				___/___/___	o
DOT				___/___/___	o
Detective				___/___/___	o

Reports Verified: o Fire o Police o State Patrol o EMS o DOT o Detective o Do official reports contain corrections? Y/N

Discrepancies: o Fire o Police o State Patrol o EMS o DOT o Detective (o Discrepancies Listed in report)

o Scene examined by reconstruction specialist on: Day:________ Date: ___/___/___ o Photo/Video made o Measurements

Witnesses (Not involved in accident):

Name:	Phone:	Notes:	File
			o
			o
			o

Figure 11.1 Incident report—auto accident. (continued)

insurance have been such that major investigations of the insurance industry have taken place, many of which resulted in reformed legislation that is currently reflected in the regulatory environment.

Insurance traditionally has been regulated by the individual states. Each state has an insurance department and an insurance commissioner who has several specific duties. The National Association of Insurance Commissioners

INCIDENT REPORT – AUTO ACCIDENT pt.2 of 3: Driver / Passengers

Vehicle is #____ from official diagrams. This vehicle: o Cause of wreck o Victim of wreck o Pedestrian report
Type: Make: Model: Year: Colors: Body: Roof:
VIN: Marks/Features: Tag: County:
This vehicle: o Private/Personal o Commercial:________ o Public/Gov.:__________ o Military:__________
Use/Cargo: o Verified
Driver: Age:____ Sex:____ o File Started
Address: SSN:
City: County: State: Zip: -
Phone: Pager: Website/ICQ/UIN:
Cell Phone: Fax: E-Mail:
License #:________________________ License Class:____ CDL?___ State:____ o Driver history attached
Vehicle Owner: (if not driver): o File Started

This vehicle's role in accident: o Verified

This vehicle initial collision with:
Specific maneuver:
Direction of Travel: Vision obscured?___ By:__________ o Vehicle Forensics report attached
Total $$s: Damage to this vehicle: $$____________ To property by this vehicle:$$____________
Citations Issued:
Criminal charges filed:
DUI tests performed: o Breathalizer o Blood o Other: o Other testing performed:

Insurance agent interviewed: ___/___/___ o Report attached
Insurance Agency: Policy #: $$ Coverage:
Address: Apt./Ste.: ICQ/UIN:
City: St: Zip: - Contact:
Phone: Pager: Website:
Cell Phone: Fax: E-Mail:
Date loss reported: ___/___/___ Date investigated:___/___/___ Date claim settled:___/___/___ $$:________

o Litigation filed against / by this: 1. Driver 2. Owner 3. Passenger(s):________________ o File started
o This litigation filed against / by:________________ o File started

Occupants: (see seating diagram pt. 3)

P	Name:	Age	Sex	Phone:	Injury:	SB	Ejct	Hsp	File
						o	o	o	o
						o	o	o	o
						o	o	o	o
						o	o	o	o
						o	o	o	o
						o	o	o	o
						o	o	o	o
						o	o	o	o

o All passengers interviewed. o All info verified on official reports o Vehicle Forensics sheet filled and attached.
o Relationships between passengers and driver of this vehicle and those of others investigated.

Figure 11.1 (continued) Incident report—auto accident. (continued)

proposed a bill that later became known as the McCarron-Ferguson Act. This act declared that it was the intent of Congress that state regulation of insurance should continue, and the Federal Trade Commercial Act would apply to insurance, but only to the extent that the individual states do not regulate insurance.

Federal regulation of insurance is carried out by many different federal agencies. The Federal Insurance Administration (FIA), which administers several government insurance programs, was involved in an extensive federal investigation of Worker's Compensation and no-fault automobile insurance. The Federal Trade Commission (FTC) regulates insurance commission

INCIDENT REPORT – AUTO ACCIDENT pt.3 of 3: Vehicle / Forensics	
1	Vehicle is # _____ from official diagrams. o Copy of official diagram / report attached
2	Type: o Car o Pickup o Van o Bus o Panel Van o Logging Truck o Tractor trailer o Other:
3	Make: Model: Year: Colors: Body: Roof:
4	VIN: Marks/Features: Tag: County:
5	Configuration:
6	This vehicle: o Private/Personal o Commercial o Public/Gov.:_____________ o Military:_____________
7	Use/Cargo: o Verified
8	Number of axles:______ Number wheels:______ GVWR:______ USDOT#:______________
9	Placard?: re:______________ 4 digit # on diamond or box:__________ 1 digit # bottom of diamond:______
10	Note:
11	Vehicle Towed by: Co.: Driver:
12	Address: Box: Suite:
13	City: County: State: Zip: -
14	Phone: Pager: Cellular:
15	Fax: E-Mail: Website/ICQ/UIN:
16	Interviewed on: ___/___/___
17	Notes:
18	Repair Shop: Contact:
19	Address: Box: Suite:
20	City: County: State: Zip: -
21	Phone: Pager: Cellular:
22	Fax: E-Mail: Website/ICQ/UIN:
23	Interviewed on: ___/___/___
24	Notes:

Seating Chart & Damage Diagram	Diagram:	Gen. Forensics	Safety Equipment
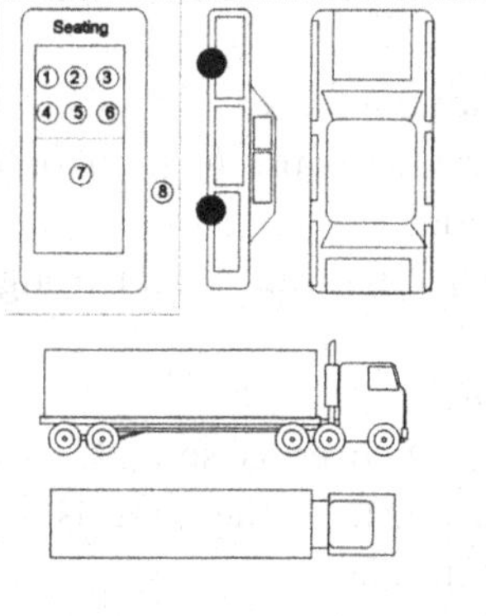	o Draw arrow to show Initial point of impact o Add numbers to show subsequent points of impact in order of event. o Shade areas & draw lines to show damage. o Use seating chart as reference for part 2. o Copy of official Diagram attached showing this vehicle's Route & final position. **Reconstruction(s):** o Computer animation of this vehicles actions o Computer animation of entire accident	MPH:________ # Times rolled:_____ Skid length:__________ **Tests Performed On:** o Light bulbs o Fuses o Gauges o Odometer o Brakes o Steering o Tires o Air Bag o Engine o Body o Frame o Axles o Drive Train o Other:	o Air Bag Deployed / Not Deployed o Seat Belts o Child Seat o Anti Lock brakes **Mechanical Failure:** o Brakes o Steering o Tires o Axles o Wheel(s) o Drive Train o Engine o Transmission o Clutch o Safety Equipment o Other

Figure 11.1 (continued) Incident report—auto accident.

mergers, mail-order advertising, and other trade practices affecting competition. Regulations of the Securities and Exchange Commission (SEC) governed the insurance of variable annuities and some aspects of insurer accounting practices. The U.S. Department of Labor (DOL) influences coverage for coal miners with black lung disease. It also operates with OSHA, which affects risk management practices. The DOL together with the Internal Revenue Service (IRS) administrates the Employee's Retirement Income Securities Act (ERISA) under which the operations of private pension plans, many of which are insured, are carefully regulated.

Insurance Fraud

Despite the ever-rising cases of insurance fraud, merely being aware of the indicators of insurance fraud will certainly help fraud investigators detect and break the cycle of the criminal activity.

Red Flags of General Insurance Fraud

- A claim is made soon after a policy's inception or a change in coverage (e.g., the purchase of a new policy just before the loss).
- The insured has a history of making numerous claims and losses.
- The insured is eager to settle a claim and seems to be very knowledgeable about the coverage and claim procedures.
- There is provider pressure for rapid adjudication of claims.
- There are threats of legal action for delaying payments.
- Frequent telephone inquiries are made on claim status.
- The insured posed a hypothetical claim to the insurer before a similar claim arrived.
- The applicant fails to sign an application for coverage.
- Important questions on an application are left blank (e.g., income, other insurance policies, hazardous activities).
- The insured handles all the business in person, rather than through the mail.
- The insured has excess insurance coverage.
- Earned income does not merit the amount of coverage sought.
- A signature on an application does not appear to be the same as that shown on an authorization at the time of the claim.
- The applicant appears to have many declined applications.
- Documents have been altered (look for erasure or white-out marks).
- Photocopies of documents are used instead of originals.
- Payroll figures reported to insurers are disproportionate to those reported elsewhere.
- The address on the claim form is a P.O. box.

Red Flags of Healthcare Insurance Fraud

- The physician's report is vague regarding details of past medical history and does not coincide with information listed on an application.
- Care plans never change.
- Multiple surgeries or office visits are claimed.
- Claims are made resulting from injuries occurring outside of the country.

- Medical records exist designating continuous need for home health visits.
- Repeated x-rays are claimed.
- Treatment was prescribed before a history and physical were taken.
- There is physician solicitation of family members.
- The physician advises against child immunization.
- There are no out-of-pocket expenses for physician visits.
- The physician or provider demands same-day claim payment and special handling.
- Charges were submitted for payment without supporting documentation (e.g., x-rays, lab results).
- The insured's address on the claim is the same as that of the physician or provider.
- Routine treatment was provided for long-distance patients (rather than specialized treatment).
- The referring physician and provider of service are linked to the same professional organization or corporation.
- Medical records were altered.
- Medical records contain "additional information attached," which would make an obvious noncovered service covered.
- Medical record pages are missing that would cover the period under review or investigation.
- Medical or dental terms are misspelled.
- Unusual charges for a particular service are claimed.
- Bill headings are typed.
- The insured and the provider appear to have the same handwriting.
- The insured describes a lower service level than that which was provided.
- Claims have irregular columns.
- Hospital bills are typed or handwritten.
- Prescription receipts from the same pharmacy are printed on papers of different colors.
- The claim form lacks the provider's signature.
- The provider's medical degree is absent (i.e., "Dr. John Black" instead of "John Black, M.D.").
- Claims were submitted for surgeries independent of related services (i.e., routine hospital charges).
- The physician's specialty is different from that which normally determines diagnosis, or services billed do not agree with diagnosis.
- There is billing for services or equipment that are clearly unsuitable for a patient's needs.
- Foreign claims show charges in U.S. dollars when such is not the currency of the foreign country.

- Multiple foreign claims are submitted from the same subscriber or the same physician or provider.
- Billing exists for experimental procedures.
- Improper contractual relationships exist with physicians.
- The length of a treatment program is extended or discharge is delayed because a patient has additional insurance benefits remaining.
- Illegitimate treatment programs are claimed (e.g., "fat farms," art therapy, music therapy).
- There is excessive treatment for psychiatric patients (e.g., thyroid testing, drug testing).
- The physician or provider has multiple tax identification numbers.

Red Flags of Property Insurance Fraud

- A claim for bulky, expensive, or recently purchased property is made following a burglary or fire.
- Commercial loss is claimed involving seasonal inventory or equipment, which takes place following the selling season.
- An insured insists that property was the best or most expensive model yet cannot provide documentary proof of purchase.
- The insured has multiple policies covering similar (or the same) losses.
- Following a burglary or fire, sentimental property is notably missing rather than partially destroyed.
- The insured cannot recall where or how property was acquired and cannot provide documentary proof of purchase.
- The remaining contents of a business or home are of an inferior quality than that which is being reported stolen, damaged, or destroyed.
- The insured has documentary proof of purchase, photographs, and witnesses for all of the missing or destroyed property.
- For arson, specifically, emergency fire doors are propped open; the fire alarm was turned off; the sprinkler system was turned off; there was an unusual presence of flammable chemicals near the scene; locked doors were unlocked; there was evidence of burglary or fraud; property value in the area is on the decrease; structural problems existed in the building before the fire; the owner is experiencing financial difficulties; the insured appears calm; the building or business was recently purchased; and so forth.
- For burglary or theft, specifically, the claim amount seems outrageously high; precious items of the insured were not taken; the insured paid cash for all missing items; receipts are missing or photocopied; no evidence of forced entry was found; the alarm system was turned off; the insured was seen moving claimed objects in and

out of the building prior to the burglary; receipts were incorrect or missing; the loss inventory does not match that in the police report; losses were questionable; and so forth.

Red Flags of Life Insurance Fraud

- Information on a life insurance application is vague as to an applicant's health history (i.e., dates, places of treatment, names of physicians and hospitals, specific diagnoses).
- A death claim resulting from a death outside of the country was presented.
- An attorney is immediately involved in a contestable death claim and tries to interfere with an investigation.
- A contestable death claim reported as an accidental death may be a suicide (e.g., one-vehicle accident, hunting accident, accidental shooting while cleaning a weapon, etc.).
- An autopsy report discloses different height and weight measurements than shown on a recent application.
- Records of a patient confined to a hospital are missing.

Fire and Arson Investigation

Co-written with Rich Harris

Arson has been identified as the fastest-growing type of crime in the United States today. National statistics show that when measured on a cost-per-incident basis, arson is the most expensive crime committed. Less than 20% of arson arrests result in convictions. Arson for profit is responsible for approximately one half of all fire-related property damage in the United States. Insurance fraud is the most common target for an arson-for-profit scheme. Insurance fraud has been referred to as "the modern way to refinance."

The primary role of the fire investigator, as with any criminal investigator, is to determine the truth. In seeking the truth, the investigator must complete a post-fire examination of the structure or vehicle that is the subject of a suspicious fire and determine the cause and origin of the fire. Interviews must be conducted, evidence must be collected, and comprehensive reports of all findings must be prepared. If, during the initial stages of inquiry, actions indicating criminal conduct or evidence of criminality are uncovered, the fire investigator must immediately shift to his or her secondary role to identify and move against those responsible.

Investigative Checklist

An investigative checklist is used to ensure that every pertinent fact about the case has been identified. It is also used to identify those cases to be assigned to case management. Finally, it may serve as a supervisory tool in evaluating an investigator's performance and in the assignment of additional cases based on caseload. An investigative checklist should include the following types of data:

- Identity of the assigned investigator
- Victim identification
- Suspect/defendant information
- Detailed information relating to the incident, including time, address, identity of the fire chief, first firefighter, and police officer at the scene, and so forth
- Classification of the offense (e.g., arson, occupied or abandoned, etc.), arson/homicide
- Detailed information relating to the investigative procedures and steps taken (e.g., photos, sketches, canvas, etc.)
- Identification of physical evidence and follow-up procedures (e.g., laboratory analysis results)
- Identification relating to prosecution of the case (e.g., grand jury, assigned prosecutor)
- Witness information
- Types of data to be determined from related reports, including a chronological listing of incidents; date and time; classification, including whether residential or commercial, occupied or abandoned, forest or brush; point of origin (where fire started); type of accelerant used or suspected; classification of damage; and death or other injury

Commercial Fires

It is important to start gathering information as soon as possible after the fire. The investigator should ask to see business records and tax returns and should check the answers to the following questions:

- What is the relationship among owners of the business?
- What are the names and addresses of the suppliers?
- What is the dollar value of the business on a weekly basis?
- What are the owner's gross earnings per week?
- Does the owner have any financial interest in other businesses nearby?

- Were the storeroom and shelves checked for merchandise that is the most expensive?
- Were the suppliers asked if bills were overdue or if checks were bouncing?
- How much money is owed to suppliers?
- What is the name of the owner's insurance company and the extent of the coverage?
- Has the owner applied to the Small Business Administration or any other agency for a loan?
- Is the business protected by an alarm? What time of day is it turned on? Was it on or off at the time of the fire? Was it circumvented?
- Was the sprinkler system working?
- Are any flammable liquids kept on the premises? What type, and why?

The elimination of all possible accidental causes of the fire is one of the most difficult duties of the fire investigator. Unless all of the relevant accidental causes can be eliminated, the fire must be declared accidental, the presence of direct evidence to the contrary notwithstanding.

Vehicular Fires

The overwhelming majority of vehicular fires are intentionally set. The primary motive seems to be economic. For the most part, automobile arsonists are "selling" their cars to the insurance company.

Investigation of a vehicular fire requires a two-part approach. The first part involves completion of a post-fire automotive salvage examination to determine the cause and origin of the fire. The second part, which hinges upon the determination made during the first part, involves interviewing or interrogating the vehicle's owner. The purpose of the interview is to elicit statements that would implicate the vehicle's owner.

Suspicious Indicators

Any fire in which fire damage extends "bumper-to-bumper" should be considered highly suspicious. A fire that accidentally starts in one of the three interior compartments will tend to stay in that compartment. A person intending to burn his or her car may remove good tires and replace them with old or worthless tires before starting the fire.

The presence of either separate (distinct) or primary and secondary burn patterns on the vehicle's exterior is highly suggestive of intentional damage. If the ignition key is found in the debris, this fact alone may be enough to rebut a statement or claim that the vehicle had been stolen. Any time the driver of a vehicle sustains or is treated for burns associated with a vehicular fire that is under investigation, the investigator should attempt to obtain the doctor's or other official diagnosis regarding the patient, the degree, and the location of such burns.

Arson

Arson is defined as the willful and malicious burning of the dwelling of another. Today, statutes define arson as the willful burning or destruction by explosion of a structure of another, the personal property of another, or for the property of arson if done for the purpose of defrauding an insurer. The main task of the investigator is to determine whether a fire or explosion was intentionally (incendiary) set or accidental. The investigation and prosecution of incendiary acts are similar to the investigation of other crimes.

Most fires are started by accident. If an accidental cause cannot be readily established, the investigator should assume that the fire was set on purpose. Unintentional destruction of property, while not punishable as a crime, may still be the object of legal liability in a civil suit. It is estimated that 150,000 fires are set intentionally each year. Property losses from incendiary fires account for more than 10% of all fire losses and also account for about $2 billion per year. Thus, annual dollar losses from arson are higher than losses from any other crime except larceny. In addition, approximately 1000 people die each year because of incendiary fires.

Crimes of arson have a very low solution rate, approximately 10%. Similarly, the percentage of conviction for those arrested is quite low. A large percentage of intentional burnings is the work of juveniles who generally are not processed through the normal criminal justice system. Juveniles are usually not required to make restitution for the loss. No reliable data exist on recidivism (repeat rate) for arson.

Motives of Arson Offenders

As with other serious crimes, arson is committed for a reason. Determining the motive of the offender may help to narrow the suspect list. There are several basic motives for arson fires. The first motive is fraud. Because the cost of fire insurance is slight in comparison to the value of the property covered, a fire to collect from the insurer may be profitable to the owner. Fires to defraud insurers are sometimes used to dispose of buildings that are not easily marketable, to recover cash for obsolete machinery, or to liquidate business enterprises.

Fire may be the result of political activities. In the 1960s, this was a frequent motive for the massive burnings that accompanied inner-city riots. The likelihood of political motive depends upon the social and political situation in the community in question.

Because an intense fire and the means to control it (water, chemicals, etc.) often alter or destroy property, arson may be used to cover up the commission of another crime. Similar to any destructive act, an incendiary fire may be a means of gaining revenge (spite) against an enemy. Anger, jealousy, and ill will toward another may be sufficient motivation for the destruction of property by arson.

On occasion, an arsonist may set a fire in order to attract attention to him- or herself. Often, this takes the form of setting a fire and then saving lives or property by reporting the blaze in hope of recognition (vanity) for such actions. Pyromania may also be a motive. Finally, a large percentage of incendiary fires are set by vandals and juveniles seeking a thrill. Many small fires are started for this reason.

Procedures for Investigating Arson

Incendiary fires can pose many problems for the investigator. The following steps should be observed when conducting an arson investigation. During the fire, observe the scene to the extent possible. The arson investigator should respond to all major fires at commercial establishments, because observations during the fire are often as valuable as a later search of the property. The investigator should be alert to the following characteristics.

Location, Extent, and Direction of Flames Focusing on the specific area of the fire and direction of spread helps pinpoint the point of origin of the fire. Due to variations in construction materials and wind direction, fires rarely burn equally in all directions. The existence of two or more separate blazes may indicate an intentional fire.

Color and Height of Flames Observing the appearance of flames at the fire will aid in determining the intensity of the fire and the presence of accelerants. Flame color is a function of temperature, which, in turn, depends upon the nature of the fuel. Flame color will range from red to yellow to blue to white, depending on the temperature. The caloric value of certain substances causes them to emit a distinctive color when burned.

Color of the Smoke Fire produces a vapor that contains minute particles of the fuel being burned. The color of this vapor, commonly called smoke, can indicate the nature of the burning fuel. Thick black smoke indicates a heavy carbon fuel, such as gasoline, oil, tar, or paint. These substances are popular accelerants for arsonists. Gray or white smoke is evidence of burning dry wood. Gray smoke with blowing ash is evidence of loosely packed organic matter, such as straw or wastepaper. Yellow or brown smoke is evidence of nitrate compounds, such as farm fertilizer.

Odors at the Scene Odors at the scene may also provide evidentiary clues. Kerosene and gasoline have distinctive odors. The investigator should also be familiar with the odor given off by other popular accelerants, such as lacquer and paint thinner.

Weather Conditions Weather conditions at the site should be noted by the investigator. Warm, humid days are more conducive to spontaneous combustion and the likelihood of an accidental fire than are hot days. The local weather bureau can provide information concerning relative humidity at the time of the fire. Wind direction and intensity should also be noted.

Witnesses The investigator should identify and, if time permits, interview any witnesses at the fire scene. At the scene, the investigator should be alert to anyone who appears out of place because of dress, mannerisms, or the time of day.

Photographs of the Fire If practical, the investigator should take color photographs of the fire scene. Such photos report flame color, wind direction, smoke color, and other visual details. Attempts should be made to record the fire's pattern and progress with photos. Photographs of onlookers should be made, especially if pyromania appears to be a possible motive. If the arson investigator arrives at the scene after the fire has been extinguished, he or she may contact local newspapers or television stations to determine whether they photographed the scene.

Photographs of the Scene After the fire is extinguished, the charred remnants of the fire should be photographed. Because most remains from the fire have a dark color, greater exposure time and aperture openings are generally required to obtain high-contrast quality photos.

Search of the Scene A search of a fire scene should be conducted by the fire investigator. The investigator should dress for safety and comfort in clothing that will resist smut and water. Boots, raincoat, gloves, and safety helmet are mandatory. The search should be conducted after the fire is extinguished but before any cleanup efforts begin. The investigator should be alert to the possibility that fire personnel may have accidentally moved or destroyed evidence while fighting the fire.

Normally a fire area is treated as a zone, so the search begins at the exterior and moves toward the interior. During the exterior search, the investigator should be especially alert to evidence of outside activity indicating an incendiary fire, such as footprints or empty gas containers. During the interior search, the point of origin of the fire should be the focus. Any pertinent evidence, such as soot, ashes, charred paper, and matches, should be collected. The presence of vapors from possible accelerants may be detected by using a sniffer (an instrument for detecting hydrocarbon gases that is commercially available). Vapors and chemically saturated lumber should be collected at the scene.

Point of Origin of the Fire The key to determining whether a fire was intentionally set requires identifying its point of origin. The point of origin is most likely to yield evidence on the cause of the fire. The presence of an igniter, an unnatural kindling agent, or a delay fuse is strong evidence of an incendiary fire. All fires must be started in some manner. If non-accidental igniters, such as matches, candles, or cigarette lighters, are found, arson is likely. Because a high temperature must be reached before most substances will burn, a strong sustained flame is often necessary to cause standard building materials to ignite. An arsonist may use kindling or accelerant to start the fire. The presence of unnatural kindling agents would indicate arson.

The point of origin of a fire may be found in several ways. The firefighters should be interviewed, because they may have observed the point of ignition while fighting the fire. Observation based on recognized principles of combustion may elicit clues. A fire burns in a triangular pattern away from its source in the direction of prevailing air currents. The point of origin is generally on the windward tip of this triangle.

Fire burns upwards rapidly but downwards slowly. Thus, the lowest level of destruction will be near the source of the fire. Where a roof or floors have collapsed, the investigator must separate fallen debris from stationary burned objects in order to determine the point of origin. The point of origin tends to be the place at which maximum destruction and charring have occurred. This general principle may vary under special circumstances.

Once the crime scene has been searched, the investigator should complete his or her investigation as follows.

Interview of Owner A comprehensive interview of the owner and occupants of the structure involved should be conducted. In particular, the investigator should try to determine where the owner was at the time of the fire, the size of the loss, whether the victim had any enemies, whether the victim had received threats to his or her life or property, and whether the victim experienced vandalism to his or her property in the past.

Insurer The investigator should find out the name of the owner's insurance carrier. The insurance company should be contacted to determine the scope and value of the owner's coverage and any limitations on payment. Arson may be likely if the building is overinsured, if the insurance coverage in the owner's policy is greater than the market value of the building and its contents, or if the investigator discovers the existence of coinsurance (two or more policies covering the same risk). Normally, the owner can lawfully collect on only one policy.

The Property Insurance Loss Register (PILR) is a cross-check of policyholders and claimants maintained by the insurance industry to detect fraudulent schemes, such as collection on the same property from several companies, phony ownerships, false claims, and people who suffer fire losses more than once.

Cause of Fire The physical cause of the fire should be determined by the investigator. This is a necessary element in proving arson, because an incendiary act is required. The cause of the fire may be obvious once the investigator examines the point of origin. The cause may be established by examining possible accidental causes and either accepting or eliminating them as the cause of the fire. If an accidental source is not apparent but no evidence of an intentional fire is located, one must assume the fire is of unknown origin until the cause can be established by proof outside the scene.

Motive for Setting the Fire Establishing a motive may aid in developing a suspect list. Evidence of elaborate preparations (i.e., gasoline-soaked walls, delayed ignition) indicates fraud as a motive. Minor preparations may indicate spite or revenge as a motive. Use of combustible materials normally at the scene (i.e., rags, newspapers) would indicate vandalism. The presence of pornographic material at the scene strongly suggests pyromania.

Liability Claims Investigation

Liability is a present or potential duty, debt, obligation, or responsibility to pay or do something, which may arise out of a contract, tort, statute, or otherwise. The rules for investigating liability involving questions of negligence are basically as follows:

1. What is the duty owed?
2. Was there a breach of that duty?
3. Was that the proximate cause of the resulting damage?
4. Was the other party guilty of any contributing negligence?

Duty Owed

Duty is that which a person is obliged to do or refrain from doing, a responsibility that arises from the unique relationship between particular parties, or what one should do based on the probability or foreseeability of injury to a party. Statutes affect "duty owed," and the claims adjuster should be aware of the laws that affect duty. A very important law is the statute of limitations. Duty owed is also limited or affected by exculpatory notices, contracts and subcontracts, leases and subleases, declarations of condominiums, indemnity agreements, certificates of insurance, rental forms, warranties, guarantees, covenants, deeds, bills of lading, and so forth.

Proximate Cause

The proximate cause is something that produces a result, and without which a result could not have occurred; it is any original event, which in natural unbroken sequence produces a particular foreseeable result, without which the result would not have occurred. The question to resolve is whether the alleged breach of duty is the proximate cause of the resulting damage. The adjuster must be prepared to show who (if not the insured) or what was the proximate cause of the loss.

Contributory Negligence

Contributory negligence is the failure to exercise care by a plaintiff, which contributed to the plaintiff's injury. Even though a defendant may have been negligent, in the majority of jurisdictions, contributory negligence will bar a recovery by the plaintiff.

Any claim, when properly investigated, can result in decreased exposure for the primary culprit. Implied reasonable assumption of risk is a defense when the injured party had knowledge of the risk or danger. Establishing the status of the party will help in this process (e.g., determining whether the claimant was an invitee or a trespasser).

No-Fault Law

The no-fault law is intended to eliminate contributory negligence. A loophole in the law called "tort threshold" made it necessary to incur at least $1000 of legal expenses before a tort claim could be made.

Appendix 11.1: Sample Investigative Report

Investigation Report

Privileged and Confidential

Prepared for:

Fire & Casualty
39 NE 163rd Street
North Miami Beach, Florida 33160
Owner: ____
Loss Location: Tampa, Florida
Claim Number: ____
Loss Date: July 11, 2005
Prepared By: Richard Harris
Report Date: September 13, 2005
Case Number: ____

This report was prepared for Fire & Casualty who will be responsible for further distribution. The opinions contained in this report are based on personal observations at the fire scene, the statements of witnesses, as well as depositions and other documents reviewed as of the date on this report and were developed to a reasonable degree of certainty. The author agrees to a reconsideration of the conclusion if new evidence becomes available. This investigation was conducted using NFPA 921 as a guide.

Assignment

This assignment was received from ____. Instructions were to conduct an origin and cause examination of the loss site; obtain statements of the insured, neighbor, ____, who reported the fire to the husband of the insured, and of the husband of the insured, ____; determine the date and time of arrest of the insured's brother, _; and determine the presence of utilities at the time of the fire with a verbal report to ____. This investigator contacted the insured and conducted the investigation on Wednesday, September 7, 2005. The insured gave me consent to conduct my investigation and was present during the examination. A verbal report was given to ____, at which time she requested a written report be completed and sent to her.

Background Information

The loss site, located at _, Tampa, Florida, is an elevated one-story, single-family dwelling, of wood frame construction, on wood pilings approximately 10 high. It is approximately 21 years old and measured approximately 25 wide by 35 deep, and faced a northerly direction toward 68th Street. The structure is owned and occupied by insured ____, DOB: November 1951, and her brother ____, DOB: February 24, 1954. The insured resided at the loss location for approximately 13 years, with one previous incident, prior to this incident. She claims her brother accidentally left a pan of grease on the stove, which overheated and ignited approximately 2 weeks prior to this incident causing minor damage above the stove. She did not file a claim regarding that incident.

Structure Information

The structure involved is of protected wood frame construction, with exterior walls of wood siding construction. Interior walls and partitions were of 2 ≤ × 4 ≤ true dimensional framing on 16 ≤ centers covered with 5/8 ≤ sheet rock. Roof construction was of 2 ≤ × 6 ≤ true dimensional framing on 24 ≤ centers, covered with ¾ ≤ plywood and asphalt shingles.

An electric heat unit provided heat, and a window unit provided air-conditioning. Hot water was provided by an electric water heater. Electricity was provided by a three-wire overhead service that entered the structure at the east side into the residence, and provided power to a 150 A General Electric breaker panel. All breakers were in the off position at the time of my examination.

At the time of this investigator's scene examination, the property appeared to have been adequately maintained and appeared to have been being remodeled and painted prior to the fire.

Incident Information

The fire was reported to the Hillsborough County Fire Department on Monday, July 11, 2005, at approximately 4:20 p.m. First arriving firefighters reported heavy smoke conditions coming from under the eaves and vents of the residence. The first entering firefighters found the door to the residence ajar and found signs that it had been previously kicked or pried open. They found fire in the middle bedroom on the floor. It was easily extinguished.

Fire Scene Security

The structure was closed but unlocked upon my arrival and was not secure.

Alterations to the Fire Scene

The fire suppression and overhaul activities performed by firefighting personnel as well as the investigation activities performed by local investigative personnel and the previous private fire investigator had altered the fire scene. The insured had also begun to clean up the floor of the room of origin and removed much of the fire debris prior to my arrival. These activities did not hinder this investigator's fire scene examination; however, the evidence had been moved about.

Exterior Observations

The exterior examination was conducted by working in a counterclockwise manner starting at the front portion of the residence. There was no visible fire damage to the exterior (see photos 1 through 5). The entrance door was examined, and it was noted that the lower three panes of glass were broken out and boarded up. The insured advised this had occurred years ago. The doorjamb was cracked, and the latch plate and door edge were damaged as well (see photos 6 through 10).

Interior Observations

The interior examination of the insured's property was conducted by working from the least damaged areas to the most severely damaged areas (see photos 11 through 13). The residence had smoke damage throughout and fire damage contained to the middle bedroom. The fire damage was on the floor where combustibles had been and were ignited. The debris had been removed prior to my examination; therefore, I am unable to comment on the type and form of combustible (see photos 14 through 18). Fire patterns present indicate that the fire originated within the middle bedroom on the floor in an unknown combustible material. This area sustained extremely severe damage to both building and contents due to fire, heat, smoke, and water.

Interview of ____

Neighbor ____ indicated that on the date of the loss, he was in his residence at _ 68th Street when two white men came to his door and asked him to call the fire department, as the house next door was on fire. Mr. ____ stated he had been in poor health due to a stroke and did not notice anything at the residence prior to being alerted to the fire by the two men. He could not identify either of the men. He called 911 and then called ____, the insured's estranged husband, and told Mr.____ to find _ and tell her about the fire. Mr. ____ stated that ____ and her brother ____ usually occupied the house. He said he was on his front porch the day prior to the fire and overheard Ms. ____ and Mr. ____ arguing and saw Ms. ____ leave the house with a bag of some sort. He said she got in her truck and left and did not come back to the residence until after being notified of the fire.

Interview of _

____, of Big John's Bail Bonds, at 2100 Orient Road, Tampa, Florida, (813) 641-8400, said she is ____ bondsperson. She stated that on the date of the fire, Monday, July 11, 2005, she and one of her bounty hunters arrested Mr. ____ at his work, Tampa Tire, at approximately 10:30 a.m., and that he was booked into Hillsborough County Jail by 1:00 p.m. the same day. She said he is currently incarcerated in State Prison for 1 to 3 years on drug-related charges. She said she has known Ms. ____, Mr. ____, and their family for over 20 years. She said that she has heard from other people she has on bond that Mr. ____ owes several individuals money for illegal drugs, and that one of these people may have set the fire.

Origin and Cause Summary

Based on a careful and detailed examination of the fire scene and interviews conducted, this investigator's fire scene examination resulted in the determination that the fire originated in the middle bedroom. Unknown person or persons ignited the fire in combustibles on the floor.

Attachments

Photo descriptions
Scene photos
Transcribed taped statement of____

September 13, 2001

Richard Harris, CFEI, CFII, CFC, FCI

This report was prepared for Argus Fire & Casualty who shall be responsible for further distribution. The opinions contained in this report are based on personal observations at the fire scene, the statements of witnesses, as well as depositions and other documents reviewed as of the date on this report, and were developed to a reasonable degree of certainty. The author agrees to a reconsideration of the conclusion if new evidence becomes available. This investigation was conducted using NFPA 921 as a guide.

Appendix 11.2: Sample Vehicle Fire Report

Investigation Report

Privileged and Confidential

Preparers:
McMahon & Associates
Forensic & Insurance Services Division
Orlando/North Florida: (407) 382-2403
Tampa/St. Petersburg/Sarasota: (813) 299-8066
Broward/Palm Beach: (954) 341-2001
Dade/Fort Myers/Keys: (954) 341-2001
Statewide, national, and international toll free: (800) 211-5092

Prepared for:
United States of America Insurance
1234 Main Street
Anywhere, Florida 12345

Owner: Jane Doe
Loss Location: Anywhere, Florida
Claim Number: ____
Loss Date: June 11, 2005
Date Received: June 20, 2005
Prepared by
Richard Harris
Report date:
June 23, 2005
Case number: ____

This report was prepared for United States of America Insurance Company, who will be responsible for further distribution. The opinions contained in this report are based on personal observations at the fire scene, the statements of witnesses, as well as depositions and other documents reviewed as of the date on this report and were developed to a reasonable degree of certainty. The author agrees to a reconsideration of the conclusion if new evidence becomes available. This investigation was conducted using NFPA 921 as a guide.

Assignment

This assignment was received from United States of America Insurance Company Special Investigator Jessica Smith on Monday, June 20, 2005, at approximately 3:45 p.m. Instructions were to conduct an origin and cause analysis of the loss vehicle. This investigator traveled to the loss vehicle on Wednesday, June 22, 2005, and completed the examination.

Background Information

The loss vehicle is a 1997 Navistar-International 4700 Wrecker Unit, with the vehicle identification number ABCDEFGH123456789. Eddy Jones, owner of Acme Towing, owns the vehicle. The vehicle was located at Acme Towing, 4839 Citrus Avenue, Anywhere, Florida. It was in his locked impound lot and had been moved approximately 50 feet away from the site where it had burned. Per the insured, he was contacted by his wife at approximately 10:50 p.m. on the night of the occurrence and was told the wrecker was on fire. The Anywhere Police Department had notified her at about 10:40 p.m.

Exterior Observations

Examination of the exterior revealed that the fire originated on the engine compartment hood and on and in the cab of the vehicle. Further examination of the exterior revealed that prior to this event, the exterior was in overall good condition. The window glass was broken and gone due to the fire, as well as the windshield being melted, down toward the hood of the vehicle. The front tires and wheels were also present and damaged by the fire. The rear tires and wheels were in good condition. The tire tread depth on the rear tires was 5/32, and the front was less. No components were noted as being missing from the exterior of this vehicle. The vehicle identification number was not located on the unit.

Interior Observations

Examination of the interior of this vehicle revealed that the fire caused total destruction to the cab area interior. No components were noted as being missing.

Engine Compartment Observations

Examination of the engine compartment revealed that the fire originated on the hood of the engine compartment causing extensive fire damage. Further examination of the engine compartment, and the burn patterns found, revealed that the point of origin was on the hood, as well as the cab and interior cab. It was intentionally set. I also noted that the head for the engine, as well as the oil pan, were missing from the vehicle. The hood was made of fiberglass and was almost totally consumed by the fire. Two debris samples of pieces of the hood and carpeting from the cab were removed and placed in nylon bags and then in metal evidence cans and sent to our forensic lab for analysis on the date of this examination.

All other causes were eliminated as a cause for this fire. This investigator conducted a recall search, which found no recalls for this vehicle. I also conducted a search through Navistar-International Company for maintenance records and found none available.

Insured Interview

The insured, Eddy Jones, met me at the scene, as did Jessica Smith, United States of America Insurance Company Special Investigator. Mr. Jones advised that his lot, as well as buildings and tow trucks, had been burglarized and vandalized often for a long period of time. He has filed complaints with the Anywhere Police Department who have made an arrest; however, the suspect is free at this time and has, per the insured, continued to burglarize Mr. Jones' business. Ms. Smith will be following up on this information.

Conclusion Summary

This investigator's examination of this vehicle resulted in the determination that fire started on the cab of the vehicle, as well as in the vehicle. A flammable liquid was poured and ignited. It is an intentional act. All other causes were eliminated.

June 23, 2005

Richard Harris, CFEI, CFII, CFC, FCI
Fire Investigator

This report was prepared for United States of America Insurance Company who shall be responsible for further distribution. The opinions contained in this report are based on personal observations at the fire scene, the statements of witnesses, as well as depositions and other documents reviewed as of the date on this report, and were developed to a reasonable degree of certainty. The author agrees to a reconsideration of the conclusion if new evidence becomes available. This investigation was conducted using NFPA 921 as a guide.

Appendix 11.3: Car Theft, Past, Present and the Future

Richard Harris, CFEI, CFII, CFC, CPI, FCI, FLPI

Many years ago in the mid 1980s I attended an Automobile Fire and Theft Class in Detroit. I was a newly assigned lieutenant and fire explosion investigator. I was a naïve and young officer eager to learn as much as I could about my new position. During this 2-day-long course, several vehicles from the "Big 3" were brought in and burned, caused to burn, broken into, and had their ignitions defeated and driven away without keys.

The vehicles were easily entered even when locked. The windows were smashed, or to quietly steal the car we used the "Slim Jim" car door opening devices (which back then were and still are easily available at auto parts stores and truck stops across the country) as well as the good old "Wire Coat Hanger" fashioned into a long wire with a hook on the end of it to slide between the window and the weather stripping to pull up the old-fashioned lock knobs on the doors. Nowadays the knob tops of the door locks have been removed so they cannot be hooked and pulled up unnaturally.

As for defeating the ignition, this was easy—we simply broke the ring off the key lock on the steering column and inserted a screwdriver into the key pathway, gave it a "tap" or two with our fists or a hammer, and turned the screwdriver clockwise and started the car just as if we had the key to the car in the ignition. I got so good at this that I was able to enter a locked car, start it, and drive away in under a minute, "Gone in Sixty Seconds." Vehicles in the 1980s and well into the 1990s could be stolen in this fashion.

Well, in the past 25 or so years since this class, vehicle security has evolved into a kind of game. The auto manufacturers and their experts through technology come up with a new security feature to stop car theft and the thieves figure out how to defeat it. Now remember, I am talking about the true car thieves, not those who are attempting insurance fraud. True car thieves do not take the time to defeat vehicle security systems and sometimes use high-end, expensive equipment to do so and then drive the vehicle somewhere and set it on fire. The true car thief steals the vehicle and it ends up in a cargo container at the local port of call to be shipped to another country for resale or you may find the frame of the vehicle somewhere totally stripped of all of its components.

Components such as airbags can be sold for as much as $800 on the black market, where they would sell for $1000 through the manufacturer. Seats, tires and wheels, shocks/struts, fenders, doors, engines, transmissions, trunk lids, drive shafts, transfer cases, dashboards and components, center consoles, carpeting, headliners, etc., are all resalable at a total profit to the car thieves. Catalytic converters are highly sought after vehicle components on the black market due to their platinum and palladium contents. The average car can be professionally stripped by a team of four thieves of all components listed above leaving only the frame and attached uni-body in about 20 to 30 minutes. Sometimes these thieves strip these vehicles on the street in a secluded or industrial area of cities with the use of air tools, hydraulic jacks, lifts, etc. The profit is huge to car thieves in sales of the vehicles and parts.

The Federal Bureau of Investigation's full year totals for 2010 show over a 7% decrease in car thefts nationwide from the previous year. This is the seventh straight year of decline for auto thefts across the country. The forecasted figures for 2011 show over a 3% decrease at this time. In Detroit the 2010 statistics for auto theft were 14,111 vehicles stolen, in 2011 13,010 vehicles were stolen, and stats in 2012 indicate a year-end figure of about 12,457 stolen vehicles in the city. New York City reports auto thefts in 2011 totaled 9,300 down from about 150,000 in 1990. It is definitely more difficult to steal a car nowadays and will be even more difficult in the future.

Thieves did, however, steal more than 735,000 vehicles nationally in 2010, valued at about $4.5 billion. There are also signs that the electronic theft systems present on some vehicles may not be as daunting as advertised. Some high-end cars have been shown in online videos being stolen in less than 3 minutes by supposed car thieves, apparently after defeating the cars' alarm and anti-theft systems. They are shown supposedly cloning the vehicles' electronic key fobs using easily accessible diagnostic ports on the vehicles. There are numerous other videos online showing how to supposedly defeat anti-theft systems on vehicles using laptop computers and diagnostic ports on vehicles.

The more sophisticated the manufacturers get inventing, manufacturing, and installing vehicle anti-theft systems on new cars, the more sophisticated the true car thief becomes. In Europe auto manufacturers are required by law to make the diagnostic ports on vehicles easily accessible for service and allow independent mechanics and locksmiths to cut and reprogram keys and onboard computers for keys. In the United States most high-end manufacturers as well as some domestic auto manufacturers allow only a factory licensed dealer to reprogram their systems and cut keys for their vehicles. Obviously there are still some aftermarket programmable keys and companies who program them, other than the dealerships.

The National Insurance Crime Bureau (NICB), a non-profit organization in the United States, lists most stolen vehicles each year. Their figures show that thieves mainly are looking for older cars for the used part market where mass-market models are among more valuable cars than luxury cars.

The most frequently stolen automobile in 2010 was the 1994 Honda Accord, second was the 1995 Honda Civic, and third the 1991 Toyota Camry. The larger pickup truck 1999 Chevrolet Silverado was fourth with the 1997 Ford F-150 coming in at number five. All of these vehicles were among the top-selling cars and trucks in the United States. Advanced electronic anti-theft technology has decreased thefts of some model vehicles. NICB data show that in 2010, 5331 Honda Accords built in 1997 were stolen, and only 533 1998 model year Honda Accords were stolen. The later model cars had new electronic anti-theft ignition immobilization systems in them. Only the key assigned to the vehicle could be used to start it.

Even though thefts of vehicles have gone down, recovery rates have also gone down. In 2004 63% of all stolen vehicles were recovered in the United States, while only 56% were recovered in 2010. True auto thieves now move quickly to strip and sell parts or export the whole vehicle to other states and countries.

Modern electronic ignition systems, which reset the codes every time they are started, and stronger immobilizer systems for the steering wheel and shifter made it much harder for unskilled thieves to steal a vehicle in less than 8 minutes, which is the average longest time an expert car thief will take to successfully steal a vehicle. Obviously, the more skilled and equipped the thief is, the more probable it will be for the thief to be successful in stealing a car. Most vehicles' steering and shifter locks can be broken by a strong individual. I can grab a steering wheel of most locking columns on cars and with my 250 pounds of weight can turn the wheel with such force to break the locking pin. The same can be accomplished usually one handed on the shift lever on the column or console.

Unfortunately we cannot currently stop the true auto thief who uses highly sophisticated electronic equipment to replicate key codes and tow trucks and flatbed trucks to steal vehicles. These thieves usually target luxury vehicles and after changing the vehicle identification numbers on them and changing the onboard computers sell them in other states or countries from where they were stolen.

The future of vehicle anti-theft systems will include stronger hardware to stop the breaking of the steering column and shifter lever of vehicles. New locking systems will stop the defeating of these systems by cordless drills and even brute force by using electric motors that respond to signals from keyless starter and remote keyless entry systems to lock down the steering and shifter.

Appendix 11.4: Car Insurance Scam

Shady Clinics Bilk $1.3 Billion in Bogus Car Insurance Claims Scam

Michele Henry
Toronto Star, July 13, 2011

Ontario's car insurance industry is under attack by bogus medical clinics that use fake accident treatment charges to milk the system.

$1,247 for a portable acupuncture machine.
$2,363 for "aqua fitness therapy."
$450 for pain-relieving massages.

Michele Henry.

Then there was the $1,293 invoice submitted to an insurer for a long-handled Swiffer and other equipment to help a Toronto man with a minor injury clean his house.

None of these treatments or machines were provided to accident victims.

Doctors, chiropractors and physiotherapists are unwitting dupes in what some insurers claim is a $1.3-billion scam. Fraudsters steal their credentials to make fake invoices appear legitimate. The victims of the scam are drivers across the province, who annually see their rates hiked to pay for fraudulent claims.

Insurance investigators claim more than 300 clinics loosely connected in fraudulent rings are working this system.

"This is the bane of my existence for the last year," Dr. Tajedin Getahun, a Mississauga physician, said in an interview.

His stolen signature was on treatment plan invoices for a series of costly devices he said he would never prescribe. One was a "whole body vibrating plate," priced at $1,980, the other a $998 "biofeedback device."

Travel around Toronto and you will see more and more of these rehabilitation clinics popping up. Anybody can open one and they are not regulated. One New York man with an auto insurance fraud conviction is listed as administrator of a Mississauga clinic.

Some people who visit bogus clinics are legitimate victims.

Others are part of the scam, either faking injuries or claiming for injuries that are the result of staged accidents.

Here's how it typically works.

Tow truck drivers or paralegals direct accident victims—drivers and passengers—to rehab clinics. They might get a finder's fee of $1,000 cash or, in the case of paralegals, a percentage of the payout. It is not uncommon for a clinic to bill an insurer $40,000 over the life of a claim.

The accident victims the Star found often spoke little or no English. At the clinic they were handed forms to sign that gave the clinic the right to submit claims to their insurance firm and receive payments.

Insurance companies only pay out if treatment is given by a regulated health professional—a doctor, chiropractor, physiotherapist, or massage therapist. It appears that clinics sometimes steal a professional's information. In other cases, a professional briefly worked in the clinic and left behind a college-issued registration number and electronic signature.

"It's sort of a murky world out there when it comes to these assessment clinics," said Rocco Neglia, vice-president of Economical Insurance Group.

It's tough to police a system where clinic owners and staff do not need any accreditation or credentials and get unrestricted access to confidential health information. Insurance investigators say clinics swamp insurance claim departments with hundreds of claims, often late on a Friday, figuring that while some will be rejected, many will be paid.

"They're really treatment mills and for the longest time they've been operating with impunity.... This is why insurance rates can give you whiplash," Neglia said.

Woodbridge realtor Steve Moustakas suffered minor back pain after his Cadillac was T-boned in June 2010. A tow-truck driver at the crash scene suggested a local paralegal firm could "help" push Moustakas's claim through the "complicated" insurance system.

Moustakas visited paralegal firm Lofranco Scarola Wentzel, where a client relations manager provided a list of four clinics. Moustakas chose Osler Rehabilitation in northern Etobicoke.

Moustakas said Osler staff booked him for three to five treatments a week and he visited the clinic for two months, then quit. He recalls on each visit being pressured to sign many documents.

Months after he stopped visiting the clinic, his insurance company told him thousands of dollars of treatments were billed using his name as a patient and a series of doctors who, Moustakas said, he never saw.

"I didn't know what I was getting into," he said.

The invoices claimed he had not only attended Osler, but also another clinic called Assessment Direct where, the papers said, various doctors gave him numerous, costly treatment assessments.

One invoice from Assessment Direct totalled $995.69 for eight services such as "documentation support activity" and "counselling, promoting health and preventing disease," which Moustakas never had and knows nothing about. Another for nine services, including "other" and "assessment mental health," totalled $1,959.90.

In total, Economical Insurance estimates that $37,000 in assessment and treatment costs were submitted by clinics in Moustakas's name. Economical became suspicious and only paid out about $2,500.

Moustakas said he never went to Assessment Direct and never saw any of the doctors (plus a psychologist and a dentist) named as providers on the claims.

Bombarded by bills from the clinics, Economical sent Moustakas to its own professionals to determine whether the invoices were legitimate.

In October they sent him to a dentist, who asked to see Moustakas's X-rays.

"What X-rays?" Moustakas asked. "My teeth were never injured in the accident."

To sort out the mess he was in, Moustakas went back to the paralegal firm for advice. Paralegal Joseph Corriero, whom he had previously dealt with, responded by sending Moustakas a batch of blank insurance expense forms, instructing him to sign—but not date—the documents and return them to him "as soon as possible."

Moustakas became suspicious, alerted his insurance company and wrote Corriero a scathing letter, terminating their relationship.

When the Star contacted Corriero about this story, he sighed, "Oh God." Corriero said his job is to "handle claims" and he declined to comment on the blank invoice allegation. He said there was "a breakdown in communication" between him and his client.

Corriero works on a contingency basis, claiming a percentage of everything an insurer pays. He has been sending Moustakas bills, asking him to "kindly remit" 20 per cent of the money he believes his client received from the insurance company for caregiver and housekeeping benefits. One of Corriero's bills was for $1,270.12.

Officials at the two clinics would not answer questions from the Star.

Loreto Scarola, head paralegal at Lofranco Scarola Wentzel, says that sending blank expense forms for client signature is common practice at the firm.

"It saves the client from having to come in every two or three days" to sign papers. He said the firm gives the client copies of everything it sends to insurance companies so the "client is fully apprised of what's been submitted on their behalf."

Scarola said "there's no basis for any accusation" lobbed at his firm. Moustakas is "barking up the wrong tree here. As far as we're concerned this is all absolutely false."

While there is no regulation or accreditation of clinics, the province has recently created a registration system called HCAI—Health Claims for Auto Insurance.

Registration is required to submit a claim, and 6,771 clinics or individuals are registered, three-quarters of them clinics and half of them in the GTA. There is no cost to register and no vetting of registrants.

The Insurance Bureau of Canada has created a tracking system that loosely links 300 GTA clinics.

The IBC has in the last two years passed on information on suspected cases of fraud to the Financial Services Commission of Ontario, leading to four convictions of clinics for providing false information to obtain payment from an insurance company.

The punishment is a fine; in one case the clinic was ordered to pay $50,000.

Meanwhile, insurance companies have started suing clinics and their owners.

In one case, a lawsuit by Economical Insurance alleges Toronto Regional Medical Assessment Centre director Danny Grossi and other defendants used the information of 55 car accident victims, the majority of whom do not speak English, to submit fake invoices to three insurance companies.

The alleged fraudsters then ripped off the electronic signatures of health care professionals and pasted them onto the invoices.

Grossi, an anesthetist in training, is under investigation by the College of Physicians and Surgeons. The college would not reveal the allegations it is investigating.

On invoices the insurance company says are fake, Grossi's name appears as a "provider" of service.

In his statement of defence, Grossi denies "any role in the conspiracies alleged" and in a letter to the Star his lawyer, Joseph Falconeri, writes that Grossi has himself been exploited and "there are serious and significant concerns with respect to Dr. Grossi's signature being misappropriated by third parties."

Grossi directed the Star to his lawyer when a reporter tried to interview him at his Dufferin St. clinic.

Before publication of this article, Grossi sued the Star, seeking $10 million in damages, claiming that the Star reporter's "aggressive manner" of researching caused doctors the reporter interviewed to resign from the clinic where Grossi is director.

Getahun is one doctor the Star interviewed as part of its research on the Toronto Regional Medical Assessment Centre. He said he discovered his signature was stolen last year when insurance investigators called to question him about out-of-character treatment recommendations that bore his name.

Getahun briefly worked for Grossi's clinic and provided a statement to insurance investigators.

"It has been an absolute nightmare," Getahun said. "I can't understand how someone would have the audacity to do this."

Health care professionals from all disciplines say the province must do something to stop their credentials from being misused.

In a case related to a different series of clinics, chiropractor Nasim Husnani discovered last year her signature was being pasted onto hundreds of fake invoices.

After she left a short stint at a clinic in 2009, her signature was used on invoices submitted to State Farm Insurance Co. by two other clinics where she had never worked. "I went to school for eight years and then someone comes along and decides to rub your name in the mud," Husnani said.

One Toronto man, 78-year-old George Antoniadis, was confused about his entire experience at a mid town clinic after he suffered shoulder and knee pain following a rear-end collision.

A lawsuit alleges the clinic filed dozens of fake invoices worth more than $6,000 in Antoniadis's name. When a Star reporter interviewed Antoniadis, he said the only treatment he received came in the form of a "Magic Vibro Belt" that is advertised on the web as a "slimming device" at $99.

Domestic Investigations 12

Domestic investigations are the least favorite and most dangerous of all investigations conducted by professional investigators. They are the basis of most of the stereotyping of investigators found in the media, movies, and television: the private investigator jumps out of the bushes to photograph the cheating spouse. That stereotype does not portray private investigators in the most favorable light. Does that mean that domestic investigations are not worthwhile? Absolutely not. They are very necessary and a major source of income for many investigators.

Some investigators will not do domestic investigations that have the purpose of "catching" the cheating spouse. In some states, such as Florida, divorces are no-fault—there does not have to be an allegation of wrongdoing to obtain the dissolution of the marriage. Therefore it is not necessary to determine if one of the parties is unfaithful. However, it is human nature for the parties to want to know if their spouse is committing adultery.

There are many other types of domestic investigations, including determination of custody, locating children abducted by their noncustodial parent, and asset investigations of the parties involved. In the custody issue investigation, the role of the investigator is to document the fitness of one or both of the parties to obtain primary custody. The location of abducted children usually revolves around the location of the missing parent. The asset investigation is designed to uncover all assets, hidden and obvious, of one or both of the parties. All of these investigations result in evidence being presented on behalf of one of the marital parties to support his or her position.

Like most of the investigations described in this book, domestic investigations are in essence legal investigations designed to produce testimony at some point in time that will be used in court by one or both parties. See Figure 12.1 for a sample data report. The investigator may be called upon to refute or confirm claims on a financial statement or present testimony and evidence regarding the suitability of a parent seeking custody of a child.

One area that sometimes requires investigation in domestic matters is the duration of residence. Most states have a residency requirement, usually 6 months, before a party may file for divorce. Therefore, among the issues that the investigator must clarify is whether both parties have resided in the state for the required time period. This may be accomplished by determining ownership of property within the state, date that a driver's license was issued

MATRIMONIAL PRELIMINARY DATA REPORT

FILE#__________ DATE:__________ TYPE OF CASE:__________

CLIENT:__________ TELEPHONE:__________

ADDRESS:__________

BUSINESS ADDRESS__________ TELEPHONE:__________

OTHER PERSON TO CALL:__________ TELEPHONE:__________

VEHICLE DESCRIPTION:__________

SUBJECT:__________ MAIDEN NAME:__________ AGE:______ DOB:______

HT:____ WT:____ RACE:____ HAIR:____ EYES:____ BUILD:____ GLASSES:____ DISTING. FEAT. FACIAL HAIR:__________

RELATIONSHIP TO CLIENT:__________ YEARS MARRIED:__________

OF CHILDREN:__________ NAMES/AGES/SEX:__________

HOME ADDRESS:__________ TELEPHONE:__________ LISTED/UNLISTED:______

DIRECTIONS:__________

VEHICLE DESCRIPTION:__________ CAR TELEPHONE:__________

OCCUPATION & ADDRESS:__________ TELEPHONE:__________

SS#__________ CREDIT CARDS:__________

PARENTS NM/ADD:__________ BESTS FRIEND(S):__________

ADDITIONAL INFORMATION:__________

____

OTHER PARTY INFORMATION:__________ AGE:______ DOB:______

HT:____ WT:____ RACE:____ HAIR:____ EYES:____ BUILD:____ GLASSES:____ DISTINQ. FEAT. FACIAL HAIR:__________

MARITAL STATUS:__________ NAME OF SPOUSE:__________ #/NMS CHILDREN:__________

HOME ADDRESS:__________ TELEPHONE:__________ LISTED/UNLISTED:______

DIRECTIONS:__________

VEHICLE DESCRIPTION:__________ CAR TELEPHONE:__________

OCCUPATION & ADDRESS:__________ TELEPHONE:__________

ADDITIONAL INFORMATION:__________

REFERRED BY:__________ RECD BY:__________ ATTORNEY/TELE:__________

FINANCIAL ARRANGMENTS:__________ RETAINER CONTRACT:__________

Figure 12.1 Sample data report.

in the state, date that the party registered to vote, whether there has been extensive travel outside the state by either party, and any other proof that can be identified by the investigator.

State law usually requires some ratio for the distribution of assets, called the equitable distribution of assets. In some states, the requirement is that assets be "equitably distributed" between the parties. However, in order to equitably distribute the assets, both sides need to determine what assets are to be divided. This is where the investigator can help one party determine the existence of the marital assets of the other party. This becomes significant in the case of a nonworking wife in a marriage with a husband who may attempt to hide assets. In particular, the court takes into consideration any intentional dissipation, waste, depletion, or destruction of marital assets that has taken place after the filing of the Petition for Dissolution (divorce). The investigator may be looking for spending sprees (clothes buying, cruises, etc.), unexplained major expenditures, consistent expenditures for things such as controlled substances, excessive alcohol consumption, and gambling, as well as unexplained missing or stolen assets.

In some states, the court must decide whether alimony is appropriate and if so, what the appropriate award should be. Factors the court considers include the standard of living established during the marriage; duration of the marriage; ages and physical and emotional conditions of each party; financial resources of each party; contributions of each party to the marriage, including but not limited to services rendered as a homemaker, child care, education, and career building of the other party; and all sources of income available to either party. In many cases, the role of the investigator would include investigation of the physical and emotional conditions of each party (i.e., is the party claiming emotional and physical damage able to conduct normal activities, such as tennis, jogging, nightlife, etc.?), discovery of the financial resources of each party and standard of living of each party while the divorce is pending, and finding of any proof of marital infidelity, especially where it has resulted in substantial expenditures (such as jewelry, trips, cars, living accommodations, flowers, etc.).

The issues the court must consider in determining the best interests of the children are which parent is more likely to allow the children frequent and continuing contact with the nonresident parent; the love, affection, and emotional ties existing between the parent and the children; the capacity and disposition of the parents to provide the children with food, clothing, medical care, and other remedial care as needed; the length of time the children have lived in a stable, satisfactory environment; and the desirability of maintaining this continuity. Other issues include permanence, as a family unit, of the existing or custodial home; the moral fitness of a parent; the mental and physical health of the parents; and the home, school, and community records of the children. The reasonable preferences of the children, if they are of sufficient age and intelligence in the opinion of the court, the willingness and ability of each parent to facilitate and encourage a close and continuing parent-child relationship between the children and the other parent, and any other factor considered by the court to be relevant would also be included in determining the best interest of the children.

The role of the investigator in providing evidence related to any of the aforementioned issues could determine the outcome in a custody case. The investigator may be required to conduct surveillance of the child and parent together, determine the moral fitness and the mental and physical stability of the parent, investigate school records, and check any other records that may exist with respect to the children.

Not only do the issues described previously need to be investigated by a qualified individual, there is a recent development within the area of domestic or family law that needs to be considered. In the new age of the private investigator, people are not conducting background checks of their dates. According to an article in *The New York Times*, many single women in this age of risky romance are hiring private detectives to check the backgrounds of their suitors.

It is the choice of each investigator working in the field to decide whether domestic investigations are appropriate for his or her agency. Based upon my personal experience, they are very lucrative; however, they can be heart-wrenching. One is dealing with heightened emotions on both sides, and therefore, there may be danger not only to the investigator but also to any of the parties involved.

Appendix 12.1: Sample Activity Report

Domestic Surveillance

Privileged and Confidential

December 22

8:00 a.m. Investigator ____ arrived at the subject's home address and minutes later gained access to the gate, and the investigator searched for the vehicle; however, the vehicle was not present. The investigator then departed from the area to the subject's business.

9:03 a.m. The subject's vehicle was present at the business, and video was taken.

10:13 a.m. The subject exited the office. He retrieved an unknown object from the vehicle and entered the office out of view.

10:53 a.m. The subject exited the building, accompanied by an unknown white female. They drove around the building. Minutes later, the female entered the building out of view.

12:29 p.m. The subject and the female departed from the business area, and mobile surveillance continued.

12:42 p.m. The couple arrived at ____ Pizza, located on the ____ block of Atlantic Boulevard, Delray Beach, Florida. They remained inside the restaurant for an extended period of time.

1:37 p.m. They departed from the restaurant, and minutes later they arrived at the subject's business. They sat inside the vehicle for a period of time, apparently talking.

2:46 p.m. The female entered the subject's business.

3:42 p.m. The subject arrived at Starbucks, located on _, Delray Beach. Minutes later, another unknown white female entered the store, and the investigator observed them talking for an extended period of time.

4:06 p.m. They returned to the nursing home, and the unknown female was observed standing and smoking outside the building. She then entered the building out of view.

4:56 p.m. Surveillance was maintained.

6:00 p.m. Surveillance was terminated.

December 23

7:37 a.m. Investigator ____ arrived at ____. He assumed a tactical surveillance position. (Video was taken.)

8:10 a.m. The investigator observed the subject depart from his residence driving a maroon Ford Expedition.

8:11 a.m. Video was taken of the subject as he proceeded northbound on Powerline Road toward Atlantic Avenue.

8:13 a.m. The subject arrived at ____, Delray Beach, Florida. (Video observation [VO] was conducted.)

8:15 a.m. He departed from his vehicle and entered the building (VO).

11:29 a.m. The investigator observed the subject standing outside talking on his cell phone. Shortly after, he returned into the building (VO).

11:45 a.m. The subject exited the building and approached the passenger side of a white Chevrolet Blazer, where he spoke with an unknown white female. He then walked toward his vehicle out of view (VO).

11:46 a.m. The subject drove to 5858 Heritage Park Way, where he remained inside of his vehicle (VO).

11:48 a.m. He departed from his vehicle and walked with an unknown female toward the building out of view (VO).

11:56 a.m. The subject entered his vehicle and returned to his office.

12:19 p.m. The subject departed from the area (VO).

12:32 p.m. The subject arrived at Walgreens Delray Beach and remained inside of his vehicle (VO).

12:35 p.m. The investigator observed a white Lexus bearing FL tag# ____ parked next to the subject's vehicle. A white female, subsequently identified as ____, exited her vehicle and entered his, and they departed from the area (VO).

12:36 p.m. Video was taken of them leaving the Walgreen's parking lot.

12:37 p.m. Video was taken of them kissing each other at a red light on the corner of Congress Avenue and Atlantic Avenue (VO).

12:46 p.m. Video was taken of the subject after his vehicle exited on Glades Road in Boca Raton, Florida.

12:55 p.m. The investigator followed the subject to Town Center Mall, where he parked in the garage and began to make physical contact with the female. Shortly after, they departed from the area (VO).

1:03 p.m. The subject parked his vehicle, and he and female walked toward Nordstrom out of view (VO).

1:31 p.m. The subject walked the unknown white female to the passenger side of the vehicle, where he opened the door for her, and she entered the vehicle. He then entered the vehicle, and they departed from the area (VO).

1:35 p.m. The subject parked in the upper level of the garage, where he and female continued to make physical contact (VO).

1:38 p.m. The investigator relocated his surveillance position and observed that the subject and female went to the rear seat of the vehicle, where they performed unknown activities (VO).

2:09 p.m. The investigator observed the female and the subject go from the rear seat to the front seat of the vehicle, and then he departed from the area (VO).

2:10 p.m. The investigator proceeded to Walgreen's to wait on the subject's arrival (VO).

2:32 p.m. The investigator observed and videotaped the female's vehicle.

2:36 p.m. The subject arrived at Walgreen's, and he and female remained inside of the vehicle as they conversed with each other and kissed several times.

2:52 p.m. The female exited the subject's vehicle. She then entered her vehicle and departed from the area (VO).

2:54 p.m. The investigator lost the subject's vehicle in traffic.

3:19 p.m. The investigator returned to the ____ and searched for the subject's vehicle, but he was not there.

3:50 p.m. The investigator was instructed to terminate surveillance, to meet with CLI McMahon.

4:20 p.m. The investigator provided tape to CLI McMahon to review with the client.

Appendix 12.2: Indicators of Online Marital Infidelity

Here are some signs that one's spouse may be committing infidelity online.

1. Alternate E-Mail Accounts—Have you noticed that your spouse has a new e-mail account registered in his or her name that he or she does not allow you to have access to? Many people involved in

Internet infidelity will have several e-mail addresses, because sometimes they will use a unique e-mail address for each person they communicate with. Couples with nothing to hide should not be hiding e-mail accounts from each other.

2. Erased History—Does your partner frequently erase incoming or sent e-mails or Internet history? This could be a signal that your partner is visiting sites he or she would rather you didn't know about, which could be adult in content, or the places they go to talk with strangers or participate in Internet infidelity. Does your partner delete text messages, or the call list on his or her cell phone? It's just not normal behavior to randomly erase lists of calls, and often doing so may be a sign that there's someone sending those texts besides work or family.
3. Privacy—Is the door to the home office or computer room *always* closed when your partner is online? Does your partner frequently shut down the computer when you come into the room or hide the screen when you approach the computer? A demand for privacy while online is often an indication of Internet infidelity.
4. Excess Computer Usage—Is your spouse hooked to the Internet and in fact would be doing something on the computer until late in the night or early in the morning? Is your partner defensive when questioned about his or her online usage? With today's technology some affairs don't ever have to include meeting a person face-to-face (although more often than not, rendezvous do happen eventually). Your spouse may be going on sites to "meet" people or to pornographic sites that involve live chat.
5. Gut Feeling—If you have to ask yourself these questions, chances are infidelity is being committed.

In my 20-plus years of working domestic cases I have found that in 97% of cases where women believe that their spouses are cheating, our investigation revealed that they were correct.

Due Diligence and Background Investigations

13

- Fifty percent of all résumés and applications contain fabrications.
- Employee theft causes 33% of all business failures.
- Employee theft costs U.S. business $60 billion.
- Over 20% of lawsuits for premises liability result in awards of over $1 million.
- Approximately 75% of people who perpetrated white-collar crime in a given company did so previously at another company.

These are some very good reasons for corporate America to conduct background investigations prior to acquiring new companies or businesses, hiring new employees or executives, or investing time and money in a new venture. It is a good idea to know who you are doing business with before you become involved. See Figure 13.1 for a sample background checklist. These are some of the reasons that investigators who specialize in background investigations can be very busy. Let us look at some of the different types of investigations that can be conducted.

Due Diligence Investigations

A growing number of court decisions have deemed that an employer can be held liable for the criminal actions and negligent behavior of an employee. The failure of an employer to thoroughly investigate an employee's background can result in a judgment against the company.

Checking the asset quality of a prospective business partner or senior-level employee before a deal is consummated or an individual is hired may prevent future losses or lawsuits for businesses and financial institutions. Checking the asset quality of an individual involves research to determine if there are any "skeletons" or problems in his or her background that could financially impact the company following the acquisition.

A due diligence investigation is by nature a search for negatives. In contrast to investigations conducted in the context of litigation, due diligence inquiries are usually conducted in a friendly, cooperative atmosphere of an anticipated business deal. This does not mean that the investigative agency should not do a thorough search for the facts. Regardless of whether the deal

BACKGROUND INVESTIGATION CHECK LIST

FILE#: ______________________ DATE: ______________ FEE INFO: ______________

CLIENT: ______________________________________ TELE: ______________

ADDRESS: ______________________________________ FAX: ______________

SUBJECT: ______________________________________

ADDRESS: ______________________________________ TELE: ______________

COUNTY: ______________ MARITAL STATUS: __________ SPOUSE: ______________

DOB: ______________ SS#: ______________ DL#: ______________

POSITION DESIRED: ______________________________________

____/____ DATE INT	CONFIRM ADDRESS/ DATA ON APPLICATION			
____/____	CONFIRM EDUCATION/ APPLICATION			
____/____	CONFIRM EMPLOYMENT/ APPLICATION			
____/____	PERSONAL REFERENCES/ APPLICATION			
____/____	PROFILE	____/____	DMV RESEARCH	
____/____	CRIMINAL	____/____	____________	
____/____	CIVIL	____/____	____________	
____/____	WORKERS COMP	____/____	____________	
____/____	PHYSICAL SURVEILLANCE/ PERSONAL VISIT			

Figure 13.1 Background investigation checklist.

succeeds or fails, the investigation will be scrutinized to determine appropriateness and fairness.

In addition to pursuing leads suggested by public records research, an investigator should seek information from the company's competitors, labor unions, and other potentially knowledgeable groups, after weighing the obvious risks involved. Former high-level employees of companies are often premium sources of adverse information about the company that would not otherwise be disclosed.

When hired to conduct a due diligence investigation, the recommended steps to be taken are to first establish ground rules and strategies. Cost (budget) and time frame (deadlines) are two factors that must be considered with or without the subject's (target's) knowledge. Obtain a signed release. Next, interview key executives and other important personnel within the company. The investigator should search public records, including local newspapers and business publications, secondary magazines and industry newsletters, and federal, state, and local courthouses for civil suits, liens, judgments, divorces, criminal cases, Universal Commercial Code (UCC) filings, bankruptcies, property tax assessments, land records, mortgages, and so on. The investigator should also check courts where federal agencies file suits such as U.S. district courts, tax courts, bankruptcy, and so on. The investigator may check filings by companies and individuals at relevant federal agencies (Securities and Exchange Commission [SEC], Federal Trade Commission [FTC], Federal Communications Commission [FCC], etc.) as well as public materials generated by those agencies—that is, complaints or consent decrees; incorporation and other filings with the secretary of state, including articles of incorporation, amendments, and annual reports; motor vehicle and driving records; the Better Business Bureau, consumer protection agencies, and the state attorney general's offices for complaints or other indications of investigations; state and local licensing agencies; and other related state and federal agencies with regulatory oversight responsibility (i.e., the state comptroller's office).

To complete the profile, check the target business. The investigator needs to identify significant business, partnership, or ownership interests of parties involved, verify business and banking references, and identify and interview anyone who has left senior management within the last 5 years and include reason for departure and current whereabouts. Identify the principals and ascertain whether they have been arrested or convicted of crimes, are the target of any criminal investigation, are the target of an SEC (or other regulatory agency) litigation, signatory, or consent decree or any other type of administrative investigation. Check for personal or corporate bankruptcy. Determine whether the individual was a plaintiff or defendant in any civil litigation, including suits alleging fraud or misrepresentations, and whether the individual was the subject of any suits brought by creditors or any government agency.

Follow up the investigations and write a final report. Include the interviews of the sources. The professional investigator selectively interviews persons who have been identified as having adverse information about the target. It is important to determine the motives of these people for providing the information. Re-interview key personnel to clarify problems or discrepancies that have arisen during the course of the investigation. It is important to carefully report interim results to the client, and stress that only preliminary conclusions are to be drawn. Credibility of sources providing critical information must be carefully assessed. The interim report should contain a recommendation as to what extent each item of information should be relied upon.

The final report of the investigation should include a review of all investigative steps taken, the overall results, and an assessment of the credibility of the information gathered. If further investigation is needed, it should be described in detail with a plan for implementation.

Business Background Investigation

Before entering into any business deal or partnership arrangement or hiring a senior executive, it is strongly recommended that a thorough background investigation be conducted. This may well prevent future losses and lawsuits. In fact, the success of the business may depend on this investigation.

Any history of personal litigation, including small and large suits, management track record, personal and business credit problems, criminal history, including convictions, association with organized crime offenders, drug traffickers, and white-collar criminals; material misrepresentation; conflict of interest; and character defects all need to be investigated.

Applicant Background Investigation

The chief reason for a background or screening investigation is to establish that the applicant has truthfully related all relevant information. Prospective employers have the option of rejecting applicants for employment at their own discretion except for reasons dealing with ethnic or racial origins, religious preferences, age, or sex, or further requirements of the National Labor Relations Act. Similar state laws say that there shall be no discrimination based on workers' rights to collective bargaining. The employer is otherwise unregulated with respect to reasons for rejecting employment applications. Many kinds of personal behavior and activities might be considered unsuitable for a prospective employee. See Figure 13.2 for a sample background investigation form.

The employer has an obligation to be prudent and reasonable in the selection of an employee. The company has no information about the applicant until he or she applies, and then it has only what the applicant provides. To make a decision about potential employment on the basis of such information alone would be foolish. No testing will confirm statements about past history or any other information unless the employer goes beyond the applicant's statements. A variety of relationships arise with employment that can threaten the employer's assets. Short of self-inflicted injuries, the developing trend in compensation law is to permit awards for any and all injuries

MCMAHON & ASSOCIATES

PRE-EMPLOYMENT SERVICES

EXPLANATION OF SERVICES

APPLICATION/RELEASE FORM Use your company employment application and release form or our standard release form.. Form must include applicant's SSN, Date of Birth, Driver's License Number (State), and proper release consent language.

CREDIT HISTORY This is an excellent tool to evaluate if an applicant is able to handle his or her own finances. These reports not only reflect the applicant's financial stability but can also contain other useful information as prior addresses, employment information and civil law suits that may have been filed against the applicant.

CRIMINAL HISTORY Performed per state (per county in some states). We recommend a minimum search of a five year history. Information returned will be on prior convictions - not arrests. Many negligent hiring cases have been successful where it was established that the assailant/employee had a prior record of a violent crime. Based on the trend in negligent hiring case law, the failure to obtain, or to attempt to obtain criminal history data is the single most common reason for employer liability.

DRIVER'S RECORDS Driver's records will be obtained through our sources for those applicants who may be driving company vehicles. This will demonstrate previous records of accidents, DUI charges, tickets, etc. Such reports can identify such high risk applicants, particularly individuals who have had a series of serious violations.

Figure 13.2 Due diligence and miscellaneous intel. (continued)

sustained at, in the course of, going to, or leaving the business. An applicant's history with respect to unsafe practices and prior injuries is important.

Employers with health insurance programs beyond Worker's Compensation coverage are in even greater jeopardy from malingerers who may have already demonstrated by past record taking maximum advantage of such programs. Hiring people with active histories of alcohol or drug addiction can be the start of a widespread and continuing problem.

Suitability of employment should be evaluated. It would be a disservice to a person convicted of a larceny, who served a prison term, to assign that person to a position involving responsibility for access to cash, not necessarily

DRUG SCREENING PROGRAM We do not perform drug screening. However, we can establish a screening program for applicants and current employees that will support the ADA guidelines.

EMPLOYMENT HISTORY Up to three different employers will be contacted by us through our office for previous employment verification. It is almost too obvious to suggest that the applicant's references be checked, yet many employers have been found negligent in not doing so. All information obtained should be well documented and placed in the applicant's personnel folder.

PROFESSIONAL~ EDUCATIONAL VERIFICATION Usually performed on applicants for management positions. When researched some information given by the applicant may be embellished or false and cannot be verified through the educational institutions as given by the applicant.

WORKERS COMP HISTORY Will be performed in our office on a separate per-state' search. This information is needed to insure that the applicant is not a "professional claimant." It also insures that the applicant has no physical impairment that could lead to further claims. Proper consent forms, etc. will be provided.

Figure 13.2 (continued) Due diligence and miscellaneous intel.

because the employee might steal again, but because if a loss should occur after his or her hiring, he or she would be a natural suspect.

Criteria for Employment

Major attention should be given to a company's initial establishment of standards under which suitability for employment will be judged. The final determination of those criteria should be a function of management, because the criteria will reflect basic business policy. Such criteria are important, because they deal with aspects of personal suitability, integrity, sobriety, truthfulness, financial responsibility, and so on.

The purpose of a background investigation is to determine whether an applicant has been complete and truthful in his or her answers and whether his or her past history shows the presence of any relevant unfavorable information. The purpose of the employer making the final hiring decision is to be sure there is no information concerning the applicant's technical qualifications or past history that would deem him or her unsuitable for employment.

Application Form

The application form is the most important document that an applicant will submit. It should be designed to draw the maximum amount of lawful, relevant information from the applicant and to prevent omission or misstatements. Included on the application form should be the following:

- Name
- Residence
- Education
- Employment
- Licenses and special qualifications
- Military service
- Personal and business references
- Criminal convictions

With respect to criminal information, there is a trend toward narrowing the scope of such questions. A significant decision was made by the U.S. District Court in California in the case of *Gregory v. Litton Systems Incorporated* (316 F.S. 401, 1970). This case held that a policy of rejecting employment applicants because of multiple arrests was a violation of Title 7 of the Federal Civil Rights Act of 1964, because it had the foreseeable effect of denying applicants an equal opportunity for employment. The court held that the question was discriminatory.

Preemployment investigations can be a prudent precaution, provided that such investigations comply with the law, are not the basis for improper discriminatory practices, and serve their primary purpose of providing confidence in a prospective employer's decision about an applicant.

Authorizations and Agreements

In addition to questions related to specific employment requirements, it is useful to have the applicant, when he or she signs the application form, execute an authorization and release regarding the investigation of his or her statements. The applicant should be advised about the nature of the relationship created by his or her submission of the application and the effect of providing false or misleading information. This caution should appear close to the authorized release and near the applicant's signature. See Figure 13.3 for a sample disclosure and release authorization.

The most carefully designed employment application will fail its purpose if the applicant is permitted to not complete it adequately. Prior to being accepted, the completed application form should be reviewed with the applicant by a staff member. Each field should be completed. If review of the application reveals any questionable items, prompt follow-through can save hours of investigative labor and much cost.

DISCLOSURE AND RELEASE

In connection with my application for employment (including contract for services) with you, I understand that consumer reports, which may contain public record information, may be requested from (YOUR COMPANY NAME HERE), Chicago, Illinois. These reports may include the following types of information: names and dates of previous employers, reason for termination of employment, work experience, credit history, accidents, etc. I further understand that such reports may contain public record information concerning my driving record, workers compensation claims, credit, bankruptcy proceedings, criminal records, etc., from federal, state and other agencies which maintain such records.

I AUTHORIZE, WITHOUT RESERVATION, ANY PARTY OR AGENCY CONTACTED BY (YOUR COMPANY NAME HERE) TO FURNISH THE ABOVE-MENTIONED INFORMATION.

I have the right to make a request to (YOUR COMPANY NAME HERE) upon proper identification, to request the nature and substance of all information in its files on me at the time of my request, including the sources of information; and the recipients of any reports on me which (YOUR COMPANY NAME HERE) has previously furnished within the two-year period preceding my request. I hereby consent to your obtaining the above information from (YOUR COMPANY NAME HERE) and I agree that such information which (YOUR COMPANY NAME HERE) has or obtains, and my employment history with you if I am hired, will be supplied by (YOUR COMPANY NAME HERE) to other companies which utilize (YOUR COMPANY NAME HERE)

I hereby authorize procurement of consumer report(s). If hired (or contracted), this authorization shall remain on file and shall serve as ongoing authorization for you to procure consumer reports at any time during my employment (or contract) period.

PRINT NAME	SOCIAL SECURITY NO.
APPLICANT'S SIGNATURE	DATE

Figure 13.3 Business data file.

Scope of Investigations

Three considerations will affect the extent to which investigations are carried out: cost, available time, and investigative resources.

The cost of the background investigation should be regarded in the same way as any other cost in recruitment and hiring. It should be held to a minimum, be consistent with objectives, but not be allowed to lessen the need for investigation. The absolute cost in dollars will depend upon how much investigation is conducted and by whom. Costs extend from $25 for an abbreviated report by a credit agency to $1000 or more for a comprehensive report by a professional investigator. Arriving at the appropriate amount of investigation and related cost is the task of the employer or personnel manager. Knowledge of resources available and how to utilize them comes from experience and training in the field of investigation.

Content of Investigations

Education

For positions that do not require a specific educational background, no investigation of education is necessary. When specific education is required for a position or is a basis upon which wage rate is determined, education should be verified.

For each school checked, the following items are significant: inclusive dates of attendance; the program or course in which the applicant was enrolled; the degree, diploma, or certificate awarded; student's conduct; reason for withdrawal or termination if prior to graduation or completion; and applicant's class standing and grade point average.

Prior Employment

Most unfavorable information about applicants will come from sources connected with prior employment. A sufficient period of time should be investigated to allow for developing information. For an entry-level employee, a suggested minimum is the preceding 5 years or last two employers, whichever is longer. For technical or supervisory employees, the period should be extended to 10 years or the last three employers, whichever is longer. For management and executive personnel, the entire business career should be investigated or a minimum of 15 years.

Information to be obtained from each place of former employment includes dates of employment, type of work performed, previous employment noted on application (applicant may have omitted positions from the application for reasons unknown), reason for termination, evaluations by former supervisors, eligibility for rehire, interviews with previous supervisors and coworkers, attendance records (whether the person was usually on time or chronically late), and work habits (amount of supervision required, responsibility, honesty, and reliability). Was the employee considered an asset to the company?

The investigator is interested not only in verifying the exact dates of employment but also in determining whether there were any periods of unexplained unemployment. Anything over 30 days may be looked upon with suspicion. Where was the applicant during this time? Did the applicant include reasons for periods of unemployment?

Residence

In conducting an investigation with neighbors, be certain to impress upon them that the purpose of the interview is for employment screening. Factors that the interviewer should focus on are how long neighbors have known the applicant; whether they know the applicant's family; whether they hesitate in answering any specific questions; whether their recommendations are sincere, lukewarm, or enthusiastic; whether they appreciate the nature of the investigation you are undertaking; and whether they offer assistance in answering questions or appear cautious in responding.

If neighbors do not know the applicant well enough to answer specific questions, can they furnish names of anyone who might know the applicant better? In the event that a neighbor furnishes derogatory information regarding the applicant, such statements must be verified through other neighbors or discounted as unverified. A particular neighbor may not get along with the applicant and thus provide negative information. At least three neighbors should be interviewed to complete this phase of the investigation. Derogatory information will require a more intensive search and interviews.

References

Personal and business references listed by an applicant should be interviewed thoroughly. Business references can be asked about the applicant's character and reputation. Would they recommend the person for the position to be filled? References are also good sources of information for any family problems that may have been uncovered in some other phase of the investigation. Social references are individuals who may be closer in age and better able to provide information relative to the applicant's reputation and peer relationships. Furthermore, they may know whether the applicant has a history of drug or alcohol abuse.

Credit History

Without signed releases, most companies will not cooperate in making these available. Credit bureau information is useful with respect to the history of trade account delinquencies, suits or judgments, and personal or business bankruptcies. Care must be exercised, because these records are often partial or preliminary and can be used as leads for further checks.

Medical History

Signed releases by the applicant are essential for examination of medical records. The investigator needs to determine any physical problems that could be chronic and preclude hiring. It is presumed that information obtained from these records and from any physical examination can determine the applicant's fitness for employment.

Criminal History

It is important to determine whether the applicant has any criminal history and whether any arrests in the past 5 years have resulted in convictions.

Legal Constraints

The Privacy Act of 1974 controls the gathering and dissemination of personal information by certain federal agencies. Some states have or are enacting similar legislation. This act ensures the individual's right to obtain information written about him or her. The individual can then contest the accuracy of the information. The Privacy Act requires the hiring agency that has gathered the information to notify the applicant, on request, of the uses it has made of the information, and the applicant may refuse to disclose his or her social security number unless it is required by federal statutes.

The Family Education Rights and Privacy Act of 1974, also known as the Buckley Amendments, guarantees parents' access to the school records of their children and places restrictions on dissemination of this information to third parties.

In addition to various state laws dealing with credit reporting agencies, Congress passed a comprehensive measure in March 2004, revising the Fair Credit Reporting Act (FCRA) and enacting the Fair and Accurate Transaction Act (see excerpts below).

Fair Credit Reporting Act (FCRA)

The section of the Fair and Accurate Transactions Act of 2003 that exempts employers from some disclosure requirements of the FCRA for conducting misconduct investigations took effect on March 31, 2004. Other sections of the act will have different effective dates.

Investigators who donated funds, wrote letters, and lobbied are to be congratulated for their perseverance during the 5-plus years it took to get Congress to remedy a serious error.

Representative Pete Sessions, R-TX, also persevered, introducing bills in three consecutive sessions of Congress before getting his last version included in the omnibus reauthorization bill.

Preemployment investigations are still covered by the FCRA. It is highly recommended that you or your client seek counsel from a qualified attorney before initiating investigations based on this law change.

The pertinent section of HR 2622 states:

Title VI—Protecting Employee Misconduct Investigations

Sec. 611. Certain Employee Investigation Communications Excluded from Definition of Consumer Report

(a) IN GENERAL—Section 603 of the Fair Credit Reporting Act (15 U.S.C. 1681a), as amended by this Act is amended by adding at the end the following:
  (x) EXCLUSION OF CERTAIN COMMUNICATIONS FOR EMPLOYEE INVESTIGATIONS—
  (1) COMMUNICATIONS DESCRIBED IN THIS SUBSECTION—A communication is described in this subsection if—
    (A) but for subsection (d)(2)(D), the communication would be a consumer report;
    (B) the communication is made to an employer connection with an investigation of—
      (i) suspected misconduct relating to employment; or
      (ii) compliance with Federal, State, or local laws and regulations, the rules of a self-regulatory organization, or any preexisting written policies of the employer;
    (C) the communication is not made for the purpose of investigating a consumer's credit worthiness, credit standing, or credit capacity; and
    (D) the communication is not provided to any person except—
      (i) to the employer or an agent of the employer;
      (ii) to any Federal or State officer, agency, or department, or any officer, agency, or department of a unit of general local government;
      (iii) to any self-regulatory organization with regulatory authority over the activities of the employer or employee;
      (iv) as otherwise required by law; or
      (v) pursuant to section 608.
  (2) SUBSEQUENT DISCLOSURE—After taking any adverse action based in whole or in part on a communication described in paragraph (1), the employer shall disclose to the consumer a summary containing the nature and substance of the communication upon which the adverse action is based, except that the sources

of information acquired solely for use in preparing what would be but for subsection (d)(2)(D) an investigative consumer report need not be disclosed.

(3) SELF-REGULATORY ORGANIZATION DEFINED—For purposes of this subsection, the term "self-regulatory organization" includes any self-regulatory organization (as defined in section 3(a)(26) of the Securities Exchange Act of 1934), any entity established under title I of the Sarbanes-Oxley Act of 2002, any board of trade designated by the Commodity Futures Trading Commission, and any futures association registered with such Commission.

(b) TECHNICAL AND CONFORMING AMENDMENT—Section 603(d)(2) (D) of the Fair Credit Reporting Act (15 U.S.C. 1681a(d)(2)(D)) is amended by inserting "or (x)" after "subsection (o)."

Preemployment Screening

Approximately 30% of employees from retail, restaurant, manufacturing, and healthcare industries admit to theft.

Approximately 60% of salaries reported on résumés are inflated, 5% of personal references are nonexistent, and 14% of educational references are bogus.

Job candidate deception must be considered in hiring an employee. Studies have shown that application and résumé fraud are at an all-time high—30% of all résumés are fraudulent. Employers cannot afford the luxury of hiring the wrong employees. Lost money from training and paying unsuitable employees makes a dramatic difference in the year-end profit and loss statement.

The instability of operation caused by high turnover rates, internal theft, losses owing to worker-related litigation (i.e., sexual harassment, Worker's Compensation cases, etc.) all impact on the stability of a business and the bottom-line profit and loss statement.

Screening Problems

A thorough review of the résumé and interview of the candidate are not sufficient in today's marketplace. A more exhaustive investigation is required of the finalists for positions in order to determine the most appropriate and best-qualified candidate for each position.

Due diligence and background investigations are an integral part of investigations including legal, domestic, and fraud investigations. Well-trained investigators have a comprehensive understanding of all the components of conducting thorough background investigations.

[illegible] information about [illegible] (e.g., [illegible]) in investigative [illegible] had [illegible].

[illegible] RECLASSIFICATION [illegible] [illegible] this [illegible] [illegible] regulations [illegible] [illegible] (Controlled Substances [illegible]) [illegible] [illegible] [illegible] (Controlled [illegible])

[illegible]

[illegible] Screening

Approximately [illegible] of employees [illegible] health care [illegible] [illegible] [illegible] [illegible] [illegible]

[illegible] [illegible] [illegible] [illegible] [illegible] [illegible] [illegible] [illegible] [illegible] [illegible] [illegible] [illegible] make [illegible] [illegible] [illegible] [illegible] [illegible] [illegible] [illegible] [illegible] [illegible] [illegible] [illegible] [illegible] [illegible] [illegible]

[illegible]

Although [illegible] [illegible] [illegible] [illegible] [illegible] required of the [illegible] to determine the [illegible] [illegible] [illegible] [illegible] each [illegible]

[illegible] [illegible] [illegible] an integral part of [illegible] investigations [illegible] [illegible] [illegible] [illegible] [illegible] [illegible] [illegible] [illegible] [illegible] through [illegible] investigations.

14 Locates and Skip Tracing

The Basics of Skip Tracing

What Is Skip Tracing?

Skip tracing is the art of locating someone. A skip is a person who, for whatever reason, chooses to leave a given area. Most skips eventually leave paper trails, verbal trails, or both.

There are many reasons for a person to skip, such as marriage, divorce, and revenge; escaping debt; boredom and frustration; amnesia; rebellion or adventure; and running from the law.

Skips Can Be Divided into Four Main Groups

- Unintentional skip—The person is not intentionally hiding but is secretive about his or her location.
- Intentional skip—The person intentionally conceals his or her location to avoid creditors or others.
- Marital skips—One party is overwhelmed by the pressures and stress of a divorce.
- Criminal skip—The person is hiding to avoid apprehension by law enforcement.

Relevant Federal and State Statutes

The Fair Credit Reporting Act (FCRA), a federal statute, governs the investigation of information on debtors as well as the rules for the collection of debt. The FCRA was revised in July 1999 and includes amendments to the Consumer Credit Reporting Act of 1997 and the Consumer Reporting Employment Clarification Act of 1998. For complete information, refer to the FCRA.

In some states, for example, in Florida, according to statute 119 (Public Records Law), "it is the policy of this state that records shall at all times be open for a personal inspection by any person."

Some of the exemptions to this statute are criminal records (open cases), informant information, and intelligence information. All other records are open for review. According to the Sunshine Law in Florida, public officials must maintain records of official meetings and make these records available for inspection to the public.

Beginning the Process

The first step in locating a skip is to review all information currently available on the skip from in-house records. Second, profile sheets should be prepared and a search undertaken for any information that is not complete through public records searches, database searches, government records, and Internet sites. That will be discussed in a later section of this book.

A skip trace should start with the basics—telephone directory information, criss-cross directories, and directory assistance for new listings. A skip tracer should keep a flowchart to track information, searches, and leads. This will prevent him or her from becoming sidetracked. The tracer should also keep an activity log so that if the records are subpoenaed or used in court, his or her documentation will be unchallenged. Finally, when all public and database sources have been exhausted, interviews with family, friends, employers, and enemies (i.e., ex-wives) should be conducted to try to obtain leads to the current whereabouts of the skip. See Figure 14.1 for a skip trace check list.

Researching Public Records

This is often the beginning to any investigation. Use telephone books, records, and listings; cross-reference books; and do neighborhood and employment investigations. Check postal records and public records, including a search of microfiche; voter registration; birth, death, and marriage records; real property records; fictitious business files; municipal, county, state, and federal civil court records; state and federal criminal records; corporate and partnership filings; Department of Motor Vehicle (DMV) records; church, medical, and dental records; credit history records; and union records. Also check state licensing boards and law enforcement agencies. And, check the trash (dumpster diving).

Interviews

After searching public records, if you are still unable to find the person, you must seek other sources of information. It is now time to polish your interpersonal skills and call or visit anyone who may have information about the whereabouts of the person you are trying to locate. Start with the people you have identified: ex-wives, ex-employers, former friends, and so forth. Ask if they have any knowledge about the person, or who else might have contact with the person. Follow all leads, and interview as many people as necessary to get the information you need.

Skip Tracing Resources

Public Records

A driver's license (DL) often contains all the identifying information required to find someone. The most important pieces of information are Social Security number (SSN) and date of birth (DOB). If the SSN is not shown on the DL, at least you will have the DOB to distinguish people with the same or similar names. This is the single most useful resource of the skip tracer.

If you cannot find the subject via his or her driver's license, a search of motor vehicle registrations is suggested. With the large number of seasonal visitors and tourists in a state such as Florida, for example, sometimes people do not obtain driver's licenses, preferring to maintain the license of their home state. However, the person may keep a car registered in a seasonal home. From that registration, you will obtain the DOB if it is not a leased car, and you may obtain the SSN.

Depending on the type of case you are working on, and whether you have legal process (i.e., judgments, liens, etc.) or a signed release, you can obtain a credit report or, alternatively, a header report. The FCRA is specific as to who is entitled to obtain credit reports. Penalties are severe for violations; criminal and civil penalties may be imposed. Exclusions to the act include court orders—that is, judgments or process (604(1))—or use of information in connection with a credit transaction or "collection of an account"—that is, judgments (604(3)(A) #5). In the absence of a credit report, you can obtain credit header reports (address information only) from certain database providers.

Many people are found by simply looking them up in the phone book. You can use a reverse directory, by phone number (name and address provided), or a cross directory, by address (name and phone number provided). You can even go back and use the city directories if you have old addresses for the subject.

One of the most useful searches on the local level is searching traffic offenses. Search of these records in the local courthouse may reveal a traffic infraction. Search of the court docket will provide the subject's home address. Search of the state and federal civil records will provide names and addresses of all plaintiffs, defendants, and witnesses in lawsuits. On the criminal side, records will provide names and addresses of defendants in criminal cases, as well as witnesses called to testify.

The Division of Corporations at the Department of State provides the names of all officers and registered agents of all corporations doing business in the state. Out-of-state corporations doing business are required to register in some states. The address provided might only be the corporate address, but by law, the officers are responsive to process served on the registered agents.

Searching occupational records in the county offices and city hall will reveal the names and address of business owners.

Skip Tracing Individuals versus Corporations

The same searches that you conduct on individuals would be used in searching for corporations. However, the first step would be to go online to the state in which the corporation is filed and obtain the information registered by the company, including the current status (active or inactive), present location (both mailing and physical addresses), and list of officers and directors.

After you finish searching information on the corporation, then you should follow up by doing searches on the individual officers and/or directors in the same manner as you would conduct the individual person search.

The Division of Corporations at the Department of State provides the names of all officers and registered agents of all corporations doing business in the state. Out-of-state corporations doing business are required to register in some states. The address provided might only be the corporate address, but by law, the officers are responsive to process served on the registered agents.

Searching occupational records in the county offices and city hall will reveal the names and address of business owners.

Searching for Financial and Business Information

Information regarding finance and business can generally be located within proprietary, local, state, and federal records. The following searches are helpful in locating such information:

- Property information at the county level
- Assumed business name or sales tax registration to locate sole proprietorship business information
- Uniform Commercial Code (UCC) filings at the state level to find general business information
- Business incorporation documents at the state level
- Bankruptcy filings, tax liens, and judgments
- Business reports from the Better Business Bureau
- Google search for both the business and the individual

Searching for Legal Information

The skip tracer can search most state court records by visiting the county court's Web site, or federal records by visiting the district court's Web site for the particular area or the Public Access to Court Electronic Records (PACER). PACER is an online database that provides users with a means to obtain case and docket information from the federal courts. Some states provide statewide searches for criminal convictions. The type of information provided varies (e.g., whereas one state provides information on arrests, charges, and misdemeanor and felony convictions, another state may only provide information on felony convictions).

Database Resources

Records Service Companies

Records service companies search public records for you online. Generally, the company will locate and provide the fraud examiner with information regarding businesses (financial statements, corporate status, UCC filings, contact names, history, etc.), date of birth and death, asset searches, court documents, newspaper and magazine articles, and the like. Costs to access these records vary. Some companies allow a subscriber to pay for a particular search, while others may charge a monthly fee for the use of their services.

The following companies provide valuable access to information online:

- *Factiva* (www.factiva.com): business information; news; publications.
- *LexisNexis* (www.lexisnexis.com): news (global); publications.
- *infoUSA* (www.infousa.com): business information, including sales volume, corporate linkage, contract names and titles, company history; can search by business size, location, length of time in operation, and industry
- *Dialog* (www.dialog.com): article abstracts, references, and full documents; statistical tables; business and financial information.
- *D&B* (www.dnb.com): business information (global); America's corporate families; industry norms; key business ratios.
- *Experian* (www.experian.com): direct marketing; real estate information.
- *Hoovers* (www.hoovers.com): comprehensive company, industry, and market intelligence.
- *People Lookup* (www.peoplelookup.com) and *Yahoo* (www.yahoo.com): provide information and directory of the Internet as well as individuals, business, and finance.

Other useful resources are:

- *IRB*—International Resource Bureau (irbsearch.com) is one of the most widely used databases in the nation, if not the world. It offers the most current addresses and up to a 30-year-plus address history. Links to relatives, neighbors, and associates are also available in Comprehensive Reports. Billions of records are updated daily. A sample comprehensive custom report is shown in Appendix 14.1.
- *IRB Search, LLC*, is the largest and most powerful database of people, businesses, and their assets.
- *TLO* (www.tlo.com): TLOxp for professional investigators leverages the largest, most powerful online database of public and proprietary records available providing information about people, businesses, assets, and locations. Private investigators, detectives, bail agents, and process servers use TLOxp to conduct deep investigations to find missing persons, locate and recover debt, and find more bail fugitives faster and at less expense than ever before. Our investigative database is updated constantly, ensuring that investigators find the most accurate phone numbers, SSNs, and location information to solve investigations faster. Built on an architecture of advanced linking algorithms and cutting-edge supercomputing, the TLOxp Online Investigative System allows investigators to quickly identify interrelationships between people, their relatives and associates, businesses, assets, and locations so they can easily connect the dots and solve their cases.
- *IQ Data Online* is another database that provides access to billions of records. They also offer document retrieval services.
- *Locateme.com* is an online database search company that accesses approximately 422 million records. They also specialize in adoption searches.
- *Tracers Information Specialists, Inc.*, is a tool for employment screening, collections, legal research, investigations, and insurance (www.tracersinfo.com).
- *Information America* is a very large database that provides access to over 800 million records (infoam.com). They have both "person locator" and "skip tracer" database information resources. It is also a subscription service database.
- The *KnowX.com* database is a subsidiary of ChoicePoint. They specialize in low price information on the Internet. Their "Ultimate People Finder" searches telephone directories, real property databases, and death records. They have access to millions of records.

- *Merlin* is a database company that also offers CD-ROMS for sale with lists of names taken from public records—that is, voter registration lists, property records, and so on. They also offer online services at merlindata.com

Searching for Financial and Business Information

Information regarding finance and business can generally be located within proprietary, local, state, and federal records. The following searches are helpful in locating such information:

- Property information at the county level
- Assumed business name or sales tax registration to locate sole-proprietorship business information
- UCC filings at the state level to find general business information
- Business incorporation documents at the state level
- Bankruptcy filings, tax liens, and judgments
- Business reports from the Better Business Bureau

Searching for Legal Information

- State and federal records—The fraud examiner can search most state court records by visiting the county court's Web site, or federal records by visiting the district court's Web site for the particular area or the Public Access to Court Electronic Records (PACER) database. PACER is an online database that provides users with a means to obtain case and docket information from the federal courts.
- Criminal convictions—Some states provide statewide searches for criminal convictions. The type of information provided varies (e.g., whereas one state provides information on arrests, charges, and misdemeanor and felony convictions, another state may provide information only on felony convictions).
- Laws and court cases—FindLaw and MegaLaw are search engines that allow fraud examiners to locate most laws and big cases for free. For more in-depth information, you can subscribe to a commercial database, such as Lexis or Westlaw. Such databases provide fraud examiners with search tools such as federal and state statutes, international law, case decisions, and professional publications regarding particular subject matters. Subscriptions can be costly but are invaluable tools for quickly searching for a particular law or case.
- Security- and fraud-related information (QuickFind).

- Insurance information (FraudTracer).
- Criminal record information at the county level, and other services, including employment screening, corporate due diligence, fraud and private investigations, and tenant screening (G.A. Public Records Services).
- Publications and news and history, images, and maps (HighBeam Research).
- Publications (Data Times).

Search Engines

The cheapest and most basic way to find information online is to use an Internet search engine. Search engines allow the fraud examiner to type in a single keyword or multiple keywords describing a particular subject. The search engine then searches the Internet and locates pages that contain your keywords.

The following search engines are favorites for locating information in a fraud examination or investigation:

- Google
- Yahoo
- Bing
- Beaucoup!
- Excite
- Lycos
- Alta Vista

To efficiently use search engines, the fraud examiner must know how to construct the proper queries. Most searching allows the use of keywords, but simply typing in "fraud" and then "insurance" probably will give you much more information than you will need, including information that has nothing to do with insurance fraud. In order to successfully search for a topic, it is important to make use of Boolean operators.

Boolean operators are symbols that help the search engine yield more accurate results based on a more precise search. For example, using quotation marks around "insurance fraud" will ensure that a search engine will search for the two words together rather than all sites that contain "insurance" and/or "fraud." Common Boolean operator symbols and connectors include the following:

+ Designates words that must appear right next to each other when you use this symbol between two or more search keywords (e.g., Insurance + Fraud)

— Designates words that should not appear on a Web page when you put this symbol between two or more search keywords (e.g., "Pyramid Scheme" Egypt)

"" Designates a list of words that must appear together when you put a phrase in quotation marks (e.g., "insurance fraud")

OR Designates two connected words, one of which must appear on a page, when you use OR between two or more search keywords (e.g., "insurance fraud" OR "insurance scams") (Note: "OR" should be capitalized.)

Limitations of Online Searches

To avoid inefficient research when searching for public records, the professional investigator must know the appropriate jurisdiction in which the search should be conducted. For example, when looking for land titles, liens, divorce records, etc., the investigator must search records in the county in which the suspect's information exists. Though a multijurisdictional database can help you find general information when you lack specifics, it can also lead to records of another individual with the same name. Be aware that most online public records are mere summaries of the full, original public record. Thus, if you need the full record for additional details or evidentiary purposes, you should contact the county clerk or records office to obtain a certified copy of the original document.

Search Engines—Business

- Business Information—LibrarySpot (www.libraryspot.com)
- Business.com—business portal to public records of companies, plus more (www.business.com)

Search Engines—Geographic

- American Community Network (www.ScienceCentral.com)
- International Chamber of Commerce and City-State-Province Directory (www.chamber-of-commerce.com)

Search Engines—Government (United States)

- gov.search (www.usa.gov)

- CataLaw—catalogs of worldwide law on the Internet; indexes of law and government (www.catalaw.com)
- Center for Immigration Studies (www.cis.org/)
- EPA; Envirofacts (www.epa.gov/enviro)
- GovStartPage.com (www.govstartpage.com)—your start page to government on the Web
- Office of Justice programs (www.ojp.usdoj.gov)—links to Office of Justice bureaus, program offices, and support offices
- OSHA statistics and data (www.osha.gov/oshstats/)
- Middletown Thrall Library government information: GovSites (www.thrall.org/govsites/htm)

Search Engines—How to Search

- Search Engine Showdown—compares search engines, gives advice on use of search engines for specific needs, and provides suggestions as to when to use multiple search engines.
- 1997 Investigators Guide to Sources of Information.
- Answering Reference Questions Using the Internet (www.bcpl.gov.bc.ca/workshop/table.htm
- How to Effectively Locate Federal Government Information on the Web

Telephone and E-Mail Directories

- National Cellular Directory
- Telephone Area Code Finder© by MMIWORLD
- SuperPages Yellow Pages
- 411 Locate (www.411locate.com)
- Area Code Changes
- Area Decoder (If you know the area code but do not know the city name, enter the area code in the "City or Area Code" field. If you know the city name, state name, and/or country name, enter those into the appropriate fields.)
- Bigfoot (search.bigfoot.com)
- BigYellow—Online Yellow Pages Directory
- Reverse Lookup—555-1212.com
- PC411—The North American Phone Book
- Fone Finder (www.primeris.com/fonefind)—use area code and prefix to find city and carrier
- Switchboard—telephone and e-mail directory, people locators, skip tracing
- Ultimate Email Directory—reverse email search

- Ultimate White Pages
- Yahoo! People Search

Telephone and E-Mail Directory—Reverse

- ThreeClicks.com
- MyFreeemailsearch.com
- AnyWho.com

Competitive Intelligence and Business Research

- Intelliscope (SM) Service
- *Sun Tzu and the Art of Business*, Mark R. McNeilly
- Enviroknow: health and environment resource center
- Minnesota Public Radio—The Surveillance Society
- The Economist Intelligence Unit
- 1Jump.com—The ultimate business portal. 1,000,000 selected companies. 50 interlinked content databases
- The Benchmarking Exchange and Best Practices Homepage
- The CI Resource Index—a search engine and listing of sites by category for finding Competitive Intelligence resources (information sources and the vendors of CI services and products). (CIseek.com)
- Cipher (www.cipher-sys.com/)
- CMSWire—business intelligence
- *Competitive Intelligence Handbook*, Richard Coombs Associates
- Deadline Online (www.deadlineonline.com/)
- Hoovers—company information (www.hoovers.com/)
- Science news (www.eurekalert.org/)
- Competitive Intelligence Research Center—Fuld & Company Inc.
- Internet Prospector Reference Desk
- Locating U.S. Copyright Holders (www.copylaw.com/)
- Omniquad Security Blog
- Strategic and Competitive Intelligence Professionals (scip.org/)

Databases—Health; Business

- Health Information Resource Database (www.health.gov/nhic/newssrch.htm)
- RBB Reuters Business Briefing

Document Retrievers

- National Association of Background Investigators (ACBI.net)

- BRB Publications, Inc.—information broker
- The Pettit Company—UCC and other filing and search services

Investigator Portals

- Reddy's Forensic Page—links to sites of general forensic interest, forensic science organizations, forensic science journals, and colleges and universities with forensic programs (www.forensicpage.com/)
- Bombsecurity.com—central source for information on explosive-related protection issues; explosives, forensics
- Crime Spider—national directory of private investigators and protective services listed by city/state and/or services offered; free resource center offering an extensive database of investigative tools
- MyRecords.com—investigative bookmarks locate reference resources
- Council of Private Investigators-Ontario (www.cpi-ontario.com/)
- eInvestigator.com—private investigator resources
- Firearms ID (firearmsid.com)—firearm identification, references, forensics
- VirtualGumshoe.com
- Loc8fast—investigative bookmarks locate reference resources
- Attorney's Toolbox—competitive intelligence and business research, skip tracing, form letters (www.macattorney.com/tools.html)
- Investigative Links Directory—investigative bookmarks locate reference resources
- Forensic Law and Science—investigative bookmarks locate reference resources (www.pimall.com/nais/links-forensic.html)
- PI Portal—investigative bookmarks locate reference resources (osp.osu.edu/portalguide/portalguide.pdf)
- Sheila Lowe & Associates—handwriting analysis software, forensics (www.sheilalowe.com/)

Other Internet Sites

The following additional Web sites may be helpful in locating skips and other missing persons:

www.ancestry.com/ssdi/advanced.htm
www.crimetime.com
www.cyberspydetective.com
www.ftc.gov/os/statutes/fcra.htm

www.iaf.net
www.infospace.com
www.infousa.com
www.interagencyla.com
www.iqdata-inc.com
www.militaryusa.com
www.onestopinfo.com
www.pimall.com
www.tracersinfo.com
www.virtuallibrarian.com/it
www.well.com/user/fap/foia.htm
www.whowhere.com

Government Records

Government records that may be used to locate people include driver's licenses, motor vehicle registrations, and the U.S. Postal Service. Previously, investigators could obtain change of address information under Freedom of Information Act (FOIA) requests. Since that practice has been discontinued, you can obtain the new address from the post office by sending a letter marked "Do Not Forward. Address Correction Requested" to the previous, known address.

Civil and criminal records can be reviewed at the county clerk's office. By checking the Department of Health, Office of Vital Statistics, birth and death records can be obtained under certain circumstances.

The Department of State, Division of Corporations may have records on corporations, officers and registered agents, partnerships, and fictitious names for businesses. The Board of Elections, Voter's Registration has the names and addresses of all registered voters in the county. The Property Records Office maintains the names and mailing addresses of all property owners.

The FOIA will reveal the present duty assignments of military personnel, as well as information on discharged personnel. You may contact the U.S. Locator Service 10, at P.O. Box 2577, St. Louis, MO 63114; telephone (314) 423-0860; or send e-mail to uslocator@earthlink.net. See Figure 14.2.

Under certain circumstances, addresses can be obtained from the Social Security Administration or provided to other government agencies (i.e., deadbeat dads, etc.). You may also obtain information from the U.S. Passport Office. Civil, criminal, and bankruptcy information is available from the courts.

In the county recorder's office, official index, deeds, liens, and judgments are available for review. From the Bureau of Alcohol, Tobacco, and Firearms, you may obtain the names and addresses of all owners and operators of establishments where alcohol and tobacco are sold. The Federal Aviation Administration will provide the names and addresses of all pilots or owners of aircraft.

Public Records Information

Bureau of Vital Statistics

- Records are maintained on deaths, births, and marriages. Aside from parties' names, records will also show addresses, relatives, and witnesses.

Property Assessor's Office

- Maps of real property are on file, including dimensions, addresses, owners, taxable value of property, and improvements.

Street Department

- Maps of the city are kept on file, showing widths of streets, locations of conduits, drains, sewers, and utility lines. Also listed are current street numbers, abandoned streets, and rights-of-way.

City and County Business Licenses and Permit Offices

- These records contain the name, address, phone, owner, type of business, date filed, and expiration or renewal date on a license.

Local Police and Fire Departments

- Local law enforcement may know the subject and may even run a check for you, if you approach them correctly. The fire department might tell you if they have ever received a fire zoning violation.

Fictitious Filings (DBA)

- These records are kept by owner's name and cross-referenced by the business name. They will give you the name and address of any business the subject is involved in. Also, the names and addresses of all registrants and the date of filing are available. For a small fee, they will also certify this information for use as a court document.

Building Department

- This department issues building permits, maintaining applicants on file, addresses of construction sites, amount and cost of construction, and the names of builders. Blueprints and diagrams showing construction details are also available.

Fire Marshal and Sanitary Engineer

- These are the officials who conduct inspections on businesses to check for possible violations of code. They have the right to inspect all premises.

County Recorder's Office

- This office maintains official index records. All instruments are required to be recorded; all papers pertaining to real estate transactions, marriage certificates, contracts (prenuptial), petitions for separation and divorce decrees (lots of information contained), notice of lien and attachment on real estate, certified copies of decrees and judgments of courts of record, official bonds, and, occasionally, birth and death records.
- Also available in the County Recorder's Office is the General Index to Official Records. It is cross-indexed as to plaintiffs and defendants, grantors and grantees. The General Index shows the date that the instrument was filed, the defendants and the plaintiffs, the type of instrument, and the book and page of official records where the instrument may be found.

County Clerk's Office

- This office may be checked for naturalization records, marriage license applications, petitions for divorce, and criminal files.
- The Naturalization Records and Record Book provides the names of applicants for citizenship, port and date of entry, manner of arrival, declaration of intent, and miscellaneous information relating to the naturalization process.
- Marriage license applications provide pertinent information about applicants.
- Petitions for Divorce include information on the grounds or charges, place and date of marriage, children, and community property.
- Criminal files provide information about the complaint, the arresting officer's report, a description of preliminary proceedings, and other pertinent information.

Property Assessor's Office

- This office maintains plats or maps of real property in the county; with dimensions, address of owner, taxable value, and legal description. Files also include information on buyers and sellers of the property.

County Tax Collector

- Records of names and addresses of property owners, legal descriptions of property are kept, as well as a record of the amount of taxes paid on real and personal property, and whether or not taxes are delinquent.

Registrar of Voters or Board of Elections

- The affidavits of registration that include some biographical information on registrants are kept on file here. They have a file that lists registered voters according to precincts and a roster of voters. Listings are maintained on microfiche and include subject's name, address, telephone number, date of birth, date registered, and voter registration number. This is free. Also on file are the nomination papers of candidates for public office.

Department of Motor Vehicles

- Provides information regarding operator's licenses, verification of certificates of title, motor or serial numbers, license plate, and vehicle ownership.

Health and Rehabilitative Services
Social Service Agencies and State Unemployment

- These offices maintain information concerning individuals receiving assistance from these agencies. This information may be obtained for legitimate investigative purposes.

Professional and Licensing Bureaus (Department of State and Department of Agriculture)

- These bureaus set professional and vocational standards for the state and issue licenses or certificates to individuals who qualify. Professional and vocational groups licensed by such agencies include doctors, dentists, social workers, real estate agents and brokers, funeral directors, cosmetologists, contractors, pest control specialists, dry cleaners, chiropractors, accountants, teachers, architects, attorneys, and private investigators.

Florida Department of Law Enforcement (FDLE)

- Maintains criminal records on all individuals who have been arrested in the state of Florida. Other states have State Police Agencies that keep criminal records of individuals arrested in that state.

State Bureau of Alcohol, Beverages, and Tobacco

- Governs the issuance of licenses to establishments that sell alcoholic beverages and tobacco. They are usually a valuable resource of information about such establishments.

Appendix 14.1: IRB—Custom Comprehensive Report (Sample)

Subject Information:
Name: RORY J MCMAHON DOB: 7/11/1XXX
SSN: xxx-xx-xxxx issued in New York between *1/1/19xx* and *12/31/19xx*
Names Associated With Subject:
KORY J MCMAHON DOB: 7/11/1__ Age: __
Liens and Judgments:
    [None Found]
Phones Plus(s):
    Name: RORY MCMAHON
    Address: ____ NW ____ -RD TER, COCONUT CREEK
    FL 33066-2225
    Phone Number: 954-956____ - EDT
    Phone Type: Residential
    Carrier: BELLSOUTH SO BELL - (POMPANO BEACH, FL)
Email Address:
Name:
  RORY MCMAHON
SSN: xxxx-xx-xxxx
Email Address(es):
  RORYM@__________ -.COM
Street Address(es):
  1451 W CYPRESS CREEK RD, FT LAUDERDALE FL 33309-1961
People at Work:
  Name: RORY J MCMAHON
  Gender: Male
  Title: CHIEF EXECUTIVE OFFICER
  Company: INVESTIGATION EDUCATION CONSULTANTS INC.
  Address: ____ W CYPRESS RD SUITE __ -, FT LAUDERDALE
    FL 33309
  FEIN: 20-1304244

Dates: May 4, 2007 - Jul 18, 2008
Company: R. J. MCMAHON & ASSOCIATES, INC.
Address: 1451 W CYPRESS CREEK RD STE 300, FT LAUDERDALE FL 33309-1953
Phone: 954-956-9066
FEIN
Dates: Sep 30, 2003 - Jul 18, 2008

Driver's License Information:
Name: RORY J MCMAHON
State: Florida
License Address: 78 NW, __, __ FL 33067
DOB: 07/11/1__ -
Gender: Male
Ethnicity: WHITE
Expiration Date: 07/11/2__ -
Issue Date: 06/02/2008
License Type: Renewal
License Class: Non-Commercial - Regular Operator License
Height: 6'02

Address Summary:
7800 NW ____, PARKLAND FL 33067-2498, BROWARD COUNTY (May 2005 - Oct 2008)
1451 W CYPRESS CREEK RD APT 300, FORT LAUDERDALE FL 33309-1961, BROWARD COUNTY (Feb 2000 - Aug 2008)
NW— RD TER, COCONUT CREEK FL 33066-2225, BROWARD COUNTY (May 1999 - Jul 2006)
____ N OAKLAND FOREST DR APT 15, OAKLAND PARK FL 33309-7652, BROWARD COUNTY (1999 - 2001)
____ N OAKLAND FOREST DR APT 101, OAKLAND PARK FL 33309-7632, BROWARD COUNTY

Active Address(es):
78 NW ____, __ FL 33000-BROWARD COUNTY (May 2005 - Oct 2008)
Current Residents at Address:
F L E
RJM

MCMAHON & ASSOCIATES 954-341-2001

Motor Vehicles Registered To Subject:
Vehicle:
Description: 2002 BMW 325I - Sedan 4 Door
VIN: WBAEV ________________
Owner(s)
Name: RORY J MCMAHON

Possible Criminal Records:
[None Found]
Professional License(s):
[None Found]
Possible Associates:
____ CHOUIE DOB: 10/9/1959 (Aug 1989)
__: 5/18/1949 DOD: 9/4/2007 Age at Death: 58 (Born 59 years ago) - Proof
Issued in Kentucky between 1/1/1966 and 12/31/1967
Names Associated with Associate:
C F DOB: 5/18/1949 DOD: 9/4/2007 Age at Death: 58 (Born 59 years ago)

Appendix 14.2: Sample Forms

MCMAHON & ASSOCIATES DETECTIVE DIVISION

SKIPTRACE OR BACKGROUND CHECKLIST

SUBJECT ____________________ OUR FILE : ____________________

CLIENT ____________________ INV ____________________

CLIENT ____________________ TYPE ____________________

ATTY/CONTACT ____________________ THEIR FILE ____________________

CLIENT PHONE ____________ FAX ____________ EMAIL ____________

DATE	F/U	ACTIVITY/SEARCH/DATABASE/CALLS/VERIFICATION—TYPE OF SEARCH OR ACTION TAKEN
		SUMMARIZE DATE/ACTION TAKEN-CHECK IF FOLLOWUP (F/U) NEEDED-COPIES OF SEARCHES IN FILE
		Master Files-Merlin Criss-Cross-Telephone Directories-Web Telephone Directories-Detail Searches
		General Web Searches-Google-Copernic Pro-Note Others
		Mail Address Forwardings -Detail Addresses-USPS.com-Fax Form
		IRB-Computer Name Searches-Detail Databases Searched
		Motor Vehicles-Use In-House-Locate Plus
		Drivers License-Softech Int. or Detail Other
		Property Checks-Online Sources-Tax Assessor-Recorder Offices- Searchsystems.net
		Litigation Searches-Criminal-Civil-Traffic –brppub.com
		Recorder Info-Tax Liens-Judgments-UCCs –Searchsystems.net
		Utilities Search
		-
		Newspapers-Factiva-Google News-thelocatlnewspapers.com
		Incarceration Records-Death Records-IL Penal (State)-Vinelink (County)-Bureau of Prisons (Fed)
		Death Records-Kadima-Legacy-Local Newspaper Websites

X* - Denotes Follow-up required

Figure 14.1 Sample skiptrace or background checklist. (continued)

PAGE ____

SKIPTRACE CHECKLIST/

PHONE CALL/CONTACT REGISTER

SUBJECT: ______________________________ **OUR FILE:** __________________________

DATE	F/U	ACTIVITY/SEARCH/DATABASE/CALLS/VERIFICATION---TYPE OF SEARCH OR ACTION TAKEN
		SUMMARIZE DATE/ACTION TAKEN-CHECK IF FOLLOWUP (F/U) NEEDED-COPIES OF SEARCHES IN FILE
		NOTE YOUR TECHNIQUE USED TO VERIFY INFORMATION-SKIPTRACY TYPE NUMBERS LEFT/USED WITH EXTENSION
		Contacts- -Detail Pretext & Call Back Number Used- Relatives-Neighbors-Landlords-Friends-References-Past Employers

X* - Denotes Follow-up required

Figure 14.1 (continued) Sample skiptrace or background checklist. (continued)

PAGE ____

SKIPTRACE CHECKLIST/

PHONE CALL/CONTACT REGISTER

SUBJECT: ______________________ **OUR FILE:** ______________________

DATE	F/U	ACTIVITY/SEARCH/DATABASE/CALLS/VERIFICATION—TYPE OF SEARCH OR ACTION TAKEN
		SUMMARIZE DATE/ACTION TAKEN-CHECK IF FOLLOWUP (F/U) NEEDED-COPIES OF SEARCHES IN FILE
		NOTE YOUR TECHNIQUE USED TO VERIFY INFORMATION-SKIPTRACY TYPE NUMBERS LEFT/USED WITH EXTENSION
		Contacts- -Detail Pretext & Call Back Number Used- Relatives-Neighbors-Landlords-Friends-References-Past Employers

X* - Denotes Follow-up required

Figure 14.1 (continued) Sample skiptrace or background checklist. (continued)

Bypassing Barriers:
Sharing Information on Military Personnel

The Bottom Line (Simple Approach to getting it all):

Send one written request to the facility's credentials office:
**Request the privileging/risk management information you need.
**If they refuse, get written explanation.
**May need to work through higher headquarters.
**Use exception to Title 10 to force release (see notes on privacy act).

Send second written request to the facility's legal office:
**Request copies of all "command directed formal and informal investigations of allegations of misconduct against (person's name)"
**Include personnel's waiver of Privacy Act, if you have one.
**If legal office refuses, ask for written explanation of denial.

[Using a subpoena makes requests more powerful; If denied information, your recourse is to go to a Federal Judge with the agency's written explanation of denial and get the Judge to force them to release info]

Terms to Know:

DOD or DoD—Department of Defense

MTF—Medical Treatment Facility—Marines do not have Medical
—only Air Force, Army and Navy

JAG—Judge Advocate General—the Legal Office or Officer(s)
CJA—Center Judge Advocate—Lead Attorney for a specialized center
SJA—Staff Judge Advocate—Attorney for a major command/installation

FOIA—Freedom of Information Act

"Protected under Title 10"—refers to confidentiality of medical quality assurance records—under Title 10, US Code, Section 1102.

Article 15—non-judicial punishment used by military commanders
--May be used in lieu of court martial for some offenses
--Serious for an officer to have one (usually a career killer)
--Virtually automatic for DUI, illegal drug use
--Used for shoplifting, breech of ethics, false statements
--Max punishment for officer; ½ month pay for 2 months, 30 days house arrest, 60 days restriction, and reprimand

Figure 14.2 Information on military personnel. (continued)

--known as "Captain's Mast" in the Navy

Court Martial—used for a wide range of violations of military law
--Enforces the Uniform Code of Military Justice (UCMJ)
--Includes typical criminal actions, but also others (conduct unbecoming)
--Used for larceny, child abuse/pornography, spouse abuse w/injury and typical major crimes (murder, etc.)
--Used if command is seeking officer's dismissal from service (Extremely Serious—result is like "Branded")
--This is a federal conviction; however, since some of the "crimes" in the military (such as Article 133) do not fit in the scheme of civilian laws, they may not appear in an NCIC report.

Conduct Unbecoming an Officer (Article 133 of UCMJ)—unique to military law
--Used for broad range of breaches of discipline
--Inappropriate conduct that brings disrepute to the military
--Includes offenses not covered in civilian law, for example
--Cursing at a neighbor
--Associating with people involved with drugs
--Male dancing at a club as female impersonator
[--Selling items to a subordinate (such as multilevel marketing)—Art 92]

OMPF—Official Military Personnel File (provided on microfiche)—has complete service record and military can get it.
--Any service member (present or past) may bet a copy
--Obtained from service personnel command
--Contains efficiency reports, disciplinary actions, but not privileging info
--Efficiency reports are highly inflated; if not glowing, look for a problem* "OERs" (tend to be inflated)
--If average or below average report—read the verbiage carefully
--However, with new army reports (>1998), center of mass is OK
--With a waiver of Privacy Act, agency may obtain a copy.

DD 214—Documents release from active military service (everyone on active duty get a green card and not on active anymore has one)
--Includes courts-martial convictions, awards, time of service
--Copy given to every service member when leaving military
--Used as proof of past military service for government agencies

15-6 Investigation (Army) – (might not be used by Navy) —command directed administrative investigation; statements made or sworn statement in a 15-6)
--Other military services have similar informal investigation systems

*If OER says anything negative, it is a huge event.

Figure 14.2 (continued) Information on military personnel. (continued)

--Can be done by individual or tribunal (done by a senior officer who has knowledge of the incident)

Need to know who denial authority is – appeal to them – get denial in writing.

<u>**Excuses for not releasing information.**</u>

"That's Quality Assurance information and it's protected under Title 10" (National Defense Authorization Act for Fiscal Year 1987—Public Law no. 99-661, Section 1102, Title 10, US Code)

--provides that records created by or for DOD in a medical or dental QA program are confidential and precludes release, EXCEPT **disclosure** of records or testimony **is allowed** to government boards, agencies, or professional health care societies/organizations **if needed to perform licensing, credentialing, or monitoring of the professional standards of any present or former member of the DOD (Title 10, Section 1102, para (c)(1)(C).**

--Local MTF may say they cannot release information, however, it may (and should) be released by their higher headquarters [such as MEDCOM (US Army Medical Command), BUMED—HLTHCARE SUPPO (US Navy Bureau of Medicine and Surgery—Healthcare Support Office), or AFMOA (US Air Force Medical Operations Agency). Expect this for any adverse information. If local level tries to be non-responsive, push them that they must give you written denial of release from their denial authority (if still balking, suggest that <u>denial authority</u> review the law—remind them of the exception).

"That's protected under the Privacy Act" (5 USC Section 552A)

--If they are claiming they are protecting the personnel's privacy, get a waiver of the privacy act from the personnel. Have the personnel sign a statement saying "I hereby waive my rights under the Privacy Act of 1974 to allow the XYZ medical board access to any records concerning my medical privileges/practice during the period of (date) to (date)". Alternatively, apply for the information under as above under QA Information or via the FOIA (below).

--Privacy Act should not be used as an excuse for non-release of QA information to a government licensing agency.

--If they claim they are protecting patient privacy, request they simply blacken out the patient's name and identifying number, but leave all other info.

"We can't release that under the Freedom of Information Act (FOIA) because it is medical/personal information" (5 USC Section 552)

--Although medical/personal information is generally thought of as protected from release, the regulation actually only excludes information where disclosure would clearly be an invasion of privacy. The agency who receives the request for release of information should do a balancing act between the invasion of privacy and the public's interest in disclosure. If you suggest that it is in the best interest of the public to release the information, it may help. The local MTF is typically NOT the denial authority—they have to send the FOIA request to a higher level for denial.

Figure 14.2 (continued) Information on military personnel. (continued)

--Requesting information via FOIA is the common man's subpoena—anyone may request information under FOIA; however, the government may turn down the request for a variety of reasons outlined in the act.

Ways to request information:

Send request to MTF Credentials office – They typically release routine favorable information, but will refer the request to higher headquarters if there is adverse information. This is a good route to request "QA" information (credentials, risk management). Generally, a written request for release of the privileging or risk management information you need should get you what you need, though it may be slow because of needing to go through higher headquarters. [May choose to sight the exception to Title 10 (see next page)]

Send FOIA Request to the MTF JAG—You may NOT request QA information via a FOIA request. Needs to be done as separate requests.

Note: Privacy Act waiver by personnel should help you get what you want; however, see next page.

Note: Subpoena for "command directed formal and information investigations of allegations of misconduct against (person's name)" will help you get non-QA documents that may have useful information for your investigation. If you do not ask for this information separately, you may not get it—it may not be in the credentials file if credentials office is unaware or didn't use it to take action. (Judge signature = most powerful; if only agency subpoena, may not get the information—since military is federal, might not readily respond to state agency) Non-QA documents that might be useful could include EO investigations, criminal investigations, 15-6 investigations, and other administrative inquiries. (These are places to look for smoke that you might not usually encounter in a credentials file) If Subpoena is denied, contact the JAG office for a written explanation

In some states, you can get an inexpensive and rapid background check by requiring the individual to get a permit for a handgun—if issued a permit, the individual has no felonies or misdemeanors involving domestic relations (Lautenberg Act, 1976)

Figure 14.2 (continued) Information on military personnel. (continued)

Contact/Reference information:

Credentials/Privileging information:
US Army MEDCOM (Medical Command)—210-221-6195
US Navy HLTHCARE SUPPO—904-542-7200 (might try ext. 8111)
US Air Force MOA (Medical Operations Agency): 202-767-4077

DOD:
Information and links: http://defenselink.mil
Publications: http://www.defenselink.mil/pubs/
Directives, instructions, and memos: http://web7.whs.osd.mil/corres.htm
DD 214 information: http://members.aol.com/usregistry/warlib25.htm
DD 214 codes: http://members.aol.com/usregistry/warlib45.htm

Army:
http://www.armymedicine.army.mil
Copies of regs: http://www.usapa.army.mil/
Personnel: http://www-perscom.army.mil/
AR 40-68 Quality Assurance Administration
AR 40-48 Non-physician Healthcare Providers
AR 40-66 Medical Records Administration

Navy:
Info and publications: http://navymedicine.med.navy.mil/
BUMED Instruction 6320.66B Credentials Review and Privileging Program
BUMED Instruction 6320.67 Adverse Privileging Actions, Peer Review Panel Procedures, and Health Care Provider Reporting

Air Force:
Copies of publications: http://afpubs.hq.af.mil/ (electronic publications)
Personnel info: http://www.afpc.randolph.af.mil/
AFI 44-119 Medical Service Clinical Quality Management

Miscellaneous:
CFRs: http://www.access.gpo.gov/nara/cfr/cfr-retrieve.html
(Code of Federal Regulations)
Military Law info: http://www.freeyellow.com/members5/uppmlj/main.html
Administrators In Medicine: http://www.docboard.org/

Figure 14.2 (continued) Information on military personnel. (continued)

Sue Abreu MD - Colonel
Military Personnel/Communications

St. Louis is the depository for information in the military
-will take awhile to get information from this depository
-ORB—officer record brief – is kept at local level

PA's are not required to be licensed
NP's are not required to be licensed—but has to be licensed as an RN and meet qualifications of NP.

Figure 14.2 (continued) Information on military personnel.

Surveillance

15

General Rules

The three general rules to follow are obey the law, your life is more important than the assignment, and never tell anyone who you are.

It is better to lose your subject than to burn the case. Never forget that if a subject is lost, he or she can be found again later. However, once the suspect is aware that he or she is being followed, your case is finished. Many subjects become hot (suspicious), but with careful tail work, you can still keep contact without burning the case.

Dress in ordinary clothes that will match your environment. If you must change your appearance, do it by taking off or putting on a hat, a pair of glasses, or a coat. Never dress in conspicuous clothes, but always dress conservatively. If you are using a car, carry a change of street clothing and some work clothes. At night, dress in dark clothing so you will blend in with a dark background.

Presurveillance

Certain activities should be carried out by the investigator before a surveillance. The two most important are as follows:

- Obtain information pertaining to the subject, including a physical description (photo, if possible), the subject's name and current home address (this is useful for locating the subject if contact is lost during the course of surveillance), details of any vehicles that the subject might use, and any mannerisms or other characteristics that might be helpful for identification or other purposes.
- Perform relevant reconnaissance, taking in the target area, including traffic conditions, transportation that could be used by the subject, and determination of suitable sites for surveillance.

Most of these activities can now be performed online where you can find background information on the target, his or her family, vehicles, maps of his or her residence and all surrounding areas, etc.

Foot Surveillance

Never, under any circumstances, lose sight of your subject. If you are following him or her in very heavy sidewalk traffic, stay about 8 to 9 feet behind him or her. If the streets are not crowded, remain further back and, if possible, on the other side of the street. Change position frequently behind the subject so that you are not always directly behind him or her. Try to use other pedestrians as cover.

If your subject turns around, do not panic. He or she is probably looking for an address or something else. Never jump into a doorway or behind a tree or make any other sudden or obvious movement. If the subject stops and turns around, pretend to tie your shoe, look into a store window, buy a paper, or do anything else that would not look out of place. Do not be afraid to talk to people on the street if the subject glances your way. Most individuals are friendly, and this would make the subject think that you live in the area and are not tailing him or her. If you are too close, pass your subject and then pause at a window and slowly look back. Never look your subject directly in the eyes. If you do, he or she will probably remember you the next time he or she sees you, because you have made an impression.

One person alone can do a successful foot surveillance, but a better foot surveillance can be accomplished with two or more people. Never signal to the other investigator by obvious gestures such as waving or shouting.

On a close tail, do not hesitate to follow your subject into an elevator. If he or she gives a floor number, you can give the floor below or above it. Then run up or down the stairway, and cautiously open the door to his or her floor. You will probably see what room your subject enters. Then proceed to the main floor and watch the most likely exit.

If the subject enters a restaurant and you have been instructed to enter also, sit to one side or behind him or her. Ask for the check when your food arrives and carry change so you can pay the bill in the exact amount if your subject leaves in a hurry. Leave a few minutes before he or she does, if possible, so that you will not be delayed when you pay the cashier.

At all times, carry a sufficient reserve of money and credit cards for any emergency. You never know when a subject will take a bus, plane, or train to another city.

Automobile Surveillance

Never take any unnecessary chances. Do not instruct others to do so. A bad accident may mean a jail sentence, cancellation of insurance, loss of a driver's license, plus a life of misery if anyone was seriously hurt or killed. No reputable agency should expect this of employees, and no one should work for an agency that expects such performances. Each person pays his own traffic tickets, insurance, and repair bills.

Use a medium-priced late-model car in a neutral color—light blue, tan, white, or black. Avoid two-tone paint jobs. Never have a car painted in loud colors or drive a car with a noisy muffler or excessive chrome trim. Do not put decals, stickers, or other identifying marks on the car body or windows.

At all times, keep your motor, tires, and brakes in excellent working order. Make sure your headlights are properly adjusted so they will not be noticed at night.

In any type of surveillance, three important factors to be remembered are patience, practice, and relaxation. Reading books and articles on surveillance will not make you an expert. It takes many years of practice to acquire a feel for following people. A great deal of patience is required to wait hours for a subject to appear. Never become discouraged or leave the stakeout position. The minute you leave will be the time the subject decides to take off. Keep in mind that there is no easy way to watch a subject. You can do a better job when you are relaxed than when you are tense and nervous.

Before starting a new surveillance, have your car thoroughly checked. A full tank of gas is essential. You never know where the subject will go. If your gas tank is full, chances are the suspect will need gas before you do.

If for any reason you feel that you might have been detected, or if you will be on a case for a long time, try to change cars. If only one car is employed, try to use two people in it. In this manner, one can drive while the other watches the subject. Also, one person can follow the subject on foot while the other parks the car.

In car tailing, as in foot surveillance, do not remain directly behind the subject. Change lanes frequently, but never change at the same time the subject does. Attempt to keep a car or two between you and the subject (called a cover car). If the subject makes a turn before you can get into the turn lane, go to the next street and turn in the same direction as he or she does. This is called paralleling. Also parallel if your subject is driving on narrow residential streets. If you are on the same street, try to stay at least a block or two behind the subject, depending on traffic.

Be very careful when turning corners, because the subject may have parked immediately around the corner. In such a case, do not panic and stop in the middle of the street or make any other overt actions. Pass the subject and come back around. The same applies to pulling behind the subject at a red light. Few drivers (unless they are hot) watch their rearview mirrors. Also, even hot drivers are usually only hot when they leave their homes for a rendezvous or when they approach the rendezvous spot.

If a subject goes slowly then fast, circles a block, looks in the rearview mirror, or makes a U-turn, it does not mean he or she is hot. Let the subject prove it. If he or she continues such tactics, then drop the surveillance unless you have enough cars to handle the situation.

Familiarize yourself with the city in which you are working. Knowing the area makes it easier to pick up your subject if you should lose him or her. In addition, acquire as much information as you can about your subject so that you can figure out where he or she might have gone if you lose him or her.

When using several tail cars, be sure to alternate cars in a prearranged method. Plan every possible eventuality in advance. The blinking of brake lights may be used for signals. However, the best way to communicate is to use two-way radios or cell phones.

If you use your own car, you should have field glasses (binoculars), city and county maps, a camera, a camcorder, and a change of clothing. It is also a good idea to keep some old clothes in the car. Common sense and good planning will tell you what is essential in all cases.

Stakeouts

Often, obtaining a fixed observation post proves impractical, so the perfect answer is a stakeout truck. Stakeout trucks are usually old panel trucks or vans. However, a milk-type or walk-in delivery truck is recommended. This will allow you to stand up and stretch. Trucks suitable for this purpose can usually be purchased for very little money, if they are 6 to 9 years old or older. It is not essential that the truck be new, because trucks are usually only driven to the scene and left there until the stakeout is over. Trucks are seldom used for tailing, although if a truck is in good running order, it could be used occasionally as a second vehicle.

All locks on the truck must be in working order. A heavy curtain should be placed across the front of the truck, separating the driver's compartment from the rear of the truck. The curtain should be light-proof so that no light may be admitted to the back of the compartment. The rear windows should have hinged light-proof doors over them. The same type of window should be installed on both sides of the truck. One-way glass should be used for the windows. Mirrors of this type could be used, although many people are aware of those, and you might be spotted.

When observing, use only one window at a time, and keep all other window doors firmly closed. Keep a piece of tinted or shaded celluloid over the window you are using, and stand back at least a foot. If the rear compartment is light-free, you will never be detected inside the truck.

Ordinarily, it is recommended to panel the inside of the truck and insert insulation behind the paneling. The truck will then remain cooler in the summer and warmer in the winter. A light-colored truck will reflect the sun's rays and be noticeable, whereas a dark color will absorb them and be less conspicuous. A carpet on the floor is mandatory, not only for insulation, but also to absorb noise and foot movement and render the truck more comfortable.

At night, it is essential to be close to the subject. It is advisable to sit low in the seat or in one of the corners of the back seat where you will not be silhouetted by passing cars. Your windshield will often reflect light, so park in a good spot, then get out and walk a short distance to determine if you can see into your own car. Also ensure that street lights are behind your car rather than in front of it.

Before starting a stakeout, it is advisable to let the local police know you are in the vicinity (not the exact spot), how long you will be there, your license number, and the car's description. This may save your stakeout from being ruined when some nosy neighbor calls the police. If neighbors approach your car, tell them your tag number and to call the police to verify that they know you are there. As with any type of assignment, keep your credentials and business cards on your person at all times.

Tactics

A major problem that may develop is how to weigh the possible loss of contact with a subject against the risk of being detected or exposed. A quick, believable response is called for when a subject takes some action to determine if he or she is under surveillance. It is easier to drop a surveillance before being confronted than to respond to a confrontation by convincing the subject that he or she is mistaken.

If your subject comes directly to you and asks if you are following him or her, never admit it. Tell the suspect that you do not know what he or she is talking about, and walk away. Do not follow him or her again. Always make your subject prove to you that he or she is hot. Just because he or she looks or walks in your direction does not mean that you have been spotted. Make certain before you give up.

Hot subjects will seek to discover a tail by reversing their course of direction, watching mirror and window reflections of individuals following them, dropping a slip of paper to see if it is picked up (pick it up only if you can do so without detection), and driving or walking around a corner and then stopping suddenly. If the subject pauses, keep on going. Do not stop and turn around until it is safe to do so without being detected. A subject also may use another person as a lookout to spot a tail. He or she may drive into a theater, restaurant, or hotel parking lot. If several investigators are assigned, one should enter and the others watch the main exits. A subject also may drive into a residential area where a tail can be easily detected because of lack of concealment.

Surveillance Equipment

Numerous items are required to conduct surveillances. Most surveillances require the basics, which are a flashlight, binoculars, pen and paper or a tape recorder to take notes of the investigator's activities, a camera, and a camcorder.

Microphones

The built-in microphone is located above or to the side of the lens. The sound quality recorded will vary considerably, ranging from poor- to good-quality hi-fi sound. The sound being recorded can be monitored using headphones. Never record during surveillance. It is illegal to record conversations in most states without the consent of both parties.

Formats

The primary format for most surveillances today is digital. Your camcorder should record with the day, hour, and date, for evidentiary value. The camcorder should be able to operate in low light and should have extended battery life.

Holding the Camcorder

Steadiness when holding the camera by hand is an important technique to master. Video cameras and camcorders weigh little more than a 35 mm camera. Their light weight makes them difficult to hold steady. The problem is greater with cameras that offer no shoulder support and must be held in front of the eye. A steady grip is important and comes with practice and concentration.

First, adopt a comfortable stance with legs slightly apart and elbows tucked into your sides to give firm support to the camera. The right hand does the steadying, leaving the left free to adjust the lens. If you must move to follow the action, turn from the waist at half speed, making your movements steady and deliberate, not jerky. Minimize your movements as much as possible. Adopt a camera position that allows for full coverage of the action you wish to record. The more the action develops in view of the camera and the less obtrusive your movements, the more natural the result will be.

Another good technique when taking handheld shots is to look for extra support, such as a wall, doorway, or the back of a chair. For low-angle work, kneel and rest your right elbow on your knee, or lie prone with the camera resting on a pile of books.

There will always be a degree of unsteadiness to handheld shots, but this will be far less apparent using the wide-angle end of the lens, particularly when close to the subject. No matter how skilled you become at handholding the camera, you will never achieve the absolute steadiness that comes with using a tripod.

Technical Surveillance

Technical surveillance involves the use of electronic and visual enhancement devices to view or eavesdrop on subjects in the conduct of their daily affairs.

Bugs, Pen Registers, and Beepers

Ways to obtain investigative information in addition to wiretapping include using bugs to eavesdrop on private conversations; pen registers to record all numbers dialed; and beepers attached to a person, an automobile, or anything being transported, to track the movement of a person or a piece of merchandise. The Fourth Amendment's impact on these devices ranges from a total ban to outright approval.

Unless there is a physical invasion of a constitutionally protected area, it would appear that electronic eavesdropping is permissible under the Fourth Amendment. However, the *Katz v. United States* decision of 1967 negates this theory. In this case, the suspect, placing a call from a public phone, had his conversation recorded by government investigators who had attached a listening device to the outside of the telephone booth. The court held that the right to claim Fourth Amendment protection was not dependent upon the property right in the invaded place but on a reasonable expectation of freedom from government intrusion. Katz is important because it provides the court's view on legitimate electronic surveillance.

In *Smith v. the State of Maryland*, the court ruled that individuals have no expectation of privacy in dialing phone numbers. The installation and use of a pen register, therefore, was not a search, and no warrant was required.

Monitoring Movement of Vehicles and Items of Commerce

The beeper is a device that tracks the movement of contraband, vehicles, or persons usually suspected of or engaging in crime. The beeper must be hidden in advance on the subject to be tracked to follow and trace to its ultimate destination. In 1982, the Supreme Court in *United States v. Knotts* (460 U.S. 276) ruled that monitoring the beeper signals did not invade any legitimate expectation of privacy, and thus there was neither a search nor a seizure under the Fourth Amendment. The beeper surveillance amounted principally to following an automobile on public streets and highways. The court approved the use of a beeper to monitor the movement of vehicles only on public roads. It refused to allow the government to monitor beepers on private property.

Electronic Communications Privacy Act of 1968

The investigative practices permitted by the New York Telephone Company were limited by federal legislation enacted in 1968. The law regulates the use of beepers and pen registers. The statute requires police to obtain a prior court order for any evidence obtained to be admissible in court. It also provides for criminal and civil penalties.

Visual Enhancement Devices

Other technical devices used to observe a subject, vehicle, or other object without detection can be quite simple (binoculars, camera, or telescope), while others are more intricate (infrared snooper scope) and expensive (helicopter or airplane). There have been constitutional challenges to their use, although none have been challenged successfully.

Lower courts have ruled in some cases that visually enhanced observations may be viewed as searches under the Fourth Amendment. The issues of importance are as follows:

- The nature of the area
- The kind of precautions taken by the subject to ensure privacy
- Whether an enhancement device is used to avoid detection of the surveillant after having first made observations with the unaided eye
- Whether the investigator must do something unusual to make the observation, such as climb a fence to be high enough to view the activity or use a telescope
- The distance between the investigator and the behavior or activity of the subject under observation
- The level of sophistication of the viewing device

Practical Considerations

Surveillance should seldom be the task of one person. Vehicles equipped with direct communications systems are generally essential. Less expensive equipment such as CBs, high-quality binoculars, and infrared optical devices may assist in locating suspects without detection and in making a determination as to their activities.

Procedures for Interception of Wire or Oral Communications

Title III, Section 2518 of the Omnibus Crime Bill describes how to obtain an order from a judge authorizing interception of a wire or oral communication. In federal cases, the order must be approved by the Attorney General (or his designate); state cases require the approval of the principal prosecuting officer of the state or its political subdivisions. The applications must be in writing and sworn or affirmed, then submitted to the appropriate federal or state judge for approval.

The order may not remain in effect longer than is necessary to achieve its objectives, and no longer than 30 days. It must be executed promptly, minimizing any interference with communications not subject to interception. There is no limitation on the number of extensions that may be granted, but each must provide the required information and show probable cause. In executing the order, the investigator must avoid all unnecessary intrusions upon innocent communications, thereby respecting the right of privacy.

Appendix 15.1: Notes on Surveillance

JP Merlano

In this section, I will share with you what was never taught to me as a field investigator when I ventured into the surveillance realm of real-time intelligence gathering. Surprisingly, my employers at that time let me loose in "the streets" without much training. The high quality of skill that I developed is being shared with you so you can become a master in the craft of *stealth, invisibility,* and most important, *real-time intelligence gathering.*

Shadowing: "The Craft of Pattern Recognition"

In this section, I discuss the principles of *shadowing*, whereby you will be able to track and predict your target's every move using pattern recognition applications without compromising the integrity of the case or getting burned.

Shadowing is the systematic approach that in the end when properly executed will fuse together the informational pieces, accordingly giving you clear understanding of your target's day-to-day activities commonly referred to as "Pattern Recognition" or "Human-Intelligence Gathering/HUMINT [HUMan INTelligence]."

As a professional, shadowing is the surveillance model that you most likely use the most once you learn how to master all of the surveillance models. Shadowing and pattern recognition are inherently fused together. The common denominators that govern the underlying principles of shadowing in my opinion are various. There is nothing complex about this surveillance model; confidence and general know-how will be your co-pilots.

In shadowing sometimes the informational pieces that you are observing in surveillance stand alone—I refer to this as *fragmentation*—without you having the relevant subcategories to connect the pieces together. Do not allow this to alarm you. Human beings do things all the time that make no logical sense. In pattern recognition you must learn to identify these so-called "illogical pieces" and try to equate them into an entirely different puzzle. However, if a piece does not fit, put it aside. Never discard the piece of information as irrelevant. Make no mistake, all information is relevant, even the information that has no merit. Start a whole new puzzle with pieces that make no sense, for instance. At times, the illogical pieces will make perfect sense. Maybe your target is simply illogical at times. For instance, your target takes the longest route home from work. This might seem illogical to you. However, you must contemplate every reason and option permissible to entertain your wildest imagination. Your target might be taking the longest route home because he or she does not enjoy being at home alone after work because he or she is depressed, or maybe because the target enjoys the scenic route, or maybe your target is smoking marijuana and is trying to conceal this from other members in his or her household. The reason is unknown to you. Do not allow the fragmented pieces of irrelevant information to distract you. Learn to let go of them and move on to bigger pieces that are more relevant to you and your investigation.

As in all surveillance models, an underlying objective is not to get caught or alert your target that he or she is being monitored. Do not do anything while out in the field that is going to draw attention to yourself and ultimately compromise the integrity of your case. Shadowing is a fascinating technique that when mastered accordingly, you will never get burned.

I know you have heard it before, "All professional investigators get burned." That is a fallacy. You will not get burned if you are careful. I will show you how to employ an arsenal of surveillance models that I have crafted throughout the years which will make you invisible and a master in the art of stealth.

One of the reasons I don't get burned by my target is because I know when to let go. I am watching my target so closely that at times I can feel what the target is feeling. While on mobile surveillance I may see my target tapping the steering wheel with his fingers at a traffic light while he is listening to hip-hop with the sunroof open. This normally suggests to me that everything is okay and I am being paranoid if I suspect something is wrong.

As a professional investigator we need to trust our sixth sense and allow our intuition to take control of our modus operandi while out in the field, especially in surveillance where timing is of the essence and hesitation can cost you plenty.

In shadowing, if your intuition is telling you to break off, listen to your inner voice and break off. If you don't, you might be compromising the integrity of the case. Shadowing is about getting closer to your target using various surveillance models. You can always employ the Cool Down Surveillance Model and get back on your target's trail. However, in shadowing time is on your side. In due time, all the informational pieces will fuse together, and you will literally be doing circles around your target, as in the Circular Surveillance Model.

One of the most important operational challenges shadowing brings into play is your willingness to act without hesitation in demanding operational circumstances where timing is of the essence; your ability as a professional will be tested over and over in a matter of a tenth of a second. In shadowing three key factors come into play. The first is *staying cool*, not losing your composure or control no matter what happens in the field. This can be labeled as the *operational equilibrium* or *status quo* in every field investigation where gradual progress is being made. Second is *timing*—you need to know when and how to act without hesitation, with confidence and the utmost professionalism. The more you practice this technique, the easier it will be. It will eventually become second nature to you and you will do this swiftly without drawing attention to yourself. And last, your *operational game plan*. What's your contingency plan? Okay, so you let your target go because he made an illegal U-turn or was braking erratically and you thought letting him go was your best option to preserve the integrity of the case. Was this a good judgment call? The answer to this question will always be yes. As long as the status quo in relation to the preservation of your case remains intact, allowing your target to go will always be a safe operational setback. No regrets. Move on and get over it. If your target does not return home and you have to squash the case for the remainder of the day, it is not as bad as if you had compromised the integrity of the case because you didn't trust your instincts.

Most of your clients have very little idea about the operational challenges that we encounter in the field and what we need to employ to improvise to overcome and adapt to circumstances and operational challenges. Clients are usually busy and do not have the time to listen to the mechanics and operational game plan you have in case something goes wrong. Remember that your clients are driven by results, period. Don't be a cowboy. If you update your client and tell him that you let your target go because you wanted to preserve the integrity of the case rather than get burned, your client will most likely respect you more and will gradually begin to accept your discreet mode of operation and value your service as a professional.

In shadowing, every day is a win-win outcome for the operative no matter what the circumstances are. Nothing can go wrong if the principles of shadowing are being executed accordingly. Shadowing is about putting the pieces together and mostly monitoring from a distance, documenting what is being observed and reinforcing and confirming your observations by simply monitoring your targets do the same things over and over again over a period of time—pattern recognition. In shadowing letting your target go can be a good thing. In employing various surveillance models from our arsenal, we must strive to be as Machiavellian as we are trained to be. Surveillance is like a game of chess between two worthy opponents, and you must respect your opponent and never underestimate his or her actions. In the end only one of you will be the better player.

Shadowing is one of my favorite surveillance models. I perfected the craft of shadowing years back thanks to surveillance assignments from Uncle Sam. These surveillance assignments went on for years, and luckily for me pattern recognition was evident mainly because humans are predictable. I was able to shadow targets for years without ever getting burned or compromising the integrity of the case. Shadowing takes the edge from doubt and uncertainty.

Static Surveillance: "The Craft of Acquisitions of Surveillance Positions"

As a surveillance operative you will spend most of your time inside the confines of your vehicle. I personally spend more time inside my vehicle than I do in my own bed. This has been the case for over a decade now. I'm not complaining. I would not change anything about my life if I had the opportunity.

Static surveillance refers to surveillance positions that are maintained for a prolonged time—hours, days, months, and even years in some cases—with breaks in between. The acquisitions of your surveillance positions will be one of the most important techniques that you will employ during the commencement of your surveillance assignment and throughout the interim of your field investigation. This includes when your target is mobile, whether your target is operating a vehicle or traveling as a passenger, or whether your target is on foot walking to a bus stop or elsewhere, or whether your target boarded a boat, cruise ship, jet ski, or any other kind of water vessel, whether your target is peddling a bicycle or riding a motorcycle or in some cases boarding a small aircraft or commercial airliner. The canvassing and acquisitions of surveillance positions will determine what kind of operative you will be.

There is no manual out there that can effectively tell you which will be the best operational surveillance position for you to acquire without risking detection. However, if you feel comfortable from the surveillance position that you acquired, most likely the surveillance position is a durable one for you to maintain and keep eyes on your target. Canvassing for a surveillance position takes strategy and general know-how concerning logistics.

Always think of your target as being at least a fairly intelligent person worthy of detecting your presence. Do not underestimate your target because of his or her age, background, culture, disability, etc.

Most of your targets will increase their vigilance when they are departing from their home operating their vehicle. This is not because they are on to you or because they think they are being monitored. Targets also increase their vigilance when something draws their attention as being out of place. For instance, when they see a vehicle that is not parked in a residential driveway but rather is parked on the street facing their home. Your target may depart on his or her way to work and say to him- or herself, "I have never seen this vehicle parked on my street." (First mental photo.) Seconds later you begin to follow your target and you are done. You just got burned. Rookie mistake.

Operationally speaking, if you decide to park on the road because there are a lot of other vehicles parked on the road—clusters of vehicles that can actually camouflage you—and you think this is a suitable surveillance position, by all means take it. That sounds like a safe operational move. Maybe there is a cluster of vehicles because it is a weekend and people are home from work. However, during the weekdays this may not be a suitable surveillance position because most people are at work and there are no clusters of vehicles during the work hours. So basically, you have acquired one surveillance position that may be suitable for you on weekends and not weekdays.

While clusters of vehicles are great for surveillance, residential driveways are even better. However, if your engine is turned on while you are parked in someone's driveway, make sure that the puddle of water your radiator is leaking is not too evident, informing others of your presence.

While in static surveillance you need to constantly maintain your vigilance at an equilibrium. For instance, if you see someone walking his or her dog and the person is approaching your location, shut off your engine before the person can hear you do so. If someone hears you shut off your engine and doesn't see anyone get out of the driver's side, that person may call the police and alert them of a suspicious car in the neighborhood. If you are shooting video of your target, shut off the engine so your video will not be shaky.

You continue to canvass the community to search for more surveillance positions and you find a residence that has landscaping that has not been trimmed in months. Maybe there is a lockbox on the door handle to the front entrance, maybe there is a "for sale" sign, or maybe the home is being renovated; whatever the case may be, you decide to use this home as another suitable surveillance position at your disposal.

As a field operative you are not out there to make friends. You are there to get a job done, period. I normally commence my surveillance efforts no later than 6:00 a.m., including weekends. I have no problem arriving to my surveillance site and parking on a stranger's driveway without asking for permission. Sometimes I will hear the garage door behind me open and the tenants will literally freak! Or they may back up without noticing you, and hit your car. If something like this happens, you should exit your car with a badge in your hand and identify yourself, and tell them that the police know that you are out here working on an assignment. Politely ask if you can park on their driveway for the remainder of the day. Sometimes they will think that you are investigating them. If this is the case tell them that if you were investigating them you would not be having this conversation with them. Make up a lie. It is not illegal to lie to people. As a matter of fact, if you have a problem lying to people in this line of work, you might as well quit now.

Pretexting people is the best way to acquire suitable surveillance positions. The best surveillance positions that I have obtained are mostly because of my pretexting abilities. Just make sure that the neighbor is not your target's friend or family. In most cases you will not know this. Your best operational bet is to choose a neighbor's house a few houses down from your target. The farther your surveillance position is from your target's home, the less likely you are of being made or burned by your target. If your target begins to walk toward your car, you had better have a pretext ready. First, hide all of your equipment, especially your video camera. Don't make contact with your target anticipating his or her approach. I have had targets get out from the driver sides of their vehicle, wave at me, and withdraw items from their truck. Do not make contact with your target unless they make contact first. The golden rule is: Never, under any circumstances, admit to your target that you are a private investigator. Never mention the word "surveillance" when you are pretexting people.

If your target approaches your vehicle, cautiously open your window, give the target a big smile, make up a name, and ask, for instance, "Are you Larry from ReMax? I've been for you." Or you can tell your target that you are a student working on a dissertation and you are observing driving patterns in middle-class neighborhoods. Always have an excuse ready, but remember that the more you talk the bigger your hole becomes for you to climb out from. If the situation becomes unbearable, simply turn on your engine and get out of Dodge. You do not have to tell your target anything by law, not even your name, and if your target blocks you in with their car, videotape this and call the authorities; most likely your target will get arrested.

A variety of surveillance positions can be used. Facing your target from the front end of your vehicle is what I recommend. I have seen an investigator secure a surveillance position and monitor the target from the rearview mirror, from the front passenger side of the window, from the back, seated in the back seat. Those positions are okay if you are working against a small window of opportunity and you know that your target will surface within the next 30 minutes. Those positions can work if you increase your vigilance to 2- to 3-second intervals. What I mean by 2- to 3-second intervals is that you glance in the direction once every 2 to 3 seconds; otherwise, your target may depart undetected. I use two-tone front sun shields: black on one side and gray on the other. These sun shades are safe to use; they do not draw attention because they are neutral colors, and you can combine both colors that at a distance gives the illusion of being a different vehicle because of the different colored shades.

What moves draws people's attention. What stays still does not draw people's peripheral vision. I have worked hundreds of surveillance assignments utilizing vehicles with no tints, and I have had people standing right next to my vehicle who did not notice that anyone was inside because they did not detect any movement from inside the confines of the vehicle. If you are utilizing a surveillance vehicle with no tints, simply get yourself some hangers and hang a dark color shirt on the back passenger side (both sides) and recline your seat (driver's seat). If someone looks in your direction, it appears as if no one was inside the vehicle. Get used to wearing a dark color shirt, preferably black, always. Remember that black is your best ally in surveillance. Black blends in well with everything and most importantly, at night a black shirt will fade in with the shadows. Always keep your windows fully closed to block sunlight. Sunlight puts you in the spotlight no matter how tinted your windows are. Cracking the windows will be necessary at times to allow for air to ventilate your car, especially if your engine is off. However, ventilate your vehicle in most cases if your vehicle engine is off by turning on your ignition and putting your air-conditioning on full blast and going out for a 3-minute drive to cool down your vehicle. If your vehicle is like an oven because of the hot summer rays, go and hose it down or get a $6 car wash. This will cool down your vehicle immediately. I normally just drench myself with a gallon of water and that decreases my body temperature immediately. If you begin to hallucinate, that is because you are about to pass out. The heat will do this to you. When you are not hydrated and your body temperature is over the top, you will fall asleep. Do not allow this to happen. Do something. No assignment is worth your life.

Be very cautious of children. Children will ruin your day on any surveillance assignment. Children will surround your car and ask what you are doing in the neighborhood, and if they do not buy into it, they will alert other children, those children will alert their parents, those parents will alert their neighbors, and those neighbors will alert the police.

Lie to whomever you think is justified while out in the field, with the exception of police. Always check in with the local police department when you are settled in at your surveillance position. Give the dispatch call taker for the police department a physical description of what you look like and what you are wearing and also whether there is a firearm in your vehicle. Let the dispatcher know even if he or she does not ask. Also ask for the dispatcher identification number or name, and ask when the shift recycles so you can call back an hour after the new shift comes in and check in again. This may sound troublesome, but it is well worth the time, and it should take you no more than 5 minutes. The only times that I have not checked in with the police are when I am investigating one of their deputies and do not want to risk dispatch informing the subject of investigation of my presence in their neighborhood.

Parking underneath a shade tree is perfect. It keeps your car cool, and you become invisible at a distance.

As in a game of chess, you must anticipate your target's actions. You must learn to cover all probable routes of departure from any vantage position. For instance, if your target is going to be walking out from a supermarket pushing a metal grocery cart and the target is claiming some kind of injury, you want to position your vehicle where you can document your target pushing the metal grocery cart and depositing the groceries into his or her vehicle. This means that you must also anticipate whether your target is going to deposit the grocery bags inside the trunk or the back passenger side. Anticipate everything, because if you do not you will lose your opportunity and you will have to wait until your target goes grocery shopping again. Most surveillance assignments are 2 to 3 days if related to insurance defense on behalf of an insurance carrier, self-insured, or third-party administrator.

Okay, so you obtained video of your target pushing the grocery cart and depositing the groceries inside of the vehicle. What then? I normally break off surveillance and meet my target at his or her home, anticipating the target's arrival so I can document my target unloading groceries, as well. This means that I have to have a surveillance position in mind beforehand. This is why the acquisition of surveillance positions plays such a vital role in surveillance. You must secure those positions when timing is of the essence, secure your video, and fall back to another surveillance position that is less aggressive.

To be an effective field operative, you must know when securing an aggressive surveillance position is warranted. In other words, you should not secure an aggressive surveillance position parked across your target's home to videotape your target withdrawing his or her mail. If your target is pushing a lawn mower and is claiming multiple injuries, securing a surveillance position from across the home when he or she is not looking, or maybe has gone inside the house for a few minutes to cool down, may be a worthy risk—the gains supersede the risk. What are you going to do? Whatever the case, you must figure it out before it is too late.

Surveillance acquisitions at night or early in the morning are less challenging because you can blend in more discretely with low light visibility. You can also get closer to your target without too much risk. Be careful with cell phones and laptops or anything that radiates sound or brightness. Sounds travel farther at night because your surroundings are mostly silent, and pedestrians walking dogs and exercising are more receptive to anything that draws their attention; for instance, your engine running, shadows or noises stemming from your vehicle, and most importantly lights, especially those from cell phones or your laptop. Keep them turned off, because light travels far, particularly at night, even the light from your radio. Dim all of your components on your dashboard to the lowest setting, crack open your window with the radio off, and listen to a garage open, a car engine turning on, the voices of people, a window closing, a dog barking, anything that will give you the heads up that your target is leaving. If you are following your target in low light visibility, make sure your high beams and fog lights are turned off. You can switch on and off your fog lights when your target is out of view to give the illusion that the vehicle behind your target is another vehicle. However, do this only a few times if you feel that you are drawing attention. If you are following your target in your vehicle and you are weaving back and forth, you are going to get burned by your target. Stay linear without switching lanes constantly unless you see your target doing something that suggests that he or she is turning elsewhere. "The nail that sticks out gets hammered."

Open Surveillance: "The Craft of Changing Outcomes"

Most of your surveillance assignments will be *closed surveillance*. In closed surveillance your target does not know that you are monitoring his or her activities periodically and is unaware of your presence. In contrast, in open surveillance you deliberately make yourself known at a distance so your target can catch on and realize that he or she is being watched. In open surveillance you are indirectly intimidating your target to deter certain actions or outcomes. In open surveillance you are in a way preventing your target from engaging in certain activities or actions that can be of interest to your client.

Here are some examples of why you would recommend or employ an open surveillance model. There may be a disgruntled employee who was fired and has threatened his employer that he is going to return to the workplace and go ballistic. You may want your presence to be known to basically discourage the individual from engaging in certain actions. You may want to secure a surveillance position at the target's employment and let your presence be known. Open surveillance is not always conducted at your target's place or home. The kind of message you want to send to your target will dictate where you want the open surveillance to be conducted. For instance, if you want to let your target know that other family members close to them may also be at risk, you may set up your surveillance position near the parents' home or even children. This is legal as long as you do not approach your target or the target's family.

Legally, private investigators are not law enforcement, and therefore probable cause is not required. What this means is that you do not need to show cause to investigate someone as long as you are not criminally liable.

This is why private investigations are private. We are bound to a different standard that law enforcement and the courts can't infringe upon. Take for instance the example mentioned above. Why would you want to use scare tactics involving your target's parents or children? People judge by what they see on the surface. However, the reality of the case is unknown to mostly everyone. Maybe the parents and children are involved in serious matters that require immediate intervention by a private party because the police have no probable cause or resources to investigate; a private investigator may be your only option to settle matters, legally speaking.

Consider open surveillance as sending out a message. In most cases one of two things will happen: your target will realize the severity of his actions and be deterred from engaging in certain actions, or your target will perceive open surveillance as a violation of his privacy and make matters worse for your client. As a professional operative you need to inform your client of the pros and cons; you can be held liable if someone gets hurt.

In open surveillance you should stick to these rules so as to not derail your efforts. Your acquisitions of surveillance positions must always be on a public street, and if you position yourself on private property make sure that you have permission to be there. Check in with the police. Do not carry a firearm in your car in open surveillance. This could send out the wrong message if your carrying a firearm becomes a matter of public record. In open surveillance, your target is going to call the police and tell them that there is a suspicious vehicle following them or monitoring their activities. If you checked in with the police, as you should have, the police dispatch will tell your target that "we know of his presence already." Checking in with the police does not mean that police will not be dispatched to your location. If the police think that making contact with you to verify your identity is warranted, they will be dispatched to your location and you will be approached by a law enforcement officer. In most cases the police are attempting to maintain the peace. Be courteous and explain that you are a private investigator; show police your credentials. The police can tell you to leave or you will be arrested. However, they can only tell you this if you are parked on private property and the tenant is not present to tell police you have their permission to be on their property. If you are parked in a public place like a street, the police can't legally force you to leave. If no law has been broken this does not mean that the police will not make one up. Unfortunately, I have been victimized by police in the past and as a rule of thumb every time that police approach my vehicle, I always have a recording device playing. In Florida, it is illegal to record someone's conversation without his or her consent unless one of the two people is a law enforcement officer conducting an investigation. Guess what—when a police officer approaches your car to conduct an investigation, you are legally permitted to record his voice without his consent because it meets the statute criteria. To date, four law enforcement officers have been suspended from the police department because I chose to record their voices when they were interacting with me while I was out on surveillance. However, most police officers will treat you with respect if you treat them with respect. Then again, some police officers may simply not like your tone of voice or responses, and railroad you. This is why a recording device comes in handy when you are filing your complaint with internal affairs.

Do everything by the book in open surveillance. Your target may call the police and tell them that you are brandishing a firearm or exposing yourself. As a private investigator you must think of the worst-case scenario and be ready for it. This is why you should not carry a firearm in open surveillance. If the police find a firearm in your car, this gives your target's allegations more validity. So be ready. Open surveillance can get ugly.

Lock all vehicle doors while out in the field. I once had my target's neighbor attempt to throw a pit bull into my vehicle. Luckily for me, my doors were locked. I saw him walking toward me with the pit bull and I had no idea he was planning to deposit the dog inside the car. I thought he was going to walk his dog. So always stay vigilant around your surveillance position.

In open surveillance, if you are pulled over by the police while you are following your target, there is no reason to panic. You are a professional and no law has been broken. When the police approach your car, turn on your recording device. If you have no recording device, call your cell number and allow your answering service to go on. Place the phone audio up and place the phone out of view where the mic has no obstructions. Turn off the radio and the air conditioning, roll down all your tinted windows for your safety and the officer's, and respectfully communicate with the officer. The officer will ask you whether you are following your target. You have two options at this point. You can tell the officer that yes, you are following your target. If you do tell the officer that you are following your target, it will become a matter of public record, plus now there is a witness—in this case the police officer—to you following your target and your target can file a restraining order in court to keep you away. Your second option is the most professional choice. Tell the police officer that you are not following your target and that you have no idea what he is talking about. The officer will probably not believe you, and fill out a contact card with your information, run your name through FCIC/NCIC, and let you go. In this case you must break off surveillance immediately, or you can risk arrest for stalking; if you are armed with a firearm, you can be arrested for aggregated stalking. Legally, you don't have to disclose to police who your client is or whom you are monitoring. Moreover, in private investigations, you do not have to tell authorities anything that will be a conflict of interest with your client. This is the beautiful aspect about private investigations. In Florida, privileged communication is protected under F.S. Chapter 483.

Last, in the acquisition of surveillance positions be aware that your position may welcome onlookers who may consider your presence suspicious. For instance, if you are parked in a multi-apartment complex that is gated, and you decided to secure your surveillance position in front of a roof that contains all of the mailboxes to the community, this may draw attention. Onlookers may wonder why your engine has been idling for hours. They may call the police to respond to a suspicious vehicle in the area. If you see someone looking in your direction intensely and then you see that person dialing from a cell phone or walking behind your vehicle, most likely to obtain your license plate number, this will be as good a time as ever for you to contact the dispatcher who took your call. Have the dispatcher check you in with police and inform them that someone from the community may be calling them because they noted your license plate number, and try to diffuse the complainant's nature for peace of mind.

Be careful when following a school bus with children inside or securing a surveillance position at a day care center or elementary school. If you hear over the public announcement systems for teachers not to allow their students to exit from the class, probabilities suggest that the police are on their way to your location.

In the acquisition of surveillance positions pay close attention to everything and take mental notes of what you observe. For instance, when you bypass or tailgate someone inside a gated community to gain access, do not take the same route that person is taking even if it takes you off course. Most drivers are aware when someone tailgates their vehicle, and most people allow this to happen without making contact with you. However, if they do make contact, calmly let them know that you are an investigator and that the police know that you are out here doing a job. Do not let them know anything else. Take a mental note if you see a security car parked near the guard house; count how many vehicles there are. In most cases there will be only one and it will most probably be electric and not a gas engine. Take a mental note of clubhouses, designated areas for car wash, mailboxes for the community, laundry areas, trash bins, and so forth. Most important is how many routes of departure there are to the community, where surveillance efforts are taking place, and what the probabilities are that your target may take each route of departure so you can anticipate your target's route of egress. Your target will most likely take the same route as his or her neighbors, i.e., the most commonly followed route, so follow the neighborhood trend in pattern recognition.

You need to find the best way to work the case by being receptive to the layout. In rural areas you may secure a surveillance position at a local gas station or the only grocery mart in the area, hoping that your target is going to pass by your surveillance position. In surveillance as in all of the models, the main objective is to stay undetected. At times this means parking hundreds of yards away from your target's primary place of departure and tracking the target ahead of the road.

If the layout is literally impossible, let's say your target lives in the middle of nowhere surrounded by 5-acre tracts in agricultural zoning, you can set up a fruit stand. I am not kidding, this is an option—buy yourself a folding table and lots of fruit and bill your client for the expenses. Put up a large sign and sit in your car anticipating your target passing by. Take note of your target's license plate number, and whatever you do, do not follow the target. Stay there to see if your target returns. Your target may be testing you. Do not underestimate him. You may also want to secure a suitable surveillance position along the primary route of departure and put a "For Sale" sign on the windshield of your car. If someone approaches your vehicle and starts poking inside (which they will), exit from the driver's side and extend your arms and call the person any name you would like as if you were waiting for him or her to test drive the car. The person will think this behavior is odd, but as long as this is not your target or a relative of the target it doesn't matter.

Routes of Departure

Routes of departure are routes that your target is most likely to take when departing from a specific place; this can be the target's home, place of employment, shopping center, airport, etc. Routes of departure are mostly secured in the surveillance realm when the operative can't gain access to a certain location, where you know or suspect that your target may be frequenting or visiting. For instance, a high-rise condominium with a vigilant security guard is not going to allow you in even with a creative pretext. Routes of departure are also convenient when you elect as an operational move not to gain entry to a certain area because you think it may jeopardize the integrity of the case and it would be a safer operational move to secure a surveillance position at the route of departure, anticipating your target's departure or appearance. Acquiring a subject at routes of departures is popular because they are convenient and easy to find in most challenging layouts. Most importantly, when you secure a surveillance position at a route of departure, the element of surprise is optimum and your target will be oblivious to your presence, mainly because by the time your target passes by your surveillance position, the target's guard will be down even if he or she is surveillance conscious.

Routine Spot-Checks

Routine spot-checks are conducted to detect a change in exterior activity and for pattern recognition. For instance, you conducted a routine spot-check of your target's home at 5:00 a.m. and noticed that your target's vehicle was present, suggesting that your target was home. You then conducted a routine spot-check at 8:00 a.m., and again your target's vehicle was present. You then conducted a routine spot-check at 10:00 a.m., and your target's vehicle was not present, suggesting that your target departed anywhere from 8:00 a.m. to 10:00 a.m.; therefore, you schedule the surveillance to commence at 8:00 a.m., and increase your vigilance upon arrival because you suspect that your target will be departing anywhere from 8:00 a.m. to 10:00 a.m.

Spot-checks are a convenient way to save your client money rather than sitting at an empty house not knowing whether your target is present or not. At times, there will be no other option than to sit at an empty house anticipating your target to arrive; maybe the target's home has a two-car garage and your target is probably parking his or her vehicle in the garage, so when the spot-checks are being conducted, they do not reveal any change in exterior activity. In such a case, a spot-check would not have an operational utility.

Determining What Your Target Is Driving

Most of your targets will be commuting from point A to point B operating some kind of a vehicle. A few of your targets may be riding a bicycle to commute; others may be riding a motorcycle; and some may be using public transportation—a bus, metro mover, or train. However, 95% of your targets will be commuting operating their personal or company vehicle. A background check will usually tell you what vehicles your target has owned or current vehicle registrations. However, most information broker databases don't have current vehicle information if the vehicle was purchased within 90 days (3 months). So you must question everything that you have observed as well as what you have read.

It is imperative for you to know what vehicle your target is operating in order to effectively monitor the target's activities. Does your target have access to one vehicle or multiple vehicles? Knowing the primary vehicle that your target is operating is the top requirement in any given surveillance assignment. This may sound like an easy task, but it can become an operational nightmare in some cases.

Take for instance that you arrive at your target's most recent address as reported and you are almost certain that your target resides there because the utility bill is under his or her name. However, a records check revealed no vehicles registered there in your target's name, and to make matters worse once you arrive at your address you notice in your preliminary field investigation that the front door is not observable from any vantage point—there is no suitable surveillance position that you can acquisition with a view of your target's front door. You were hoping to observe your target exiting from his home and proceeding to enter one of the vehicles in the tenant parking lot. However, this is not the case and you have no idea what your target looks like, and a diligent search of social networks did not reveal any hits with your target's name. You are now faced with a challenging task.

Here's what you do. Conduct an online search query and determine whether your target has received a traffic violation in the past 3 years. If you are lucky and your target was in fact cited in the past 3 years, drive to the courthouse and obtain a duplicate copy of the traffic citation. The traffic citation will note the license plate number of the vehicle that your target was operating, and then you can cross-reference the license plate number with the vehicles in the tenant parking lot where surveillance efforts are taking place. However, if a records search revealed that your target was not cited, or maybe your target was cited but the vehicle was sold or transferred, follow this suggestion. Canvass the tenant parking lot and document all of the license plates to the vehicles in the tenant parking lot starting with the vehicles parked closest to your target's home. In Florida, all license plates have the registration sticker visible, attached to the plate. The visible registration sticker notes the month that the registrant of the vehicle was born and the expiration of the year that the vehicle registration needs to be renewed. For instance, 12-13 means that the registered owner of the vehicle was born in December and that the vehicle registration will expire December 2013.

If you know your target's date of birth (*you should*), you can then canvass the parking lot and selectively note the license plates of vehicles that show that the owners were born in December. I recommend that you walk with your cell phone and text yourself all of the license plates in question. If someone is looking it will appear as if you are texting.

Second, if your target is claiming some kind of an injury, record the license plates of the vehicles parked in disability parking spaces; if you spot a vehicle with a disability hanger and the vehicle is not parked in a disability parking space, note that vehicle license plate number as well. If you know that your target is, for instance, a student, record the license plate numbers of the vehicles that have student decals, even if the decals are expired. Also, if you know that your target has children or a toddler, be on the lookout for baby seats and booster seats in the vehicles. If your target is a female, be on the lookout for feminine colors and anything that may be hanging from the windshield mirror that may suggest the sex of the driver of the vehicle. People are also in the habit of leaving behind correspondence, letters, employee badges, and many other identifying documents in open view inside their vehicles. If your target was involved in prior car accidents maybe the vehicles with dents and damage in the tenant parking lot will draw your attention.

The bottom line is that you should use your observational skills and correlate what you are observing, and then use trial and error to determine which vehicle your target is operating. You are conducting a preliminary field investigation at this point in time because surveillance efforts can't commence until you determine what vehicle your target is operating.

During the initial field investigation you must correlate and use what is readily available to you. This may include a deposition that was taken of your target on behalf of your client. Depositions, no matter when they were taken, are filled with pertinent information and little details that are very useful when assembling the pieces in the interim of your field investigation. A recent deposition taken of your target may reveal whom your target resides with, where your target works, and what vehicle your target is operating. It does not surprise me that many of my clients do not e-mail me copies of depositions when they assign a surveillance case unless I ask them or their assistants to do so if any are on file. With my insurance-related clients, I ask for the diary of the file from inception to end. Use every tool at your disposal.

Foot Surveillance: "The Craft of Staying with Your Target's Every Move"

Unfortunately, some private investigators do not like to get out of their vehicles and conduct foot surveillance, mostly because of complacency. Some feel that they are not dressed properly and this would draw attention and risk compromising the integrity of the case. The bottom line is that as a field operative you need to get out of your car when it is warranted and continue to gather information.

Foot surveillance is the craft of staying with your target no matter where the target goes. I was recently conducting a two-man surveillance operation for a client. We had followed our target to Starbucks every day. We would not follow the target inside the Starbucks because she would leave after 5 to 15 minutes, and we would resume mobile surveillance. One day our target, while supposedly at Starbucks, did not exit after 30 minutes. As a rule of thumb, this should tell you to get out of your car and find out what it is that is going on. To my surprise our target was now at a nearby salon getting her hair straightened. This may not appear to be significant, but it is significant to me because now I am thinking that our target may be going out tonight or meeting with someone she wants to impress, because it is a Saturday and she is known to dine out on weekends. Case in point—get out of your vehicle and gather information.

Principles in Foot Surveillance

When you are visibly in motion you will draw attention. It is important that you do not stand out in a crowd. The initial stage in foot surveillance is to determine whether it is worth the risk of detection. In most cases you will not be detected by your target if you are gradually following him or her. The golden rule is do not pass by your target's field of vision unless you have the ability to change your attire by maybe changing the color of your shirt, putting on a golf cap, glasses, or whatever you have at your disposal. The likelihood is that when you elect to conduct foot surveillance you will only be wearing the shirt on your back and you will not have the option of changing your attire.

Tracking your target on foot is fairly simple as long as you stay away from his or her field of vision. This can be accomplished by trailing behind your target and not to your target's side, or in front of your target. If your target is walking at a fast pace, you need to pick up your pace as well. Walk adjacent to walls or clusters or crowds of people who can disguise your physical presence. If your target suddenly looks back in your direction, whatever you do, do not stand there like a portrait, continue moving forward and simply head in a different direction. This may mean walking past your target. Make sure that you do not bump into your target or make eye contact. Eye contact is a deal breaker in foot surveillance. Any time that you make eye contact with your target you are drawing way too much attention to yourself and your target will take mental snapshots of your physical appearance. If your target appears to be in a hurry, look at your watch. If the time is nearing or passed the hour, your target may be meeting with someone and is probably running late.

Do not do something illogical, like taking off your shirt or pretending that you are on the phone speaking, within distance of your target. Taking off your shirt may be appropriate if you are at the beach or pool area and you do not have a bathing suit. However, speaking within distance from your target is not a good idea. Your voice travels and may reach your target, and then you will be exposing yourself mainly because you are the only person on the cell phone.

Wear dark colors, and not loud or fluorescent colors that will draw the attention of others. My favorite is black because it blends in well at a distance and with shadows.

Intelligence Gathering inside Restaurants

In foot surveillance getting too close is not recommended. It all depends on the setting. People have a certain comfort zone, which is normally a circumference of 5 to 6 feet. This means that if you are 5 feet or less from your target, you are drawing attention to yourself. However, this principle may not always fit. For instance, you follow your target to a restaurant, you wait a few minutes, and you spot your target seated at a table with an unidentified person. You get the feeling that this is a business meeting because you see files or documents on the table. You feel that this meeting might be of importance to your client and therefore decide to move in closer. You tell a waiter that you prefer to be seated at a certain table; make up an excuse—for instance because that is where you proposed to your wife who has passed away, and today is your anniversary, and every year you return to the same table because of its sentimental value. No restaurant manager will deny your request. If there is a wait time because you have no reservation, ask to be seated at the bar and keep your eyes on your target if their table is visible from that vantage point. If your target goes to the bathroom do not follow him or her. This will draw too much attention. Sitting near your target at a nearby table is do-able. However, there may be too much noise that makes it difficult to hear your target's conversation. This is fine. At times your target may say things that your client will need to know. Even if most of what you are listening to is hard to understand, at least some of the words may be clear. You can text whatever you can make out to yourself using your cell phone, or write down the words that you can hear on a piece of paper for future reference. This will be useful when updating your client.

Your target's body language is very important. By looking at your target from afar you can determine by your target's hand gestures, facial expressions, and nodding of the head whether what the target is communicating in a business luncheon is being sold or not. Did your target's luncheon appear to be successful? If so, inform your client of your investigative findings.

In intelligence gathering, your client will often want to know who the target was speaking with, for instance at a luncheon such as described. Follow the unidentified person with whom your target was having lunch out of the restaurant when their luncheon is over. If they go to a car, get the license plate number. If the person works nearby and walked to the luncheon, determine the person's place of employment by following him or her there. Gather whatever intel you can so that you can follow up and identify that person in the future.

Always pay for your bill before you commence to eat or before your plate is brought to your table. This way if your target suddenly rushes out or asks for the bill, you will be ready to stay with your target. If you run out without paying your bill you can be arrested. So plan ahead.

Transitioning Targets

Foot surveillance, as with any other kind of surveillance model being discussed, will transition into something else. Transitioning from one target to another is what professional investigators do without the need to ask their clients or secure their clients' authority. The bottom line is that there is no time. As a field operative it is your job to determine operational decisions without hesitation. If you hesitate you risk losing both targets. Keep your eyes on one and follow through. In most cases you will be able to go back to your target once the identity of the person of interest has been established.

Foot Surveillance in Airports

Airports are high-security areas and are vulnerable to terrorist acts of violence. So if you track your target to an airport, whether commercial or not, make sure that you are not carrying a concealed weapon and that you do not attempt to infiltrate or bypass Transportation Security Administration (TSA) checkpoints. If your target is going to board a flight, attempt to follow him or her to the check-in counter and note the airline, and the flight number if possible. Pay close attention to your target's luggage—the color, size, any visible markings or distinguishing features. Note what your target is wearing. Is your target carrying a jacket or sweater? If so, what color? This will be important to the field operative who will intercept your target once you call it in. Also make note of whether your target is traveling with a laptop or briefcase. Details of this nature will help the identification process when your target lands. If you can, videotape your target at the TSA line and e-mail your client a real-time picture of what your target is wearing so your client can be better equipped when relaying the information. If you point a video camera at a TSA checkpoint, you will be told to stop recording. Just point, shoot the video, and wave. It will look as if you are waving good-bye and video recording someone you know who is departing. If a TSA employee notices you doing this, stop video recording immediately. If you do this quickly enough you will not draw any attention. Do it at a distance and then leave the premises and call it a day.

Foot Surveillance inside Gymnasiums

Obtaining video documentation of your target in a gymnasium while the target is working out requires three things. First, you need a day pass if you are not a member. Waive the tour and tell the sales employee that you reside elsewhere and are only in town for a few days. Most gymnasiums will sell you a day pass for $5 to $10. Second, you need a pair of sneakers/tennis shoes. You will not be allowed inside if you are wearing dress shoes. Last, you need a spy-cam or any other kind of a recording device whereby you can record and document your target without drawing attention to yourself. Remember that 5- to 6-foot rule. Do not invade your target's space. Stay away and record mostly at a medium range standing anywhere from 6 to 25 feet away. If your target is using a stationary bike or a treadmill, try to secure the adjacent bike or treadmill. If your target is benching or performing some kind of strenuous exercise, move in closer. The gain outweighs the risk. Your target may think you are gay, but remember that you are doing a job. Just walk away and give your target the space that he or she needs, or the target may ask you something to see how you react.

Foot Surveillance at Supermarkets

As an insurance fraud field investigator, I've made a science of following and documenting my targets inside supermarkets, wholesale clubs, big box stores, you name it, I've been there. Here are the golden rules that you must follow. Insurance carriers love it when you document their claimants pushing a metal grocery cart, leaning and reaching into shelves, carrying large dispensable grocery items, like a 50-pound bag of dog food, a 24-pack of beer, or a gallon of milk or bottled water. If your target is a claimant, it would be most beneficial for you and your client for you to document your target's physical capabilities and range of motion inside the facility.

The minute that you observe your target enter a supermarket or other such facility, park your vehicle close to the target's vehicle with a view of the trunk, hatch, and back passenger side doors. Keep in mind that not everyone deposits their groceries in the back. Some people use the back passenger side of their vehicle. Position your vehicle in the right spot. Don't rush out of your car. Allow for your target to get settled in. Don't be surprised if your target exits from the supermarket a few minutes later with a lottery ticket or a pack of smokes. If a suitable surveillance position is not available outside, just wait; supermarkets are high-density parking lots where people are constantly coming and going. Wait a few minutes until someone leaves and you can take that parking space for the perfect surveillance position. If it takes you more than 10 minutes to canvass for a surveillance position, simply secure whatever position is readily available to the best of your abilities anticipating your target's departure.

Next, enter the supermarket. As soon as you are inside look at all the cashier counters and lines to make sure that your target is not cashing out. If your target is cashing out, hurry to your vehicle and watch the exit so you can start recording your target depositing the groceries inside the vehicle, assuming that this is the case. If your target is not at the checkout line, visually inspect the pharmacy and the cash services and lottery lines. Not everyone who frequents a supermarket is going grocery shopping. Once you confirm that your target is not at any of these locations, conduct a canvass of the entire supermarket.

Canvassing for Your Target in Symmetrical Buildings

To conduct a canvass of the entire supermarket or any building, follow these principles. First, do not look in the restroom or bathrooms; this will only expose you and when you are near your target, the target may suspect that something is amiss. Second, do not look for your target by walking the aisles or walking with no apparent destination. Walk the entire perimeter of the building, staying close to the wall and continue to walk in the same direction moving forward; never backtrack unless you believe that you missed something or that your eyes are playing tricks on you. Don't walk in quadrants. Walk the perimeter of the building and turn your neck in only one direction and visually canvass and dismiss every aisle. Do not turn your head clockwise and counterclockwise while in motion; turning your neck in both directions will draw attention because it will appear as if you are looking for someone (and indeed you are), and doing so also deters the quality of your visual acuity, because you are not allowing your peripheral vision to set in and detect movement in the aisles. Most buildings are symmetrical in width and length. It should not take you more than 10 minutes to canvass the inner shell of a WalMart Superstore, for instance. When making your first round, if you find a quadrant that you can walk and canvass and visually dismiss as a place of interest, go ahead and do it; however, if you start walking down that path, then continue to dismiss the following quadrants adjacent to each other systematically and in order, otherwise, you are going to make another round and end up where you started without knowing where your target is. If this happens, continue canvassing by walking the perimeter; however, every round you need to close the gap 35 to 70 feet, at least until you detect the location of your target. Simply close the gap and move in closer to the center.

It is extremely important to remember what your target is wearing. This is an advantage when looking in a crowd. However, remember that there exists a probability that your target may now be alone but will meet up with people later. This is why knowing what your target is wearing, your target's walk, mannerism, and tone of voice is important. If your target is speaking, you may detect your target's dialect or tone of voice and be able to draw closer to the target's location.

Videotaping the Target inside Buildings and Close Environments

Videotaping your target in a building is tricky. If the building where your target is located is not congested with people because it is early in the morning, you must be extra cautious. If you are in motion and your target's peripheral vision notices a silhouette in the background or from afar, this will not be a problem if there are many other people in the building. However, if there are only a few people around, this may draw attention and the target may look in your direction. If this happens, look away—remember, no eye contact under any circumstance.

There are only two ways to videotape your target inside a building or closed environment without being detected. The first option is what I refer to as *fishing*. This is described only in the context of a grocery store here. In *fishing* let's say you are going to use an actual video camera and not a spy-cam. Get yourself a grocery cart and place the lens of your camera facing forward looking at the direction in which you are steering the cart. Hit the *record* button and run continuous video whether you are recording your target or not. This is not something that you want to set up near people and especially not near your target. Secure your camera in the cart at the highest elevation—where babies sit. Your video camera will be facing forward and the metal grills will be in front of your lens. Look at the side viewfinder and make sure that your camera is in focus by setting the focus to infinity, not auto focus—otherwise your lens will focus on the grill of the cart and the background will be distorted.

Once you confirm that your video camera is recording and the image in the background is clear, locate a few nonperishable items and cover the body of your video camera. A word of caution: People in public places may react to people with video cameras similar to people with guns. If people see you with a video camera they may think you are a pedophile, a pervert, or something worse, and they may contact the authorities or inform the person whom you are videotaping. So be sure that your camera is completely disguised. I normally use rolls of paper towels or toilet paper from the supermarket aisle and build a tower covering both sides of the camera, so if someone were to see my cart from the left or right side, they would not notice the video camera between the paper towels or toilet paper. Use something to cover the top of the video camera, like a newspaper or magazine, whatever is readily available. Your lens will be visible, however, and this is why in *fishing* you must videotape your target at a distance, from either the beginning of the aisle from the front or the back, not from the middle or near the subject. At that distance your target will not see the lens of your camera. If your target is approaching you, push your cart out of view, and do not allow your target to see you looking in his or her direction. Do not push your cart past your target. Give your target space.

In *fishing* you usually position your camera in view of your target and you abandon your target and stand near your grocery cart reading the labels of food items, speaking on the cell phone, reading a magazine while standing in the aisle, or simply paying attention to something that has caught your attention, a can of beans or whatever is handy, simply make it look credible at a distance. In the meantime your video camera is recording your target. You can zoom in and out when your target has his or her back to you or is pushing the cart away from you, and then do the entire process again in the next aisles. Your target will probably follow the same paths, canvassing each food aisle. This is why you want to abandon your cart facing in your target's direction at the beginning of the aisle. This way your target does not see you in every aisle. You can peek and determine whether you want to zoom in or not in many cases, depending on what your target is doing. You can also use items from the grocery store to elevate your camera as well as to better adjust your image and quality of your video. You may need to place a book or something else underneath your camera to elevate it so you will not catch both grills while your camera is recording. Last, please use non-perishable items, because once you see that your target is headed toward the checkout line, this will be your cue to abandon your grocery cart, grab your video camera, and head out to your vehicle to anticipate your target's departure. Document your target, in this case being your claimant, loading the groceries in his or her vehicle and break off surveillance and rush to your target's home to secure a suitable surveillance position there. Once your target arrives home and begins to unload the groceries, you can document this too. This is a home run for you and your client.

Foot Surveillance at the Beach

Videotaping your target at the beach is fairly simple if you stay below the radar. Once my target has chosen a spot at the beach to lay out his or her towel or place a chair, this tells me that my target will be located at that spot throughout his or her stay at the beach. I can go about my business, eat lunch, and take a dip in the water, and when I return, my target will most likely be in the same location. However, as a professional you try to position yourself where it is most beneficial to you. For instance, I can be in the water taking a dip and have my target in view from there. Do not go into the water when your target is there. One look at each other and there goes the first mental photo of what you look like. I can be at a nearby food vendor at the beach and maintain a visual of my target.

Videotaping someone at the beach has its advantages. I normally secure my video camera on top of a cloth, preferably my shirt, on top of the hot sand with my target in view, and hit the record button and allow the camera to record my target for hours while my target is tanning, using the cell phone, etc. When I see that my target is rising and walking toward the water for a dip, I just reposition my video camera to continue recording my target while he or she is in the water. I cover my video camera with any piece of apparel and no one notices anything. I look like a guy at the beach tanning, no different than anyone around me.

Advantageous Surveillance Positions

As a professional field operative you will often find yourself monitoring your target from a very advantageous surveillance position. At times this will warrant allowing your target to walk away from your field of view without you having to follow, but simply waiting for your target to return.

It is late in the evening and you are parked across the street from your target's home. Your target has the garage open and is working on his vehicle with the engine compartment open. You are documenting your target, in this case your claimant, performing numerous strenuous activities; you are documenting his physical capabilities on behalf of your client. Your target suddenly decides to test drive the vehicle and leaves the garage door open at 11:00 p.m. You elected not to follow your target because you suspect that your target will return to the residence soon and resume working on the vehicle. This is an intelligent operational decision because you do not want to turn on your headlights, or for neighbors to notice that a vehicle in the neighborhood departed and returned minutes later and no one exited the vehicle. As a common denominator in the operational mechanics of all surveillance models, assume that someone is always watching you. Just because you cannot see someone watching you does not mean that no one is. The sooner you accept this, the better you will be accustomed to it in the art of *stealth* and *invisibility.*

Securing an advantageous surveillance position requires time, vigilance, and patience. For instance, you want to secure a surveillance position on a parking space that has a view to your target's front door from a distance, and this is the best surveillance position available based on the layout of your target's community. However, there is a car parked in this space for days and the vehicle has not moved. You notice that the car parked in the spot that you want is for sale and there is phone number on the windshield. You call the number and pretext the owner into meeting with you down the road so you can test drive the car. Minutes later you observe the owner of the vehicle leaving the parking space and you move in and take the space. You allow 5 minutes to pass and then call back the owner of the car and tell him that you had an accident and will not be able to meet with him. You will then see him return to the community a few minutes later. By then you are out of your car and you have secured your position. When the owner walks past your car and notices no one inside, you can then enter your vehicle and will have accomplished what you wanted.

A few hours go by and you are ready to eat lunch, but if you go get lunch you know someone will take your spot. You decide to order food to be delivered to the location. This is an intelligent operational decision.

Foot Surveillance at Public Parks

Tracking people in public or state parks is possible as long as you keep eyes on your target and maintain your distance. If your target happens to enter the premises before you secure a parking space and by the time that you enter the park your target is nowhere to be found, simply look at the layout of the park and follow the path that makes the most sense.

Many state parks are immense, ranging anywhere from 5 acres to over 100 acres. If this is the case, remember that most of your targets will be walking. Some parks offer mini-shuttles to and from buildings and theme attractions. However, your target will most likely be walking at a slow pace and bonding with nature, making him or her a slow moving target. This means that your target may not be far from you. There may be some operational challenges like visual obstructions, trees, bushes, buildings, or sun glare, but walk in a direction that makes sense. For instance, if your target is accompanied by his or her children, check the playgrounds first and visually inspect anything where you as a parent might take your child in similar circumstances. Take note of weather conditions, for instance, if it begins to rain suddenly, your target may be en route to a building that has a roof; therefore, your target may not be mobile and may be confined to one place waiting for the rain to stop. This is an opportunity for you to canvass buildings in the park and conduct a process of elimination.

Not all targets who attend parks are there to visit the attractions or walk and tour the grounds. Some targets visit public parks to dine or visit the café. I once followed my target to *Ringling Museum of Art* in Sarasota, Florida. The park was immense. By the time I secured a parking space, my target had already entered the park. As soon as I paid my admission and proceeded to enter the park, I noticed two immense buildings. I also noticed that the guests at the park were heading in that direction. I followed and canvassed one building and my target was nowhere to be found. I walked to the information booth and asked, "If I wanted to take my girlfriend someplace romantic in this beautiful park in today's weather where would you suggest?" The park employee mentioned a restaurant that overlooks a lake. I checked the restaurant and strike two; my target was not there. I then took a complimentary ride to one of the buildings that was the biggest. The minute I arrived the tour guide recommended that I start my tour on the east side and work my way around. I kindly turned down the tour guide's recommendation and started the tour on the fourth floor and worked my way down, clearing the entire building. Strike three, my target was not in that building either. Eventually, I exited the park and maintained a visual of her car. I did not want to risk my target departing from the park undetected while I was in the grounds looking for her.

Foot Surveillance in Government Buildings

Foot surveillance in courthouses and local, state, and federal buildings is mostly about intelligence gathering and not videotaping your target. If you are caught videotaping someone in a federal building, simply say that you are a licensed private investigator and that you followed your target inside. Legally, the worst-case scenario is that they tell you that you will be arrested for trespassing if you come back. If you decide to lie from the start, they may think that you are shooting a video of the building to commit some kind of terrorist act, and your day could turn ugly really fast. Your tape can be confiscated and reviewed as a matter of national security. This is why telling them the truth is the best way of getting out of the situation you put yourself in.

In intelligence gathering in government buildings, you may see your target walking to certain departments. For instance, if in a courthouse, your target may walk into the Family Division or may search the computer to request documents. In the latter instance, wait until your target walks away from the computer and go fish for a name or other information in the computer the person was using. Most people who conduct online queries do not refresh the computer. If you see your target entering a courtroom, look at the day calendar and look for the target's name.

Tracking targets in government buildings is okay as long as you keep your distance and do not make eye contact. Do not look at your target from corners or shadows like you see in the movies. Blend in with the rest of the people in the building. Do not answer your cell phone or talk to anyone near your target. This may draw your target's attention. If your target is sitting in a room full of people, sit behind your target so you can keep an eye on him or her. Do not sit in front of your target. Do not expose yourself by being in your target's field of vision. If your target throws away papers or documents, try to retrieve for them if there are any identifying marks. Just make sure your target does not see you fishing for papers in a trash bin.

Foot Surveillance in Gated Communities and Tracking Joggers

Foot surveillance in gated communities is high risk. The only place where this is recommended is in clubhouses, lakes, and parks inside the community, and anywhere else there are groupings of people. For instance, following your target while the target is walking the dog, jogging behind your target while the target is jogging, walking behind your target when the target is exercising and walking inside his or her community, are all not recommended. If your target is walking or jogging and you need to obtain video of this for your client, do so from the confines of your car. Shoot video of your target's back at a distance. When your target turns, you will be able to shoot a photo identification from the surveillance video feed by zooming in. When your target walks out of view, reposition your surveillance position someplace closer to your target. You can even "hi-jack" (as I refer to it) a surveillance position. This term basically means to acquire surveillance positions on private property without the permission of the owner. This is not illegal nor is it trespassing. In order for trespassing to take place you must be warned by a law enforcement officer. In the hi-jacking of surveillance positions, you will only be there for a few minutes and your presence will not be noticed in most cases.

Foot Surveillance in Shopping Centers and Theme Parks

Foot surveillance in shopping centers and theme parks can be exhausting. The most important operational objective for you to remember is what your target is wearing. In most cases your target will not be alone. Also remember what your target's party is wearing. This way you can spot the party at a distance. This will come in handy if you lose your target and you come upon one of your target's company. You can follow them, hoping they will lead you back to your target. In most cases they will. Bear in mind that your target may change clothes, if shopping for clothes. Or your target may put on a jacket or sweater. Take note if your target is carrying a jacket, for instance. If your target's wife is carrying a jacket, do not assume that she will be wearing that jacket. Assume that there is a possibility that anyone in the party will be wearing that jacket.

Normally in theme parks, particularly here in Florida, your target, if traveling with the family, will stay with them. This makes your job easier. The larger the crowd, the slower moving they will be. Simply blend in and keep a safe distance where you feel comfortable. I normally wait at the exits of the rides. This works best. Do not anticipate your target exiting if you did not see your target board the ride. This is very important. In theme parks do not be surprised if your target does not board the ride because the wait time is too long. Also take note of whether your target has an express passport that allows him or her to go to the beginning of the line.

Foot Surveillance in Public Transit

Foot surveillance in a public transit bus, metro rail, or train is considered high risk mainly because you are too close to your target, and your target will probably see you and take his or her first mental snapshot of you. This is why it is important for you to not make any eye contact with your target, but avert your gaze so your target can only see one side of your face. If you have a book or newspaper that will cover your face, this will help you disguise yourself. Make sure that if you are reading the newspaper that it is not an old paper and most importantly, that you are reading the paper in the right direction and not upside down. If you have a hood or golf cap, have it on and take it off the minute you exit the public transit and resume foot surveillance. You can switch back and forth and maintain the integrity of the case. Most targets who take public transit take more than just one bus. If this is the case and you find yourself close to your target on several occasions, have a pretext ready in case your target asks where you are going. As mentioned earlier, if your target is sitting, sit behind your target, never in the target's field of view if this is an option.

Foot Surveillance in Low Light Areas

Foot surveillance in low light areas is considered high risk. Just imagine someone following you in a low lit area. This will make you panic and you might become confrontational. Foot surveillance in a low light area probably has the highest risk of detection and may lead to a confrontation as well, so be extremely careful in this scenario.

Surgical Surveillance: "Open Roof Applications in High Security Areas"

Several years ago I shadowed a target suspected of insurance fraud for the federal government. I followed the target to one of the most secured ports in the United States: Port Canaveral, on the east coast of Florida near Satellite Beach. I shadowed the claimant at least four times a month for approximately a year and a half.

Cape Canaveral Port was not easy to bypass at first. There were numerous security guards on the premises roving, directing traffic, and moving through the parking garage at irregular intervals with no pattern recognition, making the port's internal security unpredictable. Second, there were numerous sheriff's deputies assigned to the port by Brevard County Sheriff's Office. I was not too concerned about the deputies because they mainly remained confined to one area and were mostly visible and predictable. I had other security matters to keep in mind. For instance, Port Canaveral is adjacent to a Navy dock that houses nuclear submarines. Florida Marine Patrol are constantly patrolling the bay. To make matters more challenging, the Brevard County Sheriff's Office was conducting periodic aerial spot-checks of the port in a marked helicopter.

My objective was clear. Monitor my target at the port without being detected by anyone, including port authorities. I would hate to call my client up and say: "I was booted out from the port with a trespass warning and if I return to the port I can go to jail."

I was instructed by one of the parking attendants to park in a designated spot. This parking attendant was the person whom I was investigating. I followed the flow of traffic, tailgating the car in front of me. The parking attendant walked up to my window and asked me if I was picking up a passenger from one of the cruise ships. I responded "yes" without hesitation. I then proceeded to exit from the front driver's side and followed what other drivers were doing. I walked toward the terminal where passengers were waiting to be picked up with luggage ready standing underneath the shade of the bus terminals. I approached one of the passengers and spoke with her for a few seconds to give the impression that we were related in case someone was watching me. I turned around and all the parking attendants were oblivious of their surroundings, minding their own business. There was a lot going on at one time; this was obviously an advantage.

I was mostly concerned about where I was going to position for the remainder of the day, not knowing where my target was going to be for the remainder of his shift. I was not familiarized with the layout of the port and was scanning everything like a hawk to determine what would be the most beneficial surveillance position to monitor and videotape my claimant.

I then noticed a parking garage that was approximately six stories high that I learned houses the vehicles from the cruise ship passengers. The parking garage faced the entire parking lot where my target seemed to be confined. I thought to myself that securing a surveillance position above ground level would be most beneficial to secure an aerial view of the entire parking lot and remain discreet without compromising my surveillance position.

I immediately walked toward the front driver side of my car and entered the vehicle swiftly without drawing attention to myself. I sat in my vehicle waiting for my cue. I noticed that the parking attendants were instructing the vehicles that were departing from the parking lot where to go by using hand gestures. I noticed that there was a security guard standing adjacent to the ramp that leads into the upper levels of the parking garage. I needed to infiltrate and gain access with my vehicle to this secured access point that leads to the upper floors of the parking garage. However, I needed to sit patiently behind the steering wheel and hope that the security guard would abandon his post, at which point I could start my engine and drive in as if I was lost, in case anyone was watching. I did not observe any closed circuit television cameras anywhere; however, I knew there was CCTV, but I could not locate the cameras from my field of view.

I knew I had only a few minutes until the parking attendants would wonder why my vehicle continued to be there. I also knew it was only a matter of minutes until the security guard posted at the ramp leading to the upper parking levels of the garage area would abandon his post. A common vulnerability in private security is that security guards periodically abandon their posts to go to the bathroom, smoke a cigarette, or have their lunch, but mostly to help people who are in need of their assistance.

A few minutes later the security guard posted at the ramp began to walk away from his post. I waited a few seconds more for my cue; I waited until the security guard walked away from my field of vision. A rule of thumb is that if you can't see your target, your target probably can't see you. I then opened and closed loudly the front driver side door of my vehicle to give the illusion that someone had entered the vehicle. I turned on the engine and proceeded to follow the flow of traffic exiting from the port parking lot. I paused for a few seconds and with precise timing drove up the ramp leading into the multi-tier parking levels of the parking garage and gained entry. Upon entering the garage level, I was overwhelmed with relief. I knew that if someone was watching it was through CCTV.

All the vehicles were symmetrically parked and no spaces were readily available. I did not see a single person or roving security inside the enormous parking building. I was alone. I immediately noticed that the vehicles parked in the garage did not have any type of indication on the windshield or dash for overnight parking. This was a security risk to the port but good news for me. I also noticed that there were no closed circuit television cameras in most common areas. The only cameras in the parking garage were pointing to the primary pedestrian entrance to every elevator on every floor—another security flaw. I continued to drive to the upper floor of the parking garage to have a better field of view and where I expected there would be plenty of parking spaces available. On the upper floor I immediately secured a parking space facing east and secured a vantage field of view overlooking my claimant's range of mobility covering the entire parking lot to the port. The view showed everything and I knew that my target would not go undetected.

However, there were unexpected problems. The elevation of the VW Jetta that I was operating was too low to the ground, and even if I were operating an SUV with higher elevation, I would have probably encountered a similar elevation challenge. Remember that there are no such things as problems in the field. I prefer to call them operational challenges. The operational challenge here was that the concrete wall surrounding the parking garage in front of the parking spaces was approximately 4 feet tall, standing erect from the concrete slab of the parking garage. I would encounter the same operational challenge no matter where I parked in the garage. I had visual obstructions and could not monitor my target from my vehicle. My only option was to document my target from outside of my vehicle and risk being detected by a roving helicopter, roving security, or onlookers. My biggest concern was that if I could see people from this aerial view, they could see me standing out there with a camera in my hand.

I had to improvise. The German soldier and military theorist, Carl von Clausewitz, referred to unexpected developments as "the fog of war" which called for rapid decisions by alert commanders. My game plan was simple. I secured a primary surveillance position on the top floor of the parking garage vulnerable to all the security mechanisms at the port. I knew that sometimes you are so visible that this actually makes you invisible. I also know that at a distance things become apparent when you move or are in motion. Remember that what is motionless does not draw attention, no matter the proximity. The clothing you wear can disguise you further. In this case, I was going to be standing adjacent to a concrete wall that was white and light gray. I was able to use a long-sleeved light beige shirt to blend in with the concrete and to protect my arms from the sun. I taped my entire tripod with beige adhesive tape, changing the color to blend in with me and the concrete wall. I made certain that my video camera and tripod did not have any reflective material that would bounce off from the sunlight. I took off all of the reflective stickers that manufacturers place on their devices.

I returned to the Cape Canaveral Port and bypassed the entire security repeatedly for over a year, obtaining endless hours of video documentation evidencing my claimant doing many activities that were contradictory to his claim. I would simply secure my camera on a tripod and run continuous video of my claimant in a predetermined area that was the focal view of my video camera. I would remain in my car, out of view, keeping myself cool and hydrated and checking my video camera periodically to determine whether my claimant remained in the predetermined area or had walked out of view. I would also zoom in and out periodically for a face identification shot. It was a beautiful thing. If helicopters were checking the upper level of the parking level, they would see only a bunch of cars parked symmetrically. My camera remained screwed to the tripod out of view.

As time progressed with this surveillance assignment, I was beginning to feel uneasy because I continued to pretext my way into this port too regularly. No one had detected my presence for over a year. I had infiltrated the port over 26 times. I was so efficient in infiltrating the port's security that by then I could even hear and differentiate the security car metal chassis scraping against the speed bump located on the first floor ramp that leads into the upper levels, alerting me that security was on their way up. This would give me a window of opportunity of approximately 5 minutes to take down my tripod and camera and get them out of view, and get into my car lying dormant with the engine shut off. I would wait until roving security drove past me canvassing the upper level, and would wait for the same scraping noise alerting me that roving security was out of the parking garage and I could resume monitoring and videotaping my target.

I had my driver-side window open an inch or two to allow air to ventilate my car and to listen to the chassis scraping noise, too. If the security guard knew what to look for, it would be obvious that my radiator was leaking water from having my engine on for continuous hours.

On one occasion the roving security caught me with my video camera mounted on the tripod on the top floor. I immediately exited from my vehicle and proceeded to take down my camera and walk toward the elevator as if I were a cruise passenger on my way to a vacation. At a glance this looked normal. The security guard never bothered to stop me and question me as to why I was not carrying any luggage or whether I had my boarding pass.

Surgical Surveillance

Through surgical surveillance, I have been able to obtain evidence of my target by securing surveillance positions from various vantage points including major highways, fishing parks, clandestine hot spots, and rooftops.

This technique requires some "fishing" as well positioning your video camera on a tripod with the primary focal point directed at an area where you have predetermined that your target will be surfacing periodically, based on pattern recognition of your target from previous surveillance efforts. Press the record button and allow the video feed to continue. Eventually your target will appear and your video camera will record him or her. If the authenticity of your target ever comes into question by the plaintiff's attorney, stand your ground.

Through surgical surveillance techniques in one case, I was able to document my target arriving to work and walking away from my field of vision early in the morning when few people were present at the workplace. As the day progressed, without entering the premises, I was able to spot my target by extracting him from hundreds of people, approximately one-quarter mile away. I used an old-school Sony video camera that is heavy and bolts in your hand firmly keeping the camera as steady as a surgeon's hand. High-definition video cameras today are small, and keeping them stable is difficult even with an image stabilizer. For surveillance purposes, I prefer old-school Sony's, mostly available on eBay.

In surgical surveillance, claimant mannerisms come into play, specifically in long distances. For instance your claimant may have a habit of spitting, or running his hand through his hair. Many women have a habit of securing their long hair with a band or moving their hair away from their face when speaking with others, especially when flirting. Look at your target's upper extremities. Does your target use his or her hands expressively when interacting with others? Does your target walk distinctively?

Does your target move vigorously or with debilitated motion, or is your target unpredictable? Put the pieces together and label them accordingly. Pattern recognition is not only about intelligence gathering but can also be applied to profiling, and should be applied to all surveillance models.

Pattern recognition is accomplished through the acquisition of visual sensory connectivity when mastered effectively, but pattern recognition to be used effectively uses all of your human senses: sense of touch, smell, hearing, sight, and feel. For instance, through pattern recognition you are able to recognize the perfume your target wears or the distinct ring of your target's cell phone, drawing in your visual acuity. In a crowded bar if your target receives a phone call and you are able to hear the distinct ring tone, this will draw you closer to your target. The same goes for the perfume. All the surveillance models that we are discussing are interdependent of each other and are inherently fused together.

Vehicular Surveillance: "The Craft of Vehicular Stealth in Intelligence Gathering"

As a professional field operative you must master the craft of stealth in intelligence gathering when following your targets in a vehicle. There are no shortcuts in mobile surveillance. Mobile surveillance will account for most of the intelligence gathering that you obtain. If you are not stealthy in mobile surveillance and continue to get "burned" by your target, you will not be doing this for long. You will create a reputation for this and you will not be hired because potential clients will consider you a risk.

I had a potential client ask me how many of my investigators were law enforcement. Being a former law enforcement officer myself, having graduated at the top of my corrections and police academy, I can tell you that they did not teach me anything about surveillance in either academy. Surveillance is a one-man show. There will be no helicopters hovering above your surveillance vehicle for aerial support; you will not have multiple vehicular units dispatched to your aid when you lose a visual of your target; you will not have an electronic device that will enable you to locate your target using global positioning satellite (GPS), and your employer or operations manager can do little to help you. Basically you are on your own, and as a professional investigator the faster that you accept this, the faster you will become efficient in mobile surveillance. Break loose from your operations manager and conduct all of your investigations on your own from inception to end. Be receptive to intel offered by others who are on your side and pay close attention to information that is offered by other intelligence sources. Conduct a retroactive investigation if the investigation has been fouled. Remember that you are only as good as your last case, and live by this standard.

Two-Man Operations in Mobile Surveillance

Sometimes you may be assigned to work with a second investigator—a two-man surveillance team. It is possible that both of you will lose your target in traffic while conducting mobile surveillance if one of the team loses the visual of the other investigator and the target, and is preoccupied trying to figure out where they are. I hear this from my buddies who are federal agents all of the time, too. If one member of the team is not keeping his eyes on the ball, he may call the other member to see where he is, which leads to multi-tasking and the target may be lost in the confusion. So a good rule of thumb is to only work a two-man surveillance when you have prior knowledge that you can work with the other investigator and will not be distracted while you are both in mobile surveillance mode.

The best way to handle two-man surveillance is to say very little when conducting mobile surveillance. The less you both say while in mobile surveillance, the better you will work together. My rule in two-man surveillance is simple: pretend that I am not out here with you and call me if you need me. I sometimes use handheld radios, too, but communication remains limited. Remember that two-man assignments should not baby-sit each other. Keep your eyes on the ball and pretend that it is a one-man operation and you will do just fine.

Operational Challenges in Mobile Surveillance

The *operational constant* that makes mobile surveillance challenging is that your target is in constant movement. Your target is mobile most of the time except when traffic control devices dictate what your target will be doing next. This is a good thing. For instance, your target is approaching a traffic light that is about to turn red, and your target will probably slow down to a complete stop until the light turns green. You must learn to systematically identify and label the operational constants in mobile surveillance as *predictable constants* or *unpredictable constants*. Traffic control devices are predictable constants because most drivers follow the traffic rules. In mobile surveillance this gives you time to improvise, adapt, and overcome road conditions and situations you will encounter while in mobile surveillance. Consider your target in mobile surveillance predictably unpredictable. Unpredictable because you do not know your target's final destination and your target will be making unpredictable turns and traffic maneuvers on public streets that you will not always be able to anticipate. However, in many cases this will not matter because you will learn to systematically identify a predictable flow of vehicular patterns and clusters, and sometimes you will know what your target's next move will be before the target knows him- or herself, based on gauging his or her speed, braking, turn signaling, and traffic control devices that are helping you stay with your target.

Pattern Recognition in Mobile Surveillance

Pattern recognition is fused together with all the surveillance models discussed here. For instance, let's say that your target is a safe driver and based on pattern recognition identifiers you have observed your target traveling 10 miles above the speed limit as his or her comfort area. Suddenly you view your target slowing down and continuing to travel in the middle lane. You should be anticipating that your target is getting ready to turn within the next quarter mile. This prediction would be considered unpredictable because you are anticipating a move that your target may be executing soon. However, you will not know with certainty until your target actually executes the move within the time constraint of your predictions.

It is best to track your target to their right. Always be on the right-hand side, not to their left and not directly behind them. There are exceptions to this rule, of course. If you are tracking your target on the highway, you can give your target more space and be vigilant in searching for exit ramps and vehicles that are the same make, model, and color that are traveling in close proximity to your target vehicle. However, following your target vehicle while staying on the right is the safest operational decision, because most drivers are more vigilant in looking at their driver side mirror than the mirror on the front passenger side. If by chance the vehicle you are tracking is missing a rearview mirror, this is good news because the likelihood of the driver spotting you is decreased.

Stay in the middle lane when uncertain as to whether the vehicle you are tracking is going to turn left or right. Put more space between you and the vehicle you are tracking to allow for ample time to not make an abrupt turn and draw attention to yourself. You should learn to drive safely even if you sometimes have to make reckless maneuvers. Be careful not to speed in school districts and never run a school bus stop or a school crossing guard, and be extremely alert in residential communities for children, pedestrians, and vehicles backing up from residential driveways.

I see mobile surveillance in relation to the flow of traffic in general as a predictable constant. Your target will be following the same flow of traffic regardless of where your target is going. Your target is restrained by the same traffic control devices that we must all obey and will most likely be obeying the traffic control devices as most drivers on the road do. This operational constant limits your target's mobility, and it should be used as an operational advantage.

Circular Surveillance: "The Craft of Literally Doing Circles Surrounding Your Target Unbeknownst to Them"

Sometimes I may be intentionally going in the opposite direction of the flow of traffic from my target while conducting mobile surveillance. Why am I on the opposite side of the road when my target is going the other way, gaining distance away from me? I am most likely going to lose a visual of my target's vehicle once in motion. In circular surveillance the odds are against you. The probability of losing your target while in mobile surveillance is as high as 85%. Why employ circular surveillance? Because at times you will have no option but to employ this technique to preserve the integrity of the case, rather than go home because you got "heated" or "burned."

So here I am stuck at a traffic light in a four-way intersection facing my target head on from the opposite direction across the street, anticipating the light changing. When my light turns green, I will be heading east, and simultaneously my target will be heading west. I am obviously defying the rules of the game. You are supposed to follow and stay close to your target and not gain too much distance from your target vehicle going further in the opposite direction.

In circular surveillance, things do not make sense in a linear world. The circular surveillance model is tailored only for seasoned professional investigators who have been conducting mobile surveillance for years. Circular surveillance is the most challenging model being discussed in this chapter. Do not allow this to discourage you. I encourage you to take this model out for a test drive. It is a great way to boost your ego and broaden and strengthen your mobile surveillance techniques.

Let's start by discussing *when* to employ circular surveillance. You should be thinking of this surveillance model when you are following your target and your target makes an abrupt U-turn. You may also select this model when you do not want to follow your target into a residential neighborhood or streets where there is no traffic flow or a dead end. If you make an illegal U-turn in unison with your target, your target will probably snap a mental photo of your vehicle and think to him- or herself, "Hey, that driver was bold, cool! We both violated the law together." Your target will now create a *vehicular bond* between the two of you. This is not a good thing. Your target may feel that the two of you are driving in a caravan and will be glancing in the direction of your vehicle when the opportunity arises. Sooner or later you will draw too much attention and risk getting burned by your target. There are exceptions to this rule; for instance, rush hour traffic, an accident down the road whereby drivers are making illegal U-turns to avoid getting stuck in gridlock, legally making a U-turn, or a cluster of vehicles breaking the law in unison to get out of a certain traffice situation. In this case, you might have no choice but to make an illegal U-turn with your target or risk losing your target in traffic.

Circular surveillance is a surveillance model that you have very little control over. That's okay, though. This model will teach you to trust your instincts and your expertise. It will teach you the art of *absolute execution without hesitation*. You will be manning your surveillance vehicle in a rhythmic tempo with the traffic flow, anticipating traffic control devices while gauging your speed and using clusters of vehicles to camouflage your position.

As in all surveillance models discussed here, do not be afraid to put this to the test. Take all the surveillance models out for a test drive, and challenge yourself! Practice makes perfect. Follow anyone. Get it right. Most important, familiarize yourself with the feeling of the operational constants and break away from any phobia that is working against you.

Imagine yourself doing circles around your mobile claimant while driving your vehicle. You and your claimant will be in constant movement unless one of you is stationary. The operational constants that will be limiting both you and your claimant's movements will be governed by a symmetrical and parallel world fused together with traffic control devices, unpredictable weather conditions, flow of traffic, the presence of law enforcement vehicles, and buffers that can camouflage you or cause you to lose your claimant. You must use everything around you to your advantage.

You must become one with the terrain. Clock and gauge the traffic light intervals. I know at times exactly how long it will take for my target's traffic light to switch because I have been gauging the intervals of the traffic lights. I know how long it takes for my traffic light to switch in case I am stuck at a light and my target is stuck at another light in front of me. I know how many seconds my target has gained in distance from me.

Let's talk about symmetrical and linear constants. When you are conducting mobile surveillance, you are following your target along symmetrical and parallel paths ranging from south to north or from east to west. Circular surveillance if not executed efficiently will cause you to lose your claimant. However, remember that it is always a better operational setback to lose your target than to get burnt.

Circular surveillance is composed of several double-edged operational constants. Each of these is fused with other operational constants, both predictable and unpredictable, that you will encounter while conducting mobile surveillance. Each constant is interdependent with other constants regardless of their classification, because they all connect at one point.

You must learn to identify and classify each operational constant as either a predictable or an unpredictable mechanism that governs the flow of vehicular traffic patterns. You will identify these constants depending on the circumstances dictating the traffic flow patterns for that particular time of day. For instance, one variable might be that it recently stopped raining and the asphalt roads on which you are traveling are wet. When asphalt gets wet it becomes slippery because oil residue rises to the top. In such a case you must take into consideration that braking abruptly may cause your vehicle to hydroplane. Therefore, you might want to get closer to your claimant's vehicle and maintain your speed limit maybe 10 miles slower than your claimant's and allow one buffer car at the most to get between you and your claimant's vehicle. I would classify some buffers as unpredictable because you never know whether the driver is an aggressive driver who will drive through a yellow light instead of stopping in front of you and causing you to lose a visual of your claimant's vehicle. Predictable buffers are police cars, waste management trucks, school buses, public transit buses, and senior citizens driving their personal cars; these are considered predictable because their speed remains the same most of the time. These types of vehicular buffers are fantastic when you want to give the impression that you are slowing down without the need to brake and draw attention to yourself.

Here are two scenarios of circular surveillance. Your claimant turns into a residential neighborhood and continues to follow a road heading south. You continue to follow the same direction but using a street that runs parallel close to the street on which your claimant is traveling. You may not always have this option, but assume in this case that you do. You confirm that your claimant continues to head south because you can see your claimant in the gaps between the homes to your side. A few seconds later, you and your claimant are each at a stop sign, a few streets apart. You continue to follow the same path and come to another stop sign. You glance over to your right side, and you see the claimant approaching the stop sign a few streets away from you. You are cautiously waiting for your claimant's presence to determine whether he will be turning left or right, or continue heading south. In the meantime, the people in the vehicle behind you are getting impatient and honking their horn. You quietly maintain your position and let that vehicle pass. By this time, your claimant is turning toward you and you resume your mobile surveillance.

What are your options at this time? It depends. What does the terrain and symmetrical/linear world have to give you? Take into consideration all of the operational constants that will make this particular model and operational challenge.

Here's another scenario: you are facing your claimant at a four-way intersection and you are on the opposite side of the road, stuck at a light. Your claimant's traffic light turns. Your traffic light turns at the same time. You continue driving until you see a legal U-turn marker or traffic light. You make the U-turn and continue driving. You have no visual of the claimant at this time. You choose your best bet and continue to go in the same direction your claimant was traveling. Then you get stuck at another traffic light. A few yards away there's a ramp leading to a major highway going east and west bound. With binoculars in hand, you glance at traffic flow in front of you and you don't see your claimant. You decide to take the highway ramp to increase the probabilities of recovering your claimant and salvaging your surveillance. What direction will you take, east or west? You decide to go west because it's farther from your claimant's residence and your clamant recently departed from the residence, so it makes no sense that your claimant will be traveling east unless he or she was headed back home. You take the west-bound ramp, gun your vehicle in excess of 70 MPH, continue this speed for approximately 2 to 3 minutes, and a few miles down the road you spot your claimant's vehicle traveling in the middle lane and cross-reference the license plate number with what you have on file. It checks out. Congratulations, fantastic work—you recovered your claimant!

In circular surveillance you are using symmetrical and parallel streets to literally go in circles around your claimant. Your options are endless depending on what street you choose, keeping in mind all the operational constants that will be working with you and against you. In circular surveillance you are defying the traditional mode of operation when following your claimant. You are increasing the probabilities of losing your claimant, but you are also increasing the probabilities of preserving the integrity of the case by electing a stealth mode that will keep the claimant from being alerted of your presence.

You may decide to follow your claimant who is traveling northbound using alternate paths and crisscrossing from all possible directions to include west, east, and south. It will not be unusual for you to retract your distance from your claimant by going the opposite direction to ultimately discover where your claimant destination is going to be. You will then recover a direction that is in the same path that your claimant is traveling on, based on where the streets lead or dead end.

In circular surveillance time is of the essence. You can buy yourself some time by driving faster. However, be mindful in residential zoning where children and pedestrians are present, school zones, or where there might be anything that is moving into your path such as other vehicles backing out of driveways.

You need to buy yourself time to increase the probability of rectifying your selected routes while following your claimant. This way if you are following your claimant in the same direction, a few streets north or east of the claimant, and if you encounter a dead end street or cul-de-sac, you will have a few seconds to rectify your choice of routes and keep your claimant in your sights.

The circular surveillance model is tailored for advanced techniques in mobile surveillance applications. I would not recommend taking this model out for a test drive on a real claimant unless you feel confident you can get this done effectively and know what you are up against.

To practice the technique, you can select any moving vehicle on the street and see how long you can stay with it until the driver does something that will warrant this particular model to be exercised.

I put this model to the test whenever I have the opportunity. My percentage rate of success for this model is high, ranging anywhere from 50% to 70%. This means that whenever I put this model to the test, I do not lose my claimant 7 times out of 10. I am constantly challenging my stealth modes by creating different models of surveillance techniques and raising my own bar and that of those with whom I work or train.

What about circular surveillance while stationary? This mode of operation is less challenging and is essentially what most investigators are accustomed to. It is basically the acquisition of suitable and transient surveillance vantage points. For example, let's say your claimant is taking a dip during a warm summer day in the pool located in the back patio. Is there a suitable surveillance position that you can acquire to monitor your claimant's activities without risking detection or drawing attention from nearby neighbors? Or let's say your claimant is washing a vehicle. Is there a surveillance position you can acquire to avoid any visual obstructions that block your view? Surveillance vantage points surrounding your claimant must be acquired as soon as your claimant frequents a new location. By acquiring different surveillance positions with different vantage points, you can literally do circles around your claimant.

When you begin to master all the surveillance models discussed here, you will feel confident in your professionalism. You will truly feel you are an accomplished investigator, distancing yourself from the conventional investigator and solidifying your true modus operandi signature.

Gradual Surveillance: "The Craft of Uncovering Surveillance Conscious Target's Final Destination"

Sometimes being very obvious makes you invisible. Something that is obviously visible means it has no reason to hide. This is called hiding in plain sight. In *gradual surveillance* the model is tailored for surveillance-conscious targets or investigators who continue to lose a visual of their targets on public streets. The approach is fairly simple but can take longer than other models, so it will depend on how much time and money your client is willing to invest in you. This surveillance model can be a slam dunk when executed correctly.

Humans are creatures of habit and are fairly predictable day in and day out. Gradual surveillance along with pattern recognition is therefore useful.

Let's say you have a target who burned you while he was on his way to work. You observed the target wearing what appeared to be a uniform but you could not make out the corporate markings on the uniform due to the brevity of the target's appearance, proximity, or visual obstructions. A follow-up surveillance a few days later reveals that your target continues to be surveillance-conscious and now he has burned your two-man surveillance team. Your client is not happy. What do you do?

To employ the gradual surveillance model, first you need to know where you are going to secure a surveillance position, anticipating your target's appearance. This surveillance position will be within close proximity to where you last observed your target, or where you know that your target will be driving past. I recommend that you change into a different surveillance vehicle, preferably with no tints. Canvassing for your surveillance position in gradual surveillance is the first step to beat a surveillance-conscious target.

For instance, if you discontinue a surveillance to preserve the integrity of your case, or got burned by your target as he was nearing a major highway, you may want to employ the gradual surveillance model and conduct a process of elimination to determine in which direction your target is headed by parking near the highway ramp that your target approaches on his or her way to work in the morning, or, my favorite, parking where toll booth attendants park their personal vehicles during their work shift. These employee parking lots are accessible to the public and are strategically visible any time you are nearing a toll booth on any major highway. You may want to secure your position a few blocks down the road where your target is going to drive past you. If you are working the surveillance assignment you can contact your backup investigator and inform him that the target is headed in his direction. You can connect a chain of investigators in a predetermined area assuming you suspect that your target is going to drive past one of your assets, and then you can all scramble and catch up to your target and follow the target to his or her destination. However, in most cases gradual surveillance will be employed solo.

Second, you need to identify and become familiarized with most of the possible routes of departure leading to and from your target's place of departure, in this case their place of residence. You also need to become familiar with nearby highways and most major streets on which your target may be traveling to get to and from work. Also become familiar with any nearby Starbucks, Dunkin' Donuts, or cafeteria that your target stops at for coffee. Google Earth is a great investigative tool giving you operational preparedness with the layout of the target's community without your being there physically.

Once you have identified and are familiarized with nearby major streets and highways within close proximity of your target's residence, it is time to put your gradual surveillance model to the test.

Scout for the golden surveillance position. If you can't see your target, this means that your target can't see you. If the surveillance position that you secured allows you to see your target, you need to look for another surveillance position. You may need to pretext a tenant to allow you to park in their driveway. But before you ask a tenant for permission, check in with the local police, approach the tenant's door, knock politely, stand 7 feet away from the door so the tenant won't become nervous by your presence, have a cup of coffee in your hand and look friendly; give the appearance that you are on the job and have your shield ready, and as soon as the tenant opens the door say authoritatively while flashing your badge, "Good morning sir/madam, my name is Detective (your last name) and the (county) Sheriff's Office knows that I am out here conducting an investigation. Do you mind if I park on your driveway for a few hours so I can remain discreet?" Note that I did not use the term "private investigator." Most tenants will not cooperate when they hear the words "private investigator" and do not want to get involved in private matters. Most people will assume that you are a detective because you have a badge and you used the Sheriff's Office name. By the way, you are not impersonating anyone. If the tenant asks whether you are a law enforcement officer, you then have no choice but to tell the tenant the truth—that you are a licensed private investigator. Most tenants will allow you to park on their driveway if you follow this approach. If not, scout for another surveillance position and repeat the process until someone allows you to park on their property. One or two attempts should suffice. You do not want to alert the entire neighborhood of your presence. Always compose yourself when dealing with the public; tuck in your shirt, comb your hair, and do not chew gum.

Now that you have secured your predetermined surveillance, keep your eyes peeled for your target to drive past you. In gradual surveillance you will not be putting in an entire day, maybe 1 to 2 hours at the most. You will be going back to the area multiple times, keeping in mind that you have a small window of opportunity, knowing approximately when your target departs from a certain point, i.e., from home in the morning, from work during lunch time, from a doctor visit, deposition, court date, etc., and you will gradually get closer and closer to your target depending how stealthy you are. Often in gradual surveillance, once your target drives past your position he or she is done, mainly because people are most surveillance conscious close to their homes. Surveillance conscious claimants will be on the lookout to any tail when they are leaving their neighborhood. However, the farther the claimant gets from his or her residence, the lower his or her defenses, giving you an operational edge. People who are surveillance conscious will be more likely to notice vehicles with dark window tints, the makes and models of the vehicles that they suspect are following them, dark color vehicles, drivers traveling alone, and most importantly anyone who appears to be looking in the claimant's direction. This is why gradual surveillance and shock surveillance are like peanut butter and jelly, because your target will not be looking out for surveillance assets once he or she reaches the comfort area away from the home and workplace. Most of your targets will hit their comfort area 30 seconds to a minute from the time they leave a place. In gradual surveillance the element of surprise is on your side.

Remember that most targets are probably going to follow the same flow of traffic. This is pattern recognition. Knowing the dominant routes of departure based on what you observe on surveillance will facilitate the process by eliminating other probable routes of departure that your target might take.

Did your target pass by your surveillance position? Was it the street that you expected? Pattern recognition comes into play. Whether your target took the route that you expected or not, you now have a piece to the puzzle. Invoice your client for a 2-hour minimum and scout for a secondary surveillance position that you will secure for the follow-up surveillance.

During your follow-up gradual surveillance, your target drives past your surveillance vehicle, and his guard is up, so you elect not to follow him. Your target drives past you, and you let him go, good for you. Now, you have two pieces to the puzzle. You are gradually forming pattern recognition in an effort to uncover your target's final destination. Repeat the process until you uncover your target's final destination. Gradual surveillance is a tedious process, but it works. This is why it is called gradual surveillance, because you gradually get closer to knowing your target's final destination by being stealthier than what the target estimated you to be. If you commence gradual surveillance efforts, let's say on a Monday, I would feel confident to say that by Friday you will uncover your target's final destination and satisfy your client. There's nothing to it—it simply takes patience and general know-how.

Operational Preparedness

Always have a full fuel tank before you commence your surveillance. Make sure that your headlights are off. If you operate a vehicle that automatically keeps the headlamps lit, get a kill switch, or in case of emergency turn your emergency brake lever one increment and that should work.

Make sure that your windshield and windows in your surveillance vehicle are clean with no bugs or insect body parts. If you are shooting video from inside your car with the windows up, which will be the case in most assignments, and you have your camera set to auto-focus, your camera will auto focus on your windshield if there are objects such as bugs on the windshield, and the target you are trying to videotape will be blurred. Take pride in your work and clean all your windows prior to the commencement of your surveillance assignment.

Do not reset your day and time stamp with the exception of at the end of the seasons. Turn down the volume and recording light on your video camera. Use mini-DV cassettes. Do not use video cameras that record on DVDs or hard drives. Set your video camera to LP (long play) and turn on your image stabilizer and set your zoom to 20× amplification, preferably not digital but optical.

Check in with the local police department and give the dispatch call taker your physical description and what you are wearing even if the call taker does not ask for the information. Ask for the name of the call taker and write it somewhere where it will be readily available. Don't be surprised if police respond to a suspicious vehicle call and approach you anyway. Give the police the call taker's name and time that you were logged in and usually the police leave without incident. Sometimes during change of shift there will be a breakdown in communication and dispatch will not relay the information to the relieving shift.

Preliminary Investigation—Open Source Intelligence (OSINT)

Every investigative assignment consists of a three-tier phase. First there is the preliminary investigation, which consists of an online investigation that will be discussed shortly in greater detail. This may involve Facebook, Google Earth, GPS, TLOs, Lexis-Nexis, and smart phones. Second is your field investigation, which consists of the surveillance that you conducted and what you witnessed. Last is your report writing and packaging your entire work product, and providing it to your client.

Social Networks

Once I have become familiar with the layout of the area where my surveillance efforts are going to begin, I move on to social networks. I start with Facebook and that usually does the trick. If I strike out on Facebook, I check Myspace or Spokeo or other social networks. When I find my target on Facebook, however, the profile will often be set to private settings. In this case, I look at the profile picture and copy the picture onto my media report that will include satellite imagery (discussed below) as well. When a profile is set to private, I can still see the target's list of friends and can access their profiles, mainly the ones with the same last name, and hope that their profiles are set to public view. In many cases they are. I will access my target's network of friends and look for that needle in the haystack. Maybe I will find a picture of my target or a vehicle in the background with visible license plates that I can run. Maybe I will find a shirt with a company logo or an employment uniform that I can identify at a first glance. In addition to looking at the photos, I comb through all of the wall posts. This takes time and patience. The comments on Facebook need to be expanded. I look for comments that my target has posted and I will be able to read those comments and label them as Exhibits in my investigative report if the comment helps my client.

Comprehensive Reports

A thorough online investigation should take you 15 minutes to an hour if you are really digging for clues. Whenever I receive an investigative assignment, the first thing that I do is run the name in TLO (an information broker in Florida) to determine where my target lives by looking at the most recent address that my target reports. Usually, I can look at the comprehensive report and know whether the information is reliable. Remember that information does not mean anything unless you get out there and see it for yourself. You can then transition what was obtained in a comprehensive report into factual information. Bear in mind the fallacy constant in field investigations. Don't believe everything that you see, and constantly challenge and question what is observed. In due time, you will question yourself less and will learn to trust your instincts more.

Imagery Intelligence (IMINT)

Once I have an address for the target, I continue my online investigation using Google Earth to see the satellite imagery of the area where surveillance efforts will take place. I love this application. I can now walk in the front of my target's home and even canvass their backyard and see whether there is a boat, jet-ski, off-road bikes, etc. without physically being there. I can also see the vehicles parked at the residence and look at the layout of the community and nearby highways, shopping centers, schools, hospital, and airports at a click of a button. Note that Google Earth is not real-time satellite imagery. What you are looking at was photographed by a satellite in orbit with immense resolution capabilities, in most cases within a year. Satellite imagery has an exceptional operational advantage for professional investigators, and if you have not implemented this application in your preliminary search you are missing out on all of the fun.

Multiple Online Databases

I have saved favorite Web sites on my desktop so I can swiftly navigate the Web and access numerous sites in an effort to reveal pertinent information about my target. I check criminal records (not the real Mc Coy—not FCIS/NCIS), prior claims, driving records, county clerk of court, recorder's office, Division of Corporations, Division of Licensing, and many more. You may be thinking, Isn't that information picked up by the comprehensive report? In most cases, yes, however, don't believe everything that you read, and question everything. Remember that there is a drag time of approximately 3 months, for instance, in vehicle registrations, and comprehensive reports don't pick up this data. Therefore, check and recheck, and eventually the information will surface.

Pretexting

As a professional investigator you must have a *contingency plan* if your target disappears from your field of view and you maintain your position and your target does not return within about 30 minutes. What are you going to tell the Florida Highway Trooper when he knocks on your window and offers to assist you because he thinks you are pulled over to the side of the road in need of assistance? What are you going to tell onlookers if approached while seated behind the front driver side of your vehicle in a public park for hours and your radiator is creating a puddle under your engine compartment and people are noticing your idling engine? Did you check in with the police? What pretexts are you going to use that will allow you to salvage your acquisition of surveillance positions without insulting someone's intelligence. And last, and most importantly, will your investigative findings, evidence, and exhibits hold up in court? Will you be able to discuss your investigative findings in a collected manner with nothing to hide? If the answer is yes, then best of luck to you and happy hunting.

Appendix 15.2: Glossary and Sample Logs

Glossary

Be burnt: To have your subject know that he or she is being followed, and who is following him or her.

Be hot: To have your subject suspect that he or she is being followed.

Be made: To be detected or suspected of being a surveillant by the subject.

Bugging: Eavesdropping by electronic means, such as a hidden microphone or radio transmitter.

Bumper beeper: A battery-operated device that emits radio signals that permit it to be tracked by a directional finder-receiver; also called a beacon, transponder, or electronic tracking device.

Burn the surveillance: When the surveillant's behavior causes the subject to know he or she is under surveillance.

Close or tight surveillance: The subject is kept under constant surveillance. The aim is not to lose the subject even at the risk of being made.

Convoy: A countermeasure to detect a surveillance.

Loose surveillance: A cautious surveillance, because the loss of the subject is preferable to possible discovery.

Moving surveillance: The surveillant moves about in order to follow the subject.

Open surveillance: A surveillance with little or no attempt at concealment.

Pen register: A device that records all numbers dialed on a telephone.

Shadow: To follow secretly.

Stakeout: Also called a plant or fixed surveillance—the surveillant usually remains in a fixed position or location.

Subject: The party under surveillance.

Surveillance: The secretive, continuous, and sometimes periodic watching of persons, vehicles, places, or objects to obtain information concerning the activities and identities of individuals. Observation of people to determine information relevant to an investigation without the subject being aware of the observation. Watching and following a person.

Surveillant: The person conducting the surveillance.

Tail: To follow and keep under surveillance.

Tailgating: A form of open surveillance in which the subject's vehicle is closely followed.

Technical surveillance: Surveillance involving the use of scientific devices to enhance hearing or seeing the subject's activities.

Photograph Log Cover Sheet

*****PHOTOS TAKEN*****

By ____________________ Case # ____________________

Date ____________________

Location ____________________

Incident ____

____

____

____

____

____

Figure 15.1 Photograph log cover sheet.

Type of Film: ____________________

Photo #	Description	Shutter/f Stop	Time	Lighting	Weather

Figure 15.2 Photograph log.

PHOTOGRAPHS

Case Title:

Attorney:

Date/Loss:

VTS File:

FILM: 35mm **LENS:** 50mm

ISO: 100ASA **FLASH:**

Photo No.: 0001

Date taken:

Location:

Photographer:

DESCRIPTION:

Case Title:

Attorney:

Date/Loss:

VTS File:

FILM: 35mm **LENS:** 50mm

ISO: 100ASA **FLASH:**

Photo No.: 0001

Date taken:

Location:

Photographer:

DESCRIPTION:

Figure 15.3 Sample display sheet.

Service of Process 16

Process is defined as a formal document, authorized by law, directed to a person named in the document and commanding him or her to do or refrain from doing a certain act. Process is a form of writ and is sometimes called a Writ of Process. The purpose of process and its service is to notify the defendant that he or she is being sued, tell the defendant the nature of the litigation, give the defendant an opportunity to defend him- or herself, and confer jurisdiction of the court over the defendant's person.

In some states, Florida, for example, state law authorizes service by the sheriff in the county. It authorizes the sheriff to appoint process servers. The appointee is called an elisor. If the sheriff is unable to serve process for any reason, the court may appoint any competent person who has no interest in the action to make service.

Types of Service

Service of process is classified as personal, substituted, or constructive. Personal service is the physical delivery of a copy of the process and initial pleading to the person to be served by a person authorized by law to serve process. Substituted service is a similar delivery to someone other than the defendant who is authorized by law or contract to be served for the defendant. Constructive service is made by publication of notice of the litigation in a qualified newspaper or by posting of notice in the places required by law with the mailing of a copy of the notice and the initial pleading to the defendant if his or her whereabouts are known.

In some types of constructive service, only the publication is required. Both personal and substituted service give the court personal jurisdiction over the defendant so a judgment can be entered. Constructive service gives jurisdiction over some things that the court can act on to give relief to the parties seeking it. After the process has been properly served, the court can adjudicate the matter.

Service of process can be waived in two ways. The defendant can voluntarily serve responsive pleadings, motions, or papers prior to being served, or the defendant may authorize his or her attorney to accept the initial pleading without service of process.

The method of service of process is a procedural matter. Service of original, cross-claim, and third-party process is made by delivering a copy of the process and initial pleading to the person to be served. This method applies to all personal service, whether the person served is a defendant, officer, agent, or representative of an organization. Service of process on Sunday is prohibited unless a court order authorizing service is obtained.

Proof of Service

The court cannot proceed in the action until proof of valid service has been made. The proof must specify the papers served; the person who was served; the date, time, address, or place; and the manner of service. Facts must be set forth that show that the service was made by an authorized person in an authorized manner. Proof of service shall contain a description of the person served, which will include sex, color of skin, hair color, approximate age, height, weight, and any other identifying features. See Figures 16.1 and 16.2 for sample forms used by process servers to verify service of a process. Figure 16.3 shows a sample request for change of address.

Pitfalls to Avoid

The following points should be followed to avoid pitfalls:

- Do not make service on Sunday (unless by permission of the trial judge).
- Do not state anything about a certificate or affidavit of service that is not true.
- Do not conceal process in any way or for any reason.
- Do not conceal a summons in an envelope when delivering it.
- Do not use deceit to effect service. Process servers should be resourceful but must not misrepresent the process.
- Do not give legal advice to anyone you may serve.
- Do not take back the process after making service.
- Do not use any force in effecting service.

Service of Subpoenas for Witnesses in Federal Courts

- The rules that apply to subpoenas in federal court are found in Fed. R. Civ. P. 45 and are similar to the state rules. The subpoenas are issued by the clerk of the federal court and will be served by a federal

AFFIDAVIT OF SERVICE

IN THE CIRCUIT COURT OF THE FIFTEENTH
JUDICIAL CIRCUIT IN AND FOR PALM BEACH COUNTY
STATE OF FLORIDA

Plaintiff

v. Case No.: 200 CA 000000

Defendant

The Subpoena Duces Tecum was received by McMahon & Associates Detective Division on June 15, 2006 to be served on_______..

I, __________, who, being duly sworn, deposes and says that on the 16th day of June, 2006, I made substitute service on __________. by serving __________) at _______________., Suite 5200, West Palm Beach, FL. with a Copy of the Subpoena Duces Tecum For Deposition.

I certify that I am over the age of eighteen, and that I have no interest in the above action.

____

Server #

Sworn to and subscribed before me
this ____ day of June, 2006

____
Notary Public

MCMAHON & ASSOCIATES
DETECTIVE DIVISION
1451 W. Cypress Creek Road
Suite 300
Ft. Lauderdale, FL 33309
(954) 341-2001

Figure 16.1 Return of service affidavit.

marshall, deputy marshall, or any person who is 18 years old or older who is not a party to the case. A subpoena will set out the name of the case, where one is to appear, and whether any documents or other evidence are to be produced with the witness. Unlike the state rules, there is no time mandated before the appearance in which one must be served. However, one may object if the time is such short notice as to be unreasonable. Like the state rules, a witness fee ($40.00 for federal cases) for one day and mileage must be tendered when the subpoena is served. If the subpoena is issued on behalf of the United States, then no fee need be tendered.

AFFIDAVIT OF SERVICE

IN THE DISTRICT COURT OF THE 383rd
JUDICIAL CIRCUIT IN AND FOR EL PASO COUNTY
STATE OF TEXAS

In the matter of

Cause No.: 2003CM0000

The Writ of Attachment _________ were received by McMahon & Associates Detective Division on July 23, 2004 to be served on __________.

I, _________, who, being duly sworn, deposes and say that on the 29th day of July, 2004, I made personal service on __________ at his residence, ___________________., Pompano Beach, FL with a Copy of the Writ and Order to __________.

I certify that I am over the age of eighteen, and that I have no interest in the above action.

____

Server # 545

Sworn to and subscribed before me
this 29th day of July 2004.

____
Notary Public

MCMAHON & ASSOCIATES
DETECTIVE DIVISION
1451 W. Cypress Creek Road
Suite 300
Ft. Lauderdale, FL 33309
(954) 956-9066

Figure 16.2 Field sheet return of service.

- The person requested to appear has ten days to object to the subpoena, or until the time designated in the subpoena for compliance with its request if that time is less than ten days.

The witness may be ordered to appear at a deposition at any place within 100 miles of residence, employment, or the place of service or at any convenient place ordered by the court. A subpoena for a hearing or trial must be served within the district (in Nebraska, this is the entire state) or within 100 miles of the place of the hearing or trial if outside the district, or at another place if the court finds cause to do so. Failure to obey the subpoena without adequate excuse will result in contempt of the court.

MCMAHON & ASSOCIATES DETECTIVE DIVISION

1451 W. CYPRESS CREEK ROAD,
SUITE 300
FT. LAUDERDALE, FL 33309
954 341-2001
954 796-0209 (FAX)

FLORIDA LICENSE
A 91-000261

E-MAIL
rorymcmahon@bellsouth.net

Please Fax Results as Court Date May Be Pending
(Fax) 954 796-0209

WEBSITE
www.mcmahonpi.com

Postmaster

______________________________ Date

City, State, ZIP Code

Request for Change of Address or Physical Address to Serve Boxholder
Information Needed for Service of Legal Process

Please furnish the new address or the name and street address (if a boxholder) for the following:

Name:______________________________

Address:______________________________ Apartment or Unit No:______________

NOTE: The name and last known address are required for change of address information. The name, if known, and post office box address are required for boxholder information.

The following information is provided in accordance with 39 CFR 265.6(d)(6)(ii). There is no fee for providing boxholder information. The fee for providing change of address information is waived in accordance with 39 CFR 265.6(d)(1) and (2) and corresponding Administrative Support Manual 352.44a and b.

1. Capacity of requester (e.g., process server, investigator, attorney, party representing himself): ***State Licensed Investigator/Process Server***
2. Statute or regulation that empowers me to serve process (not required when requester is an attorney or a party acting *pro se* - except a corporation acting *pro se* must cite statute): ***Illinois Compiled Statutes 735 5/2-202***

3.The names of all parties to the litigation: ______________________________

4. The court in which the case has been or will be heard: ______________________________

5.The docket or other identifying number if one has been issued: ______________________________

6. The capacity in which this individual is to be served (e.g. defendant or witness): ______________________________

WARNING

THE SUBMISSION OF FALSE INFORMATION TO OBTAIN AND USE CHANGE OF ADDRESS INFORMATION OR BOXHOLDER INFORMATION FOR ANY PURPOSE OTHER THAN THE SERVICE OF LEGAL PROCESS IN CONNECTION WITH IN CONNECTION WITH ACTUAL OR PROSPECTIVE LITIGATION COULD RESULT IN CRIMINAL PENALTIES INCLUDING A FINE OF UP TO $10,000 OR IMPRISONMENT OR (2) TO AVOID PAYMENT OF THE FEE FOR CHANGE OF ADDRESS INFORMATION OF NOT MORE THAN 5 YEARS, OR BOTH (TITLE 18 U.S.C. SECTION 1001.)

I certify that the above information is true and that the address information is needed and will be used solely for service of legal process in connection with actual or prospective litigation.

____
Signature
Your Name/Your Title
Printed Name

State License # A91-000261
McMahon & Associates Detective Division
1451 W. Cypress Creek Road, Suite 300
Ft. Lauderdale, FL 33309

FOR POST OFFICE USE ONLY

BOXHOLDER'S POSTMARK

______ Mail is delivered to address given.
______ No change of address order on file.
______ Not known at address given.
______ Moved, left no forwarding address.
______ No such address.

NEW ADDRESS OR NAME AND STREET ADDRESS

______________________________ Unit No:

City State Zip

COMMENTS: **(Please provide any information that may assist us in serving this witness or defendant)**

____

Figure 16.3 Request for change of address from post office.

Appendix 16.1: Florida Statutes Governing Service of Process

48.021 Process; By Whom Served

(1) All process shall be served by the sheriff of the county where the person to be served is found, except initial non-enforceable civil process may be served by a special process server appointed by the sheriff as provided for in this section or by a certified process server as provided for in ss. 48.25–48.31. Witness subpoenas may be served by any person authorized by rules of procedure.

(2)

(a) The sheriff of each county may, in his or her discretion, establish an approved list of natural persons designated as special process servers. The sheriff shall add to such list the names of those natural persons who have met the requirements provided for in this section. Each natural person whose name has been added to the approved list is subject to annual recertification and reappointment by the sheriff. The sheriff shall prescribe an appropriate form for application for appointment. A reasonable fee for the processing of the application shall be charged.

(b) A person applying to become a special process server shall:

1. Be at least 18 years of age.
2. Have no mental or legal disability.
3. Be a permanent resident of the state.
4. Submit to a background investigation that includes the right to obtain and review the criminal record of the applicant.
5. Obtain and file with the application a certificate of good conduct that specifies there is no pending criminal case against the applicant and that there is no record of any felony conviction, nor a record of a misdemeanor involving moral turpitude or dishonesty, with respect to the applicant within the past 5 years.
6. Submit to an examination testing the applicant's knowledge of the laws and rules regarding the service of process. The content of the examination and the passing grade thereon, and the frequency and the location at which the examination is offered must be prescribed by the sheriff. The examination must be offered at least once annually.
7. Take an oath that the applicant will honestly, diligently, and faithfully exercise the duties of a special process server.

(c) The sheriff may prescribe additional rules and requirements directly related to subparagraphs (b)1.–7. regarding the eligibility of a person to become a special process server or to have his or her name maintained on the list of special process servers.

(d) An applicant who completes the requirements of this section must be designated as a special process server provided that the sheriff of the county has determined that the appointment of special process servers is necessary or desirable. Each special process server must be issued an identification card bearing his or her identification number, printed name, signature and photograph, and an expiration date. Each identification card must be renewable annually upon proof of good standing.

(e) The sheriff shall have the discretion to revoke an appointment at any time that he or she determines a special process server is not fully and properly discharging the duties as a special process server. The sheriff shall institute a program to determine whether the special process servers appointed as provided for in this section are faithfully discharging their duties pursuant to such appointment, and a reasonable fee may be charged for the costs of administering such program.

(3) A special process server appointed in accordance with this section shall be authorized to serve process in only the county in which the sheriff who appointed him or her resides and may charge a reasonable fee for his or her services.

(4) Any special process server shall be disinterested in any process he or she serves; and if the special process server willfully and knowingly executes a false return of service or otherwise violates the oath of office, he or she shall be guilty of a felony of the third degree, punishable as provided for in s. 775.082, s. 775.083, or s. 775.084, and shall be permanently barred from serving process in Florida.

48.031 Service of Process Generally; Service of Witness Subpoenas

(1)

(a) Service of original process is made by delivering a copy of it to the person to be served with a copy of the complaint, petition, or other initial pleading or paper or by leaving the copies at his or her usual place of abode with any person residing therein who is 15 years of age or older and informing the person of their contents. Minors who are or have been married shall be served as provided in this section.

(b) Employers, when contacted by an individual authorized to make service of process, shall permit the authorized individual to make service on employees in a private area designated by the employer.

(2)

(a) Substitute service may be made on the spouse of the person to be served at any place in the county, if the cause of action is not an adversary proceeding between the spouse and the person to be served, if the spouse requests such service, and if the spouse and person to be served are residing together in the same dwelling.

(b) Substitute service may be made on an individual doing business as a sole proprietorship at his or her place of business, during regular business hours, by serving the person in charge of the business at the time of service if two or more attempts to serve the owner have been made at the place of business.

(3)

(a) The service of process of witness subpoenas, whether in criminal cases or civil actions, shall be made as provided in subsection (1). However, service of a subpoena on a witness in a criminal traffic case, a misdemeanor case, or a second degree or third degree felony may be made by United States mail directed to the witness at the last known address, and the service must be mailed at least 7 days prior to the date of the witness's required appearance. Failure of a witness to appear in response to a subpoena served by United States mail that is not certified may not be grounds for finding the witness in contempt of court.

(b) A criminal witness subpoena may be posted by a person authorized to serve process at the witness's residence if three attempts to serve the subpoena, made at different times of the day or night on different dates, have failed. The subpoena must be posted at least 5 days prior to the date of the witness's required appearance.

(4)

(a) Service of a criminal witness subpoena upon a law enforcement officer or upon any federal, state, or municipal employee called to testify in an official capacity in a criminal case may be made as provided in subsection (1) or by delivery to a designated supervisory or administrative employee at the witness's place of employment if the agency head or highest ranking official at the witness's place of employment has designated such employee to accept such service. However, no such designated employee is required to accept service:

1. For a witness who is no longer employed by the agency at that place of employment;
2. If the witness is not scheduled to work prior to the date the witness is required to appear; or
3. If the appearance date is less than 5 days from the date of service.

The agency head or highest ranking official at the witness's place of employment may determine the days of the week and the hours that service may be made at the witness's place of employment.

(b) Service may also be made in accordance with subsection (3) provided that the person who requests the issuance of the criminal witness subpoena shall be responsible for mailing the subpoena in accordance with that subsection and for making the proper return of service to the court.

(5) A person serving process shall place, on the copy served, the date and time of service and his or her identification number and initials for all service of process.

(6) If the only address for a person to be served, which is discoverable through public records, is a private mailbox, substitute service may be made by leaving a copy of the process with the person in charge of the private mailbox, but only if the process server determines that the person to be served maintains a mailbox at that location.

48.041 Service on Minor

(1) Process against a minor who has never been married shall be served:
  (a) By serving a parent or guardian of the minor as provided for in s. 48.031 or, when there is a legal guardian appointed for the minor, by serving the guardian as provided for in s. 48.031.
  (b) By serving the guardian ad litem or other person, if one is appointed by the court to represent the minor. Service on the guardian ad litem is unnecessary when he or she appears voluntarily or when the court orders the appearance without service of process on him or her.

(2) In all cases heretofore adjudicated in which process was served on a minor as prescribed by any law heretofore existing, the service was lawfully made, and no proceeding shall be declared irregular or illegal if a guardian ad litem appeared for the minor.

48.042 Service on Incompetent

(1) Process against an incompetent shall be served:
  (a) By serving two copies of the process to the person who has care or custody of the incompetent or, when there is a legal guardian appointed for the incompetent, by serving the guardian as provided in s. 48.031.
  (b) By serving the guardian ad litem or other person, if one is appointed by the court to represent the incompetent. Service on the guardian ad litem is unnecessary when he or she appears voluntarily or when the court orders the appearance without service of process on him or her.

(2) In all cases heretofore adjudicated in which process was served on an incompetent as prescribed by any law heretofore existing, the service was lawfully made, and no proceeding shall be declared irregular or illegal if a guardian ad litem appeared for the incompetent.

48.061 Service on Partnerships and Limited Partnerships

(1) Process against a partnership shall be served on any partner and is as valid as if served on each individual partner. If a partner is not available during regular business hours to accept service on behalf of the partnership, he or she may designate an employee to accept such service. After one attempt to serve a partner or designated employee has been made, process may be served on the person in charge of the partnership during regular business hours. After service on any

partner, plaintiff may proceed to judgment and execution against that partner and the assets of the partnership. After service on a designated employee or other person in charge, plaintiff may proceed to judgment and execution against the partnership assets but not against the individual assets of any partner.

(2) Process against a domestic limited partnership may be served on any general partner or on the agent for service of process specified in its certificate of limited partnership or in its certificate as amended or restated and is as valid as if served on each individual member of the partnership. After service on a general partner or the agent, the plaintiff may proceed to judgment and execution against the limited partnership and all of the general partners individually. If a general partner cannot be found in this state and service cannot be made on an agent because of failure to maintain such an agent or because the agent cannot be found or served with the exercise of reasonable diligence, service of process may be effected by service upon the Secretary of State as agent of the limited partnership as provided for in s. 48.181. Service of process may be made under ss. 48.071 and 48.21 on limited partnerships.

(3) Process against a foreign limited partnership may be served on any general partner found in the state or on any agent for service of process specified in its application for registration and is as valid as if served on each individual member of the partnership. If a general partner cannot be found in this state and an agent for service of process has not been appointed or, if appointed, the agent's authority has been revoked or the agent cannot be found or served with the exercise of reasonable diligence, service of process may be effected by service upon the Secretary of State as agent of the limited partnership as provided for in s. 48.181, or process may be served as provided in ss. 48.071 and 48.21.

48.071 Service on Agents of Nonresidents Doing Business in the State

When any natural person or partnership not residing or having a principal place of business in this state engages in business in this state, process may be served on the person who is in charge of any business in which the defendant is engaged within this state at the time of service, including agents soliciting orders for goods, wares, merchandise or services. Any process so served is as valid as if served personally on the nonresident person or partnership engaging in business in this state in any action against the person or partnership arising out of such business. A copy of such process with a notice of service on the person in charge of such business shall be sent forthwith to the nonresident person or partnership by registered or certified mail, return receipt requested. An affidavit of compliance with this section shall be filed before the return day or within such further time as the court may allow.

48.081 Service on Corporation

(1) Process against any private corporation, domestic or foreign, may be served:
  (a) On the president or vice president, or other head of the corporation;
  (b) In the absence of any person described in paragraph (a), on the cashier, treasurer, secretary, or general manager;
  (c) In the absence of any person described in paragraph (a) or paragraph (b), on any director; or
  (d) In the absence of any person described in paragraph (a), paragraph (b), or paragraph (c), on any officer or business agent residing in the state.

(2) If a foreign corporation has none of the foregoing officers or agents in this state, service may be made on any agent transacting business for it in this state.

(3)
  (a) As an alternative to all of the foregoing, process may be served on the agent designated by the corporation under s. 48.091. However, if service cannot be made on a registered agent because of failure to comply with s. 48.091, service of process shall be permitted on any employee at the corporation's principal place of business or on any employee of the registered agent.
  (b) If the address provided for the registered agent, officer, director, or principal place of business is a residence or private mailbox, service on the corporation may be made by serving the registered agent, officer, or director in accordance with s. 48.031.

(4) This section does not apply to service of process on insurance companies.

(5) When a corporation engages in substantial and not isolated activities within this state, or has a business office within the state and is actually engaged in the transaction of business there from, service upon any officer or business agent while on corporate business within this state may personally be made, pursuant to this section, and it is not necessary in such case that the action, suit, or proceeding against the corporation shall have arisen out of any transaction or operation connected with or incidental to the business being transacted within the state.

48.091 Corporations; Designation of Registered Agent and Registered Office

(1) Every Florida corporation and every foreign corporation now qualified or hereafter qualifying to transact business in this state shall designate a registered agent and registered office in accordance with chapter 607.

(2) Every corporation shall keep the registered office open from 10 a.m. to 12 noon each day except Saturdays, Sundays, and legal holidays, and shall keep one or more registered agents on whom process may

be served at the office during these hours. The corporation shall keep a sign posted in the office in some conspicuous place designating the name of the corporation and the name of its registered agent on whom process may be served.

48.101 Service on Dissolved Corporations

Process against the directors of any corporation which was dissolved before July 1, 1990, as trustees of the dissolved corporation shall be served on one or more of the directors of the dissolved corporation as trustees thereof and binds all of the directors of the dissolved corporation as trustees thereof. Process against any other dissolved corporation shall be served in accordance with s. 48.081.

48.111 Service on Public Agencies and Officers

(1) Process against any municipal corporation, agency, board, or commission, department, or subdivision of the state or any county which has a governing board, council, or commission or which is a body corporate shall be served:
  (a) On the president, mayor, chair, or other head thereof; and in his or her absence;
  (b) On the vice president, vice mayor, or vice chair, or in the absence of all of the above;
  (c) On any member of the governing board, council, or commission.
(2) Process against any public agency, board, commission, or department not a body corporate or having a governing board or commission shall be served on the public officer being sued or the chief executive officer of the agency, board, commission, or department.
(3) In any suit in which the Department of Revenue or its successor is a party, process against the department shall be served on the executive director of the department. This procedure is to be in lieu of any other provision of general law, and shall designate said department to be the only state agency or department to be so served.

48.121 Service on the State

When the state has consented to be sued, process against the state shall be served on the state attorney or an assistant state attorney for the judicial circuit within which the action is brought and by sending two copies of the process by registered or certified mail to the Attorney General. The state may serve motions or pleadings within 40 days after service is made. This section is not intended to authorize the joinder of the Attorney General or a state attorney as a party in such suit or prosecution.

48.151 Service on Statutory Agents for Certain Persons

(1) When any law designates a public officer, board, agency, or commission as the agent for service of process on any person, firm, or corporation, service of process thereunder shall be made by leaving two copies of the process with the public officer, board, agency, or commission or in the office thereof, or by mailing said copies to the public officer, board, agency, or commission. The public officer, board, agency, or commission so served shall file one copy in his or her or its records and promptly send the other copy, by registered or certified mail, to the person to be served as shown by his or her or its records. Proof of service on the public officer, board, agency, or commission shall be by a notice accepting the process which shall be issued by the public officer, board, agency, or commission promptly after service and filed in the court issuing the process. The notice accepting service shall state the date upon which the copy of the process was mailed by the public officer, board, agency, or commission to the person being served and the time for pleading prescribed by the rules of procedure shall run from this date. The service is valid service for all purposes on the person for whom the public officer, board, agency, or commission is statutory agent for service of process.

(2) This section does not apply to substituted service of process on nonresidents.

(3) The Chief Financial Officer or his or her assistant or deputy or another person in charge of the office is the agent for service of process on all insurers applying for authority to transact insurance in this state, all licensed nonresident insurance agents, all nonresident disability insurance agents licensed pursuant to s. 626.835, any unauthorized insurer under s. 626.906 or s. 626.937, domestic reciprocal insurers, fraternal benefit societies under chapter 632, warranty associations under chapter 634, prepaid limited health service organizations under chapter 636, and persons required to file statements under s. 628.461.

(4) The Director of the Office of Financial Regulation of the Financial Services Commission is the agent for service of process for any issuer as defined in s. 517.021, or any dealer, investment adviser, or associated person registered with that office, for any violation of any provision of chapter 517.

(5) The Secretary of State is the agent for service of process for any retailer, dealer or vendor who has failed to designate an agent for service of process as required under s. 212.151 for violations of chapter 212.

48.161 Method of Substituted Service on Nonresident

(1) When authorized by law, substituted service of process on a nonresident or a person who conceals his or her whereabouts by serving a public officer designated by law shall be made by leaving a copy of the process with a fee of $8.75 with the public officer or in his or her

office or by mailing the copies by certified mail to the public officer with the fee. The service is sufficient service on a defendant who has appointed a public officer as his or her agent for the service of process. Notice of service and a copy of the process shall be sent forthwith by registered or certified mail by the plaintiff or his or her attorney to the defendant, and the defendant's return receipt and the affidavit of the plaintiff or his or her attorney of compliance shall be filed on or before the return day of the process or within such time as the court allows, or the notice and copy shall be served on the defendant, if found within the state, by an officer authorized to serve legal process, or if found without the state, by a sheriff or a deputy sheriff of any county of this state or any duly constituted public officer qualified to serve like process in the state or jurisdiction where the defendant is found. The officer's return showing service shall be filed on or before the return day of the process or within such time as the court allows. The fee paid by the plaintiff to the public officer shall be taxed as cost if he or she prevails in the action. The public officer shall keep a record of all process served on him or her showing the day and hour of service.

(2) If any person on whom service of process is authorized under subsection (1) dies, service may be made on his or her administrator, executor, curator, or personal representative in the same manner.

(3) This section does not apply to persons on whom service is authorized under s. 48.151.

(4) The public officer may designate some other person in his or her office to accept service.

48.181 Service on Nonresident Engaging in Business in State

(1) The acceptance by any person or persons, individually or associated together as a co-partnership or any other form or type of association, who are residents of any other state or country, and all foreign corporations, and any person who is a resident of the state and who subsequently becomes a nonresident of the state or conceals his or her whereabouts, of the privilege extended by law to nonresidents and others to operate, conduct, engage in, or carry on a business or business venture in the state, or to have an office or agency in the state, constitutes an appointment by the persons and foreign corporations of the Secretary of State of the state as their agent on whom all process in any action or proceeding against them, or any of them, arising out of any transaction or operation connected with or incidental to the business or business venture may be served. The acceptance of the privilege is signification of the agreement of the persons

and foreign corporations that the process against them which is so served is of the same validity as if served personally on the persons or foreign corporations.

(2) If a foreign corporation has a resident agent or officer in the state, process shall be served on the resident agent or officer.

(3) Any person, firm, or corporation which sells, consigns, or leases by any means whatsoever tangible or intangible personal property, through brokers, jobbers, wholesalers, or distributors to any person, firm, or corporation in this state is conclusively presumed to be both engaged in substantial and not isolated activities within this state and operating, conducting, engaging in, or carrying on a business or business venture in this state.

48.193 Acts Subjecting Person to Jurisdiction of Courts of State

(1) Any person, whether or not a citizen or resident of this state, who personally or through an agent does any of the acts enumerated in this subsection thereby submits himself or herself and, if he or she is a natural person, his or her personal representative to the jurisdiction of the courts of this state for any cause of action arising from the doing of any of the following acts:

(a) Operating, conducting, engaging in, or carrying on a business or business venture in this state or having an office or agency in this state.

(b) Committing a tortious act within this state.

(c) Owning, using, possessing, or holding a mortgage or other lien on any real property within this state.

(d) Contracting to insure any person, property, or risk located within this state at the time of contracting.

(e) With respect to a proceeding for alimony, child support, or division of property in connection with an action to dissolve a marriage or with respect to an independent action for support of dependents, maintaining a matrimonial domicile in this state at the time of the commencement of this action or, if the defendant resided in this state preceding the commencement of the action, whether cohabiting during that time or not. This paragraph does not change the residency requirement for filing an action for dissolution of marriage.

(f) Causing injury to persons or property within this state arising out of an act or omission by the defendant outside this state, if, at or about the time of the injury, either:

1. The defendant was engaged in solicitation or service activities within this state; or

2. Products, materials, or things processed, serviced, or manufactured by the defendant anywhere were used or consumed within this state in the ordinary course of commerce, trade, or use.

(g) Breaching a contract in this state by failing to perform acts required by the contract to be performed in this state.
(h) With respect to a proceeding for paternity, engaging in the act of sexual intercourse within this state with respect to which a child may have been conceived.

(2) A defendant who is engaged in substantial and not isolated activity within this state, whether such activity is wholly interstate, intrastate, or otherwise, is subject to the jurisdiction of the courts of this state, whether or not the claim arises from that activity.
(3) Service of process upon any person who is subject to the jurisdiction of the courts of this state as provided in this section may be made by personally serving the process upon the defendant outside this state, as provided in s. 48.194. The service shall have the same effect as if it had been personally served within this state.
(4) If a defendant in his or her pleadings demands affirmative relief on causes of action unrelated to the transaction forming the basis of the plaintiff's claim, the defendant shall thereafter in that action be subject to the jurisdiction of the court for any cause of action, regardless of its basis, which the plaintiff may by amendment assert against the defendant.
(5) Nothing contained in this section limits or affects the right to serve any process in any other manner now or hereinafter provided by law.

48.194 Personal Service Outside State

(1) Except as otherwise provided herein, service of process on persons outside of this state shall be made in the same manner as service within this state by any officer authorized to serve process in the state where the person is served. No order of court is required. An affidavit of the officer shall be filed, stating the time, manner, and place of service. The court may consider the affidavit, or any other competent evidence, in determining whether service has been properly made. Service of process on persons outside the United States may be required to conform to the provisions of the Hague Convention on the Service Abroad of Judicial and Extrajudicial Documents in Civil or Commercial Matters.
(2) Where in rem or quasi in rem relief is sought in a foreclosure proceeding as defined by s. 702.09, service of process on a person outside of this state where the address of the person to be served is known may be made by registered mail as follows:
(a) The party's attorney or the party, if the party is not represented by an attorney, shall place a copy of the original process and the complaint, petition, or other initial pleading or paper and, if applicable, the order to show cause issued pursuant to s. 702.10 in a sealed envelope with adequate postage addressed to the person to be served.
(b) The envelope shall be placed in the mail as registered mail.

(c) Service under this subsection shall be considered obtained upon the signing of the return receipt by the person allowed to be served by law.

(3) If the registered mail which is sent as provided for in subsection (2) is returned with an endorsement or stamp showing "refused," the party's attorney or the party, if the party is not represented by an attorney, may serve original process by first-class mail. The failure to claim registered mail is not refusal of service within the meaning of this subsection. Service of process pursuant to this subsection shall be perfected as follows:

(a) The party's attorney or the party, if the party is not represented by an attorney, shall place a copy of the original process and the complaint, petition, or other initial pleading or paper and, if applicable, the order to show cause issued pursuant to s. 702.10 in a sealed envelope with adequate postage addressed to the person to be served.

(b) The envelope shall be mailed by first-class mail with the return address of the party's attorney or the party, if the party is not represented by an attorney, on the envelope.

(c) Service under this subsection shall be considered obtained upon the mailing of the envelope.

(4) If service of process is obtained under subsection (2), the party's attorney or the party, if the party is not represented by an attorney, shall file an affidavit setting forth the return of service. The affidavit shall state the nature of the process; the date on which the process was mailed by registered mail; the name and address on the envelope containing the process; the fact that the process was mailed registered mail return receipt requested; who signed the return receipt, if known, and the basis for that knowledge; and the relationship between the person who signed the receipt and the person to be served, if known, and the basis for that knowledge. The return receipt from the registered mail shall be attached to the affidavit. If service of process is perfected under subsection (3), the party's attorney or the party, if the party is not represented by an attorney, shall file an affidavit setting forth the return of service. The affidavit shall state the nature of the process; the date on which the process was mailed by registered mail; the name and address on the envelope containing the process that was mailed by registered mail; the fact that the process was mailed registered mail and was returned with the endorsement or stamp "refused"; the date, if known, the process was "refused"; the date on which the process was mailed by first-class mail; the name and address on the envelope containing the process that was mailed by first-class mail; and the fact that the process was mailed by first-class mail with a return address of the party or the party's attorney on the envelope.

The return envelope from the attempt to mail process by registered mail and the return envelope, if any, from the attempt to mail the envelope by first-class mail shall be attached to the affidavit.

48.195 Service of Foreign Process

(1) The service of process issued by a court of a state other than Florida may be made by the sheriffs of this state in the same manner as service of process issued by Florida courts. The provisions of this section shall not be interpreted to permit a sheriff to take any action against personal property, real property, or persons.
(2) An officer serving such foreign process shall be deemed as acting in the performance of his or her duties for the purposes of ss. 30.01, 30.02, 843.01, and 843.02, but shall not be held liable as provided in s. 839.19 for failure to execute any process delivered to him or her for service.
(3) The sheriffs shall be entitled to charge fees for the service of foreign process, and the fees shall be the same as fees for the service of comparable process for the Florida courts. When the service of foreign process requires duties to be performed in excess of those required by Florida courts, the sheriff may perform the additional duties and may collect reasonable additional compensation for the additional duties performed.

48.20 Service of Process on Sunday

Service or execution on Sunday of any writ, process, warrant, order, or judgment is void and the person serving or executing, or causing it to be served or executed, is liable to the party aggrieved for damages for so doing as if he or she had done it without any process, writ, warrant, order, or judgment. If affidavit is made by the person requesting service or execution that he or she has good reason to believe that any person liable to have any such writ, process, warrant, order, or judgment served on him or her intends to escape from this state under protection of Sunday, any officer furnished with an order authorizing service or execution by the trial court judge may serve or execute such writ, process, warrant, order, or judgment on Sunday, and it is as valid as if it had been done on any other day.

48.21 Return of Execution of Process

Each person who effects service of process shall note on a return-of-service form attached thereto, the date and time when it comes to hand, the date and time when it is served, the manner of service, the name of the person on whom it was served and, if the person is served in a representative capacity, the position occupied by the person. A failure to state the foregoing facts invalidates the service, but the return is amendable to state the truth at any time on application to the court from which the process issued. On amendment, service is as effective as if the return had originally stated the omitted facts. A failure to state all the facts in the return shall subject the person effecting service to a fine not exceeding $10, in the court's discretion.

48.27 Certified Process Servers

(1) The chief judge of each judicial circuit may establish an approved list of natural persons designated as certified process servers. The chief judge may periodically add to such list the names of those natural persons who have met the requirements for certification provided for in s. 48.29. Each person whose name has been added to the approved list is subject to annual recertification and reappointment by the chief judge of a judicial circuit. The chief judge shall prescribe appropriate forms for application for inclusion on the list of certified process servers. A reasonable fee for the processing of any such application must be charged.
(2) The addition of a person's name to the list authorizes him or her to serve initial non-enforceable civil process on a person found within the circuit where the process server is certified when a civil action has been filed against such person in the circuit court or in a county court in the state. Upon filing an action in circuit or county court, a person may select from the list for the circuit where the process is to be served one or more certified process servers to serve initial non-enforceable civil process.
(3) Nothing herein shall be interpreted to exclude a sheriff or deputy or other person appointed by the sheriff pursuant to s. 48.021 from serving process or to exclude a person from appointment by individual motion and order to serve process in any civil action in accordance with Rule 1.070(b) of the Florida Rules of Civil Procedure.

48.29 Certification of Process Servers

(1) The circuit court administrator and the clerk of the court in each county in the circuit shall maintain the list of process servers approved by the chief judge of the circuit. Such list may, from time to time, be amended or modified to add or delete a person's name in accordance with the provisions of this section or s. 48.31.
(2) A person seeking the addition of his or her name to the approved list in any circuit shall submit an application to the chief judge of the circuit or to the chief judge's designee on a form prescribed by the court. A reasonable fee for processing the application may be charged.
(3) A person applying to become a certified process server shall:
    (a) Be at least 18 years of age;
    (b) Have no mental or legal disability;
    (c) Be a permanent resident of the state;
    (d) Submit to a background investigation, which shall include the right to obtain and review the criminal record of the applicant;
    (e) Obtain and file with his or her application a certificate of good conduct, which specifies there is no pending criminal case against

the applicant and that there is no record of any felony conviction, nor a record of a conviction of a misdemeanor involving moral turpitude or dishonesty, with respect to the applicant within the past 5 years;

(f) If prescribed by the chief judge of the circuit, submit to an examination testing his or her knowledge of the laws and rules regarding the service of process. The content of the examination and the passing grade thereon, and the frequency and location at which such examination shall be offered shall be prescribed by the chief judge of the circuit. The examination, if any, shall be offered at least once annually;

(g) Execute a bond in the amount of $5,000 with a surety company authorized to do business in this state for the benefit of any person wrongfully injured by any malfeasance, misfeasance, neglect of duty, or incompetence of the applicant, in connection with his or her duties as a process server. Such bond shall be renewable annually; and

(h) Take an oath of office that he or she will honestly, diligently, and faithfully exercise the duties of a certified process server.

(4) The chief judge of the circuit may, from time to time by administrative order, prescribe additional rules and requirements regarding the eligibility of a person to become a certified process server or to have his or her name maintained on the list of certified process servers.

(5)

(a) An applicant who completes the requirements set forth in this section and whose name the chief judge by order enters on the list of certified process servers shall be designated as a certified process server.

(b) Each certified process server shall be issued an identification card bearing his or her identification number, printed name, signature and photograph, the seal of the circuit court, and an expiration date. Each identification card shall be renewable annually upon proof of good standing and current bond.

(6) A certified process server shall place the information provided in s. 48.031(5) on the copy served. Return of service shall be made by a certified process server on a form which has been reviewed and approved by the court.

(7)

(a) A person may qualify as a certified process server and have his or her name entered on the list in more than one circuit.

(b) A process server whose name is on a list of certified process servers in more than one circuit may serve process on a person found in any such circuits.

(c) A certified process server may serve foreign process in any circuit in which his or her name has been entered on the list of certified process servers for that circuit.

(8) A certified process server may charge a fee for his or her services.

Please check for the rules and procedures in your federal, state, and local jurisdictions to ensure that all the correct procedures are followed.

Testifying in Court 17

Proper presentation of the professional investigator's testimony can be the deciding factor in a case. The first step in impressing the jurors is the initial appearance presented by the investigator or any other witness. How he or she dresses and carries him- or herself sets the tone for his or her testimony on the stand. The witness should dress in well-fitting, conservative clothes. Testimony should be easily audible, concise, and crisp.

The Investigator Pretrial

As a witness, the investigator should do pretrial preparation. He or she should familiarize him- or herself with all material pertaining to the case. The professional investigator should meet with the attorney representing his or her client and review the material covering all questions that will be asked. The investigator should review with the attorney for his or her client any material that is likely to be covered by the opposing attorneys. The investigator should concentrate on how to correctly answer any difficult questions that may arise. The investigator must learn what areas the attorney wants to avoid discussing. While waiting to testify and after testifying, he or she should avoid conversations with any other witnesses or members of the jury.

The Investigator during Trial

During the trial, the investigator should be well dressed, well groomed, and without excessive jewelry, makeup, or provocative clothing. In the witness chair, the investigator should be calm and confident and should sit upright with his or her feet planted on the floor and arms resting on both chair arms. Testimony should be presented in a well-organized, logical, and orderly fashion. All questions should be answered completely and as simply as possible. Information should never be volunteered. If the investigator does not hear or understand the question, he or she should ask that it be repeated. The investigator, as any witness, should speak loudly, clearly, slowly, and use proper grammar without resorting to slang or jargon (i.e., the subject, suspect, "perp," etc.). Proper names and titles—that is, Mr. (the defendant's name) or Dr. (witness), and so on—should be used.

When on the witness stand, the investigator should be serious yet relaxed in order to show that he or she is in command of the situation. He or she must always be truthful and as accurate and precise as possible. A witness should think carefully before answering. On cross-examination, the investigator should allow time before answering to allow the attorney to object to the question if he or she so wishes. The investigator should look at the attorney asking the questions before answering (to avoid the appearance of being coached).

The investigator should try to avoid yes or no answers that require additional clarification. The investigator should ask the judge to allow him or her to answer the question more completely. He or she should not play games or try to outsmart the opposing attorney.

The investigator should be professional in both demeanor and testimony. Remember, jurors view investigators as unbiased witnesses with valuable information. They should continue to feel that way after the investigator gives his or her testimony.

Preparation of Witnesses by Investigator

Pretrial Re-Interviewing of Witnesses

During the trial preparation, it may be necessary to re-interview witnesses, particularly when:

- The witnesses were interviewed by other investigators and their information is not fresh in your recollection.
- Considerable time has elapsed since your last interviews.
- The witnesses may also be called to testify and/or produce important documents.
- The witness is expected to provide complex (or expert) testimony.
- The reliability of the witness is doubtful (i.e., reluctant or hostile witness).

Procedures in Re-Interviews

During the re-interview, the investigator wants to obtain all the pertinent facts. Focus on the most significant aspect of the information the witness has. Make sure the witness understands how this information will best be conveyed by both you and him or her, if the witness is to testify.

Review the facts of the entire case with the witness. Explain your theory of the case and the theory of the other side (defense or prosecution) and show where the witness' information and testimony fit into the overall picture. Both the investigator and the witness will be able to testify with greater effectiveness if you both understand the significance of the information held by the witness.

Familiarize the witness with trial procedures. Explain the purpose of direct and cross examination. Tell the witness about the trial so that the witness feels more comfortable when he or she takes his or her place on the witness stand.

- Make sure that the witness can identify the parties involved, if it is material.
- Make sure the witness provides the documents or physical evidence about which he or she will testify.
- Make sure the witness is familiar with the facts, dates, and times, and can identify the time and place of the occurrence.
- Check the facts of the witness' testimony.
- Allow the witness to review any reports of the interview or any other significant reports about information about which he or she will testify.
- Discuss the areas of attack anticipated during cross-examination.
- Discuss any possible rebuttal witnesses.

Preparation of Evidence

Be sure that there is a witness to produce and identify each document or piece of evidence. The custodian of records may be required to produce certain documentary records in his or her possession, such as a clerk of court. Arrange for all physical evidence to be available at trial. Arrange for the witness to produce and identify it. Make sure the witness can document the chain of custody, thereby making it admissible.

The Investigator as a Witness

Preparation is the key to being an effective witness. The amount of preparation that an investigator needs for a given case will depend on the complexity of the case, the seriousness of the event investigated, and the investigator's comfort level with testifying in court. Preparation should begin with reading and reviewing the case report and activities that were conducted in furtherance of the investigation. You should get to a point where you are familiar enough with the case to carry on a detailed and spontaneous conversation about it. You may want to revisit scenes that were part of the investigation, so they are fresh in your mind. Sometimes physically being in a place may jog your memory and cause you to remember something you otherwise would have forgotten.

Preparation

Another way for the investigator to prepare is to have a pretrial, or preconference meeting with the attorney or representative who will be asking you the questions. These pretrial meetings are beneficial for both parties. You should prepare for the meeting in order to maximize the time spent reviewing your testimony. While attorneys sometimes portray these meetings as unlawful or inappropriate, they are beneficial and helpful, providing both parties with a better understanding of the subject matter.

Presentation

- Proper presentation of the professional investigator's testimony can be the deciding factor in a case. The first step in impressing the jurors is the initial appearance presented by the investigator. How he dresses and carries himself sets the tone for his testimony on the stand. The investigator should dress in fashionable, well-fitting, conservative clothes. While in the witness chair, the investigator should exhibit an aura of professionalism. Testimony should be easily audible, concise, and crisp.
- As a witness, the investigator should do pretrial preparation. He should familiarize himself with all material pertaining to the case. The professional investigator should meet with the attorney representing his client and review the material covering all questions that will be asked. The investigator should review with the attorney for his client any material that is likely to be covered by the opposing attorneys. He should concentrate on how to correctly answer any difficult questions that may arise. The investigator must learn what areas the attorney wants to avoid discussing. While waiting to testify and after testifying, he should avoid conversations with any other witnesses or members of the jury.

Testifying

- During the trial, the investigator should be well dressed, well groomed, and without excessive jewelry, makeup, or provocative clothing. While in the witness chair, the investigator should be calm and confident and should sit upright with his feet planted on the floor and his arms resting on both chair arms. Testimony should be presented in a well-organized, logical, and orderly fashion. All questions should be answered completely and as simply as possible. Information should never be volunteered. If he does not hear or understand the question, he should ask that it be repeated. The investigator, as any witness, should speak loudly, clearly, slowly, and use proper grammar without resorting to slang or jargon (i.e., the subject, suspect, "perp," etc.). Proper names and titles (i.e., Mr. [the defendant's name] or Dr. [witness], and so on) should be used.

- On the witness stand, he should be serious yet relaxed in order to show that he is in command of the situation. He must always be truthful and as accurate and precise as possible. A witness should think carefully before answering. On cross-examination, he should allow time before answering to allow the attorney to object to the question if he so wishes. The investigator should look at the attorney asking the questions before answering (to avoid the appearance of being coached).
- If he does not understand the question, he must seek clarification. He should try to avoid a yes or no answer that requires additional clarification. He should ask the judge to allow him to answer the question more completely. He should not play games or try to outsmart the opposing attorney.
- The investigator should be professional in both demeanor and testimony. Remember, jurors view investigators as unbiased witnesses with valuable information. They should continue to feel that way after his testimony.

Cross-Examination

During the cross-examination, the professional investigator should maintain composure. He should not be impatient or lose his temper. If he does, the attorney will have shown the jury that his testimony is biased. Some tactics an attorney may employ include rapid-fire questions and not allowing time to answer each question; a condescending manner; a benevolent, oversympathetic, or friendly manner; and courteous, polite questions to lull the witness into a false sense of security. The attorney also may badger the witness. Other tactics used by attorneys include suggestive questions to lead or confuse the witness; asking yes-or-no questions framed to produce a desired answer that is not necessarily the complete answer; reversing the witnesses' testimony in framing additional questions; repetitive questions designed to elicit conflicting answers; conflicting answers designed to show inconsistencies in the investigation; and staring after the witness has answered, provoking the witness to add more information than the answer called for.

Trial Tactics Used by Attorneys

Attorneys may try the following tactics:

- Mispronounce or misstate your name. Ignore it and answer the question just asked. Before taking the witness stand you will be asked by the clerk to state your name and spell it for the court. The attorney who continually mispronounces your name will lose credibility with the jury.
- Try to get you to argue with him/her so you lose your composure. Your polite demeanor and calm disposition will win the hearts of the jury.
- Deliberately misstate some of your previous testimony and get you to agree with their version. This may cause you to become confused and disoriented. Listen to the question and do not allow the attorneys to put their words in your mouth.
- Quote some of your previous testimony and then ask you, "Why did you leave that out of your report?" If you find yourself in this spot, answer truthfully. Your response may simply be, "I forgot," "It did not occur to me," or "I put in the information I knew was important at the time."
- Cause you not to look at the jury, focusing your attention on him/her while you are testifying. Often an attorney will get up from his/her seat and move to a position that will cause you to look at him/her while answering questions. When this happens, look at him/her as you begin your answer, and then turn to the jury as you complete your response.
- Try to get you to do two things at once, for instance draw a picture and answer a question at the same time. If you are asked a question while you are drawing a diagram, stop drawing, face the attorney, and answer the question. If you did not hear the whole question, say, "I did not hear all of the question you asked."
- Question your professional experience and training. Anticipate this. Take a written record of your training experience or a résumé with you to court.
- Attack your credibility as a witness through some error in your report and/or exploit your failure to recollect the facts of the case. Remain calm; innocent mis-recollection is not uncommon.
- Interrupt your answer to their question by asking you another question. If you are interrupted for any reason, stop talking. Likewise, do not interrupt the attorney before s/he has finished asking his/her questions.

- Try to get you to play attorney by subtly placing you in a position to refuse to directly answer the attorney's question(s), give evasive answers, or pose your own question(s). Avoid trying to be something you are not—another attorney. Avoid giving flippant or sarcastic answers.
- Try to get you to speculate or testify to things that you did not actually see, hear, or otherwise experience. You are not there to guess. You are there to tell what you know. Avoid answers such as "I suppose so," "I think so," or "If you say that is correct."
- Try to get you to "fill in the gaps" by giving testimony for which you were not specifically asked. Avoid volunteering information. After you have completely answered the question, stop talking.
- Try to get you to guess the answer to technical questions related to your field. Even if you think you are right, never guess.
- Make a statement during cross-examination that is not a question and wait a moment or two to see if you'll react to it in front of the jury. Avoid falling for this trick. If there is not a question posed to you, say nothing.
- Use words like "generally," "slightly," "frequent," and "often" to avoid being specific. These words can mean different things to different people. Make sure that your answer is specific, regardless of the attorney's tactics.
- Use words that you may not understand in an effort to embarrass you. If you do not fully understand the question, do not answer it. Say "I do not understand the question," or "I do not understand the word."
- Treat you so nicely that you will agree with him/her on the next question. Listen to the entire question and understand it before answering.
- Talk to you during breaks so that you will not see him/her as an adversary.
- Pretend to be reading to you from a document of some unknown origin and then ask you a question beginning with the phrase, "Is it not true that ..." Don't believe that "If it is on that paper, it must be true." The document may or may not have anything to do with the case.

Testifying in Court for Law Enforcement Officers

Many law enforcement officers cite testifying in court as one of the most stressful aspects of their job, perceiving it as an adversarial system where defense attorneys may skewer them during aggressive cross-examination.

While many patrol officers will testify only a few times in their careers, for others, such as traffic cops and criminal investigators, court testimony constitutes a regular part of their work routine. As witnesses, law enforcement officers must ensure that the facts they present communicate the complete story and that their delivery of those facts makes their testimony clear and credible.

Types of Witnesses and Testimony

- A *fact witness* has personal knowledge of events pertaining to a case and can only testify to things he personally has observed (e.g., "Fred told me he was mad at his boss." "I saw Fred reach for something in his glove compartment."). He may not offer opinions (e.g., "Based on Fred's behavioral profile and history of violence, he is likely to seek revenge for even small slights."), such as those expected from an expert witness retained either by the prosecution or defense or appointed by the court to make statements about aspects of the case.
- *Expert witnesses* only offer opinions that may assist the judge or jury in understanding specialized technical knowledge that would otherwise be beyond their knowledge (typically credentialed specialists in forensic-related fields, such as a medical examiner, crime lab expert, firearms specialist, or forensic psychologist). Although experts usually are allowed more leeway in testimony than fact witnesses, the court carefully evaluates the content of their testimony for admissibility.
- *Police officers* may find that their testimonies sometimes straddle the domains of fact and expert witness. For example, an officer may be queried about what he did and what the defendant did (like a fact witness) and then be asked to state an opinion (like an expert witness). Or, he may state an opinion that the opposing attorney challenges, and the judge must decide whether or not to admit it in the record.

Attorney: Officer Jackson, can you tell us how you first approached the defendant while undercover?

Officer: Well, actually, he first approached me.

Attorney: What do you mean?

Officer: I was undercover as a local high school student, and the defendant came over and asked me if I needed directions.

Attorney: And what did you answer?

Officer: That I was going uptown.

Attorney: Can you explain to this court what that conversation means?

Officer: Well, in that neighborhood, "needing directions" means that you want to buy drugs, and "uptown" is coke or sometimes crystal meth—some kind of stimulant drug.

Attorney: But, at no time did the defendant actually ask you if you, quote-unquote, "wanted to buy drugs," did he?

Officer: Not in those words.

Attorney: So, you don't know for sure if he really intended to sell you drugs or was just trying to help out.

Officer: Of course I knew. That's the language they use.

Attorney: Officer Jackson, are you an expert in linguistics?

Officer: No, but I'm an expert on that neighborhood—I've worked undercover there for 5 years.

Preparation

Officers should understand the importance of proper record keeping and develop a well-organized, standardized, and readable style for reports. This will help them clarify, organize, and remember particular points if the case goes to trial. Officers can draw pictures to help their description and to jog their memories in court. They can supplement standard forms and checklists with their own words and illustrations to help explain a potentially confusing scenario.

Officers should review their cases several times—the more thoroughly they know the facts and theories about the case, the easier they can answer questions without relying on rote memorization. Their knowledge and recollection will be an organic, automatic process against cross-examination. An officer should meet with the prosecutor several times to review testimony. Together, they should clarify the officer's testimony, agree on how the officer should best express himself, and discuss what the prosecution and defense sides will ask.

Officers should mentally rehearse for their case, going over the facts and testimony out loud while standing in front of a mirror or driving. If unfamiliar with delivering testimony, they should visit a courtroom and observe other trials in progress. But even for the seasoned witness, no substitute exists for adequate preparation. Many veteran experts have let overconfidence hinder their testimony.

On the Stand

Most important aspects of courtroom demeanor cannot be programmed; each witness brings his or her unique style to the stand. Nevertheless, officers can apply a few principles of effective testimony. They should have an attitude of confidence without being arrogant. To the average juror, police officers convey an air of authority and respect; therefore, they should maintain their composure and dignity at all times and remember that their job is only to present the facts and evidence.

Body language is important. Officers always should sit up straight. If a microphone is present, officers should sit close enough to not have to lean over every time they speak. They should keep presentation materials neatly organized in front of them to find documents and exhibits when needed. While testifying, officers should look at the attorney questioning them and then switch eye contact to the jury when answering. They should establish a connection with the jurors because jurors tend to find witnesses who look straight at them more credible.

Officers should remain open, friendly, and dignified and speak clearly, slowly, and concisely. They should keep sentences short and to the point and maintain a steady tone, as in a normal conversation. Their general attitude toward the jury should convey collegial respect (i.e., they are there to present the facts to a group of mature adults who will make the right decision). Officers should carefully listen to each question before they respond.

If they do not fully understand the question, they should ask the attorney to repeat or rephrase it, taking a couple of seconds to compose their thoughts, if necessary. If an officer does not know the answer to the question, he should state plainly, "I don't know."

They should not try to bluff their way out of a difficult question. Officers should not become defensive, and above all, they must be honest. If anyone in the courtroom detects even a somewhat dishonest answer, especially from police officers, it can ruin the rest of their testimony.

Attorneys may phrase questions in a way that constrains answers in a particular direction. If officers feel they cannot honestly answer the question with a simple yes or no, they should respond: "Sir, if I limit my answer to yes or no, I will not be able to give factual testimony. Is that what you wish me to do?" Sometimes the attorney voluntarily will reword the question. But if he presses for a yes or no answer, at that point, either the opposing attorney will voice an objection or the judge will intervene. The latter may instruct the cross-examining attorney to allow the officer more leeway in responding, to rephrase his question, or to simply order the officer to answer the question as asked.

Officers should not preface answers with such phrases as "I believe...."; "I estimate...."; "To the best of my knowledge/recollection...."; "As far as I know...."; "What I was able to piece together...."; or "I'm pretty sure that...." They should be as definite in their answers as possible or honestly state that this particular piece of testimony may not be a clear perception or recollection, but they should remain firm about what they are sure about.

Officers should try not to answer beyond the question. For example, if the attorney asks an officer to phrase answers in precise measurements that are not relevant or that the officer cannot accurately recall, officers should not speculate unless actually asked to do so.

Attorney: Officer Jackson, you say you saw the defendant take two drug vials out of his jacket pocket. How far away from the defendant were you when you made this observation?
Officer: About half a block away.
Attorney: How many feet away would that be?
Officer: I don't know.
Attorney: Surely, officer, you can estimate the distance. Was it a hundred feet? Two hundred? Fifty? Ten?
Attorney: Officer, could you see how much cocaine the defendant had in the plastic bag? Could you see exactly how many ounces it was?
Officer: Exactly how many ounces, no.
Attorney: So, you can only guess what the amount was, is that correct?
Officer: Obviously, I couldn't measure the cocaine in the suspect's hands. But I could clearly see that he was holding an 8-ounce plastic bag and that the amount of powder in the bag almost filled it. So, that's got to be at least 6 or 7 ounces, well above the 2-ounce limit for felony possession and sale.

An Officer as the Defendant

If an officer becomes the defendant in a criminal or civil case, he may have to testify in court; the general principles of testimony still apply. But this time the personal stakes are higher and the rules are a little different. Now the officer's role switches from dispassionate fact or expert witness to the person on trial. The officer may not be afforded the same deference and respect he received as a witness. Accordingly, the officer's demeanor, while still professional, should lean slightly more to the deferential and humble side with an attitude conveying confidence in putting his fate in the jury's hands and trusting them to do the right thing. Otherwise, the principles of effective court testimony are the same.

Psychologist Testimony

A special issue relates to the role of psychologists in the legal process. Officers criminally charged or civilly sued may have undergone psychological counseling, stress debriefing, a psychological fitness-for-duty evaluation, or other mental health services. This raises issues of confidentiality and admissibility of psychological records. In the author's experience, rarely do courts order the release of confidential mental health records, except under the most extreme circumstances. Still, because this may happen, officers undergoing any kind of legal charge should feel free to tell the psychologist about their feelings, symptoms, and efforts to cope with their ordeal. But if an officer is not sure whether to reveal a piece of factual case evidence, the officer should ask the lawyer first. If the lawyer advises the officer not to tell the psychologist, the officer should comply with that advice. Psychologists still can administer effective psychotherapy without knowing every technical detail. Accordingly, neither the officer nor the psychologist will be put in the position of revealing a secret.

Psychologists may still be subpoenaed to testify, and the line of questioning can be skillfully used to make it look like the clinician is hiding something or, at least, that he is incompetent.

Attorney: Dr. Lopez, during the course of your psychological treatment of Officer Jackson, did he render to you a history of the events he is charged with and a description of what took place?

Psychologist: He pretty much told me what's in the record regarding the circumstances of the charges against him.

Attorney: Did he tell you how many times he struck Mr. Williams after he had been handcuffed and restrained?

Psychologist: No.

Attorney: Isn't that something you would want to know when taking a clinical history from Officer Jackson?

Psychologist: The exact number of strikes isn't really an important detail at that point.

Attorney: Did he tell you how he felt during his struggle with Mr. Williams? Was he mad? Frightened? Enraged? Was he looking for revenge?

[At this point, the officer's attorney will probably object.]

Psychologist: We really didn't discuss that in our first session. I was more concerned with his mental status at that time.

Attorney: And, how was he feeling, doctor? Did he express remorse? Was he sorry for what he'd done? Or was he glad Mr. Williams got what he deserved? [Probably another objection.]

Psychologist: He was generally upset about the injuries Mr. Williams received as that was not his intention. As it already has been well documented in the record, Officer Jackson maintains that the injuries were accidental, sustained while Mr. Williams was violently resisting arrest in a state of extreme intoxication.

Attorney: And that's it, doctor? You mean to say that you spent an hour with Officer Jackson, and all he told you was what was in his initial statement?

Psychologist: I believe I just answered the questions you asked me.

In such cross-examinations from aggressive opposing counsel, officers should try to maintain as much composure and dignity as possible. An important part of trial testimony is the impression an officer makes on the jury by his demeanor, language, and grace under pressure. Therefore, officers should avoid either being cowed into submission or baited into an angry overreaction. Consistently reviewing testimony before the trial can help officers anticipate challenges and become comfortable with the substance of the case.

Conclusion

Most citizens, including jurors, want to believe that the people they place their trust in—such as doctors, police officers, and public officials—have their best welfare in mind. Many people give law enforcement officers the benefit of the doubt if they offer a credible reason to do so.

In contrast, if officers cross jurors through dishonesty or flagrant disrespect, jurors may reciprocate especially hard for betraying that trust. Law enforcement agencies should ensure that officers prepare carefully for their cases, present clear and honest testimonies, and maintain dignity and decorum. As a result, officers may find that testifying in court need not rank among the most stressful aspects of their duties.

Expert Witnesses

Expert witnesses are called because they have special qualifications to give an informed opinion about something relating to their field, such as economics, surgical procedures, or the design of buildings.

It is common for expert witnesses to be hired to testify and receive pay from one party to the lawsuit. For example, in a medical malpractice suit, the plaintiff who claims to be injured will hire one doctor as an expert who is expected to testify that the defendant doctor did not act with the proper care, while the defending doctor will hire another doctor as an expert witness who is expected to testify that the defendant acted as he/she should have. These hired witness doctors would be treated as experts regarding the standard of care that a doctor must use. Such a matter is something about which a well-qualified doctor would have the ability to testify while the average person would not. In such instances, each side pays for the services of its own expert.

Should the witness prefer to be subpoenaed, the rules regarding subpoenas in state and federal courts discussed above would then apply and the witness would only receive the statutory witness fees applicable to any non-expert witness. Because such amounts are insignificant and are no more than any other witness appearing, accusations of bias are difficult to make. These problems are not as likely to be encountered when one is called upon to testify outside one's state of employment, which is often the case with experts who are well known or highly regarded in their field.

Finally, both the state and federal evidence rules (Rule 706) provide that a judge may appoint an expert witness either upon the judge's own motion or the motion of any party to the suit, if the witness consents to the appointment. The witness is paid whatever sum the judge deems reasonable. This is a process separate from the subpoena procedures and is somewhat unusual as parties generally prefer to select their own experts.

How to Prepare Expert Witnesses

Many of the general rules regarding preparing witnesses above apply also to expert witnesses. The investigator's job is to make the expert feel comfortable and relaxed on the witness stand. You must see to it that an expert comes across to the jury as a knowledgeable, honest, and impartial witness.

The following instructions will help expert witness testimony. Tell your witness to:

- Be calm without appearing overconfident or arrogant.
- Explain technical terms to the jury in language that members of the jury can understand. Avoid the use of technical jargon.
- Know the rules of evidence—testimony that is deemed irrelevant and unsubstantiated will benefit no one.
- If objections are raised, don't answer until instructed to do so by the judge.

Tips for Testifying in Court

- Behave professionally. This applies both on the witness stand and off. As well as the fact that this influences the jurors, you never know who is sizing you up for the other side while you're waiting in the hall.
- Dress professionally. Studies have shown that blue for men and black for women are the most appropriate colors for looking believable. Both men and women should dress in a conservative fashion. If you are a peace officer, your uniform will enhance your credibility. Avoid flashy colors and loud ties; wear minimal jewelry.
- Before the trial starts, walk into the courtroom and familiarize yourself with where the witness chair is located and the path you need to take to get to it. This will enable you to walk directly to the stand in a forthright manner to be sworn in.

- When you are sworn in, look at the jury and say, in a loud, clear voice, "I do." Stand up straight when taking the oath. Once you are seated, sit up straight and look at the questioning attorney, and when answering make eye contact with the jurors.
- Answer all questions clearly; do not nod. If you nod the court reporter or the judge will tell you to answer audibly, and this will make it appear that you're not sure what you're doing.
- Speak toward the jurors and look at them during testimony; speak frankly and openly as to a friend, in a tone of voice clear and loud enough to be heard by all the jurors.
- Keep your hands in your lap. Keep them away from your mouth. Don't fidget.
- If you need to ask the judge a question, look at the judge and say "Your Honor" and wait until the judge gives you permission before you ask the question.
- Listen carefully to each question. Be sure you understand it before you answer. If you don't understand the question, ask for clarification.
- If either attorney objects, stop talking immediately and let the judge rule on the objection, and then continue when told to do so.
- Avoid being combative. Let the attorneys get as nasty as they want. They're probably trying to bait you. Stay cool, don't be intimidated, and answer the questions.
- If you make a mistake, admit it. Don't try to cover it up. Nobody is going to hold it against you that you made a mistake, but they will certainly hold it against you if they think you're lying.
- Clarify at once an answer that may be unclear.
- Explain answers if a "yes" or "no" is not adequate.
- Remain polite, even under intense cross-examination, and avoid appearing cocky or overconfident.
- Never memorize your testimony. Know your facts, but don't try to say things word for word. You will look rehearsed during your testimony and then will not be able to handle cross examination, where the questions are out of sequence.
- If the other side asks a question that you think is objectionable, pause before answering and give your attorney a chance to object. If he doesn't, answer the question. If either attorney objects, stop your answer and wait for the judge to tell you to proceed.
- Avoid looking at your attorney when answering questions. This looks like you're asking for help and jurors might interpret this as a damaging question, even though your answer makes sense.
- Most important, tell the truth, the whole truth, and nothing but the truth. Avoid temptation to embellish the truth. If you're caught doing this it will make your whole testimony suspect.

- Be yourself.
- Your role is to testify, not to convince the jury.
- Do not cover your mouth or rest your chin on your hand while you are speaking.
- Speak at a normal rate of speed so that the court reporter and the jury can hear your words.
- When asked a question, pause, think about the question, and think about your answer before you start talking.
- Simple "yes" or "no" answers should be directed to the person who asked the question. Longer, narrative answers, however, should be directed to the jury (or the judge if a jury is not present).
- Answer questions with a "yes" or "no," if possible, and then explain.
- Be brief and to the point if a narrative answer is requested.
- Avoid answering any question that you do not understand completely; ask to have the question clarified.
- "I do not know" or "I do not remember" are valid answers, if appropriate. "I do not know" means that you do not and never did know something. "I do not remember" means that you may have known something at some previous time, but do not remember it now.
- Use terms like "approximately" when asked for measurements of time and distance.
- Do not allow yourself to be talked into false testimony or affirm incorrect statements. If a question begins with "Isn't it true that...," be sure everything stated is true before agreeing.
- If you realize that you have made an error in your testimony, immediately ask the judge for permission to correct the error.
- Do not volunteer information. Remember to only answer the question asked of you.
- If you have any apparent interest in the outcome, your credibility may be reduced in the minds of the jury.
- Avoid testifying, reading from, or otherwise referring to your report without first asking for permission from the judge to refresh your recollection by looking at it.
- If you are asked to read a document out loud by an attorney or the judge, read it slowly so the court reporter can record your testimony.
- Keep in mind that any document taken by you to the witness stand can be examined by either attorney.
- You cannot offer or volunteer your opinion unless you are testifying as a court-qualified expert witness. An expert witness (e.g., a DNA expert) is entitled to express an opinion in the area of his/her expertise.
- Do not hesitate to ask for clarification if you are uncertain about a question.

- Speak up! Remember that everyone must hear your answers (judge, jury, court reporter, clerk, interpreters, attorneys, and clients).
- Avoid answering a question with the phrase "I believe...," "I think...," or "I am not sure...."
- You are to testify only as to what you saw, heard, smelled, tasted, or felt, unless you are an expert witness qualified by the court to give your opinion(s).
- Be prepared! You should know days or weeks ahead of time that you will be testifying in court. Think about the incident and what happened so that you can recall the details accurately when you are asked in court. If you need help remembering these details, write the facts down. If you have already written a statement for the police, ask the assistant prosecutor for a copy; reading it may jog your memory on some details. Think ahead of time about the answers you will give to the questions you expect will be asked.
- Stick to the facts! The judge (or jury) only wants to hear the facts as you know them to be, not what someone else told you.
- Expect to be questioned by several people. One of the basic rules in a criminal case is that both sides have a chance to question every witness. Questions asked by both sides have the same goal—to find out what is true.
- Never attempt to talk to a juror about the case or any other matter while the case is being tried. This includes chance meetings during recesses, in hallways, at lunch, or any other place.

Your Rights as a Witness

Legal Rights

Witnesses play an important role in the search for justice. As a witness you have legal rights:

- An employer cannot discipline or discharge you because you are subpoenaed to testify.
- A separate waiting area away from the defense witnesses is available.
- You will not be required to disclose your home or employment address unless ordered by the court.
- It is also against the law for any person to use force, threats, or coercion to prevent or dissuade a person from testifying in a legal proceeding or reporting a crime to law enforcement.

When You Receive a Subpoena

- A subpoena is an order of the court and serious penalties can attach for your failure to appear.
- *If you have been issued a subpoena, read it carefully.* A subpoena always gives directions on when and where you are to appear.
- The subpoena may also be a "duces tecum" which requests you to bring something with you. The item(s) you are to bring will be listed on the subpoena underneath the box marked "duces tecum."

If you are requested to come to the (State's)/County Attorney's Office,

- Should you have any questions, change your name or address during the course of a case, or should any exceptional circumstances arise, please call the State's/County Attorney's office.
- Bring your subpoena with you to court. It must be signed by a representative of the County Attorney's Office and returned to Court Administration.
- You may be eligible for some expense reimbursements; please read the back of the subpoena. Collect receipts for expenses such as child care, loss of wages, meals, or mileage. Reimbursements should be mailed to you within a few weeks of the court hearing.

Before You Appear in Court

- If you have previously given a formal statement to a law enforcement officer or an investigator and have a copy, please review it carefully before coming to court.
- Don't try to memorize what you are going to say. Go over in your mind those matters that will help you recall the incident when you do testify. Try to mentally picture the matters about which you will be testifying, such as the place of the incident, the objects and people present, what happened, what was said, to whom, at what time, or other circumstances which may aid you in recalling the events.
- A neat appearance and proper dress in court are important—remember, the jury will be affected by first appearances.

Cross-Examination by the Defense Attorney

- Take time to think through your answer before speaking. If you don't understand the question, say so.

- Should you be asked if you were paid for coming to court and you are receiving some reimbursement for mileage expenses or other witness fees, tell the defense attorney about this reimbursement fee.
- Do not be afraid to say you discussed the facts of the crime with other people. At a minimum, you talked with a law enforcement officer or an attorney; otherwise your name would not be known to the state.
- Remember to stay calm and not lose your temper, even if the defense attorney seems rude or makes you angry. She or he is testing your ability to accurately remember the facts about the crime.
- Never argue with the defense attorney. It is the job of the prosecuting attorney to object to any improper questions asked by the defense attorney.
- When your testimony is completed and you have been excused, do not discuss your testimony with other witnesses.

Types of Evidence

Attorneys present cases in court by introducing evidence. There are two basic types of evidence:

- *Physical evidence*: Things that support the attorney's argument. This could be the "smoking gun," a photograph, or in the case of computer crimes, a firewall log or a computer hard disk holding data.
- *Direct evidence*: Testimony of a person who has direct (first-hand) knowledge of what happened. Hearsay evidence (second-hand testimony from someone who was told something by a person who had direct knowledge) is generally not admissible except in special cases such as dying declarations, in which the person with the first-hand knowledge told the witness the information before dying.

Physical evidence must always be accompanied by direct evidence. That is, when a physical object is introduced as evidence, someone must testify as to its relevance to the case. As a network administrator or IT worker, you might be asked to testify that the firewall log introduced into evidence is the one you printed out immediately following an intrusion or attack.

There is a third type of evidence, intangible evidence, which refers to something that cannot be seen or touched.

Testifying as a Witness or Victim, or an Expert Witness

Testifying as a Witness or Victim

- When you testify as a witness or victim, it's important that your knowledge be firsthand—not something you heard from someone else. If it's a jury trial, speak to the jury, not just to the attorney posing the question. If you don't understand the question, ask for clarification. If you don't know the answer to a question, say so. Don't just make something up.
- The opposing attorney may try to shake you up, make you contradict yourself, or cast doubt on your testimony. That's his/her job. Don't take it personally. Even if the attorney shouts at you or derides you, just calmly answer the questions. Remain professional at all times. Not only does this lend more credibility to your testimony, but if you get angry and say things that are inappropriate, you could be found in contempt of court and fined or even jailed.
- If no question has been asked (the attorney simply makes a statement, especially a provocative one such as "I don't think you really know how to read a firewall log") say nothing. Wait for a question. When being questioned by the opposing attorney, answer only the question that's asked, and no more. Don't volunteer anything. Don't try to explain things. Stick to just the facts. If you think a question is improper, pause long enough to give the prosecutor time to object.
- If you are testifying as a witness or victim, you should meet with the prosecutor or a member of the prosecution team prior to giving your testimony. They should not tell you *what* to say, but they can give you advice on *how* to say it. If your testimony is used to introduce physical evidence, be sure you know exactly when the evidence left your hands and to whom it was given. This is important in establishing the *chain of custody*, a record of where the evidence was and who had control of it from the time it was collected until the time it is presented in court.
- If testifying as a witness or victim, you can give only facts, not opinion.

Testifying as an Expert Witness

- If testifying as an expert witness, your opinion is about the purpose of the testimony. An expert witness does not have personal knowledge of the offense but testifies based on his or her expertise in the subject matter about the facts given by other witnesses and provided by the physical evidence.

- Keep in mind that jury members (and the judge, for that matter) are probably not technology experts. Make sure your answers are clear and simple enough for non-techies to understand. Avoid jargon and acronyms, even ones that seem obvious to you. Don't "talk down" to the jury.
- If you are testifying as an expert witness, you are actually *working for* one side or the other. Expert witnesses are hired by either the prosecution or the defense, and are usually paid (often quite well) for their testimony at a per-diem rate. Professional expert witnesses provide testimony for either prosecution or defense.
- The most important aspect of testifying as an expert witness is establishing your credentials. The court must accept your qualifications as an expert in order for you to be allowed to testify. The attorney on whose side you're called as an expert will ask you a series of questions designed to show your qualifications as an expert. You might be asked about your formal education in computer science, how many years you've worked in the tech business, specifics about your experience in the technical area the case involves (for example, encryption), books and articles you've published, awards you've received, courses you've taught, and so forth.
- The opposing attorney will usually attempt to attack your credentials to get your testimony excluded or to cast doubt on its credibility if it is admitted.
- The job of the expert witness is also to help simplify highly technical material so that non-technical people (judge and jury) can understand it and make decisions based on it.

There are books and training courses available for those who want to be expert witnesses in the computer crimes area. New Technologies, Inc. (NTI), which makes computer forensics software, offers training in presenting expert testimony on electronic evidence. Books such as *Expert Witness Handbook* (Dan Poynter, 2011) offer tips on becoming a successful expert witness.

Some experts don't take the stand and testify but instead act as consultants to the attorneys on the case. To get hired as an expert witness or consultant, you need to establish a reputation in the field of expertise and then make known your interest in participating in the judicial process. There are a number of services that locate expert witnesses for attorneys. You can register as an expert with these services (for a fee).

Testifying as a Private Investigator

Here are a few pointers for private investigators which will make you a professional witness and a hit with your attorney client.

- Don't volunteer anything! Respond thoughtfully to the question that is asked but keep it brief AND answer only what is asked. That applies to your client as well as to the cross-examination. If your client wants more, he will guide you with his questions.
- Respect....for the court, the judge, the opposing counsel, and for yourself.
- Have confidence in your testimony. Remember that you are there to talk only about what you know to be the truth to the best of your knowledge...nothing else. You're not going to be asked to give a speech, sing, or dance. That will inspire self-confidence and goes a long way to help with the "jitters."
- Do not....let me repeat that....do not...take your investigative file to court. Anything you have in your hand on the stand, and sometimes anything you bring to the courtroom, can be admitted into evidence at the request of opposing counsel. That will not make your client happy, since you will be, in essence, revealing part of his "attorney work product." In short, your client does not want the other side to have your notes. If a bunch of dates are involved or something else that would otherwise require handwritten notes, ask your client about this before trial. My answer on the stand to such questions is, "I would have to look at the file to give you the exact date (name, time, address, etc.)."
- Talk to your client before trial. Let him guide you with regard to any special circumstances that may come up in advance.
- Do not be combative. It is the lawyer's job to get you riled and make you look like an unprofessional witness...see rule no. 2.
- Finally, what may seem the most obvious....Tell the truth. I know you are not going to lie, but there may be the temptation to "touch-up" the truth just a little to make yourself or your client look better. Don't do it. You may not get caught, but in the end, your client will know you lied to the court and will always wonder, in future dealings, if you are lying to him. A private investigator's ethics, honor, and integrity are not for sale.

Self-Evaluation as a Witness

Following your testimony as a witness it is important that you obtain feedback from anyone who witnessed your testimony. It is most critical to obtain suggestions from the attorney and your client. Ask them for comments on what you did that was good, what could be improved and how, and what you did that you shouldn't have done. As with most lessons in life you learn from your mistakes.

The critical areas that should be evaluated are:

- Pretrial preparation. Were you fully prepared to testify?
- Did you dress appropriately/professionally?
- Did you answer questions satisfactorily without becoming emotional?
- Did you handle cross-examination well?
- Did you allow time for your attorney to object before answering questions?
- Did you speak to the jury?
- If you conduct a thorough evaluation of your testimony after each event, it will help you improve each and every time.

Remember, nobody starts out as an expert. You become one over time as you improve and sharpen your skills. Becoming a good witness is an invaluable tool for the professional investigator!

Personal Experience

- Be prepared—prior preparation and review with your client prior to testimony are essential!
- Don't take it personally.
- Don't follow your instincts; do what your lawyer tells you.
- How you look and act really matter.

Summary

The most important thing to remember, in all cases, is to be sure you know your stuff inside and out. The judicial process is an adversarial one, which means there are attorneys on both sides attempting to build their own case and tear down the opposition's case. As a witness, you are called by and seen as part of one side or the other, and you must be prepared for questions from the opposing side that will challenge your testimony and perhaps even attempt to cast doubt about your honesty, integrity, and expertise.

Your testimony as a victim or eyewitness could be instrumental in bringing a computer criminal to justice or recovering damages for your organization. Your testimony as an expert witness could be the deciding factor in a criminal or civil trial and could also result in a lucrative career for you.

WITNESS EVALUATION

Name:

Home Address: Home Phone:

Employer:

Work Address: Work Phone:

Occupation:

DOB: SSN: CDL:

Close Relative: Address: Phone:

Marital Status: Spouse:

Educational Background:

Military Experience: Branch __________; Rank _____; Type Discharge __________

Court Martials _______; Time Period of Service ____________

Criminal History:

Driving History:

Drug/Prescription Medication/Alcohol History:

Attitude Regarding Case:

Relationship to Case:

Personal Appearance: Ht._ ____ Wt _____ Hair _____ Eyes _____ Glasses ______

Scars/Marks/Tattoos _________________________________

General Impression:

Interviewer: Date:

Figure 17.1 Screening witnesses and experts.

Ethics 18

The values that guide our behaviors are called ethics. Many ethical guidelines of the past have become the laws and regulations of today. Businesses stress their ethical considerations in their promotional material or mission statements, but what do they really mean? They all state that they have a commitment to business ethics, but how should a client interpret a business's professional code of ethics, and what should that code state? Ethical behavior goes beyond knowing what is right and what is wrong. It is simply doing what is right. The purpose of ethical business practices is to provide, in conjunction with laws, a structure that will promote and protect the greatest interests of the profession and the public from illegal or unethical performance. Making ethical choices in business ensures legal behavior and promotes a strong public image.

The uniqueness of the professional investigation industry—that is, as legal and fraud investigators—must be recognized. The conduct of professional investigators must be ethical at all times. A professional investigator must observe and adhere to the principles of honesty, goodwill, accuracy, discretion, and integrity. He or she must be faithful, diligent, and honorable in carrying out assignments, and in the discharge of his or her professional responsibilities. Intelligence gathering is not without controversy. It may be legal, but is it ethical? Because highly diverse values exist, managing ethics in the workplace is a difficult task.

Today's corporate intelligence operatives tread a fine line between honest inquiry and deception. For companies, it is legal to call competitors' sales departments to acquire information about rates, lead times, and product availability, but it is unethical to misrepresent yourself. At trade shows, it is ethical that you wear an accurate name tag like everyone else. Where companies draw the line in their intelligence gathering is hard to document, and they are reluctant to discuss it.

Some agencies have little real-world private-sector investigative experience and lack even basic knowledge of applicable legalities and ethics. Many are uninsured. Other agencies may rely on one experienced supervisor to direct and correct the activities of a high-turnover staff of low-paid, inexperienced investigators who are sent into the field with little or no training. Do not leave yourself open to these mistakes. You are judged by how you conduct your business, and how you are judged will affect your income. Assuming the principles of professional conduct with legal and ethical standards of practice is necessary for success in today's competitive business environment.

The purpose of promoting an ethical business practice is to establish and promote clearly defined standards required by all investigators. These standards will assist in protecting the profession, the clients, and the public at large. Maintaining integrity and trust should be a continuing endeavor by professionals in accordance with the highest moral principles.

Outlined next are the major areas of concern to an investigator who conducts business with honesty, legality, integrity, and a code of ethics. Practice of these tenets will avoid conduct detrimental to the profession and to an agency's or an individual's reputation. Additionally, individuals and agencies should adhere to all applicable standards and practices common to the general business community.

Confidentiality and Privacy

The purpose of confidentiality is to safeguard privileged communication and information obtained in the course of business. Disclosure of information is restricted to what is necessary, relevant, and verifiable with respect to the client's right to privacy. An investigator must not disclose, relate, or betray in any fashion the trust placed in him by the client, employer, or associate. In accepting instructions from clients, an investigator guarantees confidentiality and his or her protection and promotion of the interests of his or her clients.

When a third party is involved, the key when considering personal or confidential information is to make certain that the client is notified. To further a truthful and legitimate manner of operation, the rights of your clients must be respected. Refraining from divulging confidential information to newspapers, publications, or other media will protect your clients and prevent interference in the administration of justice or a fair trial in the courts.

A client's confidence must also be preserved beyond the term of employment. The disclosure or use of confidences for the private advantage of the investigator or his or her employees, or to the disadvantage of the client without knowledge or consent (even though there may be other available sources of information), would be a breach of confidentiality. Professional files, reports, and records should be maintained under conditions of security, with provisions made for their destruction when appropriate.

Truth

The obligation of commitment to the client's interest is primary but does not eliminate the obligation to determine the facts and render honest, unbiased reports. Investigators are dedicated to the search for truth and the furtherance of employers' or clients' interests. The search for that truth enables the establishment of ideals of fairness and justice for the benefit of the client in every case. The intention of every professional investigator should be to treat honestly, justly, and courteously all with whom they come in contact.

Keep Informed

Investigators have an obligation to maintain technical competency at such a level that the client receives the highest quality of services that the investigators' discipline is capable of offering. It is important to keep informed of developments and changes in matters of law, proposed legislation, public policies, forensic or technical advances, and techniques that affect the profession. Local, state, and federal levels of information must be current so that investigators are able to offer an informed opinion and advise clients properly in an area of expertise and the feasibility of proposed assignments.

Promote Education and Advocacy

Industry programs must be promoted and supported. The educational intent should be designed to raise standards, improve efficiency, increase effectiveness, and enhance the private investigation industry. Direct and determined efforts should be made toward the support, advancement, and furtherance of high personal and professional conduct. An endeavor to provide the opportunity, training, and education for the professional development and advancement of investigators will raise the standards of performance and improve the perception of the industry.

Business Conduct

Do not be party to any practices that are damaging to the good of the public or the profession. Do not engage in illegal or unethical practices as defined under the statutes and legal precedents in your respective jurisdiction. Never maliciously injure or defame the professional reputation or practice of colleagues, clients, or employers. When appropriate, explain to the public the role of your profession in the promotion of the administration of justice.

Guard against employing those techniques, or utilizing such equipment or devices, that may threaten the life, limb, or safety of another. Carry professional liability insurance for your own protection and the protection of affected third parties.

Labor diligently and unceasingly to elevate the standards of practice, and do not tolerate unscrupulous invasion of business contracts by anyone who intrudes knowingly and willfully for his or her own private advantage or financial gain to the detriment or injury of another investigator.

Avoid Conflicts of Interest

Refrain from accepting an assignment or employment if the mission will create a personal or professional conflict of interest. Extend the effectiveness of the profession by cooperating with other investigators and related professions, provided that this exchange does not violate the interests of their clients and employers. Respect the integrity of people with whom you work. When there is a conflict of interest, the nature and direction of loyalty and responsibilities must be clarified, and all parties must be kept informed of that commitment. Private investigators should not enter into fee arrangements that would be likely to create conflicts of interest or influence testimony in any matter.

Fair Representation to Clients

Do not misrepresent or embellish your services to clients. Clients should receive a factual report or summary of the services provided. Respect the best interests of your clients by maintaining a high standard of performance and reporting to your clients the complete facts ascertained as a result of the work and effort expended, whether advantageous or detrimental to the interest of the client; nothing should be withheld from the client. Do not knowingly misrepresent yourself, your duties, or your credentials.

Treatment of Competitors

Never publicly criticize the business practice of a competitor or volunteer an opinion of a competitor's practice unless your opinion is sought. When asked to comment on cases being actively managed by another investigative organization, you should make every reasonable effort to conduct an in-person evaluation before rendering a conclusion, and give the other member an opportunity to respond. When an investigator deems it appropriate to respond, such opinion should be rendered with strict professional integrity and courtesy. Do not directly or indirectly injure the professional reputation, prospects, or practice of another investigator. Any discussion, comments, or criticism directed toward a fellow investigator or organization should be positive and constructive. Promote and protect the interest of fellow professional investigators.

However, when you have knowledge that another investigator has acted in an unethical, illegal, unprofessional, or unfair manner, present the information to the proper authority so that disciplinary action can be taken. Actively assist any regulatory agency charged with monitoring the profession.

Do not compete illegally or unfairly with other investigators in the solicitation of work. Do not seek any unfair trade advantage as deemed improper or illegal by state or federal laws or regulations. A private investigator working for one agency is forbidden to contact the client of another agency directly, unless instructed in writing to do so.

Legal Issues

Perform services within the boundaries of the law, and do not permit or demand of any employee or fellow member any violation of the law or any manner of fraud. Do not knowingly violate any right or privilege of any individual which may be guaranteed or provided for by the U.S. Constitution or the laws of the state and federal governments. Cooperate with all recognized and responsible law enforcement and governmental agencies in matters within the realm of their jurisdiction. Investigators should not engage in illegal or unethical claim practices as defined under the statutes and legal precedents in their respective jurisdictions. Do not suggest, condone, or participate, in any fashion or degree, for any purpose whatsoever, in entrapment. Perform professional duties and business operations in accordance with the laws, and be familiar with what the laws are.

Render Services That Match Your Qualifications

Render only those services that you are competent and qualified to perform. Do not undertake to provide specialized professional services concerning something that is outside your field of competence unless you engage the assistance of someone who is competent in such service. Do not engage in the unauthorized practice of law. Do not promise or offer services or results that you cannot deliver or have reason to believe you cannot provide.

Reporting

All your reporting should be based on truth and fact, and you should express only honest opinions. The services and submission of reports should be provided in a timely fashion and should respond to the purpose of the investigation and include recommendations, if appropriate. All reports should reflect objective, independent opinion based on factual determinations within the provider's area of expertise and discipline. Reports of services and findings should be distributed to appropriate parties and be in compliance with all applicable legal regulations.

Compensation

Do not accept commissions or allowances, directly or indirectly, from independent contractors or other parties dealing with your client, employer, or associate in connection with work for which you are responsible. Do not solicit clientele for an attorney. Uphold, and never abuse, the principle of appropriate and adequate compensation for those who engage in investigative work.

A professional investigator is responsible for all proper fees and expenses incurred by another agency for work undertaken under written instruction. Pay invoices in accordance with normal payment practices. Deal fairly and equitably with your client or employer, and clearly explain your duties and the basis for your charges in each undertaking. The investigator should advise the client of the fee structure in advance of rendering services and should furnish, upon request, detailed, accurate time records. Avoid all controversies concerning compensation by using some form of written agreement or letter that states terms or fees as agreed upon by both parties. At all times, remember that the business of investigation is a profession, and all financial dealings with clients should be handled on that basis. The professional investigator should accept no compensation, commission, rebate, or other advantage from others without the knowledge and consent of his or her client.

Advertising

When marketing services or products, advertising should be factually accurate and should avoid exaggerated claims as to costs or results. Refrain from using unprofessional media for advertising. Personal communications or interviews that fail to qualify you in a professional capacity can be detrimental. Do not misrepresent or exaggerate available services to clients. Do not advertise your work, skill, or merit in an unprofessional manner or in dramatic, misleading fashion, and avoid all conduct or practice likely to discredit or do injury to the dignity and honor of your profession. Competitive advertising should be factually accurate.

Client Relations

Do not accept instructions from any client in situations in which the proposed inquiries are judged not to be viable. Refuse to participate in practices that are conflicting with standards established by regulatory bodies regarding the delivery of services to clients. At the time of initial referral, identify to the client what services are available. All instructions both to and from clients should be acknowledged. Counsel clients against any illegal or unethical courses of action. Provide an efficient procedure for dealing with any client complaints, and comply with any decision determined by an arbitrator or court.

Testimony

Investigators have the responsibility, when requested, to provide objective testimony. Investigative professionals provide services within the legal system and are called upon to testify to facts of which they have knowledge or to render a professional opinion on questions or factors affecting the outcome of a case. The testimony of an investigator should be limited to the specific fields of expertise of that individual as demonstrated by training, education, and experience. The extent of proficiency needed to testify is determined by the legal jurisdiction in which the professional is testifying.

Equal Rights

Do not deny equal professional services to any person for reasons of race, color, religion, sex, handicap, sexual preference, or national origin, and do not be party to any plan or agreement to discriminate against a person on the basis of the preceding characteristics. Do not allow personal feelings or prejudices to interfere with factual and truthful disclosures.

Appendix 18.1: U.S. Association of Professional Investigators (USAPI) Code of Ethics

- To continually strive to increase the recognition and respect of the investigative profession.
- To support the principle of due process of law and comply with all applicable laws.
- To avoid conflicts of interest in fulfilling one's duties.
- To perform our professional duties in accordance with the highest ethical and professional standards.
- To maintain in the strictest of confidence all aspects of any investigation undertaken by me or my employer unless legally authorized or required to release such information.
- To strictly observe the precepts of truth and accuracy and provide honest reports, recommendations, and conclusions.
- To faithfully adhere to and abide by one's agency/company policies, objectives, and guidelines.
- To always maintain and uphold my professional reputation and that of my professional colleagues.
- To promote this code of ethics within one's own agency/company, with third-party contractors, and within the entire profession.

Appendix 18.2: Ethics

- To maintain an attitude of independence and impartiality in order to ensure an unbiased analysis and interpretation of the evidence.
- To be an impartial advocate of the truth.
- To maintain a safe distance from the emotional hazards of investigative work (to be emotionally detached).
- To strive to avoid preconceived ideas or biases regarding my clients, potential suspects, victims or witnesses from influencing a final profile or crime analysis when appropriate.
- To conduct myself in my profession with honesty, sincerity, integrity, fidelity, morality and good conscience in all my dealings with clients and/or my employers.
- To provide only those services which I am competent to perform.
- To respect and protect confidential and privileged client information except in those instances contrary to state or federal law.
- To concentrate and perform my duties and obligations as a Professional Investigator in accordance with all applicable state and federal laws and regulations.
- To strictly observe the precepts of truth, accuracy and prudence.
- To prepare and present my investigative reports based upon truth and fact.
- To not exaggerate, embellish, or otherwise misrepresent qualifications when testifying, or at any other time, in any form.

- To only render expert opinions and conclusions strictly in accordance with the evidence in the case.
- To not side with either of the two scales of justice. To gather the facts, and then only hold those scales as does the Lady of Justice.

Appendix 18.3: Investigative Ethics

Though it is values that guide our behaviors, the process of how these values are applied is considered ethics. Many ethical guidelines of the past have become laws and regulations of today. Businesses stress their ethical considerations in their promotional material or their mission statements, but what do they really mean? They all state that they have a commitment to business ethics ... so what? How should a client interpret a business's professional code of ethics and what should that code state? Ethical behavior goes beyond knowing what is right and what is wrong. It is simply doing what is right. The purpose of ethical business practices is to provide, in conjunction with laws, a structure that will promote and protect the greatest interests of the profession and the public from illegal or unethical performance. Making ethical choices in business ensures legal behavior and promotes a strong public image.

The uniqueness of the private investigation industry, working as independent fact finders, must be recognized. The conduct of professional investigators must be ethical at all times. Intelligence gathering is not without controversy. It may be legal, but is it ethical? Because highly diverse values exist, managing ethics in the workplace is a difficult task.

Today's corporate intelligence operatives tread a fine line between honest inquiry and deception. Calling other companies' sales department to get information about rates, lead times, and product availability is legal, but misrepresenting oneself is unethical. Likewise when conducting investigations is it ethical to provide a false name, or present a business card of someone else, giving the reader the impression you are that person named on the card? Where investigators and their agencies draw the line in their intelligence gathering is hard to document, as they are reluctant to discuss it.

Some agencies have little private sector investigative experience and lack even basic knowledge of applicable legalities and ethics. Many are even uninsured. Other agencies rely on one experienced supervisor to direct and correct the activities of a high turnover staff of low-paid inexperienced investigators, who are sent into the field with little or no training.

Do not leave yourself open to these mistakes. You are judged by how you conduct your business, and how you are judged will affect your ability to be successful.

Assuming the principles of professional conduct with legal and ethical standards of practice is necessary for success in today's competitive business environment.

The purpose of promoting an ethical business practice is to establish and promote ethics that are clearly defined standards, required by all investigators. These ethics will assist in protecting the profession, the clients, and the public at large. Maintaining the integrity and trust of the private investigative profession should be a continuing endeavor by professionals in accordance with the highest moral principles.

Appendix 18.4: Summary of the Rules of Professional Conduct[1]

Kitty Hailey, CLI*

Maintaining the Integrity of the Profession

Rule 1:1 licensing

Proper registration and approval by applicable licensing authorities should be met before one seeks to initiate work in the field of professional investigation.

Rule 1:2 certification

The investigator must not utilize credentials that do not apply and have not been earned and maintained.

Rule 1:3 highest professional standards

To sufficiently serve the public, the investigator should maintain the highest professional standards. All investigations are to be conducted with integrity, honesty and excellence.

Rule 1:4 abiding by the law

The investigator must, at all times, adhere to those legislated rules and regulations that apply to all other citizens.

Rule 1:5 cooperation with law enforcement

An investigator should cooperate with all recognized and responsible law enforcement and governmental agencies, not interfering with ongoing investigations or knowingly promoting criminal activity.

Rule 1:6 advertising and the investigator

Advertising of services by the investigator should be truthful, tasteful, and in compliance with the laws of the state in which he or she is licensed.

* From Kitty Hailey, CLI, *Code of Professional Conduct; Standards and Ethics for the Investigative Profession* (Lawyers & Judges Publishing, Tucson, Arizona, 2006). Reprinted with permission from the author.

Rule 1:7 solicitation for attorneys

An investigator should not solicit clients on behalf of an attorney or attorneys.

Rule 1:8 misconduct

Investigators should not engage in professional misconduct, or fail to report the misconduct of others. Professional misconduct extends to criminal acts, falsification of information or violation of the *Code of Professional Conduct.*

Investigator-Client Relations

Relations with the Public

Rule 2:1 scope of employment

The investigator works at the will of others. The services to be provided and the rules of engagement should be defined and delineated prior to the inception of any work.

Rule 2:2 competence

An investigator shall provide competent service for a client.

Rule 2:3 diligence

An investigator shall act promptly and with reasonable diligence for all clients.

Rule 2:4 communication

An investigator should keep a client reasonably informed.

Rule 2:5 fees

All fees should be reasonable. Fees should be mutually agreed upon prior to initiating work and should be adequately explained to the client.

Rule 2:6 confidentiality

Discretion and confidentiality by an investigator are expected and anticipated.

Rule 2:7 conflict of interest

An investigator should not work for a client if that employment jeopardizes an investigation for another client.

Rule 2:8 truthfulness and accuracy

It is incumbent upon the investigator to be truthful and accurate in advertising, in dealings with clients, in reporting of findings, and to any tribunal, court or law enforcement agency.

Rule 2:9 to do no harm

The investigator should be constantly mindful of the welfare of others, taking care to not knowingly do harm to any person.

Rule 2:10 courtesy to the client and to the public

Courtesy and civility are to be extended to all clients and to the public.

Rule 2:11 personal bias

Personal prejudice, bias, political or religious beliefs should not be permitted to interfere with the faithful and honest discharge of an investigator's duty.

Rule 2:12 records maintenance

Property of the client should be maintained in a separate and safe manner, apart from the possessions of the investigator. Investigators should retain a system of record maintenance that allows for retrieval of information up to a reasonable time after the work has been completed.

Rule 2:13 terminating a working relationship

An investigator's service for a client shall cease when either party has withdrawn from the working relationship and has clearly informed the other that all work should be terminated. The relationship may be terminated by either the investigator or the client.

Investigator-Investigator Relations

Rule 3:1 responsibilities of an investigator, agency owner, or license qualifier

The investigator must make reasonable effort to ensure that all persons working with or for him or her adhere to the same rules and abide by the law in the same manner as the investigator.

Rule 3:2 partner, employee or subcontractor responsibilities

All individuals working with or for an investigator are expected to adhere to the same rules of conduct demanded of the investigator.

Rule 3:3 subcontractor regulations

A subcontractor is forbidden to contact the primary client directly unless authorization is first obtained from the contracting firm.

Rule 3:4 reputation of other investigators

An investigator will not inhibit the future prospects or adversely affect the practice of another investigator by direct or indirect means.

Rule 3:5 payment of work by other investigators

Investigators should compensate each other appropriately and expediently for work performed.

Rule 3:6 multiple investigators working in concert

A delineation of all work, reimbursement and responsibilities should be clarified and confirmed prior to the initiation of the assignment. Responsibility and credit should be shared with all parties.

Rule 3:7 competition between investigators

An investigator should not engage in unscrupulous invasion of business contracts with clients of another investigator.

Rule 3:8 assistance and guidance between and for investigators

Assistance and guidance should be offered to investigators with lesser experience or those in need of help to complete an assignment.

Transactions with Other Persons

Rule 4:1 respect for rights of third persons

The legal rights of all persons are to be respected by the investigator in the pursuit of evidence and information for a client.

Rule 4:2 communication with person represented by Counsel

An investigator working for an attorney or a client who is represented by counsel is precluded from contacting an individual represented by opposing counsel. An investigator should not violate any rules regarding pro-se contact during an investigation.

Rule 4:3 communication with witnesses and persons being interviewed.

All persons with whom an investigator must communicate regarding a matter under investigation are to be afforded all rights and privileges of any citizen. An investigator should respect and not infringe upon the rights of any person.

Rule 4:4 communication regarding investigative services

An investigator should truthfully and accurately represent his or her services to the public. Investigative services and the investigator's abilities should be honestly portrayed.

19 Finding a Niche

Contrary to what you may want to believe, the entire planet is not your market. Only one part of the world is your customer, and another part is your competitor. The difference between success and failure in the professional investigative agency business is based on more than just being an exceptional investigator. Marketing techniques, management skills, and the ability to find your niche are the secrets to developing a lucrative private investigative practice.

The most common error made by amateurs in any business is thinking that by increasing the variety of their offerings, they will acquire additional business. The opposite is true: specializing and narrowing one's focus will increase the probability of getting more business. When presented with a choice, consumers will go to a business that specializes in the unique area for which they have a need. Specialization is also an essential element of the marketing process. It is remarkably effective in creating "top-of-mind" consciousness in a target market.

The private investigator fits into an intriguing niche in our culture, filling the gap between crimes committed and serving the investigative needs of the legal industry, the public, and numerous government agencies short on personnel or resources dedicated to investigation. Law enforcement typically spends much of its time on crimes against people (rapes, murders, and robberies). They do not always have the time for civil issues or crimes against property, such as burglary, theft, and larceny. This has created a void that professional investigators fill. Further defining that void into a specialized area will benefit not only an agency but also society as a whole.

Fifty years ago, investigators created a niche for themselves based on people's needs. The idea was, "If the police and Uncle Sam cannot help me, maybe Sam Spade can." The work was laborious and challenging, and sometimes perilous. For years, the investigator's primary focus was matrimonial, fraud, and insurance investigations. In the 1970s, things changed. Computer databases made it simple to find people, and in some states, no-fault divorce laws made pursuing most infidelity cases unnecessary. The role of the detective was changing. Today, professional investigators work for an increasing number of corporate clients, and the stakes are high. Methods of detection range from the simple to the sublime, from undercover intuition to undercover with a body wire. There are even more opportunities for specialization in today's market.

A niche or target market is a group of potential customers who share common characteristics, making them especially receptive to your service. Think of your niche as an area of business that is uniquely yours, and your niche market as a targeted group of individuals who need or want what you have to offer. A niche does not rule out any prospects, but it gives a specific foundation and a place to concentrate your efforts. A niche can change over time as your range of experience grows or as market trends and needs dictate. You might find yourself with more than one niche as your business develops. By breaking out of the ordinary offerings in professional investigative work and adding your own areas of expertise, you will increase the size of your agency.

As companies, Web sites, e-mail, and the media inundate us with information, and with limited time to shop around for the best product from the best company at the best price, we will usually go to the store that pops into the mind first, and we do so only when the need presents itself. For example, we can purchase a toaster from a department store, a home furnishings store, an appliance store, a grocery store, a drugstore, and even a bank. If there was a store selling only toasters, we would probably go there first. Your job is to find your niche and to narrow it down as much as possible.

Success is hard to come by in a wide-ranging category like professional investigation. You are competing with thousands of others, making it difficult for potential clients to locate you. Over one million people are privately employed in positions such as security officer, private investigator, security manager, and computer security. That is a huge choice for businesses or individuals in need of service. A prospective client will know exactly what he or she needs to accomplish or what information he or she needs gathered. Having your own niche allows you to have an individual identity, to stand out from the droves of investigators going after the same business. If there is an offer available, an agency that specializes in filling that person's specific need gets the job, not the agency that does it all.

Specialization projects an impression of authority and exclusivity. When dealing with a specialist, people assume that he or she has superior expertise and knowledge about the discipline, and thus offers a better service, because catering to a unique market implies that the specialist will have a better understanding of the situation, needs, and concerns. This perceived impression has a major influence on people's business choices.

Identifying a target market makes it easy to plan effective marketing and to develop a winning sales message. When you know the specific concerns of your market, you can tailor your message to focus on solutions to those concerns. Different sales messages can be created for different target markets. By defining your niche market you will be able to maximize your ad budget by targeting only those in your niche market. You will know exactly where to advertise. You can design a marketing campaign to convey precisely how and why you can help solve the specific problems. Moreover, you will have the opportunity to develop additional new services that inherently appeal to your niche market, while establishing yourself as a leader in your industry.

You must not only become expert in the usual and customary desired services of an investigation firm, you must also place an emphasis on your forte. There is a specific group with an intense need or desire for the benefits you offer. Find that niche market, and commit your efforts to getting business from it.

How to Find Your Niche

Answer the following questions and apply the information to help find your target market and create your sales material. Genuine opportunities require preparation in the form of establishing objectives and organizing priorities. You will make apparent the benefits you can present to this market and why these benefits are important. By structuring your advertising and sales material around these benefits, you will appreciate the proceeds from successfully targeting that niche market.

Who Are You?

What are your skills? Doing what you naturally do best is an easy way to find your niche. What is your passion? You must feel good about how you will spend most of your waking hours. Your positive attitude will motivate you. Where would you fit in? Where would you not fit in? Where people have to or are prohibited from doing certain things or are required to dress a certain way, do you agree? Are those people on the same wavelength as you? With whom and for whom do you want to spend time working? Working and being with intelligent people who share your passions and understand your sense of humor will have a strong effect on your attitude and success.

Who Is Your Competition?

Small business owners need to be concerned about competition from both small and large businesses. Identify your competitors, gather information on them, find out how they operate, and then apply the information to develop your unique niche in the market. Be aware of what your competition does—both positive and negative. Competing businesses push each other to be better. Look for ways to find your competitive niche. Find ways to capitalize on the strengths of your own business. Be a follower or improver of your competitors' service.

Though it is atypical for a small company to be a market leader, by considering its own resources versus those of its competitors, a small company can be innovative by concentrating on market segments that have the lowest probability of attracting larger competitors. Some of these segments may be too small for a larger company to specialize in, or some segments may just not receive the local or regional exposure from larger companies. Smaller companies possess unique strengths that must be applied to enhance their niche market offerings.

Is There an Untapped Market?

Find profits in one of the least-known commercial ventures, something innovative and new. Be a groundbreaking leader. Can you offer services in a niche that have not been filled before? If you can fill a void in the marketplace and build a business around it, you cannot go wrong.

What Are You Offering?

Start by listing all of the benefits, not the features, offered by your service. You must know the difference between benefits and features to market anything successfully. A feature is what something is, and a benefit is what it does. For example, a large agency may employ 20 investigators, which is a feature. The fact that the investigators are on call 24 hours a day is a benefit. Understanding this difference is important. People never buy something to get a feature. They always buy something to get the benefit produced by the feature.

Who Are Your Prospects?

Can you list some of the characteristics of prospects whose current situation would be dramatically improved by your benefits? You should begin to see a definable group emerging as a niche or target market. Determine if the target group you identified is a market you can reach and develop profitably. If it is, you will be able to answer yes to all of the following questions. Can you identify prospects with enough contact information to communicate with them? Can you deliver your sales message to these prospects in an acceptable and positive way? Do your potential prospects have a strong need or a strong desire for your services? Do your prospects have the financial ability to pay for what you are offering? Is the group of prospects large enough to produce the volume of business you need? Can you identify the biggest problem and offer a solution to it?

Double-Check Your Choices

Ask yourself the following questions: Is your emerging niche something you know how to do? Can you do it well? Is it something you like to do and would not mind doing day after day? Is it something with a broad enough appeal to sell on a steady basis? Can it be sold at a price that will cover all of your expenses and overhead plus return a healthy profit? Do not waste your time on this market if you have answered no to any of these questions. It is not a niche market for you.

Do you have or can you raise enough funds to get the business started and keep it running until it becomes a profitable venture? You want to be the leader in your unique area of expertise. By doing so, free publicity will come to you fairly easily, because the media loves anything out of the ordinary. In a frenzied and cutthroat marketplace, specializing causes people and companies, along with specialized publications and cable, to seek you out. You arouse interest by offering a unique and expert public service and, thereby, generate indirect advertising.

Identifying the right niche market is crucial to your success. When you define your niche, you can focus your time, energy, and money on reaching people who will most likely become your clients. Specialization is the wave of the future, and the greater the competition becomes, the greater is the need for more specialists. As more ventures get started (and more Web sites populate cyberspace), the less time, energy, and money potential clients will have to spend in making choices about with whom they will do business. Finding your niche can make the difference between frustrating disappointment and a prosperous venture that shines above the competition.

Niche Markets in the Investigative Industry

When I started my agency in 1991, I conducted all types of investigations:

1. Insurance claims (primarily surveillance)
2. Domestic (primarily surveillance following cheating spouses)
3. Background investigations: pre-employment, due diligence, asset searches, criminal checks, etc.
4. Legal—working with criminal defense attorneys representing accused defendants, and plaintiff and defense attorneys working civil suits. Cases involve locating and interviewing witnesses, taking pictures of accident or crime scenes, reviewing discovery, and finding evidence that helps your client attorneys.

5. Fraud—working usually with companies or corporations that have uncovered evidence of fraud. Finding those responsible, helping to identify and recover stolen assets, and providing evidence to police for prosecution of those responsible, or to the attorneys who will file civil suits to try to recover lost assets.

Other types of case work may include loss prevention, security, executive protection, skip tracing, and auto repo and bail bond bounty hunting.

Each person needs to decide what type of work best suits his or her experience and interest, and what will make you better at it than your competitors.

Getting Licensed 20

In most states, it is mandatory to obtain licensing in order to become a private investigator. In Florida, for instance, there is a double requirement—the applicant must be sponsored by a private investigator (C license holder) who works for a private investigative agency (A license holder). The agency is required to maintain liability insurance. In Florida, you are eligible to obtain a C license if you have 2 years' provable investigative experience (e.g., a prior law enforcement officer). If you do not, then you may apply for a CC license (intern), under which you will be required to work with a C license holder for 2 years and will then become eligible to obtain a C license. The State of Florida recently passed legislation requiring that prior to license issuance the intern must take a 40-hour class at an approved school and pass a written test. To obtain a C license you must pass a written test. To become an intern you must take 40 hours of training from a state-approved school.

Each state has its own requirements, although some states do not license investigators. There is a wide disparity in requirements, from mandatory background checks and insurance bonding to training requirements and testing prior to license issuance. However, there has been an increasing trend to require prior training and testing to become licensed and to attend continuing education to maintain the license.

All states that require licensing have a regulatory authority charged with license issuance, regulation, and enforcement. Some states, such as Pennsylvania, have licensing on the county level. The eight states that do not require licensure recommend that applicants contact local and county municipalities for possible business license requirements.

A number of books are available that provide information on obtaining licenses in all states. I recommend *How to Become a Professional Private Investigator* by John M. Lajoie, a fellow Certified Legal Investigator. This book is available through his Web site at www.privateinvestigator.com. (Needless to say, Lajoie has a veritable gold mine in owning that domain name.)

Lajoie has also written *Trials and Tribulations of a Real Life Private Eye* about his experiences in owning and operating an agency in Massachusetts. I recommend this book highly as an example of what it is like to be a professional investigator.

Good luck to all of you who have read this book and aspire to be professional investigators. I can tell you that it is the greatest job that I have ever had. I cannot even picture doing something else as a career. Being a professional investigator is never boring and can be very profitable for those who are true professionals.

Operating a Professional Investigative Agency 21

Choosing a Name

The first decision to be made is the name of the agency. Do you want to create a catchy sounding name, a name that will describe what your business does, or something simple? Pick a name that you are comfortable with and that will help you market your agency.

Form of Operation

There are four forms of operation to choose from: sole proprietorship, partnership, corporation, and an "S" corporation. Each has its advantages and disadvantages.

Sole Proprietorship

This is a business owned by one person. The advantage is that one person has complete control of the business. It is the easiest form of business to start. It can be set up and run any way the proprietor wants. The major disadvantage is that the liabilities and obligations of the business belong to the sole proprietor alone. The sole proprietor has personal liability for all business debts. If the business fails, it can bring financial ruin to personal finances.

Partnership

A partnership is an association of two or more persons for the purpose of business for profit. The advantages of forming a partnership are that more money, more knowledge, and more talent are available to get the business going. Also, liabilities are spread out among all the partners. The disadvantages are that all profits are shared, all partners have a voice in managing the business, each partner is personally liable for the actions of the other partners, and a change in the relationship between the partners can, like a marriage, have a devastating effect on the business.

Corporation

A corporation is an artificial person. It is a method of organizing a business where the business has a separate legal existence from its owner or owners. The major advantage of creating this distinct entity is that it protects the owners from personal liability. Debtors can obtain only the assets of the corporation and cannot go after the owners' personal assets. The disadvantage is possible double taxation. First, as the owner and employer, you must pay taxes. Second, any profits the corporation makes are taxable.

"S" Corporation

The subchapter "S" corporation is given special income tax treatment by the Internal Revenue Code. Although the owners of the business enjoy the same protection from liability as a corporation, the "S" corporation does not pay tax. Only profits passed through to the owners are subject to income tax, which makes the "S" corporation the preferable form of business where the corporation has less than 75 shareholders.

Location

The first rule is to keep your overhead down. When you first start your business, you will want to keep basic monthly expenses to a minimum. You may consider operating the agency from your home and using a mailing address until you get your business established. Many economical business identity programs will provide you with a mailing address and some may provide an office at which to meet clients when the need arises. This will provide your agency with an address other than your home.

A great deal of thought should be given to determining what type of location is best suited for your operation. A site in a central shopping district will provide very high traffic but requires very high rent, and all other operating costs are high. Competition may be considerable, and most businesses are well established. Shopping centers provide modern interiors and exteriors with a medium amount of traffic. Rents are medium to high. Neighborhood shopping centers may also be chosen. Only light traffic can be expected, but rents are generally lower, and overall operating expenses will be lower. The other stores will be small. Strip malls usually have very low rental rates, so the total operating cost will be much lower, and there will be abundant parking space.

The requirements for different types of businesses may vary considerably, but some common areas to consider when choosing a location, regardless of the kind of business you are setting up, are accessibility to transportation;

availability of manpower; proximity to clients; local ordinances and regulations; quality of local services (police, fire, etc.); water supply, power, and other utilities; space for future expansion; and tax structure.

Pricing

The price concept is closely affiliated with products and services and service management. Price involves the buying and selling process that is affected by the law of supply and demand. The way price is structured is a useful tool in promotion and can help or hinder sales. Price can affect your bottom-line figure for better or worse. Price can be a valuable tool when used as a competitive weapon.

To the consumer, the price of a service represents the seller's interpretation, expressed in monetary terms, of the product's usefulness—its ability to satisfy a consumer's wants and needs. Consumers may regard the price of an item as fair (consistent with his or her perception of its worth in dollars and cents) or higher or lower than fair. If the price is considered too high, customers resist purchasing the item; if the price is considered low, then it becomes a bargain (although a low price can also cause consumers to doubt the quality of the product). In pricing your services, take into consideration competitors' prices, local economic conditions, level of demand, desired profit return, other market factors, and the price-quality relationship.

Determine the best pricing strategy to employ relative to your competition. Logically, there are three ways to go. You may set your prices on the level with your competitors. You may deliberately price above the competition (if seeking a quality image for your firm) and use pricing to distinguish your product. You may also undercut your competitors to secure a foothold in a new market, to create a discount image, or to obtain a heavier volume.

Bookkeeping

Bookkeeping is an orderly method of recording financial information. Financial statements are formalized reports summarizing financial data previously recorded. There are two basic reports. A balance sheet lists the agency's assets. Assets minus liabilities equals the agency's net worth. The agency's worth may also be determined by compiling a total of assets plus liabilities for net worth as of a specific date. The second basic financial report is a statement of income and expenses (profit and loss statement). Gross profit is the difference between sales and the cost of sales. Net pretax is the profit—that is, the difference between gross profit and expenses.

As you are running your business, you will rely on the monthly statement of profit and loss to determine if you made or lost money during the month. Consecutive months operating at a loss could mean the start of a "cash flow crunch." The business may appear to be running smoothly, when suddenly receivables are high and cash outlay is great because you are busy working new cases. This means that you may not have enough cash to pay your present expenses until your past-due receivables arrive. You may need a line of credit or a loan from the bank to carry you through.

Purpose of Financial Statements

You cannot effectively plan for the future unless you have a sense of past history and know where you are at the present. If you do not control your business, it will control you. Proper use of your financial reports is the basis for control.

You should keep the following basic records. An income of receipts record should contain your total sales, listed by department, and should include all income received in cash, by check, or paid by credit card as well as the clients' names. Any other or sundry income, such as commissions, rebates (cash discounts, etc.), or interest earned, should be included in the records. All payouts should be recorded, including cash payouts or cash disbursements, such as postage, trucking, tips, and so forth. All merchandise pickups and capital expenditures, including furniture, equipment, and machinery, should be recorded, as should all payroll records. Be sure to keep actual records of hours for each person.

Record all payments made by check, including expense items; merchandise; capital investments, including furniture, equipment, and machinery; payroll (check register should show gross pay and itemized deductions, such as taxes, etc.); and paid taxes, including federal, state, county, and city taxes.

Records are kept not only for dealing with tax collectors. They are also a tool that can lead you to success. The best-kept records are of no value if you do not use them to manage your business.

Business Problems

Insurance coverage that is too high can be expensive, while undervalued insurance coverage can be devastating in case of loss. In the case of tax problems, you are required to prove any statements made on tax forms. You are guilty until proven innocent by the Internal Revenue Service (IRS). Other common problems include excessive expenses, such as payroll, advertising, overhead, and so forth; a low volume of new cases; high advertising cost versus case volume; low net profit versus high costs; financial overreaching or expansion; and bad debts.

Additional problem areas may include poor debts collection, high interest costs, and difficulty in borrowing. Banks will require a detailed profit and loss statement, a balance sheet, and sometimes a cash-flow chart. Make business comparisons to see how your business is operating as compared to other businesses of a similar type.

Keep an updated list of furniture and equipment already owned as well as that purchased as you go along. These items can be depreciated and represent a tax savings. Keep accounts payable current to avoid the loss of cash discount. Keep accounts receivable current to avoid collection expenses. Funds should be placed in a separate account to pay any taxes owed. If possible, a perpetual inventory of equipment, supplies, and other such items should be kept.

The good news is that there is a wide variety of software programs available to keep track of all your financial record-keeping. Programs such as Quicken and Quickbook Pro will solve your financial record-keeping needs.

Licenses and Permits

Private Investigator (PI) Licenses

- Agency license
- Investigator license
- Intern license

Occupational License

- County
- City

Taxes

In the state of Florida, investigators' agencies are required to pay sales tax for services in most cases for work done for Florida clients. Certain types of cases are exempt, such as courthouse records research and cases for the insurance industry. Otherwise, we have to charge anywhere from 6% to 7.5% for hourly investigative services rendered. This requires that you register with the Florida Department of Revenue and obtain a monthly coupon book for filing. Businesses are also required to pay tangible and intangible taxes in Florida.

Forms

See Figures 21.1 through 21.10 for examples of some forms that you may want to use in your business.

Keys to Success

1. Find your niche.
2. Be a professional in everything you do.
3. Join a professional association.
4. Treat your clients and employees with respect.
5. Provide a quality product for a fair price.
6. Get a mentor—someone you know and trust.

There are a lot of professional investigative agencies. However, there are not many good quality private investigative agencies in existence. The key to success is quality professional personalized services in your area of expertise.

MCMAHON & ASSOCIATES
DETECTIVE DIVISION

Dear:

Thank you for employing _______________ (hereinafter referred to as___________) to provide you with professional investigative services. We will do our best to provide you with efficient, economical and effective service. In order to confirm the terms of engaging________ concerning the above referenced matter we forward this letter, which sets forth those terms, for your signature.

SCOPE OF EMPLOYMENT:

You have requested that __________Investigations conduct an investigation of :

We will undertake all aspects of attempting to investigate said matters and will do so at our sole discretion, by way of any lawful and ethical means deemed appropriate, and necessary, in accordance with state and federal law, and accepted industry practices. You will indemnify and hold harmless____________, its agents, employees, and sub-contractors from, and against, any and all liability, loss or damage, including reasonable attorneys fees, that_________ may sustain as a result of any claims, demands, costs or judgments which may be brought against___________ as a result of the investigation that you have requested.

You will be kept apprised of the progress of the investigation via telephone and/or written reports. All reports, documents, tapes, photographs, video tapes and other exhibits prepared and presented as part of this investigation are deemed to be confidential, and are for the use of the client only. Any legal counsel, retained by you, is authorized to have access to said materials, at your discretion. The investigative materials may not be copied or released to the media or any other individual or entity without the express written permission of the client, and _______.

COMPENSATION/FEES:

This office will represent you at an hourly rate of _____ per hour. Depositions, statements and appearances in court, or any administrative hearing or meeting, by ________, its agents and employees shall be billed at the stated hourly rate.

EXPENSES:
In addition to the above hourly rate, you are responsible for payment of all out of pocket expenses which are necessary to conduct the investigation. A mileage expense for travel associated with this investigation, will be charged at the rate of $.___ per mile.

Figure 21.1 Sample client financial contract. (continued)

Other out of pocket expense may include, but shall not be limited to: copies, overnight or priority postage, long distance and cellular telephone calls, database research fees, public records research fees, video tape, photographs and overnight accommodations.

Out of pocket expenses that shall be borne by _______shall include gasoline, local telephone calls, tolls, and meals (unless on an overnight stay).

RETAINER:

You will be responsible for a retainer balance in the amount of $_____ in order for work to commence on your case. The remainder of any unused portion of a retainer will be sent to you with the final report.

BILLING:

You will receive periodic billing statements listing services performed and time and expenses incurred in your case. The present retainer will be applied to the initial billing. Payment of invoices which are normally prepared weekly, are due in full upon receipt. Any unpaid balance, outstanding over thirty days, may be assessed an interest charge of 2% per month.

We reserve the right and in all likelihood will cease work on any case where bills have not been paid in strict accordance with the above. In the event of any default of payment of the sums here under, and if this agreement is placed in the hands of an attorney, collection agency, or the small claims court, you will be responsible for all costs of collection, including but not limited to attorneys fees, court costs, sheriffs' costs and time necessarily spent by_____ in the collection of said moneys at the above mentioned hourly rate and expenses.

If the foregoing terms are acceptable to you, please indicate by signing below and return this letter to our office, with the retainer. You should keep the enclosed duplicate original for your own records.

BINDING EFFECT:

This agreement shall be binding and inure to the benefit of the respective successors, heirs, executors, administrators and assigns of_____, and you, the client.

Very Truly Yours

I have reviewed the foregoing and agree and accept all of its terms and conditions.

Signature: Date:

Figure 21.1 (continued) Sample client financial contract.

The Nature of Investigations As an aid to help our clients better understand the nature of the Private Detective industry, the processes by which we work, and the regulations by which we are governed, we have prepared this informational sheet so you may have more realistic expectations regarding the work **MCMAHON & ASSOCIATES** will conduct on your behalf.

1. We have no more authority than does a private citizen. We are not police officers. The training, testing, background checks, and certification process we go through in order to obtain our licenses is meant to set us apart as individuals who are committed to unbiased professionalism. As such, we are bound to rigid codes of conduct dictated by the State of Florida.
2. We are not magicians. Ours is an industry revolving around detail gathered through available information, the understanding of this detail, and the working knowledge of how to follow the trails we uncover. This detailed information is generated through diligence and knowing where to look. Just as librarians are not geniuses, they simply are trained on where and how to find the information.
3. Sometimes the information generated is contrary to what the client hopes to find. We cannot guarantee results. We can only guarantee that the necessary information, documentation, etc. will be searched for diligently, legally, expediently, and as economically as possible.
4. If surveillance is necessary we feel obligated to inform you of the "real life caveats." Surveillance, especially moving surveillance, is a hit and miss science. We can perform these observations under agreed upon time and location parameters but cannot promise activity on behalf of the subject. Similarly, moving surveillance carries with it inherent obstacles such as the unpredictable nature of traffic. There is no guarantee that contact with the subject can be maintained as we cannot predict traffic flow, traffic conditions, weather, or other unforeseen problems. As in number one above, we have no more authority than an ordinary citizen. This includes traffic laws.
5. **MCMAHON & ASSOCIATES** can, however, make a promise that most of the other agencies can't. That is, that we will do everything in our power to reach the goal of obtaining the information you need in a timely and economical fashion and conduct ourselves in a professional and discreet manner while representing you in your case.

INVESTIGATOR:____________________, **Signature:**____________________ **Date:**___/___/___

Figure 21.2 Sample information disclosure.

MCMAHON & ASSOCIATES

Activity Checklist - PI

Case#: Client:: Re:

Case Start					
Date	**IN**	**Activity**	**Date**	**IN**	**Activity**
		Initial contact with client			
		Contract signed			
		All necessary releases signed			
		Info listed in case roster			
		Agent			

Case Final Disposition	
Case: o Closed o Terminated o Suspended on: ___/___/___ Re:	
Synopsis of final result:	
Reopened on: ___/___/___ Re:	
Court date of: ___/___/___ Court: ______________ Judge: ______________	
Subject / Suspect	**Notes:**
Other disposition of main subject:	

Disposition of Evidence			
Date	**IN**	**Activity**	**Note**
		Police reports	
		Forensics reports	
		Witness Interview Tapes and Transcripts	
		Surveillance Reports and Materials	
		Number of audio cassettes:	
		Number of video cassettes:	
		Still photos: Total # rolls:	
		Courthouse or other legal doc. Copies:	
		Misc. items from trash run:	

Billing and Accounting					
Date	**IN**	**Activity**	**Date**	**IN**	**Activity**
		Retainer of: $______ collected w/contract			
		Case conclusion balance of:$________			30 day notice sent
		Retainer refund or first bill of: $________			60 day notice sent
		Payment of:$__________ rec'd			90 day notice sent
		Payment of:$__________ rec'd			Collection activity initiated
		Payment of:$__________ rec'd			

Final Communication		
Date	**IN**	**Activity**
		Final synopsis/report mailed to: o Client o Client's attorney o Other:
		Thank you notes sent to all applicable people (client, attorney, LEOs, stellar witnesses, etc.)
		All computer files copied to floppy and stored in evidence envelope inside The Case File itself.
		Case entered into master log and/or database o Case details entered into spreadsheet

Figure 21.3 Sample activity checklist.

MCMAHON & ASSOCIATES

OUTGOING CORRESPONDENCE / DOCUMENTATION

	Sent to:	Re:	Date Sent	Deliv ID#	[illegible]	Author	Comp File Nm	[illegible]	Copies (	Copies .	Copies (	Copies I	File
1													
2													
3													
4													
5													
6													
7													
8													
9													
10													
11													
12													
13													
14													
15													
16													
17													
18													
19													
"Copies" Column above: C = Client, J = "Judge" (Court), O = Opposing Counsel, I = "In house"													

INCOMING CORRESPONDENCE

	Source	Re:	Author	Date Rec'd	Date Sent	Sent Via	RSVP	File
1								
2								
3								
4								
5								
6								
7								
8								
9								
10								
11								
12								
13								
14								
15								
16								
17								
18								
19								

MASTER CORRESPONDENCE LOG; INCOMING AND OUTGOING MAIL

Figure 21.4 Sample correspondence log.

MCMAHON & ASSOCIATES

Journal Entry Starter Page. Place plain notebook paper behind this page and use this sheet as a model for entering lengthy notes. These entries should directly correspond with day-date-time entries on "Daily Activity Log" located on top of these notes. No length limit here.

Date	Time	Notes
Date	**Time**	**Notes**

Journal Entry Starter Page

Figure 21.5 Sample journal entry starter page.

MCMAHON & ASSOCIATES
Investigator Assignment Log Sheet

Client or Case # ____________

	Agent	Start Date	End Date	Hours	Tot Exp	Mil	Assignment, Results, Notes
1.							
2.							
3.							
4.							
5.							
6.							
7.							
8.							
9.							
10							
11							
12							
13							
14							
15							
16							
17							
18							
19							
20							
21							
22							
23							
24							
25							
26							
27.							
28							
29							
30.							

Figure 21.6 Sample daily activity log.

MCMAHON & ASSOCIATES

CASE "TO DO" LIST

"**P**" is Priority, "**?**" column is for your personal code symbols; "4" is to mark item completed

P	Due by:	2	3	Item	Assigned to:
P	Due by:	?	3	Item	Assigned to:

"**P**" is Priority, "**?**" column is for your personal code symbols; "4" is to mark item completed

CASE "TO DO" LIST

Figure 21.7 Sample case "to do" list.

MCMAHON & ASSOCIATES

Case Final Disposition Checklist - PI

Case#: ______________________ Re: ______________________

	Date	Int	Process
1			**Case**: o Closed o Terminated o Suspended:
2			**Re**:
3			Final synopsis mailed to o Client o Client's attorney o Other:
4			
5			Pertinent documentation sent to client. **Via:** **Doc.#:**
6			Pertinent documentation sent to attorney. **Via:** **Doc.#:**
7			Financial status report sent. o Balance due us: o Refund due Client:
8			**Billing details:**
9			First Bill:
10			Second Bill:
11			Third Bill:
12			**Paid in full via:** Cash $: Check #: MO.#:
13			Visa,MC, Amex, Discover Card #: Exp: ___/___/___
14			Thirty day notice sent.
15			Sixty day notice sent.
16			**Notes:**
17			
18			
19			
20			
21			
22			
23			
24			
25			
26			
27			
28			
29			
30			
31			
32			
33			
34			**Double check "Evidence Tracking Sheet" for these items:**
35			Number of audio cassettes: Copy sent? Y N
36			Number of video cassettes: Copy sent? Y N
37			Still photos: Total # rolls: Total useable unique prints: Copy sent? Y N
38			Courthouse or other legal doc. Copies: Copy sent? Y N
39			Misc. items from trash run: Copy sent? Y N
40			Cross-checked for all info: o Daily Activity Chart, o To-Do list o "Report To Client" o Contract
41			Additional follow-up. **Re:**
42			
43			o **Thank you notes sent to all applicable people** (client, attorney, LEOs, stellar witnesses, etc.)
44			o **All evidence from Evidence Tracking Sheet accounted for**
45			o **Case entered into master log and/or database** o **Case details entered into spreadsheet**

Figure 21.8 Sample final disposition checklist.

RJM **MCMAHON & ASSOCIATES**
1451 W. CYPRESS CREEK ROAD
SUITE 300
FT. LAUDERDALE, FL33309
(954) 341-2001
(954) 796-0209(FAX)
www.mcmahonpi.com

CASE
TIME / EXPENSE
RECORD

☐ MASTER
☐ INVESTIGATOR

CASE NR. ______________________
CLIENT NAME ______________________
CASE NAME ______________________

6 MIN = .1 HR	36 MIN = .6 HR
12 MIN= .2 HR	42 MIN = .7 HR
18 MIN= .3 HR	48 MIN = .8 HR
24 MIN= .4 HR	54 MIN = .9 HR
30 MIN= .5 HR	60 MIN = 1.0 HR

DATE	INV. NAME	OFF.	INV.	SURV.	MISC	MILES	EXPENSE	EXPLAIN
Totals								

Signature

______________________ **Date:** __________

______________________ **Date:** __________

Figure 21.9 Case time sheet.

RJM
1451 W. Cypress Creek Rd.
Suite 300
Ft.Lauderdale, FL 33309
954 341-2001
954 796-0209 Fax

TIME SHEET

Employee Name: ______________________
Address: ______________________

Pager: ______________________
Phone ______________________
SS NR. ______________________

Week Beginning __/__/__ End __/__/__

Date	Case #	Case Name	Location	Activity	Mileage	Hrs.	Description
					Totals		

Dates: ______________________
Employee ID # ______________________
Date Submitted: ______________________

Signature Employee ______________________ **Date:** ____________

Signature Manager ______________________ **Date:** ____________

Figure 21.10 Investigator time sheet.

Appendix 21.1: Tips for Operating Your Agency*

Steve Mallon

Marketing

It's very clear, by virtue of the fact that you are reading this book on professional investigation, that you are either in the investigative business already and want to improve yourself, or you are new to this field and are hungry for information. Either way, I congratulate you and wish you all the best. While many people will refer to this field of investigation as a profession, the fact remains that it is a business and your survival depends upon your skills and abilities, not only as an investigator, but as a salesman for your business. Remember this, you cannot maintain your profession without the power of the business concept. Striving to grow and be the best starts with the one at the top: you. In my first book on marketing entitled *Building Your Professional Agency Practice*, I stated that building a solid business isn't a frivolous, part-time activity. If you begin to find that your marketing activities take a back seat to other responsibilities, do whatever it takes to shift your priorities back into focus. It doesn't matter how good you are at being an investigator, if new business is not flowing into your agency, you will soon find yourself in a panic mode to survive. Facing that kind of dilemma is not how you want to start your business or maintain it over the long haul. Sales and marketing should not be considered a 50-yard dash. Quite the contrary, building your agency through effective sales and marketing would be better compared to a 26-mile marathon, for which you are always in training.

Always Start with a Great Plan

Insurance companies, attorneys, and businesses that you know and use are the best sources of new business. Get involved in networking groups, chambers of commerce, bar associations, rotary, and so on. Go to breakfast meetings, luncheons, and dinners, and tell people about your business and what you do.

Marketing Tips

The more specifically you can target your efforts at publicity, the better your chance of success. Each magazine, newspaper, TV, and radio station represents

* Reprinted with permission from Steve Mallon, *Building Your Professional Investigative Agency Practice*, 2005, Thomas Investigative Publications, Austin, TX.

a wide variety of targets. If you simply send a press release to a magazine editor, it could get lost before it arrives at the appropriate department. Mailing your release to the appropriate editor or section of the magazine or newspaper will most likely produce more favorable results. Do not make cold calls.

Ideally, your Web site should pop up every time a prospective customer uses a search engine to locate your type of service. To make your Web site as visible as possible to every search engine, consider all the specific words and phrases that people might use to search for it, and then make sure those words (key words) appear somewhere in your site's text.

Appendix 21.2: The Paperless Office

1. Of course e-mail is a mainstay of our business; it's easy to go paperless if your clients will accept reports as attachments through e-mail. Our choice for e-mail is Google Apps http://www.google.com/a because it allows you to use your own custom domain (i.e., president@whitehouse.gov) and it gives you almost unlimited storage and ties in nicely with Google's other features like Google Docs which is where this article was written and all of our reports and video are stored. This service is free; however, a professional version is also available which most don't need.
2. I recently received a great gift—a Samsung 10 Tablet. This hybrid between an iPhone and a computer is an unbelievable tool. My favorite feature is it now allows me to read my magazines paperless. If you think you will miss holding the newspaper or a magazine, give it a week and you will not turn back—trust me. So now that I no longer need to receive magazines in the mail, this service that scans your old-fashioned snail mail and e-mails you the contents makes a lot more sense. Earth Class Mail (www.earthclassmail.com) offers P.O. boxes and street addresses all over the country in major cities just like Mail Boxes Etc. used to. However, instead of going to pick up your mail, they will notify you by e-mail with a picture of the envelope and give you the option to open the document (fee applies), shred it, or recycle it at no charge. This is a great tool because most of the mail we receive is junk mail anyway. For those of you who still receive payments by check from your clients, Earth Class Mail offers an optional deposit feature where they deposit the check in your bank for you. My bank now accepts a scanned copy of a check for deposit (similar to the iPhone app that allows you to take pictures of checks for deposit), so we just upload the PDF version of the check that Earth Class Mail provides.

3. This service is our newest edition and might be one of my favorites. Now that you are receiving all of your invoices by e-mail or scanned e-mail, you can forward these invoices to a special e-mail address or fax number provided to you by Bill.com (www.bill.com). For a small fee they will enter the vendor's information into your account and automatically pay the bill for you through a method of your choice such as debiting your bank account or PayPal service. This service is similar to your bank's Bill Pay service; however, there is no data entry. For a dollar per invoice the service will enter all of your vendor and invoice details into the service for you. You can set it up to approve the payment or automatically pay it for you. This may sound like a lot, but if you consider how long it takes you or your employees to enter bills into QuickBooks and print out a check, plus the cost of a stamp and compare this with your hourly rate you are in good shape. The service also syncs your payments with QuickBooks.
4. With regard to invoices, one of the ways most of you have started going paperless is because of QuickBooks' great feature of e-mailing invoices to your clients. Most clients love this because they can forward the invoices to their accounting department. If you have clients that still need to be mailed an invoice, check out Freshbooks (www.freshbooks.com) which has most of the features that QuickBooks has in relation to invoices and offers a few extras like printing and mailing an invoice to a client for you. They also have great mobile apps for iPhone and Blackberry to access invoices and add entries for those of you who are out in the field and need to record billable hours.
5. One other long-time obstacle for truly going paperless was the need for clients to sign contracts. For the longest time we would just e-mail clients our contract and they would fax it back to our virtual fax number that e-mailed us the fax. Now we have a little bit more advanced and professional service called Echosign (www.echosign.com). Echosign is a digital signature service that is recognized by banks, courts, and corporations through a federal law that basically says a digital signature is as good as an in-person signature. We have all clicked on "Agree" to terms of services for almost every Web service out there. Echosign takes it a bit further where the client can type in his or her name and an identifying number (like a driver's license number) or sign using his or her finger on an iPhone or using a mouse. It's not pretty, but it works and has many more features that will help you go paperless similar to a PDF.

Other services that can help on the quest to go paperless are a PDF converter and Adobe Acrobat (www.acrobat.com). It has some really useful features like inserting video into your reports. Salesforce (www.salesforce.com) is a service to keep track of leads, phone calls, and cases. It is expensive but is highly customizable.

For those of you still worried about security and having so much information about you and your clients up on the Web (or in the "cloud") you should relax. Data breaches are possible but the risk is the same as accessing your financial information through your bank's Web site. The skip tracing databases that many of us use every day have everyone's Social Security number listed with the same level of security as the ones mentioned above.

Appendix 21.3: Managing and Marketing Your Investigative Practice: An Interactive Discussion*

John M. Lajoie, CLI, CCDI, CII
Lajoie Investigations, Inc.

- How did you select your specialty?
- What's in a name?!
- How did you select your business structure?
- S/C Corp; LLC; SP; Partner
- Accountant/Financial Advisor
- Liability and Insurances
- How did you establish your identity? Branding!
- Agency Brand = Reputation!
- Tagline (slogan)—We Focus on the Real Picture!
- What makes you different and distinguishes you from the next PI?
- Brand by logo; taglines; and all marketing materials associated with your agency

Business and Marketing Plans

- Did you/do you have a business/marketing plan?
  - Written
  - Current
  - I CAN do that turns into I WILL do that!
  - I shall achieve certain goals
  - Describes the company; the market; the competition; profitability; marketing and sales
- Business/marketing plan outline

* Presented at the Florida Association of Licensed Investigator's (FALI) Annual Conference in June 2011 by Massachusetts professional investigator John Lajoie.

- Business/Marketing Plan
- The company
  1. Describe the business
  2. Describe the business structure
  3. Describe the company location(s) and area of business operation
  4. Describe the business specialties and core competencies. BRAND!
     - The market
       1. List your target market segments
       2. Describe why they need your services
       3. Marketing strategies outlined
     - The competition
       1. Who is the competition?
       2. Describe their business
       3. Compare and contrast
     - Profitability
       1. Describe how you will make money—sales
       2. Include financial projections
       3. Assure profitability based on 4 fundamental business principles:
          1. Low start up cost/overhead
          2. Client paid expenses
          3. Quick turnaround and invoicing
          4. Minimal accounts receivables
- Set realistic goals and continue to update your business and marketing plans as needed

Business Plan

How do you write a plan for:

- Operation and Product
  - Employees and time management
  - Do you have database
- Management for case work and assignments?
  Investigative *Case Works* (www.case-works.com)
- Money matters! Rates? Invoicing? Collection?
- Reporting—delivering the final product?
- How do you go about it?
  - Time Lines—surveillance
  - To/From—lengthy and detailed reports
  - Letter Reports—short reports with result but no detail

    - Letter subject heading and subheadings—long and detailed w/ summary and results of investigation
    - Memorandums—corporate style overview but lacks details
- Investigator's Notes—chronologically

  28,210 PI's in USA/21% SE
  6,000 Agencies in USA
  $42,870 Median Income ($20.61 p/h)
  $25,760 Starting Salary ($12.38 p/h)
  $75,000+ top 10%
  Fast Growth—22% (advancement limited)
  Female Investigators in Demand
  9/11 Factor

Note: Sources for above numbers come from the U.S. Bureau of Labor Statistics and Occupational Outlook Handbook; numbers are approximate.

Appendix 21.4: Case File Management*

Paul Purcell
Infoquest

As case management is one of my specialties, my good friend Rory asked me to add an intro to his case management chapter in this latest edition of *Practical Handbook for Private Investigators.* To do this right, I need to tell you a little about the importance of good case management, and its effect on your agency and your future.

Though one of my specialties is case management, our agency's main focus is security analysis. Naturally, since 9/11, the work we've done has drastically increased in importance. As a post-9/11 contribution, InfoQuest has contributed vulnerability studies to the CDC [Centers for Disease Control and Prevention], FAA [Federal Aviation Administration], 2001 World Series Games (where we made drastic changes in the security lineup), 2002 Super Bowl, and 2002 Winter Olympics. As an analyst, I've been privileged to have meetings with former Senator Sam Nunn, H. Ross Perot, and Col. David H. Hackworth. I've also served on the board of Col. Hackworth's "Soldiers For The Truth" foundation, I served on the original DeKalb County Office of Homeland Security as a member of the Executive Planning Panel (the first non-federal homeland security office in the country formed after 9/11), I did work for the 2004 G-8 Summit held here in Georgia, and lately, I've been asked to help with various aspects of

* Reprinted with permission of the author.

Pandemic Influenza planning at both the state and county levels. In the process of doing all this, I also authored "Disaster Prep 101," an individual and family preparedness manual (www.disasterprep101.com).

So, why is all this important to you? Here's why: I always want students of the private investigation industry to know the vast potential open to them. Everything I have done, *any* of you can do. I've worked with some of the larger law enforcement agencies in the state, though I have no law enforcement experience. I've been a board member for one of the most recognized military figures in the country even though I have no military experience. And, I've been asked to participate in influenza planning though I have no medical degree. I do, however, have a strong aptitude and considerable work experience in these areas, but the *most* important thing of all is that *whenever I communicate with any of these people or groups, I'm able to do so in a clear, concise, accurate, organized, and professional manner, and* ***that*** *is the very essence of good case management, your personal and company image, and the foundation on which your future as a PI rests!*

Therefore, if there's any one thing you do as a private investigator, whether you're a beginner in the process of learning, or an old pro brushing up on your skills, you should take a long hard look at your case management and information/communication systems and make sure you can guarantee the highest degree of professionalism, clarity, and accuracy.

"The Case File" (www.thecasefile.com) is certainly one of the tools that can help you do this, and you'll find excerpts from some of this document throughout this book. The system is very straightforward and simple, but it's also very powerful. It can be used as hardcopy in the field, softcopy on your computer, and it can be used as a stand-alone system, or as the initial organizer for a fully integrated software package you may use back at the office. In any event, the detail of the system acts a massive checklist for the new PI and as an organizer for the seasoned vet. Its organized and detailed layout enhances your professional image in front of your client and others, and the accounting elements interwoven in the system will make sure you don't miss any billable hours that should go on your invoice.

The most important things though, whether you use "The Case File" or not, are good case management, a detailed report, an accurate invoice, and thereby a professional image, a respected agency, and a bright future as a private investigator.

Appendix 21.5: "PI" Should Also Mean "Professional Image"*

Paul Purcell

Let's face it. Our financial bottom line is affected by the fact that we live in a world that judges a book by its cover. Pretty singers sell more records than plain ones, missing persons stories rank higher in the news if the person is attractive, and politicians are elected based on their image as much as any other factor.

It's not right, but this issue of image is one we have to live with and one that we have to learn to work with.

Looking at our own industry, don't we have to fight the public's perceptions of our profession? We see it on TV and in movies every day. More often than not, private investigators are portrayed as cheap, petty, low-rent, and usually alcoholic. Whenever I meet a new client for the first time, I usually hear, "Wow, you're not what I expected" when they see that I'm in a suit and tie and conduct myself in a professional manner.

Besides potential clients, who else might be basing their opinion on the Hollywood stereotype? How about the legislators who are constantly chipping away at our rights to do our jobs? Or the database companies with poor cyber security who try to shift focus to us when hackers steal their data? How would they be able to get away with that if the world saw us for the true professionals the vast majority of us are?

Let's cut to the bottom line which is this: In today's business climate, all of us should realize that "PI" should also mean "Professional Image" and that all of us could stand to improve ours to some degree or other. It's what we need to do to keep our individual agencies thriving, and it's what we need to do collectively to keep our profession **A.L.I.V.E.**

Appearance—Our physical persona and the way we present ourselves.
Letterhead—The level of professionalism demonstrated in our printed marketing materials.
Information—Accuracy and honesty; the keys to presenting the data we gather during a case.
Voice—How we communicate to everyone we're associated with.
Education—The continual improvement to our professional knowledge base.

* Reprinted with permission from the author.

Appearance

People base a large percentage of their first impression on your appearance. When a client meets us for the first time, they're sizing up our credibility, our ability as investigators, and deciding just how well we might conduct ourselves in public. As the saying goes, you only get one chance to make a good first impression, so let's look at a few pointers.

- First, dress the part. For men and women both, the attire should be "business professional," which for men means suit and tie whenever possible, and for women, business suits, nice skirt and blouse, or dresses. If you look unkempt or "second rate" the client will probably wonder how you will represent them while working their case.
- A close cousin to dress is personal grooming. Simply put, make sure your hair, facial hair, hands, nails, and teeth are all clean and well kept. By the way, how's your breath? Always keep some mints handy.
- Keep jewelry at a minimum. Jewelry should follow the rule on colognes or scents. It's better to smell of nothing than to overpower with the wrong thing. A general jewelry guideline is no more than 2 rings per hand, no more than 2 thin necklaces, and either post or small-ring earrings. And … you guessed it, visible exotic piercings are out if you're going to be taken seriously by the investigative and legal community. The "Professional Image Dress" website at http://www.professionalimagedress.com seems to have some good articles and checklists. Also, you might find some good books on business and professional image at your local library.

Letterhead

In some cases, the first contact someone may have with you might be one of your business cards. For our purposes though, "letterhead" refers to any printed material (paper or electronic) anyone outside your office might see.

- Business cards are a must. Make them distinctive, but with minimal content. Let your website or brochure carry the detailed content.
- On business cards, stationery, and your website stay away from trite or cliché icons such as magnifying glasses, silhouettes of Sherlock Holmes, or the use of "007" in your web address, phone numbers, or email addresses. These might be cute to some of your colleagues, but to many potential clients, they're a turnoff.
- For stationery, choose an economical yet quality paper and have your letterhead and envelopes, as well as your contracts, professionally

produced by the same people who do your business cards. Make sure their color themes match. Your local print shop or office supply store should have everything you need. If there's any one place you want to spend a little money, this is near the top of the list.

- Websites. If your stationery has a particular logo or color scheme, it should be reflected on your website, or vice versa. As with business cards, your website should be an exercise in minimalism after it's done its job of relaying all the necessary information about your agency. Avoid animation, sound files, heavy graphics, flash, or anything else that some web developers think is cool but which actually makes your site slow to load. Slow loading or "busy looking" sites are more an annoyance than an attraction. Additionally, though they might provide a tiny bit of pocket change per year, try to stay away from banner ads and other outside links on your home page. If you have outside links, put them all on your links page. You don't want your client clicking off into cyberspace before they've read what a good job you can do for them.
- While working a case, stay away from blank notepads and manila folders. They'll both get too messy too soon and not only will that make you look unprofessional and disorganized, but blank notepads make you look unprepared. Too, lost or disorganized notes lead to inaccurate reports and invoices. Invest a little time and/or money into buying or developing a comprehensive set of forms or an organizer system to use in the field, especially in front of people involved in your case. Note: You can get a no-cost ebook called "Case Management 101" at http://www.thecasefile.com/ebook.htm.

Information

In our business, the glass is neither half full nor half empty. It's at 50%. And, unless we know what's in it, we don't speculate. "Just the facts Ma'am." One of the biggest opportunities for a good impression, and naturally the most important, is the timely delivery of honest, accurate, information. Nothing will kill our image, our reputations, and therefore our livelihood, like an incomplete, inaccurate, biased, or late report. Likewise, an inaccurate invoice can either cost us by being too low, or cost us by being too high.

- Rule one is, always has been, and always will be, "Use a good case management system." Make sure everyone working for you uses the same system, and that your standards of accuracy start in the field, and proceed through not only the creation of the report and invoice, but through any follow-up you may ever have with that client. Then treat all of your other clients the same way.

- Use a nice looking presentation folder for all your reports; even the "small dollar" ones. Each client is important to you from a marketing standpoint and therefore deserves to be treated with respect. Putting your report and invoices on better stationery, in a well-organized format, and in an attractive presentation folder will provide a greater perceived value to your client. These people have probably paid a hefty sum for your service and a more professional report will help assure them that it was money well spent.
- With any kind of information transfer, the key word in today's legal climate is "PRIVACY!" Reassure your clients in your contract, and in your final report that your relationship with them is as private as the law allows, and everything you do in connection with their case, before, during, or after the fact, will remain confidential. Loose lips not only sink ships, they destroy good client relationships.

Voice

Voice describes not only the actual verbal communication you have with your clients and others, but the "tone" your business has with those it deals with.

- When you answer the phone, do so cheerfully and actually smile. You can tell when someone's not happy to be on the phone and so can others. This phone call might be your first contact with the next big client, so make it count.
- If you can't personally answer every call, the next best thing is to have a receptionist or answering service. A person is always better than voice mail. Go with what you can afford, but since the phone call is one of your opportunities for a first impression, anyone answering the phone should be trained to be courteous, cheerful, informative, and as professional as possible.
- If voice mail is your only option, make the best of it. First, be smiling and cheerful when you record the message. Second, have the message convey your high standards. Say something like "As we're extremely devoted to all our clients, we're probably out working a case on their behalf right now. However, YOU are just as important to us so please leave us your name and number and we'll get back to you within the hour." Then, if you say you'll be back to them within the hour, you should actually do it. Prompt personal attention is a major plus in any business.
- Education and intelligence are just as necessary as a cheerful hello. When speaking with people you want them to know that you are every bit as qualified and capable as they could hope for. Therefore, when speaking with people, speak clearly, and choose your words

carefully. They don't have to be big words, but they do have to make sense, and grammar is important.

- The written word should follow the same rule. Make sure your business cards, letterhead, brochures, reports, invoices, and all other written documents use correct spelling and proper grammar. Though your client may be enamored enough with your abilities as an investigator to overlook a minor grammatical error, you never know who else of importance might see your report or correspondence.

Education

Here we continue where your writing skills leave off and we cover the actual knowledge or skill base upon which your investigative expertise is founded. Experience is the best teacher, but classroom education can certainly help keep you informed and up to date. Also, the fact that you are continually updating your training is impressive to most potential clients.

- Many states require continuing education for private investigators. If your state does, you should publish this fact in your agency's literature. If your state does not require CEU, you should still take it upon yourself to keep your own training updated and make that fact a prominent component of your marketing materials.
- Join professional organizations where possible. Many of them will offer various classes and training programs and, if nothing else, many of the functions will prove educational to you though you might not be able to list the experience on your résumé. At the bare minimum, if your state has a private investigation association you should join.
- Many online communication forums are professionally dedicated and will provide educational information and opportunities through either on-site or on-line courses, or through the hints, tips, and suggestions offered by members. One good online communication forum is found through "Yahoo Groups" at www.yahoogroups.com and others through "Linked-In" at www.linkedin.com. The free registration for either is easy to complete, and all you'll need to do is search through the groups using the phrase "private investigator" or other keywords associated with your specialty.
- Keep your library stocked. Many people learn as much from books and videos as they do in a classroom setting. Two really good sources of books are "PI Magazine," found online at www.pimagazine.com, and "Thomas Publications" which can be found through www.pimall.com.

As you attend some of these educational functions, take the opportunity to look around you and either further your own education on this issue of appearance by studying your colleagues, or help improve the way they represent you by helping educate them as to the benefits of a more Professional Image.

Appendix 21.6: Three Ways to Raise Prices without Losing Customers

Charging more for your products and services can be easier than you think. For many business owners, linking price and product seems natural. Consumers, however, are often willing to break this link and pay more for a product or service, if given sufficient motivation.

If product and price were tightly linked in consumers' minds, companies such as Starbucks Corp. or Rolls Royce Motor Cars would never sell their products over the cheaper generic equivalents on the market. But Starbucks isn't just about coffee and Rolls Royce isn't only about transportation. Instead, these products are about a brand identity that adds to price, but adds little or nothing to intrinsic value.

The association between your product and the price you've assigned it most likely is not fixed in your consumers' minds the way it might be in yours. Business owners can and should think creatively when it comes to pricing their products and experiment with various price points that are different from what they initially think they can charge.

The sooner you break free of rigid pricing models, the easier it may be for you to sell more to affluent customers and, ultimately, make more money. Here are three ways to charge more for your products or services.

1. **Target more affluent customers.** Who is buying the product is an important factor when it comes to pricing a product. Different people often buy the same product or service at different prices because of who they are, rather than what the product is. For example, an ambitious mid-level executive might prefer to drink Starbucks coffee at work rather than a coffee from a less-regarded brand. Some people refuse to shop at stores like Walmart even though it likely carries the same brands they purchase elsewhere for considerably more money.

   Another factor is life stage. For example, parents often spend more money on their first baby than on their second or third. Price is automatically separated furthest from product if you are selling to them while the couple is pregnant with or raising their first child compared to later children.
2. **Become a leader in your field.** Who is selling a product or service can makes a big difference to many customers. A seller's reputation,

financial stability and leadership position in its market have been made more valuable as competitive assets than they were several years ago. Customers often prefer trendy, talked-about restaurants over others to the extent that the prices at those restaurants, and the prices at other restaurants, are sometimes made irrelevant. In the financial services sector, recent investment and banking fall-outs have caused a number of customers to seek out trustworthy institutions over those that only claim to be able to make the most money.

As a business owner, your goal should be to make your company the go-to authority in your industry or area.

3. **Upgrade your venue.** The importance of context when it comes to buying can't be underestimated. The difference in price between a face cream sold at a Walgreens Co. store and one sold in the home by Mary Kay, or at a cosmetic counter at higher-end stores such as Saks or Neiman Marcus, or at an exclusive Parisian boutique can be disproportionate to the difference in the product's ingredients. The price is governed by the expectations of the consumer largely based on where they are buying it, the brand and the expertise of the salesperson—not the product.

Also consider changing presentation. A chiropractor, for instance, relocated from a small, messy office to a well-appointed professional office, and switched his attire from casual to conservative clothes. These two minor changes allowed him to increase his average fee from $2,000 to $5,000, with no change to the end product.

Considering these three aspects can help you separate price from product—and hopefully make more profits in the process.

Professional Associations

22

There is a wide variety of private investigator, private detective, and related professional associations, including national organizations, international associations, statewide associations, and local groups. Doctors have the American Medical Association; lawyers have legal associations such as the National Association of Criminal Defense Attorneys (NACDL) and the American Trial Lawyers Association (ATLA). Investigators have numerous choices related to their areas of expertise.

In addition to enhancing your stature as a professional by belonging to a professional association, it is also a great method of obtaining additional business. Networking with other investigators around the state or around the world will result in referrals to your business. I receive numerous new cases monthly from other investigative agencies throughout the United States as a result of my membership in professional associations. Membership also keeps me current on trends in the industry, legislation that may impact my business, and training conferences and seminars.

National Associations

National Association of Legal Investigators, Inc. (NALI)

The National Association of Legal Investigators (NALI; www.nalionline.org) was formed in 1967 with its primary focus on conducting investigations related to litigation. Membership in NALI is open to all professional legal investigators who are actively engaged in negligence investigations for the plaintiff or criminal defense, and who are employed by investigative firms, law firms, or public defender agencies. An applicant must have a minimum of 24 months of documented full-time employment in this endeavor.

Membership in NALI currently exceeds 650 professional legal investigators located throughout the United States and in several other countries. The common bond of these legal investigators is the arena of litigation and the ability to work with attorneys to prepare a case for trial.

If you are an investigator involved in litigation-oriented matters, you should seriously consider membership in the NALI. The association is recognized internationally as the standard bearer in the realm of litigation investigation.

The Legal Investigator

Legal investigators are licensed private investigators or law firm staff investigators who specialize in preparing cases for trial for attorneys. Their job is to gather information and evidence that advance legal theories to benefit the client's case. The legal investigator must possess knowledge of statutory and case law, local rules of court, civil procedure, forensic sciences, techniques of evidence collection, and techniques concerning the preservation and admissibility of evidence.

Legal investigators assist attorneys by reviewing police reports and discovery materials, analyzing and photographing crime or accident scenes, interviewing parties and witnesses, obtaining signed or recorded statements, performing background investigations, preparing documentary and demonstrative evidence, recommending experts, and testifying in court. Legal investigators must exhibit the highest standards of professional and ethical conduct.

The NALI sets national standards for legal investigators and confers the designation of Certified Legal Investigator (CLI) upon those who meet professional requirements and those who successfully pass stringent written and oral examinations. For this reason, the designation of CLI is an honored and sought-after credential. Once conferred, CLIs must advance their professional careers by earning continuing educational credits and by maintaining the high standards of the CLI program.

You are encouraged to read the requirements and to submit an application to become a Certified Legal Investigator.

The NALI Certification Program

The NALI offers a CLI program that certifies that qualified investigators possess superior knowledge in the field of legal investigation. There is no certification in any specialty field of investigation.

The criteria to become a CLI include the following:

- An applicant must devote the majority of his or her practice to negligence investigations for the plaintiff or to criminal defense and must be employed by either a law firm or an investigative firm.
- An applicant must be licensed, if required, by the state in which he or she is practicing or employed.
- An applicant for the CLI designation must have a minimum of 5 years of verifiable work experience as a full-time negligence investigator for the plaintiff or as a criminal defense investigator. An applicant may substitute 1 year of work experience for successful completion of 60 semester hours or 90 quarter hours of course work at an accredited college or university.

- An applicant must write a minimum 1000-word research "white paper" on any investigative subject. The research paper does not have to accompany the application and fee, but the original and two copies must be submitted to the Chairperson of the CLI Committee at least 30 days prior to the established test date.
- An applicant must submit the application for examination and the appropriate fee to the CLI Chairperson at least 30 days prior to the established test date. The Chairperson of the CLI Committee will complete a confidential background investigation on each candidate and determine his or her eligibility to take the CLI examination.
- The applicant will take the CLI examination. CLI tests will be administered by the CLI Chairperson annually at the Mid-winter and National Conferences. Regional testing will be made available where there are five eligible candidates to sit for the CLI examination.
- The applicant must receive a minimum passing score of 70% in each examination section, including the white paper, the written examination, and the oral examination, in order to receive the designation of Certified Legal Investigator.
- Should the candidate fail one or more sections of the CLI test, the candidate must retake and pass any failed section. It is not necessary for the candidate to retake any section that was previously passed. The candidate may retake any failed section no sooner than 6 months, but must successfully complete all portions of the exam within 3 years of the date the candidate submits his or her application.
- The application fee is $200 for members of NALI and $300 for non-members. Payment of the application fee, or retest fee (one-third of the application fee per section retaken) must be received by the Chairperson of the CLI Committee at least 30 days prior to the established test date.

The CLI test scores and white paper scoring shall be destroyed by the CLI Committee Chairperson immediately upon confirmation of the designation of the candidate as a Certified Legal Investigator. The CLI Chairperson will retain the tests and scoring for any candidate who failed to pass all portions for a period of 3 years from the date of the candidate's original application. The candidate's original application will be maintained in his or her file after confirmation of the CLI designation. No scores will be made public.

Certified Legal Investigators must adhere to the Code of Ethics established by the National Association of Legal Investigators, Inc. Complaints concerning Certified Legal Investigators who are members of the NALI will be investigated by NALI's Disciplinary Committee. A complainant will have the opportunity to file a complaint with the Certified Legal Investigator Committee following the Disciplinary Committee's investigation and final resolution. Complaints concerning a Certified Legal Investigator who is not a member of the NALI will be filed with and investigated by the Certified Legal Investigator Committee.

Criminal Defense Investigation Training Council (CDITC)

The Criminal Defense Investigation Training Council (CDITC) was established to encourage a dialogue among professionals and scholars involved in various aspects of criminal defense investigation. The council exists as an open forum in which investigative philosophy, methodology, education, and principles of ethical inquiry can be considered via academic training programs, discussions, debate, and writings. The council is actively pursuing the goals of professional competence and academic excellence via the Board Certified Criminal Defense Investigator program and the Training Accreditation Program. The council encourages professionals actively engaged in the discipline of Criminal Defense Investigation to join the council and pursue the designation of Board Certified Criminal Defense Investigator.

Board Certified Criminal Defense Investigator (CCDI)

Certification Requirements The following standards have been approved by the Executive Council of the Criminal Defense Investigation Training Council as the minimum requirements for being awarded the designation of Board Certified Criminal Defense Investigator (CCDI). The CCDI designation is awarded to professional criminal defense investigators who have met the minimum training and experience requirements required to perform effectively within the discipline of criminal defense investigation as an expert. Investigators seeking the CCDI designation are evaluated by the Academic Director and Executive Council on an individual basis. The applicants must meet the minimum requirements enacted by the board in order to qualify for the CCDI designation.

CCDI Requirements

- Successfully complete 40 hours of formal training in the discipline of criminal defense investigation. The training program must be approved and accredited by the CDITC.
- Provide documentation supporting the successful investigation of a minimum of 25 criminal defense assignments. The assignments must be comprehensive in nature and not merely single-task oriented. A notarized affidavit from a supervisor or defense counsel attesting to the fact must be provided to the Advisory Board.

- Provide two written recommendations from defense counsel noting the investigator's reputation, intellectual acuity, ability, accomplishments, and skill level as a criminal defense investigator.
- Possess a minimum of 2 years professional experience as a criminal defense investigator, either working for a state public defender's office or as a licensed private investigator.
- Sign a sworn affidavit attesting to the investigator's dedication and commitment to conducting impartial, objective, and ethical investigations as an advocate of the truth.
- Adhere to the continuing education requirements mandated to maintain the CCDI designation. Ten continuing education units must be satisfied every 2 years. Continuing Education Units (CEU) requirements must be obtained from approved programs providing training in the discipline of criminal investigation.

Investigators seeking the CCDI designation who have successfully investigated a minimum of 50 comprehensive criminal defense assignments may attend an 8 hour approved and accredited training program in place of the 40 hour program. Applicants who possess extensive education and experience may qualify for an independent evaluation. Applicants who qualify for this option will be required to attend the 8 hour academic training program at a later date. A written test and interview may be required for those individuals who opt for the 8-hour program.

National Council of Investigation and Security Services (NCISS)—www.NCISS.org

Association of Certified Fraud Examiners (ACFE)—www.AFCE.com

The Association of Certified Fraud Examiners (ACFE) is a 36,000-member-based global association dedicated to providing antifraud education and training. Together with its members, the ACFE is reducing business fraud worldwide and inspiring public confidence in the integrity and objectivity of our profession.

U.S. Association of Professional Investigators (USAPI)—www.USAPI.org

This is the only national organization representing the interests of all professional investigators. (See Figure 22.1)

USAPI Focusing On
Education • Certification • Membership Benefits

Welcome to the United States Association of Professional Investigators, the only National organization representing the interests of all Professional Investigators.

ABOUT USAPI

USAPI is quite different from other organizations in that it will be an inclusive rather than exclusive group. The first difference that you will see is that membership is open to all "professional investigators." A membership requirement will be a minimum of one-year full-time employment as a investigator. Law Enforcement, PI's, Insurance, Child Welfare, Military, etc., are all welcome.

The Focus of USAPI is:
Education • Certification • Membership Benefits

EDUCATION AND CERTIFICATION:

The education and certification programs are linked and our developing relationships with universities such as Nova Southeastern and the University of New Haven will certainly enhance the quality and reputation of our programs. USAPI will be offering on-line learning through our website, the content of which is under development in conjunction with some of the most noteworthy experts in the world. Additional education will occur through USAPI conferences and specialty seminars throughout the year, and I am currently working to develop regional classroom learning centers in the northeast and the south.

USAPI has developed and will be seeking brand recognition of the Board Certified Professional Investigator (BCPI registered trademark) designation. This is not just a phrase that I developed, rather I have assembled a very impressive Certification Board, with board member positions for each of our specialty tracks:

1. Criminal Investigation
2. Civil Investigation
3. Insurance Investigation
4. Computer Forensic and Internet
5. Security
6. Special Victims/Child Abuse/Nursing Homes
7. Investigative Law and Ethics
8. Investigative Business Administration
9. Terrorism & Intelligence
10. Criminology and Behavioral Sciences

The current Certification Board consists of Dr. Henry Lee, Lt. Vernon Geberth (Ret. NYPD), Barry Zalma, Esq, Dr. Maurice Godwin, Warren G. Kruse II, CISSP,CFCE, Cynthia Hetherington, MLS,MSM, and Rory McMahon,CLI. I am actively seeking additional World Class experts to sit on the USAPI Certification Board to insure that the BCPI will become recognized as the preeminent certification for investigators in much the same way as the American Board of Medical Specialties (ABMS) has in board certifying doctors.

In order for a USAPI member to sit for the BCPI examination, that member must demonstrate 3 years of full-time employment as a professional investigator, and there will be a Continuing Education Credit (CEC) requirement that must be met every year as well.

In addition to the BCPI certification, USAPI will also be offering Expert Certifications based upon the works of our Board Members, or developed in conjunction with our university partners.

Figure 22.1 USAPI information. (continued)

THE BOARD CERTIFIED PROFESSIONAL INVESTIGATOR PROGRAM® (BCPI®)

The United States Association of Professional Investigators, Inc® (USAPI®) has established a certification program known as the Board Certified Professional Investigator (*BCPI*). The *BCPI* Program offers a professional certification designation, as well as Specialty and Expert Certificates. To allow for sufficient preparation and/or study the administration of the Specialty Examinations will begin in October of 2005, with the first BCPI Examination anticipated for January 2006.

The USAPI Certification Board consists of prominent, proven experts in the various fields of professional investigation and forensic sciences.

The Certification Board will evaluate candidates who voluntarily seek certification. To accomplish this function, the USAPI eligibility requirements determine whether the candidate possesses the prerequisite experience, training, and professional standards that are required to sit for the examinations. The Certification Board will evaluate candidates with comprehensive examinations, and certify those candidates who have satisfied the Board requirements.

The *BCPI* is a stringent examination administered by the USAPI Certification Board. The Board seeks to test candidates who possess superior knowledge in the ten (10) core tracks of professional investigation (see below). The Board also offers Specialty and Expert examinations in a number of professional investigative categories as prerequisites to the *BCPI*.

These tests are difficult, but designed to fairly and accurately evaluate the knowledge possessed by each candidate, and seek to raise the bar for all investigative professionals. The *BCPI* study materials establish high educational and practical standards for the investigative sciences.

Candidates who pass a Specialty or Expert examination will prove his or her advanced knowledge and skill in one or more of the ten (10) Core Tracks of professional investigation. The candidate who passes the *BCPI* test will have unquestionably demonstrated a superior proficiency in professional investigations.

Upon the successful completion of an examination the Certification Board will issue a Certificate to the candidate. Candidates will be deemed qualified to sit for the Board Certified Professional Investigator examination upon the attainment of three (3) or more Specialty or Expert Certificates, and upon meeting the remaining prerequisite requirements as described below. The USAPI Certification Board will recognize a candidate's successful completion of the BCPI examination by bestowing upon them the following designation:

- Board Certified Professional Investigator (***BCPI***)

Figure 22.1 (continued) USAPI information. (continued)

Three (3) Specialty or Expert Certificate(s) in one or more of the following Core Tracks are a prerequisite for the BCPI Examination:

- Criminal Investigation (CRI)
- Civil Investigation (CVI)
- Insurance Investigation (INI)
- Computer Forensic and Internet (CFI)
- Security (SEC)
- Special Victims/Child Abuse/Nursing Homes (SVI)
- Investigative Law and Ethics (ILE)
- Investigative Business Administration (IBA)
- Terrorism & Intelligence (TII)
- Criminology and Behavioral Sciences (CBS)

BOARD CERTIFIED PROFESSIONAL INVESTIGATOR PROGRAM
TEST ELIGIBILITY AND CERTIFICATION BOARD REQUIREMENTS

1. USAPI requires that all candidates for the Specialty, Expert, and BCPI certification tests be active members of the USAPI, in good standing.
2. Candidates may take Specialty or Expert examinations at any time, however candidates for the BCPI examination must prove at least three (3) years of full time employment as an investigator in any one of the 10 core tracks of professional investigation and/or a related field prior to taking the examination. Candidates may substitute 60 semester/credit hours of education at a USAPI endorsed institution of higher learning for one year of full time employment.
3. Candidates must submit an application along with the established application fee for any test prior to receiving test authorization. Applications will be available on-line at www.USAPI.org, or by phone to (202) 393-5900, or (866) 95USAPI. Study materials for the BCPI, as well as all other Expert and/or Specialty certification tests, are available for purchase at the USAPI website.
4. To insure the integrity of the exams, all tests must be taken within four (4) months of receiving the study materials, or if no study materials are purchased the tests must be taken within four (4) months of the completed registration.
5. The tests will be administered On-line and will be time sensitive. Candidates must pledge that they alone are taking the test, and that they will complete the examination without the use of study materials or assistance of any form.
6. The candidate must pass any Specialty examination taken by a score of at least 70%, and the BCPI examination by a score of at least 80%. The candidate must acknowledge and agree that the USAPI will be the final arbiter of the test grade.
7. Should a candidate fail the test, the candidate will be allowed one free re-take of the failed examination, which must be completed within forty-five (45) days of the initial exam. Any test retaken after this forty-five day period will require a new application and fee.
8. All test materials are the property of the USAPI, Inc. Test scores will be held in strict confidence. USAPI will not publish the names of any candidate that fails an examination, and reserves the right to announce the names of those candidates who have passed.
9. The BCPI designation must be renewed annually through the USAPI Continuing Education Credit Program, which will be published on the USAPI Website. The minimum number of Continuing Education Credits (CEC's) will be set at twelve (12) per annum. These CEC's will be developed from the knowledge and material base produced by the members of the USAPI Certification Board. The BCPI designation will not be renewed unless there is full compliance with this requirement.
10. The BCPI Program, the BCPI Designation, and the BCPI CEC program are the sole properties of the USAPI, and are Copyrighted and Trademarked. Candidates must agree not to utilize any BCPI materials without the express written consent of the USAPI.
11. Candidates acknowledge that any and all complaints or disciplinary actions against a BCPI designee will be administrated by a three (3) member panel of the Certification Board. The Certification Board will have exclusive rights to determine if a complaint has merit prior to commencing an inquiry. Non-meritorious complaints will not be processed.

ENDORSEMENTS

University of New Haven
Nova Southeastern University - Criminal Justice Institute

Figure 22.1 (continued) USAPI information.

Personal and Career Development

Take advantage of the educational and networking opportunities available online and at USAPI sponsored seminars and conferences. USAPI's developing relationship with major universities and their Certification Board Experts produce some of the most innovative educational programs seen in the industry.

Certification

The USAPI Certification Board is made up of world-renowned, proven experts in the various fields of professional investigation and forensic sciences. To those members who successfully pass this program of stringent exams, the Board will award the designation of "Board Certified Professional Investigator" (BCPI). See BCPI for more information.

Additional Specialty Associations of Interest

National Association of Background Investigators
National Association of Investigative Specialists (NAIS)
Women Investigators Association
Association of Security and Investigative Specialists (ASIS)

International Associations

Council of International Investigators (CII)
Global Investigative Network (GIN)
World Association of Detectives (WAD)

State Associations

Alabama
- Northern Alabama Investigators Association (NAIA)
- Alabama Professional Investigators Association (APIA)

Alaska
- Alaska Investigators Association (AIA)

Arizona
- Arizona Association of Licensed Private Investigators (AALPI)

Arkansas
- Private Investigators Association of Arkansas (PIAA)

California
  California Association of Licensed Investigators (CALI)
Colorado
  Professional Private Investigators Association of Colorado (PPIAC)
Connecticut
  Connecticut Association of Licensed Private Investigators (CALPI)
Delaware
  Delaware Association of Detective Agencies (DADA)
Florida
  Florida Association of Licensed Investigators (FALI)
  The Florida Association of Licensed Investigators was founded to advance the investigative profession. These goals are met for Florida licensed and in-house investigators through education, networking, and government and legislative advocacy in Tallahassee. The Florida Division of Licensing reports the following statewide statistics as of the end of February 2012:
  - Private Investigator (Class "C" License) - 7911.
  - Private Investigator Intern (Class "CC") - 1581.
  - Private Investigation Agency (Class "A") - 2919.
Georgia
  Georgia Association of Professional Private Investigators (GAPPI)
Idaho
  Idaho Private Investigators Association (IPIA)
Illinois
  Associated Detectives of Illinois, Inc. (ADI)
Indiana
  Indiana Society of Professional Investigators (INSPI)
  Indiana Association of Private Detectives (IAPD)
Iowa
  Iowa Association of Private Investigators (IAPI)
Kansas
  Kansas Association of Private Investigators (KAPI)
Kentucky
  Kentucky Professional Investigators Association, Inc. (KPIA)
Louisiana
  Louisiana Private Investigators Association, Inc. (LPIA)
Maine
  Maine Licensed Private Investigators Association (MLPIA)
Maryland
  Professional Investigators Alliance of Maryland (PIAM)
  Maryland Investigators and Security Association (MISA)
Massachusetts
  Licensed Private Detectives Association of Massachusetts (LPDAM)

Michigan
- Michigan Council of Private Investigators (MCPI)
- Michigan Association of Private Detectives (MAPD)

Minnesota
- Minnesota Association of Private Investigators (MAPI)

Mississippi
- Mississippi Professional Investigators Association (MPIA)

Missouri
- Missouri Association of Private Investigators (MPIA)

Montana
- Montana Association of Private Investigators (MAPI)

Nebraska
- Nebraska Association of Professional Investigators (NAPI)

Nevada
- Nevada Investigators Association (NIA)

New Hampshire
- New Hampshire League of Investigators (NHLI)

New Jersey
- New Jersey Licensed Private Investigators Association, Inc. (NJLPIA)

New Mexico
- New Mexico Private Investigators Association (NMIA)

New York
- Associated Licensed Detectives of New York State (ALDONYS)
- Society of Professional Investigators (SPI)

North Carolina
- North Carolina Association of Private Investigators (NCAPI)

Ohio
- Ohio Association of Security and Investigation Services (OASIS)

Oklahoma
- Oklahoma Private Investigators Association (OPIA)

Oregon
- Oregon Association of Licensed Investigators (OALI)

Pennsylvania
- Pennsylvania Association of Licensed Investigators, Inc. (PALI)

Puerto Rico
- Society of Private Investigators of Puerto Rico

Rhode Island
- Licensed Private Detectives Association of Rhode Island

South Carolina
- South Carolina Association of Legal Investigators (SCALI)
- South Carolina Association of Private Investigators

Tennessee
- Tennessee Professional Investigators Association (TPIA)

Texas
- Texas Association of Legal Investigators (TALI)

Utah
- Private Investigators Association of Utah, Inc. (PIAU)

Vermont
- Vermont Association of Licensed Detectives and Security Services

Virginia
- Private Investigators Association of Virginia, Inc. (PIAVA)

Washington
- Washington Association of Legal Investigators (WALI)
- Pacific Northwest Association of Investigators (PNAI)

West Virginia
- Private Investigators and Security Professionals of West Virginia

Wisconsin
- Wisconsin Association of Professional Private Investigators (WAPPI)
- Professional Association of Wisconsin Licensed Investigators (PAWLI)

Appendix 22.1: Recommended Associations

The following are associations that I belong to and recommend:

National Association of Legal Investigators (NALI)

To become a member of NALI, you must specialize in either criminal defense or civil plaintiff investigations conducted for attorneys. You are screened by the regional director, and it must be demonstrated that at least 51% of your caseload fits the requirement. In addition to outstanding seminars and conferences and training sessions, NALI conducts certification testing resulting in the designation of Certified Legal Investigator (CLI). This was one of the most rigorous testing processes that I have ever undertaken. I am proud that I was able to complete the requirements and pass the test in January 1997. The NALI CLI certification is recognized throughout the investigative industry as a badge of honor.

Association of Certified Fraud Examiners (ACFE)

This national association is made up of people in the accounting and fraud investigation professions. The association also conducts screening for certification in becoming a Certified Fraud Examiner (CFE). This was another very difficult testing process that required almost one year of study and review to pass the very difficult exam. I passed it on the first try in May 2005 as a result of taking the recommended prep course. ACFE presents great national and regional training conferences. There are also chapters in many of the larger states, including one in South Florida.

U.S. Association of Professional Investigators (USAPI)

This organization was formed in 2005. It is different from all other investigative associations in that it is open to all investigators—police, public, private, corporate, and so forth. It is an effort to have all the investigative community under one umbrella. USAPI also does certification in many areas. I am a member of their Certification Board and the author of two of the specialty tests. A number of renowned experts in the investigative field also serve on the board, including Dr. Henry Lee, forensics expert; Vernon Geberth, homicide investigator; and many other well-known and well-regarded professionals.

Criminal Defense Investigation Training Council (CDITC)

The CDITC was established to encourage a dialogue among professionals and scholars involved in various aspects of criminal defense investigation. The council exists as an open forum in which investigative philosophy, methodology, education, and principles of ethical inquiry can be considered via academic training programs, discussions, debate, and writings. The council is actively pursuing the goals of professional competence and academic excellence via the Board Certified Criminal Defense Investigator program and the Training Accreditation Program. The council encourages professionals actively engaged in the discipline of criminal defense investigation to join the council and pursue the designation of Board Certified Criminal Defense Investigator. I serve as a member of this board.

Florida Association of Licensed Investigators (FALI)

As one of the founding fathers of FALI in 1994, my colleagues and I created an association based upon the ideas and successes of a number of smaller associations around the state. By combining into one group, our hope was to create one voice for the industry. In a state of over 9000 licensed investigators, membership accounts for less than 10% of that large base, which is extremely disappointing. However, we are able to speak with a united voice to the state legislature, and we conduct training conferences that address the needs of the industry in Florida. FALI also has a Certification that is administered by a certification board. Upon successful completion, the designation of Florida Certified Investigator (FCI) is conferred (www.flacertinvestigator.com).

Index

A

ACFE, *see* Association of Certified Fraud Examiners
Advance fee scheme, 103–104
Adversary system, objective of using, 69
Agency operations, 485–515
bookkeeping, 487–488
cash flow crunch, 488
description, 488
financial statements, 488
purpose of financial statements, 488
records, 488
business problems, 488–489
accounts receivable, 489
debts collection, 488
excessive expenses, 488
list of furniture and equipment, 489
tax problems, 488
case file management, 507–508
choosing a name, 485
Echosign, 504
form of operation, 485–486
corporation, 486
partnership, 485
"S" corporation, 486
sole proprietorship, 485
licenses and permits, 489
occupational license, 489
private investigator licenses, 489
location, 486–487
managing and marketing your investigative practice, 505–507
business and marketing plans, 505–506
business plan, 506–507
paperless office, 503–505
pricing, 487
professional image, 509–514
appearance, 510
business cards, 510
education, 513–514
information, 511–512
letterhead, 510–511
voice, 512–513
websites, 511
taxes, 489–490
forms, 490, 491–501
keys to success, 490
tips for operating your agency, 502–503
marketing, 502
marketing tips, 502–503
start with a great plan, 502
ways to raise prices without losing customers, 514–515
become a leader in your field, 514–515
change of presentation, 515
target more affluent customers, 514
upgrade your venue, 515
AltaVista, 166, 340
Arson investigation, *see* Insurance and arson investigation
Association of Certified Fraud Examiners (ACFE), 521, 528–529
ATF, *see* Bureau of Alcohol, Tobacco, and Firearms
Attorney
defense, 456–457
trial tactics used by, 444–445
Attorney's Toolbox, 344
Automobile insurance coverage, 276–280
assigned risk, 278
automobile insurance claims, 279–280
collision and comprehensive, 280
liability coverage, 279–280
medical payments, 280
collision coverage, 277
comprehensive coverage, 277
conditions in order to collect under the contract, 277
damage to your own auto, 277
factors in fatal accidents, 276
general provisions, 277
liability, 276
medical payments, 276
no-fault insurance plans, 278

personal auto policy, 276
uninsured motorists, 276–277, 278–279
Autopsy, 225–227, *see also* Death investigation
diagnosed medical condition, 225
example cases, 225–226
natural deaths, 225
non-natural event, 227
"obvious" cause of death, 225
scenarios, 226

B

Background investigations, *see* Due diligence and background investigations
Beaucoup!, 340
Better Business Bureau, 123, 321, 339
Bing, 340
Blackmail, 116
Body language
reading, 47
grooming gestures, 47
gross body movement, 47
supportive gestures, 47
summary of skills, 47–49
distance, 48
eye contact, 48
gesture, 48–49
posture, 48
touch, 48
use of voice, 48
testifying in court for law enforcement officers, 448
Boiler rooms (telemarketing fraud), 119–130
"bleeding" of bank accounts, 127
cold calling, 121
court hearing, 127
"deck packs," 122
detection, 123
"fraud du jour," 119
"green peas," 122
investigation, 123
lead companies, 122
mail-in cards, 121
obtaining customers, 121–122
report of investigation, 128
script, 120–121
secondary rip-offs, 129
steps in investigation of telemarketing, 124–129
steps in investigative process when internal fraud is involved, 129–130
"stokes," 122
sworn law enforcement officers, 126
training, 120–121
what boiler rooms sell, 119–129
what goes on in a boiler room, 122–123
"yaks," 122
Bombsecurity.com, 344
Books of original entry, 116
Brady v. Maryland, 205
Bribery, 116
Buckley Amendments, 329
Bureau of Alcohol, Tobacco, and Firearms (ATF), 24, 196

C

Car theft, 302–305
anti-theft systems, 304
catalytic converters, black market purchase of, 303
defeating the ignition, 303
electronic ignition systems, 304
keyless entry systems, 305
recovery rates, 304
"Slim Jim" car door opening devices, 302
statistics, 303
vehicle security, 303
wire coat hanger, 302
Cash flow crunch, 488
Cause of Death (COD), 221
CDITC, *see* Criminal Defense Investigation Training Council
Ceding company, 266
Chain referral scheme, 107
City hall (as sources of information), 20–22
building department, 20
city attorney, 20
county auditor, 21
county clerk's office, 21
county recorder's office, 20–21
county records, 20
county tax collector, 22
fire marshal and sanitary engineer, 20
health department, 20
medical examiner or coroner's office, 22
property assessor's office, 20, 21–22
registrar of voters or board of elections, 22

sanitation department, 20
street department, 20
COD, *see* Cause of Death
Component Method™ of criminal defense investigation, 212–213
components, 213
developer, 212
execution, 213
management tool, 213
purpose, 213
Computer crime, 153–173
areas of computer abuse, 156–159
accounts receivable, 157
computer losses, 158
computer manipulation crimes, 157
disbursements, 157
hardware and software thefts, 158
inventory, 157
methods of attack, 158–159
operations information, 157
payroll, 157
telecommunications crimes, 157
computer crime, 163–166
conducting external investigations, 165
conducting internal investigations, 165
indications of suspicious behavior by employees, 164
investigative procedures on malicious e-mail, 163–164
investigator, 155–156
profiling the computer criminal, 163
report writing, 165–166
risk matrix, 165
computer forensics, 167–173
advanced searches, 170
advantages of digital evidence, 171
Cyclical Redundancy Checksum algorithm, 169
DOS environment, 169
effective strategies for electronic discovery, 171–172
file allocation table directory, 168
forensic software, 170
hex/text viewer, 170
how data is stored, 167–168
how hard drives work, 167
network audit programs, 172
online security primer for recovering electronic digital evidence, 167–173
PowerPoint file, 171
process of recovering electronic evidence, 169–170
reading and writing digital data, 168–169
searching digital evidence, 170–171
steps to preserve (or destroy) electronic evidence, 172
summary, 172–173
why "deleted" is not always deleted, 169
WinFax, 171
computer fraud, 154–155
institutional vulnerability, 159–163
areas of computer abuse, 161
computer system and electronic transactions security, 160–161
conducting thorough background investigations, 162–163
design and personnel rules for security, 160
guidelines for conducting investigation (insider suspect), 162
tip-offs to possible computer fraud, 161
Internet and the World Wide Web, 166–167
e-mail messages, 166
FAQ section, 166
legendary hacker, 167
meta search engines, 167
newsgroups, 166
search engines, 166
subject directory engines, 166
Universal Resource Locator, 166
investigation of computer fraud, 163
investigative methodology, 156
investigative process, 156
methods of attack, 158–159
data diddling, 158
logic bombs, 159
piggybacking and impersonation, 159
salami slicing techniques, 158
scavenging, 159
trap doors, 158–159
trashing (dumpster diving), 159
Trojan horse, 158
Constructive service, 417
Consumer Product Safety Commission, 111

Consumer Reporting Employment Clarification Act of 1998, 333
Corporate espionage, 36
Council of Private Investigators-Ontario, 344
Counterfeiting, 116
Court testimony, 439–462
  expert witnesses, 451–452
  investigator during trial, 439–440
  investigator pretrial, 439
  investigator as a witness, 441–443
    case report, 441
    cross-examination, 433
    preparation, 442
    presentation, 442
    testifying, 442–443
  preparation of evidence, 441
  preparation of witnesses by investigator, 440–441
    pretrial re-interviewing, 440
    procedures in re-interviews, 440–441
  summary, 461
  testifying in court for law enforcement officers, 445–451
    body language, 448
    expert witness, 446
    fact witness, 446
    officer as defendant, 449
    on the stand, 447–449
    police officers, 446
    preparation, 447
    psychologist testimony, 449–451
    types of witnesses and testimony, 446–447
    veteran experts, 447
  testifying as expert witness, 458–459
  testifying as private investigator, 460–461
    personal experience, 461
    pointers, 460
    self-evaluation as witness, 460–461
  testifying as witness or victim, 458
  tips for testifying in court, 452–455
  trial tactics used by attorneys, 444–445
  types of evidence, 457
    direct evidence, 457
    intangible evidence, 457
    physical evidence, 457
  your rights as a witness, 455–457
    before you appear in court, 456
    cross-examination by defense attorney, 456–457
    legal rights, 455
    when you receive a subpoena, 456
CRC algorithm, *see* Cyclical Redundancy Checksum algorithm
Credit card fraud, 108
Crime Spider, 344
Criminal Defense Investigation Training Council (CDITC), 520–521, 529
Criminal investigation, 175–217
  case studies, 206–212
    federal case (*U.S. vs. Albert Takhalov*), 206–211
    reliance on informants (*United States v. Bruce Bertman*), 211–212
  Component Method™ of criminal defense investigation, 212–213
    components, 213
    developer, 212
    execution, 213
    management tool, 213
    purpose, 213
  conducting a criminal investigation, 197
  development of a set of suspects, 182
  elimination of nonsuspects, 182
  government agencies, 196
    Bureau of Alcohol, Tobacco, Firearms, and Explosives, 196
    Drug Enforcement Agency, 196
    Federal Bureau of Investigation, 196
    Immigration and Naturalization Service, 196
    Internal Revenue Service, 196
    INTERPOL, 196
    Scotland Yard, 196
    Secret Service, 196
  grand jury, 214–217
    evidence, 215
    Fifth Amendment, 214, 215
    latitude, 215
    negative consequences, 216
    Organized Crime Control Act, 216
    presentments, 214
    probing, 216
    use immunity, 217
    U.S. Supreme Court, 214
    witness, 216
  investigative function, 175–176
    basic elements of investigative process, 175–176
    collection, 175
    evaluation, 176
    preservation, 175

recognition, 175
investigative theory and methods, 180–181
crime and information theory, 180–181
physical forms of information, 180
sensory forms of information, 180
written forms of information, 180
investigator's pretrial responsibility, 197–206
anonymous sources of background information, 203
art of the background investigation, 202–203
Brady material, 205
burden of proof, 204–205
civil or criminal trial, 197
court preparation, 203–204
exhibit list, 198
file, 197–198
investigating your witnesses, 201–202
investigator trial witness responsibilities, 199
obtaining evidence in a criminal case, 204–206
order of proof, 199
organization of file, 199
prosecutor has ultimate authority, 206
rules for approaching adverse witnesses, 200–201
subpoenas, 199
trial notebook, 198
witness list, 198
limitations on solving cases, 180
lack of ability to solve a crime, 180
petty offenses, 180
unknown crime, 180
unreported crime, 180
methods of investigation, 182–184
absence of eyewitnesses, 183
corpus delicti, 182
information, 183
instrumentation, 184
interrogation, 183–184
novice investigator, 183
three Is, 182
nuts and bolts, 196–197
phases of the investigation, 184–187
circumstantial evidence, 185
communicating with informant, 187
confidential informant, 186
corpus delicti, 185
elements of the offense, 186
evaluating the informant, 187
eyewitnesses, 184
identifying the criminal, 184–185
informants, 186–187
information volunteered, 186
protecting the informant, 187
proving guilt, 185
tracing and locating the criminal, 185
treatment of informant, 187
procedure for gathering evidence, 192–194
chain of custody, 192–194
collection, 193–194
identification, 194
preservation, 193
protection, 192–193
reasons for investigating crime, 179
role of the criminal investigator, 176–179
determine that a crime has been committed, 176
identify the offender, 176
legally admissible evidence, 179
locate and apprehend the accused, 176–177
present evidence of guilt, 178–179
proof beyond reasonable doubt, 179
recover property that is wrongfully held, 179
role of the police, 194–195
detectives, 195
operations, 195
patrol, 195
role in society, 19
selection and training, 195
specialized operations, 195
SWAT units, 195
rules of evidence, 188–194
admissibility, 188
burden of proof, 189
care of evidence, 192
classification, 188
competency of witness, 188
entrapment, 191
evidence concerning character and reputation, 190
exceptions to the hearsay rule, 191
hearsay evidence, 191
impeachment of witness, 189
judicial notice, 189

opinion evidence, 190
physical evidence, 191
presumption, 189
privileged communications, 191
procedure for gathering evidence, 192–194
rules of exclusion, 189
types of evidence, 181
documentary, 181
physical, 181
testimonial, 181
uses of evidence, 181–182
Cunningham v. Brown, 105
Cyclical Redundancy Checksum (CRC) algorithm, 169

D

Database resources (skip tracing), 337–339
D&B, 337
Dialog, 337
Experian, 337
Factiva, 337
Hoovers, 337
Information America, 338
infoUSA, 337
IQ Data Online, 338
IRB, 338
IRB Search, LLC, 338
KnowX.com, 338
LexisNexis, 337
Locateme.com, 338
Merlin, 339
People Lookup, 337
TLO, 338
Tracers Information Specialists, Inc., 338
Yahoo, 337
Data diddling, 158
Date of birth (DOB), 335
DEA, *see* Drug Enforcement Administration
Death investigation, 219–245
autopsy, 225–227
diagnosed medical condition, 225
example cases, 225–226
natural deaths, 225
non-natural event, 227
"obvious" cause of death, 225
scenarios, 226
decedent investigation, 229–233
autopsy reports, 230
blunt force injuries, 229
clothing, 230–231
fatal incident and medical history, 231–233
perforating injury, 229
postmortem interval, 233
serious bodily injury, 229
sharp force injuries, 229
time of death, 233
traumatic injuries, 229–230
description of death, 220–222
categories of death, 220
Cause of Death, 221
Manner of Death, 221
medical determination of homicide, 221
natural deaths, 220
obvious signs of death, 220
suicide, 222
determine the cause and manner of death, 241–245
forensic autopsy, 235–241
drug and alcohol overdoses, 240–241
gunshot wounds, 236–237
mechanisms of death and injury causation, 235–236
motor vehicle incidents, 237–238
negligence and personal injury, 240
pedestrian incidents, 238–239
workplace incidents, 239
wrongful death, 239–240
investigative protocol, 223–224
analyze, 223–224
document, 224
inquire, 223
prepare, 223
report, 224
key concepts to review and analyze, 227–233
decedent investigation, 229–233
duties of medical examiner, 227–228
evidence, 228–229
examples of evidence, 229
history of decedent, 233–235
medicolegal death investigations in criminal cases, 222
overview, 219–220
Debt consolidation, 107–108
Decedent investigation, 229–233, *see also* Death investigation
autopsy reports, 230
blunt force injuries, 229

clothing, 230–231
corresponding injuries, 230
evidence, 230
Locard's Theory, 231
trace evidence, 230–231
fatal incident and medical history, 231–233
perforating injury, 229
postmortem interval, 233
serious bodily injury, 229
sharp force injuries, 229
time of death, 233
traumatic injuries, 229–230
"Deck packs," 122
Department of Motor Vehicle (DMV) records, 334
Departments of the Army, Navy, Marines, and Air Force, 24
Digital signature service, 504
Direct evidence, 457
District of Columbia v. Brooke, 63
DMV records, *see* Department of Motor Vehicle records
DOB, *see* Date of birth
DOL, *see* U.S. Department of Labor
Domestic investigations, 311–317
alimony, 313
children, 313
equitable distribution of assets, 312
indicators of online marital infidelity, 316–317
alternative e-mail accounts, 316–317
erased history, 317
excess computer usage, 317
gut feeling, 317
privacy, 317
marital assets, 312
missing assets, 313
sample activity report, 314–316
sample data report, 312
state law, 312
stereotyping of investigators, 311
testimony, 311
types, 311
Drug Enforcement Administration (DEA), 24, 196
Due diligence and background investigations, 319–331
applicant background investigation, 322–326
application form, 324–325
authorizations and agreements, 325
compensation law, developing trend in, 322
criteria for employment, 324
employer obligation, 322
malingerers, 323
relationships, 322
content of investigations, 327–329
credit history, 328
criminal history, 329
entry-level employee, 327
information obtained, 327
medical history, 329
references, 328
residence, 328
supervisory employees, 327
unexplained unemployment, 327
due diligence investigations, 319–326
adverse company information, 320
applicant background investigation, 322–326
asset quality of prospective business partner, 319
business background investigation, 322
business data file, 326
employer liability, 319
interviews, 321
public records research, 320
recommended steps, 321
"skeletons," 319
target business, 321
legal constraints, 329–331
Fair Credit Reporting Act, 329–331
Family Education Rights and Privacy Act of 1974, 329
preemployment screening, 331
employee theft, 331
job candidate deception, 331
screening problems, 331
reasons for conducting, 319
scope of investigations, 326–327
Dumpster diving, 159
Duress, forms of, 60
coercion, 60
duress, 60
psychological constraint, 60

E

Echosign, 504
Economic crime schemes, 103–108
advance fee scheme, 103–104

chain referral scheme, 107
credit card fraud, 108
home improvement, debt consolidation, and mortgage loans, 107–108
merchandising schemes, 107
bait and switch, 107
deceptive sales contest, 107
phony sales, 107
short weighting, 107
planned bankruptcy scheme, 106–107
Ponzi scheme, 104–106
pyramid scheme, 104
e-infoseek, 166
eInvestigator.com, 344
Electronic Communications Privacy Act of 1968, 368
E-mail
directories, *see* Telephone and e-mail directories
package, electronic discovery and, 171
Employee's Retirement Income Securities Act (ERISA), 283
Employee theft, 331
Equitable distribution of assets, 312
ERISA, *see* Employee's Retirement Income Securities Act
Escobedo v. Illinois, 72
Ethics, 463–475
advertising, 468–469
avoid conflicts of interest, 466
business conduct, 465–466
client relations, 469
compensation, 468
confidentiality and privacy, 464
equal rights, 469
ethics, 470–471
fair representation to clients, 466
investigative ethics, 471–472
controversy, 471
knowledge of legalities, 471
public image, 471
standards, 472
keep informed, 465
legal issues, 467
mistakes, 463
promote education and advocacy, 465
render services that match your qualifications, 467
reporting, 468
summary of the rules of professional conduct, 472–475
testimony, 469
treatment of competitors, 466–467
truth, 464–465
uniqueness of industry, 463, 471
U.S. Association of Professional Investigators code of ethics, 470
Evidence, 85–88
chain of evidence, 86–88
collection and identification, 86
discovery, 86
important issues, 88
packaging, 86
vouchering and transmittal, 87
circumstantial evidence, 86
death investigations, 228–229
direct evidence, 85
documenting of crime scene, 88
original handwritten notes, 88
photography, 88
sketches, 88
preparation of for trial, 441
types of, 181, 457
direct evidence, 457
documentary, 181
intangible evidence, 457
physical evidence, 181, 457
testimonial evidence, 181
uses of, 181–182
Evidence (rules of), 188–194
admissibility, 188
burden of proof, 189
care of evidence, 192
classification, 188
competency of witness, 188
entrapment, 191
evidence concerning character and reputation, 190
exceptions to the hearsay rule, 191
hearsay evidence, 191
impeachment of witness, 189
judicial notice, 189
opinion evidence, 190
physical evidence, 191
presumption, 189
privileged communications, 191
procedure for gathering evidence, 192–194
chain of custody, 192–194
collection, 193–194
identification, 194
preservation, 193
protection, 192–193
rules of exclusion, 189

Excite, 166, 340
Expert witness, 446, 451–452, 458
Extremist groups, 248–249
ALF (Animal Liberation Front), 248, 253
anti-abortion, 249
ELF (Earth Liberation Front), 248, 253
identity movements, 249
lone wolf problem, 249
Phineas Priests, 249
some tax protesters, 249
white supremacist, 249, 252

F

FAA, *see* Federal Aviation Administration
Facebook, 411
Fact witness, 446
Fair Credit Reporting Act (FCRA), 329–331, 333
FALI, *see* Florida Association of Licensed Investigators
Family Education Rights and Privacy Act of 1974, 329
FAT directory, *see* File allocation table directory
FBI, *see* Federal Bureau of Investigation
FCC, *see* Federal Communications Commission
FCRA, *see* Fair Credit Reporting Act
FDLE, *see* Florida Department of Law Enforcement
Federal Aviation Administration (FAA), 24
Federal Bureau of Investigation (FBI), 24, 196
car theft numbers, 303
definition of terrorism, 247
Federal Civil Rights Act of 1964, 325
Federal Communications Commission (FCC), 24
Federal Insurance Administration (FIA), 282
Federal sources of information, 23–24
Bureau of Alcohol, Tobacco, and Firearms, 24
Departments of the Army, Navy, Marines, and Air Force, 24
Drug Enforcement Administration, 24
Federal Aviation Administration, 24
Federal Bureau of Investigation, 24
Federal Communications Commission, 24
Social Security Administration, 24
U.S. Coast Guard, 24
U.S. Department of Homeland Security, 23
U.S. Immigration and Customs Enforcement, 24
U.S. Postal Service, 23
Federal Trade Commercial Act, 282
Federal Trade Commission (FTC), 282
Felonies, 67, 70, 114
FIA, *see* Federal Insurance Administration
Fifth Amendment, 214, 215
File allocation table (FAT) directory, 168
Financial crime, 97
Financial investigations, *see* Fraud investigation
Finding a niche, 477–482
double-check your choices, 481
how to find your niche, 479–480
competition, 479–480
prospects, 480
untapped market, 480
who you are, 479
methods of detection, 477
most common error, 477
niche markets in investigative industry, 481–482
specialization, 477, 478
success, 478
target market, 478
"top-of-mind" consciousness, 477
FindLaw, 339
Firearms ID, 344
Fire insurance, 271–273
assignment, 272
direct loss, 272
examples of losses, 272
excluded perils, 272
insurable interest, 272
misrepresentation, 272–273
perils insured against, 272
purpose, 271
Fishing, 389
Florida Association of Licensed Investigators (FALI), 529
Florida Department of Law Enforcement (FDLE), 23, 349
Fog of war, 398
FOIA, *see* Freedom of Information Act
Food and Drug Administration, 111
Forensic accounting, 128
Forensic autopsy, 235–241, *see also* Death investigation

drug and alcohol overdoses, 240–241
gunshot wounds, 236–237
mechanisms of death and injury causation, 235–236
motor vehicle incidents, 237–238
negligence and personal injury, 240
pedestrian incidents, 238–239
workplace incidents, 239
wrongful death, 239–240
Forensic Law and Science, 349
Foundations of investigation, 9–39
asset protection, loss prevention, access control, 36–39
corporate espionage, 36
identification badges, 37–38
laptops, 38
assignments performed by professional investigator, 11–14
bank fraud, 12
"day in the life" productions, 14
domestic, child custody, or divorce cases, 13
drug investigations, 13
employment investigations, 12
homicide, suicide, and missing persons investigations, 13
insurance claims/insurance fraud, 11
interviews and statements, 12
malpractice defense, 12
private family investigations, 13
reconstruction of accidents; vehicular and personal injury, 13
service of legal process, 12
shopping services, 13
skip tracing, 14
slip-and-fall accident claims, 13
trademark and patent infringements, 13
undercover Investigations, 14
witness location, 11–12
worker's compensation claims, 12
city hall, 20–22
building department, 20
city attorney, 20
county auditor, 21
county clerk's office, 21
county recorder's office, 20–21
county records, 20
county tax collector, 22
fire marshal and sanitary engineer, 20
health department, 20
medical examiner or coroner's office, 22
property assessor's office, 20, 21–22
registrar of voters or board of elections, 22
sanitation department, 20
street department, 20
federal sources of information, 23–24
Bureau of Alcohol, Tobacco, and Firearms, 24
Departments of the Army, Navy, Marines, and Air Force, 24
Drug Enforcement Administration, 24
Federal Aviation Administration, 24
Federal Bureau of Investigation, 24
Federal Communications Commission, 24
Social Security Administration, 24
U.S. Coast Guard, 24
U.S. Department of Homeland Security, 23
U.S. Immigration and Customs Enforcement, 24
U.S. Postal Service, 23
information from people, 15–17
demeanor of the investigator, 17
experts, 16
informants, 15–16
paid informants, 16
personal references, 16
missing persons, 27–34
follow-up investigation, 30–31
initial interview (phase one), 27–29
investigation (phase two), 29–30
runaway juveniles, 31–34
private organizations and agencies, 25
credit reporting agencies, 25
public utility companies (gas, electricity, and water), 25
telephone companies, 25
private sources of information, 25–26
funeral directors, 26
hospitals, 26
insurance reporting agencies, 25
jewelers, 26
moving companies, 26
personnel offices, 26
private investigative organizations, 26
real estate agencies, 26
school records, 26

shipping companies, 26
transportation companies, 25–26
travel agencies, 26
records and documents as investigative sources of information, 17–22
Bureau of Vital Statistics, 19
city and county business licenses and permit offices, 19
city hall, 20–22
court records, 19
cross-reference directories, 18
fictitious filings (DBA), 19
local newspapers and magazines, 19
local police and fire departments, 19
public library, 17–18
telephone directories, 18
runaway juveniles, 31–34
conducting investigations, 32–33
located runaway, 34
locating runaways, 33–34
motives, 32
profile, 31
sources of information, 14–26
city hall, 20–22
federal sources of information, 23–24
information from people, 15–17
physical evidence, 14
private organizations and agencies, 25
records and documents, 14–15, 17–22
scientific examinations, 14
state regulatory agencies, 22–23
state regulatory agencies, 22–23
department of motor vehicles, 22
Florida Department of Financial Services, 23
Florida Department of Law Enforcement, 23
Florida Division of Alcoholic Beverages and Tobacco, 23
health and rehabilitative services, 22
professional and licensing bureaus (Department of State), 22
types of investigation, 9–11
civil actions, 10
civil investigations, 10
corporate Investigations, 10
criminal investigations, 9–10
general investigations, 11
negligence investigations, 10
personnel and background checks, 11
security, 11
undercover operations in business settings, 34–35
cover story, 34
goodwill of the "straights," 35
roping, 35
Fragmentation, 370
Fraud investigation, 97–151
boiler rooms (telemarketing fraud), 119–130
"bleeding" of bank accounts, 127
cold calling, 121
court hearing, 127
"deck packs," 122
detection, 123
forensic accounting, 128
"fraud du jour," 119
"green peas," 122
hawks, 123
investigation, 123
lead companies, 122
mail-in cards, 121
obtaining customers, 121–122
report of investigation, 128
script, 120–121
secondary rip-offs, 129
steps in investigation of telemarketing, 124–129
steps in investigative process when internal fraud is involved, 129–130
"stokes," 122
sworn law enforcement officers, 126
training, 120–121
what boiler rooms sell, 119–129
what goes on in a boiler room, 122–123
"yaks," 122
case studies, 138–151
internal fraud investigation, 138–146
United States v. Roby Dudley, 147–148
corporate accounting systems/records, 116–117
cash disbursements journal, 117
cash receipts journal, 116
journals, 116
ledger, 117
purchase journal, 117
sales journal, 117
corporate crime, 109–119
administrative violations, 111
blackmail, 116
books of original entry, 116

bribery, 116
business crime, 111
compounding a felony, 114
controlling crime/accountability for asset protection, 114
corporate accounting systems/records, 116–117
corporate crime, 111
cost of, 109
counterfeiting, 116
crimes with financial aspect, 116
difficulties in use of criminal sanctions, 109–110
environment of corporation, 110
federal and state fraud statutes, 110–111
financial investigative skills, 114–115
financial violations, 111
fraud audit, 117
fraud detection techniques, 117–118
goal of financial investigator, 115
insider trading, 116
interrogation, 113–114
kickback, 116
labor violations, 111
management fraud, 110
manufacturing violations, 111
money laundering, 116
objectives for investigation into suspected fraud, 111–112
primary rule, 117
Principle of Occam's Razor, 118
proving corporate fraud, 114
Qui Bono, 118
Racketeer Influenced and Corrupt Organizations Act, 110
reasons for fraud investigations, 118
reasons for leniency in corporate frauds, 114
records, 115
steps in conducting fraud investigation, 113
steps in fraud investigations, 118–119
steps in investigation process, 112–113
types of violations, 111
unfair trade practices, 111
what is involved in financial investigative approach, 115–116
white-collar crime, 111

corporate fraud, 99–102
audit trail, 101
corporate fraud detection, 101
corporate fraud investigation, 100–101
definition of fraud, 99
detection techniques, 101–102
embezzlement, 100
financial fraud, 100
individual net worth investigations, 102
M.O.M.M., 101
social cost, 99

defense investigations for complex fraud cases, 131–138
component one (case review and analysis), 131–133
component two (client interview), 133–134
component three (crime scene examination), 134
component four (witness background investigations), 134–135
component five (witness interviews), 135–137
component six (reports and testifying), 137–138
premise, 138
timelines, 132–133

economic crime schemes, 103–108
advance fee scheme, 103–104
chain referral scheme, 107
credit card fraud, 108
home improvement, debt consolidation, and mortgage loans, 107–108
merchandising schemes, 107
planned bankruptcy scheme, 106–107
Ponzi scheme, 104–106
pyramid scheme, 104

financial crime, 97
fraud, definition of, 98
how to conduct a criminal fraud defense investigation, 130
important rules, 99
intent to gain a benefit, 98
knowledge of false statement, 98
merchandising schemes, 107
bait and switch, 107
deceptive sales contest, 107
phony sales, 107
short weighting, 107

reasons for, 98

sample activity reports, 148–151
divorce and property timeline, 150–151
fraud investigation activity report, 148–150
steps, 99
victim, 98
white-collar crime, 108
FraudTracer, 340
Freedom of Information Act (FOIA), 12, 20, 345
FTC, *see* Federal Trade Commission
"Fundamental rights" theory, 65
Furman, Mark, 201

G

Gitlow v. New York, 66
Global positioning satellite (GPS), 400
Google, 166, 340
Google Earth, 411
Government agencies, 196
Bureau of Alcohol, Tobacco, Firearms, and Explosives, 196
Drug Enforcement Agency, 196
Federal Bureau of Investigation, 196
Immigration and Naturalization Service, 196
Internal Revenue Service, 196
INTERPOL, 196
Scotland Yard, 196
Secret Service, 196
Government records, 345–349
building department, 347
Bureau of Vital Statistics, 346
city and county business license and permit offices, 346
civil and criminal records, 345
county clerk's office, 347
county recorder's office, 345, 347
county tax collector, 348
department of motor vehicles, 348
fictitious filings, 346
fire marshal and sanitary engineer, 347
Florida Department of Law Enforcement, 349
Freedom of Information Act, 345
health and rehabilitative services, 348
local police and fire departments, 346
professional and licensing bureaus, 348
property assessor's office, 346, 348
Property Records Office, 345
public records information, 346–349
registrar of voters or board of elections, 348
social service agencies and state unemployment, 348
state bureau of alcohol, beverages, and tobacco, 349
street department, 346
U.S. Postal Service, 345
GPS, *see* Global positioning satellite
Grand jury, 214–217
evidence, 215
Fifth Amendment, 214, 215
latitude, 215
negative consequences, 216
Organized Crime Control Act, 216
presentments, 214
probing, 216
use immunity, 217
U.S. Supreme Court, 214
witness, 216
"Green peas," 122
Gregory v. Litton Systems Incorporated, 325

H

Hawks, 123
Healthcare insurance fraud, 284–286
Health Insurance Portability and Accountability Act (HIPAA), 232, 233
Hex/text viewer, 170
HIPAA, *see* Health Insurance Portability and Accountability Act
Home improvement, 107–108
Hotbot, 166

I

ICE, *see* U.S. Immigration and Customs Enforcement
Illinois v. Allen, 176
Imagery intelligence (IMINT), 412
IMINT, *see* Imagery intelligence
Immigration and Naturalization Service (INS), 196
Incarceration, 82
concurrent sentences, 82
consecutive sentences, 82
length of sentence, 82
location of, 82
Informants, 186–187

communicating with informant, 187
confidential informant, 186
evaluating the informant, 187
information volunteered, 186
protecting the informant, 187
treatment of informant, 187
INS, *see* Immigration and Naturalization Service
Insider trading, 116
Institutional vulnerability (computer crime), 159–163
areas of computer abuse, 161
computer system and electronic transactions security, 160–161
conducting thorough background investigations, 162–163
design and personnel rules for security, 160
guidelines for conducting investigation (insider suspect), 162
tip-offs to possible computer fraud, 161
Insurance and arson investigation, 263–309
automobile insurance coverage, 276–280
assigned risk, 278
automobile insurance claims, 279–280
collision coverage, 277
comprehensive coverage, 277
conditions in order to collect under the contract, 277
damage to your own auto, 277
factors in fatal accidents, 276
general provisions, 277
liability, 276
medical payments, 276
no-fault insurance plans, 278
personal auto policy, 276
uninsured motorists, 276–277, 278–279
car insurance scam, 305–309
accident victims, 306
bogus medical clinics, 305
HCAI system, 308
invoices, 307
lawsuit, 309
stolen signature, 306, 309
car theft, 302–305
anti-theft systems, 304
catalytic converters, black market purchase of, 303
defeating the ignition, 303
electronic ignition systems, 304
keyless entry systems, 305
recovery rates, 304
"Slim Jim" car door opening devices, 302
statistics, 303
vehicle security, 303
wire coat hanger, 302
fire and arson investigation, 287–294
arson, 290–294
cause of fire, 294
color and height of flames, 291
color of smoke, 291
commercial fires, 288–289
insurer, 293–294
interview of owner, 293
investigative checklist, 288
location, extent, and direction of flames, 291
motives of arson offenders, 290–291, 294
national statistics, 287
odors at the scene, 291–292
photographs of the fire, 292
point of origin of the fire, 293
primary role of fire investigator, 287
procedures for investigating arson, 291–294
search of the scene, 292
suspicious indicators of vehicular fires, 289
vehicular fires, 289–290
weather conditions, 292
witnesses, 292
fire insurance, 271–273
assignment, 272
direct loss, 272
examples of losses, 272
excluded perils, 272
insurable interest, 272
misrepresentation, 272–273
perils insured against, 272
purpose, 271
government regulation of insurance, 280–283
abuses of power, 280
characteristics of insurance, 280
Employee's Retirement Income Securities Act, 283
Federal Insurance Administration, 282
insurance costs, 280
McCarron-Ferguson Act, 282

National Association of Insurance Commissioners, 281
Securities and Exchange Commission, 283
state regulation, 281
U.S. Department of Labor, 283
ideal requirements for insurability, 265–266
ceding company, 266
potential loss, 265
reinsurance, 266
insurance, 263–264
description of insurance, 263
how insurance works, 263–264
purpose of insurance, 263
risk assumption, 263–264
what insurers do, 263
insurance adjusting, 270–271
liability insurance claims, 271
loss payment, 270
insurance contracts, 266–268
basic legal principles, 266–267
buying insurance, 266
components of insurance contract, 268
concealment, 267
estoppels, 267
indemnity, 266
insurable interest, 266
policy, 266
representations, 267
requirements of insurance contracts, 267–268
subrogation, 267
underwriting, 267
waiver, 267
warranties, 267
insurance fraud, 284–287
general insurance fraud, 284
healthcare insurance fraud, 284–286
life insurance fraud, 287
property insurance fraud, 286–287
liability claims investigation, 294–295
contributory negligence, 295
definition of liability, 294
duty owed, 294
no-fault law, 295
proximate cause, 295
negligence, 269–270
comparative negligence, 269–270
court action, 269
imputed negligence, 270
liability claims, 269
losses from fraudulent claims, 269
presumed negligence, 270
requirements for negligence liability, 269–270
probability, 264–265
adverse selection, 265
deductive and inductive reasoning, 264–265
law of large numbers, 265
risk, 264
sample investigative report, 295–299
alterations to fire scene, 297
assignment, 296
attachments, 299
background information, 296
exterior observations, 297
fire scene security, 297
incident information, 297
interior observations, 298
interviews, 298
investigation report, 295–296
origin and cause summary, 299
structure information, 296–297
sample vehicle fire report, 299–302
assignment, 300
background information, 300
conclusion summary, 302
engine compartment observations, 301
exterior observations, 301
insured interview, 301–302
interior observations, 301
investigation report, 299–300
types of insurance, 271–280
automobile insurance coverage, 276–280
employer's liability, 273–276
fire insurance, 271–273
general liability insurance, 273
individual health insurance, 271
professional malpractice liability, 273
Worker's Compensation, 273–276
Worker's Compensation, 273–276
benefits, 275
employer and employees, 275
financing of benefits, 274–275
injuries covered, 275
occupational disability, 273, 274
Occupational Safety and Health Act, 275–276
theory behind legislation, 273

types of laws, 274
willful misconduct, 274
Intangible evidence, 457
Internal Revenue Service (IRS), 196, 283, 488
Internet infidelity, 317
Internet search engines, 340–344
Alta Vista, 340
American Community Network, 341
Beaucoup!, 340
Bing, 340
business search engines, 341
CataLaw, 342
Center for Immigration Studies, 342
competitive intelligence and business research, 343
databases, 343
document retrievers, 343–344
Excite, 340
geographic search engines, 341
Google, 340
government search engines, 341–342
how to search, 342
International Chamber of Commerce and City-State-Province Directory, 341
investigator portals, 344
Attorney's Toolbox, 344
Bombsecurity.com, 344
Council of Private Investigators-Ontario, 344
Crime Spider, 344
eInvestigator.com, 344
Firearms ID, 344
Forensic Law and Science, 349
Investigative Links Directory, 349
Loc8fast, 344
MyRecords.com, 344
PI Portal, 349
Reddy's Forensic Page, 344
Sheila Lowe & Associates, 349
VirtualGumshoe.com, 344
LibrarySpot, 341
Lycos, 340
Office of Justice programs, 342
OSHA statistics and data, 342
telephone and e-mail directories, 342–343
AnyWho.com
Area Code Changes, 342
Area Decoder, 342
Bigfoot, 342
BigYellow, 342
Fone Finder, 342
411 Locate, 342
MyFreeemailsearch,com, 343
National Cellular Directory, 342
PC411, 342
Reverse Lookup, 342
SuperPages Yellow Pages, 342
Switchboard, 342
Telephone Area Code Finder© (MMIWORLD), 342
ThreeClicks.com
Ultimate Email Directory, 342
Ultimate White Pages, 343
Yahoo! People Search, 343
Yahoo, 340
Internet and the World Wide Web (computer crime), 166–167
e-mail messages, 166
FAQ section, 166
legendary hacker, 167
meta search engines, 167
newsgroups, 166
search engines, 166
subject directory engines, 166
Universal Resource Locator, 166
INTERPOL, 196
Interviews, interrogation, and taking statements, 41–60
admissions, confessions, and written statements, 54–60
admissibility of confessions, 59–60
admissions, 55
coercion, 60
confessions, 55–56
contents of statements, 58
depositions, 56–57
duress, 60
forms of duress, 60
forms of statement, 59
methods of taking statements, 58
psychological constraint, 60
witness to confession, 59
written statements, 57
interviews, introduction to, 41–45
attitude and demeanor of investigator, 44
common interviewing errors, 42
control over interviews, 44
controversy, 41
criminal investigation techniques, 43
empathy, 43

interview of complainants, victims, and witnesses, 45
interviewing guidelines, 43
preparation for interview, 44
purpose of interview, 43–44
relevant questions, 41
role playing, 42
strategies, 42
types of approach, 44–45
purpose of interrogation, 45–52
appearance, 49
attitude of investigator, 46
body language skills, 47–49
detecting insincerity, 51–52
direct approach, 46
distance, 48
emotional approach, 46
eye contact, 48, 50
gesture, 48–49
grooming gestures, 47
gross body movement, 47
indirect approach, 46
interrogation, 46
nonverbal leakage, 52
posture, 48
postures of agreement and disagreement, 49–50
pupil signals, 51
reading body language, 47
reading facial expressions, 51
subterfuge, 47
supportive gestures, 47
tip-off movement of body, 52
touch, 48
types of approaches, 46–47
use of voice, 48
taking statements, 52–54
Investigative Links Directory, 349
Investigator portals (Internet search engines), 344
Attorney's Toolbox, 344
Bombsecurity.com, 344
Council of Private Investigators-Ontario, 344
Crime Spider, 344
eInvestigator.com, 344
Firearms ID, 344
Forensic Law and Science, 349
Investigative Links Directory, 349
Loc8fast, 344
MyRecords.com, 344
PI Portal, 349
Reddy's Forensic Page, 344
Sheila Lowe & Associates, 349
VirtualGumshoe.com, 344
IRS, *see* Internal Revenue Service
Islamic terrorism, 253

J

Job candidate deception, 331
Journals (financial information), 116

K

Katz v. United States, 367
Kickback, 116

L

Law, *see also* Legal investigations; Legislation; Litigation
sources of, 67–68
types of, 66–67
administrative law, 67
constitutional law, 66–67
criminal law, 67
international law, 67
private law, 67
public law, 66–67
Law of large numbers, 265
Ledger, 117
Legal investigations, 61–95
appeals, 82–82
appeal process, 82–83
decision of the court, 83
authority to arrest, 71
Bill of Rights, 64–66
due process of law, 65–66
First Amendment, 64
Second Amendment, 64
Third Amendment, 64
Fourth Amendment, 64
Fifth Amendment, 64
Sixth Amendment, 65
Seventh Amendment, 65
Eight Amendment, 65
Ninth Amendment, 65
Tenth Amendment, 65
case study
United States v. Nancy Walter, 90–91
United States v. Pedro Huezo, 91–95
circuit court, 66
concept of crime, 70

crime classification, 70
felony, 70
misdemeanor, 70
treason, 70
conducting legal investigations, 89–90
criminal and civil procedure, 66–70
administrative law, 67
adversary system, objective of using, 69
basic components of criminal offense, 69–70
bench trial, 68
case law, 67
causation, 70
civil procedures, 68
civil trials, 68
constitutional law, 66–67
criminal law, 67
criminal procedure, 68–69
criminal state of mind, 69–70
felonies, 67
goal of criminal justice, 68–69
international law, 67
misdemeanors, 67
private law, 67
proximate cause, 70
public law, 66
sources of law, 67–68
types of law, 66–67
wrongful act, 69
effective limits of criminal law, 70–71
honesty and morality, 71
personal morality, 71
regulatory crime, 71
vice crimes, 71
evidence, 85–88
chain of evidence, 86–88
circumstantial evidence, 86
collection and identification, 86
direct evidence, 85
discovery, 86
documenting of crime scene, 88
important issues, 88
original handwritten notes, 88
packaging, 86
photography, 88
sketches, 88
vouchering and transmittal, 87
habeas corpus, 66
interrogating the accused, 72
investigative detention short of arrest (stop and frisk), 71
jury trial and jury selection, 75–76
peremptory challenge, 76
qualifying of jury panel, 75–76
selection of jury panel, 75
voir dire examination, 76
legal investigations, 83–85
civil investigations, 84–85
criminal investigations, 83
defendant, 85
plaintiff, 84
legal investigator, 61–62
preliminary proceedings in trial court, 72–74
Motion for a Bill of Particulars, 73
Motion for Change of Venue or Judge, 73
Motion for Continuance, 74
Motion for Discovery, 73
motion to suppress state's evidence, 73
pleas, 72–73
role of legal investigator, 85
searches, 72
trial, 72–83
appeals, 82–82
closing arguments, 80
concurrent sentences, 82
consecutive sentences, 82
cross-examination of witness, 77
defense's case, 79
executive review, 83
guilty plea, 74
incarceration, 82
instructions to the jury, 79–80
jury deliberations, 80–81
jury trial and jury selection, 75–76
motion for judgment of acquittal, 78
motion for a new trial, 81
opening statements, 77
preliminary proceedings in trial court, 72–74
probation, 81–82
rebuttal and surrebuttal, 79
sentencing decision, 81–82
State's case, 77–78
trial, 76–82
Writ of Certiorari, 83
trial by ambush, 91
U.S. Constitution, structure of, 62–63
Article I, 62
Article II, 62
Article III, 62

Article IV, 63
Article V, 63
Article VI, 63
Article VII, 63
limitations on state powers, 63
powers retained by state, 63
Legislation
Consumer Reporting Employment Clarification Act of 1998, 333
Electronic Communications Privacy Act of 1968, 368
Employee's Retirement Income Securities Act, 283
Fair Credit Reporting Act, 329–331, 333
Family Education Rights and Privacy Act of 1974, 329
Federal Civil Rights Act of 1964, 325
Federal Trade Commercial Act, 282
Freedom of Information Act, 12, 20, 345
Health Insurance Portability and Accountability Act, 232, 233
McCarron-Ferguson Act, 282
National Firearms Act, 24
National Labor Relations Act, 322
Occupational Safety and Health Act, 275–276
Organized Crime Control Act, 216
Racketeer Influenced and Corrupt Organizations Act, 110, 166
Securities Exchange Act of 1934, 331
Lexis, 339
Lexis-Nexis, 411
Liability claims investigation (insurance and arson investigation), 294–295
contributory negligence, 295
definition of liability, 294
duty owed, 294
no-fault law, 295
proximate cause, 295
LibrarySpot, 341
Licensing, 483–484, 489
Life insurance fraud, 287
Litigation
Brady v. Maryland, 205
Cunningham v. Brown, 105
District of Columbia v. Brooke, 63
Escobedo v. Illinois, 72
Gitlow v. New York, 66
Gregory v. Litton Systems Incorporated, 325
Illinois v. Allen, 176
Katz v. United States, 367
Mallory v. United States, 72
Mapp v. Ohio, 72
McNabb v. United States, 72
Miranda v. Arizona, 72
Smith v. the State of Maryland, 367
Terry v. Ohio, 71
United States v. Bruce Bertman, 211-212
United States v. Knotts, 367
United States v. Nancy Walter, 90–91
United States v. Pedro Huezo, 91–95
United States v. Roby Dudley, 147–148
U.S. v. Albert Takhalov, 206–211
U.S. v. Gelbhart, 216
Weeks v. United States, 72
Williams v. Florida, 75
Locard's Theory, 231
Locates and skip tracing, 333–360
basics of skip tracing, 333
criminal skip, 333
definition of skip tracing, 333
intentional skip, 333
marital skips, 333
skip groups, 333
unintentional skip, 333
beginning the process, 334–335
basics, 334
DMV records, 334
interviews, 334–335
researching public records, 334
database resources, D&B, 337
database resources, 337–339
Dialog, 337
Experian, 337
Factiva, 337
Hoovers, 337
Information America, 338
infoUSA, 337
IRB, 338
IRB Search, LLC, 338
KnowX.com, 338
LexisNexis, 337
Locateme.com, 338
Merlin, 339
People Lookup, 337
TLO, 338
Tracers Information Specialists, Inc., 338
Yahoo, 337
government records, 345–349
building department, 347
Bureau of Vital Statistics, 346

city and county business license and permit offices, 346
civil and criminal records, 345
county clerk's office, 347
county recorder's office, 345, 347
county tax collector, 348
department of motor vehicles, 348
fictitious filings, 346
fire marshal and sanitary engineer, 347
Florida Department of Law Enforcement, 349
Freedom of Information Act, 345
health and rehabilitative services, 348
local police and fire departments, 346
professional and licensing bureaus, 348
property assessor's office, 346, 348
Property Records Office, 345
public records information, 346–349
registrar of voters or board of elections, 348
social service agencies and state unemployment, 348
state bureau of alcohol, beverages, and tobacco, 349
street department, 346
U.S. Postal Service, 345
IRB (custom comprehensive report, sample), 349–351
other Internet sites, 344–345
relevant federal and state statutes, 333–33
Consumer Reporting Employment Clarification Act of 1998, 333
Fair Credit Reporting Act, 333
Sunshine Law, 333
sample forms, 351–360
search engines, 340–344
Boolean operators, 340
business search engines, 341
competitive intelligence and business research, 343
databases, 343
document retrievers, 343–344
favorites, 340
geographic search engines, 341
government search engines, 341–342
how to search, 342
investigator portals, 344
LibrarySpot, 341
limitations of online searches, 341
query construction, 340
symbol designations, 341
telephone and e-mail directories, 342–343
searching for financial and business information, 339
assumed business name, 339
bankruptcy filings, 339
Better Business Bureau, 339
property information, 339
UCC filings, 339
searching for legal information, 339–340
criminal convictions, 339
criminal record information, 340
FindLaw, 339
FraudTracer, 340
insurance information, 340
laws and court cases, 339
Lexis, 339
MegaLaw, 339
publications, 340
QuickFind, 339
security- and fraud-related information, 339
state and federal records, 339
Westlaw, 339
skip tracing resources, 335–339
database resources, 337–339
driver's license, 335
financial and business information, 336
individuals versus corporations, 336
legal information, 337
occupational records, 336
out-of-state corporations, 336
public records, 335
records service companies, 337–339
reverse directory, 335
Uniform Commercial Code filings, 336
Loc8fast, 344
Logic bombs, 159
Lone wolf problem, 249
Lycos, 166, 340

M

Madoff, Bernie, 97
Mallory v. United States, 72
Manner of Death (MOD), 221
Mapp v. Ohio, 72

McCarron-Ferguson Act, 282
McNabb v. United States, 72
MegaLaw, 339
Merchandising schemes, 107
 bait and switch, 107
 deceptive sales contest, 107
 phony sales, 107
 short weighting, 107
Meta search engines, 167
Miranda v. Arizona, 72
Misdemeanors, 67, 70
Missing persons, 27–34
 follow-up investigation, 30–31
 initial interview (phase one), 27–29
  description, 29
  motive, 29
  previous disappearances, 28–29
 investigation (phase two), 29–30
  check the bad news sources, 30
  check personal belongings, 30
 runaway juveniles, 31–34
  conducting investigations, 32–33
  located runaway, 34
  locating runaways, 33–34
  motives, 32
  profile, 31
MOD, *see* Manner of Death
Money laundering, 116
Mortgage loans, 107–108
MyRecords.com, 344
Myspace, 411

N

NALI, *see* National Association of Legal Investigators
National Association of Insurance Commissioners, 281
National Association of Legal Investigators (NALI), 517–520, 528
 certification program, 518–520
 legal investigator, 518
National Council of Investigation and Security Services (NCISS), 521
National Firearms Act, 24
National Highway Traffic Safety Administration, 111
National Labor Relations Act, 322
Natural deaths, 220, 225
NCISS, *see* National Council of Investigation and Security Services
Negligence (insurance and arson investigation), 269–270
 comparative negligence, 269–270
 court action, 269
 imputed negligence, 270
 liability claims, 269
 losses from fraudulent claims, 269
 presumed negligence, 270
 requirements for negligence liability, 269–270
Network audit programs, 172
Niche, *see* Finding a niche
Nonverbal leakage, 52

O

OCCA, *see* Organized Crime Control Act
Occam's Razor, 118
Occupational disability, 273, 274
Occupational Safety and Health Act (OSHA), 275–276
Online marital infidelity, indicators of, 316–317
 alternative e-mail accounts, 316–317
 erased history, 317
 excess computer usage, 317
 gut feeling, 317
 privacy, 317
Open source intelligence (OSINT), 411
Organized Crime Control Act (OCCA), 216
OSHA, *see* Occupational Safety and Health Act
OSINT, *see* Open source intelligence

P

PAP, *see* Personal auto policy
PCP, *see* Primary care physician
Personal auto policy (PAP), 276
Personal service, 417
Petty offenses, 180
Phineas Priests, 249
Physical evidence, 457
Piggybacking, 159
PI Portal, 349
Planned bankruptcy scheme, 106–107
PMI, *see* Postmortem interval
Police, 194–195
 operations, 195
  detectives, 195
  patrol, 195
  specialized operations, 195

SWAT units, 195
role in society, 19
selection and training, 195
Ponzi, Charles, 104
Ponzi scheme, 104–106
Postmortem interval (PMI), 233
Predictable constants, 401
Primary care physician (PCP), 232
Principle of Occam's Razor, 118
Private sources of information, 25–26
funeral directors, 26
hospitals, 26
insurance reporting agencies, 25
jewelers, 26
moving companies, 26
personnel offices, 26
private investigative organizations, 26
real estate agencies, 26
school records, 26
shipping companies, 26
transportation companies, 25–26
travel agencies, 26
Professional associations, 517–529
additional specialty associations of interest, 525
international associations, 525
national associations, 517–525
Association of Certified Fraud Examiners, 521
Criminal Defense Investigation Training Council, 520–521
National Association of Legal Investigators, 517–520
National Council of Investigation and Security Services, 521
U.S. Association of Professional Investigators, 521–525
recommended associations, 528–529
Association of Certified Fraud Examiners, 528–529
Criminal Defense Investigation Training Council, 529
Florida Association of Licensed Investigators, 529
National Association of Legal Investigators, 528
U.S. Association of Professional Investigators, 529
state associations, 525–528
Professional investigation, introduction, 1–2
earnings, 2
job outlook, 1–2
Professional malpractice liability, 273
Property insurance fraud, 286–287
Proximate cause, 70
Psychologist testimony, 449–451
Pyramid scheme, 104

Q

Query construction, 340
Qui Bono, 118
QuickFind, 339

R

Racketeer Influenced and Corrupt Organizations (RICO) Act, 110, 166
Records service companies (skip tracing), 337–339
D&B, 337
Dialog, 337
Experian, 337
Factiva, 337
Hoovers, 337
Information America, 338
infoUSA, 337
IQ Data Online, 338
IRB, 338
IRB Search, LLC, 338
KnowX.com, 338
LexisNexis, 337
Locateme.com, 338
Merlin, 339
People Lookup, 337
TLO, 338
Tracers Information Specialists, Inc., 338
Yahoo, 337
Reddy's Forensic Page, 344
Regulatory crime, 71
Reinsurance, 266
RICO Act, *see* Racketeer Influenced and Corrupt Organizations Act
Risk matrix (computer crime), 165
Runaway juveniles, 31–34
conducting investigations, 32–33
friends, activities, and so forth, 33
home situation, 32–33
located runaway, 34
locating runaways, 33–34
all-night public places, 33

automobiles, 34
campgrounds, parks, and beaches, 34
carnivals and circuses, 34
friend's house, 33
lobbies, vestibules, and basements, 33
skid row, 34
vacant buildings, 34
motives, 32
desire to avoid criticism or punishment, 32
eloping, 32
fear of being apprehended by the police for an offense, 32
lack of security in new surroundings, 32
poor home conditions, 32
rigid, overstrict home discipline, 32
profile, 31

S

Salami slicing techniques, 158
SBI, *see* Serious bodily injury
SEC, *see* Securities and Exchange Commission
Securities Exchange Act of 1934, 331
Securities and Exchange Commission (SEC), 283
Serious bodily injury (SBI), 229
Service of process, 417–437
Florida statutes governing service of process, 422–437
pitfalls to avoid, 418
proof of service, 418
service of subpoenas for witnesses in federal courts, 418–421
types of service, 417–418
constructive service, 417
personal service, 417
procedure, 418
waived service, 417
Shadowing, 369–372
fragmentation, 370
getting burned, 370
intuition, 371
operational challenges, 371
win-win outcome, 372
Sheila Lowe & Associates, 349
Simpson, O.J., 201, 239
Skills needed, 3–7
attributes of successful investigator, 4–7
ability to obtain the cooperation of others, 6
ability to play a role, 5
ability to put people at ease, 6
ability to speak at the level of the audience, 7
curiosity, 5
flexibility, 7
good listening skills, 6
good manners, 7
interest in your work and pride of accomplishment, 6
intuitive understanding of human nature, 7
memory, 5
observation, 5
persistence and capacity for hard work, 5
resourcefulness, 5
self-confidence, 7
street sense, 6
suspicion, 4
unbiased and unprejudiced mind, 5
understanding of body language, 7
description of investigator, 3–4
methods used to obtain information, 3
Skip tracing, *see* Locates and skip tracing
"Slim Jim" car door opening devices, 302
Smart phones, 411
Smith v. the State of Maryland, 367
Social Security Administration (SSA), 24
Social Security number (SSN), 335
Special weapons and tactics (SWAT) units, 195
Spokeo, 411
SSA, *see* Social Security Administration
SSN, *see* Social Security number
Statements, *see* Interviews, interrogation, and taking statements
State regulatory agencies (as sources of information), 22–23
department of motor vehicles, 22
Florida Department of Financial Services, 23
Florida Department of Law Enforcement, 23
Florida Division of Alcoholic Beverages and Tobacco, 23
health and rehabilitative services, 22
professional and licensing bureaus (Department of State), 22
"Stokes," 122

Sudden unexpected infant death syndrome (SUIDS), 222
SUIDS, *see* Sudden unexpected infant death syndrome
Sunshine Law, 333
Surveillance, 361–416
  automobile surveillance, 362–364
    accident, 362
    car color, 363
    corners, 363
    hot drivers, 363
    knowledge of area, 364
    maintenance, 363
    position, 363
  circular surveillance, 403–407
    absolute execution without hesitation, 404
    challenge of, 403
    double-edged operational constants, 404
    scenarios, 405
    stationary, 407
    symmetrical and linear constants, 404
    time, 406
    when to employ, 403
  closed surveillance, 377
  equipment, 366–367
    basics, 366
    formats, 366
    holding the camcorder, 366–367
    microphones, 366
  foot surveillance, 362, 384–395
    advantageous surveillance positions, 391–392
    airports, 386–387
    beach, 391
    close tail, 362
    distance, 362
    emergency money, 362
    fishing, 389
    gated communities, 394
    government buildings, 393–394
    gymnasiums, 387
    joggers, 394
    low light areas, 395
    principles, 384–385
    public parks, 392–393
    public transit, 395
    restaurants, 362, 385–386
    risk of detection, 384
    shopping centers, 394–395
    supermarkets, 387–388
    symmetrical buildings, 388–389
    theme parks, 394–395
    transitioning targets, 386
    videotaping of target inside buildings and close environments, 389–390
  general rules, 361
  glossary and sample logs, 413–416
    glossary, 413–414
    sample logs, 414–416
  gradual surveillance, 407–413
    comprehensive reports, 411–412
    follow-up surveillance, 407
    golden surveillance position, 408
    how to employ, 408
    imagery intelligence, 412
    integrity of case, 408
    multiple online databases, 412
    operational preparedness, 410–411
    pattern recognition, 409–410
    preliminary investigation (open source intelligence), 411
    pretexting, 412–413
    purpose, 407
    routes of departure, 408
    social networks, 411
  open surveillance, 377–384
    determining what your target is driving, 382–384
    examples, 377
    message, 378
    onlookers, 380
    probable cause, 377
    routes of departure, 381
    routine spot-checks, 381–382
    school bus, 380
    standard of law enforcement, 378
    worst-case scenario, 379
  practical considerations, 368
  presurveillance, 361
    information pertaining to subject, 361
    reconnaissance, 361
  procedures for interception of wire or oral communications, 369
  shadowing, 369–372
    fragmentation, 370
    getting burned, 370
    Human-Intelligence Gathering, 369
    intuition, 371
    operational challenges, 371
    Pattern Recognition, 369

shadowing, 369–372
win-win outcome, 372
stakeouts, 364–365
closeness to subject, 365
mirrors, 364
police, 365
trucks, 364
windows, 364
static surveillance, 372–377
aggressive surveillance position, 376
children, 375
description, 372
hallucination, 375
light, 377
police, 375
positions, 374
pretexting people, 374
surveillance position, 372
target vigilance, 373
videotaping, 376
surgical surveillance (open roof applications in high security areas), 395–400
case, 395
claimant mannerisms, 399
fog of war, 398
objective, 396
parked vehicles, 397
pattern recognition, 400
women, 399–400
tactics, 365
hot subjects, 365
risk of being detected, 365
talking to suspect, 365
technical surveillance, 367–368
bugs, pen registers, and beepers, 367–368
Electronic Communications Privacy Act of 1968, 368
monitoring movement of vehicles and items of commerce, 367–368
visual enhancement devices, 369
vehicular surveillance, 400–402
flow of traffic, 402
global positioning satellite, 400
law enforcement, 400
operational challenges, 401–402
pattern recognition, 402
predictable constants, 401
retroactive investigation, 400
two-man operations, 401
unpredictable constants, 401

SWAT units, *see* Special weapons and tactics units

T

Taking statements, *see* Interviews, interrogation, and taking statements
Telemarketing fraud, 119–130
"bleeding" of bank accounts, 127
cold calling, 121
court hearing, 127
"deck packs," 122
detection, 123
"fraud du jour," 119
"green peas," 122
investigation, 123
lead companies, 122
mail-in cards, 121
obtaining customers, 121–122
report of investigation, 128
script, 120–121
secondary rip-offs, 129
steps in investigation of telemarketing, 124–129
steps in investigative process when internal fraud is involved, 129–130
"stokes," 122
sworn law enforcement officers, 126
training, 120–121
what boiler rooms sell, 119–129
what goes on in a boiler room, 122–123
"yaks," 122
Telephone and e-mail directories, 342–343
AnyWho.com
Area Code Changes, 342
Area Decoder, 342
Bigfoot, 342
BigYellow, 342
Fone Finder, 342
411 Locate, 342
MyFreeemailsearch,com, 343
National Cellular Directory, 342
PC411, 342
Reverse Lookup, 342
SuperPages Yellow Pages, 342
Switchboard, 342
Telephone Area Code Finder© (MMIWORLD), 342
ThreeClicks.com
Ultimate Email Directory, 342

Ultimate White Pages, 343
Yahoo! People Search, 343
Terrorism investigations, 247–261
case study, 255–261
criminal activity by terrorist, 252–253
ALF/ELF, 253
Islamic terrorism, 253
entrapment, 251–252
extremist groups, 248–249
ALF (Animal Liberation Front), 248
anti-abortion, 249
ELF (Earth Liberation Front), 248
identity movements, 249
lone wolf problem, 249
Phineas Priests, 249
some tax protesters, 249
white supremacist, 249, 252
government approach to terrorism, 249–251
government tactics, 251
terrorism defined, 247–248
common definition, 247
distinctions, 248
FBI definition, 247
history, 247
types of terrorism, 248–249
domestic terrorists, 248–249
extremist groups, 248–249
state-sponsored terrorism, 248
violent global jihadists, 248
your client, 254
Terry v. Ohio, 71
Time of death (TOD), 233
TOD, *see* Time of death
"Top-of-mind" consciousness, 477
Trap doors, 158–159
Trashing (dumpster diving), 159
Treason, 70
Trial by ambush, 91
Trojan horse, 158
Turner Diaries, The, 252

U

UCC filings, *see* Uniform Commercial Code filings
UM, *see* Uninsured motorist
Underwriting, 267
Uniform Commercial Code (UCC) filings, 336, 339
Uninsured motorist (UM), 276–277, 278–279
United States v. Bruce Bertman, 211–212
United States v. Knotts, 367
United States v. Nancy Walter, 90–91
United States v. Pedro Huezo, 91–95
United States v. Roby Dudley, 147–148
Universal Resource Locator (URL), 166
Unknown crime, 180
Unpredictable constants, 401
Unreported crime, 180
URL, *see* Universal Resource Locator
U.S. v. Albert Takhalov, 206–211
USAPI, *see* U.S. Association of Professional Investigators
U.S. Association of Professional Investigators (USAPI), 521–525, 529
certification, 525
code of ethics, 470
information, 522–524
personal and career development, 525
U.S. Coast Guard, 24
U.S. Department of Homeland Security, 23
U.S. Department of Labor (DOL), 283
U.S. v. Gelbhart, 216
U.S. Immigration and Customs Enforcement (ICE), 24
U.S. Postal Service, 23, 345

V

Vice crimes, 71
VirtualGumshoe.com, 344
Virtual Reference Desk, 166
Visual enhancement devices, 369
Voir dire examination, 76

W

WebCrawler, 166
Weeks v. United States, 72
Westlaw, 339
White-collar crime, 108
Willful misconduct, 274
Williams v. Florida, 75
WinFax, 171
Witness(es)
arson, 292
cross-examination of, 77
expert, 446, 451–452, 458
fact, 446
grand jury, 216
investigator as, 441–443

police officers, 446
preparation of for trial, 440
your rights as, 455–457
before you appear in court, 456
cross-examination by defense attorney, 456–457
legal rights, 455
when you receive a subpoena, 456
Worker's Compensation, 273–276, 323
benefits, 275
employer and employees, 275
financing of benefits, 274–275
injuries covered, 275
laws, 273–274
occupational disability, 273, 274
Occupational Safety and Health Act, 275–276
theory behind legislation, 273
types of laws, 274
willful misconduct, 274
Writ of Certiorari, 83

Y

Yahoo, 166, 340
"Yaks," 122

Printed in the United States
by Baker & Taylor Publisher Services